The More Excellent Way

And I will show you a still more excellent way.

If I speak in the tongues of men and of angels,
but have not love,
I am a noisy gong or a clanging cymbal.

And if I have prophetic powers,
and understand all mysteries and all knowledge,
and if I have all faith, so as to remove mountains,
but have not love,
I am nothing.

If I give away all I have,
and if I deliver my body to be burned,
but have not love,
I gain nothing.

Love is patient and kind;
love is not jealous or boastful;
it is not arrogant or rude.
Love does not insist on its own way;
it is not irritable or resentful;
it does not rejoice at wrong,
but rejoices in the right.

Love bears all things, believes all things,
hopes all things, endures all things.
Love never ends; . . .
So faith, hope, love abide, these three;
but the greatest of these is love.

Make love your aim, . . .

Paul,
An Apostle and Servant of Christ Jesus

(1 Corinthians 12:31-14:1 RSV)

Also by Harold F. Roellig

The God Who Cares:
A Christian Interpretation of
Time, Life, and Man

The More Excellent Way:

2000 Years of Jesus' New Way of Life

And I will show you a still more excellent way
. . . Make love your aim.
First Corinthians 12:13, 14:1

by **Harold F. Roellig**

✠ **Crucifer Press** ✠
P.O. Box 205
Independence, Oregon
97351

Published by Crucifer Press,
P.O. Box 205, Independence, Oregon 97351
www.cruciferpress.com

First Edition

Library of Congress Control Number: 2006904795

Ten Digit ISBN (paperback) 0-9779853-0-X
Thirteen Digit ISBN (paperback) 9780977985302

Table of Contents

Introduction

This book is the result of requests from readers that I expand a portion of a previously written book into a book of its own. That previous book was *The God Who Cares: A Christian Interpretation of Time, Life, and Man*. It was a book that summed up the twenty years I had spent both in the study of theology and that of paleontology, which is the study of fossils and what they may tell us of the results of God's design of the universe established at the time of its creation. The book gave a historical and synthesizing survey of God's revelation in His created works, the geological record, and of God's revelation in His inspired Scriptures, the Bible.

In order to bring the story of God's revelations up to the present, the last chapters of the book summarized Jesus' teachings concerning His way of life and also the response of the Church over the past two thousand years to His teachings. I briefly discussed St. Paul's and St. John's defense of Jesus' way of life against those who would turn Jesus' way of life into a legalistic system. I followed this by a discussion of how Jesus' way of life nonetheless faded from the life of the Church over the centuries.

A few readers of my previous book commented that although they bought the book for its holistic vision of God's actions in past ages, they found the discussion of the history of Jesus' way of life particularly interesting. They suggested that I write a book just on this subject. With such encouragement, I decided to take on the task. The task was enormous, for it meant the study of all significant documents dealing with how Christians should live written over the past 2000 years. This present book is the answer to their request as well as an interest of my own.

The major question that concerned me was why Christianity appears to make so little difference in the way many Christians live their lives. This is certainly a major hindrance to bringing others into Christ's Church. What does it mean to the non-Christian if he sees Christians as uncaring and self-serving as the general population? Is there any hope of bringing others into the Christian faith when the lives of so many Christians do not reflect their faith? This book seeks to answer the question of why at the present time so little difference is seen between the lives and behavior of Christians and non-Christians.

x

Prefatory Notes

This book is written for the intelligent Christian laity and their clergy. It is for the Christian who wishes to have a greater understanding of the Jesus' way of life and why it is so little in evidence today. I have tried to write so that a Christian with a good high school education will have little difficulty understanding the text. The book, however, has the documentation necessary to meet the needs of the professional theologian.

Footnotes rather than endnotes provide the documentation for the text. In order to check a reference, it is an annoyance to have to page through the book to find the endnotes—end of chapter or end of book. Footnotes do not have that problem. Footnotes fell into bad repute because they became so abbreviated with their *op. cits.*, *loc. cits.*, and *ibids,* along with abbreviated authors' names and book titles that they were more a source of frustration than enlightenment. These abbreviations were demanded by publishers and printers because footnotes added immensely to the trials and expense of setting type either by hand or linotype machine. With present technology this is no longer a problem. Therefore, this book gives complete footnotes readily available at the bottom at the page. The only concession to abbreviation is that the place of publication and the name of the publisher are omitted after their first use in a chapter.

To make references to time periods readily understandable, I use the terms, the 200s, 600s, etc., for the centuries rather than the terms third century or seventh century, respectively. For example, many people have to think twice before realizing that the "Reformation of the Sixteenth Century" actually occurred in the fifteen hundreds.

The translations of the Bible primarily used for quotations are the NKJV, the New King James Version; the NASB, the New American Standard Bible; and the RSV, the Revised Standard Version. These translations try to render accurately the literal meaning of a verse in the Greek and Hebrew texts even if the translation is somewhat inelegant. They also appear to be the least affected by the liberal bias found in some modern translations of the Bible. My choice of a translation for a quotation was based on which of the translations best reflected the meaning of the original Greek or Hebrew text.

The liberal, theological bias mentioned above is most evident when it comes to the very late dating of many of the books of the New Testament by some academics found in university departments of religion or theology. It appears to be an unalterable prejudice among such academics that except for a few of Paul's letters no book of the New Testament could possibly have been written by the writer ascribed to it by the earliest Christians. As an antidote to such bias, the following is from W.H.C. Frend, the eminent Professor of Ecclesiastical History at the University of Glasgow. With the balanced and objective judgment of a disciplined historian, he wrote:

> The Gospels and epistles were circulating in Asia, Syria, and Alexandria (less certainly in Rome), and being read and discussed in the Christian synagogues there by about 100. In Polycarp's short letter [c. 107 A.D.] there is an astonishing amount of direct and indirect quotation from the New Testament; Matthew, Luke, John, Acts, the letters to Galatians, Thessalonians, Corinthians, Ephesians, Philippians, Colossians, Romans, the Pastorals, 1 Peter particularly, and 1 and 2 John are all used; and "the blessed and glorious" apostle Paul's letters to the Philippians are recalled specifically. Ignatius [c. 107 A.D.] is influenced through and through by John and Paul.
>
> The Christian Scriptures were quoted so familiarly as to suggest that they had been in regular use a long time. It is difficult therefore to place the final form of the Gospels or collection of Pauline letters much later than A.D. 80, with perhaps the Fourth Gospel a decade or so beyond.[76] (W.H.C. Frend, 1984, *The Rise of Christianity* (Philadelphia: Fortress Press), pp. 134-135.)
>
>> Footnote 76. The emphasis is on "final form." I am inclined to follow C.F.D. Moule, *The Birth of the New Testament,* HNTC, BNTC (New York: Harper and Row; London: A. & C. Black, 1962), pp. 121ff., that there may be "extremely little of the New Testament" later than A.D. 70. . . .

Because of the general ignorance of the Bible that is also found among Christians, in this book even such well-known parables as The Good Samaritan are written out in full rather than just cited. One cannot take for granted that the parable is known to the reader.

The thirty-eight volumes of the Ante-Nicene, Nicene, and Post-Nicene Fathers are the source of many quotations in this book. A few translators of texts in these volumes admit to imitating the words and sentence structure of the King James Version of the Bible for aesthetic reasons. I have taken the liberty of recasting a few texts into more easily read orthography while being careful not to change the meaning of the text.

When I began this book, I thought that only a small chapter would be on Luther's view of the Christian way of life because of his emphasis on salvation by faith and not works. During the year I spent reading Luther, the small chapter expanded into two large chapters. I apologize for this seeming chauvinism. However, after over two decades studying what was taught in Christendom for the past 2000 years on the way Christians should live, I have concluded that, outside of the New Testament writers, it is John Chrysostom and Martin Luther who best understood the way of life taught by Jesus. They deserve the pages given to them.

Acknowledgements

It is my inestimable teammate and wife, Ruth, who has been my greatest aid in researching and writing this book. She has joined me in library research searches, read and criticized the content, orthography, grammar, punctuation, as well as correcting typos in the numerous drafts of each of the chapters over the past many years. Indeed, since our marriage all that I have written--letters, essays, dissertations, instruction manuals, sermons, etc., I have gratefully subjected to her discerning and critical eye. If she is not the *sine qua non,* she is certainly the *sine qua parum* of my writing. This book would have been much more difficult to complete without her aid and enduring support.

My daughter Laura carefully critiqued earlier drafts of the book. I thank her for her many suggestions for improving the text. Two others who made thoughtful and extensive comments on an early draft were Joel Nichols and Scott Wycherly.

Others who gave helpful suggestions, encouragement, or advice after reading a draft or parts of the book were: Victor Albers, David Chamberlain, William and Lois Drews, Lawson Knight, William and Beverly Monroe, John Nelson, Orval Prothe, Frederick Roellig, and Lawrence Rolfing. I thank them all for their assistance.

In chapter one, the quotations denoted by footnotes 4, 5, and 6 are reprinted by permission of the publishers and trustees of the Loeb Classical Library from *The Works of the Emperor Julian*, volumes II and III, Loeb Classical Library, volumes 29 and 157, translated by Wilbur Cave Wright, Ph.D., Cambridge, Mass.: Harvard University Press, 1953, The Loeb Classical Library ® is a registered trademark of the President and Fellows of Harvard College.

Submitted excerpts found on pages 125 and 146 in the text are from THE APOSTOLIC FATHERS by EDGAR J. GOODSPEED, Copyright 1950 by Harper & Brothers, renewed © 1978 by Stephen Goodspeed and Foster B. Rhodes. Reprinted by permission of HarperCollins Publishers.

Excerpts from series *The Fathers of the Church*, Vols. 23, 11, 31 found respectively on pages 197-198, 279, and 338 are reprinted with permission from The Catholic University of America Press.

The many citations in chapter twelve concerning the penitentials are from *Medieval Handbooks of Penance* by John T. McNeill and Helen Gamer © 1938 Columbia University Press and are reprinted with the permission of the publisher.

The quotation in chapter 13, denoted by footnote 7, is reprinted from LUTHER'S WORKS, Volume 34, edited by Lewis Spitz, copyright ©1960 Muhlenberg Press, Used by permission of Augsburg Fortress.

The quotations in chapter 14, denoted by footnotes 22 and 37, are

Chapter One

THE CHRISTIANS, ARE THEY REALLY DIFFERENT?

The Early, Rapid Growth of Christianity

Why does Christianity today seem to make so little difference in the way many Christians live their lives? Evidently, this was not the case in the early years of Christianity when the faith was known as "The Way." One reason it was known as "The Way" is that the way of life of the Christians contrasted sharply with that of the non-Christians.

Christianity grew explosively after the resurrection of Jesus. Pliny the Younger, the Roman governor of Bithynia, a province in Asia Minor (modern Turkey), wrote to the Roman Emperor Trajan in 110 A.D. that Christianity had swept through his province. He complained that the temples of the Roman gods were almost deserted; the sacred rites were seldom performed; and hardly anybody purchased animals for sacrifice.[1] It is remarkable that only eighty years after Jesus' resurrection this situation prevailed almost seven hundred miles from Jerusalem. A reason often cited for this explosive growth is that the non-Christians could not help noticing the difference between their own behavior and that of the Christians. Those who followed the way of life that Jesus taught were making a major impact.

The Impact of Jesus' Way of Life upon the Ancient Roman World

The emphasis in the New Testament on Christian love expressed in lives of self-forgetful service to others made a major difference in the lives of many Christians in the first centuries. There is considerable

---

1 Pliny the Younger, *Letters of Gaius Plinius Caecilius Secundus*, in the *Harvard Classics*, bk. 9 (New York: P. F. Collier & Son), pp. 427.

documentary evidence that this was so from both early Christian and non-Christian sources. One might expect such testimony from faithful, life-long members of the early Church. Those, however, who as adults converted to Christianity from paganism could be considered valid witnesses as to what had brought them to their new faith.

Justin Martyr (100?-165?) became a convert to Christianity after spending many years studying and teaching the various Greek philosophical systems of his time. After a thorough study, he came to conclude that true knowledge was not to be found in them. It was in Christianity that he said he found true philosophy; and, therefore, he continued to wear the distinctive philosopher's cloak of a professional teacher of philosophy after becoming a Christian. Accused of being a Christian before the authorities because of teaching the truths of Christianity in a classroom in Rome, he died a martyr around 165.

In writing a defense of Christianity to the Roman Emperor around 150 A.D., Justin describes the care for those in need by the Christians in connection with a description of the Sunday worship service:

> And they who are well to do, and willing, give what each thinks fit; and what is collected is deposited with the president, who succours the orphans and widows, and those who, through sickness or any other cause, are in want, and those who are in bonds, and the strangers sojourning among us, and in a word takes care of all who are in need.[2]

The funds gathered by the Church thus went primarily to those in need. The Christians were keeping faith with their Lord's words that what you have done for even the least of these My brethren, you have done it unto Me (Matthew 25:40).

Tertullian, a highly educated adult convert to Christianity, around 200 A.D. wrote similarly about how the Church showed its love to others in deeds and not only words:

> There is no buying and selling of any sort in the things of God. Though we have our treasure chest, it is not made up of purchase-money, as of a religion that has its price. On the monthly day, if he likes, each puts in a small donation; but only if it be his pleasure, and only if he be able: for there is no

---

2 Justin Martyr, *The First Apology of Justin*, chap. 67, in *The Ante-Nicene Fathers* (Grand Rapids: Wm. B. Eerdmans Publ. Co.), vol. 1, p. 186.

compulsion; all is voluntary. These gifts are, as it were, piety's deposit fund. For they are not taken thence and spent on feasts, and drinking bouts, and eating-houses, but to support and bury poor people, to supply the wants of boys and girls destitute of means and parents, and of old persons confined now to the house; such, too, as have suffered shipwreck; and if there happen to be any in the mines, or banished to the islands, or shut up in the prisons, for nothing but their fidelity to the cause of God's Church, they become the nurslings of their confession. But it is mainly the deeds of a love so noble that lead many to put a brand on us. "See," they say, "how they love one another,". . .[3]

Tertullian, in quoting the observation of the non-Christians, "See, how they love one another," shows that the Christians were fulfilling the words of their Lord spoken on the night before his death: "A new commandment I give to you, that you love one another; as I have loved you, that you also love one another. By this all will know that you are My disciples, if you have love for one another" (John 13:34-35 NKJV).

One hardly would expect the pagan persecutors of Christianity to give evidence concerning the outgoing love of the early Christians. And yet, the writings of the emperor Julian the Apostate (331-363) give evidence from an antagonistic and hostile source that the way of life of the Christians was a major reason for many coming to faith in Christianity. Julian was a nephew of Constantine, who in 312 became the first Christian Roman Emperor. Julian succeeded to the emperorship in 361 after the death of Constantine and his sons. Although he had been raised as a Christian, Julian early in life rejected Christianity. With a fierce hatred and contempt for Christianity, Julian vigorously attempted to make once more the worship of the ancient Roman gods and goddesses the state religion of the Roman Empire. In 362 Julian wrote to Arsacius, the pagan high priest of Galatia, concerning the progress made in his attempt to restore the ancient Roman and Hellenic religion. Terming the Christians and Jews atheists and their religion atheism because they believed in one God and denied the existence of the multitude of Roman, Greek, and other gods, Julian analyzes the situation by writing:

The Hellenic religion does not yet prosper as I desire, and it is the fault of those who profess it; for the worship of the

---

3 Tertullian, *Apology*, chap. 39, in *The Ante-Nicene Fathers*, vol. 3, p. 46.

gods is on a splendid and magnificent scale, surpassing every prayer and every hope. May Adrasteia [a goddess] pardon my words, for indeed no one, a little while ago, would have ventured even to pray for a change of such a sort or so complete within so short a time. Why, then, do we think that this is enough, why do we not observe that it is their [the Christians] benevolence to strangers, their care for the graves of the dead and the pretended holiness of their lives that have done most to increase atheism? I believe that we ought really and truly to practice every one of these virtues. . . . For it is disgraceful that, when no Jew ever has to beg, and the impious Galilaeans [the Christians] support not only their own poor but ours as well, all men see that our people lack aid from us.[4]

In another letter Julian wrote to a pagan priest urging him to give an example of charity to his people. He exhorts him to share cheerfully, even from small resources, with those in need. He encourages him to try to do good to as many people as possible. He then gives his reason for urging such charity by continuing:

We must pay especial attention to this point, and by this means effect a cure. For when it came about that the poor were neglected and overlooked by the priests, then I think the impious Galilaeans observed this fact and devoted themselves to philanthropy. And they have gained ascendancy in the worst of their deeds through the credit they win for such practices. . . . the Galilaeans also begin with their so-called love-feast, or hospitality, or service of tables,--for they have many ways of carrying it out and hence call it by many names,--and the result is that they have led very many into atheism.[5]

The love feast was the Christians' practice from New Testament times of meeting on a Sunday evening for a meal provided by the members and to which the poor and destitute were invited also to take part.

When Julian came to the large and prosperous Syrian city of Antioch, he was incensed that only a goose from the personal property of an

---

4 *The Works of the Emperor Julian*, translated by W. C. Wright (Loeb Classical Library, Cambridge: Harvard U. Press), vol. 3, pp. 67-71.

5 *The Works of the Emperor Julian*, translated by W. C. Wright, vol. 2, pp. 337-339.

aged priest was offered as a sacrifice to the Roman gods at the time of the festival of the city's founding. He scolded the senate of the city for slighting the gods of the city's ancestors. He raged against them for squandering large sums of money on themselves for dinners and feasts, but yet could not bring themselves to give even one ox or bull as a sacrifice in the temple. He is angered in that

> every one of you allows his wife to carry everything out of his house to the Galilaeans, and when your wives feed the poor at your expense they inspire a great admiration for godlessness [Christianity] in those who are in need of such bounty--and of such sort are, I think, the great majority of mankind,--while as for yourselves you think that you are doing nothing out of the way when in the first place you are careless of the honours due to the gods, and not one of those in need goes near the temples--for there is nothing there, I think, to feed them with--and yet when any one of you gives a birthday feast he provides a dinner and a breakfast without stint and welcomes his friends to a costly table; . . .[6]

No matter how imperfectly, it is obvious many Christians did strive to follow the high ideals of their founder. It must be admitted that Christianity as a religion of unselfish love made a deep impression on the pagan world in the first centuries after Christ's resurrection. The perhaps preeminent twentieth century historian of Christian faith, Professor Kenneth Scott Latourette of Yale University, in describing Christian life in the first centuries wrote:

> It is men's response in humble faith and love to God's love in Christ, so the New Testament says, which should be the well-spring of Christian living. . . . Here is not a set of commands through obedience to which men can earn anything from God. Men, so the New Testament sees, can never fully comply with God's commands, and even if they could and did they would deserve nothing from Him, but would only, like good servants, have done what it is their duty to do. The Christian Gospel is, rather, the good news of God's love and of that kingdom of God which is God's free gift to men and into which men can enter

---

6 *The Works of the Emperor Julian*, translated by W. C. Wright, vol. 2, pp. 489-491.

here and now by accepting that gift. Christians are to determine their actions, not by legalistic rules, but by the love of God which itself is the gift of God through His Holy Spirit and by its inevitable corollary, love for their neighbours. As *The Epistle of James* says, "Thou shalt love thy neighbor as thyself" is the "royal law." As Paul emphatically states: "Love worketh no ill to his neighbour, therefore love is the fulfilling of the law." [7]

William Lecky, a rationalist who with considerable understatement was described as "one not too well disposed towards the Gospel,"[8] in his influential two volume study, *A History of European Morals*, published in 1900, nonetheless sums up the works of love by the early Christians as follows:

> There can, indeed, be little doubt that, for nearly two hundred years after its establishment in Europe, the Christian community exhibited a moral purity which, if it has been equaled, has never for any long period been surpassed. . . .
>
> Christianity for the first time made charity a rudimentary virtue . . . it effected a complete revolution in this sphere, by regarding the poor as the special representatives of the Christian Founder, and thus making the love of Christ rather than the love of man, the principle of charity. Even in the days of persecution, collections for the relief of the poor were made at the Sunday meetings. The agapae or feasts of love were intended mainly for the poor, and food that was saved by the fasts was devoted to their benefit. A vast organization of charity, presided over by the bishops, and actively directed by the deacons, soon ramified over Christendom, till the bond of charity became the bond of unity, and the most distant sections of the Christian Church corresponded by the interchange of mercy. Long before the era of Constantine, it was observed that the charities of the Christians were so extensive--it may, perhaps, be said so excessive--that they drew many impostors to the Church; and when the victory of Christianity was achieved, the

---

7 Kenneth S. Latourette, 1953, *A History of Christianity*, (New York: Harper and Bros.) p. 214.

8 *The Ante-Nicene Fathers*, vol. 5, p. 563.

enthusiasm for charity displayed itself in the erection of numerous institutions that were altogether unknown to the Pagan world. A Roman lady, named Fabiola, in the fourth century, founded at Rome, as an act of penance, the first public hospital, and the charity planted by that woman's hand overspread the world, and will alleviate, to the end of time, the darkest anguish of humanity.[9]

Lecky sums up:

Imperfect and inadequate as is the sketch I have drawn, it will be sufficient to show how great and multiform have been the influences of Christian philanthropy. The shadows that rest upon the picture, I have not concealed; but, when all due allowance has been made for them, enough will remain to claim our deepest admiration. The high conception that has been formed of the sanctity of human life, the protection of infancy, the elevation and final emancipation of the slave classes, the suppression of barbarous games, the creation of a vast and multifarious organization of charity, and the education of the imagination by the Christian type, constitute together a movement of philanthropy which has never been paralleled or approached in the Pagan world. The effects of this movement in promoting happiness have been very great. Its effect in determining character has probably been still greater. In that proportion or disposition of qualities which constitutes the ideal character, the gentler and more benevolent virtues have obtained, through Christianity, the foremost place. In the first and purest period they were especially supreme; but in the third century a great ascetic movement arose, which gradually brought a new type of character into the ascendant, and diverted the enthusiasm of the Church into new channels.[10]

---

9 William E. H. Lecky, 1900, *History of European Morals* (New York: Appleton and Co.), vol. 2, p. 11, 79-80.

10 William E. H. Lecky, 1900, *History of European Morals*, vol. 2, p. 100-101.

The Contrast between the Early Church
and the Church Today

What a contrast there is between the Christianity of the early Church and that of today. Unlike in the early church, the money set aside today in many church budgets to aid the needy is typically one of the smallest items in the budget. In the days of early Christianity, the faithful met in modest house churches. Today often great sums are spent to build expensive and ornate edifices. The buildings are often in stark contrast to the poverty and poor housing of the people who worship within them. In the early church, the clergy led the people in worship dressed in the common clothes of the day. Today in some churches, the clergy and especially the hierarchy wear sumptuous, highly decorative, and expensive vestments. They are vestments more fitting for the grandiose court of the Sun King, Louis XIV of France, rather than for the followers of the wandering preacher from Nazareth who had no home He could call His own.

Christian life today has typically become centered on the piety of serving the church as an institution. The early church existed as a gathering of Christians dedicated to worshiping their Lord by also serving their fellow humans as Christ served them. What seems most important today is that Christians serve the institution of the church by taking part in its churchly activities. One shows his Christianity by singing in the choir, attending the Women's Guild, sitting on the various boards of the congregation, and so forth. One also gets the feeling that ten dollars given to the church is considered more worthy than twenty dollars given to the "Save the Children Fund." The local church, at least in the United States, seems to be primarily concerned with its numerical and financial success. Seemingly of secondary importance is Jesus' major emphasis that His followers are to live in the world giving their lives in service to their neighbor and loving one another as He loved them.

Perhaps one reason there is today so little difference between the lives of Christians and non-Christians is that the way of life taught by Jesus and His apostles is almost unknown to Christians today. The teaching materials of the various Christian churches primarily use the Ten Commandments in attempting to teach the Christian way of life. But the Ten Commandments are not an emphasis in the New Testament. The Christian way of life goes far beyond following the mainly negative laws of the Commandments. The Ten Commandments are not abolished. Rather they are secondary to the way of life that Jesus taught of loving others in the same selfless way as He loved us. For Christians, living a life of unselfish love is the way the Ten Commandments are to be observed and fulfilled.

Therefore, why is there so little observable difference in the lives of Christian and non-Christians? It is because few Christians are taught the way of life found in the New Testament. During my nine years as a college chaplain in New York City, I made a practice of asking incoming Lutheran students the question, "What do you think is the Christian way of life?" Without exception they answered, "The Ten Commandments." Perhaps one in ten also mentioned the Golden Rule. The Ten Commandments had been taught to them from earliest childhood. The students remembered the commandments from Luther's catechism, but they typically had forgotten Luther's short explanations to the commandments that emphasized love for one's neighbor. Almost unknown to them was the New Testament's emphasis on a life of Christian love shown in unselfish deeds done for others following the example of Jesus. And so it is with many Christian denominations. Too many churches define being a Christian in a negative way. The good Christian is one who does not commit the gross sins condemned in the Ten Commandments. Also added by many churches is that he is also one who doesn't smoke, drink alcohol, dance, play cards or engage in sports on Sunday, and so forth. The Christian is not defined as one who in following his Savior's example gives himself in self-denying love to the welfare of his neighbor.

How did it come about that today you can't tell Christians from non-Christians by the way they live? Over the past two thousand years, the ethics of the Christians have been diluted down to little more than the Ten Commandments. In the same two thousand years, most non-Christian people have come to give at least lip-service to the Ten Commandments. Thus, the difference between the lives of Christians and non-Christians is no longer to be seen.

This book will explain and document how this change came about over the past two millenia. It will show how after the first few centuries an emphasis on personal purity and avoidance of evil came to predominate and eclipse the life of outgoing love for others that Jesus taught. As Lecky wrote in the quotation above: "but in the third century a great ascetic movement arose, which gradually brought a new type of character into the ascendant, and diverted the enthusiasm of the Church into new channels." The book will document how negative church law grew to restrict the lives and choices of Christians and thereby undermined the Christian's God-given freedom to act positively in unselfish love as led by the Holy Spirit and guided by God's Word. And, finally, it will demonstrate how Christians came to much prefer to offer God lives of personal piety rather than the lives of goodness He also asks.

The way of life that Jesus taught, however, cannot be studied apart from the overall purpose of God for human life. To gain this understanding, the following two chapters will consider what God has revealed as His will and purpose for humankind and the response of humans to His revelation.

Chapter Two

TO WALK WITH GOD

The Purpose of God for His Creation

The Bible when read from cover to cover for the first time can be a perplexing and somewhat difficult book. When the book of Revelation is finished, the last book of the Bible, one can be puzzled by the variety of literature and the many and varied accounts found in the sixty-six books of the Bible.

It may be that only some months after reading the Bible that its overall message comes into focus. The Bible is not, as many people expect, an account of humans seeking after God, but rather of God seeking a relationship of love and trust with the creatures He had brought into being. The Bible is actually one long, manifold, and involved account of God's struggle to bring humans into a living and vital relationship with Himself. That the Creator desires humans to live in harmony and communion with Him is one of the main points of the creation story in Genesis, the first book of the Bible.

Also found in the first chapters of Genesis, however, is the story of Adam and Eve's disobedience in not following the guidance of their Creator. This waywardness is symbolic of the inclinations of their descendants. Yet for all of mankind's stubborn willfulness, the Bible early makes it clear that God will not give up on humans. The remainder of the Scriptures details how God attempted to make it possible for His straying creatures to come back into an active relationship of love with their Creator.

The Bible tells us that God calls us to live as His sons and daughters. We may well stand in awe of our Creator and His concern for us. We may feel it presumptuous even to bring ourselves to His attention. The Bible, however, clearly teaches that God wills that we be His beloved children.

Servants and soldiers may have to act unknowingly and unquestioningly at their master's command. However, insofar as we are capable, our Creator takes us into His confidence. Jesus made this point when He said to His disciples: "No longer do I call you servants, for a servant does not know what his master is doing; but I have called you friends, for all things that I have heard from My Father I have made known to you" (John 15:15 NKJV).

God's revelation of Himself through the New Testament gives insight into God's overall plan for this world. In one of the most illuminating and instructive sections of the Scriptures, the apostle Paul wrote to the church at Ephesus:

> Blessed be the God and Father of our Lord Jesus Christ, who has blessed us with every spiritual blessing in the heavenly places in Christ, just as He has chosen us in Him before the foundation of the world, that we should be holy and without blame before Him in love, having predestined us to adoption as sons by Jesus Christ to Himself, according to the good pleasure of His will, to the praise of the glory of His grace, by which He made us accepted in the Beloved. In Him [Christ] we have redemption through His blood, the forgiveness of sins, according to the riches of His grace which He has made to abound toward us in all wisdom and prudence, having made known to us the mystery of His will, according to His good pleasure which He purposed in Himself, that in the dispensation of the fullness of the times He might gather together in one all things in Christ, both which are in heaven and which are in earth. (Ephesians 1:3-10 NKJV)

This is God's purpose for His creation: that He might gather together and unite all things in Christ, "both which are in heaven and which are in earth." We do not know all that this entails, but we do know that His plan for the "fullness of the times" includes the humans on this earth. We are to be united with our God in Christ. During our lifetime, our Creator calls us to be His sons and daughters. He wills that we acknowledge Him as God and that we respond to His love for us, as Paul in the above quotation wrote: "having predestined us to adoption as sons by Jesus Christ to Himself, according to the good pleasure of His will."

Our God has adopted us as His children. Paul explained, "But when the fullness of the time had come, God sent forth His Son, born of woman, born under the law, to redeem those who were under the law, that we might receive the adoption as sons" (Galatians 4:4, 5 NKJV). As adopted sons and daughters of our God, we are to follow in the ways of our Father. While on this earth, we are to walk in the ways that God would lead us. We are to seek out God's direction for our lives. Paul further instructed, "For we are His workmanship, created in Christ Jesus for good works, which God has prepared beforehand that we should walk in them" (Ephesians 2:10 NKJV), and also, "Therefore be imitators of God, as beloved children; and walk in love, just as Christ also loved you, and gave Himself up for us, an offering and a sacrifice to God as a fragrant aroma" (Ephesians 5:1-2 NASB).

The Bible Reveals a God of Steadfast Love

Walking in love following the example of Christ during our short life does not end our relationship with our Creator. When our pilgrimage through this life ends, those who in faith in Christ walked with their God are to be united with Him through all eternity. We are to dwell in His presence forever.

We may well wonder at the concern of the Creator for the inhabitants of such a small speck of dust as is our earth in this vast universe. Need a being as complete in itself as the Deity have any concern for humans? By definition, we can add nothing to the Godhead. In a very absolute sense, God is the only reality. All else, including the whole of the universe is only an act of His will, a result of the thought of God.

Scripture, however, gives us some insight into why our Creator is concerned with us. The Bible portrays the Deity as a God of steadfast love. The Old Testament prophet Nehemiah wrote, "But thou art a God ready to forgive, gracious and merciful, slow to anger and abounding in steadfast love" (Nehemiah 9:17b RSV). Indeed, almost two hundred times God is described in the Old Testament as being a God of "*chesed*," a Hebrew word variously translated as "goodness, steadfast love," "mercy," or "loving kindness." Then, of course, there is that succinct verse of John's: "He who does not love does not know God, for God is love" (1 John 4:8 NKJV).

If the essential nature of God is love, would one expect God to exist without objects of His love? To draw an analogy, if a man chose to describe himself as a loving person, would one expect him to choose a solitary life on a desert island? The early Christian teacher Irenaeus (130?-202?), who studied under the bishop Polycarp (65?-155?), who in turn was a disciple of the apostle John, wrote:

> In the beginning, therefore, did God form Adam, not as if He stood in need of man, but that He might have [some one] upon whom to confer His benefits.[1]

---

1 Irenaeus, *Against Heresies*, bk. IV, 14:1, in *The Ante-Nicene Fathers* (Grand Rapids: Wm. B. Eerdmans Publ. Co.), vol. 1, p. 478.

It appears reasonable that our God, whose being is defined as love, would by His very nature have objects of that love. Perhaps for this reason we have the creation in which we find ourselves, a creation governed by a God who benevolently watches over man, beast, and plant (Psalm 104). We humans were created so that we might dwell in the love of our Creator.

Is this idea really so startling? Why does a young man or woman seek to be married if not to give to another the fullest expression of his or her love? There may be many motivations that lead to marriage, but surely the desire to enter into a relationship of deep and steadfast love with the beloved is a major compelling desire. And isn't this also a primary reason why a couple wishes to have children—a desire to build a circle of love? Isn't it the hope of most parents that their children respond to the love they have shown to them? How saddened are human parents when a child rejects their love. And, on the other hand, how gladdened are the hearts of parents if their children respond with love and concern.

Just as a child of human parents has no say as to whether he wishes to be born, so also humans were not consulted as to whether they wished to be brought into existence. God willed the human race into existence so that we might become His children. Perhaps just as parents are disappointed when their children do not respond to their love for them, so also is God saddened if we reject His love for us. Jesus gave evidence of this when grieving for His people He lamented, "O Jerusalem, Jerusalem, the one who kills the prophets and stones those who are sent to her! How often I wanted to gather your children together, as a hen gathers her chicks under her wings, and you were not willing" (Matthew 23:37 NKJV)!

It should not be thought odd that God's love and human love are considered to a degree comparable. The Bible certainly gives us ample instances of this. Our God, for example, chose to reveal Himself as our "Father" with all the concern, warmth, and love the word implies. Indeed, even human married love is often used as an analogy to indicate the love of God for His people, for example, in the text that follows:

> You [the people of Israel] shall be a crown of beauty in the hand of the Lord, and a royal diadem in the hand of your God. You shall no more be termed Forsaken, and your land shall no more be termed Desolate; but you shall be called My delight is in her [*Hephzibah*], and your land Married [*Beulah*]; for the Lord delights in you, and your land shall be married. For as a young man marries a virgin, so shall your sons marry you, and as the bridegroom rejoices over the bride, so shall your God rejoice over you. (Isaiah 62:3-5 RSV)

When we read in the Scriptures that God destines us in love (Ephesians 1:5) to be His children, is it, therefore, really so far from our understanding that our God wishes to have a close relationship with us? God has placed us on this bountiful and beautiful planet and has enveloped us with His kindly providence. He has revealed Himself to us as our heavenly Father who, as the Psalmists never tire of telling us, is a Lord who is merciful and gracious, slow to anger and abounding in steadfast love (Psalm 103:8). Our Creator placed us upon this earth so that we might walk with Him during our lifetime and finally be united with Him for all eternity.

Our Freedom to Reject God's Love

There is, however, something that our God will not do. He will not force us to enter into a relationship of love with Himself. It was obviously in His power to have created us in such a way that we had no choice except to "love" Him, to follow His guidance, and to do His will in all our actions. If He had done so, this planet would certainly have been a far different one on which to live. However, the difference would have been critical. It would not have been a world of self-determining humans. It would not have been in our power to reject His love. It would have been a world of robots. Those who criticize God for the imperfections of this present world are but wishing that God would have created them automatons.

Actually, if all humans loved their God and only did good deeds, would you not suspect that we really were only robots, programmed by the Creator to act only in that fashion? Our God, however, would not force upon us a relationship of love with Himself. In some unknowable way, He gave us freedom—freedom to reject or ignore Him if we would so choose.

A world of humans that were only capable of following the will of their Creator would undoubtedly be a world in which the distress and sufferings that humans inflict upon themselves and others would be absent. But who would want such a world? It would be a cold world, as cold and antiseptic an environment as walking into a room full of computers; activity, but no sensibility—motion, but no emotion. If people were programmed only to love their Creator and to do His will, they would not be what we consider human. Their "love" would be as meaningless as that of a recording one might make for oneself endlessly crooning, "I love you." Would God be any more entranced by a recording of His own making mindlessly singing His praises than we would be?

Isn't much of the delight and beauty of married love due to the free commitment and choice of the couple for one another? True love is founded on the willingness to love. To "make love" to an unwilling or unresponsive partner may satisfy lust but never love. Love delights in the choice of the one for the other. Certainly, the poets, if not our own experience, have taught us the agony of love that is not returned. Love directed to another normally wills a response from the other.

Therefore, God invites us to be His children and enter into a relationship of love with Him. He would have us know Him as our loving Father. He sends His Holy Spirit into our lives to give us the gift of faith so that we might enter that circle of love in which He would "unite all things" in His Son, Jesus Christ (Ephesians 1:9-10). God does not will our disobedience, but on the contrary, we read in Ezekiel:

> "Do I have any pleasure at all that the wicked should die?" says the Lord God, "and not that he should turn from his ways and live?" . . . "For I have no pleasure in the death of one who dies," says the Lord God. "Therefore turn and live!" (Ezekiel 18:23, 32 NKJV)

God's Gift of Forgiveness through Christ, His Son

Just as human parents are willing to forgive a disobedient child, so also our heavenly Father is willing to forgive a sinful child of His. The parable Jesus told of the prodigal son who was welcomed back into the arms of his father brings home this message of forgiving love (Luke 15:11-32).

Jesus' sacrificial death on the cross was made to reconcile us with our heavenly Father. Through faith in Jesus' sacrifice of Himself for our insubordinate and sinful lives, we obtain pardon for our rebelliousness against the will of our heavenly Father. God is willing to grant us this forgiveness even up to our last moments of life. Remember Jesus' words to that repentant criminal who was crucified beside Him, "Assuredly, I say to you, today you will be with Me in Paradise" (Luke 23:43 NKJV).

The whole of Scripture portrays the nature of God as one of steadfast love. It was out of steadfast love that God called Israel to be His means of revelation to the world. In a charge to the people of Israel, Moses declared:

> "The Lord did not set His love on you nor choose you because you were more in number than any other people, for you were the least of all the peoples; but because the Lord loves you, and because He would keep the oath that He swore to your fathers, the Lord has brought you out with a mighty hand, and redeemed you from the house of bondage, from the hand of Pharaoh king of Egypt. Therefore know that the Lord your God, He is God, the

faithful God who keeps covenant and mercy for a thousand generations with those who love Him and keep His commandments; and He repays those who hate Him to their face, to destroy them. He will not be slack with him who hates Him; He will repay him to his face." (Deuteronomy 7:7-9 NKJV)

When Israel failed to keep their covenant with their God, it also was out of steadfast love that God sent His Son into the world to establish a new covenant with His errant people. In the book of Jeremiah is the prophecy:

Behold, the days are coming, says the Lord, when I will make a new covenant with the house of Israel and with the house of Judah--not according to the covenant that I made with their fathers in the day I took them by the hand to lead them out of the land of Egypt. My covenant which they broke, though I was a husband to them, says the Lord. But this is the covenant that I will make with the house of Israel after those days, says the Lord: I will put My law into their minds, and write it on their hearts; and I will be their God, and they shall be My people. (Jeremiah 31:31-33 NKJV)

Jesus, the Christ, came to establish the New Covenant with the house of Israel in keeping with the above prophecy. On the night Jesus instituted the Lord's Supper, He referred to this new covenant in saying, "This is My blood of the new covenant, which is shed for many" (Mark 14:24 NKJV). He first sent His disciples to declare the good news of the coming of the kingdom of Heaven to the people of Israel (Matthew 10:5-7). Later in His ministry, Jesus made it clear that the good news of God's love was to be preached to all nations. Jesus brought the Holy Christian Church into existence to be His means through which the Holy Spirit would bring men and women into a vital relationship of forgiveness and love with God the Father. The whole of the Scriptures can be summed up in Jesus' words: "For God so loved the world, that He gave His only begotten Son, that whoever believes in Him should not perish, but have eternal life" (John 3:16 NASB).

Walking with God in His Ways

God wills that we be His children. He would have us walk in His ways. He desires that we follow His guidance through our lives; that we cheerfully make His will, our will.

God willed that His Old Testament people be a people of love and kindness just as He Himself was. Not only did He give them laws to curb human selfishness, He told them: "You shall love your neighbor as yourself" (Leviticus 19:18 NKJV). He therefore instructed them to leave the gleanings of their fields for the poor and traveler, not harvest their fields to their edge, to forgive all debts owed to them on the sabbatical seventh year, to care for the poor, the orphan, the widow, and the sojourner, to pay the laborer a just wage, and many other similar laws. God willed that His new chosen people be a model for the rest of world as to how humans were to live in peace, love, and harmony with one another (Deuteronomy 4:5-8).

The Old Testament men or women of God were to walk before their God keeping the laws and ordinances He gave in the books of Moses. This was not to be a reluctant or sullen following of the law of God. It was to be a source of delight to humans to know God's will and to walk in the paths He showed them. Numerous texts from the Old Testament attest to the joy of following God's will and law. See, for example, Psalm 1 or 119.

In the New Testament God leads us into the new way of life that His Son Jesus taught (1 John 3:21-24). Starting with chapter four of this book, we will consider Jesus' new way of life; and how especially Paul and John fought to keep it as the way of life for the Church.

Walking with God through life is like living in a marriage. It is a positive life of love and communication together. The Bible, in fact, as was noted earlier, often uses marriage as a comparison for God's love for His people. Paul, referring to the Corinthian Christians wrote: ". . . for I betrothed you to Christ to present you as a pure bride to her one husband." (2 Corinthians 11:2 RSV).

Living in a marriage is much more than following a series of negative prohibitions such as: do not commit adultery, do not desert your spouse, or do not abuse your mate. God intended human marriage to be a positive and joyful life stressing willing commitment, mutual trust, amiable cooperation, pleasant companionship, all founded upon a deep love for one's mate. Similarly, walking with God in His paths is also far more than obeying negative restrictions. God's way is not a difficult path hemmed in by rules, ordinances, and laws applied to fearful travelers. Walking with God through life is a delightful journey in which we share our concerns, joys, and difficulties with Him as we travel through the years in the sunshine of His love. If the Twenty-third Psalm is so beloved by God's people, it is because it so well reflects what they have experienced as they followed in the paths of the Good Shepherd.

God's people rightfully have a certain awe of their Creator. They, however, are not afraid of Him; for He has taught them to think of Him as their benevolent Father. Just as a human father wishes his children to follow his direction and guidance out of love rather than fear or a sense of duty, so also our God wishes us to follow His benevolent guidance out of love and not out of fearfulness or hope for reward.

The Fulfillment of God's Eternal Plan for His Creation

The time comes when our last years on this earth are over. Then God's purpose for our presence on this earth is realized. Those who walked in faith with their Lord through this life are finally united with Him to dwell in His presence forever.

The humans on this planet are not necessarily unique in possessing such a relationship with their Creator. The Scriptures record that those non-material beings, the angels, also had their time of freedom to reject their Creator. Some used their freedom to rebel against their Maker and were cast out of His presence (2 Peter 2:4). Those angels who did not reject their Creator now live in the presence of God and are confirmed in their commitment to their Lord. They too are part of the Creator's plan to unite all things in Christ, both in heaven and on earth (Ephesians 1:10).

God does not wish that any of His creation die the spiritual death that is the result of separation from Him. As mentioned at the start of this chapter, the Scriptures are one long account of God's struggle to bring humans into a living relationship with Himself.

Through the descendants of Abraham, Isaac, and Israel God brought into existence a people whom He set on the crossroads of the ancient world. They were to be an example for the nations of the world to follow. He gave the ancient Israelites the knowledge of Himself that we find recorded in the Old Testament, the ancient covenant that God made with the people of Israel at Mt. Sinai.

When God's Old Testament people began falling away from their covenant relationship with Him, He sent prophet after prophet to try to restore them to being a people holy unto Himself. Even when His people abused and killed the prophets He sent them, God did not give up on them. He desired to save a remnant of the people and continue His witness to the world through this remnant.

This remnant, however, was to be a people under a new covenant that would be established by the Messiah. Isaiah prophesied that this Servant of God, the Messiah or Christ, would come to offer Himself for the sins of mankind (Isaiah 53). The New Covenant would be made with all the peoples of the earth who would accept God's Son, Jesus the Christ, as their Lord and Savior. Through faith in the redeeming death of God's Son, the rebelliousness and sinfulness of a man or woman would be forgiven.

Jesus, however, did more than save humans from the curse of their rebellion against God. During the years of His ministry, Jesus by word and example gave the people who would belong to His new covenant a unique way of life to follow and a much enlarged revelation of God's will for humans.

After the ascension of Christ into heaven, God sent His Holy Spirit to be with His New Testament people, the people who constitute the Holy Christian Church. God's Spirit was sent to give power to the words and lives of those within the Church—and empower them, He did!

The Holy Christian Church became the mightiest movement among humans that this planet has ever seen. From any point of view, no other institution has even come close to making the impact upon history as has the Holy Christian Church. What other movement has had the power so fundamentally to change the lives of men and women upon this earth? The power of the Holy Spirit is still with us today, working through the lives of those who are God's children.

Could any group of reasoning beings ask more from their God than the revelation that God has given to the people of this earth? He has certainly not left Himself without witnesses. The Bible, for example, is by far the most widely published book in the earth's history. The story of the Creator's love and concern for us has been spread far and wide. God's invitation for us to be His children, to walk with Him during our lives, and finally to be united with Him at the fullness of time, could hardly have been more abundantly given. As the writer of the New Testament book, Hebrews, observed, "how shall we escape if we neglect so great a salvation" (Hebrews 2:3a RSV)?

Unfortunately, the majority of people upon this earth apparently do not feel the need for what the apostle calls "so great a salvation." Humans, more often than not, have turned their backs on their Creator as they have come to know Him through the creation and the Scriptures. We will concern ourselves with this in the next chapter.

Chapter Three

TURNING AWAY FROM GOD

The Good Will of the Creator

When the first pictures of our earth taken from outer space were published, many of us were astonished at the serene beauty of our blue planet. But then, we have always known that we lived on a beautiful planet. Every landscape seems to have its own charm—the awesome massiveness and towering heights of the mountains, the shaded quiet of the forests, the peaceful expanses of the meadows, and the tranquil melancholy of the deserts. Certainly, there are few people living today who would disagree with the final verse of Genesis 1, "Then God saw everything that He had made, and indeed it was very good" (Genesis 1:31 NKJV).

Upon this well-favored planet, human life came to be. And how richly the planet sustains and provides for us. Our natural foods such as grains, nuts, edible roots, fruit, game, etc., are produced in abundance. If there is hunger upon the earth, it is typically the result of human mismanagement or selfishness and not any lack of the Creator's generosity. Is it any wonder that humans love life when they find themselves in such a pleasant and wholesome environment?

The Natural Knowledge of God

It is thus not surprising that primitive peoples came early to the conclusion that a powerful and benevolent Being must exist who was responsible for the earth on which they lived. The Old Testament affirmed this ancient insight when the Psalmist wrote, "The heavens are telling of the glory of God; and their expanse is declaring the work of His hands" (Psalm 19:1 NASB). The New Testament also attests to the natural knowledge of God. Paul wrote:

> For the wrath of God is revealed from heaven against all ungodliness and unrighteousness of men, who suppress the

truth in unrighteousness, because what may be known of God is manifest in them, for God has shown it to them. For since the creation of the world His invisible attributes are clearly seen, being understood by the things that are made, even His eternal power and Godhead, so that they are without excuse. (Romans 1:19-20 NKJV).

This natural knowledge of God is found in just about every society of humans and is a true cultural universal. The creation stories of the first chapters of Genesis reaffirm the ancient insight of primitive man: God is good, and He gave us a good earth on which to live.

The Origin of Sin and Human Striving after God's Forgiveness

God, however, willed an even greater benefit upon His human creatures. The intelligence and reasoning ability of humans make them unique among all the creatures of this earth. As noted above, they early came to realize that there must be a benevolent Creator. It is also plausible that the first reasoned morality grew out of the insight that as God was good, as was evident from His generously proportioned creation, so also humans should be good.

One of the earliest recorded prayers from around 4000 years ago and before the birth of Abraham indicates that humans early came to the insight that the deity disapproves of selfish and wrongful actions. A prayer to the Mesopotamian goddess Ishtar implores her to "forgive my sin, my iniquity, my shameful deeds and my offense . . . that thy great mercy be upon me.[1]

When the dawn of history broke with the invention of writing some 5000 years ago, highly evolved and complex religions were already in existence. Humans over the earth were seeking a relationship with the Creator whom they felt surely must exist. The apostle Paul in his speech to the philosophers of Athens mentions this human need to search for God:

. . . and He made from one, every nation of mankind to live on all the face of the earth, having determined their appointed times, and the boundaries of their habitation, that they should seek God, if perhaps they might grope for Him and find Him, though He is not far from each one of us; . . . (Acts 17:26-27 NASB)

---

1 John B. Noss, 1963, *Man's Religions* (New York: The Macmillan Company), p. 73.

The abundance of religions we see in the world today is the result of this very natural attempt of humans to build a relationship with the Great Spirit of whose existence they have become aware.

The knowledge of God, however, as divined from observing the natural world gives an incomplete understanding of God. Religions in times past often degenerated into inhumane and grotesque teachings and practices both in the old and new worlds. Human sacrifice was widespread in the ancient world. Even some of the people of Israel had reverted to paganism and were sacrificing their children to the god, Molech, as late as 600 years before Christ (2 Kings 17:17 and Jeremiah 32:35). Humans also came to project their own passions and vices upon the deities they invented as seen in Mesopotamian, Greek, and Roman mythology.

God's Entry into Human History through His Chosen People

It was to this confused and degraded religious world that the Creator chose to reveal His true nature. Out of a steadfast love for His reasoning creatures, God chose to give the ancient world knowledge of Himself and a relationship with the Deity as He truly is. The Old Testament is the record of God's revelation to His Chosen People and through them to the nations of the world. The following poem portrays the response of the people of Israel to God's revelation:

> Sing to the Lord, all the earth;
>> Proclaim the good news of His salvation from day to day.
> Declare His glory among the nations,
>> His wonders among all peoples.
> For the Lord is great and greatly to be praised;
>> He is also to be feared above all gods.
> For all the gods of the peoples are idols,
>> But the Lord made the heavens.
> Honor and majesty are before Him;
>> strength and gladness are in His place. . . .
>
> Let the heavens rejoice, and let the earth be glad;
>> And let them say among the nations, "The Lord reigns."
> Let the sea roar, and all its fullness;
>> Let the field rejoice, and all that is in it.
> Then the trees of the wood shall rejoice before the Lord,
>> For He is coming to judge the earth.
> Oh, give thanks to the Lord, for He is good!

for His mercy endures forever.
(1 Chronicles 16:23-27,31-34 NKJV. See also
Psalm 96)

The Children of Israel, God's Model for the World

God chose to accomplish this revelation of Himself by bringing into being a new nation who would be His ambassadors to the world. From the descendants of Abraham a people were to grow who in their national life would be a model for all the world. Through them God would reveal His true nature. He placed His Chosen People in Palestine, at the center of the ancient world, strategically situated between the great nations and empires of Africa, Europe, and Mesopotamia. As Ezekiel wrote: "Thus says the Lord God, 'This is Jerusalem; I have set her in the midst of the nations and the countries all around her'" (5:5 NKJV). The twelve tribes who would descend from the sons of Abraham's grandson, Israel, were to be God's means of revelation. Through the descendants of Abraham all the families of the world would be blessed (Genesis 12:3, 18:18, 22:18, 26:4, 28:14).

Early in their history, God gave His people a code of laws that would direct their way as individuals, as families, and as a nation. These laws are found in the Old Testament books of Exodus, Leviticus, Numbers, and Deuteronomy. The laws encouraged the people of Israel to live unselfish and loving lives for each other and especially for the poor, the widow and orphan, and also for the foreigner residing in their land (see pages 28-30). The laws were strict and punished those who preyed on their fellowman or acted against the general welfare of the people. God intended to lead his people by such collections of law and also by charismatic and inspiring leaders whom He would raise up from among His people as the need arose. For many years God guided His people with such judges as Joshua, Gideon, and Deborah. Israel was to become a flourishing and holy people. By their example, they would lead the nations of the world in the ways of the true God. Israel was to be the means of God's revelation to the ends of the earth. Moses said to his people before they entered Canaan:

"Surely I have taught you statutes and judgments, just as the Lord my God commanded me, that you should act according to them in the land which you go to possess. Therefore be careful to observe them; for this is your wisdom and your understanding in the sight of the peoples who will hear all these statutes, and say, 'Surely this great nation is a wise and understanding people.' For what great nation is there that has God so near it, as the Lord our God is to us, for whatever reason we may call upon Him? And what great nation is there that has such statutes and righteous judgments as are in all this law which I set before you this day?" (Deuteronomy 4:5-8 NKJV)

Non-Israelites were to be welcomed into the worship of Yahweh, Israel's God. At the dedication of the Temple, King Solomon recognized Israel's call to be a light of revelation to the nations of the world. Solomon prayed to Yahweh:

"Moreover, concerning a foreigner, who is not of Your people Israel, but has come from a far country for Your name's sake (for they will hear of Your great name and Your strong hand and Your outstretched arm), when he comes and prays toward this temple, hear in heaven Your dwelling place, and do according to all for which the foreigner calls to You, that all peoples of the earth may know Your name and fear You, as do Your people Israel, and that they may know that this temple which I have built is called by Your name." (1 Kings 8:41-43 NKJV)

The book of Isaiah records the words of the Lord inviting the nations to come to Him, the true Savior of the nations:

"Assemble yourselves and come, draw near together, you survivors of the nations! They have no knowledge who carry about their wooden idols, and keep on praying to a god that cannot save. Declare and present your case; let them take counsel together! Who told this long ago? Who declared it of old? Was it not I, the Lord? And there is no other god besides me, a righteous God and a Savior; there is none besides me. Turn to me and be saved, all the ends of the earth! For I am God, and there is no other." (Isaiah 45:20-22 RSV)

God's Covenant with Israel

So there would be no misunderstanding of what God expected of His people and what they could expect from Him, God made a covenant or testament with the descendants of Israel. It is from this formal agreement that the collected religious books of the Israelites take their name, the Old Testament. God's people ratified the covenant at the beginning of their national life during their journey and sojourn in the Sinai Peninsula.

The covenant that God made with His people contained both

positive and negative conditions. The positive terms of the covenant could be summarized as follows: if they would be His people, worship only Him, and walk in the way that He directed by observing the laws and ordinances that He gave, then He would truly bless and prosper them as His Chosen People. The actual words of the covenant that tell of God's blessings upon His people if they fulfill the covenant are found in Leviticus 26:3-13 and Deuteronomy 28:1-14. Moses' charge to the Israelites before they entered the Promised Land also repeats the blessing that will be theirs if they live by the Covenant:

> "If you obey the commandments of the Lord your God which I command you this day, by loving the Lord your God, by walking in his ways, and by keeping his commandments and his statutes and his ordinances, then you shall live and multiply, and the Lord your God will bless you in the land which you are entering to take possession of it." (Deuteronomy 30:16 RSV)

What an astounding event, the Creator coming into human history to reveal Himself as a loving Father! He invites His people to walk with Him so that He might guide them through life. He directs their footsteps in the way they should go, leading His people to a life in which justice, mercy, tolerance, and love would be foremost. Having revealed His will for humans, God desired the Israelites to bring their wills into harmony with His, to study His laws and ordinances, and to walk "with joy and gladness of heart" (Deuteronomy 28:47) in the paths in which He would lead them. With what joy and delight we might expect God's people to respond to this revelation of His will. And many throughout the history of Israel did so respond.

However, when the august Creator of this universe chose to reveal Himself and His will to His human creatures, He asked for and expected a wholehearted response from His people. God would not tolerate the continued worship of idols. He would not share His people's affection or worship with "gods" that were foreign gods. In his farewell address, Joshua admonished the people:

> "You cannot serve the Lord, for He is a holy God. He is a jealous God; He will not forgive your transgressions nor your sins. If you forsake the Lord and serve foreign gods, then He will turn and do you harm and consume you, after He has done you good." And the people said to Joshua, "No, but we will serve the Lord!" (Joshua 24:19-21 NKJV)

Thus, if God's people became idolaters, if they disobeyed His laws and ignored His ordinances, then they would have to reckon with the negative conditions of the Covenant (Leviticus 26:14-39 and Deuteronomy 28:15-68, 29:1). If the Israelites broke the Covenant by disobeying God's commandments and spurning His statutes, God would bring punishments upon them until they repented and followed His way once more. If they continued to persist in going their own way, He promised that they finally would be scattered over the face of the earth. It was the task and burden of the Old Testament prophets to warn God's people to return to Him and to do His will and not follow their own ways.

The Nature of Sin

The general view of sin today is that it is primarily the breaking of one of God's laws. What is often not understood is that it is also sin to spurn, neglect, or ignore God's will whether or not one violates God's commandments. When out of steadfast love God revealed the way in which He wished people to walk and live, He would not tolerate being ignored. He did not wish His people only to go through the motions of following His law. God wanted their heartfelt observance of His laws and ordinances. He wanted them to look to Him for guidance through life. They were to be a God-centered people. Moses stressed this in his words to the Israelites:

> "Hear, O Israel! The Lord is our God, the Lord is one! And you shall love the Lord your God with all your heart and with all your soul and with all your might. And these words, which I am commanding you today, shall be on your heart; and you shall teach them diligently to your sons and shall talk of them when you sit in your house and when you walk by the way and when you lie down and when you rise up." (Deuteronomy 6:4-7 NASB)

A people who were to meditate on God's word day and night (Psalm 1:2) were not to be a people who would stubbornly follow their own counsels and devices with everyone turned to going his own way. However, it is in just these terms that the prophets of the Old Testament described the behavior of God's people as the following texts portray:

> "But My people would not heed My voice, and Israel would have none of Me. So I gave them over to their own stubborn heart, to walk in their own counsels. Oh, that My people would listen to Me, that Israel would walk in My ways!" (Psalm 81:11-13 NKJV)

. . . "They are a people who err in heart, and they do not regard my ways." Therefore I swore in my anger that they should not enter my rest. (Psalm 95:10b-11 RSV)

I was ready to be sought by those who did not ask for me; I was ready to be found by those who did not seek me. I said, "Here am I, here am I," to a nation that did not call on my name. I spread out my hands all the day to a rebellious people, who walk in a way that is not good, following their own devices; . . . (Isaiah 65:1-2 RSV)

But this command I gave them, "Obey my voice, and I will be your God, and you shall be my people; and walk in all the way that I command you, that it may be well with you." But they did not obey or incline their ear, but walked in their own counsels and the stubbornness of their evil hearts, and went backward and not forward. From the day that your fathers came out of the land of Egypt to this day, I have persistently sent all my servants the prophets to them, day after day; yet they did not listen to me, or incline their ear, but stiffened their neck. They did worse than their fathers. (Jeremiah 7:23-26 RSV)

"Now, therefore, say to the men of Judah and the inhabitants of Jerusalem: 'Thus says the Lord, Behold, I am shaping evil against you and devising a plan against you. Return, every one from his evil way, and amend your ways and your doings.' "But they say, 'That is vain! We will follow our own plans, and will every one act according to the stubbornness of his evil heart.'" (Jeremiah 18:11-12 RSV)

The verses above do not necessarily speak of a people who are violating one or more of God's laws or ordinances. Rather, they describe a people who have turned away from their God to follow their own wills, desires, and hearts.

The Consequences of Israel's Sin

God's covenant people only sporadically were what God intended, a people wholly committed to Him, a people who kept the Covenant by obeying God's laws and ordinances. They obviously, therefore, did not become the light to the gentile nations that God contemplated. Rather, the negative strictures of the Covenant came to be applied to the Israelites. We read in Jeremiah:

> And the Lord said, "Because they have forsaken My law which I set before them, and have not obeyed My voice, nor walked according to it, but they have walked according to the dictates of their own hearts and after the Baals, which their fathers taught them," therefore thus says the Lord of hosts, the God of Israel: "Behold, I will feed them, this people, with wormwood, and give the water of gall to drink. I will scatter them also among the Gentiles, whom neither they nor their fathers have known. And I will send a sword after them until I have consumed them." (Jeremiah 9:13-16 NKJV)

If the reader would doubt the seriousness of this indictment and prophecy, let him reflect upon and ponder the truly unique history of the people of Israel over the past three thousand years. Let him ask himself in the light of the terms of the Old Covenant or Testament found in texts of the covenant cited above (p. 26) to what degree the negative terms and prophecies of the Covenant have come to pass. Unless one is ignorant of the history of the people of Israel over the past millennia, how can one possibly deny the existence of God and of His activity in times past? And yet there is still hope for Israel as found in Leviticus 26:40-45 and Romans 9-11.

However, these prophecies give no people or persons a reason to persecute Israel. On the contrary, if as Christians all that we do is to be done in love, this self-giving love must extend in deeds of love to each descendant of Israel. To gain some understanding, however, of how evil people and nations can act so sinfully against the unfaithful people of Israel in fulfillment of such prophecies, read the book of Habakkuk. Although the Lord chastises, still God will save the faithful among His people.

The Coming of the New Covenant

A remnant, therefore, of God's people were to be preserved. After the time of Jeremiah's words written above, Israel's national existence flickered on for another 600 years. But Israel was no more to be the nation through whom God would reach out in love to the peoples of the world. The Old Testament was to be replaced or superseded by a new covenant or testament. The Old Testament prophets Jeremiah, Isaiah, and Daniel looked forward to a new age and a new covenant that would include all the peoples of the earth. Jeremiah wrote of the new covenant:

"Behold, the days are coming," says the Lord, "when I will make a new covenant with the house of Israel and with the house of Judah--"not according to the covenant that I made with their fathers in the day that I took them by the hand to lead them out of the land of Egypt, My covenant which they broke, though I was a husband to them, says the Lord." (Jeremiah 31:31-32 NKJV)

Isaiah in speaking of the Messiah, the Servant who would be sent to save His people, saw Him as a universal Savior:

Indeed He [God] says, 'It is too small a thing that You should be My Servant to raise up the tribes of Jacob, and to restore the preserved ones of Israel; I will also give You as a light to the Gentiles, that you should be My salvation to the ends of the earth,'" (Isaiah 49:6 NKJV)

Jesus repeatedly identified Himself with the prophet Daniel's prophecy of the universality of the Messiah's kingdom. Jesus answered the high priest who asked Him whether He was the Messiah by saying, "I am, and you will see the Son of Man sitting at the right hand of the Power, and coming with the clouds of heaven" (Mark 14:62 NKJV and Luke 21:27). It is obvious that Jesus was referring to Daniel who long before had written:

"I kept looking in the night visions, and behold, with the clouds of heaven One like a Son of Man was coming, and He came up to the Ancient of Days and was presented before Him. And to Him was given dominion, glory and a kingdom, that all the peoples, nations, and men of every language might serve Him. His dominion is an everlasting dominion which will not pass away; and His kingdom is one which will not be destroyed." (Daniel 7:13-14 NASB)

God would not give up His intention to bring a saving revelation to the humans on this planet. Once more out of His steadfast love for His reasoning creatures, God tried to bring humans into a vital and loving relationship with Himself.

Our God took on our form in the person of His Son, Jesus, and came to live among us. He spent years teaching us the way He would have us live; showing us by His own example how we should live with one another. He spoke to us plainly of His great love for us and revealed His plans and purposes for us. Finally, He paid the price of our debt of guilt.

Christ brought home to us the seriousness of our rebellion against our Creator by dying the cruel death of crucifixion as a sacrifice for our offenses against our God.

The greatest of all the Messianic texts of the Old Testament depicts the Messiah as the servant of God suffering for the sins of His people. Jewish rabbis before the time of Jesus regarded it as a Messianic prophecy.[2] Chapter fifty-three of Isaiah prophesies that the Messiah would be rejected by His own people, suffer and die for their sins, and see the result of His life and death for humankind. It is a text often quoted in the New Testament as referring to Jesus (Matthew 8:17, John 12:38, Acts 8:30-33, Romans 10:16). Isaiah prophesied many hundreds of years before the life of Jesus:

(Christ's Life)
Who has believed what we have heard? And to whom has the arm of the Lord been revealed? For he grew up before him like a young plant, and like a root out of dry ground; he had no form or comeliness that we should look at him, and no beauty that we should desire him. He was despised and rejected by men; a man of sorrows and acquainted with grief; as one from whom men hide their faces he was despised and we esteemed him not.

(Christ's Suffering Early Good Friday)
Surely he has borne our griefs and carried our sorrows; yet we esteemed him stricken, smitten by God, and afflicted. But he was wounded for our transgressions, he was bruised for our iniquities; upon him was the chastisement that made us whole, and with the marks of his beatings we are healed. All we like sheep have gone astray; we have turned every one to his own way; and the Lord has laid on him the iniquity of us all.

(Christ's Trial, Crucifixion and Burial)
He was oppressed, and he was afflicted, yet he opened not his mouth; like a lamb that is led to the slaughter, and like a sheep that before its shearers is dumb, so he opened not his mouth. By oppression and judgment he was taken away; and as for his generation, who considered that he was cut off out of the land of the living, stricken for the transgression of my people?

---

2 Edersheim, Alfred, 1886, *The Life and Times of Jesus the Messiah,* vol. 2, Appendix IX, List of Old Testament Passages Messianically Applied in Ancient Rabbinic Writings (Chicago: W.P. Blessing Co.), p. 727.

And they made his grave with the wicked and with a rich man in his death, although he had done no violence, and there was no deceit in his mouth. Yet it was the will of the Lord to bruise him; he has put him to grief; when he makes himself an offering for sin.

(The Result of Christ's Passion, His Church)
He shall see his offspring, he shall prolong his days; the will of the Lord shall prosper in his hand; he shall see the fruit of the travail of his soul and be satisfied; by his knowledge shall the righteous one, my servant, make many righteous; and he shall bear their iniquities. Therefore I will divide him a portion with the great, and he shall divide the spoil with the strong; because he poured out his soul to death, and was numbered with the transgressors; yet he bore the sins of many, and made intercession for the transgressors. (Isaiah 53 RSV)

Christ's life ushered in the New Covenant. No longer were God's Chosen People to be of one ethnic group. Rather, the new people of God would be all who through their faith in the sacrifice of God's Son receive God's pardon for their sins. They are God's new Chosen People, chosen to bring the light of God's revelation to all the world (1 Peter 2:9-10). By their lives they are to reflect God's love in their love for others. By their words, they are to tell all people of God's love and concern for His creatures.

God would have humans know Him as a God of love and compassion. He would walk with them through life, lead them in the path their lives should take, and guide them in the way that they should live with one another. Finally, as men and women who walked with their God through life, their destiny is to dwell in the presence of their God through all eternity. This is God's purpose for humankind (Ephesians 1:3-14).

The World's Rejection of God's Love in Christ

Nonetheless, the vast majority of this world's inhabitants still refuses or ignores the invitation of their God to be His children. They, as the Israelites of old, choose to follow their own devices and counsels through life. They do not feel that they need to seek out the will of the Creator for their lives. They guide their lives by their own desires. In the attempt to escape their God, they devise numerous rationalizations for their rebellious and self-centered behavior.

The arguments used by people today to avoid confronting the invitation of their gracious God range from the naive to the tortuously sophisticated. All, however, have the same end in view—to maintain the rebellion of the creature against the Creator. The sin of the story of Adam and Eve is endlessly repeated.

Many people on this earth insist on maintaining their independence from God. Like willful children ignoring the guidance of their parents, they insist on being self-determining in everything. Like arrogant children who consider themselves their parents' equals if not superiors, they maintain that man, not God, is the measure of all things.

This is the basic sin—to ignore, to disregard, to disparage, to argue with, or to scorn one's God and His revelation. It is the sin of human pride; what the Greeks called "*hubris*," that is, arrogant impudence. It is the sin of those who cannot bear to give glory to any but themselves, who feel diminished if they must acknowledge their Creator or a wisdom beyond their own. It is the sin of idolatry of one's self—the grasping for self-glorification that eclipses any desire to give glory to God.

Self-righteousness in One's Own Eyes

It is the sin of those people who say that they don't have to be religious to lead a "good" life. They insist that their lives will bear comparison to any of those who follow the Christian way of life. In their own view, they feel that they are living as exemplary a life as any one. In the estimation of many people, they well might be. They may seek out good causes for which to work. They may contribute to the welfare of their communities. They may be good citizens in their own eyes and in the eyes of the world. They do not break the Ten Commandments—well, at least in no major way. From a human standpoint, their righteousness in civil affairs may be beyond reproach. That anyone would consider them to any degree sinful, they regard as rather amusing.

The "religion" of civil righteousness so prevalent today, however, is still a false religion. When our Creator gives guidance and direction as to how we should live our lives, when He invites us to walk with Him and to follow His way through our life, it is an act of pride and arrogance to ignore His guidance and to insist on doing things our way. The writer of the book of Hebrews wrote in this connection, "without faith it is impossible to please Him" (Hebrews 11:6 NKJV).

The sin of civil righteousness lies in that it substitutes our own values, goals, and definitions of what is good for those of God's. When our God asks that we walk in His way, we insult and rebuff our Creator when we turn our back on Him and devise our own way. In their pride, humans would define for themselves what is good and evil. They feel no necessity to defer to their God. They wish to acknowledge no greater intellect or higher authority than themselves. In their conceit, they set themselves up as judges over what their Maker has revealed concerning His purpose and will for them as found in the Scriptures.

The Pervasiveness of Sin

Thus, sin exists. It exists for all who are aware of God's law, for the Scriptures plainly teach that knowingly to violate a commandment is to sin against one's Creator. As was discussed above, however, sin also exists in a much more basic sense. No matter how upright an individual may be, to ignore God's revelation is to sin. No matter with what care we may plan our lives, to disregard God's desire to have us walk with Him in His chosen paths is to sin. No matter how ethical an individual may consider himself to be, to ignore God's way of life for him as set forth in the Scriptures is to sin against one's Creator. The basic sin of humans is pride—pride of self, pride of intellect, pride of attainment. They all set one apart from the Creator and His purposes for us, for "Man's determination to manage by himself is really striving against God's will."[3]

This then is sin:
When we come to know God's law for us—
we disobey it.
When we come to know God's love for us—
we spurn it.
When we come to know God's will for us—
we ignore it.
When we come to know God's way for us—
we insist on going our own way.

The Consequences of Unforgiven Sin

If a person, however, insists on going his own way in this life, separating himself from his God during his lifetime, then he also has set himself apart from the love of God and His presence for all time and eternity. God has not condemned him. Rather, the individual has chosen of his own free will to separate himself from his God. Our God through Christ has reached down to us to save us from drowning in the sea of our sin. If we shake off His saving hand, rebuff His aid, and drown in our sin, is He to

---

3 Gottfried Quell et al., 1951, *Book III*, Sin, in *Bible Key Words from Gerhard Kittel's Theologisches Woerterbuch Zum Neuen Testament* (New York, Harper and Brothers, Publishers), p. 76.

blame? Jesus said in this regard:

> He who believes in me, believes not in me but in him who sent
> me. And he who sees me sees him who sent me. I have come as
> light into the world, that whoever believes in me may not remain
> in darkness. If any one hears my sayings and does not keep
> them, I do not judge him; for I did not come to judge the world
> but to save the world. He who rejects me and does not receive
> my sayings has a judge; the word that I have spoken will be his
> judge on the last day." (John 12:44-48 RSV)

Our Lord honors the decision of those who reject Him and His
Word during this life. Nor will He force them to live in communion with
Him in the next life. Unfortunately, for such people, eternal separation from
God is also the basic definition of hell.

The Love of God for Sinners

However, as was discussed in chapter two, God does not wish the
spiritual death of the sinner. On the contrary, in the book of Ezekiel He
pleads: "For I have no pleasure in the death of anyone, says the Lord God;
so turn and live" (18:32 RSV).

Therefore, God made a New Testament or Covenant with
humankind. He sent His Son to bring into existence the New Testament to
be made with us. Its conditions are plain: We are to repent and turn away
from our sinful lives to new lives of self-giving love for others; through our
faith in the sacrifice made by God's Son for the forgiveness of our sin, we
become God's children and heirs of His eternal kingdom. Paul summed up
his message to his hearers as: "that they should repent and turn to God,
performing deeds appropriate to repentance" (Acts 26:20).

Those who become part of the New Covenant with their God are
called to follow the new way of life that God promised that He would write
upon their hearts (Jeremiah 31:33). Jesus spent his ministry teaching this
new way of life by word and action. In the evening before He was crucified,
He summed up His teaching by asking that we love one another with the
same love that He had for us, a love He showed by coming to this earth to
lay down His life for us. It is a way of life that Paul described so well in a
chapter he began and ended by writing: "And I will show you a still MORE
EXCELLENT WAY.... Make love your aim" (1 Corinthians 12:31b-14:1a
RSV).

Faith and love sum up the Christianity of the New Covenant. It is
faith in the love of God for us expressed in the life, death, and resurrection

of His Son, Jesus Christ who died to reconcile us with the Father. It is a life of love for our neighbor following the example of Jesus in loving one another as He loved us; for greater love has no man than this, that a man lay down his life for his friends (John 15:12-13).

Chapter Four

THE NEW COMMANDMENT OF JESUS CHRIST: A NEW WAY FOR A NEW AGE

Jesus and His New Commandment

The evening before He was crucified, Jesus finally finished His teaching about the way of life His followers were to live. He summed up His new way of life by saying:

> "A new commandment I give to you, that you love one another; as I have loved you, that you also love one another. By this all will know that you are My disciples, if you have love for one another." (John 13:34-35 NKJV)

In this new commandment, Jesus gave a fundamental and cardinal principle to guide His people in the way they should live. Just a little later during that last supper, Jesus repeated His commandment to that quiet circle of disciples:

> "As the Father loved Me, I also have loved you; continue in My love. If you keep My commandments, you will abide in My love, just as I have kept My Father's commandments and abide in His love. . . . This is My commandment, that you love one another as I have loved you. Greater love has no one than this, that he lay down his life for his friends." (John 15:9-14 NKJV)

For obvious emphasis, just a few words later, Jesus added:

> "These things I command you, that you love one another." (John 15:17)

The next day, Good Friday, Jesus' disciples were to see just how great His love was for the humans on this earth.

With these final words about the way of life He would have His followers live, Jesus brought into existence a way of life, an ethic, unknown before His time. His instruction about the way humans should live with one another was revolutionary. These teachings, considered by many of His fellow Jews to be scandalous new ideas, helped bring Him to the cross on which He was crucified. Jesus' new way of life was so revolutionary that He had to slowly introduce it over the three years of His ministry. It was only with the giving of the New Commandment on the night before His crucifixion that Jesus brought to completion His instructions on how His followers were to live.

It is a common belief among many Biblical theologians that almost everything in Jesus' ethical teaching can be found in the Old Testament or in the surrounding cultures.[1] Therefore, the ethics of Christ have been considered only derived from other sources and thus hardly original. The contention of the present writer is that this is most assuredly not so. However, if one takes the ethical teachings of Christ found in the Gospels as all of equal importance without realizing the progressive revelation involved, perhaps one can be so led astray.

The Old Testament Portrays a God of Steadfast Love

In many ways, Jesus' new way of life was in marked contrast with that of the Old Testament; yet it did not repudiate the Old Testament. Jesus' way of life was meant to go beyond and fulfill the Old Testament's moral law, not to abolish it.

The stress that Jesus put on love in the New Commandment had its forerunner in the Old Testament. When a scribe asked Jesus which commandment was first of all, Jesus, quoting from both Deuteronomy 6:4 and Leviticus 19:18 responded:

> "The first of all the commandments is: 'Hear, O Israel, the Lord our God is one Lord. 'And you shall love the Lord your God with all your heart, with all your soul, with all your mind, and with all

---

1 An excellent example of this is to be found in the 1993 book by Wayne A. Meeks, the Woolsey Professor of Biblical Studies at Yale University, entitled: *The Origins of Christian Morality: The First Two Centuries* (New Haven: Yale University Press), 275 pp. Meeks contends on page 227 that "Jesus did not arrive in Galilee proclaiming a complete, systematic, and novel Christian ethic, nor even a compact set of fundamental principles that only had to be explicated by his disciples. There was not even, I have argued, any such thing as 'New Testament ethics.'"

your strength.' This is the first commandment. "And the second, like it, is this: 'You shall love your neighbor as yourself.' There is no other commandment greater than these." (Mark 12:29-31 NKJV)

The primary way in which God guided His Old Testament people in this love was with the laws, ordinances, and statutes found in the first five books of the Old Testament, the Torah of the Jewish people. God set up His law to direct His people in the way that they should walk. The Jews count 613 of these laws. The laws were to guide the lives of the Israelites in a rather detailed fashion. God expected His people to walk joyfully in His laws. Through these laws, Israel was to be God's model for the nations of the world.

Many of the laws dealt with the ceremonial life and religious activity of God's people. There were laws that set up the major religious holy days: the festival of Passover, and the thanksgiving holidays of Pentecost and Tabernacles. There were many laws that governed the observance of the Sabbath, the seventh sabbatical year, and the fiftieth year of Jubilee. The Law of Moses sets up detailed instruction of how temple worship and the sacrifices were to be carried out. There were many laws that were concerned with ritual uncleanness, religious purity and rites of purification, the types of food to be eaten, and so forth. God wanted His people to live pious lives that recognized His governance and authority over them.

A great many laws of the Old Testament forbade various selfish, violent, or criminal acts. They were given so that God's people could live in peace and tranquility. The general welfare of the whole society was more important than any personal interests of individuals that might harm the well-being of the community. Because the happiness and well-being of humans, both of the adults but especially of the young, is so dependent on a stable family structure, strict laws were given to protect the stability of family life. Those individuals, for example, whose selfishness led them through adultery to destroy the happiness of another person's family life were dealt with severely.

There were laws that prescribed how people should carry out God's will that "you shall love your neighbor as yourself" (Leviticus 19:18). The God of Israel especially declared his care and compassion for the strangers in the land, the widows and orphans, the hired help, women, and the poor. The following is an example that illustrates God's concern with the welfare of all the individuals within the society:

"And you shall not wrong a stranger or oppress him, for you were strangers in the land of Egypt. You shall not afflict any widow or orphan. If you afflict him at all, and if he does cry out to Me, I will surely hear his cry; and My anger will be kindled, and I will kill you with the sword; and your wives shall become widows and your children fatherless. If you lend money to My people, to the poor among you, you are not to act as a creditor to him; you shall not charge him interest. If you ever take your neighbor's cloak as a pledge, you are to return it to him before the sun sets, for that is his only covering; it is his cloak for his body. What else shall he sleep in? And it shall come about that when he cries out to Me, I will hear him, for I am gracious." (Exodus 22:21-27 NASB)

The laws given by Israel's God singled out His concern for the foreign visitor or sojourner in the land:

"The stranger who dwells among you shall be to you as one born among you, and you shall love him as yourself; for you were strangers in the land of Egypt: I am the Lord your God." (Leviticus 19:34 NKJV)

As an aid to caring for those in need, God instructed the farmers not to glean their fields or vineyards but to leave the gleanings for the poor and the stranger. Nor were they to harvest their fields to the very border that the poor might be fed:

When you reap the harvest of your land, you shall not reap your field to its very border, neither shall you gather the gleanings after your harvest. And you shall not strip your vineyard bare, neither shall you gather the fallen grapes of your vineyard; you shall leave them for the poor and for the sojourner: I am the Lord your God. (Leviticus 19:9-10 RSV)

Anyone who was hungry could eat as much as he liked of the crops in a field or the grapes in a vineyard, but he was not to gather the produce into a container:

When you enter your neighbor's vineyard, then you may eat grapes until you are fully satisfied, but you shall not put any in your basket. When you enter your neighbor's standing grain, then you may pluck heads with your hand, but you shall not wield a sickle in your neighbor's standing grain. (Deuteronomy 23:24-25 NASB)

God asks that His people be open-handed with those who are less prosperous than they are. They are not to enrich themselves at the expense of the poor, but rather out of reverence for their God to aid and sustain them:

> Now in case a countryman of yours becomes poor and his means with regard to you falter, then you are to sustain him, like a stranger or a sojourner, that he may live with you. Do not take usurious interest from him, but revere your God, that your countryman might live with you. You shall not give him your silver at interest, nor your food for gain. I am the Lord your God, who brought you out of the land of Egypt to give you the land of Canaan and to be your God. (Leviticus 25:35-43 NASB)

Every seventh year was a Sabbatical year. It was a year of rest for all in the household: family, servants, and even the domestic animals. In that year, the lands were neither to be sown nor reaped (Leviticus 25:1-7). The farmer's household was to live on the abundant harvest promised in the year before the Sabbatical year (Leviticus 25:20-22). The poor were to be free to take what they needed during the Sabbatical year of what had grown by itself in the fields or of the grapes in the unpruned vineyard:

> "And you shall sow your land for six years and gather in its yield, but on the seventh year you shall let it rest and lie fallow, so that the needy of your people may eat; and whatever they leave the beast of the field may eat. You are to do the same with your vineyard and your olive grove." (Exodus 23:10-11 NASB)

At the time of the Sabbatical year, a Hebrew debtor was freed from the debts he incurred in the past six years (Deuteronomy 15:1-11):

> "At the end of every seven years you shall grant a remission of debts. And this is the manner of remission: every creditor shall release what he has loaned to his neighbor; he shall not exact it of his neighbor and his brother, because the Lord's remission has been proclaimed. From a foreigner you may exact it, but your hand shall release whatever of yours is with your brother. . .

. If there is a poor man with you, one of your brothers, in any of the towns in the land which the Lord your God is giving you, you shall not harden your heart, nor close your hand from your poor brother; but you shall freely open your hand to him, and shall generously lend him sufficient for his need in whatever he lacks. Beware, lest there is a base thought in your heart, saying, 'The seventh year, the year of remission, is near,' and your eye is hostile toward your poor brother, and you give him nothing; then he may cry to the Lord against you, and it will be a sin in you. You shall generously give to him, and your heart shall not be grieved when you give to him, because for this thing the Lord your God will bless you in all your work and in all your undertakings.'" Deuteronomy 15:1-3, 7-10 NASB)

A Hebrew man or woman who became enslaved because of his debts was to be freed in the sabbatical year. His or her master was to provide enough initial gifts and support so that the former slave would have a new start in life:

"If your kinsman, a Hebrew man or woman, is sold to you, then he shall serve you six years, but in the seventh year you shall set him free. And when you set him free, you shall not send him away empty-handed. You shall furnish him liberally from your flock and from your threshing floor and from your wine vat; you shall give to him as the Lord your God has blessed you. And you shall remember that you were a slave in the land of Egypt, and the Lord your God redeemed you; therefore I command you this today." (Deuteronomy 15:12-14 NASB)

Every fiftieth year was the year of Jubilee. In that year, the ancestral land belonging to a family which had been lost during the previous fifty years was to be returned to them (Leviticus 25:25-28). The ancient Israelites were truly to live by the maxim, "You shall love your neighbor as yourself" (Leviticus 19:18 RSV).

The employee or hired man or woman was also under the protection of their God. Concerning these, God said:

You shall not oppress a hired servant who is poor and needy, whether one of your brethren or one of the aliens who is in your land within your gates. Each day you shall give him his wages, and not let the sun go down on it, for he is poor and has set his heart on it; lest he cry out against you to the Lord, and it be sin to you. (Deuteronomy 24:14-15 NKJV)

God's love and concern also extended to the concubine. She was to have her rights in Old Testament society:

And if a man sells his daughter as a female slave, she is not to go free as the male slaves do. If she is displeasing in the eyes of her master who designated her for himself, the he shall let her be redeemed. He does not have authority to sell her to a foreign people because of his unfairness to her. And if he designates her for his son, he shall deal with her according to the custom of daughters. If he takes to himself another woman, he may not reduce her food, her clothing, or her conjugal rights. And if he will not do these three things for her, the she shall go out for nothing, without payment of money. (Exodus 21:7-11 NASB)

In view of the above, how false is the depiction of the God of the Old Testament as a wrathful and harsh Deity. God would care for all; and especially he would oversee the welfare of those who in any society are so often oppressed and exploited—the stranger, the widow and orphan, employees, women, and the poor. As is so many times depicted in the Old Testament, God is a God of *chesed*, a Hebrew word that often is translated as kindliness or loving kindness, compassion, steadfast love, and mercy. Nevertheless, toward those who act selfishly, harshly, and harmfully toward their neighbor, God is also a God of strict justice who out of His love for the greater welfare of all His people would have such unjust or predatory behavior severely punished.

Israel's Keeping of the Mosaic Law

In the many hundreds of years between the giving of the Mosaic Law and the advent of the Christ, there were times when the people truly endeavored fully to observe God's law. However, there were other times when the law was completely neglected. According to God's prophets, there were also far too many occasions when although the Israelites might piously observe the ceremonial law and the many laws against gross evil, they were not too keen on living a life of love toward those in need in their communities.

It is commonly taken for granted that people who live pious lives are also people who live good and loving lives. However, this is not necessarily so. The French philosopher and mathematician Blaise Pascal (1623-1662) made a very discerning observation when he wrote: "Experience makes us see an enormous difference between piety and goodness."[2]

Upon reflection, Pascal's insight is one of the keys to understanding much of the tension between the people of the Old Testament and their God. Throughout their history the people of Israel were quite often willing to give their God piety, but to serve Him by treating their neighbor with goodness and love—that seems to have been asking too much. God certainly expected piety in the conduct of His people as they went about their lives and attended to their religious functions, but He also wanted *chesed*, a life of kindliness, mercy, and love towards others.

Through His prophets, God rebuked His Old Testament people for acting so piously toward Him, and so unlovingly toward their neighbor. In the first chapter of Isaiah, God admonished His people:

> "What to me is the multitude of your sacrifices?" says the Lord; "I have had enough of burnt offerings of rams and the fat of fed beasts; I do not delight in the blood of bulls, or of lambs, or of he-goats. When you come to appear before me, who requires of you this trampling of my courts? Bring no more vain offerings; incense is an abomination to me. New moon and sabbath and the calling of assemblies--I cannot endure iniquity and solemn assembly. Your new moons and your appointed feasts my soul hates; they have become a burden to me, I am weary of bearing them. When you spread forth your hands, I will hide my eyes from you; even though you make many prayers, I will not listen; your hands are full of blood.
>
> Wash yourselves; make yourselves clean; remove the evil of your doings from before my eyes; cease to do evil, learn to do good; seek justice, correct oppression; defend the fatherless, plead for the widow." (Isaiah 1:11-17 RSV)

And in one of the last chapters of Isaiah, God similarly chided:

> "Shout with the voice of a trumpet blast; tell my people of their sins! Yet they act so pious! They come to the Temple every day

---

2 Blaise Pascal, *Thoughts*, sec., VII, no., 496 in the *Harvard Classics* (New York: F.F. Collier & Son), vol. 48, p. 165.

and are so delighted to hear the reading of my laws--just as though they would obey them--just as though they don't despise the commandments of their God! How anxious they are to worship correctly; oh, how they love the Temple services!"

"We have fasted before you," they say. "Why aren't you impressed? Why don't you see our sacrifices? Why don't you hear our prayers? We have done much penance, and you don't even notice it!"

"I'll tell you why! Because you are living in evil pleasure even while you are fasting, and you keep right on oppressing your workers. Look, what good is fasting when you keep on fighting and quarreling? This kind of fasting will never get you anywhere with me. Is this what I want--this doing of penance and bowing like reeds in the wind and putting on sackcloth and covering yourselves with ashes? Is this what you call fasting?

No, the kind of fast that I want is that you stop oppressing those who work for you and treat them fairly and give them what they earn. I want you to share your food with the hungry and bring right into your own homes those who are helpless, poor and destitute. Clothe those who are cold and don't hide from relatives who need your help." (Isaiah 58:1-7 Living Bible)

Through the prophet Hosea, God also reproached His people:

"What shall I do with you, O Ephraim? What shall I do with you, O Judah? Your love is like a morning cloud, like the dew that goes early away. Therefore I have hewn them by the prophets, I have slain them by the words of my mouth, and my judgment goes forth as the light. For I desire steadfast love and not sacrifice, the knowledge of God, rather than burnt offerings." (Hosea 6:4-6 RSV)

In the book of Amos God details the sins of Israel and then tells what He truly wants:

Thus says the Lord: "For three transgressions of Israel, and for four, I will not revoke the punishment; because they sell the righteous for silver, and the needy for a pair of shoes--they that trample the head of the poor into the dust of the ground, and turn aside the way of the afflicted; a man and his father go into the same maiden, so that my holy name is profaned; they lay themselves down beside every altar upon garments taken in pledge; and in the house of their God they drink the wine of those who have been fined." . . .

"I hate, I despise your feasts, and I take no delight in your solemn assemblies. Even though you offer me your burnt offerings, I will not accept them, and the peace offerings of your fatted beasts I will not look upon. Take away from me the noise of your songs; to the melody of your harps I will not listen. But let justice roll down like waters, and righteousness like an everflowing stream." (Amos 2:6-8 and 5:21-24 RSV)

Micah was a contemporary of Isaiah, Hosea, and Amos, and through him the word of the Lord came:

"With what shall I come before the Lord, and bow myself before the God on high? Shall I come before him with burnt offerings, with calves a year old? Will the Lord be pleased with thousands of rams, with ten thousands of rivers of oil? Shall I give my first-born for my transgression, the fruit of my body for the sin of my soul?" He has showed you, O man, what is good; and what does the Lord require of you but to do justice, to show steadfast love, and to walk humbly with your God? (Micah 6:6-8 RSV)

But it was to little purpose that Isaiah, Hosea, Amos, and Micah prophesied to God's people. They did not turn from their way, and in 722 B.C., the armies of Assyria carried away the northern ten tribes of Israel into permanent exile. Around a century later, Jeremiah was called by God to save the tribe of Judah from a similar fate; and his message was similar to that of the earlier prophets:

The word that came to Jeremiah from the Lord: "Stand in the gate of the Lord's house, and proclaim there this word, and say, Hear the word of the Lord, all you men of Judah who enter these gates to worship the Lord. Thus says the Lord of hosts, the God of Israel, Amend your ways and your doings, and I will let you dwell in this place. Do not trust in these deceptive words: 'This is the temple of the Lord, the temple of the Lord, the temple of the Lord.' "For if you truly amend your ways and your doings, if you truly execute justice with one another, if you do not oppress the alien, the fatherless or the widow, or shed innocent blood in this place, and if you do not go after other gods to your own hurt, then I will let you dwell in this place, in the land that I gave of old to your fathers for ever." (Jeremiah 7:1-7 RSV)

But the people of Judah gave the same response to Jeremiah that Israel had given to Amos, who wrote, "They hate him who reproves in the gate, and they abhor him who speaks the truth, . . ." (Amos 5:10 RSV). They did not listen to Jeremiah, and the armies of Babylonia carried them into exile in 586 B.C. However, God does not give up on His people. He sent them the prophet Ezekiel. But although the people with pious, cheerful willingness listened to Ezekiel's message their heart was set on their own selfish purposes. Therefore, the Lord said to Ezekiel:

"As for you, son of man, your people who talk together about you by the walls and at the doors of the houses, say to one another, each to his brother, 'Come, and hear what the word is that comes forth from the Lord.' And they come to you as people come, and they sit before you as my people, and they hear what you say but they will not do it; for with their lips they show much love, but their heart is set on gain. And, lo, you are to them like one who sings love songs with a beautiful voice and plays well on an instrument, for they hear what you say, but they will not do it. When this [retribution] comes--and come it will!--then they will know that a prophet has been among them." (Ezekiel 33:30-33 RSV)

The Jews had set up times of mourning during the seventy years they had spent away from their ancestral home. Later after they had returned, they wondered if they should continue these mourning periods. The following is found in the book of Zechariah:

Now in the fourth year of King Darius it came to pass that the word of the Lord came to Zechariah, . . . when the people sent Sherezer with Regem-Melech and his men, to the house of God, to pray before the Lord, and to ask the priests who were in the house of the Lord of hosts, and the prophets, saying, "Should I weep in the fifth month and fast as I have done for so many years?" Then the word of the Lord of hosts came to me, saying, "Say to all the people of the land, and to the priests:

'When you fasted and mourned in the fifth and seventh months during those seventy years, did you really fast for Me--for Me? 'When you eat and when you drink, do you not eat and drink for yourselves? 'Should you not have obeyed the words which the Lord proclaimed through the former prophets when Jerusalem and the cities around it were inhabited and prosperous, and the South and the Lowland were inhabited.'?"

Then the word of the Lord came to Zechariah, saying, "Thus says the Lord of hosts:

'Execute true justice,

Show mercy and compassion everyone to his brother.

Do not oppress the widow or the fatherless, the alien or the poor.

Let none of you plan evil in his heart against his brother.'

But they refused to heed, shrugged their shoulders, and stopped their ears so that they could not hear." (Zechariah 7:2-11 NKJV)

The burden or message of the prophets remained the same down to the last prophet of the Old Testament, Malachi. The people were willing to show piety in their observance of religious rites and rituals but not goodness and love in their lives. Malachi draws this distinction in the matter of divorce:

Another thing you do: You flood the Lord's altar with tears. You weep and wail because he no longer pays attention to your offerings or accepts them with pleasure from your hands. You ask, "Why?" It is because the Lord is acting as the witness between you and the wife of your youth, because you have broken faith with her, though she is your partner, the wife of your marriage covenant. Has not the Lord made them one? In flesh and spirit they are his. And why one? Because he was seeking godly offspring. So guard yourself in your spirit, and do not break faith with the wife of your youth. " I hate divorce," says the Lord God of Israel, . . . "So guard yourself in your spirit, and do not break faith." (Malachi 2:13-16 NIV)

Things had not changed in the times of Jesus. In the years of His ministry, Jesus' words were in keeping with those of the prophets when He decried the nominal practice of religion. Matthew recorded Jesus' denunciation of those among the religious leaders who loved to go piously through the rituals of their religion but neglected goodness and love:

> "Woe to you, scribes and Pharisees, hypocrites! For you devour widows' houses, and for a pretense make long prayers. Therefore you will receive greater condemnation. . . . "Woe to you, scribes and Pharisees, hypocrites! For you pay tithe of mint and anise and cummin, and have neglected the weightier matters of the law: justice and mercy and faith. These you ought to have done, without leaving the others undone." (Matthew 23:14, 23 NKJV; see also Mark 12:38-40)

The Modification of God's Law through Tradition

In addition to the written Mosaic Law, an unwritten tradition had grown up over the centuries composed of interpretations by the rabbis of the Biblical Mosaic Law and also an oral body of additional laws. The pious belief of many Jews is that God gave this oral law to Moses at Mt. Sinai at the same time as the written law. There is, however, no Biblical support for this belief. It is far more likely that the oral law and the traditional interpretations of the Mosaic Law began to come into being about the time of the Exile, over 500 years before Christ. At that time the Babylonian conquerors of the Jews had forcibly removed many of them from their homeland and exiled them for many decades in Mesopotamia. Consequently, they were without their temple in Jerusalem that had been the center of their religious life.

Many Jews saw this exile as a punishment from God because of their previous neglect of His law. In response to this sense of guilt and perhaps because of the loss of the temple in Jerusalem, the holy books of their religion and especially the Mosaic Law became the center of Jewish religious observance. The study of the Law became a major scholarly activity. Over the next hundreds of years, a considerable literature grew up that dealt with the interpretation of the Mosaic Law. Other additions to this oral tradition were laws that regulated areas of life not covered by Mosaic Law, the interpretation of these supplementary laws, and a body of pious stories and other literature.

When Jesus spoke about the "Tradition" of His people, He was referring to this large body of oral teaching. One of the purposes of this oral tradition was to build a fence around the Law so that it would be difficult even to approach violating the Mosaic Law. This is so stated in the *Talmud*, a later version of this oral tradition finally committed to writing in the second century after Christ. For example, so as to never violate the commandment that forbids misusing God's name, it became the practice neither to utter nor write God's name. The word "*Adonai*" meaning "Lord" was substituted whenever God's name, "Yahweh," was to be used. Even today this practice of avoiding the use of God's name is carried on, for example, in some Jewish newspapers where the word "God" is written as "G-d."

To cite another example—in order to make it almost impossible ever to violate the Mosaic law: "You shall not boil a young goat in its mother's milk" (Exodus 23:19b NKJV), observant Jews follow the tradition of never having dairy and meat foods at the same meal. Observant Jews even today in their homes maintain separate sets of dishes for meals with dairy foods and for meals with meat courses. Thus, they never have dairy and meat foods at the same meal even if it is only a remnant on an improperly washed plate. They also in time came to have separate dairy and meat restaurants. Examples of this nature can be multiplied almost endlessly.

The "Tradition" of the Jews became voluminous. It took full-time scholars such as lawyers, scribes, or such wealthy men of leisure as the Pharisees, to become familiar with the Tradition in all its ramifications. Unfortunately, among those who were knowledgeable about the Tradition and the Law, this led many times to contempt toward those who did not know the Law. The common people in the essential pursuit of their daily bread had no leisure for extensive study of the Tradition. The words of the Jewish leaders to the officers who failed to carry out their orders to arrest Jesus reek with this disdain, "Are you also deceived? Have any of the rulers or the Pharisees believed in Him? But this crowd that does not know the law is accursed" (John 7:47b-49 NKJV).

Christ criticized this heaping up of law upon law far beyond what the Old Testament required. It angered Him to see the Pharisees, scribes, and lawyers binding the consciences of His people with their man-made traditions. To the lawyers He said: "Woe to you also, you lawyers! For you load men with burdens hard to bear, and you yourselves do not touch the burdens with one of your fingers" (Luke 11:46 NKJV).

Mark records a confrontation between Jesus and the Pharisees over their additions and manipulation of the Law. Jesus is also once more following in the footsteps of the prophets in rebuking the scribes and Pharisees for piously following their traditions and rituals while neglecting God's command to live in love toward their parents:

> Then the Pharisees and some of the scribes came together to Him, having come from Jerusalem. And when they saw some of His disciples eat bread with defiled, that is, unwashed hands, they found fault. For the Pharisees and all the Jews do not eat

unless they wash their hands in a special way, holding the tradition of the elders. And when they come from the marketplace, they do not eat unless they wash. And there are many other things which they have received and hold, like the washing of cups, pitchers, copper vessels, and couches. Then the Pharisees and scribes asked Him, "Why do Your disciples not walk according to the tradition of the elders, but eat bread with unwashed hands?" He answered and said to them, 'Well did Isaiah prophesy of you hypocrites, as it is written: 'This people honors Me with their lips, but their heart is far from Me. And in vain they worship Me, teaching as doctrines the commandments of men.' "For laying aside the commandment of God, you hold the tradition of men--the washing of pitchers and cups, and many other such things you do." And He said to them, "All too well you reject the commandment of God, that you may keep your tradition. "For Moses said, 'Honor your father and your mother'; and, 'He who curses father or mother, let him be put to death.' "But you say, 'If a man says to his father or mother: whatever you might have profited by me is Corban (that is, a gift [to God]), he shall be free'; "and you no longer let him do anything for his father or his mother, "making the word of God of no effect through your tradition which you have handed down. And many such things you do." (Mark 7:1-13 NKJV)

A good example of what Jesus was speaking about concerns how the Jews managed to circumvent one of the Old Testament laws concerning the Sabbatical year. As mentioned above, every seventh year the Hebrew people were to forgive all debts that they made to their fellow Hebrews (see pages 40-41).

This law appears to have been an onerous one for the Jews. They could not trust God's promise that His blessing would really make up for their forgiveness of the debts owed them. Therefore, the Rabbi Hillel (c. 70 B.C.- 10 A.D.) instituted a subterfuge called "The *Pruzbul*" in order to evade and nullify this requirement to forgive debts. *Pruzbul* was explained in a recent (1986) Jewish newspaper and is summarized as follows: The forgiving and voiding of all private debts is one of the features of the Sabbatical year. The great sage Hillel instituted *Pruzbul* so that people would continue to loan money in the years just before the sabbatical year. He did this by allowing people to transfer their debts to a rabbinical court thus making them non-private. As they are no longer private debts, they are able to be collected during the Sabbatical year. This transfer of debt can be done verbally or by signing the following form before Rosh Hashanah: "FORM FOR PRUZBUL: I, the undersigned transfer to you, Rabbis (name), (name), and (name), all debts owed to me, written or verbal, so that I may collect them at any time I so desire. Date. Signature."[3]

The above decision of the Rabbi Hillel to institute *Pruzbul* was given a few decades before Jesus' own ministry. One can hardly find a better example to illustrate Jesus' charge that the religious leaders of His people were "making the word of God of no effect through your tradition which you have handed down." Also, what an excellent illustration this is of people piously pretending to follow the letter of the law while ignoring God's will that they should show love and goodness toward their neighbor.

Jesus' New Way of Life

Jesus, however, went beyond criticizing the way the people were keeping the Law. He brought a new way of life into existence to cure the past abuses of the Law. The Sermon on the Mount (Matthew 5-7) shows how Jesus began to try to change the people's thinking about the Law and concerning the way they were to live with one another. We find Him telling His hearers:

> "Do not think that I have come to destroy the Law or the Prophets. I have not come to destroy but to fulfill. For assuredly, I say to you, till heaven and earth pass away, one jot or one tittle will by no means pass from the law till all is fulfilled. Whoever therefore breaks one of the least of these commandments, and teaches men so, he will be called least in the kingdom of heaven; but whoever does and teaches them will be called great in the kingdom of heaven. For I say to you, that unless your righteousness exceeds the righteousness of the scribes and Pharisees, you will by no means enter the kingdom of heaven." (Matthew 5:17-20 NKJV)

When Christ said that He had "come not to abolish the law and the prophets but to fulfill them," it sounds as if He is defending Himself against a charge of doing away with the Law of the Old Testament. Yet His words could not have been too enlightening to His hearers. What did He mean in saying that He had not come to abolish the Law but to fulfill it? It,

---

3 "The Chabad Times," 1986, vol. 1, no. 1, (Syracuse, New York: Chabad House at Syracuse University and Lubavitch of Central New York), p. 4.

nevertheless, must have been somewhat comforting to His listeners to hear that not one aspect of the Law would pass away and that the Law was to be taught.

Yet how disconcerting must have been Jesus' words when he said: "For I say to you, that unless your righteousness exceeds the righteousness of the scribes and Pharisees, you will by no means enter the kingdom of heaven." The scribes and Pharisees were considered among the holiest people of the land. If a man could not enter heaven except with a righteousness that exceeded theirs, what hope was there? Christ's words must have shocked His hearers. They were as astounding as if a pastor today were to tell his congregation that unless they lived holier lives than the clergy and the theologians, they had no hope for eternal life. Certainly, this statement could hardly have pleased the scribes and Pharisees.

Then Jesus moved on in His sermon to a disquieting, deepening, and enlarging of the Law:

> "You have heard that it was said to those of old, 'You shall not murder,' and whoever murders will be in danger of the judgment. But I say to you that whoever is angry with his brother without a cause will be in danger of the judgment. And whoever says to his brother, 'Raca!' [empty head], will be in danger of the council. But whoever says, 'You fool!' will be in danger of hell fire. . . . You have heard that it was said to those of old, 'You shall not commit adultery.' But I say to you that whoever looks at a woman to lust for her has already committed adultery with her in his heart." (Matthew 5:21-22, 27-28 NKJV)

Jesus is telling His hearers that not only the action of murdering or committing adultery is wrong, but also the desire to do so. He is saying that God looks at the heart, desires, intentions, and motivations of the individual and not only at what he actually does.

But Jesus does not stop with reinterpreting the laws of the Old Testament. He moves to a direct break with the Mosaic Law, for in the Old Testament we read:

> "But if any lasting harm follows, then you shall give life for life, eye for eye, tooth for tooth, hand for hand, foot for foot, burn for burn, wound for wound, stripe for stripe." (Exodus 21:23-25 NKJV; Leviticus 24:19-20; Deuteronomy 19:21)

In direct contrast, Jesus says:

"You have heard that it was said, 'An eye for an eye, and a tooth for a tooth.' But I say to you, do not resist him who is evil; but whoever slaps you on your right cheek, turn to him the other also. And if anyone wants to sue you, and take your shirt, let him have your coat also. And whoever shall force you to go one mile, go with him two. Give to him who asks of you, and do not turn away from him who wants to borrow from you.

You have heard that it was said, 'You shall love your neighbor, and hate your enemy.' But I say to you, love your enemies, and pray for those who persecute you in order that you may be sons of your Father who is in heaven; for He causes His sun to rise on the evil and the good, and sends rain on the righteous and the unrighteous. For if you love those who love you, what reward have you? Do not even the tax-gatherers do the same? And if you greet your brothers only, what do you do more than others? Do not even the Gentiles do the same? Therefore you are to be perfect, as your heavenly Father is perfect." (Matthew. 5:38-48 NASB)

Jesus taught that we are not to revenge ourselves against our enemies. Rather we are to love them. If this is so, although certain individuals or groups may view us as their enemies; it is evident from Jesus' words that we are not to view them as our enemy. What this means is: If we are to be followers of Jesus, then **the way people treat us is irrelevant as to the way we are to treat them.**

Most people may view this orientation of the Christian as unthinkably idealistic. It, however, is the way Jesus wishes us to look upon and relate to one another. We are to have the best interests of all people at heart, and that includes those who try to do us harm. Our God shows His love in the bounty of His creation for all, the good and the evil. Christ showed the love of God for even the worst of sinners by suffering in their stead. Jesus instructs us to follow our God's example who "causes His sun to rise on the evil and on the good, and sends rain on the righteous and the unrighteous." We are to live a life of love toward all people without regard for how they treat us. Although Christ's principle of love is called a "New Commandment," we are not being coerced to love. Rather our Lord is guiding us to imitate His unique way of relating to people. Our orientation toward others is always to be one of unselfish and self-denying love. We are to look upon all our fellow humans through eyes of Christian love, a love that is expressed by working for their good.

Note too, that no compromise is permitted. After telling His followers "love your enemies," Jesus brooks no weaseling. He concludes his discussion by saying, "Therefore you are to be perfect, as your heavenly Father is perfect." This is not an "evangelical counsel" meant for only His twelve disciples or for professional churchmen as bishops, pastors, monks or nuns. The Sermon on the Mount was preached to a great multitude (Matthew 4:25, 5:1-2). Jesus asks all His followers to strive for lives of perfect love.

A discourse similar to the Sermon on the Mount is found in Luke's Gospel. It is probable that this discourse is not the same sermon as Matthew's Sermon on the Mount. The locales appear to have been different, for Matthew records that "He went up on the mountain" (Matthew 5:1 NASB), while Luke writes of Jesus coming down from the hills and standing on a level place (Luke 6:12, 17).

We should keep in mind that Jesus was a wandering, itinerant teacher. As do speakers on the lecture circuit today or politicians stumping for office, Jesus most likely had a number of basic talks and parables that He repeated in different places. What Jesus considered important for His listeners in one locality most likely was equally meaningful in another. Again, as is the habit of modern speakers, the repetitions of the sermons, parables, or discourses were likely seldom identical but varied with the audience and the mood of the moment. Many of the minor variations between the different Gospels in what seem to be accounts of the same event could well be because different but similar occasions were chosen by the writers to record a given talk. At any rate, in Luke's account of one of Christ's most famous sermons he records Jesus as saying:

> "But I say to you who hear, love your enemies, do good to those who hate you, bless those who curse you, pray for those who mistreat you. Whoever hits you on the cheek, offer him the other also; and whoever takes away your coat, do not withhold your shirt from him either. Give to everyone who asks of you, and whoever takes away what is yours, do not demand it back. And just as you want people to treat you, treat them in the same way. And if you love those who love you, what credit is that to you? For even sinners love those who love them. And if you do good to those who do good to you, what credit is that to you? For even sinners do the same. And if you lend to those from whom you expect to receive, what credit is that to you? Even sinners lend to sinners, in order to receive back the same amount. But love your enemies, and do good, and lend, expecting nothing in return; and your reward will be great, and you will be sons of the Most High; for He Himself is kind to ungrateful and evil men. Be

merciful, just as your Father is merciful." (Luke 6:27-36 NASB)

Jesus' Emphasis on Positive Acts of Love

One can't help notice the emphasis on living a life of constructive and positive good in the above paragraph. We are not just to exchange loving acts with those who love us. Any unbeliever can do that and often does. Even the members of the Mafia have to have friends and family with whom they have amiable relationships or of what benefit to them is their profit from preying on society. Many an evil man buys undiscriminating friends in this fashion and thus has character witnesses attesting to his "good and generous" nature when he comes to trial for his misdeeds. The Christian, however, is to do good to all, expecting nothing in return. He is to act in the same selfless and self-forgetful way as did Christ when He was crucified for the sins of all humans.

If we are to love even those who consider themselves our enemies, then we are also to follow Christ's direction of "Be merciful, just as your Father is merciful." We are to be ready to forgive and forget injustices done to us. This is what our Lord asked of us when He gave the Lord's Prayer as an example of how we are to pray. In His prayer is the petition, "And forgive us our debts, as we forgive our debtors" (Matthew 6:12 NKJV). Jesus then explained: "For if you forgive men their trespasses, your heavenly Father will also forgive you. But if you do not forgive men their trespasses, neither will your Father forgive your trespasses" (Matthew 6:14-15 NKJV).

The Christian always is to be ready to forgive. He is to keep Jesus' words constantly in mind, "But I say to you who hear, love your enemies, do good to those who hate you, bless those who curse you, pray for those who mistreat you" (Luke 6:27-28 NASB).

Does this mean we are to speak words of forgiveness to the most brazen sinner, a person who repeatedly victimizes others and does not intend to change his ways? Are we to forgive and let him continue his evil ways without hindrance? To do so would hardly be acting in love either toward such a person or toward our society. There are times when a rebuke and admonition would be more loving than offering forgiveness that might be scornfully received. Jesus understood this when He gave the following guidance in how we are to forgive:

"Take heed to yourselves. If your brother sins against you, rebuke him; and if he repents, forgive him. And if he sins against you seven times in a day, and seven times in a day returns to you, saying, 'I repent,' you shall forgive him." (Luke 17:3-4 NKJV)

We are to offer forgiveness to the repentant person who sins against us, but not necessarily the unrepentant. This instruction, however, should not be used legalistically but rather in love. There are times when we should forgive even when a person has not in so many words repented his actions against us. Often by his later behavior, it is obvious that he regrets his action and thus should be forgiven. The important thing is to have an attitude of forgiveness and love toward all, to be always ready to forgive even those who most grievously hurt us, to be always ready to help even those who have harmed us. Jesus' prayer for those who had Him nailed to the cross, "Father, forgive them; for they do not know what they do" (Luke 23:34 NKJV), is always to be our example.

The contrast between Jesus' Golden Rule and the earlier Golden Rules of the Rabbi Hillel (60? B.C. – 10? A.D.) , Confucius (551-478 B.C.), and the Greek sage and philosopher Thales (640-546 B.C.) underscores Jesus' emphasis on a positive, outgoing way of life. Hillel, Confucius, and Thales stated their golden rules negatively. Hillel, for example, wrote: "Do not to your neighbor what is hateful to you; that is the whole law. All the rest is commentary." They were men of their times who thought of the law primarily in negative terms. On the other hand, Christ calls for an active and helpful way of life oriented toward seeking out ways of benefiting others. His golden rule reads: "And just as you want people to treat you, treat them in the same way" (Luke 6:31 NASB).

A stress on positive and beneficial acts of love towards one's neighbor is a major emphasis in Jesus' new way of life. Consider the parable of the Good Samaritan and its affirmation of a life of active love in doing good to all people and especially to those in need:

> And behold, a certain lawyer stood up and tested Him, saying, "Teacher, what shall I do to inherit eternal life?" He said to him, "What is written in the law? How do you read?" And he answered and said, "'You shall love the Lord your God with all your heart, with all your soul, with all your strength, and with all your mind,' and 'your neighbor as yourself.'" And He said to him, "You have answered right; do this and you will live." But he, wanting to justify himself, said to Jesus, "And who is my neighbor?"
>
> And Jesus answered and said, "A certain man went down from Jerusalem to Jericho, and fell among thieves, who stripped him of his clothing, wounded him, and departed, leaving him half dead. And by chance a certain priest came down that road. And when he saw him, he passed by on the other side. And likewise a Levite, when he was at the place, came and looked at

him, and passed by on the other side. But a certain Samaritan, as he journeyed, came where he was. And when he saw him, he had compassion on him, and went to him and bandaged his wounds, pouring on oil and wine; and he set him on his own donkey, brought him to an inn, and took care of him. And the next day, when he departed, he took out two denarii, gave them to the innkeeper, and said to him, 'Take care of him; and whatever more you spend, when I come again, I will repay you.'

Now which of these three do you think was neighbor to him who fell among the thieves?" And he said, "He who showed mercy on him." Then Jesus said to him, "Go and do likewise." (Luke 10:25-37 NKJV).

In answering the lawyer's question, "And who is my neighbor," Jesus' parable depicted a Samaritan acting in love and mercy toward a Jew. What made this parable all the more meaningful is that the Jews despised and had treated with contempt the neighboring people of Samaria ever since the end of the Babylonian exile, that is, for over 500 years. What an illustration Jesus gave of showing unselfish love toward those who ill-treat us!

In the vision that Jesus gives of the final judgment in Matthew 25, we again find Jesus stressing a life of love expressed in active deeds of love to those in need. To His disciples sitting with Him on the Mount of Olives, Jesus said:

"But when the Son of Man comes in His glory, and all the angels with Him, then He will sit on His glorious throne. And all the nations will be gathered before Him; and He will separate them from one another, as the shepherd separates the sheep from the goats; and He will put the sheep on His right, and the goats on the left.

Then the King will say to those on His right, 'Come, you who are blessed of My Father, inherit the kingdom prepared for you from the foundation of the world. For I was hungry, and you gave Me something to eat; I was thirsty, and you gave Me drink; I was a stranger, and you invited Me in; naked, and you clothed Me; I was sick, and you visited Me; I was in prison, and you came to Me.' Then the righteous will answer Him, saying, 'Lord, when did we see You hungry, and feed You, or thirsty, and give You drink? And when did we see You a stranger, and invite you in, or naked, and clothe You? And when did we see You sick, or in prison, and come to You?' And the King will answer and say to them, 'Truly I say to you, to the extent that you did it to one of these brothers of Mine, even the least of them, you did it to Me.'

Then He will say to those on His left, 'Depart from Me, accursed ones, into the eternal fire which has been prepared for the devil and his angels; for I was hungry, and you gave Me nothing to eat; I was thirsty, and you gave Me nothing to drink; I was a stranger, and you did not invite Me in; naked, and you did not clothe Me; sick, and in prison, and you did not visit Me.' Then they themselves also will answer, saying, 'Lord, when did we see You hungry, or thirsty, or a stranger, or naked, or sick, or in prison, and did not take care of You?' Then He will answer them, saying, 'Truly I say to you, to the extent that you did not do it to one of the least of these, you did not do it to Me.' And these will go away into eternal punishment, but the righteous into eternal life." (Matthew 25:31-46 NASB)

What an extraordinary God we have! The whole point of Christ's vision of the Last Judgment concerns how we are to serve our God. There is nothing here about a life devoted to expressing our love directly to God. Rather the whole stress is that we serve God by serving even the least of Christ's brothers. How unselfish is our Lord. If we are to show our love to Him for the love that He has showered upon us, He instructs us to do it by showing love to those in need. Jesus redirects the love that we have for our God to our fellow humans who need our help. How similar are the words of Jesus to those of Isaiah and Micah quoted earlier in this chapter. We are to serve and worship our God through acts of love toward our fellow humans. The piety of our worship in church is empty and meaningless apart from a life of love and goodness toward our fellowman.

Note too the emphasis on giving to those in true need. We are not to show love just to those who are our friends or relatives or to those who can repay a good turn we do them. Rather we are to show love toward the multitude of those who lack the basic human needs of food, water, shelter, clothing, health, and freedom. What Jesus said to a prominent Pharisee who had invited Him to dinner shows this emphasis:

"When you give a dinner or a banquet, do not invite your friends or your brothers or your kinsmen or rich neighbors, lest they also invite you in return, and you be repaid. But when you give a feast, invite the poor, the maimed, the lame, the blind, and you will be blessed, because they cannot repay you. You will be repaid at the resurrection of the just." (Luke 14:12-14 RSV) It is a sad commentary on how well we have followed Jesus' counsel in that so often our gift giving at Christmas is called "an exchange of gifts."

Jesus not only taught that His followers are to show love to all and especially to those in need. He demonstrated how His teaching should be put into action. His life was devoted to aiding those who needed help. Major portions of the Gospels are given over to telling how He healed the sick, gave sight to the blind, sanity to the insane, hearing to the deaf, wholeness to the lepers, motion to the paralyzed, food for the hungry, wine for the newly-weds, and forgiveness to the repentant. They also tell of His rising to the defense of the oppressed and resisting and exposing the hypocrisy of the wealthy and powerful who would exploit and take advantage of the weak and helpless. Jesus' actions flowed from His love and compassion. When He came across a mournful funeral procession and saw a sorrowing widow walking beside the bier of her only son, Jesus' heart went out to her (Luke 7:13 NEB). His final act of love, of course, was giving His life as a sacrifice for our sins in order to reconcile us with His heavenly Father so that we might inherit eternal life. When we observe the life of Christ, we understand His words: ". . . love one another as I have loved you, Greater love has no one than this, that he lay down his life for his friends" (John 15:12b-13 NKJV). In true piety Jesus attended the worship of the Temple and the synagogue; He exemplified how a life of piety and a life of goodness can be one.

Love Is the Fulfilling of the Law

The emphasis that Jesus placed on leading a life of selfless service to others is shown in the relationship of His New Commandment to the Ten Commandments and moral law of the Old Testament. Christ did not come to abolish the Law of the Old Testament; He came to give us a way of life that would fulfill the spirit of Old Testament Law. The primarily negative commandments of the Old Testament would not be violated if we lived by the New Commandment of loving each other as Christ loved us. What Jesus emphasized in Old Testament Law was the positive commandment in Leviticus: "You shall love your neighbor as yourself." And yet Christ very much eclipsed that commandment of loving others as we love ourselves. Not our own self-love, but rather the steadfast love of our God is to be the measure of our love. We are to imitate the Son of God's love for us, a love that far surpasses any love we could possibly have for ourselves.

But these were heady ideas for Jesus' fellow Jews, a people steeped in the observance of the 613 Mosaic laws plus what they considered the holy demands of their Tradition. Jesus had to move slowly and carefully in opening the minds of His people to the new way of life He was introducing. In the Gospel of Luke, we find Christ speaking words that must have seemed a real paradox to His listeners:

> "The law and the prophets were until John; since then the good news of the kingdom of God is preached, and every one enters it violently. But it is easier for heaven and earth to pass away, than for one dot of the law to become void." (Luke 16:16-17 RSV)

Once more Jesus was giving the impression that the time of the Old Testament Law was over. On the other hand, what could He mean that not one dot of the Law was to become void? Christ's hearers must have shaken their heads in bewilderment over the puzzle He was posing. It was too early in His ministry, however, for Jesus to speak explicitly about the ethical revolution He was making. His ministry was to be three years long. If the leaders of the Jews knew the full extent of His overthrow of their beloved "Tradition" and the new way of life in which He was instructing God's people to walk, His ministry might have been measured in months rather than years. As it was, as the text below indicates, the leaders of the Jews were taking counsel how to destroy Him. Christ, therefore, only slowly disclosed the new way of life He was bringing into being.

By Jesus' actions, we get a clearer idea of how He regarded the law of the Old Testament. According to the Mosaic Law, no work or preparation of food was to be done on the Sabbath. This law was rigidly followed. For example, the rabbis taught that a person could walk from his home no more than 2000 paces, what was called a "Sabbath's day journey" (Acts 1:12). Matthew records the following episode:

> At that time Jesus went on the Sabbath through the grainfields, and His disciples became hungry and began to pick the heads of grain and eat. But when the Pharisees saw it, they said to Him, "Behold, Your disciples do what is not lawful to do on a Sabbath." But He said to them, "Have you not read what David did, when he became hungry, he and his companions; how he entered the house of God, and they ate the consecrated bread, which was not lawful for him to eat, nor for those with him, but for the priest alone? Or have you not read in the Law, that on the Sabbath the priests in the temple break the Sabbath, and are innocent? But I say to you, that something greater than the temple is here. But if you had known what this means, 'I desire compassion, and not a sacrifice,' you would not

have condemned the innocent. For the Son of Man is Lord of the Sabbath."

Jesus was echoing the words of Hosea 6:6 (see p. 44) in pointing out that God primarily desires *chesed* (compassion, mercy, kindliness, steadfast love) rather than the piety of the observance of sacrificial rites. Matthew continues by telling how Jesus put his teaching into practice:

> And departing from there, He went into their synagogue. And behold, there was a man with a withered hand. And they questioned Him, saying, "Is it lawful to heal on the Sabbath?"--in order that they might accuse Him. And He said to them, "What man shall there be among you, who shall have one sheep, and if it falls into a pit on the Sabbath, will he not take hold of it, and lift it out? Of how much more value then is a man than a sheep! So then, it is lawful to do good on the Sabbath." Then He said to the man, "Stretch out your hand!" And he stretched it out, and it was restored to normal, like the other. But the Pharisees went out, and counseled together against Him, as to how they might destroy Him. (Matthew 12:1-14 NASB)

To violate the laws of the Sabbath was considered a grievous offense, and the Old Testament commandment about doing any work on the Sabbath was especially plain. In Deuteronomy we read:

> "Observe the sabbath day to keep it holy, as the Lord your God commanded you. Six days you shall labor and do all your work, but the seventh day is a sabbath of the Lord your God; in it you shall not do any work, . . ." (Deuteronomy 5:12-14 NASB)

For Jesus to heal on the Sabbath was considered work. Christ, however, by word and action taught that to do works of compassion out of a spirit of love does not profane the Sabbath. Moreover, even in regard to the disciples rubbing out the kernels from the heads of grain which certainly can be construed as doing work on the Sabbath, Jesus proclaimed His right to modify the Sabbath laws. He declared: "For the Son of Man is Lord of the Sabbath."

But Christ went even further. The kosher laws of the present-day Jews are based in large part on the plain texts of the Mosaic Law. Concerning the eating of various foods, the Old Testament in Leviticus 11:1-47 and Deuteronomy 14:3-21 carefully discriminates between which foods are allowed and which are forbidden. Jesus declared all foods clean in what must have been a stunning discussion with His disciples:

> And he [Jesus] called the people to him again, and said to them, "Hear me, all of you, and understand: there is nothing outside a man which by going into him can defile him; but the things which come out of a man are what defile him." And when he had entered the house, and left the people, his disciples asked him about the parable. And he said to them, "Then are you also without understanding? Do you not see that whatever goes into a man from outside cannot defile him, since it enters, not his heart but his stomach, and so passes on?" (Thus he declared all foods clean.) And he said, "What comes out of a man is what defiles a man. For from within, out of the heart of man, come evil thoughts, fornication, theft, murder, adultery, coveting, wickedness, deceit, licentiousness, envy, slander, pride, foolishness. All these evil things come from within, and they defile a man." (Mark 7:14-23 RSV)

In no uncertain terms, as we find in the comment at the close of the Sermon on the Mount, "Jesus. . . taught them as one who had authority, and not as their scribes" (Matthew 7:28-29 RSV). Jesus considered it clearly within His prerogatives to modify the laws, statutes, and ordinances of the Mosaic Law.

The Christian Life and the Love of Riches

The authority of Jesus to modify the law is also seen in the story of the rich young man. In this case, Jesus again went beyond the law of the Old Testament in asking for a life of love and service from those who would follow Him. Christ was laying to rest the ancient idea that he was a good man who only avoided doing evil:

> And behold, one came and said to Him, "Good Teacher, what good thing shall I do that I may have eternal life?" And He said to him, "Why do you call Me good? No one is good but One, that is, God. But if you want to enter into life, keep the commandments." He said to Him, "Which ones?" Jesus said, "'You shall not murder,' 'You shall not commit adultery,' 'You shall not steal,' 'You shall not bear false witness,' 'Honor your father and your mother,' and, 'You shall love your neighbor as

yourself.'" The young man said to Him, "All these things I have kept from my youth. What do I still lack?" Jesus said to him, "If you want to be perfect, go, sell what you have and give to the poor, and you will have treasure in heaven; and come, follow Me." (Matthew 19:16-22 NKJV)

It was not enough that the rich young man refrained from evil in keeping the commandments; he had the opportunity to do good to those in need through the use of his possessions. Jesus invited him to offer his life in service to his God. Christ wanted no half-hearted commitment to the way of life He wished His disciples to follow. What Jesus said to His disciples shortly before He was crucified speaks to the problem of the rich young man:

"He who loves his life loses it; and he who hates his life in this world shall keep it to life eternal. If any one serves Me, let him follow Me; and where I am, there shall My servant also be; if any one serves Me, the Father will honor him. (John 12:25-26 NASB)

But it was hard for the young man to give up his many possessions. He perhaps had a place for Jesus in his life, but Christ was not his first priority.

With considerable sadness, Jesus must have watched the rich young man depart. What He said next, however, has been a stumbling block to those who admire the wealthy down to this present day:

And Jesus said to His disciples, "Truly I say to you, it is hard for a rich man to enter the kingdom of heaven. And again I say to you, it is easier for a camel to go through the eye of a needle, than for a rich man to enter the kingdom of God." And when the disciples heard this, they were very astonished and said, "Then who can be saved?" And looking upon them Jesus said to them, "With men this is impossible, but with God all things are possible." (Matthew 19:23-26 NASB)

The Gospels give some insight as to the reasons why the wealthy dwell in spiritually slippery places. There is, for example, always the tendency to put one's trust in one's wealth rather than in God. Jesus told the following parable in this regard:

And one from the crowd said to Him, "Teacher, tell my brother to divide the inheritance with me." And He said to him,

"Man, who made Me a judge or an arbitrator over you?"

And He said to them, "Take heed and beware of covetousness, for a man's life does not consist in the abundance of the things he possesses."

And He spoke a parable to them, saying: "The ground of a certain rich man yielded plentifully. And he thought within himself, saying, 'What shall I do, since I have no room to store my crops?' And he said, 'I will do this: I will pull down my barns and build greater, and there I will store all my crops and my goods. And I will say to my soul: Soul, you have many goods laid up for many years; take your ease; eat, drink, and be merry.' But God said to him, 'You fool! This night your soul will be required of you; then whose will those things be which you have provided?' So is he who lays up treasure for himself, and is not rich toward God." (Luke 12:13-21 NKJV)

The wealthy and affluent of this world stand endangered by God's displeasure at their self-indulgent lives. As with the rich young man, it is a matter of priorities. What comes first in our lives? Jesus put the matter plainly:

"Do not lay up for yourselves treasures on earth, where moth and rust destroy and where thieves break in and steal; but lay up for yourselves treasures in heaven, where neither moth nor rust destroys and where thieves do not break in and steal. For where your treasure is, there your heart will be also. . . . No one can serve two masters; for either he will hate the one and love the other, or else he will hold to the one and despise the other. You cannot serve God and mammon [money and the things of this world]." (Matthew 6:19-20, 24 NKJV)

Our Lord expects us to make a choice between serving Him and serving money and material possessions. We cannot have it both ways.

The foolishness of being more concerned with treasure on earth rather than laying up treasure in heaven is made clear in Jesus' paired and complementary parables of The Unjust Steward and The Rich Man and Lazarus. The parables begin with Jesus saying to His disciples:

"There was a certain rich man who had a steward, and an accusation was brought to him that this man was wasting his goods. And he called him and said to him, 'What is this I hear about you? Give an account of your stewardship, for you may no longer be steward.' Then the steward said within himself, 'What shall I do? For my master is taking the stewardship away from me. I cannot dig; I am ashamed to beg. I have resolved what to do, that when I am put out of the stewardship, they may receive me into their houses.' So he called every one of his master's debtors to him, and said to the first, 'How much do you owe my master?' And he said, 'A hundred measures of oil.' And he said to him, 'Take your bill, and sit down quickly and write fifty.' Then he said to another, 'And how much do you owe?' And he said, 'A hundred measures of wheat.' And he said to him, 'Take your bill, and write eighty.' And the master commended the unjust steward because he had dealt shrewdly. For the sons of this world are shrewder in their generation than the sons of light." (Luke 16:1-8 NKJV)

Jesus in this parable is not praising the dishonesty of the unjust steward but rather his foresight in providing for his future. Jesus comments that the "sons of light" show little such foresight. Therefore, Jesus says to His disciples:

"And I say to you, make friends for yourselves by unrighteous mammon, that when you fail [die],[4] they may receive you into everlasting habitations." (Luke 16:9 NKJV)

Jesus tells His disciples to use the unrighteous mammon, the riches of this world, in aiding those who need our help. When death comes, those whom we have aided will be there to receive us into the everlasting habitations of God.

Jesus then points out that the unrighteous mammon of this life does not belong to us; it is only loaned to us for this life. If we are not faithful in its use, the true riches of the kingdom of Heaven will not be ours. Jesus continues:

"He who is faithful in what is least is faithful also in much; and he who is unjust in the least is unjust also in much. Therefore if you have not been faithful in the unrighteous mammon, who will

---

4 Some translations have "but when it fails," that is, when unrighteous mammon, the things of this world, no longer sustain life. The meaning is the same in either case.

commit to your trust the true riches? And if you have not been faithful in what is another man's, who will give you what is your own? No servant can serve two masters; for either he will hate the one and love the other, or else he will hold to the one and despise the other. You cannot serve God and mammon." (Luke 16:10-13 NKJV)

Many have struggled with trying to understand this parable.[5] The Pharisees, however, who had listened to His parable understood it plainly enough. Luke records their contemptuous reaction to Jesus' parable and its explanation:

And the Pharisees, who were lovers of money, also heard all these things, and they derided Him. And He said to them, "You are those who justify yourselves before men, but God knows your hearts. For what is highly esteemed among men is an abomination in the sight of God." (Luke 16:14-15 NKJV)

The scoffing and derision of the Pharisees obviously nettled Jesus, for just a few sentences later He tells them what will be the result of their love for the mammon of this world. In a parable that drives home the message of the story of The Unjust Steward, Jesus continues:

"There was a certain rich man who was clothed in purple and fine linen and fared sumptuously every day. But there was a certain beggar named Lazarus, full of sores, who was laid at his gate, desiring to be fed with the crumbs which fell from the rich man's table. Moreover the dogs came and licked his sores. And it came to pass that the beggar died and was carried by the angels to Abraham's bosom. The rich man also died and was buried. And being in torments in Hades, he lifted up his eyes and saw Abraham afar off, and Lazarus in his bosom. And he cried and said, 'Father Abraham, have mercy on me, and send Lazarus that he may dip the tip of his finger in water and cool my tongue; for I am tormented in this flame.' But Abraham said, 'Son, remember that in your lifetime you received your good things, and likewise Lazarus evil things; but now he is comforted

---

5 For example, notice the complete loss of the meaning of this parable in *The Living Bible's* unhappy paraphrase of Luke 16:8-9.

and you are tormented. And beside all this, between us and you there is a great gulf fixed, so that those who want to pass from here to you cannot, nor can those who want to come from there pass to us.' Then he said, 'I beg you therefore, father, that you would send him to my father's house, for I have five brothers, that he may testify to them, lest they also come to this place of torment.' Abraham said to him, 'They have Moses and the prophets; let them hear them.' And he said, 'No, father Abraham; but if one goes to them from the dead, they will repent.' And he said to him, 'If they do not hear Moses and the prophets, neither will they be persuaded though one rise from the dead.'" (Luke 16:19-31 NKJV)

True enough, Lazarus was not there to welcome the rich man into the everlasting habitations (see above Luke 16:9).

Doesn't the clue to the meaning of this parable lie in the description of the rich man in contrast to Lazarus? The rich man is described as dressed in purple and fine linen, clothes of a color so expensive that they were often reserved only for royalty. He doesn't just eat; he fares sumptuously every day. Lazarus, on the other hand, is described only as being full of sores. Also, note well, Jesus does not say that Lazarus was fed by the crumbs that fell from the rich man's table, only that he desired to be so fed.

Is not the rich man's problem that of self-indulgence, a concentration on so indulging himself that he neglects those in need? It is so easy to rationalize our own self-indulgence. We feel the need to have our homes, food, drink, clothes, cars, boats, and vacations reflect our financial status. We upgrade our standard of living in keeping with our increasing income. We finally spend on ourselves far more than is necessary to maintain a moderate and decent way of life. To our God who surveys the lives of all His children and Who sees the misery of the multitudinous poor, the lives of the rich are too often surfeited, self-centered, and callous. Christ's parable is in keeping with the words of God regarding His destruction of the city of Sodom as recorded by Ezekiel:

Behold, this was the guilt of your sister Sodom: she and her daughters had pride, surfeit of food, and prosperous ease, but did not aid the poor and needy. They were haughty, and did abominable things before me; therefore I removed them, when I saw it. (Ezekiel 16:49-50 RSV)

Also, if those who are prosperous give, so often they give only of their abundance. In fact, it is sort of a pattern in American culture that some who gained their wealth by the ruthless exploitation of their fellowman, then buy back their reputations with a fraction of their wealth by setting up charitable foundations in their names. Thus, our robber barons and unscrupulous businessmen soon are touted as "philanthropists," that is, lovers of men.

God does not look at the amount of our giving. He looks at our heart. Keep in mind, the only gift Christ praised was a gift of a penny. Mark recorded an occasion when Jesus and His disciples were in the temple in Jerusalem:

> "And He sat down opposite the treasury, and began observing how the multitude were putting money into the treasury; and many rich people were putting in large sums. And a poor widow came and put in two small copper coins, which amount to a cent. And calling His disciples to Him, He said to them, "Truly I say to you, this poor widow put in more than all the contributors to the treasury; for they all put in out of their surplus, but she, out of her poverty, put in all she owned, all she had to live on" (Mark 12:41-44 NASB).

To Live Christ's Way Is to Walk by Faith

The thought of truly following Jesus' way of life tends to make many people nervous. They don't feel that they will survive unless they make their material well-being of first importance in their lives. Jesus was aware of this anxiety. He therefore follows up His counsel of not trying to serve both God and the things of this world by gently encouraging His followers to put their trust in God. In the Sermon on the Mount He counseled:

> "Therefore I say to you, do not worry about your life, what you will eat or what you will drink; nor about your body, what you will put on. Is not life more than food and the body more than clothing? Look at the birds of the air, for they neither sow nor reap nor gather into barns; yet your heavenly Father feeds them. Are you not of more value than they? Which of you by worrying can add one cubit to his stature? And why do you worry about clothing? Consider the lilies of the field, how they grow: they neither toil nor spin; and yet I say to you that even Solomon in all his glory was not arrayed like one of these. Now if God so

clothes the grass of the field, which today is, and tomorrow is thrown into the oven, will He not much more clothe you, O you of little faith? Therefore do not worry, saying, 'What shall we eat?' or, 'What shall we drink?' or, 'What shall we wear?' For after all these things the Gentiles seek. For your heavenly Father knows that you need all these things. But seek first the kingdom of God and His righteousness, and all these things will be added to you. Therefore do not worry about tomorrow, for tomorrow will worry about its own things. Sufficient for the day is its own trouble." (Matthew 6:25-34 NKJV)

The Good Lord knows our needs. If we seek first His Kingdom and through our faith in His redeeming death obtain His righteousness, His providence envelops us. When we walk in His way, He will see that we are cared for. Our Lord wants our faith and trust to be in Him and not in our bank accounts. To live this way is what it means, "to walk by faith."

However, by living this way it does not mean that we are trying to strike a bargain with our God. We are not to live the Christian way of life for any other reason except as an expression of our love for God. We do not follow Jesus and His way of life to either earn heaven or avoid hell. When we repent our sinful lives and turn to Him for forgiveness, we become righteous in God's sight. We need nothing more to make us His children and members of His Kingdom. As Christians who have drowned our old nature in the waters of baptism and have risen to a new life, we are saved to live in His presence forever. Our response to the saving acts of our God, however, can't help being one of love and gratitude. The love and thankfulness that wells up in us in response to God's love for us are the only motivations for following Jesus' way of life.

Jesus, however, does speak at times of our receiving a reward as a result of our actions in following Him. In the Sermon on the Mount, He said:

> "Take heed that you do not do your charitable deeds before men to be seen by them. Otherwise, you have no reward from your Father who is in heaven. Therefore, when you do a charitable deed, do not sound a trumpet before you as the hypocrites do in the synagogues and in the streets, that they may have glory from men. Assuredly, I say to you, they have their reward. But when you do a charitable deed, do not let your left hand know what your right hand is doing, that your charitable deed may be in secret; and your Father who sees in secret will

Himself reward you openly." (Matthew 6:1-4 NKJV)

Our Lord speaks of God's reward, and yet we know that love for our God is to be our motivation for living a Christ-like life, not seeking a reward. As Paul said: "Let all that you do be done with love" (1 Corinthians 16:14 NKJV). How can we resolve this paradox? Think of Jesus' words concerning a reward in the light of the following example:

If parents ask their children to aid them in planting a garden, how pleased they are if the children work cheerfully out of love for them. And how often does such joy in their children's love result in the parent's taking the children out for a treat at the ice cream store. Now, did the children do their task because they hoped for a reward? Not necessarily. They may well have done it out of love for their parents, even if they were aware that as the result of their activity they would later receive a treat. Love responds to love.   Thus, it is also with our God. Jesus said, "Blessed are the pure in heart, for they shall see God" (Matthew 5:8 NKJV). It is a pureness of motivation that our God wants from us. All that we do for Him is to be done out of love. We do not do our Father's will because we calculate on His rewarding us. In addition, if we allow other motivations to creep in, such as hoping to gain the applause of our fellowman for the good deeds we do, we have rewarded ourselves. We have not acted out of love for God but have diluted our purity of motivation with a love for the praise and regard of others. The child who will only work in the family's behalf if he is paid is as loveless as the Christian who will only give generously to a good cause if he receives "proper" recognition. Both parents and the Good Lord are rightly disheartened at such a cold response to their love.

God rewards as a Father who gives generously to His children. He does not calculate His gifts as does an employer paying for piecework. We are rewarded because of God's great love. It is not based on our deserving. That God's reward is all out of relation to our deserving is seen in Jesus' words: "And whoever gives one of these little ones only a cup of cold water in the name of a disciple, assuredly, I say to you, he will by no means lose his reward" (Matthew 10:42 NKJV). And then keep in mind Jesus word's to His disciples, "So likewise you, when you have done all those things which you are commanded, say, 'We are unprofitable servants. We have done what was our duty to do'" (Luke 17:10 NKJV).

Seeking God's Will for Our Lives

Christians have long been urged to live in imitation of Christ. Paul encourages us in this way, "Therefore be imitators of God, as beloved children; and walk in love, just as Christ also loved you, and gave Himself up for us, an offering and a sacrifice to God as a fragrant aroma" (Ephesians

5:1-2 NASB). To follow the example that Jesus gave is to follow Him also in seeking out God's will for our lives.

Jesus in the Lord's Prayer taught us to pray to our heavenly Father: "Thy will be done on earth as it is in heaven." That Jesus lived by this petition Himself is seen in His prayer to His Father in the Garden of Gethsemane on the night before He was crucified: "O My Father, if this cup may not pass away from Me unless I drink it, Your will be done" (Matthew 26:42 NKJV). A striking aspect of Christ's life is how often He referred to His task as carrying out His Father's will. John's Gospel especially wrote of this:

> Jesus said to them, "My food is to do the will of Him who sent Me, and to finish His work." (John 4:34 NKJV)

> "I can of Myself do nothing. As I hear, I judge; and My judgment is righteous, because I do not seek My own will but the will of the Father who sent Me." (John 5:30 NKJV)

> Jesus therefore answered them and said, "My teaching is not Mine, but His who sent Me. If man is willing to do His will, he shall know of the teaching, whether it is of God, or whether I speak from Myself." (John 7:16-17 NASB)

Jesus lived His life endeavoring to follow His Father's will. The following texts indicate He also asked His disciples to imitate Him in striving to follow the will of God the Father:

> "Not every one who says to Me, 'Lord, Lord,' will enter the kingdom of heaven, but he who does the will of My Father who is in heaven." (Matthew 7:21 NKJV)

During the evening before his crucifixion, Jesus defined the will of the Father for those who would believe in Him:

> "If anyone loves Me, he will keep My word; and My Father will love him, and We will come to him and make Our home with him. He who does not love Me does not keep My words; and the word which you hear is not Mine but the Father's who sent Me. . . . If you keep My commandments, you will abide in My love, just as I have kept My Father's commandments and abide in His love. . . . This is My commandment, that you love one another as

I have loved you. Greater love has no one than this, that he lay down his life for his friends." (John 14:23-24; 15:10, 12-13 NKJV)[6]

That we should follow Christ in loving others as He loved us is clearly the will of God the Father for us.

Christ's New Way of Life Is One of Unselfish Service

"Greater love has no one than this, that he lay down his life for his friends." This was the ultimate service that a man could do for those He loved. Jesus did not come into this world to reap honor and glory. He did not come to live among us as a superhero, a superstar, a celebrity, enjoying the favors of the rich and influential and the idolization of the people. He came to serve, and He asks His followers, both laity and clergy, to follow His example. His disciples had a hard time understanding this. They were willing to give up their present comfort and security to follow Jesus as He wandered through Palestine, but they wanted a fitting reward. Luke records the problem Jesus had with His disciples in this regard:

But there was also strife among them, which of them should be considered the greatest. And He said to them, "The kings of the Gentiles exercise lordship over them, and those who

---

6 There are those who say that the New Commandment is to be applied only to fellow Christians and not to non-Christians because Jesus said specifically to His disciples "love one another." One could just as well contentiously argue that it really only applies to the disciples present at the last supper; for after all, it was to these He spoke His New Commandment. This is as foolish as saying that because Jesus spoke just as specifically of laying "down his life for his friends," His sacrifice on the cross was only for His friends, the disciples at the Last Supper. It ignores the common practice of Hebraic speech, well illustrated in Jesus' teaching, of preferring to speak in concrete rather than abstract terms. Could one, therefore, possibly believe that Jesus taught that the maxim "Love your neighbor as yourself" was to be applied to both non-Christian and Christians, while the New Commandment was restricted to Christians? Is the word "brother" in the New Testament only applied to fellow Christians? Did Jesus mean only needy Christians when in Matthew 25:40 He said, "to the extent that you did it to one of these brothers of mine, even the least of them, you did it to Me"? Or should the New Commandment and the brothers mentioned in Matthew 25 be interpreted in the light of Jesus saying, "But I say to you, love your enemies, bless those who curse you, do good to those who hate you, and pray for those who spitefully use you and persecute you, that you may be sons of your Father who is in heaven; for He makes His sun rise on the evil and on the good, and sends rain on the just and the unjust" (Matthew 5:43-45 NKJV). (See John Chrysostom's and Augustine's view on this same question on pages 259-260 and 278 as well as Martin Luther's view page. 359)

exercise authority over them are called 'benefactors.' But not so you; on the contrary, he who is greatest among you, let him be as the younger, and he who is chief as he who serves. For who is greater, he who sits at the table, or he who serves? Is it not he who sits at the table? But I am among you as the One who serves." (Luke 22:24-27 NKJV)

After Jesus' disciples James and John came to Him to ask for the highest places of honor in the kingdom of heaven, Jesus called together His disciples and said:

"You know that those who are considered rulers over the Gentiles lord it over them, and their great ones exercise authority over them. Yet it shall not be so among you; but whoever desires to become great among you shall be your servant. And whoever of you desires to be first shall be slave of all. For even the Son of Man did not come to be served, but to serve, and to give His life a ransom for many." (Mark 10: 42b-45 NKJV)

As Christ came not to be served, but to serve, so it is to be among His followers. The mark of Christian love, (*agape*), is the unselfish motivation that inspires it. It is a love that reflects the steadfast love of our God for us. God showed His love in that He sent His Son to be born among us, to live among us, to serve and teach us, and finally to die for us. He did this out of pure grace and unselfish love. There was no intrinsic worth in us that would demand or deserve such love.

Our Lord asks that our love for one another be as unselfish as His own. Christian love does not hope that a good turn we do to another will be returned. Christian love does not expect the applause of men. The ideal of Christian love is to love and serve our neighbor as unselfishly, dispassionately, and as unselfconsciously as possible. We are to live our love in imitation of Christ's love for us. **In the rest of this book whenever the term "Christian love" is used it will mean the type of love signified by the New Testament Greek word, "*agape*," the selfless love that we have for one another lived in imitation and emulation of Christ's love for us.**

When the apostles chose a Greek word to translate the uniqueness of the connotations that Jesus gave to the Aramaic word that He used for love, they chose *agape*, a little-used word in the Greek language. They did not choose the Greek word *eros* that primarily denoted the sexual or erotic love between man and woman. They did not want Christian love to be confused with the love between the sexes, a love that seeks its gratification from the other. They did not choose the Greek word, *philia*, which denoted the fraternal love between friends, a love based on the mutual regard and friendship between two people. Christian love was to be extended to more than friends. Rather, the apostles chose an infrequently-used and almost unfamiliar Greek word for love, *agape*. A word previously used to express a love that was somewhat colorless and indefinite. It usually meant little more than being content with the person to whom *agape* was directed. It was the "love" expressed in a courteous but formal greeting. It could also be used to denote sympathy and mutual respect. At times the word was used to value or express a preference for one person or idea above another. "Agape" as used by the pre-Biblical Greeks had neither the passion of *eros*, erotic love, nor the warm feelings of *philia*, fraternal love.[7]

The word *agape* was given new and deeper meaning by the apostles of Jesus Christ. Only with a "new" word could the apostles give full meaning to the words about love that Jesus spoke. *Agape* is translated "Christian love" in this book for it is Christ-like love. Christian love is Christ-like in that it follows the New Commandment of Jesus Christ in loving one another in the same self-giving and selfless way as Christ did when he was crucified for us. Christian love is Christ-like in that it brings us to serve our neighbor as Christ served the needs of the bridal couple in Cana, the widow of Nain, blind Bartimaeus, the hungry 5000, and the centurion's servant. It is Christ-like in rising to the defense of the exploited, victimized, and oppressed. It is Christ-like in not judging the worth of the individual but responding as Jesus did to sinful humankind's need for salvation. *Agape* is a word that also describes the pure and steadfast love of God the Father for us. John wrote: "for God is love. In this the love of God was manifested toward us, that God has sent His only-begotten Son into the world, that we might live through Him" (1 John 4:8b-9 NKJV). Christian love is the love, gratitude, and joy that Christian men and women have in their hearts as they respond to the love of God in Jesus Christ who made them holy so that He might endow them with salvation and everlasting life.[8]

It is obvious that only Christians can live the life that Jesus taught. The motivation for leading a life of Christian love is our appreciative, thankful, and loving response to God's love that we experienced when we

---

7 Gerhard Kittel, ed., Geoffrey Bromiley, trans. and ed., 1964, *Theological Dictionary of the New Testament*, vol. 1 (Grand Rapids, Mich.: Wm. B. Eerdmans Publ. Co.), pp. 35-38.

8 Ephesians 1:3-10

came to faith in Christ. As John wrote: "We love, because He first loved us" (1 John 4:19 NASB). This being so, one has to conclude that only Christians can possess this motivation. Only Christians through the Holy Spirit's gift of faith have experienced Christ's redeeming love.

The ability to lead a life of Christian love no matter how imperfectly is the result of the sanctifying work of the Holy Spirit. A Christian and a non-Christian may be doing exactly the same activity, but the motivations may hardly be the same. The non-Christian may be aiding an invalid in a wheelchair through the swinging doors of a department store because of his personal ethical philosophy and his sense of satisfaction in living that philosophy. The Christian may be doing the same action because his God taught him, and through the activity of the Holy Spirit inspired and motivated him, to have an orientation of benevolent and compassionate love toward all people and especially toward those in need. Jesus' words, "Truly, I say to you, to the extent that you did it to one of these brothers of Mine, even the least of them, you did it to Me" (Matthew 25:40 NASB), channels the love we have for our Savior to the needs of our fellowman.

Does it make a difference? Jesus stressed repeatedly that God looks at the motivation of the heart. The non-Christian has set up his own norms of personal behavior and through his ignorance or rebelliousness frustrates his Creator's desire for him to walk in His Son's way. The Christian accepts God's revelation of Himself in the person and work of Jesus and cheerfully walks in the way of unselfish love that Jesus taught.

Christian Love Is a Discerning Love

This motivation of the heart, this Christian love, is not one of mindless sentimentality. It is a discerning love. It is a love that may express itself in strong action in the protection of the weak from the oppressor. The tough words with which Jesus protested the actions of those who robbed the widows and for a pretense made long prayers (Mark 12:40) were still spoken in love. It was a love that would confront the oppressor with his sin and call for his repentance, a love that would protest injustices against the weak. Luke wrote of a time when Jesus was invited to dinner at the home of a Pharisee:

> While he [Jesus] was speaking, a Pharisee asked him to dine with him; so he went in and sat at table. The Pharisee was astonished to see that he did not first wash before dinner. And the Lord said to him, "Now you Pharisees cleanse the outside of the cup and of the dish, but inside you are full of extortion and wickedness. You fools! Did not he who made the outside make

the inside also? But give for alms those things which are within; and behold, everything is clean for you.

But woe to you Pharisees! for you tithe mint and rue and every herb, and neglect justice and the love of God; these you ought to have done, without neglecting the others. Woe to you Pharisees! for you love the best seat in the synagogues and salutations in the market places. Woe to you! for you are like graves which are not seen, and men walk over them without knowing it."

One of the lawyers answered him, "Teacher, in saying this you reproach us also." And he said, "Woe to you lawyers also! for you load men with burdens hard to bear, and you yourselves do not touch the burdens with one of your fingers." (Luke 11:37-46 RSV)

What a dinner party that must have been! It ended with the lawyers and Pharisees vehemently questioning Him. They tried to provoke Him to say something concerning which He might be accused (Luke 11:53-54).

When Jesus drove the moneychangers and sellers of livestock for sacrificial offerings out of the Temple, it was also an act of love toward those who were being victimized by such impious trade that made the house of prayer a marketplace. John recorded:

And the Passover of the Jews was at hand, and Jesus went up to Jerusalem. And He found in the temple those who were selling oxen and sheep and doves, and the moneychangers seated. And He made a scourge of cords, and drove them all out of the temple, with the sheep and the oxen; and He poured out the coins of the moneychangers, and overturned their tables; and to those who were selling the doves He said, "Take these things away; stop making My Father's house a house of merchandise." (John 2:13-16 NASB)

The portrayal of the clergy and Christians by the motion picture and television industries so often as weak-minded, naïve, foolishly sentimental types should bear no relationship to reality. Our Lord counseled that His people should be as wise (sensible, thoughtful, prudent) as serpents and as guileless (pure and innocent) as doves. (Matthew 10:16) The followers of Jesus are to love people as He loved them, not necessarily to trust them. Jesus certainly did not: John records, "While He was in Jerusalem for Passover many gave their allegiance to him when they saw the signs that he performed. But Jesus for his part would not trust himself to them. "He knew men so well, all of them, that he needed no evidence from others about a man, for he himself could tell what was in a man" (John 2:23-25 NEB).

During my life, I have observed many an evil man stumble and come to grief when he mistook the lack of deceit, cunning, and guile of a Christian for naiveté. The old adage coined by Paul "to the pure all things are pure" may mean at times that Christians in putting the best construction on another's actions will not immediately recognize evil. The converse of the saying, however, "to the corrupt and unbelieving nothing is pure" (Titus 1:15 RSV), is also true. Basic to the corrupt man's mental health is his view that all men operate as impurely and cynically as himself, that all men have their price. When he observes a person who does not operate in his own self-serving fashion, he takes it for mere stupidity and simplemindedness. The Thomas à Beckets and Thomas Mores are certainly in the minority, but they have been present all through history to trip up the King Henrys.

The New Commandment is the Key to Understanding Jesus' Previous Teachings

All that Jesus had taught previously about the way of life that His disciples were to follow makes sense in the light of the New Commandment that He gave at the close of His ministry. The ancient Christians understood the major significance of Christ's giving the New Commandment by calling the day before Good Friday, *Mandatum* Thursday, that is, Commandment Thursday. Over the centuries, the word *Mandatum* has been corrupted into "Maundy." Thus, we have Maundy Thursday in Holy Week of today.

It is in the light of the New Commandment that we can understand Jesus' healing on the Sabbath and allowing His hungry disciples to pluck and eat grain on the Sabbath. These acts of compassion and concern on Jesus' part are in keeping with His orientation of self-giving love found in the New Commandment.

The extension of the Law in the Sermon on the Mount is also best understood when Christ's New Commandment is taken into account. The New Commandment of loving others as Christ loved us is surely broken not only when we murder, but also when we hate or demean another; not only when we commit adultery, but also when we lust after another person. Christ is telling us that God looks at the motivation of our hearts as well as at our actions.

In the Sermon on the Mount, Jesus said that He had not come to abolish the Law but to fulfill it. If we follow our Lord's New Commandment of loving our fellowman as He loved us, the truth of Christ's statement will be evident in our lives; for through love the Law is indeed fulfilled. We will not dishonor our parents; we will hardly murder, commit adultery, steal, perjure ourselves, or enviously covet that which is our neighbors. Such behavior would be foreign to an attitude of showing love toward all those with whom we live or come in contact. Thus, as Jesus taught, the moral code of the Old Testament is not abolished. Rather, our Lord showed us how to fulfill the moral laws of the Ten Commandments by living a life of selfless love for our neighbor.

A New Way for A New Age

Truly, Jesus Christ brought a new age and a new way of life into existence. Nonetheless, as Jesus said: "The law and the prophets were until John; since then the good news of the kingdom of God is preached, and every one enters it violently. But it is easier for heaven and earth to pass away, than for one dot of the law to become void" (Luke 16:16-17 RSV). The way of life that Christ taught does not destroy or abolish the basic Old Testament moral law. It rather supersedes the way of life of the Old Testament. The Ten Commandments should still be taught, but they are not the focus of the New Testament way of life.

With His new way of life, Jesus made it impossible any longer to live by the letter of the law and violate the spirit of the law. If one follows Jesus' New Commandment of loving others as He loved us, there is no way of evading the spirit of the law and yet living by its letter. If we follow His preeminent commandment of loving one another in the same selfless and unselfish way that He loved us, then obviously we will fulfill the spirit of the law.

Jesus' New Commandment also overthrew the haughtiness and pride of those learned scholars in the Law who looked with condescension and disdain on the common working folk who had no leisure to study the Law. The Gospels record how this conceit of the scribes, lawyers, and Pharisees so obviously riled our Lord. When He gave the New Commandment, Jesus made it possible for even a person with limited intelligence or education to live fully the Christian life. If a Christian treats every person he encounters with the same compassionate, benevolent, and self-giving love as his Lord showed to him, he will fulfill the moral law.

Perhaps another reason Jesus waited until the end of His ministry to give His New Commandment is that only then could His disciples fully understand just how great His love was for them. Certainly, as they watched Him dying on that rough wooden cross the next day, His words of the previous evening must have rung in their ears, "This is My commandment, that you love one another as I have loved you. Greater love has no one than this, that he lay down his life for his friends" (John 15:12-13 NKJV).

In the New Commandment given to His assembled disciples during that last supper, we see the culmination of Christ's ethical teaching about the way of life He wished His people to live. Jesus slowly unfolded and gave insight into His new way of life throughout His ministry. He would have shocked and traumatized His listeners, so steeped in Mosaic Law and their Tradition, had He done otherwise.

The Lord, therefore, had slowly to reveal His teaching concerning His new way of life. The Sermon on the Mount is often taken as the high point of Jesus' instruction concerning His way of life. Rather, it is more of an introductory statement calling the Old Testament Law into question and initiating the discussion of His new way of life.[9] Until Christ gave His New Commandment, His teachings about the way of life His disciples were to follow cannot be fully understood. Giving equal weight to all of Jesus' ethical statements without regard to His progressive revelation of His new way of life is an error that makes it very difficult to understand the ethics of Jesus Christ.

Jesus Revealed His New Way of Life as He Did His Messiahship

When Jesus gave His New Commandment the evening before He was crucified, He completed His teaching about His way of life in a similar way to that of His being the Christ, the Messiah. Jesus had only slowly revealed that He was the Messiah to His disciples. When His disciples came to know that He was the Christ, He charged them to tell no one (Matthew 16:20). Although Jesus did not openly identify Himself as the Messiah to His countrymen, His constant reference to Himself as the Son of Man had strong messianic implications. The religious leaders of the Jews understood that all too well. When at Jesus' trial before the Council the high priest asked Jesus, "I adjure You by the living God, that You tell us whether you are the Christ, the Son of God?" Jesus replied to the question, "You have said it yourself; nevertheless I tell you, hereafter you shall see the Son of Man sitting at the right hand of power, and coming on the clouds of heaven." Upon hearing this the high priest threw himself into a high dudgeon, for he obviously recognized Jesus' answer as referring to Daniel's ancient prophecy: "I kept looking in the night visions, and behold, with the clouds of heaven One like a Son of Man was coming, and He came up to the Ancient of Days and was presented before Him. And to Him was given dominion, glory and a kingdom, that all peoples, nations, and men of every language might serve Him. His dominion is an everlasting dominion which shall not pass away; and His kingdom is one which will not be destroyed."[10]

---

9 This also is the view of John Chrysostom, (see page 257).

10 In Daniel 7:13-14 "Son of Man," is often perhaps tendentiously translated as "human being." See Appendix 1 for references in the early church literature concerning

Jesus' identification of Himself with this Danielic prophecy of the Messiah caused the high priest to tear his robes in anger and accuse Jesus of blasphemy. The Council responded to Jesus' words by judging Him as deserving of death and rising up vented their rage upon Him by spitting in His face, slapping Him, and beating Him with their fists (Matthew 26:63-68 NASB, also Mark 14:61-65).

One of the reasons Jesus obscured His being the Christ is evident—He had no intention of letting the people propel Him into being a political messiah whom they hoped would overthrow the Roman occupation of their country. Finally, however, Jesus did fully identify Himself as the Messiah. He did this not only at His trial but also in His reply to the woman of Samaria (John 4:25-26). Biblical scholars have called Jesus' treatment of His messiahship, "the Messianic Secret."

Christ's New Way of Life and the Opposition of the World

Jesus predicted that those who followed His way of life would find themselves resented and at times persecuted by the world. For example, the moral young man who belongs to the typical college fraternity may not find himself admired for his virtue but rather resented and ridiculed by those of his fraternity brothers who are sexually immoral. He will find himself the butt of jokes. He will find that his fraternity brothers will try to entrap him in sexually compromising situations. Their own rationale and justification for their sexually irresponsible behavior is that everyone does it. They argue that because of what they believe to be their irrepressible natural drives it is impossible and indeed unhealthy to avoid fornication. A person in their midst who lives as a Christian and who treats young women with respect contradicts their self-serving rationalizations for their exploitation of young women.

One can give examples such as the above almost endlessly. Guilty of exceptional behavior and often resented by a good number of their fellow workers is the employee who does not take advantage of his expense account, the school teacher who does not take all her sick days whether she is sick or not, the office worker who does not purloin office supplies, the policeman or politician who refuses minor if not major gifts or bribes, the executive who does not do some insider stock trading, the factory worker who does not steal tools, the student who does not cheat on tests, and the government employee who actually works at his job as if he were serving the Lord and not men. And so forth into infinity.

Jesus knew what He was talking about when He said, "Woe to you when all men speak well of you! For so did their fathers to the false prophets" (Luke 6:26 NKJV). If one lives the way that Jesus taught, it can be taken for granted that one will at times meet resentment, ridicule, and hatred just as did Jesus. A good example of this bigotry and prejudice is, as mentioned earlier, the usual depiction of clergy and Christians in the anti-Christian dominated film and television industries as weak, foolish, sentimental people. This evil world, filled with aggrandizing, exploiting, self-serving men and women, can seldom tolerate a person who lives the unselfish, self-giving love of Jesus' New Commandment. Such a person is a bother to their conscience. He is a living refutation of that grand excuse, "Everybody does it." Therefore, Christ ends His description of His followers in the Beatitudes by concluding:

> "Blessed are those who have been persecuted for the sake of righteousness, for theirs is the kingdom of heaven.
> Blessed are you when men cast insults at you, and persecute you, and say all kinds of evil against you falsely, on account of Me. Rejoice, and be glad, for your reward in heaven is great, for so they persecuted the prophets who were before you." (Matthew 5:10-12 NASB)

Living Christ's way of life, therefore, is not an easy path to take. Our Lord indicated as much when He said:

> "If anyone desires to come after Me, let him deny himself, take up his cross daily, and follow Me. For whoever desires to save his life will lose it, but whoever loses his life for My sake will save it. For what advantage is it to a man if he gains the whole world, and loses himself or is cast away? For whoever is ashamed of Me and My words, of him the Son of Man will be ashamed when He comes in His own glory, and in His Father's, and in the holy angels." (Luke 9:23-26 NKJV)

The Joy of Living the Full Christian Life

Living the Christian life may be no bed of roses, but that does not mean that life on this earth is not to be enjoyed. We may follow the example of our Lord also in this respect. Jesus was no morose, somber, long-faced, disapproving bluenose. Christ was criticized during His life for His buoyant and wholehearted approach to life. In the Gospel of Luke, we find Jesus mentioning this carping by His detractors:

"For John the Baptist came neither eating bread nor drinking wine, and you say, 'He has a demon.' The Son of Man has come eating and drinking, and you say, 'Look, a glutton and a winebibber, a friend of tax collectors and sinners!" (Luke 7:33-34 NKJV)

Now it certainly may be rightly doubted that Jesus was a glutton or over-indulged in wine, but there would have been no basis for the slurs if Jesus were not one who obviously enjoyed the fruits of the earth and the vine.

Consider too that the first of Jesus' miracles was at the wedding celebration at Cana (John 2:1-11). There may be a variety of opinions as to why Jesus turned water into wine at that reception. Certainly among them, however, is that He took pleasure in the happiness of the crowd celebrating the new marriage. Note too, the miracle took place at a time when according to the steward of the feast men had already drunk freely—to the point, obviously, where they might not be able to distinguish good wine from poorer wine. The Old Testament speaks of God's gift of "wine to gladden the heart of man" (Psalm 104:15 RSV). Jesus lived within this tradition of condemning the abuse but not the use of the fermented fruit of the vine.

The Lord created a beautiful and bountiful earth on which we are to live. How disappointed He must be if His people ignore the abundance and comeliness of the creation in which they find themselves. As Christ said, "Consider the lilies of the field. . . even Solomon in all His glory was not arrayed like one of these" (Matthew 6:28-29 NKJV). Christians may also be imitators of our Lord in the wholesome enjoyment of His plenteous creation.

But the real joy of walking in Jesus' way of life is the inner joy of knowing that you are walking in harmony with your God. You are striving, however imperfectly, to do His will. You are living the life to which your Creator calls you. You are sharing with your God His providence for the world. You are making a difference in the world in the way that your God wishes. The beauty of this way of life is that it is the road to true inner happiness. Paul quotes Jesus as saying, "It is more blessed to give than to receive" (Acts 20:35 NKJV). An equally valid translation of the Greek text is that of the New English Bible: "Happiness lies more in giving than receiving." It is only the fortunate few who have the courage to live this way and thus have realized the supreme truth of Jesus' words. The worldly may believe that getting is the way to happiness; but for all their possessions, they end up with dust in their mouths.

When one reads Jesus' words in the four Gospels about how Christians are to live, it is remarkable how little Jesus asks of his disciples: They are to keep in communion with their Lord through prayer. They are to remember His death for them by gathering to partake of His Holy Supper for the remission of their sins and its promise of eternal life (Matthew 26:27-29, John 6:52-58). They are to teach and tell others of the good news of God's great love for them (Matthew 28:18-20).

The only service that He asks of them is that they serve Him by acting in Christian love shown in deeds of service even to the least of His brethren, for what they have done unto these He will regard as done unto Him (Matthew 25:31-46). This sums up Christianity, faith in Christ and a life of Christian love to one's neighbor. It is a life of piety and equally of goodness.

Jesus never viewed His followers as ever being in the majority. They are to be the yeast in the loaf, not the whole loaf (Luke 13:20-21). They are to be the salt of the earth, not the whole roast, but that which makes the meat palatable (Matthew 5:13). Christians are to follow their Lord's words: "Let your light so shine before men, that they may see your good works and glorify your Father who is in heaven" (Matthew 5:16 NKJV). Our life of following in the way of Jesus is part of God's plan of uniting all things in Christ, things in heaven and things on earth (Ephesians 1:9-10).

Let us close this chapter on the way of life that Jesus taught with Jesus' own portrayal of the kind of disciple that He wished His followers to be as depicted in His introduction to the Sermon on the Mount:

> How blessed, happy, and fortunate* are they who know their spiritual need;
>> for theirs is the kingdom of heaven.
> How blessed, happy, and fortunate are those who mourn;
>> for they shall be comforted.
> How blessed, happy, and fortunate are the meek;
>> for they shall inherit the earth.
> How blessed, happy, and fortunate are those who hunger and thirst for righteousness;
>> for they shall be satisfied.
> How blessed, happy, and fortunate are the merciful;
>> for they shall obtain mercy.
> How blessed, happy, and fortunate are the pure in heart;
>> for they shall see God.
> How blessed, happy, and fortunate are the peacemakers;
>> for they shall be called sons of God.
> How blessed, happy, and fortunate are those who are persecuted for righteousness' sake;

for theirs is the kingdom of heaven.

How blessed, happy, and fortunate are you when men revile you and persecute you and utter all kinds of evil against you falsely on My account.

Rejoice and be glad, for your reward is great in heaven, for so men persecuted the prophets who were before you. (Matthew 5:3-11)

*(Author's translation of the Greek word *makarios* in its full meaning of "blessed, happy, and fortunate.")

Chapter Five

ST. PAUL AND THE WAY:
The Struggle to Preserve Christ's Way of Love

Paul's Interpretation of Jesus' New Way of Life

The new and revolutionary way of life that Jesus brought into existence presented in the last chapter initiated a way of life based primarily on selfless love rather than law. Christ's people were to imitate their Lord in loving one another in the same unselfish and self-denying way that He loved them. Jesus' new way of life did not abolish the moral code of the Old Testament but rather fulfilled it through lives motivated by Christian love. Christians were to go beyond living pious lives and avoiding evil; they were to engage in acts of goodness that benefited others.

One way of testing this interpretation of Jesus' way of life is by looking at how Paul and John treated Christ's way of life in their writings. Did they also see Jesus' ethical teaching as a significant departure from the approach to ethics as found in the Old Testament? This chapter and the next will consider the ethical teaching of Paul and John in part with this test in mind.

Paul's Faithfulness to the Way of Life Jesus Taught

"Love One Another, As I Have Loved You"

Jesus completed His teaching about His way of life by emphasizing three times the New Commandment during His Maundy Thursday discourse with His disciples:

> A new commandment I give to you, that you love one another; as I have loved you, that you also love one another. By this all will know that you are My disciples, if you have love for one another. . . . This is My commandment, that you love one another as I

have loved you. Greater love has no one than this, that he lay down his life for his friends. . . . These things I command you, that you love one another. (John 13:34-35, 15:12-13, 15:17 NKJV)

These words completed Jesus' emphasis on unselfish and self-denying love in the life of His followers. He had encouraged His followers to love even their enemies. His life was one of not only speaking about love but also acting in love. Earlier in His ministry, He had often cited Leviticus, ". . . you shall love your neighbor as yourself" (19:18). Paul in his letters followed Jesus' example of citing the Old Testament text of loving your neighbor as yourself (Romans 13:8-11, Galatians 5:14).

Paul's letters show the same stress on love as Jesus had in His teaching. Although Paul never quotes the wording of Jesus' New Commandment of loving one another as He loved us, he evidently knew its content. What he wrote in Ephesians is essentially a rewording of Jesus' New Commandment:

Therefore be imitators of God, as beloved children; and walk in love, just as Christ also loved you, and gave Himself up for us, an offering and a sacrifice to God as a fragrant aroma. (Ephesians 5:1-2 NASB)

How this text reminds one of Jesus' words, "Greater love has no one than this, that he lay down his life for his friends." Paul also appears to be referring to Jesus' New Commandment when he wrote to the Thessalonians, "for you yourselves are taught by God to love one another; . . ." (1 Thessalonians 4:9 NASB).

The New Testament contains thirteen of Paul's letters dated between 48 A.D. and his martyrdom in 67 A.D. The theme of Christian love abounds in them:

To the Roman church he wrote:
        "Let love be without hypocrisy. . . . Be devoted to one another in
        brotherly love; . . ." (Romans 12:9-10 NASB)
To the church at Corinth:
        "Let all that you do be done in love." (1 Corinthians 16:14 NASB)
To the Galatian Christians:
        ". . . through love serve one another." (Galatians 5:13 NASB)
In Ephesians:
        ". . . walk in a manner worthy of the calling with which you have
        been called, with all humility and gentleness, with patience,

showing forbearance to one another in love, . . ." (Ephesians 4:1-2 NASB)

To the Christians at Philippi:

"And this I pray, that your love may abound still more and more in real knowledge and all discernment, . . ." (Philippians 1:9 NASB)

To the Christians at Colossae:

"And beyond all these things put on love, which is the perfect bond of unity." (Colossians 3:14 NASB)

To the church at Thessalonica:

". . . and may the Lord cause you to increase and abound in love for one another, and for all men, just as we also do for you" (1 Thessalonians 3:12 NASB)

And to his protégé Timothy:

"But the goal of our instruction is love from a pure heart and a good conscience and a sincere faith." (1 Timothy 1:5 NASB)

If love was an emphasis of Jesus, it certainly was also that of His faithful apostle Paul. Paul was a reliable communicator and interpreter of ethical teachings of Jesus. The same emphases that Jesus had are also to be found in the letters of Paul. There is no support for the idea that Paul rather than Jesus was the true creator of Christianity when you consider the way of life as taught by Jesus and applied by Paul. In item after item, in idea after idea, Paul follows Jesus' teaching about the way of life that Christians are to live.

Christian Love Is Active in Good Deeds

Paul taught that we are saved by our faith alone in Jesus Christ and not by good works. The text that teaches this most plainly is:

For by grace you have been saved through faith, and that not of yourselves; it is the gift of God, not of works, lest anyone should boast. (Ephesians 2:8-9 NKJV).

Far too often, however, the sermons of Protestant Christians stop at the above verses. But are works therefore unimportant in our lives? That is most emphatically not the case! Paul completes the thought of the verses above in writing:

For we are His workmanship, created in Christ Jesus for good works, which God has prepared beforehand that we should walk in them. (Ephesians 2:10 NKJV).

Therefore, what is a major reason why Christ has saved us through faith? It is to the end that we should spend our life doing good works. The piety of our faith is to result in an active life of walking in love and goodness.

Paul's letters are filled with an emphasis on the Christian living a life of good works. The Galatians are to have a "faith working by love" (Galatians 5:6). He encourages them not to grow weary in doing good (Galatians 6:9). He prays that the Christians of Colossae "walk worthy of the Lord, fully pleasing Him, being fruitful in every good work . . ." (Colossians 1:10 NKJV). To Titus, his co-worker in Crete, he wrote, "And let our people also learn to maintain good works, to meet urgent needs, that they may not be unfruitful" (Titus 3:14 NKJV).

Christian Love Returns Good for Evil

Jesus in the Sermon on the Mount taught that His followers should not repay evil for evil but rather good for evil (see pages 52-54). The same thought is found in Paul's writings. To the Thessalonians he wrote, "See that none of you repays evil for evil, but always seek to do good to one another and to all" (1 Thessalonians 5:15 RSV). And to the Romans Paul wrote:

> Bless those who persecute you; bless and do not curse. Rejoice with those who rejoice, and weep with those who weep. Be of the same mind toward one another. Do not set your mind on high things, but associate with the humble. Do not be wise in your own opinion. Repay no one evil for evil. Have regard for good things in the sight of all men. If it is possible, as much as depends on you, live peaceably with all men. Beloved, do not avenge yourselves, but rather give place to wrath; for it is written, "Vengeance is Mine, I will repay," says the Lord. "Therefore if your enemy hungers, feed him; if he thirsts, give him a drink; for in so doing you will heap coals of fire on his head." Do not be overcome by evil, but overcome evil with good. (Romans 12:14-21 NKJV)

The Christian Forgives Others As Christ Forgave Him

And as did Jesus (see pages 55-56), Paul counseled forgiveness for all who sin against us. This is a theme that appears time and again in his letters. In his letter called Ephesians, he counseled:

> And do not grieve the Holy Spirit of God, by whom you were

sealed for the day of redemption. Let all bitterness, wrath, anger, clamor, and all evil speaking be put away from you, with all malice. And be kind to one another, tenderhearted, forgiving one another, just as God in Christ also has forgiven you. (Ephesians 4:30-32 NKJV)

To the Colossians he similarly wrote:

And so, as those who have been chosen of God, holy and beloved, put on a heart of compassion, kindness, humility, gentleness and patience; bearing with one another, and forgiving each other, whoever has a complaint against anyone; just as the Lord forgave you, so also should you. And beyond all these things put on love, which is the perfect bond of unity. (Colossians 3:12-14 NASB)

The Christian Follows the Father's Will, As Did Christ

Paul followed Christ in emphasizing the priority of God's will over our own. Numerous times Jesus stressed that He and His followers were to do the will of Him who sent Him (see pages 70-72). Paul's writings are in keeping with this emphasis. For example, to the church at Rome he wrote:

And do not be conformed to this world, but be transformed by the renewing of your mind, that you may prove what is that good and acceptable and perfect will of God. (Romans 12:2 NKJV).

Also he counseled the Colossians:

For this reason also, since the day we heard of it [their faith], we have not ceased to pray for you and to ask that you may be filled with the knowledge of His will in all spiritual wisdom and understanding, so that you may walk in a manner worthy of the Lord, to please Him in all respects, bearing fruit in every good work and increasing in the knowledge of God; . . . (Colossians 1:9-10 NASB)

Christians Are To Respect Lawful Government

When some Pharisees tried to trap Jesus into opposing the Roman government by asking Him "Is it lawful to pay taxes to Caesar, or not?" Jesus answered them, "Render therefore to Caesar the things that are Caesar's, and to God the things that are God's" (Matthew 22:17, 21 NKJV). Jesus would not deny the government their rightful due of taxes. Paul is often criticized for urging obedience to the Roman government and his apparent accommodation with the status quo. The firebrands of society have never been happy with his words in Romans:

> Let every soul be subject to the governing authorities. For there is no authority except from God, and the authorities that exist are appointed by God. Therefore whoever resists the authority resists the ordinance of God, and those who resist will bring judgment on themselves. For rulers are not a terror to good works, but to evil. Do you then want to be unafraid of the authority? Do what is good, and you will have praise from the same. For he is God's minister to you for good. But if you do what is evil, be afraid; for he does not bear the sword in vain; for he is God's minister, an avenger to execute wrath on him who does evil. Therefore you must be subject, not only because of wrath but also for conscience' sake. For because of this you also pay taxes, for they are God's ministers attending continually to this very thing. Render therefore to all their due; taxes to whom taxes are due, customs to whom customs, fear to whom fear, honor to whom honor. (Romans 13:1-7 NKJV)

Paul, as did Jesus, recognized the rightful place of government in society. If there is to be change in lawful governance, the Christian is to work through persuasion and by changing the heart of men and not attempting to overthrow a legitimate government by violence.

The Danger of Wealth to the Christian

Jesus dumbfounded His disciples by stating that it was harder for a rich man to enter heaven than for a camel to get through an eye of a needle. Paul followed Jesus' teaching regarding wealth. To Timothy he wrote:

> But godliness with contentment is great gain. For we brought nothing into this world, and it is certain we can carry nothing out. And having food and clothing, with these we shall be content. But those who desire to be rich fall into temptation and a snare, and into many foolish and harmful lusts which drown men in

destruction and perdition. For the love of money is a root of all kinds of evil, for which some have strayed from the faith in their greediness, and pierced themselves through with many sorrows. . . . Command those who are rich in this present age that they not be haughty, nor trust in uncertain riches but in the living God, who gives us richly all things to enjoy; that they do good, that they be rich in good works, ready to give, willing to share, storing up for themselves a good foundation for the time to come, that they may lay hold on eternal life. (1 Timothy 6:6-10, 17-19 NKJV)

The Sanctity of Marriage

Jesus stressed the sanctity of marriage. Mark recounts the following incident:

And the Pharisees came and asked Him, "Is it lawful for a man to divorce his wife?" testing Him. And He answered and said to them, "What did Moses command you?" And they said, "Moses permitted writing a certificate of divorce, and to put her away." And Jesus answered and said to them, "Because of the hardness of your heart he wrote you this precept. But from the beginning of the creation, God 'made them male and female. For this reason a man shall leave his father and mother and be joined to his wife, and the two shall become one flesh'; so then they are no longer two, but one flesh. Therefore what God has joined together, let not man divide." And in the house His disciples asked Him again about the same matter. And He said to them, "Whoever divorces his wife and marries another commits adultery against her. And if a woman divorces her husband and marries another, she commits adultery." (Mark 10:2-12 NKJV, see also Matthew 19:3-9)

Paul knew Christ's teaching well, for to the Corinthian Church he wrote:

"And to the married I command, yet not I but the Lord: A wife is not to depart from her husband. But even if she does depart, let her remain unmarried or be reconciled to her husband. And a husband is not to divorce his wife" (1 Corinthians 7:10-11 NKJV).

The Source of Evil Is Within

Jesus recognized that the source of evil in man came from within. He said to the Pharisees:

> "What comes out of a man, that defiles a man. For from within, out of the heart of men, proceed evil thoughts, adulteries, fornications, murders, thefts, covetousness, wickedness, deceit, licentiousness, an evil eye, blasphemy, pride, foolishness. All these evil things come from within and defile a man." (Mark 7:20-23 NKJV)

To the Galatians Paul wrote similarly of the evil within man:

> This I say then: Walk in the Spirit, and you shall not fulfill the lust of the flesh. . . . Now the works of the flesh are evident, which are these: adultery, fornication, uncleanness, licentiousness, idolatry, sorcery, hatred, contention, jealousy, outburst of wrath, selfish ambition, dissensions, heresies, envy, murders, drunkenness, revelry, and the like; . . ." (Galatians 5:16, 19-21 NKJV)

Conforming to the Values of the World

The difficulty of living in two cultures, one Christian and one pagan or secular, has long been a problem. It is difficult to cast aside the often-decaying (decadent) and false values of the majority culture. It is so easy to go along with the values and attitudes of the world, for it is a way to gain acceptance in one's culture. The cultures of the world so often stress pleasure, material wealth, fame, and self-indulgence as worthy pursuits. We are tempted to live by these goals as they appeal to the baser desires of our natures. Jesus warned against following the ways of the world when He said:

> Enter by the narrow gate; for the gate is wide, and the way is broad that leads to destruction, and many are those who enter by it. For the gate is small, and the way is narrow that leads to life, and few are those who find it. (Matthew 7:13-14 NASB).

Paul was also concerned that Christian people did not follow the ways of the world; he wrote:

I urge you therefore, brethren, by the mercies of God, to present your bodies a living and holy sacrifice, acceptable to God, which is your spiritual service of worship. And do not be conformed to this world, but be transformed by the renewing of your mind, that you may prove what the will of God is, that which is good and acceptable and perfect. (Romans 12:1-2 NASB)

Among the saddest words in the Bible are those in Paul's last letter to Timothy shortly before Paul's execution by the Roman authorities when he wrote concerning a onetime coworker, "for Demas has forsaken me, having loved this present world" (2 Timothy 4:10a NKJV).

The Persecution of Those Living the Christian Life

And finally, Paul as did Jesus, predicted persecution for those who would lead Jesus' way of life. To Timothy, Paul wrote, "Yes, and all who desire to live godly in Christ Jesus will suffer persecution" (2 Timothy 3:12 NKJV). These words certainly recall Christ's words concerning persecution in the Sermon on the Mount (Matthew 5:10-12).

Paul's Emphasis on the Primacy of Christian Love

Christian Love is to Govern All Our Actions

Not only are we to act in love toward all men, but in all our activities we are to live Christ's way of life. Living the Christian life does not mean living as we please, just making sure that we do not violate one of the Ten Commandments. The Christian way of life is to fill and pervade our entire life. It modifies every human relationship that we have. It is the controlling orientation of our life. Whether at home, at work, or in the community, the selfless and self-denying love taught by the New Commandment influences all our actions. The love of Christ governs all that we do. Paul wrote to the Corinthians:

For the love of Christ controls us, because we are convinced that one has died for all; therefore all have died. And he died for all, that those who live might live no longer for themselves but for him who for their sake died and was raised. (2 Corinthians 5:14-15 RSV)

That is the point of living the Christian life; we no longer live to ourselves. Paul stressed this repeatedly: "Let no one seek his own good, but that of his neighbor" (1 Corinthians 10:24 NASB). "Let each of you look out not only for his own interests, but also for the interest of others" (Philippians 2:4 NKJV). "Therefore, whether you eat or drink, or whatever you do, do all to the glory of God" (1 Corinthians 10:31 NKJV). "And whatever you do in word or deed, do all in the name of the Lord Jesus, giving thanks to God the Father through Him" (Colossians 3:17 NKJV).

Christian Love Extends to All Humans

Christian love, however, is not restricted to the love of one's Christian brothers and sisters. Christ's New Commandment includes our fellow Christians, but it certainly also is to be applied to all humankind. If we are to love our enemies, if we are to follow the teaching of the story of the Good Samaritan, then it is obvious that the New Commandment is to include everyone. It is to this end that Paul wrote:

> . . . and may the Lord cause you to increase and abound in love for one another and for all men, just as we also do for you; so that He may establish your hearts unblamable in holiness before our God and Father at the coming of our Lord Jesus with all His saints. (1 Thessalonians 3:12-13 NASB)

> See that no one repays another with evil for evil, but always seek after that which is good for one another and for all men. (1 Thessalonians 5:15 NASB)

> And let us not lose heart in doing good, for in due time we shall reap if we do not grow weary. So then, while we have opportunity, let us do good to all men, and especially to those who are of the household of the faith. (Galatians 6:9-10 NASB)

The mark of a Christian is that his love and concern does not extend to just family, clan, ethnic group, or fellow Christian. All humans on this planet are to share in that love, whomever they might be.

Christian Love Governs Every Human Relationship

Paul sees the way of life taught by Jesus governing every human relationship. It is to govern the relationship between husbands and wives. To the Colossians he wrote, Wives, surrender and yield yourselves in love to your own husbands, as is becoming in the Lord. Husbands, love your wives, and do not be severe with them" (Colossians 3:18-19, author's translation). It is with *agape* love, Christian love, that husbands are to love their wives. They are to care for them with the same selfless and self-denying love that Jesus showed to them. At the end of chapter eight of this book, Paul's views on sex and marriage will be discussed more fully.

Paul writes similarly about human relationships in Ephesians. He counsels:

> Children, obey your parents in the Lord, for this is right. "Honor your father and mother" (which is the first commandment with a promise), "that it may be well with you, and that you may live long on the earth." And, fathers, do not provoke your children to anger; but bring them up in the discipline and instruction of the Lord.
>
> Slaves, be obedient to those who are your masters according to the flesh, with fear and trembling, in the sincerity of your heart, as to Christ; not by way of eyeservice, as men-pleasers, but as slaves of Christ, doing the will of God from the heart. With good will render service, as to the Lord, and not to men, knowing that whatever good thing each one does, this he will receive back from the Lord, whether slave or free.
>
> And, masters, do the same things to them, and give up threatening, knowing that both their Master and yours is in heaven, and there is no partiality with Him. (Ephesians 6:1-9 NASB)

Nothing lies outside the Christian way of life. Our daily work certainly is included. Many Christians in the early Church were slaves. Paul did not tell them to rebel against their condition but rather to see their service as done to the Lord Jesus and not men. Thus, he could write:

> Slaves, in all things obey those who are your masters on earth, not with external service, as those who merely please men, but with sincerity of heart, fearing the Lord. Whatever you do, do your work heartily, as for the Lord rather than for men; knowing that from the Lord you will receive the reward of the inheritance. It is the Lord Christ whom you serve. For he who does wrong will receive the consequences of the wrong which he has done, and that without partiality. (Colossians 3:22-25 NASB)

If Paul could write this to the slave, how much more does it pertain to the free person. We do our work as to the Lord. If our work can be done for the benefit of our fellow humans, it can be done as if to Christ. We remember Jesus' words, "Assuredly, I say to you, inasmuch as you have done it to one of the least of these My brethren, you have done it to Me" (Matthew 25:40 NKJV).

On the other hand, if our labor is to the detriment of our fellowman, then it is not work in which a Christian should be engaged no matter how profitable it might be. But here again is where Christian freedom should reign. It is for each individual to determine for himself whether his work can be done to the glory of God. Every Christian must justify their decision before God in his or her own mind whether or not they are acting with selfless and self-denying love.

It is, however, not only to the slave that Paul addressed his counsel; he also was concerned that the master treated his slave as a Christian should. Paul continued the quotation above by writing, "Masters, grant to your slaves justice and fairness, knowing that you too have a Master in heaven" (Colossians 4:1 NASB).

In a Roman world that treated slaves as less than human, Paul sowed the seed that would in time wither and finally kill the institution of slavery. He made it plain that God showed no partiality between the slave and the free man.

The master was to consider his Christian slave as a true brother in the Lord. When the slave, Onesimus, ran away from his Christian master in Asia Minor to come to Paul, a prisoner in Rome, he felt obliged to send him back. Paul, however, penned a thoughtful and prudent letter to Philemon, the owner of the slave:

> I appeal to you for my son Onesimus, whom I have begotten while in my chains, who once was unprofitable to you, but now is profitable to you and to me. I am sending him back. You therefore receive him, that is, my own heart, whom I wished to keep with me, that in your behalf he might minister to me in my chains for the gospel. But without your consent I wanted to do nothing, that your good deed might not be by compulsion, as it were, but voluntary. For perhaps he departed for a while for this purpose, that you might receive him forever, no longer as a slave but more than a slave, as a beloved brother, especially to me but how much more to you, both in the flesh and in the Lord. If then you count me as a partner, receive him as you would me. If he has wronged you or owes you anything, put that on my account. (Philemon 10-18 NKJV)

What Paul wrote to the Galatians comes to mind:

> For you are all sons of God by faith in Christ Jesus. For as many of you as have been baptized into Christ have put on Christ. There is neither Jew nor Greek, there is neither slave nor free, there is neither male nor female; for you are all one in Christ Jesus. (Galatians 3:26-28 NKJV)

If the slave was a beloved brother, if he was equal to the free man in God's sight, the inconsistency of owning slaves became obvious to many slave owners. The Christian faith did not decree that the ancient institution of slavery be abolished. It changed the heart of the individual slave owner so that he saw the contradiction of owning slaves and living the Christian life.

This was not easy to do for many who were influenced by Christianity. Think of how such esteemed men as Thomas Jefferson and George Washington agonized over this. And it is interesting that neither could quite give up his slaves during his lifetime. It meant going against the customs and attitudes of the dominant culture in which they lived as well as their own self-interest. Indeed, it took many centuries before the institution of slavery finally ended in some Christian countries.

Christians and the Courts

Christians are to strive to live by the ethic of selfless and self-denying love. They are to seek to live in peace and harmony with one another. Where they have disputes with one another, these are to be resolved based on Christian love. They are not to follow the world's approach of running to courts of law to decide their difficulties. Paul was distressed by the Corinthian Christians' casual resort to the non-Christian courts of law and thus he wrote:

> Dare any of you, having a matter against another, go to law before the unrighteous, and not before the saints? Do you not know that the saints will judge the world? And if the world will be judged by you, are you unworthy to judge the smallest matters? Do you not know that we shall judge angels? How much more, things that pertain to this life? If then you have judgments of things pertaining to this life, do you appoint those who are least esteemed by the church to judge? I say this to your shame. Is it so, that there is not a wise man among you, not even one, who will be able to judge between his brethren? But

brother goes to law against brother, and that before unbelievers! Now therefore it is already an utter failure for you that you go to law with one another. Why do you not rather accept wrong? Why do you not rather let yourselves be defrauded? No, you yourselves do wrong and defraud, and you do these things to your brethren! (1 Corinthians 6:1-8 NKJV).

Unfortunately, in the history of the Christian faith, Paul's admonitions often have been ignored. The world has seen even groups or factions within a congregation or a church body shamelessly going to court with one another as they struggle over the ownership of church property. The church has paid a high price for ignoring the way of life that Jesus taught and that Paul so ably instilled and defended in his ministry.

We Live as Fool's for Christ's Sake

But the idea of suffering wrong or allowing oneself to be defrauded rather than bring dishonor upon the Church is viewed as laughable by many. To live according to the Christian way of life and to abstain from chasing after wealth, fame, and material possessions is viewed as foolish and bizarre by many in the world. However, the Christian is not to allow himself to be influenced by the world's ridicule. As Paul wrote to the Corinthians, "We are fools for Christ's sake . . ." (1 Corinthians 4:10a NKJV).

Jesus also was criticized by the religious leaders for ministering to the sinners and the poor. He could have had an honored place as a teacher of Israel if only He had tried to fit in with what was expected of a rabbi by the religious establishment. Like a fool, He challenged the high priests and the elders of His people in condemning their rapaciousness and distortion of the faith of Israel. For His pains, they bled out His life on the cross of Calvary. Who would have thought as He hung on that cross that He would in time be judged to have lived the most influential life that this world has seen.

It is the same with the Christian living after the time of Christ. The Christian's goals are not the goals of the world. He lives a life that would further the prayer, "Thy Kingdom come, Thy will be done on earth as it is in heaven." If living such a life means that the world looks upon him as a fool, so be it. The Christian does not live to please the world but to please his Lord. When Christians and churches seek the approval and applause of the media and the world, they have lost their way!

Paul's Struggle to Preserve Jesus' Way of Life

Opposition to Paul's Teaching of Jesus' Way of Life

Paul faithfully followed Jesus in His ethical teachings. As an apostle and pastor he had the task of interpreting and applying his Lord's teaching to the churches in his care. He especially had to defend his flocks from those who rejected Jesus' way of life and who would bind the new Christians to the laws, statutes, and ordinances of the Old Testament.

A fundamental division was developing in the Palestinian-Jerusalem church. It arose between those who saw Christianity as only a further development of Judaism and those who saw it as a truly new faith. These last followed Jesus in viewing the new covenant as the new cloth that should not be used to patch an old garment or as the new wine that should not be poured into an old wineskin (Matthew 9:16-17).

There were two questions involved in the dispute: First, were the Jews who believed in Jesus as Messiah and Savior required to continue to abide by the laws and customs of Judaism? Second, did the Gentiles who were entering the Church also have to abide by the laws and practices of Judaism?

Paul's argument in his letter to the Roman Christians, many of whom were Jewish in background, was that salvation did not come from obedience to the law of the Old Testament. Similarly, in his letter to the Galatians he wrote: "You have become estranged from Christ, whoever of you would be justified by law; you have fallen from grace" (Galatians 5:4 NKJV).

On the other hand, Christian Jews were free to observe the ceremonial law and practices of the Old Testament if they so desired. Paul did this himself at times, for example, when he took the vow of a Nazarite (Acts 18:18 and Acts 21:23-26) or when he had Timothy circumcised (Acts 16:1-3). Freedom to observe these practices, however, did not mean that they were to be viewed as necessary for salvation. This seems also to have been the position of James, Jesus' brother, and a leader in the Jerusalem church. But many Jews in the church at Jerusalem did not accept this point of view. When Paul arrived in Jerusalem after his third missionary journey, the elders of the Jerusalem church explained to him:

> "You see, brother, how many thousands of Jews there are who believe, and they are all zealous for the law; but they have been informed about you that you teach all the Jews who are among the Gentiles to forsake Moses, saying that they ought not to

circumcise their children nor to walk according to the customs."
(Acts 21:20-21 NKJV)

This, obviously, reflects a misunderstanding of Paul's message. Paul had not taught that Christian Jews should forsake Moses or their religious customs. Rather, he taught that their salvation came through their faith in Jesus Christ and not through the performance of Jewish rites and customs or through the keeping of the Law. Christian Jews were still free to follow the customs and practices of their Jewish heritage as long as they were not held to be necessary for salvation.

The life of James, Jesus' natural brother, illustrates this attitude. James kept the practices of the Jews to the degree that even non-Christian Jews knew him as "James the Just." And yet in his letter, he does not stress keeping the Old Testament law as an observant Jew. He urges rather a faith that exhibits its vitality by a life of kindness and charity in the freedom of the Christian to follow a life of love (James 1:25, 2:8, 2:12).

But there were Christian Jews who disagreed with this freedom to observe or not to observe the Law. They felt that although the Gentiles did not have to observe the law of the Old Testament it was necessary for a Jew to do so. They evidently argued that their righteousness before God came from their observance of the Law. As was mentioned above, it is the attitude of this group that Paul primarily takes up in his letter to the church at Rome, especially in Romans 2:17 to 3:31. Paul argues that the Law basically brings knowledge of sin. He points out that no one can keep the Law as God demands, and that therefore justification before God comes through faith alone. Perhaps Luke's description in Acts of those who were "zealous for the Law" included some in this category.

Finally there were those known to us by Paul's designation of them as the "Circumcision Party" (Galatians 2:12). This group insisted that all Gentiles who would be baptized into the Christian faith should first be required to conform to the laws and practices of Judaism. They have long been termed the "Judaizers." They opposed Paul's preaching and sought to undo his work among the Gentiles by visiting the churches he had founded and belittling his apostleship and message. They insisted that Paul's message was incomplete and that to become fully Christian the males had to be circumcised and the laws and ordinances of the Old Testament had to be observed. Luke records the teaching of this group to the Gentile Christians of Antioch when he writes in Acts, "And certain men came down from Judea and taught the brethren, 'Unless you are circumcised according to the custom of Moses, you cannot be saved'" (Acts 15:1 NKJV).

Paul vehemently opposed the teachings of the Circumcision party. He accused them of preaching another gospel that was really not another gospel (Galatians 1:6-7). They were teaching a way of salvation other than through faith in Jesus Christ. As will be discussed in a later chapter, the Church's final response to the teachings of this group was their excommunication.

The conflict between these opposing points of view came to a head after Paul's first missionary journey. Leaders of the early Church held a council at Jerusalem to consider the matter. Luke records that some believers of the party of the Pharisees contended concerning Gentile Christians, "It is necessary to circumcise them, and to command them to keep the Law of Moses" (Acts 15:5 NKJV). Peter argued against this position as did Paul and his coworker Barnabas. James, Jesus' brother, summed up the arguments and then concluded by deciding, "Therefore I judge that we should not trouble those from the Gentiles who are turning to God, but that we write to them to abstain from things polluted by idols, from sexual immorality, from things strangled, and from blood" (Acts 15:19-20 NKJV).

A letter was written containing James' judgments and sent to the Christians of Antioch, Syria, and Cilicia. Two men from the Jerusalem church, Silas and Judas, were sent along with Paul and Barnabas to explain the letter to the Gentile Christians.

It does not appear that Paul had a very high regard for James's decision and letter. Paul seemingly realized the pronouncements of James were contrary to the way of life taught by Jesus. The church has followed Paul in ignoring James's rulings concerning blood and things strangled. Paul in his first letter to the Corinthians (chapters 8 and 10) discusses the eating of meat offered to idols, but he does not even mention the letter of the Jerusalem Council.

Serving Not Under the Old Written Word but in the New Life of the Spirit

Paul was not going to give up the new way of life taught by Jesus and see it overwhelmed by either old or new codes of law. The Christian was not to be one who followed a written code of law in the determination of his conduct in life. He was rather to be led by the Holy Spirit and the guidance of God's Word in his conduct through life. The Holy Spirit would guide and empower him to lead the way of life that Jesus taught. Paul wrote in this vein to the Roman Christians:

> Do you not know, brethren–for I am speaking to those who know the law--that the law is binding on a person only during his life? Thus a married woman is bound by law to her husband as long as he lives; but if her husband dies she is

discharged from the law concerning the husband. Accordingly, she will be called an adulteress if she lives with another man while her husband is alive. But if her husband dies she is free from that law, and if she marries another man she is not an adulteress.

      Likewise, my brethren, you have died to the law through the body of Christ, so that you may belong to another, to Him who has been raised from the dead in order that we may bear fruit for God. While we were living in the flesh, our sinful passions, aroused by the law, were at work in our members to bear fruit for death. But now we are discharged from the law, dead to that which held us captive, so that we serve not under the old written code but in the new life of the Spirit. . . . For the law of the Spirit of life in Christ Jesus has set me free from the law of sin and death. (Romans 7:1-6, 8:2 RSV)

To live by the Holy Spirit of God means that we no longer serve the lusts of our flesh. Rather we seek to work out in our lives "the law of the Spirit of life in Christ Jesus." Thus the Holy Spirit leads and empowers our lives. Paul then compares those who serve their flesh with those who serve the Spirit:

      For those who live according to the flesh set their minds on the things of the flesh, but those who live according to the Spirit set their minds on the things of the Spirit. To set the mind on the flesh is death, but to set the mind on the Spirit is life and peace. For the mind that is set on the flesh is hostile to God; it does not submit to God's law, indeed it cannot; and those who are in the flesh cannot please God. But you are not in the flesh, you are in the Spirit, if the Spirit of God really dwells in you. (Romans 8:5-9 RSV)

In the passage above, Paul writes of submitting to God's law. That he does not necessarily mean the law of the Old Testament is shown from a text from his letter to the Corinthians:

      For though I am free from all men, I have made myself a slave to all, that I might win the more. To the Jews I became as a Jew, in order to win Jews; to those under the law I became as one under the law--though not being myself under the law--that I might win those under the law. To those outside the law I became as one outside the law--not being without law toward God but under the law of Christ--that I might win those outside the law. (1 Corinthians 9:19-21 RSV)

Paul also speaks of the law of Christ when he wrote: "Bear one another's burdens, and thus fulfill the law of Christ" (Galatians 6:2 NASB). To bear one another's burdens is to act in love toward one another. Thus, Paul's understanding of the law of Christ reflects Christ's principle of Christian (*agape*) love. Paul can say that he is not "without law toward God" even though he is not under the law of the Old Testament because he understands and lives the new way of life brought into existence by Jesus Christ. It is in this sense that he writes, "Circumcision is nothing and uncircumcision is nothing, but keeping the commandments of God is what counts" (1 Corinthians 7:19 NKJV). He understands that the commandments given by Christ were in keeping with His Father's will. Paul obviously is aware of the essence of the Maundy Thursday discourse during which Jesus gave the New Commandment. As was noted earlier, Paul doesn't use the wording of Jesus' New Commandment, but he certainly knew and taught its substance.

The End of the Law Unites Jew and Gentile in Faith in Christ

Paul in his letters follows Jesus who spoke of the end of the Old Testament law in saying: "The law and the prophets were until John (the Baptist); since then the good news of the kingdom of God is preached, . . ." (Luke 16:16 RSV). To the Galatians Paul similarly wrote:

But before faith came, we were kept under guard by the law, kept for the faith which would afterward be revealed. Therefore the law was our schoolmaster to bring us to Christ, that we might be justified by faith. But after faith has come, we are no longer under a schoolmaster. For you are all sons of God by faith in Christ Jesus. (Galatians 3:23-26 NKJV)

Paul expresses the same thought in Ephesians. There is to be no difference between Jew and Gentile. The observance of the Law is not what makes the Jew righteous. Rather, just as with the Gentile, his righteousness comes through his faith in Jesus Christ. The Law that separated the observant Jew and the Gentile no longer divides. In his letters to both the Ephesians and the Romans, he wrote in this vein:

For He Himself is our peace, who has made both one, and has

broken down the middle wall of division between us, having abolished in His flesh the enmity, that is, the law of commandments contained in ordinances, so as to create in Himself one new man from the two, thus making peace, and that He might reconcile them both to God in one body by the cross, by it having put to death the enmity. And He came and preached peace to you who were afar off and to those who were near. For through Him we both have access by one Spirit to the Father. (Ephesians 2:14-18 NKJV)

Brethren, my heart's desire and prayer to God for Israel is that they may be saved. For I bear them witness that they have a zeal for God, but not according to knowledge. For they being ignorant of God's righteousness, and seeking to establish their own righteousness, have not submitted to the righteousness of God. For Christ is the end of the law for righteousness to everyone who believes. (Romans 10:1-4 NKJV)

Love is the Fulfilling of the Law

However, although righteousness before God is no longer to be gained by the observance of the Law, this does not mean that the Law is abolished. It does not mean that the moral code of the Ten Commandments is void. Rather it is as Jesus said, "Do not think that I came to abolish the Law or the Prophets; I did not come to abolish, but to fulfill" (Matthew 5:17 NASB). It is through a life following Christ's teachings concerning unselfish love that the Law is fulfilled. Thus, Paul could write to the Romans:

Owe no one anything, except to love one another; for he who loves his neighbor has fulfilled the law. The commandments, "You shall not commit adultery, You shall not kill, You shall not steal, You shall not covet," and any other commandment, are summed up in this sentence, "You shall love your neighbor as yourself." Love does no wrong to a neighbor; therefore love is the fulfilling of the law. (Romans 13:8-10 RSV)

Paul wrote similarly to the Galatians, "For all the law is fulfilled in one word, even in this: 'You shall love your neighbor as yourself'" (Galatians 5:14 NKJV).

Christian Liberty to Follow Christ's Way of Life

Paul's Rebuke to the Galatian Church over their Return to Old Testament Law

That love is the fulfilling of the Law became the main point of contention between Paul and his critics. Paul insisted on the Christian's freedom to follow love as the Christian worked out the ethical problems he faced. Paul neither wanted Christians to serve under the "old written code" of the Old Testament (Romans 7:6) nor under a legalistic system of their own making. Paul's letter to the Galatian Christians has often been considered the "Magna Charta" of Christian liberty. It is a blunt letter to the churches he founded concerning those who would bind the Galatian Christians to the Law and practices of Judaism.

Just a short time after he had founded the churches of Galatia, a group of Jewish Christians from Jerusalem visited these churches and began leading the new Christians astray. They disparaged the apostleship of Paul. They told the Christians of Galatia that in order to make converts Paul was watering down the Christian message and giving them only part of the requirements of the new faith. They said that they were going to complete Paul's work and give the Galatians the full Christian message. They taught that for the Galatians to become full Christians the festivals and laws of Judaism had to be rigorously followed and the males had to be circumcised. The Galatians were perplexed, and it seems they half believed these new self-appointed teachers. Paul's exasperation is evident in his letter:

> I am astonished that you are so quickly deserting him who called you in the grace of Christ and turning to a different gospel–not that there is another gospel, but there are some who trouble you and want to pervert the gospel of Christ. (Galatians 1:6-7 RSV)

And a little later in the letter:

> You foolish Galatians, who has bewitched you, before whose eyes Jesus Christ was publicly portrayed as crucified? This is the only thing I want to find out from you: did you receive the Spirit by the works of the Law, or by hearing with faith? Are you so foolish? Having begun by the Spirit, are you now being perfected by the flesh? . . . Christ redeemed us from the curse of the Law, . . . so that we might receive the promise of the Spirit through faith. (Galatians 3:1-3, 13-14 NASB)

Salvation, Paul tells them, does not come through the observance of the Old Testament law; it comes through a Spirit-given faith in the forgiveness of sins gained by the crucifixion of Jesus. In fact, to rely on the keeping of the Law for salvation puts one under the curse of God, for "'Cursed is every one who does not abide by all things written in the book of the Law, to perform them'" (Galatians 3:10 NASB).

Paul wrote that to compromise and attempt to gain salvation both through faith in Christ and also by one's own righteousness achieved by living as an Old Testament observant Jew is to put one's salvation in jeopardy. He admonishes the Galatians:

> You observe days and months and seasons and years. I fear for you, that perhaps I have labored over you in vain. . . . Behold I, Paul, say to you that if you receive circumcision, Christ will be of no benefit to you. . . . You have been severed from Christ, you who are seeking to be justified by law; you have fallen from grace. For we through the Spirit, by faith, are waiting for the hope of righteousness. For in Christ Jesus neither circumcision nor uncircumcision means anything, but faith working through love. (Galatians 4:10-11, 5:2, 4-6 NASB)

The Mark of Christian Liberty — Faith Working through Love

Paul insists on the Christian's freedom to live according to "faith working through love." Jesus' new way of life did away with the legalism into which the Old Testament people had turned the Mosaic Law. Paul urges the Galatians, "Stand fast therefore in the liberty with which Christ has made us free, and do not be entangled again with a yoke of bondage (Galatians 5:1 NKJV). Christians are not only free from the Law as a way of salvation; they are free to follow love rather than law as their way of life. A few verses after the text above, Paul wrote:

> For you, brethren, have been called to liberty; only do not use liberty as an opportunity for the flesh, but by love serve one another. For all the law is fulfilled in one word, even in this: "You shall love your neighbor as yourself." (Galatians 5:13-14 NKJV)

Christian Freedom from Man-Made Religious Law

It was not only to the Galatians that Paul wrote in this manner. In his letters to the various churches, Paul wrote of many situations in which love rather than law was to guide the Christian in his daily life. These situations illustrate how Christian freedom is to be used in the Christian's daily life. Paul is very concerned that the Christian continues in his freedom to live in keeping with the law of love that Jesus taught. The Christian was not to submit to laws and ordinances, whether new or old. For example, Paul writes to the Romans:

> Receive the one who is weak in the faith, but not to disputes over doubtful things. For one believes he may eat all things, but he who is weak eats only vegetables. Let not him who eats despise him who does not eat, and let not him who does not eat judge him who eats; for God has received him. Who are you to judge another's servant? To his own master he stands or falls. Indeed, he will be made to stand, for God is able to make him stand. One person esteems one day above another; another esteems every day alike. Let each be fully convinced in his own mind. He who observes the day, observes it to the Lord; and he who does not observe the day, to the Lord he does not observe it. He who eats, eats to the Lord, for he gives God thanks; and he who does not eat, to the Lord he does not eat, and gives God thanks. For none of us lives to himself, and no one dies to himself. For if we live, we live to the Lord; and if we die, we die to the Lord. Therefore, whether we live or die, we are the Lord's. For to this end Christ died and rose and lived again, that He might be Lord of both the dead and the living.
>
> But why do you judge your brother? Or why do you show contempt for your brother? For we shall all stand before the judgment seat of Christ. For it is written: "As I live, says the Lord, every knee shall bow to Me, and every tongue shall confess to God." So then each of us shall give account of himself to God. Therefore let us not judge one another anymore, but rather resolve this, that no one put a stumbling block or a cause to fall in his brother's way. (Romans 14:1-14 NKJV)

One of the reasons some Christians wished to avoid eating meat is that much of the meat offered for sale in Paul's day previously had been offered in sacrifice to idols. Many Christians were troubled by the thought that eating such meat might mean that they were taking part in idol worship. On this question also, Paul taught that the freedom of the Christian was to be exercised. He wrote to the Corinthians:

> Now concerning things offered to idols: We know that we

all have knowledge. Knowledge puffs up, but love edifies. And if anyone thinks that he knows anything, he knows nothing yet as he ought to know. But if anyone loves God, this one is known by Him. Therefore concerning the eating of things offered to idols, we know that an idol is nothing in the world, and that there is no other God but one. For even if there are so-called gods, whether in heaven or on earth--as there are many gods and many lords--yet for us there is only one God, the Father, of whom are all things, and we for Him; and one Lord Jesus Christ, by whom are all things, and we by Him. However, there is not in everyone that knowledge; for some, with consciousness of the idol, to this hour eat it as a thing offered to an idol; and their conscience, being weak, is defiled. But food does not commend us to God; for neither if we eat are we the better, nor if we do not eat are we the worse. (1 Corinthians 8:1-8 NKJV)

To the Colossians also Paul wrote:

Therefore let no one act as your judge in regard to food or drink or in respect to a festival or a new moon or a Sabbath day-- . . . If you have died with Christ to the elementary principles of the world, why, as if you were living in the world, do you submit yourself to decrees, such as, "Do not handle, do not taste, do not touch!" (which all refer to things destined to perish with the using)--in accordance with the commandments and teachings of men? These are matters which have, to be sure, the appearance of wisdom in self-made religion and self-abasement and severe treatment of the body, but are of no value against fleshly indulgence. (Colossians 2:16-23 NASB)

Another example of Christian liberty concerns the giving of gifts for the support of the Church. Paul never mentions the Old Testament law concerning the tithe. This is understandable for Christians are "discharged from the law" and no longer serve "under the old written code" (Romans 7:6 RSV). In addition, what was appropriate for the peculiar circumstances of the twelve tribes of Israel would hardly be appropriate for the Church. The Old Testament requirement of the tithe thus cannot be the rule for Christian giving. In Christian freedom, people are to decide what to give. It is a matter between them and their Lord. Paul only asks that Christians give as God has prospered them (1 Corinthians 16:2). He counsels, "So let each one give as he purposes in his heart, not grudgingly or of necessity; for God loves a cheerful giver" (2 Corinthians 9:7 NKJV). The gift is to come from the heart and be a gift of love.

When one observes the history of the Christian Church, how true are the following prophetic words of Paul that he wrote to the young pastor Timothy:

> Now the Spirit expressly says that in latter times some will depart from the faith, giving heed to deceiving spirits and doctrines of demons, speaking lies in hypocrisy, having their own conscience seared with a hot iron, forbidding to marry, and commanding to abstain from foods which God has created to be received with thanksgiving by those who believe and know the truth. For every creature of God is good, and nothing is to be refused if it is received with thanksgiving; for it is sanctified by the word of God and prayer. (1 Timothy 4:1-5 NKJV)

The point of the above quotation is that we should not give up our Christian liberty and freedom to those who would try to govern our lives through legalistic judgments and law. This obviously does not refer to the laws made by the secular government. It refers to the continual tendency of some "religious" people to attempt to govern other people's conduct in terms of their own idea of what is right and wrong. Paul deplored this as noted previously in Romans 14:1-4. Where the Scriptures have not spoken, we are not to pass judgment on one another.

Paul also spoke to this point when he wrote to the Corinthians, "for why is my freedom judged by another's conscience?" The context in which this clause is found is as follows:

> All things are lawful, but not all things are profitable. All things are lawful, but not all things edify. Let no one seek his own good, but that of his neighbor. Eat anything that is sold in the meat market, without asking questions for conscience' sake; for the earth is the Lord's, and all it contains. If one of the unbelievers invites you, and you wish to go, eat anything that is set before you, without asking questions for conscience' sake. But if anyone should say to you, "This is meat sacrificed to idols," do not eat it, for the sake of the one who informed you, and for conscience' sake; I mean not your own conscience, but the other man's; for why is my freedom judged by another's conscience? (1 Corinthians 10:23-29 NASB)

Christian Freedom and Giving Offense to One's Brother

The text above gives us another facet of how we are to exercise our Christian freedom. All things may be lawful to the Christian, but not all things are helpful. The exercise of our Christian freedom in a given matter may offend or cause problems for the faith of a fellow Christian. If this happens, then out of love and concern for the good of our neighbor, we may willingly give up the exercise of our Christian freedom in that instance. As Paul relates in the above illustration, it is out of concern for the brother's conscience that we will not eat of the meat if the fact that it had been once offered in sacrifice to idols is troubling him.

Paul takes very seriously the possibility of giving offense to the faith of a weak brother. After the sections from Romans and First Corinthians quoted above that spoke of one's freedom regarding eating food once offered to idols, Paul nevertheless showed his concern for the weak brother. To the church at Rome, he wrote:

> Therefore let us not judge one another anymore, but rather determine this—not to put an obstacle or a stumbling block in a brother's way. I know and am convinced in the Lord Jesus that nothing is unclean of itself; but to him who thinks anything to be unclean, to him it is unclean. For if because of food your brother is hurt, you are no longer walking according to love. Do not destroy with your food him for whom Christ died.
> Therefore do not let what is for you a good thing be spoken of as evil; for the kingdom of God is not eating and drinking, but righteousness and peace and joy in the Holy Spirit. For he who in this way serves Christ is acceptable to God and approved by men. So then let us pursue the things which make for peace and the building up of one another.
> Do not tear down the work of God for the sake of food. All things indeed are clean, but they are evil for the man who eats and gives offense. It is good not to eat meat or to drink wine, or to do anything by which your brother stumbles.
> The faith which you have, have as your own conviction before God. Happy is he who does not condemn himself in what he approves. But he who doubts is condemned if he eats, because his eating is not from faith; and whatever is not from faith is sin. (Romans 14:13-23 NASB)

He wrote similarly to the Corinthian congregation concerning giving offense to the weak brother by insisting on one's Christian freedom to eat meat once offered to idols:

> However, there is not in everyone that knowledge; for some, with consciousness of the idol, to this hour eat it as a thing offered to an idol; and their conscience, being weak, is defiled. But food does not commend us to God; for neither if we eat are we the better, nor if we do not eat are we the worse. But take heed lest somehow this liberty of yours become a stumbling block to those who are weak. For if anyone sees you who have knowledge eating in a idol's temple, will not the conscience of the him who is weak be emboldened to eat those things offered to idols? And because of your knowledge the weak brother, for whom Christ died, will perish. But when you thus sin against the brethren, and wound their weak conscience, you sin against Christ. Therefore, if food makes my brother stumble, I will eat no meat while the world stands, lest I make my brother stumble. (1 Corinthians 8:7-13 NKJV)

It is thus not hypocritical when to avoid harming the faith of a weak Christian one refrains from doing that which under other circumstances one might regard as but an exercise of one's Christian freedom. For example, a Christian farmer may decide that in the exercise of his Christian liberty, he will work on Sunday harvesting his rain-threatened wheat crop rather than attending church. Now he normally does not neglect gathering with his fellow Christians (Hebrews 10:24-25). He knows, however, the words of Paul who states, "Therefore let no one act as your judge in regard to food and drink or in respect to a festival or a new moon or Sabbath day—" (Colossians 2:16 NASB), and also "One person esteems one day above another; another esteems every day alike. Let each be fully convinced in his own mind. He who observes the day, observes it to the Lord; and he who does not observe the day, to the Lord he does not observe it" (Romans 14:5-6 NKJV). He is aware, therefore, that the commandment concerning sanctifying the Sabbath no longer pertains to Christians. However, he has a neighbor who is still weak in his faith and understanding of Christianity. The farmer may well feel that his neighbor might misinterpret his exercise of Christian freedom in regard to a holy day as indifference to gathering with his fellow Christians. Thus for the sake of and out of love for his brother, he may attend his church that Sunday to avoid giving offense to his weaker brother.

The Exercise of Christian Liberty According to Paul

To sum up Paul's teaching of Christian liberty, the following conclusions might be made:

1. As the Christian no longer serves under the old written code of the Old Testament, a Christian has the liberty to use his or her freedom to live as the Spirit leads in deciding what is the most selfless and self-denying exercise of Christian love in a given instance. This freedom extends to all areas where the New Testament has not already given direction. This freedom likewise does not extend to violating the moral code found in the Ten Commandments; otherwise, love would not be the fulfilling of the law.

2. The Christian, however, will not try to enforce his own idea of what Christian love requires in a given instance or situation upon his brother or sister in the faith. He will respect the Christian liberty of others to act in Christian love as the Spirit leads them.

3. The Christian also gently and lovingly will resist those who attempt to force their scruples upon him.

4. The Christian, nonetheless, may out of Christian love willingly give up the exercise of his Christian freedom if carrying out his liberty in a given instance or situation might offend the faith of a weak brother.

In all of the above, it is evident that we are to act in selfless and self-denying love, loving others as Christ loved us. Out of Christian love, we will not seek to force our brother to abide by our views. We will respect his Christian freedom to come to his own decision as to what Christian love might demand in a given circumstance. Out of love for the brother and the way of life that Christ taught, we will amiably resist an attempt by our Christian brother or sister to restrict our own Christian freedom. And yet, when the good of our brother is at stake, we will out of Christian love cheerfully give up our exercise of Christian freedom in a given situation. Complicated? Not really. Just follow Paul in letting "all that you do be done with love" (1 Corinthians 16:14 NKJV).

The Difference between Liberty and License

Those who wish to return to a life governed by church law have long opposed the way of life that Paul taught. In Paul's own lifetime, some who believed that salvation came through the keeping of the Law maliciously distorted Paul's stress on a saving faith in Christ's sacrifice. They charged him with libertinism. They said that he taught that one could sin freely, for it only gave an opportunity for God to forgive generously. To the Romans Paul wrote:

> And why not say, "Let us do evil that good may come"? --as we are slanderously reported and some affirm that we say. Their condemnation is just. . . . What shall we say then? Shall we continue in sin that grace may abound? Certainly not! How shall we who died to sin live any longer in it? Or do you not know that as many of us as were baptized into Christ Jesus were baptized into His death? Therefore we were buried with Him by baptism into death, that just as Christ was raised from the dead by the glory of the Father, even so we also should walk in newness of life. (Romans 3:8, 6:1-4 NKJV)

Paul also recognized that the Christian might use his Christian freedom to act in love as a way of excusing and rationalizing selfish actions. He was aware that Christian liberty might degrade to license. Therefore, he wrote to the Galatians:

> For you, brethren, have been called to liberty; only do not use liberty as an opportunity for the flesh, but by love serve one another. For all the law is fulfilled in one word, even in this: "You shall love your neighbor as yourself." (Galatians 5:13-14 NKJV)

Herein, of course, lays the proper use of the moral demands of the Ten Commandments. If a person's interpretation of what is the Christian thing to do in a given instance violates one of the Commandments, then love is no longer fulfilling the Law. The individual has rationalized a selfish desire by trying to persuade himself that he is really acting in Christian love. The moral code of the Ten Commandments works as a mirror in which we recognize loveless acts.

There are novelists who devise situations in which breaking one of the Ten Commandments is depicted as done out of selfless and self-sacrificing love. The "noble" prostitute who sells herself to save her family from starvation is one such character beloved by writers. Her basic problem, however, is her lack of trust in her God. She does what her God forbids as her solution to a problem in which she can see no other alternative. It is in just such situations when we cannot see any way out that our God wills that we trust Him.

The way to avoid using one's Christian freedom as an excuse to gratify the desires of the flesh is to recognize that these cravings are too often immoral and may lead to evil and selfish actions. Paul urges the Christian to concentrate rather on the sanctifying activity of God's Holy Spirit. Paul thus writes to the Galatians:

> This I say then: Walk in the Spirit, and you shall not fulfill the lust of the flesh. For the flesh lusts against the Spirit, and the Spirit against the flesh; and these are contrary to one another, so that you do not do the things you want. But if you are led by the Spirit, you are not under the law.
>
> Now the works of the flesh are evident, which are these: adultery, fornication, uncleanness, licentiousness, idolatry, sorcery, hatred, contention, jealousy, outbursts of wrath, selfish ambition, dissensions, heresies, envy, murders, drunkenness, revelry, and the like; of which I tell you beforehand, just as I have also told you in time past, that those who practice such things will not inherit the kingdom of God.
>
> But the fruit of the Spirit is love, joy, peace, longsuffering, kindness, goodness, faithfulness, gentleness, self-control. Against such there is no law. And those who are Christ's have crucified the flesh with its passions and desires. If we live in the Spirit, let us also walk in the Spirit. (Galatians 5:16-25 NKJV)

To be led by the Spirit also means that we try to avoid those stimuli and situations that arouse the passions of the flesh. Those whose minds are lured by the entrancements of money, power, sex, or questionable pleasures may find that their actions soon follow that which occupies their minds. What we dwell upon in our minds may well influence our behavior. If we read violent or salacious books, magazines, or watch television or films that flaunt fornication, adultery, and homosexual behavior, we may find it difficult to live the Christian life. If our culture heroes are those who live selfishly and immorally, we should not be too surprised if we find ourselves seeking to imitate their lives. Constant exposure to trashy material slowly dulls and desensitizes our conscience. What a high percentage of our TV shows, books, magazines, movies, etc., would be sent to the garbage heap if Christians lived by the words of Paul to the Philippians:

> Finally, brethren, whatever things are true, whatever things are noble, whatever things are just, whatever things are pure, whatever things are lovely, whatever things are of good report, if there is any virtue and if there is anything praiseworthy--meditate on these things. The things which you have learned and received and heard and seen in me--these do, and the peace of God will be with you. (Philippians 4:8-9 NKJV)

The Old Testament Law and the Non-Christian

Although the moral law of the Old Testament is not the Christian's primary guide in life, it still is the basic moral law for those outside the Christian faith. Paul made that plain when he wrote to Timothy:

> But the goal of our instruction is love from a pure heart and a good conscience and a sincere faith. For some men, straying from these things, have turned aside to fruitless discussion, wanting to be teachers of the Law, even though they do not understand either what they are saying or the matters about which they make confident assertions.
> But we know that the Law is good, if one uses it lawfully, realizing the fact that law is not made for a righteous man, but for those who are lawless and rebellious, for the ungodly and sinner, for the unholy and profane, for those who kill their fathers or mothers, for murderers and immoral men and homosexuals and kidnappers and liars and perjurers, and whatever else is contrary to sound teaching, according to the glorious gospel of the blessed God, with which I have been entrusted. (1 Timothy 1:5-11 NASB)

There is no place in Christ's Church for the type of casuistry or arguing over the law that took up the time of rabbinical scholars. Nor is there a place for those who would make new laws to bind the consciences of Christians by erecting new canons of Church law. Paul could not have made his point any clearer. The Law is not for the individual who is counted righteous and just before God because of his or her saving faith in Jesus' sacrificial death. The Law is for those who stand unjustified before God because of their rejection of Christ's pardon for their sins. These are people not led by the Spirit to lead lives in accordance with our Lord's commandment to love one another as He has loved us.

The moral laws of the Ten Commandments are thus primarily for those outside the Christian faith. They retain their purpose of restraining the sinfulness of the unregenerate person. They also serve to show humankind its accountability before God for its actions. As has been discussed above and as Paul time and again wrote, Christians are no longer under the Law. Those, however, who are outside the Christian faith are under the Law's demands. The Law serves to show their need for a savior from sin. Paul wrote to this effect:

> Now we know that whatever the Law says, it speaks to those who are under the Law, that every mouth may be closed, and all the world may become accountable to God; because by the works of the Law no flesh will be justified in His sight; for through the Law comes the knowledge of sin. (Romans 3:19-20 NASB)

The Christian also, however, may fall so far from acting in love that he violates the moral code of the Ten Commandments. Therefore, the commandments may act as a mirror to bring home the knowledge of his sin.

The Scriptures Are Our Guide in Living to Please Our Lord

Paul did a masterful job in his attempt to preserve the way of life that Jesus taught. He struggled against those who would preach a salvation both through Christ and also through the works of the Law. The Law may aid us at times in our interpretation of what it means to act in Christian love in a given instance. The Law, however, in its constraints is not the New Testament motivation for living the Christian life. Rather we live the Christian life out of love and to the praise and glory of God. Paul wrote to the Christians of Philippi:

> And this I pray, that your love may abound still more and more in knowledge and in all discernment, that you may approve the things that are excellent, that you may be sincere and without offense till the day of Christ, being filled with the fruits of righteousness which are by Jesus Christ, to the glory and praise of God. (Philippians 1:9-11 NKJV)

Our goal in living a life to the praise and glory of God is to live a life pleasing to Him. The angels in heaven rejoice over the sinner who repents and in so doing turns for forgiveness to his Lord and to a new life in Christ. A life sanctified by the Holy Spirit flows from being justified through faith in Christ. Christians thus seek to live in a way that their Lord approves. They seek to live a life pleasing to him. When Paul heard of new converts to Christ in Colossae, he wrote to them:

> For this reason we also, since the day we heard it, do not cease to pray for you, and to ask that you may be filled with the knowledge of His will in all wisdom and spiritual understanding; that you may walk worthy of the Lord, fully pleasing Him, being fruitful in every good work and increasing in the knowledge of God; . . . (Colossians 1:9-10 NKJV)

The Christian life, although based on the New Commandment of Jesus Christ, does not ignore the revelation of God's will for humans in the rest of the Scriptures. We are to model our life after that of Jesus. As Jesus lived a life according to the will of God so also are we. And if we are to grow in understanding and knowledge of what it means to be Christian, then we are to follow the advice of Paul who wrote to his protégé Timothy:

> "All Scripture is given by inspiration of God, and is profitable for doctrine, for reproof, for correction, for instruction in righteousness, that the man of God may be complete, thoroughly equipped for every good work" (2 Timothy 3:16-17 NKJV).

To live according to the will of God means that we are to study the Scripture as our guide through life. To the Corinthian church Paul wrote, "that you may learn by us to live according to Scripture" (1 Corinthians 4:6). To live according to Scripture means to immerse ourselves in the thought, words, and attitudes of God's prophets and of Jesus and His apostles. This does not mean, however, that we are to go through Scripture in order to make up a new list of legalistic rules. We are no longer under the Law. Rather, guided by Scripture and led by the Holy Spirit we strive to live a life of generous and self-denying love, "thoroughly equipped for every good work."

How well Paul sums up the sanctified life. We are to be filled with the knowledge of God's will by the Spirit's power so that we might live worthy of the faith we profess, a life pleasing to our Lord. A life that is pleasing to God is one that is full of the fruits of faith. It is a life of doing good works and of growth in the knowledge of God through our understanding of the Scriptures. Paul encouraged the Christians of Thessalonica to this end:

> Finally then, brethren, we urge and exhort you by the Lord Jesus, that as you have received from us how you ought to walk and to please God, you would abound more and more; for you know what commandments we gave you through the Lord Jesus. For this is the will of God, your sanctification: that you should abstain from sexual immorality; that each of you should know how to possess his own vessel in sanctification and honor, not in passion of lust, like the Gentiles who do not know God; that no one take advantage of and defraud his brother in this matter, because the Lord is the avenger of all such, as we also have forewarned you and testified. For God has not called us to uncleanness, but in holiness. Therefore he who rejects this does not reject man, but God, who has also given us His Holy Spirit.
>
> But concerning brotherly love you do not need that I write to you, for you yourselves are taught by God to love one another; and indeed you do this to all the brethren who are in all Macedonia. But we urge you, brethren, that you increase more and more; that you also aspire to lead a quiet life, to mind your own business, and to work with your own hands, as we commanded you, that you may walk properly toward those who are outsiders, and that you may lack nothing. (1 Thessalonians 4:1-12 NKJV)

A life that is pleasing to God is the sanctified life. To be sanctified is to be made holy through the working of the Holy Spirit. As the above text indicates, it is a life of being led by the Spirit to do works pleasing to God and in holding in check the too often unholy lusts of one's flesh. Here Paul seems to hark back to Jesus' New Commandment when he writes, "you yourselves are taught by God to love one another."

Walking with God in Christ's Way

To walk by faith means to walk in trust, trusting in God's concern and care for us. Paul wrote, "And we know that all things work together for good to those who love God, to those who are the called according to His purpose" (Romans 8:28 NKJV). To walk by faith means that at times the Christian must walk blindly trusting in God's leading. It is in this sense Paul could write: "Therefore we are always confident, knowing that while we are at home in the body we are absent from the Lord. For we walk by faith, not by sight" (2 Corinthians 5:6-7 NKJV). In writing "for we walk by faith, not by sight," Paul shows his understanding of the life of the man or woman of God. God is the foundation Rock of the Christian's existence. God wants our absolute trust to be placed in Him and His love for us.

Paul fought hard to preserve the way of life that Jesus taught. To a considerable degree he was successful in keeping the new faith from falling back to a legalistic morass of laws and injunctions. And yet he must have wondered at times just where God was leading him. During his many years of imprisonment for being an evangelist for Christ, he probably was at a loss as to why his Lord would permit such enforced idleness of His apostle. He had spent so many years in preparation for his mission between the time of his Damascus experience and his first missionary journey. Could Paul possibly have understood what a tremendous treasure for the Church his letters from prison would become? What an enduring legacy would be his general letter to the churches of western Asia Minor, now called Ephesians, and its sister letter to the church at Colossae, as well as the letter to the church at Philippi in Macedonia. These three carefully composed letters give calm and thoughtful direction as to what it means to be and live as a Christian. His letter from prison to Philemon urging kindness toward the slave Onesimus and his second letter to Timothy have also proved of great worth to Christ's Church. With what composure Paul faced martyrdom in his second letter to Timothy!

In the book of Acts Christianity is known as "The Way." There are two senses in which this term might be understood. First, Christ is the way to God the Father. Jesus had said, "I am the way, the truth, and the life. No one comes to the Father except by Me" (John 14:6 NKJV). Second, Christianity may be known as "The Way" as its way of life was so distinctively different from that of the surrounding cultures. The term, The Way, approximates the Hebrew word *halakhah* which means walk or rule of life.[1] Perhaps in both senses the Church was known as "The Way." Certainly, the predominant message of Paul in regard to the Christian way of life could be summed up by his words, "For we are His workmanship, created in Christ Jesus for good works, which God has prepared beforehand that we should walk in them" (Ephesians 2:10 NKJV).

Paul ably defended the way of life that Jesus taught. There were many in the church, however, who could not be persuaded that Christians could be trusted with the freedom of living a faith active in love as they were led by the Holy Spirit in following Jesus' New Commandment. Jesus'

---

1 F. F. Bruce, 1952, *The Acts of the Apostles* (London: The Tyndale Press), p. 197.

new way of life would have to be defended again and again throughout history from those who would put Christian people once more under a yoke of bondage to laws, old and new. For many long centuries, the battle would appear to have been lost. The writings of Paul, however, serve as an enduring and changeless corrective to the legalistic perversion of Jesus' way of life.

Chapter Six

ST. JOHN AND THE WAY:
John's Attempt to Save Christ's Way of Life

What Prompted John to Write His Gospel and Letters?

It is remarkable what little literature has come down to us written by Jesus' disciples. There is, of course, Matthew's Gospel. One of the Apostolic Fathers, Papias, (b. 60-70, d. after 150), the bishop of Hieropolis in Phyrgia, wrote around 140 A.D. concerning Matthew's Gospel, "Matthew compiled the sayings [*logia* of Christ] in the Hebrew language, and each interpreted them as best he could".[1] Papias is called a "hearer" of the Apostle John by Irenaeus (130?-202?).[2]

The Gospel of Mark is actually Peter's account of Christ's life and teachings. A document by Papias quotes the "presbyter "(see definition in footnote[3]), probably the Apostle John, concerning the Gospel of Mark:

> The Presbyter used to say this also: "Mark became Peter's interpreter and wrote down accurately, but not in order, all that he remembered of the things said and done by the Lord. For he had not heard the Lord or been one of his followers, but later, as I said, was a follower of Peter. Peter used to teach as the occasion demanded, without giving systematic arrangement to

---

1 *Eusebius, The Church* History, c. 325, transl. by Paul L Maier, 1999, (Grand Rapids, Michigan: Kregel Publications), p. 130.

2 Irenaeus, *Against Heresies*, Book 5, chap. 33, sec. 4, in *The Ante-Nicene Fathers* (Grand Rapids: Wm. B. Eerdmans Publ. Co.), vol. 1, p. 563.

3 The term "presbyter" means elder. In New Testament times, the term "presbyter" was used interchangeably with the term "bishop" or "overseer." A little later, the two terms were differentiated and the term "presbyter" came to mean a councilor to the bishop. In time, it also came to mean a presbyter assigned to a parish by the bishop as a priest or pastor.

the Lord's sayings, so that Mark did not err in writing down some things just as he recalled them. For he had one overriding purpose: to omit nothing that he had heard and to make no false statements in his account."[4]

Peter's close relationship to Mark is depicted at the close of his first letter from Rome (Babylon) where he wrote of greetings sent by "my son Mark" (1 Peter 5:13).

Corroborating Papias' words are those of the astute Irenaeus, the predominant theologian of the 100s. Writing between 182 and 188, he noted:

Matthew also issued a written Gospel among the Hebrews in their own dialect, while Peter and Paul were preaching at Rome, and laying the foundations of the Church. After their departure, Mark, the disciple and interpreter of Peter, did also hand down to us in writing what had been preached by Peter. Luke also, the companion of Paul, recorded in a book the Gospel preached by him. Afterwards, John, the disciple of the Lord, who also had leaned upon His breast, did himself publish a Gospel during his residence at Ephesus in Asia.[5]

What finally stirred John in his old age to write to the Church in such a decisive and definitive way in his Gospel and letters? First, as an apostle of Jesus Christ he was primarily an evangelist. He makes that clear when he tells one of the reasons why he wrote his Gospel:

And truly Jesus did many other signs in the presence of His disciples, which are not written in this book; but these are written that you may believe that Jesus is the Christ, the Son of God, and that believing you may have life in His name. (John 20:30-31 NKJV)

One might also surmise that John came to realize the incompleteness of the record concerning Jesus that the Church possessed.

---

4 *Eusebius, The Church History*, c. 325, transl. by Paul L Maier, 1999, (Grand Rapids, Michigan: Kregel Publications), pp. 129-130.

5 Irenaeus, Against Heresies, bk. 3, chap. 1, sec. 1, The Ante-Nicene Fathers, vol. 1, p. 414.

Certainly, in his old age he was able to see what documents the early Church was coming to view as the authentic records of Jesus' life.

When John wrote his Gospel, it appears that he duplicates as little as possible the material to be found in the three earlier Gospels. He rather includes and emphasizes those aspects of his Lord's ministry and teaching not found in the earlier Gospels, but which he considered important enough to be preserved for the benefit of the Church. He takes five chapters, for example, to record the extended discourse that Jesus had with His disciples on the night before He was crucified. Even in that ample discourse, however, he does not include the institution of the Lord's Supper. This is in keeping with his obvious design of not covering events and sayings well-recorded in the earlier Gospels unless they were essential to his account.

In John's later years near the end of the first century, the Gnostic heresy was beginning to plague the Church. One Gnostic contemporary of John's was Cerinthus. His brand of Gnosticism taught that Jesus was the natural son of Joseph and Mary and only at Jesus' baptism did the Christ, a heavenly being, enter into the man Jesus. He also taught that the Christ left the body of Jesus before the crucifixion. Therefore, only the man Jesus suffered and died upon the cross; the spiritual Christ did not suffer. Cerinthus's heresies were a mix of Jewish, oriental, and Christian concepts.

John in his writings does not specifically identify his opponents and their false teachings or heresies. But it is obvious what his concerns were from his strong emphasis on Jesus as both true God and true man in his Gospel and letters. In his Second Letter, he wrote, "For many deceivers have gone out into the world who do not confess Jesus Christ as coming in the flesh. This is a deceiver and an antichrist" (2 John 7 NKJV). Irenaeus (130?-202?), who was a disciple of Polycarp (69?-155?), who in turn was a disciple of the Apostle John, wrote in his third book *Against Heresies*:

> 1. John, the disciple of the Lord, preaches this faith, and seeks, by the proclamation of the Gospel, to remove that error which by Cerinthus had been disseminated among men, and a long time previously by those termed Nicolaitans, who are an offset of that "knowledge" [Gnosticism] falsely so called, that he might confound them, and persuade them that there is but one God, who made all things by His Word; . . . [6]

I believe there is an additional reason why John felt moved to write

---

6 Irenaeus, 182-188 A.D., *Against Heresies*," Book III, chap. 11, par. 1, in *The Ante-Nicene Fathers* (Grand Rapids: Wm. B. Eerdmans Publ. Co.), vol. 1, p. 426.

his Gospel and letters. Jesus' New Commandment is not found in the Gospels of Matthew, Mark, or Luke. The recording of Jesus' New Commandment had to await the writing of the Gospel of John. Perhaps John also felt compelled to write his Gospel and letters because the Church was losing its understanding of Jesus' New Commandment. Although John in the early chapters of his Gospel does not stress the moral or ethical teachings of Jesus, later he records Jesus giving His New Commandment three times during the Last Supper. John also devotes almost half of his First Letter in commenting on Christian love and the New Commandment. In both his Second and Third Letters, he again writes as to how Christians are to love one another. What could have called forth such a vigorous presentation of the Christian way of life?

John certainly was aware of Paul's struggle to preserve the way of life that Jesus taught from the legalistic tendencies of some in the early Church. He was probably among the apostles mentioned as being present at the Jerusalem Council where Paul's teachings were discussed (Acts 15). He most likely knew the writings of Paul to the churches of Corinth, Rome, Galatia, Colossae, etc. These letters circulated among the churches of Asia Minor, and John spent many of his later years in Ephesus, an early center of Christianity in Asia Minor.

Legalistic Tendencies in the Early Church

As discussed in the previous chapter, many first century Christian Jews in Palestine faithfully kept the law and practices of the Old Testament. Indeed, this in time came to be deeply resented by Jews who rejected Jesus as the Christ. They especially resented the Christian Jews attending synagogue worship. Therefore, in order to flush out the Christians, they changed one of the synagogue prayers so that it read:

> For apostates let there be no hope, and the kingdom of arrogance do Thou speedily uproot in our days; and let the Nazarenes [Christians] and heretics (*minim*) perish as in a moment; let them be blotted out of the book of life and not be enrolled with the righteous. Blessed art Thou, O Lord, who humblest the arrogant.[7]

The Jewish Sanhedrin adopted the above prayer for use in the synagogues about 90 A.D. No Christian could pray the prayer. If he kept

---

7 F. F. Bruce, 1969, *New Testament History* (Garden City, N.Y.: Doubleday & Co.), p. 386.

silent during its recital, he obviously would give himself away and thus would be identified for excommunication. That the Jewish ecclesiastical authorities saw it necessary to include the prayer indicates that a significant number of Jewish Christians still wished to follow the laws and rituals of the Old Testament.

Now there was nothing wrong with a Christian Jew following various laws and customs of the Old Testament as long as he did not view them as necessary to gain salvation. However, it was perhaps with growing dismay that John saw others in the churches again tending towards a legalistic way of life.

Documents that illustrate this tendency are *The Doctrina*, known also as *The Teaching of the Apostles*, and *The Didache*, known also as *The Teaching of the Twelve Apostles*. Only Latin translations from Greek original contain *The Doctina*. *The Didache* is a later expanded version of *The Doctrina* according to the New Testament scholar Edgar Goodspeed. They were brief books of instruction used by some in the church perhaps as early as 70 A.D.[8] These documents of unknown authorship show a return to legalistic approach similar to that of late Judaism. *The Doctrina*, for example, is composed for the most part of commandments, both new and old, as the following quotation indicates:

> There are two ways in the world, that of life and that of death, of light and of darkness. Over them are set two angels, one of right, the other of wrong. Moreover there is a great difference between the two ways. The way of life is this: first, you shall love the eternal God who made you; second, your neighbor as yourself. Moreover, anything that you would not have done to you, you shall not do to anyone else.
> Now the meaning of these words is this:
> You shall not commit adultery, you shall not commit murder, you shall not bear false witness, you shall not corrupt a boy, you shall not commit fornication, you shall not practice magic, you shall not use enchanted potions, you shall not murder a child by abortion, nor kill one when it is born, you shall not desire any of your neighbor's goods, you shall not commit perjury, you shall not speak evil, you shall not hold a grudge, or show duplicity in giving advice, or be double-tongued, for the tongue is a deadly snare. Your speech shall not be vain or false. You shall not be covetous or avaricious, or rapacious or an

---

8 W. H. C. Frend, 1984, *The Rise of Christianity* (Philadelphia: Fortress Press), p. 29.

idolater, or contentious or ill-humored. You shall not entertain an evil design against your neighbor. You shall hate nobody; some you shall love more than your own soul.[9]

Note the return to the negative Golden Rule and the unremitting cascade of "You shall not." Almost with a vengeance, *The Doctrina* urges a return to a life bounded and fenced by law. It shows little understanding of the new way of life brought into existence by Jesus. *The Doctrina* and its expanded version, *The Didache*, may well have been strong reactions to the circulation of Paul's letters with their stress on Christian love and liberty as Edgar Goodspeed suggests.[10]

The writings of Papias also indicate that there were those in the church who were proposing new and strange commandments. Papias was interested in recording all he could find of the sayings and remembrances of the Apostles and other early Christians. He complains, however, of those who promulgate "strange commandments:"

> But I shall not be unwilling to put down, along with my interpretations, whatsoever instructions I received with care at any time from the elders, and stored up with care in my memory, assuring you at the same time of their truth. For I did not, like the multitude, take pleasure in those who spoke much, but in those who taught the truth; nor in those who related strange commandments, but in those who rehearsed the commandments given by the Lord in faith, and proceeding from truth itself.[11]

Thus, what Paul complained about many years earlier in his letter to the Colossians was still taking place in the church. Paul had been sorely provoked with those who would place new commandments, rules, and regulations on Christian people. Recall his words to the Colossians, "Therefore let no one act as your judge in regard to food or drink or in respect to a festival or a new moon or a Sabbath day— . . . why, as if you

---

9 *The Doctrina*, chaps. 1, 2, in E. J. Goodspeed, 1950, *The Apostolic Fathers* (New York: Harper and Bros.) p. 5.

10 E. J. Goodspeed, 1950, *The Apostolic Fathers* (New York: Harper and Bros.), pp. 2-3.

11 *Fragments of Papias*, I, in *The Ante-Nicene Fathers* (Grand Rapids: Wm. B. Eerdmans Publ. Co.), vol. 1, p. 153.

were living in the world, do you submit yourself to decrees, such as, "Do not handle, do not taste, do not touch!" (which all refer to things destined to perish with the using)—in accordance with the commandments and teaching of men?" (Colossians 2:16, 20-22 NASB).

John's Struggle to Preserve Jesus' Way of Life

If *The Doctrina* is a counterblast against Paul's letters as, for example, to the Galatians and Colossians, it is likely that John's Gospel and First Letter were written in part as strong rebuttals to such legalistic documents as *The Doctrina* and *The Didache* circulating among the churches over thirty years later.

As mentioned previously, John in his Gospel records his recollections of what Jesus taught, especially those sayings absent from the earlier Gospels of Matthew, Mark, and Luke. Is it not likely that because the New Commandment was absent from the first three Gospels, and also because John saw that Jesus' words were passing from the memory of the Church that, at least in part, he saw the necessity of writing his own Gospel? It has already been noted that Paul never explicitly quotes Jesus' New Commandment. Yet he is obviously familiar with its content as seen by his advice to live in imitation of Jesus and to walk in love as Jesus loved (1 Corinthians 11:1; Ephesians 5:1-2).

John's extended account (John 13-17) of Jesus' discourse with His disciples on the evening before He was crucified is undoubtedly a shortened account of Jesus' words. Nevertheless, John pointedly retains Jesus' emphasis by recording the three times Jesus stressed to His disciples:

> "A new commandment I give to you, that you love one another; as I have loved you, that you also love one another. By this all will know that you are My disciples, if you have love for one another. . . . This is My commandment, that you love one another as I have loved you. Greater love has no one than this, that he lay down his life for his friends. . . . These things I command you, that you love one another." (John 13:34-35, 15:12-13, 15:17 NKJV)

The First Letter of John to the churches at large is almost a commentary on these words from his Gospel. In emphatic terms, John gives his interpretation of Jesus' ethic of selfless and self-denying love. John, in his typically Hebraic way of writing, returns repeatedly throughout his letter to Christ's teaching of living a life of love as God in Christ loved us.

One of the problems that Christians today have in reading the New

Testament is that every time they see the word "commandments" they think almost immediately of the Ten Commandments. The Ten Commandments have been so emphasized in most people's early Christian training that they automatically think of them rather than Christ's New Commandment. Unlike *The Doctrina*, however, the New Testament lays little stress on the Ten Commandments. This certainly is also the case with John's letters. The commandments of which John writes are Christ's commandments, and he defines in his first letter just what the commandments of Christ are:

> Beloved, if our heart does not condemn us, we have confidence toward God. And whatever we ask we receive from Him, because we keep His commandments and do those things that are pleasing in His sight. And this is His commandment: that we should believe on the name of His Son Jesus Christ and love one another, as He gave us commandment. And he who keeps His commandments dwells in Him, and He in him. (1 John 3:21-24a NKJV)

In this John follows Jesus' own words. On the night before He was crucified, Jesus said to His disciples:

> "If you love Me, keep My commandments. . . . As the Father loved Me, I also have loved you; continue in My love. If you keep My commandments, you will abide in My love, just as I have kept My Father's commandments and abide in His love. These things I have spoken to you that My joy may remain in you, and that your joy may be full. This is My commandment, that you love one another as I have loved you. Greater love has no one than this, that he lay down his life for his friends." (John 14:15, 15:9-13 NKJV).

John in his First Letter sums up Jesus' way of life by urging Christians to live in imitation of the life of Jesus Christ—"to walk just as He walked:"

> And by this we know that we know Him, if we keep His commandments. He who says, "I know Him," and does not keep His commandments, is a liar, and the truth is not in him. But whoever keeps His word, truly the love of God is perfected in him. By this we know that we are in Him. He who says he abides

in Him ought himself also to walk just as He walked. (1 John 2:3-6 NKJV)

John does not want his readers to think that he was devising a new way of life on his own authority. He is evidently concerned that the legalistic way of life taught by such documents as *The Doctrina* and *The Didache* had become so pervasive in the Church that some would think that he was teaching a novel way of life. Therefore, he wrote in his first letter:

Brethren, I write no new commandment to you, but an old commandment which you have had from the beginning. The old commandment is the word that you heard from the beginning. Again, a new commandment I write to you, which thing is true in Him and in you, because the darkness is passing away, and the true light is already shining. He who says he is in the light, and hates his brother, is in darkness until now. He who loves his brother abides in the light, and there is no cause for stumbling in him. (1 John 2:7-10 NKJV)

What John writes about Christ's way of life in his Second Letter also indicates that the old commandment is the one given by Jesus over a half century earlier during the Last Supper. He shows in the following quotation that he is concerned that people should recognize that his stress on Christian love is not his own but Jesus' emphasis:

And now I plead with you, lady, not as though I wrote a new commandment to you, but that which we have had from the beginning: that we love one another. And this is love, that we walk according to His commandments. This is the commandment, that as you have heard from the beginning, you should walk in it. (2 John 5-6 NKJV)

John in his letters was recalling Christ's words to His disciples some sixty years after they were spoken; and, therefore, they are indeed already an old commandment. There was, however, a need to make that commandment new once more.

When John wrote his Gospel and letters, the Christians were no longer just a small group of disciples gathered in Jerusalem. Christianity had become a rapidly growing faith of which people throughout the Mediterranean world were becoming aware. The darkness of the heathen world was passing away as the only true enlightenment of the world, the good news of God's love through His Son's sacrifice, was becoming known. The good news also brought a new way of life, a way of life taught by Jesus many decades before. John reminds his readers: "For this is the message that you heard from the beginning, that we should love one another," (1 John 3:11 NKJV).

Jesus' stress on positive acts of love is also underscored by John. Recalling Jesus' words on Maundy Thursday night, "Greater love has no one than this, that he lay down his life for his friends." (John 15:13 NKJV), John points out that just as Jesus gave His life as an act of love in service to humanity, so are our lives to express the Christian way of life in action not empty words:

> By this we know love, because He laid down His life for us. And we ought to lay down our lives for the brethren. But whoever has this world's goods, and sees his brother in need, and shuts up his heart from him, how does the love of God dwell in him? My little children, let us not love in word or in tongue, but in deed and in truth. (1 John 3:16-18 NKJV)

As did Jesus and Paul, John taught that Christ-like love was to be expressed in action, in deeds of love, even, if necessary, to the extent of laying down one's life to aid others. Christian love is not a sentimental or emotional love that whispers sweet nothings. It is a selfless love that expresses itself in action, wherever and whenever one sees a need and has the available means to answer the need. It answers the need of our fellow humans just as our Lord answered our need for forgiveness so that we might be holy before God and thus able to be taken up into His presence forever.

The Motivation to Live Christ's Way of Life

The whole ethic of Christianity is built on God's love for us to which we respond. And when we turn to our God in love, He tells us to direct that love toward our fellowman; for what we do to the least of our fellow humans we have done to Him. Christian love is to be expressed in deeds that answer the needs of people. Christian love involves an all-embracing desire for the well-being of others.

Unlike the ethics of the philosophers that cannot provide the motivation to live the ethic they teach, Christianity supplies the motivation to live its way of life. The Christian has strong motivations to live Christ's New Commandment. There is the response of love and thankfulness that the Christian has for his Savior that would lead him to live a life pleasing to his Lord. There is the motivation of the sanctifying work of the Holy Spirit in the Christian's life that empowers him to live a life of love for others. Also, the Christian knows that as our Lord loved all the humans on this earth to the point of dying to gain for them eternal life, how could a Christian possibly hate what his God so loved.

The love that we have for our God in response to His love for us is the strongest motivation for living a Christ-like life. John explains this in writing:

> Beloved, let us love one another, for love is of God; and everyone who loves is born of God and knows God. He who does not love does not know God, for God is love. In this the love of God was manifested toward us, that God has sent His only begotten Son into the world, that we might live through Him. In this is love, not that we loved God, but that He loved us and sent His Son to be the propitiation for our sins. Beloved, if God so loved us, we also ought to love one another. (1 John 4:7-11 NKJV)

The Christian follows Jesus' way of life not out of any hope for reward. In the acceptance of God's pure love and pardon through Jesus, the Christian already has the promise of the resurrection and eternal life. Nor does the Christian live Christ's way of life out of fear; for what is there to fear, when one's life is cradled in the hand of God's love? He or she is a child of God; hell holds no terrors for the Christian. Either those who follow Jesus' words of loving one another as He loved them do it out of a loving, willing heart or they cannot do it at all. John wrote in his first letter:

> God is love, and he who dwells in love dwells in God, and God in him. In this our love has been made perfect, that we may have boldness in the day of judgment; because as He is, so are we in this world. There is no fear in love; but perfect love casts out fear, because fear involves torment. But he who fears has not been made perfect in love. We love Him because He first loved us. (1 John 4:16b-19 NKJV)

Love between Christians is the Mark of the Church

John is obviously aware that Christian love is to extend to all humans. The letters of Paul and the Gospels of Matthew, Mark, and Luke in which such universal love is taught would have been well known to him. The careful way in which he wrote his own gospel, avoiding the repetition of topics well covered in the other Gospels, makes it evident that he knew the content of the other Gospels. In his letters, however, John is especially concerned that, above all, Christians treat one another with Christian love. The Church is a divine, not a human, institution. It should reflect its founder's admonition that we are to love one another. Therefore, there is no place in the Church for the hardheartedness toward others seen in so many in the world: the knavery and underhandedness seen in secular politics, the often ruthless spirit of competition between businessmen, and the petty squabbling to be found in clubs and associations. A loveless church is in danger of ceasing to be Christian.

John knew that love between Christians was to be the mark of the Church. After all, Jesus had said, "By this all will know that you are My disciples, if you have love for one another" (John 13:35 NKJV). John urges that love be shown to our brothers in the Lord. He exhorts:

> If someone says, "I love God," and hates his brother, he is a liar; for he who does not love his brother whom he has seen, how can he love God whom he has not seen? And this commandment we have from Him: that he who loves God love his brother also. (1 John 4:20-21 NKJV)

There is a story about John preserved for the Church by the church father Jerome (340?-420). Although it may well be apocryphal, whether true or not, the story underscores the Church's recognition of John's strong commitment to the love between Christians that Jesus taught. The story is from John's extreme old age and tells of a time when he had to be carried into church and was too old to speak for any length of time. He was accustomed then in addressing the congregation to use simply the old commandment, "Little children, love one another." His disciples, weary of the continual repetition, asked why he always said this. His answer was, "Because it is the commandment of the Lord, and, if it alone is done, it suffices."[12]

The Tension between Christ's People and the World

The Christian does not expect to receive the plaudits of the world for living the life that Jesus taught. There is a natural tension between the values of the Christian and the values of the world. For the Christian to succeed in living Christ's way of life, he must overcome the temptation to

---

12 James Hastings, ed., 1906, *A Dictionary of the Bible* (New York: Chas. Scribner's and Sons), vol. 2, p. 681.

conform to the world's values, fads, and fancies. If he does not, he stands in danger of being overcome by the world instead of overcoming the world.

This antagonism between the world's values and Christian values has existed since the beginning of the Church. Too often Christians wish to have the praise and acceptance of the world and will ignore or compromise their Christian values to attain it. John, as did Paul, warns against being conformed to the values of the godless culture of the majority in which the Christian is ever in the minority. More often than not the following warning by John has been ignored by those who profess to be Christians:

> Do not love the world or the things in the world. If anyone loves the world, the love of the Father is not in him. For all that is in the world--the lust of the flesh, the lust of the eyes, and the pride of life--is not of the Father but is of the world. And the world is passing away, and the lust of it; but he who does the will of God abides forever. (1 John 2:15-17 NKJV)

John warns his readers that refusal to follow the ways of the world might result in their persecution. Using as an example the murder of Abel by Cain, he instructed:

> For this is the message that you heard from the beginning, that we should love one another, not as Cain who was of the wicked one and murdered his brother. And why did he murder him? Because his works were evil and his brother's righteous. Do not marvel, my brethren, if the world hates you. We know that we have passed from death to life, because we love the brethren. He who does not love his brother abides in death. Whoever hates his brother is a murderer, and you know that no murderer has eternal life abiding in him. (1 John 3:11-15 NKJV)

God's Love and Forgiveness for His Imperfect People

John, however, is aware that the Christian often has a difficult time living up to Jesus' way. Our natural self-centeredness leads us to act in unloving ways. To all of us, John wrote:

> My little children, these things I write to you so that you may not sin. And if anyone sins, we have an Advocate with the Father, Jesus Christ the righteous. And He Himself is the propitiation for our sins, and not for ours only but also for the

whole world. (1 John 2:1-2 NKJV)

Paul and John's Limited Success in Preserving
Jesus' Way of Life

This then is John's attempt to restore again in all its clarity and simplicity the way of life that Jesus taught. It must have been a powerful antidote to such documents as *The Doctrina* and *The Didache*. Perhaps the continual rapid growth of the Church during the second Christian century was because John, like Paul, once more made clear Jesus' distinctive way of life.

Unfortunately, the way of life taught by Jesus, Paul, and John did not long prevail in the Church. *The Doctrina, The Teaching of the Apostles,* and its successor *The Didache, The Teaching of the Twelve Apostles,* found their way into much Christian literature in the succeeding centuries. Such later works as *The Apostolic Church Ordinances*, *The Apostolic Constitution, The Coptic Life of Schnudi, The Didascalia*, and so forth, all show the legalistic influence of *The Doctrina* and *The Didache* according to the scholar Goodspeed.[13] The growing influence of *The Doctrina* and *The Didache*, with their peculiar mixture of Old Testament law and New Testament teachings, became a sad omen of what would happen to Jesus' way of life in the future. How widely *The Doctrina* and *The Didache* were used in the early Church is not known. However, *The Doctrina, The Teaching of the Apostles,* did have a long history of use. Athanasius (296?-373), the Archbishop of Alexandria, mentions it as having been used in the catechetical instruction of new Christians.[14]

---

13 E. J. Goodspeed, 1950, *The Apostolic Fathers* (New York: Harper and Brothers), pp. 2, 3.

14 Athanasius, *Letters of Athanasius, Festal Letters*, Letter 39, in *The Nicene and Post-Nicene Fathers* (Grand Rapids: Wm. B. Eerdmans Publ. Co.), Second Series, vol. 4, p. 552.

Chapter Seven

CHRIST'S WAY OF LIFE IN HEBREWS, JAMES, AND PETER

The Book of Hebrews

The book of Hebrews has a long and honorable record in the history of the Church. It is true that early in the Church's history some spoke against its inclusion in the New Testament. But this was because the name of its author had been forgotten. The book, nonetheless, is an early document. For example, Hebrews was known and extensively used by Clement, a leader in the Roman church, in his letter to the Corinthian Christians written around 95 A.D.

The writer of Hebrews evidently was well known to Paul's circle of co-workers. At the close of the letter, he wrote, "Know that our brother Timothy has been set free, with whom I shall see you if he comes shortly" (Hebrews 13:23 NKJV). Tertullian's speculation of Barnabas as the author or Luther's conjecture that it may have been written by Apollos, both fellow workers with Paul, are probably as close to the mark as any. It seems that the author of Hebrews was so well known to the Christians of his day that no one thought it necessary to make a record of the book's authorship. The writer himself in his humility did not presume to attach his name to the document.

The major purpose of the book of Hebrews was to strengthen the faith of Jewish Christians by showing how the Old Testament was completed in the life and sacrifice of Jesus, the Messiah, the Christ, for whom the Jews had longed. It teaches that with the coming of Christ the Old Covenant or Testament becomes obsolete and is ready to vanish away (Hebrews 8:13). Hebrews was not written primarily to instruct or exhort believers about the Christian way of life.

What little the book does have to say about living the Christian life is in tune with the emphases of Paul. He summarizes how Christians are to live by writing:

> Let brotherly love continue. Do not forget to entertain strangers, for by this some have unwittingly entertained angels. Remember the prisoners as if chained with them, and those who are mistreated, since you yourselves are also in the body. Marriage is honorable among all, and the bed undefiled; but fornicators and adulterers God will judge. Let your conduct be without covetousness, and be content with such things as you have. For He Himself has said, "I will never leave you nor forsake you." (Hebrews 13:1-5 NKJV)

The writer of Hebrews encourages his readers to remain steadfast in the faith. He encourages a life of both goodness and the piety of true worship:

> Let us hold fast the confession of our hope without wavering, for he who promised is faithful; and let us consider how to stir up one another to love and good works, not neglecting to meet together, as is the habit of some, but encouraging one another, and all the more as you see the Day drawing near .... Therefore let us be grateful for a kingdom that cannot be shaken, and thus let us offer to God acceptable worship, with reverence and awe; for our God is a consuming fire. (Hebrews 10:23-25, 12:28-29 RSV)

His stress on a life of faith working through deeds of love is also seen in his counsel, "But do not forget to do good and to share, for with such sacrifices God is well-pleased" (Hebrews 13:16 NKJV). Thus, although the book of Hebrews does not say a great deal as to how Christians are to live, what it does say is in keeping with the teachings of Christ, Paul, and John.

The Letter of St. James

As one might expect from the description of him in Acts, James, the natural brother of Jesus, does not write like one of Paul's co-workers or companions. During his lifetime as one of the main pillars of the church at Jerusalem, both Christian and non-Christian Jews knew him as James the Righteous. He was honored for his piety and for his faithfulness to the ancient customs of the Jewish people. James, however, agreed with Paul at the Apostolic Council in Jerusalem that the gentile Christians were not to be held to all the laws, rituals, and customs of the Old Testament (Acts 15).

James in his letter emphasizes unselfish love and calls the Old Testament verse, "You shall love your neighbor as yourself," the royal law (James 2:8). As did Jesus and the apostles Paul and John, James stresses beneficial acts of love as basic to the Christian life. He writes, "But one who looks intently at the perfect law, the law of liberty, and abides by it, not having become a forgetful hearer but an effectual doer, this man shall be blessed in what he does" (James 1:25 NASB).

Although James does not expand upon the subject, he also is aware of the liberty and freedom that the Christian possesses in applying the commandment of love to one's life. Not only in the text immediately above, but also later in his letter he writes of Christian freedom in stating, "So speak and so act, as those who are to be judged by the law of liberty" (James 2:12 NASB).

It is worthy of note that James does not charge his readers to follow the rituals and customs of the Jewish people although they were dear to his own heart. James cannot be claimed by those later Christians who insisted on a return to following all the laws and ordinances of the Old Testament or to a new legalistic way of life.

James' major concern was that his readers not have a superficial faith—a faith that would not be reflected in their lives. He is as interested in a faith that acts freely in love as was his natural brother, Jesus, and the apostles Paul and John. He stresses additionally, however, that a faith that is not made evident by the fruits of faith, is really no faith at all.

Paul emphasized that we are saved by faith alone, but he also taught that this faith would be "a faith working through love" (Galatians 5:6). Paul argued against those who felt that if Christians were saved through faith, they could then live as they pleased (Romans 6:1-4). James is even more vehement in decrying those who would profess the Christian faith and lead uncaring and self-serving lives:

> But be doers of the word, and not hearers only, deceiving yourselves. For if anyone is a hearer of the word and not a doer, he is like a man observing his natural face in a mirror; for he observes himself, goes away, and immediately forgets what kind of man he was. But he who looks into the perfect law of liberty and continues in it, and is not a forgetful hearer but a doer of the word, this one will be blessed in what he does. If anyone among you thinks he is religious, and does not bridle his tongue but deceives his own heart, this one's religion is useless. Pure and undefiled religion before God and the Father is this: to visit orphans and widows in their trouble, and to keep oneself unspotted from the world.

My brethren, do not hold the faith of our Lord Jesus Christ, the Lord of glory, with partiality. For if there should come into your assembly a man with gold rings, in fine apparel, and there should also come in a poor man in filthy clothes, and you pay attention to the one wearing the fine clothes and say to him, "You sit here in a good place," and say to the poor man, "You stand there," or, "Sit here at my footstool," have you not shown partiality among yourselves, and become judges with evil thoughts? . . . If you really fulfill the royal law according to the Scripture, "You shall love your neighbor as yourself," you do well; but if you show partiality, you commit sin, and are convicted by the law as transgressors. . . . So speak and so do as those who will be judged by the law of liberty. For judgment is without mercy to the one who has shown no mercy. Mercy triumphs over judgment. What does it profit, my brethren, if someone says he has faith but does not have works? That faith cannot save him, can it? If a brother or sister is naked and destitute of daily food, and one of you says to them, "Depart in peace, be warmed and filled," but you do not give them the things which are needed for the body, what does it profit? Thus also faith by itself, if it does not have works, is dead. (James 1:22-2:4, 8-17 NKJV)

James, as also Paul and Christ, knows the selfish and self-seeking nature of humans. He pleads, as did Paul, that the fruits of faith be evident in the lives of Christ's followers:

Who is wise and understanding among you? Let him show by good conduct that his works are done in the meekness of wisdom. But if you have bitter envy and self-seeking in your hearts, do not boast and lie against the truth. This wisdom does not descend from above, but is earthly, sensual, demonic. For where envy and self-seeking exist, confusion and every evil thing will be there. But the wisdom that is from above is first pure, then peaceable, gentle, willing to yield, full of mercy and good fruits, without partiality, and without hypocrisy. And the fruit of righteousness is sown in peace by those who make peace. (James 3:13-18 NKJV)

How the above remind us of Paul's words in his letter to the Galatians (5:16-24). The life of James is an excellent example of one who emphasizes both the piety of religious observance and a life of love and goodness.

As did his brother Jesus and the apostles Paul and John, James wrote of the dangers that the world posed to the life of a Christian. Jesus spoke of the devil as the prince of this world. He said that the way to destruction is wide and broad and many follow this road to their eternal sorrow. Paul warned that Christians should not be conformed to the values of this world. John wrote that Christians could expect to be hated by the world. James makes very plain that the values of the world are not Christian values by writing, "Do you not know that friendship with the world is enmity with God? Whoever therefore wants to be a friend of the world makes himself an enemy of God" (James 4:4 NKJV)

All through history, there have been people in Christendom who have tried to accommodate the Church and its teachings to the philosophies, values, fads, and sociological movements of the world. When certain truths or teachings of Scripture cause them to be uncomfortable or embarrass them before the world, they either ignore the teachings, distort their meaning by tortured interpretation, or through the often highly speculative procedures of higher criticism attack the validity of the given text or book (naturally, however, pretending disinterested objectivity and denying their real purpose). They are people who long for their religion to be approved and applauded by the world. They love the attention and praise of the media. But this was never to be!

If the Church is to be the Church that Christ intended, its teachings and values will often be found to be in conflict with those of the world. If Christians find they are loved by all, they couldn't possibly be following the way of Christ. For, as our Lord predicted, following His teachings and way of life often results in the Christian being rebuked, discriminated against, and persecuted by the ungodly of this world. Christians are not to court persecution, but they are not to avoid it by giving up the distinctive teachings of the Scriptures and way of life that Jesus taught.

The Letters of St. Peter

Peter wrote his first letter to the churches of Asia Minor that were about to undergo such persecution. They were about to experience the persecution that Christ spoke of in the Beatitudes when He said, "Blessed are you when they revile and persecute you, and say all manner of evil against you falsely for My sake. Rejoice and be exceedingly glad, for great is your reward in heaven, for so they persecuted the prophets who were before you" (Matthew 5:11-12 NKJV). Peter, echoing Christ's words, encourages his readers in the face of the impending persecution in Asia Minor by writing:

> Beloved, do not think it strange concerning the fiery trial which is to try you, as though some strange thing happened to you; but rejoice, insofar as you are partakers of Christ's sufferings, that when His glory is revealed, you may also be glad with exceeding joy. If you are reproached for the name of Christ, blessed are you, for the Spirit of glory and of God rests on you. On their part He is blasphemed, but on your part He is glorified. But let none of you suffer as a murderer, a thief, and evildoer, or as a busybody in other people's matters. Yet if anyone suffers as a Christian, let him not be ashamed, but let him glorify God in this matter. . . . Therefore let those who suffer according to the will of God commit their souls to Him in doing good, as to a faithful Creator. (1 Peter 4:12-16, 19 NKJV)

Peter is very concerned that the Christians give the pagan populations no excuse for persecuting them. He urges:

> Beloved, I beg you as sojourners and pilgrims, abstain from fleshly lusts which war against the soul, having your conduct honorable among the Gentiles, that when they speak against you as evildoers, they may, by your good works which they observe, glorify God in the day of visitation. (1 Peter 2:11-12 NKJV)

In his letter, he gives the Christians of Asia Minor a broad review of what it means to live as a Christian under the rule of a pagan government. He warns them not to fall back to their former lusts in counseling:

> Therefore gird up the loins of your mind, be sober, and hope to the end for the grace that is to be brought to you at the revelation of Jesus Christ; as obedient children, not conforming yourselves to the former lusts, as in your ignorance; but as He who has called you is holy, you also be holy in all your conduct, because it is written, "Be holy, for I am holy." (1 Peter 1:13-16 NKJV)

As did the apostles Paul and John, Peter also knows that the Christian life flows from love. He too was at the Last Supper and heard his Lord say, "By this all will know that you are My disciples, if you have love for one another." Thus, he wrote, "Seeing you have purified your souls in obeying the truth through the Spirit in unfeigned love of the brethren, love one another fervently with a pure heart" (1 Peter 1:22 NKJV).

Because they considered it idolatrous, Christians would not offer wine and incense in worship before the statue of the reigning emperor.[1] The Roman government, however, viewed their rejection of this worship as an act of disloyalty and treason. Because Peter would not compromise his belief that Christianity was the only way of salvation, he died a martyr, being crucified in Rome upside down according to a tradition in the Church. He remained true to his earlier witness to the Jewish rulers when he said to them concerning Jesus Christ, "And there is salvation in no one else, for there is no other name under heaven that has been given among men, by which we must be saved" (Acts 4:12 NASB). The early Christians held strongly to the truth that there was only one way to salvation, and that was through faith in Jesus Christ. How incredulous Peter would have been if he had known that later church rulers who claimed to be his direct successors were going to teach officially that God's plan of salvation also included non-Christian religions, such as Islam, and personal beliefs.[2] The early Christians protested that although they could not compromise their beliefs, they were not disloyal. Peter, for example, urges Christians to be loyal to the governments under which they lived:

> Therefore submit yourselves to every ordinance of man for the Lord's sake, whether to the king as supreme, or to governors, as to those who are sent by him for the punishment of evildoers and for the praise of those who do good. For so is the will of God that by doing good you may put to silence the ignorance of foolish men--as free, yet not using your liberty as a cloak for vice, but as servants of God. Honor all people. Love the brotherhood. Fear God. Honor the king. (1 Peter 2:13-17 NKJV)

Then, as did Paul in many of his letters, Peter reviews for his readers how a Christian should live with those with whom God has placed them. He writes of what servants and slaves owe their masters (1 Peter 2:18-25). He writes, as did Paul, of the love and respect that is to exist between husband and wife. He counsels wives living with non-Christian husbands to win them to the faith by their Christian conduct. He advises:

---

1 Pliny the Younger, *Letters*, Letter 97, in *The Harvard Classics* (New York: P. F. Collier and Son), pp. 426-427.

2 *Catechism of the Catholic Church*, 1994 (Liguori, Mo.: Liguori Publications), pp. 222-225.

> Likewise you wives, surrender and yield yourselves in love to your own husbands, in order that if any do not obey the Word, by their wives' conduct without a word they may be won, having witnessed your chaste and respectful conduct. Let not your manner be an outward one of braiding the hair, encircling with gold, or putting on fine garments, but may it be that of the hidden person of the heart, with the incorruptible ornament of a gentle and quiet spirit, which before God is of great value. For thus formerly also those holy women hoping in God adorned themselves, giving and yielding themselves in love to their own husbands; as Sarah obeyed Abraham, calling him lord, of whom you have become children, doing good and not fearing any intimidation. (1 Peter 3:1-6 author's translation, see page 180 for translation of *hupotasso*)

And he warns the husbands concerning their wives:

> Likewise you husbands, live together according to Christian understanding, conferring honor on the woman as the more delicate sex, as you are joint heirs of the grace of life, that your prayers may not be cut off. (1 Peter 3:7 author's translation)

Jesus' teachings concerning the life His followers were to live obviously made a deep impression upon Peter. What he wrote closely followed the teaching and emphases of his Lord:

> Finally, all of you be of one mind, having compassion for one another; love as brothers, be tenderhearted, be courteous; not rendering evil for evil or reviling for reviling, but on the contrary bless, knowing that you were called to this, that you may inherit a blessing. For "He who would love life and see good days, let him refrain his tongue from evil, and his lips that they speak no guile; let him turn away from evil and do good; let him seek peace and pursue it. For the eyes of the Lord are on the righteous, and His ears are open to their prayers; but the face of the Lord is against those who do evil." (1 Peter 3:8-12 NKJV)

As did Jesus and Paul, John, and James, Peter also warns the Christians that their way of life and values will differ markedly from the people of the world with whom they live. He wrote of the resentment the pagan friends of Christians will feel if the Christians no longer indulge in the lusts of the flesh as they did before they became Christians:

> Therefore, since Christ has suffered for us in the flesh, arm yourselves likewise with the same mind, for he who has suffered in the flesh has ceased from sin, that he no longer should live the rest of his time in the flesh for the lusts of men, but for the will of God. For it should be sufficient that we did the will of the Gentiles in the former time of our lives--when we walked in licentiousness, lusts, drunkenness, revelry, drinking parties, and abominable idolatries, in which they think it strange that you do not run with them in the same flood of dissipation, speaking evil of you. They will give an account to Him who is ready to judge the living and the dead. (1 Peter 4:1-5 NKJV)

Peter, however, like Jesus and the other apostles, does not primarily warn about avoiding evil; he stresses a life of love that selflessly serves:

> But the end of all things is at hand; therefore be serious and watchful in your prayers. And above all things have fervent love among yourselves, for "love will cover a multitude of sins." Be hospitable to one another without grumbling. As each one has received a gift, minister it to one another, as good stewards of the manifold grace of God. If anyone speaks, let him speak as the oracles of God. If anyone ministers, let him do it as with the ability which God supplies, that in all things God may be glorified through Jesus Christ, to whom is the praise and the dominion forever and ever. Amen. (1 Peter 4:7-11 NKJV)

As noted above, Peter, James, and the writer of the book of Hebrews had different concerns in writing their books than did John and Paul. And yet what they wrote about the Christian life was very much in keeping with the words of Christ concerning the way Christians were to live. Nothing in what they wrote gives any indication that they wished to return to a legalistic way of life bounded by a host of laws to restrict human behavior. Rather they also stressed a faith active in deeds of love as did Jesus, Paul, and John. They took as a given the way of love that Jesus taught and in a matter-of-fact manner discussed how it should work out in a Christian's life.

Chapter Eight

JESUS' WAY OF LIFE IN THE POST-APOSTOLIC CHURCH: 95 TO c. 175 A.D.

The Church after the Apostles' Death

What happened after the death of the apostles to the way of life taught by Jesus and so ably defended by Paul and John? Did the efforts of Paul and John prevail in the Church to preserve for the people the freedom to live a life of Christian love, led by the Holy Spirit and guided by God's Word? Or after the apostolic age did the Church slowly sink back to a Judaistic style of life overburdened by the heaping up of rules, laws, canons, and ordinances?

In this and in the following chapters, we will survey the Christian literature written in the centuries after the time of the apostles to try to understand how the church fathers and others understood the Christian way of life. So that the reader may form his or her own views of the teachings of these early Christian leaders, the primary source materials will be quoted. If the quotations at times seem lengthy, it is done in order to give the reader a feeling for the context in which the quotation is found. It is only too easy to give a false impression by quoting short sections out of context. It is a problem, I am sure, that many of us have encountered.

The century after the apostolic age was a somewhat confused time theologically. The Scriptures of the early church around 100 A.D. were still primarily the Old Testament. The Gospels and the writings of the apostles were only in the process of being recognized for what they were, the Holy Spirit inspired Scripture of the New Covenant. The task of working out a careful understanding and exposition of the teachings of Jesus and His apostles would also take a significant period of time.

There were many in the Church who strove to be faithful to the teaching that was handed down from the apostles. There were others, however, who wished to be influential innovators, seeking to impress their own ideas on the new faith. Those who tried to remain faithful to the teaching of the apostles became known as adhering to what was called in the early centuries "The Catholic Church," catholic in the sense of being the universal orthodox faith. The Catholic Church of the first centuries is not to be confused with the later Roman Catholic Church of Western Europe that developed over the demands of the bishops of Rome for authority over the whole Church, thus finally causing enduring divisions in Christianity. It is especially among the presbyters and bishops of the early Catholic Church that the foremost defenders of the apostolic faith are found.

It is evident that in the first two centuries of the Christian era the way of life taught by Jesus predominated in the life of the Church. The Christians practiced a broad hospitality. They cared for those in need. This was true from the very beginning. We read in Acts 4:34 that because of the generosity of those in better circumstances there was not a needy person among the first Christians. The love of the Christians for others was not confined to their own members. They cared for all of the poor insofar as they were able. As was noted in the first chapter, even as late as the 360s the Roman emperor Julian the Apostate, who had relapsed into paganism, commented unhappily on this care by the Christians for all who were in need, both Christian and non-Christian.[1]

The New Testament stress on a life of Christian love expressed in serving others is found in the earliest writings of the post-apostolic age. However, there is already evidence in some of these early writings of a growing legalistic spirit. It is coupled at times with an excessive concern for one's own purity and righteousness. It was, however, too often a self-righteousness that was based on one's own endeavors and not the true righteousness that results from the sinner's saving faith in Jesus.

The Christian Life according to the Apostolic Fathers

The Earliest Documents

The earliest recorded teachings of the Church in the period immediately after the time of the apostles are found primarily in a collection of writings called *The Apostolic Fathers*. These writings were given this name because their writers followed closely upon the apostolic age. The documents were first gathered and published as a collection in the 1600s. The earliest of the documents is dated between 70 and 95 A.D. and the latest around 160 A.D. The writers of the documents, when known, were primarily early leaders in the Church, some of whom had been acquainted with the apostles.

---

1 S. Neill, 1964, *History of Christian Missions* (Baltimore, Md.: Penguin Books, Inc.), p. 42.

A number of these documents deal with how the early Christians were to live their lives. The documents found in *The Apostolic Fathers* that we will consider in this connection are: *The Doctrina* and its expanded version *The Didache, The First Letter of Clement, The Letters of Ignatius, The Letter of Polycarp to the Philippians, The Shepherd of Hermas, The Letter of Barnabas, The Second Letter of Clement,* and *The Address to Diognetus.* The remaining three documents in the collection known as *The Apostolic Fathers* are not considered in this discussion for the following reasons: *The Martyrdom of Polycarp* deals only with Bishop Polycarp's last days; *The Apology of Quadratus* is one short paragraph and is all that remains of the original document; and *The Fragments of Papias* are short excerpts from various now lost writings of Bishop Papias, and they do not deal with the topic under discussion.

The Doctrina and *The Didache*

One of the earliest of these documents is a brief treatise called *The Doctrina* also known as *The Teaching of the Apostles.* According to the distinguished New Testament scholar Edgar Goodspeed, who in 1950 published his translation of *The Apostolic Fathers, The Doctrina* was expanded into the more widely known document *The Didache* also known as *The Teaching of the Twelve Apostles.*[2] *The Didache* has been dated to be perhaps as early as 70 A.D.[3] *The Didache* retained many of the negative injunctions of *The Doctrina* that were discussed in chapter six (see pages 125-126) and added to them a brief manual of church practices. It is highly unlikely that any of the apostles had any part in writing the two documents. Rather, the anonymous writer(s) of the documents wished to marshal the authority of the apostles behind their treatises by ascribing the authorship to them. Forgotten by the Church for centuries, a Greek version of *The Didache* was discovered in Constantinople in 1873. Since then a few other copies have become known.

The Doctrina showed a return to a legalistic way of life and the negative injunctions that some in the early Church desired. In his introduction to *The Doctrina* Goodspeed wrote:

> Over against Paul's bold doctrine of the all-sufficiency of faith, and probably at Antioch, about the end of the first century,

---

2 E. J. Goodspeed, 1950, *The Apostolic Fathers* (New York: Harper and Brothers), pp. 9, 10, 285-295.

3 W. H. C. Frend, 1984, *The Rise of Christianity* (Philadelphia: The Fortress Press) p. 29.

Christians more in the Jewish tradition thought it necessary to draw up a set of rules of conduct, which would make the Christian's practical moral obligations more definite. For this leaflet they claimed the authority of the Twelve Apostles, naming it *The Teaching of the Apostles*. It is predominantly negative, telling what sins to avoid. It depicts first the Way of Life in some seventy short commands, most of them prohibitions, in the style of the Ten Commandments, and then in a list of almost forty more the Way of Death, not neglecting the characteristic heathen practices of magic, astrology, and enchantment. But it is totally lacking in art or genius, and seems to attempt to foist the essence of the old legalism upon the new religion, reducing its living faith to the keeping of a set of rules.[4]

Paul's struggle, therefore, was only partially successful against those who ignored the revolutionary way of life that Jesus taught. There remained in the Church those who taught a way of life that primarily consisted of avoiding evil rather than a life of doing good.

The First Letter of Clement:

The earliest writing by a known Apostolic Father is *The First Letter of Clement*. It is a letter written from Rome to the church at Corinth. It was ascribed by the early Church to Clement of Rome (30?-100?), although the name of the author does not appear in the letter. The letter, written about 95 A.D., is most likely by the Clement who was the companion of Paul (Philippians 4:3). The writer freely uses the writings of Paul and the book of Hebrews in his letter. He addresses the problem of unrest and insubordination toward their elders among some members of the Corinthian church.

The First Letter of Clement certainly has many echoes of Paul's understanding of Christ's way of life. The following is a section on Christian love that is reminiscent of chapter thirteen of Paul's first letter to the church at Corinth as well as containing thoughts from Hebrews and First Peter.

Let him who has love in Christ keep the commandments of Christ. Who can describe the [blessed] bond of the love of God? What man is able to tell the excellence of its beauty, as it

---

4 E. J. Goodspeed, 1950, *The Apostolic Fathers*, p. 1.

ought to be told? The height to which love exalts is unspeakable. Love unites us to God. Love covers a multitude of sins. Love bears all things, is long-suffering in all things. There is nothing base, nothing arrogant in love. Love admits of no schisms: love gives rise to no seditions: love does all things in harmony. By love have all the elect of God been made perfect; without love nothing is well-pleasing to God. In love has the Lord taken us to Himself. On account of the Love he bore us, Jesus Christ our Lord gave His blood for us by the will of God; His flesh for our flesh, and His soul for our souls.[5]

Clement, as does James and Paul, asks for a faith active in love:

Let the strong not despise the weak, and let the weak show respect unto the strong. Let the rich man provide for the wants of the poor; and let the poor man bless God, because He hath given him one by whom his need may be supplied. Let the wise man display his wisdom, not by [mere] words, but through good deeds.[6]

The overall impression that one gets from Clement is that the Christian's life should be one of faith and love expressed in good works. He warns against following evil, and he would overcome evil with active deeds of love. He quotes the words of Christ in writing:

For thus He spoke: "Be ye merciful, that ye may obtain mercy; forgive, that it may be forgiven to you; as ye do, so shall it be done unto you; as ye judge, so shall ye be judged; as ye are kind, so shall kindness be shown to you; with what measure ye mete, with the same it shall be measured to you." By this precept and by these rules let us stablish ourselves, that we walk with all humility in obedience to His holy words. For the holy word says, "On whom shall I look, but on him that is meek and peaceable, and that trembles at My words?"[7]

---

5 *The First Letter of Clement*, chap. 49, in *The Ante-Nicene Fathers* (Grand Rapids: Wm. B. Eerdmans Publ. Co.), vol. 1, p.18.

6 *The First Letter of Clement*, chap. 38, in *The Ante-Nicene Fathers*, vol. 1, p.15.

7 *The First Letter of Clement*, chap.13, in *The Ante-Nicene Fathers*, vol. 1, p 8.

Clement understands, however, that works of love do not save. He teaches that in both the Old Testament and New Testament it is faith that saves. However, as did Paul in his sixth chapter of his letter to the Romans, Clement teaches that although works do not save it is no reason for forsaking a life of Christian love. In discussing the lives of the Old and New Testament saints, Clement wrote:

> All these, therefore, were highly honored, and made great, not for their own sake, or for their own works, or for the righteousness which they wrought, but through the operation of His will. And we, too, being called by His will in Christ Jesus, are not justified by ourselves, nor by our own wisdom, or understanding, or godliness, or works which we have wrought in holiness of heart; but by that faith through which, from the beginning, Almighty God has justified all men; to whom be glory for ever and ever. Amen.
>
> What shall we do, then, brethren? Shall we become slothful in well-doing, and cease from the practice of love? God forbid that any such course should be followed by us! But rather let us hasten with all energy and readiness of mind to perform every good work.[8]

The Letters of Ignatius

A contemporary of Clement of Rome was Ignatius (?-107), bishop of Antioch in Syria. Around 107 A.D. the aged and venerable bishop was condemned in Syria to die by being thrown to the lions in the Coliseum at Rome. His crime was holding to the Church's belief that the way of salvation came only through Christ. A true Catholic Christian, he denied the validity of all other religions as a way of salvation in writing to the church at Symrna:

> Let no man deceive himself. Both the things which are in heaven, and the glorious angels, and rulers, both visible and invisible, if they believe not in the blood of Christ, shall, in consequence, incur condemnation. "He that is able to receive it, let him receive it."[9]

---

8 *The First Letter of Clement*, chaps.32 and 33, in *The Ante-Nicene Fathers*, vol. 1, p.13.

9 *The Letters of Ignatius*, "To the Smyrnaeans," chap. 6, in *The Ante-Nicene Fathers*,

gnatius began the long journey from Syria to his martyrdom in

gnatius began the long journey from Syria to his martyrdom in
Rome chained and guarded by a decury, a squad of ten Roman soldiers.
Early in the journey as he traveled across Asia Minor, the present-day
Turkey, the Christians came out to greet, salute, and cheer him on his way.
The bishop Onesimus of Ephesus, a city in Asia Minor, provided Ignatius
with a scribe through whom Ignatius wrote seven letters to various churches
and also one to Polycarp, the bishop of Smyrna, another city in Asia Minor.
Polycarp later took it upon himself to see that Ignatius's letters were widely
circulated.

The squad of soldiers conveying Ignatius to Rome was seemingly
angered by the attention afforded to their condemned prisoner. Evidently
silenced by his guard, we hear no more from Ignatius after he leaves Asia
Minor to cross the Aegean Sea to Philippi in Macedonia. Ignatius refers to
the resentful truculence of his captors in writing: "From Syria even unto
Rome I fight with beasts, both by land and sea, both by night and day, being
bound to ten leopards, I mean a band of soldiers, who, even when they
receive benefits, show themselves all the worse."[10]

The letters of Ignatius do not shed a great deal of light on how he
viewed the Christian way of life. Christianity was still in its organizational
phase; and Ignatius was mainly concerned with exhorting his readers to
follow devotedly their bishops, presbyters, and deacons and to maintain
peace in the churches. He also endeavored to combat the rising Docetic
heresy that maintained that the Christ only "seemed" (in Greek, *dokeo*) to be
human, and that Christ's body was celestial and not of flesh and blood.

His letter to the Christians of Rome is especially noteworthy. The
aged bishop fears they will somehow obtain the commutation of his death
sentence, and he will be denied his opportunity to be poured out in sacrifice
to God. He wrote, "For I am afraid of your love, lest it should do me an
injury. For it is easy for you to accomplish what you please; but it is
difficult for me to attain to God, if ye spare me."[11]

What little Ignatius does have to say about the way of life of the
Christian is in keeping with the emphases of Christ, Paul, and John. He
wrote five letters to churches in Asia Minor. In each he touches on Christian
love:

---

vol. 1, p. 88-89.

10 *The Letters of Ignatius*, "To the Romans," chap. 5, in *The Ante-Nicene Fathers*,
vol. 1, p. 75.

11 *The Letters of Ignatius*, "To the Romans," chap.1, in *The Ante-Nicene Fathers*,
vol. 1, p. 74.

In a letter now called Ephesians, he wrote:

> No man [truly] making a profession of faith sins; nor does he
> that possesses love hate any one. The tree is made manifest by
> its fruit; so those that profess themselves to be Christians shall
> be recognized by their conduct.[12]

To the Christians of Magnesia, he echoed Jesus' New Commandment of loving one another in writing:

> May all of you then, imitating the same divine conduct, pay
> respect to one another, and let no one look upon his neighbor
> after the flesh (in a material way), but may all of you continually
> love each other in Jesus Christ.[13]

In his letter to the church at Tralles, he similarly wrote:

> "And may everyone of you love one another with undivided
> heart."[14]

He urged the Christians of Philadelphia to live in imitation of Jesus Christ:

> Do nothing without the bishop; keep your bodies as the temples
> of God; love unity; avoid divisions; be the followers of Jesus
> Christ, even as He is of His Father.[15] As did Paul, Ignatius saw
> faith working through love: "ll these things are good together, if
> you believe in love."

Ignatius warned the Christians of Smyrna:

---

12 *The Letters of Ignatius*, "To the Ephesians," chap. 14, in *The Ante-Nicene Fathers*, vol. 1, p. 55.

13 *The Letters of Ignatius*, "To the Magnesians," chap.6, in *The Ante-Nicene Fathers*, vol. 1, p. 61.

14 *The Letters of Ignatius*, "To the Trallians," chap. 13, in *The Ante-Nicene Fathers*, vol. 1, p. 72.

15 *The Letters of Ignatius*, "To the Philadelphians," chap. 7, in *The Ante-Nicene Fathers*, vol. 1, p. 84.

Let not [high] place puff any one up: for that which is worth all is a faith and love, to which nothing is to be preferred. But consider those who are of a different opinion with respect to the grace of Christ which has come unto us, how opposed they are to the will of God. They have no regard for love; no care for the widow, or the orphan, or the oppressed; of the bond, or of the free; of the hungry, or of the thirsty.[16]

There are both short and long versions of the letters of Ignatius. Most scholars consider the shorter versions to be the authentic letters. They consider the longer versions to be expansions of the shorter letters by unknown later writers. The longer letter to the church at Smyrna contains one of the few quotations of the New Commandment, John 13:34, found in early Christian literature:

Let no man's place, or dignity, or riches, puff him up; and let no man's low condition or poverty abase him. For the chief points are faith towards God, hope towards Christ, the enjoyment of those good things for which we look, and love towards God and our neighbour. For, "Thou shalt love the Lord thy God with all thy heart, and thy neighbour as thyself." And the Lord says, "This is life eternal, to know the only true God, and Jesus Christ whom He has sent." And again, "A new commandment give I unto you, that ye love one another. On these two commandments hang all the law and the prophets."[17]

The above text may not have come from Ignatius, but it indicates that at least some in the Church used and cited Christ's New Commandment.

Ignatius also keeps the emphasis of the New Testament on being wary of the temptations posed by those values of the world that are contrary to Christianity. He warns the Roman Christians: "Do not speak of Jesus Christ, and yet set your desires on the world."[18]

Thus, around the year 107, Ignatius gives us only a brief glimpse of

---

16 *The Letters of Ignatius*, "To the Smyrnaeans," chap. 6, in *The Ante-Nicene Fathers*, vol. 1, p. 89.

17 *Epistle of Ignatius to the Smyrnaeans*, chap. 6, in *The Ante-Nicene Fathers*, vol. 1, p. 89.

18 *The Letters of Ignatius*, "To the Romans," chap. 7, in *The Ante-Nicene Fathers*, vol. 1, p. 76.

what it means to live as a Christian. What he does say, however, is in harmony with the New Testament about how Christians are to live in the world.

The Letter of Polycarp to the Philippians

When Ignatius passed through Philippi in Macedonia, he suggested to the Christians of Philippi that they write to Bishop Polycarp of Smyrna (69?-155?) and ask Polycarp to send them copies of the letters that he, Ignatius, had written to the churches in Asia Minor. Polycarp complied with their request and sent a covering letter with Ignatius' letters. Polycarp at this time was a respected teacher of the Church having been in his youth a disciple of the Apostle John in Ephesus. Although one of the leading bishops of the Church, Polycarp shows a true humility in presuming to write to the Philippian Christians. The superior authority of the Apostle Paul is recognized in Polycarp's comment:

> These things, brethren, I write to you concerning righteousness, not because I take anything upon myself, but because ye have invited me to do so. For neither I, nor any other such one, can come up to the wisdom of the blessed and glorified Paul. He, when among you, accurately and steadfastly taught the word of truth in the presence of those who were then alive. And when absent from you, he wrote you a letter, which, if you carefully study, you will find to be the means of building you up in that faith which has been given you, and which, being followed by hope, and preceded by love towards God, and Christ, and our neighbor, "is the mother of us all." For if any one be inwardly possessed of these graces, he has fulfilled the command of righteousness, since he that has love is far from all sin.[19]

Note also how Polycarp echoes Paul's emphasis on love as the fulfilling of the law in writing that if a man has love he will fulfill the command of uprightness, "for one who has love is far from any sin." He also echoes Jesus' Sermon on the Mount in writing:

> But He who raised Him up from the dead will raise up us also, if we do His will, and walk in His commandments, and love what

---

[19] *The Letter of Polycarp to the Philippians*, chap. 3, in *The Ante-Nicene Fathers*, vol. 1, pp. 33-34.

He loved, keeping ourselves from all unrighteousness, covetousness, love of money, evil speaking, falsewitness; "not rendering evil for evil, or railing for railing," or blow for blow, or cursing for cursing, but being mindful of what the Lord said in His teaching: "Judge not, that ye be not judged; forgive, and it shall be forgiven unto you; be merciful, that ye may obtain mercy; with what measure ye mete, it shall be measured to you again; and once more, "Blessed are the poor, and those that are persecuted for righteousness' sake, for theirs is the kingdom of God."[20]

Polycarp emphasized a life of love active in doing good deeds. He summed up his counsel to the Philippians by urging:

Stand fast, therefore, in these things, and follow the example of the Lord, being firm and unchangeable in the faith, loving the brotherhood, and being attached to one another, joined together in the truth, exhibiting the meekness of the Lord in your intercourse with one another, and despising no one. When you can do good, defer it not, because "alms delivers from death." Be all of you subject one to another, having your conduct blameless among the Gentiles," that you may both receive praise for your good works, and the Lord may not be blasphemed through you.[21]

The phrase "charity delivers from death" does not mean that Polycarp is suggesting that charity is necessary for salvation and that the fear of eternal death is a motivation for doing good works. Polycarp makes it unmistakably clear that he follows Paul in teaching that one is saved by faith and not by works or deeds of love. After the salutation, he opens his letter with the words:

I have greatly rejoiced with you in our Lord Jesus Christ, because ye have followed the example of true love [as displayed by God], and have accompanied, as became you, those who were bound

---

20 *The Letter of Polycarp to the Philippians*, chap. 2, in *The Ante-Nicene Fathers*, vol. 1, p.33.

21 *The Letter of Polycarp to the Philippians*, chap. 10, in *The Ante-Nicene Fathers*, vol. 1, p. 35.

in chains, the fitting ornaments of saints, and which are indeed the diadems of the true elect of God and our Lord; and because the strong root of your faith, spoken of in days long gone by, endures even until now, and brings forth fruit to our Lord Jesus Christ, who for our sins suffered even unto death, [but] "whom God raised from the dead, having loosed the bands of the grave." "In whom, though now ye see Him not, ye believe, and believing, rejoice with joy unspeakable and full of glory; " into which joy many desire to enter, knowing that "by grace ye are saved, not of works," but by the will of God through Jesus Christ.[22]

Bishop Polycarp was martyred in 156 A.D. for the faith he taught during the eighty-six years of his life. At his trial the pagan crowd shouted their accusation, "This is the teacher of Asia, the father of the Christians, and the overthrower of our gods, he who has been teaching many not to sacrifice, or to worship the gods."[23] By his martyrdom of being burned alive at the stake for his belief in Jesus as the only way of salvation, Polycarp gave witness to the Church's faith in Christ's words, "I am the way, the truth, and the life. No one comes to the Father except through Me" (John 14:6 NKJV).

The Shepherd of Hermas

Quite unlike the writings of Clement of Rome, Ignatius, and Polycarp is the book, *The Shepherd of Hermas*. It is a book of popular religion written by Hermas, a Roman Christian prophet, sometime between 100 and 120 A.D. It was widely read in especially the Eastern Church, the churches in the countries around the eastern Mediterranean Sea. There were those who felt it should be included among the books of the New Testament. The book is composed of visions and parables and also discussions between the young man Hermas and the Shepherd, an angel of repentance assigned to Hermas.

It is a book of religiosity that is hardly informed by the writings of either the Old or the New Testament. Filled with religious moralism and platitudinous piety, it is only superficially Christian. In fact, the saving sacrifice of Christ's death for human sin is scarcely mentioned. Rather,

---

22 *The Letter of Polycarp to the Philippians*, chap. 1, in *The Ante-Nicene Fathers*, vol. 1, p. 33.

23 *The Martyrdom of Polycarp*, chap.12, in *The Ante-Nicene Fathers*, vol. 1, p. 41.

repentance for past sins and a pure life in the avoidance of evil is taught as the way of salvation. It breathes the same type of sentimental, empty, religiosity that fills so many New Age and similar books in religious bookstores in the U.S.A. today. For the most part, a negative legalism pervades the book. At times, however, the book also encourages acts of doing good to others.[24] The preeminent church historian of early twentieth century, Philip Schaff, wrote of the book's legalistic tendencies:

> The theology of Hermas is ethical and practical. . . . He views Christianity as new law and lays chief stress on practice. Herein he resembles James, but he ignores the "liberty" by which James distinguishes the "perfect" Christian law from the imperfect old law of bondage. He teaches not only the merit, but the supererogatory merit of good works and the sin-atoning virtue of martyrdom. He knows little or nothing of the gospel, never mentions the word, and has no idea of justifying faith, although he makes faith the chief virtue and the mother of virtues. He dwells on man's duty and performance more than on God's gracious promises and saving deeds. In a word, his Christianity is thoroughly legalistic and ascetic, and further off from the evangelical spirit than any other book of the apostolic fathers.[25]

The book is a forerunner of the grotesque asceticism that in later times would pervert the way of life that Christ taught. The book opens with a story in which the young man Hermas sees a beautiful woman bathing in the Tiber River with whom he was once acquainted. He gives her his hand to help her out of the river. The account continues, "The sight of her beauty made me think with myself, 'I should be a happy man if I could but get a wife as handsome and good as she is.' This was the only thought that passed through me: this and nothing more." In the vision a little later, the young woman confronts Hermas, accuses him of sinning against her and rebukes him with the words, "The desire of wickedness arose within your heart. Is it not your opinion that a righteous man commits sin when an evil desire arises in his heart? There is sin in such a case, and the sin is great."[26]

---

24 *The Shepherd of Hermas*, bk. 2, Commandment 8, in *The Ante-Nicene Fathers*, vol. 2, p. 25.

25 Philip Schaff, 1910, *History of the Christian Church*, Vol. 2, (Grand Rapids: Eerdmans Publ. Co.), p. 684.

26 *The Shepherd of Hermas*, bk. 1, Vision 1, chap. 1, in *The Ante-Nicene Fathers*, vol. 2, p. 9.

If it is indeed an evil for a man to consider a woman as a possible spouse, how early in the history of the Church has the wholesome and matter of fact acceptance of human sexuality found in the Scriptures been corrupted by a false and extreme idea of what constitutes purity. According to the account, Hermas was hardly lusting after the woman.

The way of life espoused by the author is primarily concerned with avoiding temptation and any possible opportunity for evil rather than a life of service to others as Christ served us. It can best be summed up by the following quotation in which the Shepherd, an angel assigned to Hermas, tells Hermas what constitutes a true fast:

> Listen, he continued: God does not desire such an empty fasting. For fasting to God in this way you will do nothing for a righteous life; but offer to God a fasting of the following kind: Do no evil in your life, and serve the Lord with a pure heart: keep His commandments, walking in His precepts, and let no evil desire arise in your heart; and believe in God. If you do these things, and fear Him, and abstain from every evil thing, you will live unto God; and if you do these things, you will keep a great fast, and one acceptable before God.[27]

The Shepherd of Hermas is an unhappy example of popular religion. It attracted a broad following probably because of its rather simple-minded, moralistic piety and its highly imaginative imagery in the form of parables and visions. Parable nine, for example, which depicts Hermas sporting with twelve virgins, was aptly termed by the historian Philip Schaff as "silly stuff."[28] *The Shepherd of Hermas* is theistic but only very shallowly Christian. Its muddled and often contradictory theology is in sharp contrast to the theology of the New Testament.

The Shepherd of Hermas indicates how early in Christian history the way of life taught by Christ and His apostles was being ignored. Christ's way of life of living unselfishly for others was shouldered aside by a zeal for the ascetic life. The ascetic was encouraged to seek self-centeredly after personal purity. It was a purity attained by absorbing one's self in the endeavor to avoid any possible opportunity for sin. It put its emphasis on living a pious life to the neglect of a life of goodness and Christian love.

---

27 *The Shepherd of Hermas*, bk.3, Similitude 5, chap.1, in *The Ante-Nicene Fathers*, vol. 2, p. 33.

28 Philip Schaff, 1910, *History of the Christian Church*, vol. 2, p. 403 in footnote.

The Letter of Barnabas

The Letter of Barnabas is another book that some in the early church felt should be included in the New Testament. It is a rather curious document, being wildly allegorical in its attempt to show how the Old Testament prefigures the life of Jesus Christ. The letter is thought by Goodspeed to have been written about 130 A.D. by perhaps a Christian teacher of Alexandria, Egypt.[29] It certainly is in the Alexandrian tradition of interpreting the Bible by means of far-fetched allegory. Seemingly added later to the end of the letter is a section that is a modified version of *The Doctrina*. That this version of *The Doctrina* is indeed a later addition is indicated by the existence of a Latin manuscript found at St. Petersburg that does not contain the addition. It is also indicated by the crude transitional sentences between the natural ending to the letter and the addition of the modified text of *The Doctrina*. This transition reads: "So much for that. Now let us pass to another lesson and teaching."

If the mainly negative injunctions of *The Doctrina* are disregarded as a later addition to the letter, *Barnabas* also shows an emphasis on an active life of doing good out of Christian love rather than just the avoidance of evil. Early in the letter a long section is taken from Isaiah 58 in which God urges His people to feed the hungry, house the homeless, clothe the naked, etc., rather than just hypocritically going though the rituals of their religion. Barnabas ends this section with the comment, "To this end, therefore, brethren, He is long-suffering, foreseeing how the people whom He has prepared shall with guilelessness believe in His Beloved. For He revealed all these things to us beforehand, that we should not rush forward as rash acceptors of their laws."[30] The context indicates that it is the laws of Judaism that are considered "their law." Christians are not to live under the law of the Old Testament. Rather they are to "diligently inquire into the ordinances of the Lord," . . . "that the new law of our Lord Jesus Christ, which is without the yoke of necessity, might have a human oblation [offering]."[31]

Although *The Letter of Barnabas* is not primarily concerned with the Christian way of life, what little there is is in keeping with the emphasis in the New Testament on an active life of serving others. The Christian is to

---

29 E. J. Goodspeed, 1950, *The Apostolic Fathers*, p. 19.

30 *The Letter of Barnabas*, chap. 3, in *The Ante-Nicene Fathers*, vol. 1, p. 138.

31 *The Letter of Barnabas*, chap. 2, in *The Ante-Nicene Fathers*, vol. 1, p. 138.

live a new life freely fulfilling the commandments of Jesus Christ.[32] Without the negativism of the Doctrina-like addition, there is actually little of the legalistic spirit in the letter.

The Second Letter of Clement

Early in the second half of the 100s there is a letter written from Rome to the church at Corinth called *The Second Letter of Clement*. The letter is probably misnamed, for it is thought actually to be a letter written by Bishop Soter of Rome to the church at Corinth. As the letter was preserved by the Corinthian church along with the *First Letter of Clement*, it seems in time to have become identified with it, especially as the name of the author is not found in the letter.[33] Further evidence for concluding the letter is actually Soter's is a letter written by Dionysius, Bishop of Corinth, acknowledging to Bishop Soter the receipt of his letter:

> We read your letter today, the Lord's Day, and shall continue to read it frequently for our admonition, as we do the earlier letter Clement wrote on your behalf.[34]

The Second Letter of Clement appears to be a sermon based primarily on Matthew 7:21-23. The letter was written to strengthen the Christianity of the Corinthians. It encourages them to remember their pagan past and rejoice in the light into which their Christian faith has brought them. As did the Epistle of James, Soter emphasizes a faith that results in a life of deeds:

> Let us, then, not only call Him Lord, for that will not save us. For He says, "Not every one that saith to me, Lord, Lord, shall be saved, but he that worketh righteousness." Wherefore, brethren, let us confess Him by our works, by loving one another, by not committing adultery, or speaking evil of one another, or cherishing envy; but by being continent, compassionate, and

---

32 Reinhold Seeberg, 1952, *Text-book of the History of Doctrines* (Grand Rapids: Baker Book House), p. 73.

33 E. J. Goodspeed, 1950, *The Apostolic Fathers*, p. 83.

34 *Eusebius*, *The Church* History, c. 325, transl. by Paul L Maier, 1999, (Grand Rapids, Michigan: Kregel Publications), p. 159.

good. We ought also to sympathize with one another, and not be avaricious.[35]

Later in the letter, he again writes, "Let us therefore love one another, that we may all attain to the kingdom of God."[36] John's Gospel and Epistles that preserved Jesus' New Commandment had made their impact.

Soter is intent on the church living up to the Lord's counsel that loving one another is to be the mark of the Christian Church. He warns the Corinthians of the damage they do to the Christian faith if their lives do not reflect their words. He cautions them:

> For the Lord says, "Continually my name is blasphemed among all nations," and "Wherefore my name is blasphemed; blasphemed in what? In your not doing the things which I wish." For the nations, hearing from our mouth the oracles of God, marvel at their excellence and worth; thereafter learning that our deeds are not worthy of the words which we speak, — receiving this occasion they turn to blasphemy, saying that they are a fable and a delusion. For, whenever they hear from us that God says, "No thank have ye, if ye love them which love you, but ye have thank, if ye love your enemies and them which hate you " — whenever they hear these words, they marvel at the surpassing measure of their goodness; but when they see, that not only do we not love those who hate, but that we love not even those who love, they laugh us to scorn, and the name is blasphemed.[37]

Christian love is a major emphasis in Soter's letter. Acts of Christian love are more important than acts of piety. As did Paul in 1 Corinthians 13, he writes of Christian love as the greatest of Christian virtues:

> Good, then, is alms [charitable giving] as repentance from sin; better is fasting than prayer, and alms than both; "charity

---

35 *The Second Letter of Clement*, chap. 4, in *The Ante-Nicene Fathers*, vol. 10, p 252.

36 *The Second Letter of Clement*, chap. 9, in *The Ante-Nicene Fathers*, vol. 10, p. 253.

37 *The Second Letter of Clement*, chap. 13, in *The Ante-Nicene Fathers*, vol. 10, p. 254.

covereth a multitude of sins," and prayer out of a good conscience delivers from death. Blessed is every one that shall be found complete in these; for alms lightens the burden of sin.[38]

The Second Letter of Clement also is faithful to the New Testament in teaching that the ways and values of this world are the natural enemy of the Christian. As Christ indicated in His prayer for the Church found in John 17, the Christians are to be in the world but not of the world. Bishop Soter shows his understanding of this in writing:

> And consider, brethren, that the sojourning in the flesh in this world is but brief and transient, but the promise of Christ is great and wonderful, even the rest of the kingdom to come, and of life everlasting. By what course of conduct, then, shall we attain these things, but by leading a holy and righteous life, and by deeming these worldly things as not belonging to us, and not fixing our desires upon them? For if we desire to possess them, we fall away from the path of righteousness.
>
> Now the Lord declares, "No servant can serve two masters." If we desire, then, to serve both God and mammon, it will be unprofitable for us. "For what will it profit if a man gain the whole world, and lose his own soul?" This world and the next are two enemies. The one urges to adultery and corruption, avarice and deceit; the other bids farewell to these things. We cannot, therefore, be the friends of both; and it behooves us, by renouncing the one, to make sure of the other. Let us reckon that it is better to hate the things present, since they are trifling, and transient, and corruptible; and to love those [which are to come,] as being good and incorruptible.[39]

The tension between The Way and the world is thus still being taught during the middle of the 100s in that center of Christianity, the Church at Rome. The way of life that Jesus taught was still being preached.

However, one change may have been taking place. Some have

---

38 *The Second Letter of Clement*, chap. 16, in *The Ante-Nicene Fathers*, vol. 10, p. 255.

39 *The Second Letter of Clement* chaps. 5 and 6; in *The Ante-Nicene Fathers*, vol. 10, p. 252.

considered the letter legalistic. Perhaps there is a tendency for the writer to see the motivation for living the Christian life as one of trying to obtain "the rest of the kingdom to come, and of life everlasting" through "a holy and righteous life." Or perhaps the writer is attempting to keep his sermon revolving around the same thought as is found in his primary text (Matthew 7:21) which he paraphrased from the Sermon on the Mount by writing, "Not everyone who says to me, 'Lord! Lord!' shall be saved, but he who works righteousness."[40]

The writer stresses a faith active in love and follows James' thought that a faith apart from works is dead (James 2:26b). He begins his sermon by emphasizing the salvation that a Christian has obtained through Christ. He devotes much of the remainder of the sermon to the Christian's response to God's gift of salvation by offering Him a life of loving one another.

The Address to Diognetus

A minor work included in *The Apostolic Fathers* written about the same time as *Second Clement* is a letter known as *The Address to Diognetus*. The letter was perhaps directed to the Diognetus who was a tutor of Roman emperor Marcus Aurelius (161-180 A.D.).[41] The author of this defense of the Christian faith is unknown.

The author first discusses the superiority of the Christian conception of God in comparison to the idols fashioned by human hands. Then after detailing the type of lives Christians lead in the world, he encourages Diognetus to consider Christianity by writing:

> If you also desire [to possess] this faith, you likewise shall receive first of all the knowledge of the Father. For God has loved mankind, on whose account He made the world, to whom He rendered subject all the things that are in it, to whom He gave reason and understanding, to whom alone He imparted the privilege of looking upwards to Himself, whom He formed after His own image, to whom He sent His only-begotten Son, to whom He has promised a kingdom in heaven, and will give it to those who have loved Him. And when you have attained this knowledge, with what joy do you think you will be filled? Or, how

---

40 *The Second Letter of Clement*, chaps. 4 and 5, in *The Ante-Nicene Fathers*, vol. 10, p.252.

41 E. J. Goodspeed, 1950, *The Apostolic Fathers*, p. 273.

will you love Him who has first so loved you? And if you love Him, you will be an imitator of His kindness. And do not wonder that a man may become an imitator of God. He can, if he is willing. For it is not by ruling over his neighbors, or by seeking to hold the supremacy over those that are weaker, or by being rich, and showing violence towards those that are inferior, that happiness is found; nor can any one by these things become an imitator of God. But these things do not at all constitute His majesty. On the contrary he who takes upon himself the burden of his neighbor; he who, in whatsoever respect he may be superior, is ready to benefit another who is deficient; he who, whatsoever things he has received from God, by distributing these to the needy, becomes a God to those who receive (his benefits): he is an imitator of God.[42]

The way of life taught by Jesus and His apostles is very much in evidence here. From knowledge of God's activity in the life of His Son will come a faith in that knowledge. From that faith will flow a love to God and one's fellow humans. Diognetus will be led to imitate the selfless love of God. The writer of the letter thus follows the teachings of Christ and His apostles by prompting Diognetus to love others as God loved him and to live in imitation of Christ's love. Thus in the late middle 100s a life of love that expresses itself in deeds of love is still the Christian way of life for this unknown writer.

In conclusion, *The Apostolic Fathers* are a relatively sparse collection of writings that have come down to us from the decades immediately after the apostolic age. Nonetheless, they indicate that in the late years of the first century and in the second century there were prominent Christian teachers who continued to faithfully teach the way of life taught by Jesus and His apostles.

On the other hand, such documents as *The Doctrina, The Didache*, and *The Shepherd of Hermas* indicate that there were others in the Church who continued to press for a legalistic way of life. The struggle of Paul and John to preserve Jesus' way of life had not been won. There continued to be some in the Church who felt that Christian behavior is best controlled by primarily negative laws and regulations. Unlike Jesus, Paul, and John, they appear to have had little trust in a way of life based on faith working through love. They show little confidence that Christians can live a life

---

42 *The Address to Diognetus*, chap. 10, in *The Ante-Nicene Fathers*, vol. 1, p. 29.

flowing from the motivation of selfless Christian love, sanctified and guided by the Holy Spirit and informed by God's Word.

Other Witnesses to Jesus' Way of Life from the 100s

Justin Martyr, Irenaeus, and Theophilus

The latter decades of the 100s saw writers who were still strongly influenced by the way of life taught by Jesus and His apostles. In addition, it also was a time when especially two major theological thinkers in the Church, Justin Martyr and Irenaeus, wrote major works in the defense of Church's teachings from the attacks of non-Christians and heretics.

Justin Martyr (100?-165?)

Justin was born a gentile in Samaria. He devoted much of his early life to the study of philosophy, examining and evaluating the various philosophical schools of his day. At a time when he was interested in the teachings of Plato, he met by chance an elderly Christian while walking on the eastern shore of the Mediterranean Sea. The witness of this Christian to Jesus turned Justin to an examination of Christianity, and subsequently he was converted. Throughout his life, he continued to wear his philosopher's cloak, because he maintained that in Christianity he finally found the true philosophy. Justin was scourged and beheaded in Rome around 165 A.D. because of his belief that only in Christianity is to be found the true religion—hence his name: Justin Martyr.

Justin became a strong defender of the Christian faith. He wrote two long essays in the defense of the faith to the reigning Roman emperor and the Roman Senate. His other major work, *Dialogue with Trypho*, is in the form of an imaginary dialogue between himself and one Trypho, a religious Jew. The dialogue is a debate over the validity of Christianity with arguments based primarily on the Old Testament.

The writings of Justin do not take up the Christian way of life to any extent. Four short chapters in *The First Apology of Justin* discuss Christ's way of life based mainly on Matthew's account of the Sermon on the Mount.[43] In these chapters, Justin attempts faithfully to reflect his Lord's instruction. He stresses especially Christ's teaching concerning showing love and doing good to all.

In the *Dialogue with Trypho*, Justin quotes from Isaiah 58 to illuminate the way of life that is pleasing to God. Justin tells Trypho:

---

43 Justin Martyr, *The First Apology of Justin*, chaps. 14-17, in *The Ante-Nicene Fathers*, vol. 1, pp. 167-169.

> "The new law [of Christ] requires you to keep perpetual sabbath, and you, because you are idle for one day, suppose you are pious, not discerning why this has been commanded you: and if you eat unleavened bread, you say the will of God has been fulfilled. . . . For this is the symbolic significance of unleavened bread, that you do not commit the old deeds of the wicked leaven. But you have understood all things in a carnal sense, and you suppose it to be piety if you do such things, while your souls are filled with deceit, and, in short, with every wickedness. . . . Learn, therefore, to keep the true fast of God, as Isaiah says, that you may please God."

Justin then quotes extensively from Isaiah 58 in explaining that the true fast that God desires is not one of sackcloth and ashes but rather a life spent in freeing the oppressed, dissolving and avoiding iniquitous covenants and contracts, feeding the hungry, housing the homeless, and clothing the naked.[44] Here, once again, a man of God notes that a life of going through the motions of religious piety is no substitute for a life of goodness and Christian love.

If there is a tendency toward legalism and asceticism in Justin's writings, it is more of a reflection of the somewhat unsettled and immature state of Christian thought and doctrine in early post-apostolic Christianity rather than of well-considered ideas held by Justin.

Irenaeus (130?-202?)

Irenaeus, who ended his years as the formidable bishop of Lyons in Gaul (France), was perhaps the most learned and effective defender of Christian faith in the 100s. His major work is a series of lengthy writings against the heresies of his time. He was well prepared to take up such a task, for he had been a student of the Bishop Polycarp of Smyrna in Asia Minor who in turn was a disciple of the Apostle John. With Irenaeus, therefore, we have again a direct link with the teachings of the apostles. Irenaeus wrote of this relationship in a letter to his friend Florinus:

> When I was still a boy I saw you in Lower Asia with Polycarp, . . . I remember events from those days more clearly than those that have happened recently—what we learn in childhood adheres to

---

44 Justin Martyr, *Dialogue with Trypho*, chaps. 12-15, in *The Ante-Nicene Fathers*, vol. 1, pp. 200-202.

the mind and grows with it—so that I can even picture the place where the blessed Polycarp sat and conversed, his comings and goings, his character, his personal appearance, his discourses to the crowds, and how he reported his discussions with John and others who had seen the Lord. He recalled their very words, what they reported about the Lord and his miracles and his teaching—things that Polycarp had heard directly from eyewitnesses of the Word of life and reported in full harmony with Scripture. I listened eagerly to these things at that time and, through God's mercy, noted them not on paper but in my heart.[45]

The majority of the writings of Irenaeus preserved to us are composed of arguments against the speculations and teaching of groups of heretics collectively known as the Gnostics. Only tangentially does Irenaeus write about the Christian way of life. It is in his *Against Heresies*, Book IV, that he enlarges upon the Church's teaching concerning its way of life in opposition to the distortions of Marcion, a Gnostic teacher.

Irenaeus follows John and Paul in maintaining the preeminence of love in the life of the Church. He writes against the Gnostic heresies, held by those who prided themselves on their supposed secret, special knowledge of God. Irenaeus maintains, on the contrary, that true knowledge consists of the doctrine of the apostles, a proper understanding of the Church as the body of Christ, and a faithful adherence to the Scriptures. He ends by stating: "and (above all, it consists in) the pre-eminent gift of love, which is more precious than knowledge, more glorious than prophecy, and which excels all the other gifts (of God)."[46] Irenaeus certainly appears to have in mind Paul's words to the Corinthians, "So faith, hope, love abide, these three; but the greatest of these is love" (1 Corinthians 13:13 RSV).

In emphasizing love for God and love for one's neighbor, Irenaeus follows Jesus and Paul by citing Paul's letter to the Romans (13:8-10) which teaches that love is the fulfilling of the law. In his major work, *Against Heresies*, he wrote:

Moreover, He did not Himself bring down (from heaven) any other commandment greater than this one, but renewed this very same one to His disciples, when He enjoined them to love

---

45 *Eusebius, The Church* History, c. 325, transl. by Paul L Maier, 1999, pp. 195-196.

46 *Irenaeus Against Heresies*, bk. IV, 33:8, in *The Ante-Nicene Fathers*, vol. 1, p. 508.

God with all their heart, and others as themselves. . . . And Paul
in like manner declares, "Love is the fulfilling of the law: and (he
declares) that when all other things have been destroyed, there
shall remain "faith, hope, and love; but the greatest of all is love;
. . ."[47]

Irenaeus also sees Christ as not abolishing but fulfilling the law during His
lifetime by acting as high priest in healing and performing cures on the
Sabbath.[48]

The New Testament stress on a life of doing good rather than just
the avoidance of evil is maintained by Irenaeus. A quotation from Irenaeus
found in an ancient sermon (A.D. 422) given by Maximus, the bishop of
Turin, is almost a paraphrase of 1 John 3:17:

"As long as any one has the means of doing good to his
neighbors, and does not do so, he shall be reckoned a stranger
to the love of the Lord."[49]

Irenaeus understands that the good we do is motivated by our
thankfulness to God. When we would return such thanks, God directs that
what we would do for Him, we do instead for our needy fellowman. In
commenting upon Matthew 25:34ff., Irenaeus points out that God
acknowledges and recompenses works of mercy as done to Himself:

Now we make offerings to Him, not as though He stood in need
of it, but rendering thanks for His gift, and thus sanctifying what
has been created. For even as God does not need our
possessions, so do we need to offer something to God; as
Solomon says: "He that has pity upon the poor, lends unto the
Lord." For God, who stands in need of nothing, takes our good
works to Himself for this purpose, that He may grant us a
recompense of His own good things, as our Lord says: "Come,
you blessed of My Father, receive the kingdom prepared for you.
For I was hungry, and you gave Me to eat; I was thirsty, and you

---

47 *Irenaeus Against Heresies*, bk IV, 12:2, in *The Ante-Nicene Fathers*, vol. 1, pp.
475, 476.

48 *Irenaeus Against Heresies*, bk. IV, 8:2, in *The Ante-Nicene Fathers*, vol. 1, p. 471.

49 *Irenaeus* in *The Ante-Nicene Fathers*, vol. 1, p. 569.

gave Me drink; I was a stranger, and you took Me in; naked, and
you clothed Me; sick, and you visited Me; in prison, and you
came to Me."[50]

The Sermon on the Mount is also central to Irenaeus's
understanding of Christ's way of life. He sees Jesus extending and fulfilling
the law in His condemnation of not only murder but also anger, and not
only adultery but also lust. Irenaeus teaches that we are set free from the
law so that we may act freely from love and not by constraint.[51]

Basic to Irenaeus's understanding of Christ's way of life is that
Christians no longer serve under the law of the Old Testament. Quoting
from Luke 16:16, Irenaeus wrote: "Since, then, the law originated with
Moses, it terminated with John [the Baptist] as a necessary consequence.
Christ had come to fulfill it: wherefore 'the law and the prophets were' with
them 'until John.'"[52]

Irenaeus argues in regard to the Old Testament that the law was laid
down for those in bondage in order that through obeying the
commandments humans might learn to serve God. But the Word, Christ, set
free the soul. The bonds of slavery to the law were removed. The law of
liberty in Christ was extended. Set free from obedience to the law, the
Christian gives himself wholeheartedly and completely in service to his
King.[53] Thus, for example, Irenaeus teaches, "instead of the law enjoining
the giving of tithes. (He told us) to share all our possessions with the poor; .
. ."[54]

An excerpt from a letter to one Blastus shows the understanding
that Irenaeus had concerning Christian freedom. In an evident reference to
Paul's instruction to the Colossians (2:16), Irenaeus wrote:

> The apostles ordained, "we should not judge any one in respect
> to meat or drink, or in regard to a feast day, or the new moons,
> or the sabbaths." Whence then these contentions? Whence

---

50 *Irenaeus Against Heresies*, bk. IV, 18:6-8, in *The Ante-Nicene Fathers*, vol. 1, p.
486.

51 *Irenaeus Against Heresies*, bk. IV, 13:2, 3, in *The Ante-Nicene Fathers*, vol. 1, p.
477.

52 *Irenaeus Against Heresies*, bk. IV, 4:2, in *The Ante-Nicene Fathers*, vol. 1, p. 466.

53 *Irenaeus Against Heresies*, bk. IV, 13:2, in *The Ante-Nicene Fathers*, vol. 1, p.
477.

54 *Irenaeus Against Heresies*, bk. IV, 13:3, in *The Ante-Nicene Fathers*, vol. 1, p.
477, also bk. IV, 18:2, p. 485.

these schisms? We keep the feast, but in the leaven of malice and wickedness, cutting in pieces the Church of God; and we preserve what belongs to its exterior, that we cast away these better things, faith and love. We have heard from the prophetic words that these feasts and fasts are displeasing to the Lord.[55]

Irenaeus argues that we are free from the Law and are to live in Christian liberty, loving our neighbor as we do ourselves. This does not mean, however, that the basic moral law of the Old Testament is void or abrogated. As was discussed above, love is seen as the fulfilling of the law. Irenaeus insists that the Decalogue, the Ten Commandments, is not abrogated. He wrote, "Preparing man for this life, the Lord Himself did speak in His own person to all alike the words of the Decalogue; and therefore, in like manner, do they remain permanently with us, receiving by means of His advent in the flesh, extension and increase, but not abrogation."[56] Irenaeus views the Ten Commandments as part of God's natural law written into the hearts of men. He sees them as predating the Mosaic law,[57] termed by him, "the laws of bondage, . . . canceled by the new covenant of liberty."[58]

Irenaeus quotes the negative form of the Golden Rule found as a later addition to the rules James lays down for gentiles in Acts 15:29 after the Jerusalem Apostolic Council. The addition reads, "and whatsoever you do not wish to be done to you, do not to others" . . .[59] This addition which is not found in the most reliable manuscripts of the New Testament seems to have been added early to the book of Acts; for it also is found in the writings of Cyprian (200?-258), the famous North African bishop of Carthage, and others.[60] It reflects the tendency of some within the early Church to turn from a life of doing good as taught by Jesus' positive Golden Rule to an emphasis on avoiding doing evil.

---

55 Irenaeus in *The Ante-Nicene Fathers*, vol. 1, p. 575.

56 *Irenaeus Against Heresies*, bk. IV, 16:4, in *The Ante-Nicene Fathers*, vol. 1, p. 482.

57 *Irenaeus Against Heresies*, bk. IV, 13:1, in *The Ante-Nicene Fathers*, vol. 1, p. 477.

58 *Irenaeus Against Heresies*, hk. IV, 16:5, in *The Ante-Nicene Fathers*, vol. 1, p. 482.

59 *Irenaeus Against Heresies*, bk. III, 12:14, in *The Ante-Nicene Fathers*, vol. 1, p. 436.

60 Footnote One in *The Ante-Nicene Fathers*, vol. 1, p. 436.

Noteworthy among the voluminous writings of Irenaeus is the complete absence of any reference to the New Commandment of Jesus found in John's Gospel. Nor is any reference made by Irenaeus to John's stress on the commandment of love found in his first epistle. This is hard to understand in a theologian who was the disciple of Polycarp who was in turn a disciple of John.

The Gospels of Matthew, Mark, and Luke but not the Gospel of John record Jesus' use of Leviticus 19:18: "You shall love your neighbor as yourself." The three synoptic gospels, however, do not record His giving the New Commandment. James and Paul also quote the Leviticus passage in their letters. Paul offers at most a paraphrase of Jesus' New Commandment in Ephesians 5:1-2. Thus, Jesus' emphasis on unselfish love is well recorded in the usage of the apostolic Church, but His New Commandment is not accented. It was some thirty years after the writing of the other three gospels that John wrote his gospel in which he recorded Jesus' New Commandment. It is perhaps due to the late recording of Jesus' New Commandment that for many decades Jesus' New Commandment could make little headway against the Church's already well-established practice of citing Jesus' use of Leviticus 19:18 in regard to love as found in the earlier gospels .

Irenaeus became bishop of Lyons in Gaul, the modern France, upon the martyrdom of his predecessor, Bishop Pothinus, who died under the persecution of the Christians waged by the Emperor Marcus Aurelius. A tradition of the church related by Jerome and Gregory of Tours is that Irenaeus in turn suffered martyrdom during the persecution of Christians under the Emperor Septimius Severus.

Theophilus (115?-181?)

Theophilus, although a minor figure compared to Justin and Irenaeus, also wrote in defense of Christianity from the attacks of the pagans. Eusebius (263-339) lists him in his *The History of the Church from Christ to Constantine* as the sixth bishop of Antioch.[61] Only one of his three works mentioned by Eusebius has been preserved. It is known as *Theophilus to Autolycus*. It is apparently a record of a discussion concerning Christianity between Theophilus and his pagan friend Autolycus. Only a small portion of the work concerns Theophilus's understanding of the Christian way of life. Theophilus first writes concerning the chastity and marital faithfulness practiced by the Christians. He then discusses the life of love that is to be lived by those who follow Christ's teaching:

---

61 Eusebius, c. 325, transl. by G.A. Williamson, 1965, *The History of the Church from Christ to Constantine*, bk. 4, chap. 19 (New York: Dorset Press), p. 181.

And that we should be kindly disposed, not only towards those of our own stock, as some suppose, Isaiah the prophet said: "Say to those that hate you, and that cast you out, You are our brethren, that the name of the Lord may be glorified, and be apparent in their joy." And the Gospel says: "Love your enemies, and pray for them that despitefully use you. For if you love them who love you, what reward have you? This do also the robbers and the publicans." And those that do good it teaches not to boast, lest they become men-pleasers. For it says: "Let not your left hand know what your right hand does." Moreover, concerning subjection to authorities and powers, and prayer for them, the divine word gives us instructions, in order that "we may lead a quiet and peaceable life." And it teaches us to render all things to all, "honor to whom honor, fear to whom fear, tribute to whom tribute; to owe no man anything, but to love all."[62]

The emphasis of Theophilus is on Christian love, of being kindly disposed toward all. His words are thus in keeping with the ethic of selfless love espoused by Jesus and His apostles.

The Legalistic Tendencies of some Jewish Christians

The types of response by some Christian Jews to Paul that were discussed in a previous chapter (see pages 99-101, 105-106) also continued to exist after the time of the apostles. Gentile Christians were in contact with and influenced by those Christian Jews who still practiced the rituals and dietary laws of the Old Testament and were lovers of trifling debates over its laws. Paul in his letter to Timothy had warned about this problem:

But the goal of our instruction is love from a pure heart and a good conscience and a sincere faith. For some men, straying from these things, have turned aside to fruitless discussion, wanting to be teachers of the Law, even though they do not understand either what they are saying or the matters about which they make confident assertions. (1 Timothy 1:5-7 NASB)

Thus, alongside Jesus' way of life as taught by Paul and John there

---

62 *Theophilus to Autolycus*, bk. III, chap. 14, in *The Ante-Nicene Fathers*, vol. 2, p. 115.

were Jewish groups in early Christianity who preferred a legalistic way of life rather than the freedom to live according to Christ's New Commandment.

Justin Martyr (100?-165?), discussed these groups in his work, *Dialogue with Trypho*. Justin is describing two of the groups of Christian Jews when he says to Trypho:

> "But if some, through weak-mindedness, wish to observe such institutions as were given by Moses, from which they expect some virtue, but which we believe were appointed by reason of the hardness of the people's hearts, along with their hope in this Christ, and (wish to perform) the eternal and natural acts of righteousness and piety, yet choose to live with the Christians and the faithful, as I said before, not inducing them either to be circumcised like themselves, or to keep the Sabbath, or to observe any other such ceremonies, then I hold that we ought to join ourselves to such, and associate with them in all things as kinsmen and brethren. But if, Trypho," I continued, "some of your race, who say they believe in this Christ, compel those Gentiles who believe in this Christ to live in all respects according to the law given by Moses, or choose not to associate so intimately with them, I in like manner do not approve of them."[63]

Irenaeus (130?-202?) described the Christian Jews known as the Ebionites as follows:

> Those who are called Ebionites agree that the world was made by God; but their opinions with respect to the Lord are similar to those of Cerinthus and Carpocrates. They use the Gospel according to Matthew only, and repudiate the Apostle Paul, maintaining that he was an apostate from the law. As to the prophetical writings, they endeavor to expound them in a somewhat singular manner: they practice circumcision, persevere in the observance of those customs which are enjoined by the law, and are so Judaic in their style of life, that

---

63 Justin Martyr, *Dialogue with Trypho*, chap. 47, in *The Ante-Nicene Fathers*, vol. 1, p. 218.

they even adore Jerusalem as if it were the house of God.[64]

This extreme group of Ebionites continued as a Christian Jewish faction into the 300s. They denied the virgin birth and taught that the Christ entered the man Jesus at His baptism. They are later discussed negatively in the writings of both the church father Jerome (340?-420), and the church historian Eusebius of Caesarea (260?-340?).[65] There was also another early group of Ebionites, identical perhaps to the Christian Jews known as the Nazarenes, who lived according to Judaic law but did not deny that the Messiah was born to the Virgin Mary.

As Christianity spread through the Roman world, the views of the early Palestinian and Syrian Jewish Christians slowly came to have less influence. As the Church evolved into a predominantly Gentile Church, the peculiar views of some of the Jewish Christians became less relevant to the Church. The writings of Justin Martyr, Irenaeus, and others also did much to combat their teachings.

Aspects of Christianity in the 100s

The Primacy of Christian Love

For the most part, the Christian literature of the 100s faithfully follows the way of life taught by Jesus and His apostles. The tendency, however, of some in the Church toward asceticism and a legalistic way of life is also present. Nonetheless, the apostles' emphasis on a faith active in love expressed in Christian freedom was too alive and recent for a way of life foreign to the New Testament to yet overthrow it.

The memory and oral tradition of the apostles' words, however, finally came to fade from the minds of the people, presbyters, and bishops. Irenaeus writes of how Polycarp memorized the words of John and the other apostles to whom he listened. He tells of how he himself then in turn memorized Polycarp's words. But as Irenaeus says, he did not write down these memories; and no one can say what was contained in Irenaeus's memory. Thus, unless later written down the oral tradition of the apostles' words slowly disappeared from the Church. It is as these memories were being lost that legalistic attitudes and an unhealthy asceticism came to the

---

64 *Irenaeus Against Heresies*, bk. 1, chap. 26, 2, in *The Ante-Nicene Fathers*, vol. 1, p. 352.

65 Eusebius, c. 325, transl. by G.A. Williamson, 1965, *The History of the Church from Christ to Constantine*, bk. 3, 27, pp. 136, 137.

fore. It is then that Christians came to have a fixation on inward purity instead of outgoing Christian love as a way of striving for perfection before God. Lives of extreme piety came to be more admired by the Christian populace than lives of goodness and love towards one's neighbor.

The Beginnings of a Growing Ascetic Fixation upon Sexuality

There were also those in the Church that began to regard sex and even sexual love in marriage not as a gift of God but primarily as a source of torment and temptation. Lost was the wholesome attitude toward married sexual love found in the Scriptures in which it is taught, "Marriage is honorable among all, and the bed undefiled; but fornicators and adulterers God will judge" (Hebrews 13:4 NKJV). The Biblical view came to be replaced by a zealous stress on virginity and celibacy quite out of keeping with the teachings of both the Old and New Testaments.

In the coming chapters, we will see many church leaders becoming concerned to an obsessive degree with regulating sex and marriage for themselves and the lay people of the church. Early in the church's history, the clergy were forbidden to marry unless they were married before they entered holy orders. From the four hundreds until 1075 A.D. married priests in the western Christianity, the churches in the lands around the western Mediterranean Sea, might live with their wives, but they were forbidden to have sexual relations with them. In 1075, the church in the West under Pope Gregory VII dissolved all existing clergy marriages. Concerning the laity, especially in the Middle Ages church law grew to become almost inordinately concerned with the sexual side of their lives.

In order to better understand how these attitudes and laws relate to the teaching of the Scripture, a review of what the Bible has to say about the sexual aspects of human life follows.

AN EXCURSUS ON THE BIBLICAL VIEW OF SEX AND SEXUAL RELATIONSHIPS

The Bible's View as to the Purpose of Sex

To seek a basic understanding of the Biblical view of the relationship of the sexes, one must go back to the story of the creation in Genesis. The creation story describes the making of humans as the last of God's creative acts, and then it only speaks of the male being made. The narrative, however, continues, "And the Lord God said, 'It is not good that man should be alone; I will make him a helper comparable to him'" (Genesis 2:18 NKJV). Note that the reason God gives for making woman is that man should not live alone. In God's eyes he should have a helper suited for him. Eve then is primarily intended to be a companion and to work together with him through life.

That this companionship involved more than a platonic relationship is seen in the verse, "So God created man in His own image; in the image of God He created him; male and female He created them. Then God blessed them, and God said to them, 'Be fruitful and multiply: fill the earth and subdue it. . .'" (Genesis 1:27-28 NKJV). This verse takes us to the second reason or purpose for the creation of man and woman: they are to bring children into the world.

Biblical Marriage

Marriage is the normal estate of a man and woman according to Scripture. It is in marriage and family life that they find completion, contentment, and fulfillment. It is God's will that they so live, for in the Psalms we read, "God sets the solitary in families; . . ." (68:6 NKJV). In the Psalms is also this peaceful picture of the home and family life:

> Blessed is everyone who fears the Lord,
>> Who walks in His ways.
> When you shall eat the labor of your hands,
>> You shall be happy and it shall be well with you.
> Your wife shall be like a fruitful vine,
>> In the very heart of your house,
> Your children like olive plants
>> All around your table.
> Behold, thus shall the man be blessed
>> Who fears the Lord. (Psalm 128:1-4 NKJV)

Marriage in the Old Testament is highly regarded. There is no asceticism in the Old Testament when it comes to the institution of marriage. Even the Nazarites, the Old Testament class of ascetics, were allowed marriage. One of the worst situations for a woman was to be without a husband. In depicting the coming fate of the nation of Judah, Isaiah wrote, "And in that day seven women shall take hold of one man, saying, 'We will eat our own food and wear our own apparel; only let us be called by your name, to take away our reproach'" (Isaiah 4:1 NKJV).

Marriage is so highly regarded that it is used as a metaphor many times to depict the close relationship existing between God and His people (Isaiah 62:5, Hosea 2:16-20). Marriage is the most intimate of relationships. The married couple is one flesh in the sight of God: "Therefore a man shall leave his father and his mother and be joined to his wife, and they shall become one flesh" (Genesis 2:24 NKJV).

In the Old Testament, one of the chief reasons for becoming married was to acquire an heir who would carry on the family name and inherit the family property. That a man should have no male offspring was considered a misfortune. So much importance was laid upon the misfortune of dying without a male heir that if a man died without a son, the law in Deuteronomy decreed that his brother was to marry the widow and the first son born to them was to take the deceased man's name (Deuteronomy 25:5). The crime of Onan was not *coitus interruptus*, that is, spilling his semen on the ground as some have said; but that he broke the law by withdrawing before ejaculation to avoid inseminating the widow of his dead brother (Genesis 38:1-11).

Although the Old Testament stresses the bearing of children, one should not get the impression that sexual intercourse was only for procreation. Within marriage perfect freedom of sexual expression was allowed, and sexual love for its sake alone was part of the normal life. In the book of Deuteronomy we read the law, "When a man takes a new wife, he shall not go out with the army, nor be charged with any duty; he shall be free at home one year and shall give happiness to his wife whom he has taken" (Deuteronomy 24:5 NASB). The writer of Ecclesiastes advises, "Enjoy life with the woman whom you love all the days of your fleeting life which He has given to you under the sun; for this is your reward in life, and in your toil in which you have labored under the sun (Ecclesiastes 9:9 NASB). In the book of Proverbs is found, "Let your fountain be blessed, and rejoice with the wife of your youth. As a lovely deer and a graceful doe, let her breasts satisfy you at all times; and always be enraptured with her love" (Proverbs 5:18-19 NKJV). In Exodus, we find that a man cannot deny a second wife her conjugal rights. If he does, she may leave him (Exodus 21:10-11).

The Song of Solomon, or Canticles as it is sometimes called, is a love poem of a sensuous an uninhibited nature (compare Song of Solomon 2:3-7; 5:10-16; 7:1-13). It contains a beautiful story of a young woman who refuses the attentions of the king, for she is sick with love for her beloved, a virile young shepherd. Many among both Jews and Christians were uncomfortable with the passionate sexuality of the poems and endeavored to interpret this book only in symbolical and allegorical terms. But Canticles place in Scripture needs no such justification; it is a book written in recognition of God's blessing on His gift of the joys and rapture of sexual love between man and woman.

Sex is very frankly treated in the Old Testament. It is something that is taken for granted as a gift of God, and it is to be wholesomely used. The Old Testament knows no restriction on sex play or sexual enjoyment within the marriage bond. On the other hand, homosexual behavior, fornication, and adultery are condemned (Leviticus 18:22, Deuteronomy 22:22-30). These are considered grave sins against the general welfare. They are alternatives that harm the basic structure of society—a family in which a man and woman are committed to each other. In their life together, they give to their children not only a secure and loving home but also a model of happy married and family life for the children to follow when they in turn marry. How blessed are those children who grow up in such a home. No greater earthly gift can parents give their children than such a model.

It is obvious that a homosexual couple cannot give such a model to children. It is also obvious that adulterous behavior destroys such a model. Thus, the whole community took part in the punishment of those whose self-serving behavior endangered the family as the fundamental institution of society. If the penalties prescribed in the Old Testament for sexual offenses seem severe to the modern mind, perhaps God takes a great deal more seriously than does our decadent modern culture the welfare and happiness of the family and especially that of innocent wives, husbands, and particularly children. In the Bible, the good of the society rises above the desires and willfulness of individuals.

The New Testament has a similar view to that of the Old Testament concerning family, sex, and sexual relationships. Marriage according to the writer of the book of Hebrews is honorable in all, and the marriage bed is undefiled (Hebrews 13:4). It is significant for the Christian view of marriage that the first recorded miracle of our Lord was the changing of water into wine to aid the festivities during the marriage celebration at Cana (John 2:1-11).

The family into which Jesus was born has often been taken to be a model family. In the history of the Church, however, there have been attempts to downplay the physical sexual relationship in marriage by attempting to maintain the perpetual virginity of Mary in this model family. Somehow for Mary to have had a physical relationship with her husband after the birth of Jesus was viewed as sullying the chasteness of her life. The New Testament gives no support to this view.

Jesus' family was a typical family of its day. According to the Gospel of Matthew, Mary and Joseph did not have sexual relations until after the birth of Jesus. That they later had a normal married life is made evident by Matthew writing, "And Joseph arose from his sleep, and did as the angel of the Lord commanded him, and took her as his wife, and kept her a virgin (literally in the original Greek, 'and he was not knowing her') until she gave birth to a Son, and he called His name Jesus" (Matthew 1:24 NASB). The word "until" in the phrase, "and he was not knowing her until she gave birth to a Son," should have put an end to later speculations about the perpetual virginity of the Blessed Virgin Mary. If a person says, "I did not drive my new car until after I had received driver training," it certainly implies that he later did drive his new car. Much tortured reasoning has been expended on Matthew's "until" by Jerome and others in their attempt to maintain the "perpetual virginity" of the Blessed Virgin.

The Gospels that tell of Jesus' life give insight into the growing family of Mary and Joseph. Matthew records people saying concerning Jesus, "Is not this the carpenter's son? Is not His mother called Mary, and His brothers, James and Joseph and Simon and Judas? And His sisters, are they not all with us" (Matthew 13:55-56 NASB, see also Mark 6:3)? Certainly, Matthew's words describe a nuclear family. It strains belief to consider the children that Matthew mentions to be really Jesus' cousins as some have suggested or children of the "other Mary" (Matthew 28:1).

There are other instances when the Gospels mention Jesus' family. The Gospels tell of an occasion when during His ministry Jesus' mother and brothers came to speak with Him (Matthew 12:46-47, Mark 3:31-32, and Luke 8:19-20). John records a trip made to Capernaum by Jesus, His mother, brothers, and disciples (John 2:12). John also wrote of Jesus' brothers in mentioning that during Jesus' life and ministry His brothers did not consider Him the Messiah (John 7:2-10). After Jesus' resurrection, however, His brothers did come to believe in Him as recorded in Acts 1:14. Paul speaks of visiting Jerusalem and meeting with "James, the Lord's brother" (Galatians 1:19). Jude begins his short letter: "Jude, a servant of Jesus Christ and brother of James" (Jude 1). Therefore, as is evident from the matter-of-fact treatment of Jesus' family by the New Testament, the later teaching of the perpetual virginity of Mary has no basis in the New Testament. Mary and Joseph lived a normal married life.

It is not only the New Testament that attests to Mary and Joseph having other children. The Jewish historian Josephus (37-100?) in his work, *Antiquities of the Jews*, wrote of the death of James, whom he identified as the brother of Jesus. In the early 60s, there was an interval of time between the death of the Roman governor of Judea, the procurator Festus, and the arrival from Rome of a new Roman procurator to replace him. During this interim, the high priest Ananus took advantage of the political vacuum by illegally ordering the stoning of James, the leader of the church in Jerusalem. Josephus records the event:

> Ananus was of this disposition, he thought he had now a proper opportunity. . . . so he assembled the sanhedrin of judges, and brought before them the brother of Jesus, who was called Christ, whose name was James, and some others, (or, some of his companions); and when he had formed an accusation against them as breakers of the law, he delivered them to be stoned; . .

.66

Thus, not only the Bible attests to Mary having other children, but also a contemporary non-Christian Jewish historian.

Jesus taught that a man and woman united in wedlock are in a permanent union and are one flesh (Mark 10:7-9, 1 Corinthians 7:10-11). Only for reasons of adultery or malicious desertion is the marriage to be broken (Matthew 5:31-32, 1 Corinthians 7:15).

Although one of the primary functions of marriage is procreation, Paul teaches that the enjoyment and taking pleasure in the sexual relationship is part of married life:

> The husband should give to his wife her conjugal rights, and likewise the wife to her husband. For the wife does not rule over her own body, but the husband does; likewise the husband does not rule over his own body, but the wife does. Do not refuse one another except perhaps by agreement for a season, that you may devote yourself to prayer; but then come together again, lest Satan tempt you through lack of self-control. (1 Corinthians 7:3-5 RSV)

Again, in the New Testament as in the Old, the Scriptures are silent concerning the sexual practices of a married couple.

The principle of Christian love is a vital part of the New Testament ethic concerning marriage. Christian love is distinguished from erotic love or fraternal love by its being a selfless love. It is a love showered upon another without any expectation of self-gratification. It is a love offered and given without inflicting an obligation on another. Paul paraphrased Jesus' new commandment when he wrote, "Therefore be imitators of God, as beloved children. And walk in love, as Christ loved us and gave himself up for us, a fragrant offering and sacrifice to God" (Ephesians 5:1-2 RSV). Paul expanded upon what this love means to married couples when a few sentences later he counseled:

> Submit and yield yourself in love to one another out of reverence for Christ. Wives, submit and yield yourself in love to your husbands, as to the Lord. For the husband is the head of the wife as Christ is the head of the church, His body, and is

---

66 *The Works of Flavius Josephus*, trans. by W. Whiston, bk. 20, chap. 9:1, (Grand Rapids, Michigan: Baker Book House), vol. 4, p. 140.

Himself its Savior. As the church submits and yields itself in love to Christ, so let wives also submit and yield themselves in love to their husbands in everything. (Ephesians 5:21-24 author's translation)

Husbands, love your wives, just as Christ also loved the church and gave Himself up for her; that He might sanctify her, having cleansed her by the washing of water with the word, that He might present to Himself the church in all her glory, having no spot or wrinkle or any such thing; but that she should be holy and blameless. So husbands ought also to love their own wives as their own bodies. (Ephesians 5:25-28a NASB)

Too often in the texts above relating to wives, the translation of the Greek text into English found in various versions of the Bible reads, "Wives, be subject to" . . . or "Wives be submissive to. . ." The Greek word that is thus translated is *hupotasso*. However, an authoritative and comprehensive lexicon of New Testament Greek, the Arndt and Gingrich *Greek—English Lexicon of the New Testament*, recommends that in such verses as that cited above the Greek word *hupotasso* should be translated "of submission in the sense of voluntary yielding in love." In the translation above, this recommendation is followed.

The verses above put marriage on the highest possible plane. As Christ loves the Church, husbands are to love their wives even to the extent of giving their lives for them as Christ gave His life for the Church. As Christ, however, is the head of the Church, so is the husband the head of the wife. This arrangement does not lead to tyranny; however, since if the husband loves his wife as his own body he certainly will not misuse his position as the head of the family. Although a self-gratifying erotic love is likely to be a part of any marriage and might lead to sexual exploitation, modifying this erotic love is Christian love that strives to treat one's partner as selflessly as possible. As this unselfish love is to rule all of a Christian's dealings with his fellow humans, certainly it is basic to his closest human relationship, his marriage partner.

Although there are many passages in the New Testament that speak highly of marriage, there are some passages that have been used in an effort to show that marriage is frowned upon as less worthy than being unmarried. Paul, himself being unmarried, wrote:

Now concerning the things of which you wrote to me: It is good for a man not to touch a woman. Nevertheless, because of sexual immorality, let each man have his own wife, and let each woman have her own husband. . . . For I wish that all men were even as I myself. But each one has his own gift from God, one in this manner and another in that. But I say to the unmarried and to the widows: It is good for them if they remain even as I am; but if they cannot exercise self-control, let them marry. For it is better to marry than to burn with passion. (1 Corinthians 7:1-2, 7-9 NKJV)

Paul writes that he wishes that all could be unmarried as he is. But he recognizes that this ability is a special gift from God and that not all have this gift. In fact, he acknowledges that few have the gift, for he wrote that each man should have his own wife and each woman her own husband. Why Paul wished that all were single as he is himself he explains in writing:

Now concerning the unmarried, I have no command of the Lord, but I give my opinion as one who by the Lord's mercy is trustworthy. I think that in view of the impending distress it is well for a person to remain as he is. Are you bound to a wife? Do not seek to be free. Are you free from a wife? Do not seek marriage. But if you marry, you do not sin, and if a girl marries she does not sin. Yet those who marry will have worldly troubles, and I would spare you that. I mean, brethren, the appointed time has grown very short; . . . (1 Corinthians 7:25-28 RSV)

It is in view of the "impending distress" that Paul counsels that Christians should remain as they are, whether married or single. It seems that Paul realized how, particularly in times of impending persecution (such as existed when his words were written), having a wife and family might make it more difficult to live within the faith. Also, when Paul wrote, "I mean, brethren, the appointed time has grown very short," he indicates that he also is anticipating the early return of Christ and the tumultuous end of the age. In such times, institutions such as marriage are not the first priority. Paul wants Christians to be free from unessential cares in view of the impending persecution and the hoped for early return of Christ. Therefore, he continues:

I want you to be free from anxieties. The unmarried man is anxious about the affairs of the Lord, how to please the Lord; but the married man is anxious about worldly affairs, how to please his wife, and his interests are divided. And the unmarried woman or girl is anxious about the affairs of the Lord, how to be holy in body and spirit; but the married woman is anxious about worldly affairs, how to please her husband. I say this for your own benefit, not to lay any restraint upon you, but to promote good order and to secure your undivided devotion to the Lord. (1 Corinthians 7:32-35 RSV)

Paul realizes, however, that there are many who do not have the Spirit's gift of celibacy. He would not bind consciences where His Lord has not bound them. Therefore, he continues:

If any one thinks that he is not behaving properly toward his betrothed, if his passions are strong, and it has to be, let him do as he wishes; let them marry--it is no sin. But whoever is firmly established in his heart, being under no necessity but having his desire under control, and has determined this in his heart, to keep her as his betrothed, he will do well. So that he who marries his betrothed does well, and he who refrains from marriage will do better. (1 Corinthians 7:36-38 RSV)

People have been able to accuse Paul of denigrating marriage only if they take selected verses in the above texts out of historical context.

Paul, however, made it clear that he himself had the right to be married. He wrote to the Christians at Corinth, "Do we not have a right to take along a believing wife, even as the rest of the apostles, and the brothers of the Lord, and Cephas" (1 Corinthians 9:5 NASB)? In this text, he plainly states that the normal condition of his fellow evangelists was marriage.

It is evident that Paul envisioned a church served by a clergy living with wives and families. About seven years after his letter to the church at Corinth, Paul wrote to Timothy:

An overseer [bishop], then, must be above reproach, the husband of one wife, temperate, prudent, respectable, hospitable, able to teach, not addicted to wine or pugnacious, but gentle, uncontentious, free from the love of money. He must be one who manages his own household well, keeping his children under control with all dignity; . . . (1 Timothy 3:2-4 NASB)

A deacon likewise was to be a husband of one wife and a person who managed his children and household well (1 Timothy 3:12). Paul gave similar advice concerning church leaders to his co-worker Titus, to whom he gave charge over church affairs in Crete (Titus 1:5-6).

Guided by the Spirit, Paul, however, envisions a time when a different view of marriage would arise. He wrote to Timothy:

> Now the Spirit expressly says that in latter times some will depart from the faith, giving heed to deceiving spirits and doctrines of demons, speaking lies with hypocrisy, having their own conscience seared with a hot iron, forbidding to marry, and commanding to abstain from foods which God has created to be received with thanksgiving by those who believe and know the truth. (1 Timothy 4:1-3 NKJV)

Certainly, this prophecy of Paul's about those who would forbid marriage has been amply and unhappily fulfilled too many times both in the history of Christendom and among many heretical groups.

In summary, the Bible views marriage as an institution in which normally all men and women are to take part. It is an institution set up by God for love and companionship, the bearing of children, and responding to the tension of sexual desire. In addition, upon the death of a spouse it is no sin to contemplate another marriage. Paul advises, "Therefore I desire that younger widows marry, bear children, manage the house, give no opportunity to the adversary to speak reproachfully" (1 Timothy 5:14 NKJV).

Paul advised against marriage primarily in view of the unsettled conditions of the early Christian Church. Even then, the celibate life was only for those who possessing the spiritual gift of celibacy could chastely live the single life.

Paul's words were in keeping with Jesus' observation that there would be those who would make themselves eunuchs for the sake of the kingdom of heaven (Matthew 19:12). A celibate life, however, lived for the kingdom of God can never be a source of pride. The gift of celibacy is the Spirit's gift and not our own doing just as are the other gifts of the Holy Spirit as described in 1 Corinthians 12. Thus, the celibate life and the married life can be equally chaste in the sight of God.

Sexual Morality

While sex is treated frankly by Scripture and with a wholesome openness, it is only to be regarded as a good gift of God when properly used. As with any of the appetites and needs of humans, there can be a use and an abuse. There is a very human need for food; but this appetite need not lead to the abuse of food, the sin of gluttony. There is the necessity of providing one's family with shelter, clothes, and sustenance; but caring for one's family need not lead to the sins of covetousness, theft, and the exploitation of others. It also follows that natural sexual desire may be a factor in leading a person into a God-pleasing marriage; it need not lead one into the abuse of sex through promiscuity, fornication, or adultery. Thus, on the one hand, Paul instructs Christians to make no provision for the lusts of the flesh that result in reveling, drunkenness, debauchery, and licentiousness (Romans 13:13-14). On the other hand, he advises: "If any one thinks that he is not behaving properly toward his betrothed, if his passions are strong, and it has to be, let him do as he wishes; let them marry—it is no sin" (1 Corinthians 7:36-38 RSV).

The Old Testament understanding of sexual behavior is in keeping with its view of humans not as isolated individuals but rather as members of families, clans, and communities. Those attitudes and behaviors that are for the common good were acceptable. The Old Testament considered evil any sexual behavior that was harmful to the general welfare of the larger group. Sexual promiscuity was not condoned in Hebrew culture since this would endanger the family. An illegitimate child would have no inheritance and no real place in the social structure. A girl who had an illegitimate child was a burden to the society. Few men would be willing to marry a woman whose child would confuse the rights of inheritance of their own children. Proverbs constantly speaks of sexual adventure outside of marriage as great folly, engaged in only by the immature and fools.[67] Adultery especially is considered a great evil; for one thereby sins against the bedrock of society, the integrity of the family. The necessity of having a sexual outlet was recognized. It was provided for by having an early age for marriage and by the social custom of expecting practically all members of the community to be married.

The New Testament teaches the same sexual code. The early Christians lived in a Roman/Greek culture that was a promiscuous and morally decayed society that engaged in fornication, adultery, pedophilia, and homosexual practices.[68] Because of this sexual decadence, the New Testament speaks much concerning sexual misconduct. Paul views sexual passion as natural to humans, but he recognizes that it can be disruptive to society if improperly used (Romans 1:24-32). In marriage sex has its proper expression in a way that benefits and protects the whole community. Sexual activity outside of marriage is viewed as disruptive both to the life of the community and to the lives of the people who engage in it.

---

67 Proverbs 6:24-35; 7:6-27; 9:13-18; 23:27-28

68 Not all Romans approved of such practices. For example, the Roman historian Suetonius criticized such decadence in his *The Lives of the Twelve Caesars*. See under Julius Caesar, secs. 49-52; Caesar Augustus, secs. 69, 71; Tiberius, secs.42-45.

Sexual activity outside of marriage is sinful because of the selfish, self-gratifying way it uses the sexual partner. Basic to the Christian's life is a selfless Christian love. The Christian is to live in imitation of Christ's love. Christ's love brought Him to die for the redemption of every individual. How could a Christian use for selfish sexual purposes a person for whom his Lord died?

In illicit sexual activity, there is typically little thought of the welfare of the person who is seduced or of any responsibility toward the welfare of the child who may be born. Nor is there any sense of responsibility toward the community as a whole whose welfare is based primarily on well-knit and integrated family life. The community often has no secure and honorable place for the victims of sexual practice outside of marriage, that is, the pregnant, unmarried woman or the illegitimate child. The New Testament condemns not only sexual misconduct, but censures even the desire for illicit relations. Jesus said, "But I say to you that every one who looks at a woman lustfully has already committed adultery with her in his heart" (Matthew 5:28 RSV). The letter of Paul to the church at Corinth gives an example of the serious way the New Testament views sexual immorality:

> Do you not know that the unrighteous will not inherit the kingdom of God? Do not be deceived. Neither fornicators, nor idolaters, nor adulterers, nor effeminate homosexuals, nor sodomites, nor thieves, nor covetous, nor drunkards, nor revilers, nor extortioners will inherit the kingdom of God. And such were some of you. But you were washed, but you were sanctified, but you were justified in the name of the Lord Jesus and by the Spirit of our God. (1 Corinthians 6:9-11 NKJV)

It is worthy to note, however, that the Bible is silent concerning auto-eroticism or masturbatory practices. In regard to Genesis 38:1-11, the term "onanism" for masturbation is an example of faulty Biblical interpretation. As mentioned previously, the crime of Onan was that he refused to inseminate the childless wife of his dead brother and thus perform the duty of the brother-in-law to her.

It is only late in the 300s that auto-eroticism became a concern of the church authorities[69] The first mention of masturbation in early Christian literature known to myself is found in John Cassian's (360?-435?) "The

---

69 James A. Brundage, 1987, *Law, Sex, and Christian Morality in Medieval Europe* (Chicago: Univ. of Chicago Press), p. 109.

Second Conference with Abbot Theonas." During an interview with the Egyptian monk, Abbot Theonas around 380 to 400, the question is raised whether a nocturnal emission of semen debars one from taking the Lord's Supper the next day. The abbot answers that only if the emission is involuntary can one take the Lord's Supper. One cannot come to the altar if the efflux is due to one's own fault and the result of voluptuous movement.[70] In later centuries, churchmen become highly condemnatory of any practice of masturbation.

The Place of Sex in the Total life of Humans

Sex in itself is a gift of God and among the things that God in His creation called "very good." The ultimate purpose of sex, for humans as well as for other life, is reproduction. The pleasure of the sex act, however, apart from reproduction is understood, accepted, and approved by Scripture. The basic thought in Scripture is that sexual relationships have a normal and natural place in a man and woman's life.

Sexual desire is misdirected when it violates the sexual rights of another person, or when it would assume sexual rights without the corresponding responsibility of a permanent sexual relationship between the man and woman. In marriage, sexual activities are only wrong when carried out in a selfish or loveless manner.

A sexual relationship thus is a good, useful, and pleasurable gift of the Lord if experienced within the bounds of the married state where all parties concerned are secure and protected: the woman who would have support and security during a possible pregnancy; the child who would have a secure, nurturing, and honorable home and family in which to be born; and the community whose welfare is enhanced by happy, stable, and responsible family life.

---

70 Terrence G. Kardong, translator, 1993, *Cassian on Chastity* (Richardton, N.D.: Assumption Abbey Press), p. 52.

Chapter Nine

THE EARLY GROWTH OF ASCETICISM
AND CHURCH LAW: 175 - 300 A.D.

Early Trends towards Extreme Asceticism and Legalism

The historian William Lecky wrote,

> There can, indeed, be little doubt that, for nearly two hundred
> years after its establishment in Europe, the Christian community
> exhibited a moral purity which, if it has been equaled, has never
> for any long period been surpassed. . . . Christianity for the first
> time made charity a rudimentary virtue . . . . it effected a
> complete revolution in this sphere, by regarding the poor as the
> special representatives of the Christian Founder, and thus
> making the love of Christ rather than the love of man, the
> principle of charity. . . . "but in the third century a great ascetic
> movement arose, which gradually brought a new type of
> character into the ascendant, and diverted the enthusiasm of
> the Church into new channels" (see page 7 for the full quotation).

This movement toward Christian asceticism, that is, the attempt to
achieve perfection and win God's favor primarily through self-denial, strict
discipline, and self-punishment, slowly grew as the centuries passed. There
was a similar trend during this period toward a legalistic approach to the
Christian way of life. The present chapter will demonstrate from three
sources the acceleration of these trends.

First, we will consider the writings of those church fathers that dealt
with Christian ethics and the Christian way of life. Second, we will review
the Pseudo-Clementine literature, which are writings falsely ascribed to
Clement of Rome. These documents will give insight into the trends toward
asceticism and legalism found among various groups who considered
themselves Christians. Third, we will discuss the same trends found in the

New Testament Apocrypha. The Apocrypha are composed of supposed gospels of the life of Christ, books describing the activities of the apostles and letters supposedly written by them. They often pretend to be of equal authority to the books of the New Testament and are usually from heretical or Gnostic sources. They are called Apocrypha (from the Greek "hidden away") because their authorship is either unknown or pseudepigraphic, that is, writings falsely ascribed to another more prominent individual.

As later chapters will show, the trend toward viewing asceticism as the Christian ideal will grow to ever more rigorous ascetic practices found among anchoritic hermits and in the organized asceticism of the monasteries and convents. The trend toward a legalistic approach to the Christian way of life will result with the growing dominance of church law over the lives of clergy and lay people in medieval times. The freedom of the Christian to make his own moral decisions based on Christian love as led by the Holy Spirit and informed by the Scriptures will be lost.

It is not the case, however, of Christian love ever disappearing from the life of the Church. It is rather a major change of emphasis. The Christian who gives of himself in self-less acts of Christian love for the benefit of others comes to be less valued than the person who flees the world to seek purity and perfection in the solitary life of the pious ascetic. A life based on striving for perfection through self-denial, worship, prayer, acts of penitence, avoidance of temptation, and absorption with one's own personal purity is held up as the Christian ideal. The life of the "religious," the cloistered monk or nun, is considered more saintly than the life of the "secular," the priest in a church giving himself in service to his flock. Extreme piety becomes much more highly valued than goodness and Christian love.

Christian love, nonetheless, although often overwhelmed by these trends was ever present in the life of the Church. Throughout Christian history, there have always been men and women who have followed lives of Christian love. The constant stress in the New Testament on a faith active in deeds of unselfish love served as a continuous antidote to the often-unhealthy obsession with one's own personal purity. Only when the New Testament is ignored or denigrated and its teachings replaced by human opinion and non-Biblical doctrines masquerading as "Tradition" is Christian love in danger of being lost to Christianity.

The writings of church leaders and other religious literature of the late 100s and the 200s will illustrate how these changes in emphasis slowly came about; and how asceticism and church law came to displace the New Testament's guiding principle of *agape*, Christian love.

Early Christian Writers

Athenagoras (Dates unknown)

Around 177 A.D., Athenagoras, a cultured and well-educated Christian concerning whom very little is otherwise known, wrote two treatises. One treatise was on the resurrection. The other, *A Plea for the Christians*, was written to the Roman emperors Marcus Aurelius and Lucius Aurelius Commodus. In the letter, Athenagoras argues against the slanders that the Christians eat human flesh, are atheists, and are immoral. He asks the emperors the rhetorical question, "What, then, are those teachings in which we are brought up" And he answers quoting Jesus:

> "I say unto you, love your enemies; bless them that curse you; pray for them that persecute you; that you may be the sons of your Father who is in heaven, who causes His sun to rise on the evil and the good, and sends rain on the just and the unjust."

And he adds further:

> But among us you will find uneducated persons, and artisans, and old women, who, if they are unable in words to prove the benefit of our doctrine, yet by their deeds exhibit the benefit arising from their persuasion of its truth: they do not rehearse speeches, but exhibit good works; when struck, they do not strike again; when robbed, they do not go to law; they give to those that ask of them, and love their neighbors as themselves.[1]

Athenagoras thus argues that the Christians are taught to do good works and to live according to Jesus' counsel, "You shall love your neighbor as yourself" (Mark 12:31). However, along with this stress on a life of love expressed in service to others, there is a turning away from the wholesome view of human sexuality found throughout the Scriptures. Instead, Athenagoras appears to view sex as a necessary evil. Intercourse between the sexes is to be solely for begetting children. Seen here is the continued growth of the idea that only in virginity is true chastity. Athenagoras defends the Christians from the accusation of immoral sexual conduct by writing:

---

1 Athenagoras, *A Plea for the Christians*, chap. 11, in *The Ante-Nicene Fathers* (Grand Rapids: Wm. B. Eerdmans Publ. Co.), vol. 2, p. 134.

Therefore, having the hope of eternal life, we despise the things of this life, even to the pleasures of the soul, each of us reckoning her his wife whom he has married according to the laws laid down by us, and that only for the purpose of having children. For as the husbandman throwing the seed into the ground awaits the harvest, not sowing more upon it, so to us the procreation of children is the measure of our indulgence in appetite. Nay, you would find many among us, both men and women, growing old unmarried, in hope of living in closer communion with God. But if the remaining in virginity and in the state of an eunuch brings nearer to God, while the indulgence of carnal thought and desire leads away from Him, in those cases in which we shun the thoughts, much more do we reject the deeds. For we bestow our attention, not on the study of words, but on the exhibition and teaching of actions,—that a person should either remain as he was born, or be content with one marriage; for a second marriage is only a specious adultery. "For whosoever puts away his wife," says He, "and marries another, commits adultery;" not permitting a man to send her away whose virginity he has brought to an end, nor to marry again. For he who deprives himself of his first wife, even though she be dead, is a cloaked adulterer, . . .[2]

The Church is obviously going beyond the New Testament teachings concerning the Christian way of life by adding what Athenagoras calls, "laws laid down by us." Athenagoras terms a man who marries again after his spouse has died a "cloaked adulterer." The words of Paul are ignored, for Paul wrote, "Therefore I desire that the younger widows marry, bear children, manage the house, give no opportunity to the adversary to speak reproachfully" (1 Timothy 5:14 NKJV). The church is beginning to do what Jesus said about rabbis of His time: "And in vain they worship Me, teaching as doctrines the commandments of men. For laying aside the commandment of God, you hold the tradition of men" (Mark 7:7-8 NKJV). Thus once again in the late 100s we see a movement away from the way of life taught by Jesus and His apostles toward a life based on a new legalism and asceticism.

---

2 Athenagoras, *A Plea for the Christians*, chap. 33, in *The Ante-Nicene Fathers*, vol. 2, pp. 146, 147.

Hippolytus (died 236? A.D.)

Hippolytus was a well-educated Christian especially trained in Greek philosophy. He also had been privileged to hear the discourses of Irenaeus either in Lyons or in Rome. The date of his birth is not known; however, he was active as a Christian leader and theologian in the decade before and the decades after the year 200. One tradition records his death as a martyr around 236 A.D.

A bishop in his own right, he opposed some of the doctrinal positions and also the administrative looseness of the Roman bishops Zephyrinus (202-218) and Callistus (218-223). Hippolytus was an author and a voluminous commentator on the Scriptures. In *The Apostolic Tradition*, a manual of church practice written in 217 A.D., is found the earliest known reference to the Church's tradition of using sponsors or godparents at the baptism of small children. Hippolytus writes, "And first baptize the little ones; if they can speak for themselves, they shall do so; if not, their parents or other relatives shall speak for them."[3]

Hippolytus had a keen analytical mind. In his writings, he is especially skilled at exposing and explaining the tricks and frauds of astrologers, magicians, and pagan religious leaders.[4] Many of his writings opposed the various heresies afflicting the Church. It is in these writings that Hippolytus comments on the Christian way of life in opposition to the practices of the heretical groups. He takes them to task for their views on marriage and the relationships between the sexes. In his book, *The Refutation of All Heresies,* he writes concerning a heretical group called the Encratites:

> Others, however, styling themselves Encratites, acknowledge some things concerning God and Christ in like manner with the Church. In respect, however, of their mode of life, they pass their days inflated with pride. They suppose that by meats they magnify themselves, while abstaining from animal food, (and) being water-drinkers, and forbidding to marry, and devoting themselves during the remainder of life to habits of asceticism. But persons of this description are estimated Cynics rather than Christians, inasmuch as they do not attend unto the

---

3 B. R. Easton, translator, 1934, *The Apostolic Tradition of Hippolytus* (Cambridge Univ. Press, reprinted by Archon Books, 1962), p. 45.

4 Hyppolytus, *The Refutation of All Heresies*, bk. IV, in *The Ante-Nicene Fathers*, vol. 5, pp. 24-46.

words spoken against them through the Apostle Paul. Now he, predicting the novelties that were to be hereafter introduced ineffectually by certain (heretics), made a statement thus: "The Spirit speaks expressly, in the latter times certain will depart from sound doctrine, giving heed to seducing spirits and doctrines of devils, uttering falsehoods in hypocrisy, having their own conscience seared with a hot iron, forbidding to marry, to abstain from meats, which God has created to be partaken of with thanksgiving by the faithful, and those who know the truth; . . .[5]

Unfortunately, the introduction of the novelties mentioned by Hippolytus did not turn out to be all that ineffectual. In the later history of the Church, we find some Christians once more urging these "novelties."

Hippolytus wrote similarly concerning the teachings of the heretic Marcion, "You forbid marriage, the procreation of children, (and) the abstaining from meats which God has created for participation by the faithful, and those that know the truth."[6]

Citing and following Paul, Hippolytus thus holds to Christian liberty in writing against those who would burden the Church with new laws restricting Christian behavior. Hippolytus, however, had his own rather legalistic views concerning marriage. He held to the most austere interpretation of Paul's counsel to Timothy that a bishop should be the husband of one wife. He criticized Bishop Callistus of Rome for allowing bishops, priests, and deacons who had been twice or three times married to retain their place in the clergy. He also scolded Callistus for allowing a man who married while in holy orders to continue in holy orders "as if he had not sinned."[7] Perhaps Hippolytus in this rebuke to Callistus was following canons formulated by some in the Church as found in such documents as *The Apostolic Canons* (discussed in chapter ten, see pages 229-230).[8]

---

5 Hippolytus, *The Refutation of All Heresies*, bk. VIII, chap. 13, in *The Ante-Nicene Fathers*, vol. 5, p. 124.

6 Hippolytus, *The Refutation of All Heresies*, bk. VII, chap. 18, in *The Ante-Nicene Fathers*, vol. 5, p. 112.

7 Hippolytus, *The Refutation of All Heresies*, bk. IX, chap. 7, in *The Ante-Nicene Fathers*, vol. 5, p. 131.

8 *The Ante-Nicene Fathers*, vol. 5, p. 160.

Clement of Alexandria (150?-220?)

Clement of Alexandria was perhaps the most broadly educated and learned of the early church fathers. He was a convert from pagan philosophy and possessed a vast knowledge of the literature of his day. His writings in *The Miscellanies* quote some 360 classical texts. Knowledge of many of these works would have been lost to history except for their preservation in Clement's writings.[9]

After an extensive education in Greek culture and philosophy, Clement converted to Christianity and traveled widely to hear various Christian teachers. He finally came to study under Pantaenus, the leader of the catechetical school in Alexandria, Egypt. After a few years, he succeeded Pantaenus as the head of the school. Under Clement and his successor Origen, the school became the intellectual center of eastern Christianity. Not only catechumens but also numerous future leaders of the Church studied there.

Clement was a prolific writer, and three of his writings became especially well known. They are: *The Exhortation to the Heathen*, in which he pleads the case for Christianity; *The Instructor*, in which he details what he thinks it means to live as a Christian; and *The Miscellanies*, a mixture of unrelated thoughts and ideas on the Christian faith and culture.

In many respects, Clement displays a good theoretical understanding of Christian love. This is especially seen in his work, *The Miscellanies*. Clement knows that all our good deeds are to flow from self-denying love and in imitation of Christ, not from fear of punishment or hope for reward. He thus writes about the true "Gnostic" (the Greek word for "one who has true knowledge"), for he would take over that name from the heretical groups termed Gnostics:

> The man of understanding and perspicacity is, then, a Gnostic. And his business is not abstinence from what is evil (for this is a step to the highest perfection), or the doing of good out of fear. . . . Nor any more is he to do so from hope of promised recompense. . . . But only the doing of good out of love, and for the sake of its own excellence, is to be the Gnostic's choice. . . . This, then, is the perfect man's first form of doing good, when it is done not for any advantage in what pertains to him, but because he judges it right to do good; and the energy being

---

9 W. H. C. Frend, 1984, *The Rise of Christianity* (Philadelphia: Fortress Press), p. 369.

vigorously exerted in all things, in the very act becomes good; not, good in some things, and not good in others; but consisting in the habit of doing good, neither for glory, nor, as the philosophers say, for reputation, nor from reward either from men or God; but so as to pass life after the image and likeness of the Lord.[10]

Clement thus teaches that we are to follow the example of Christ's selfless love in our lives, passing our lives "after the image and likeness of the Lord." Clement also understands that Christian love is the fulfilling of the law. He follows Paul (Romans 13:8-10) in teaching that one who loves will not disobey the Ten Commandments. Thus out of love, not out of fear of punishment, is the law is fulfilled. He instructs his readers:

"God," then, being good, "is love," it is said. Whose "love works no ill to his neighbor," neither injuring nor revenging ever, but, in a word, doing good to all according to the image of God. "Love is," then, "the fulfilling of the law"; like as Christ, that is the presence of the Lord who loves us; and our loving teaching of, and discipline according to Christ. By love, then, the commands not to commit adultery, and not to covet one's neighbor's wife, are fulfilled, (these sins being) formerly prohibited by fear.

The same work, then, presents a difference, according as it is done by fear, or accomplished by love, and is wrought by faith or by knowledge.[11]

Clement is one of the few post-apostolic writers who cites the New Commandment found in John's gospel. He cites it only in passing, however, along with a number of other texts that counsel love and mercy.[12]

Clement's practical understanding of the Christian way of life is best seen in *The Instructor*. He wrote this book to guide the Christian in the way he should live his life. It deals in exacting detail with how a Christian should conduct himself, how he should dress, what foods to eat, what

---

10 Clement, *The Miscellanies*, bk. IV, chap. 22, in *The Ante-Nicene Fathers*, vol. 2, p. 434.

11 Clement, *The Miscellanies*, bk. IV, chap. 18, in *The Ante-Nicene Fathers*, vol. 2, p. 430.

12 Clement, *The Miscellanies*, bk. II, chap. 15, in *The Ante-Nicene Fathers*, vol. 2, p. 363.

amusements to engage in, and so forth. *The Instructor* who is giving this counsel to the Christian is identified as Jesus, the Son of God, and the Word. Early in the work, Clement wrote:

> Now, O you, my children, our Instructor is like His Father God, whose son He is, sinless, blameless, and with a soul devoid of passion; God in the form of man, stainless, the minister of His Father's will, the Word who is God, . . .[13]

Thus, the moral precepts that Clement taught in *The Instructor* , he identifies to be the teachings of Jesus Christ.

In *The Instructor,* Clement shows little understanding of Christian liberty. He does not understand the freedom of the Christian to make his or her own decisions based on selfless Christian love in areas where the New Testament is silent. He makes rules for the Christian in the smallest details of life. As a judge of manners and morals, he would surround the Christian life with his own prim and censorious declarations of what is fitting and proper. Always, however, declaring that his judgments come from Jesus, *The Instructor.*[14]

In his dictates concerning Christian living we see how an austere, rigid, and narrow asceticism is developing alongside the life of self-giving love that Clement teaches in *The Miscellanies.* A few examples will illustrate Clement's attempts to regulate Christian behavior. Concerning diet and clothing Clement wrote:

> Some men, in truth, live that they may eat, as the irrational creatures, "whose life is their belly, and nothing else." But *The Instructor* enjoins us to eat that we may live. For neither is food our business, nor is pleasure our aim; . . . Wherefore also there is discrimination to be employed in reference to food. And it is to be simple, truly plain, suiting precisely simple and artless children--as ministering to life, not to luxury. . . . We must therefore reject different varieties, which engender various mischiefs, such as a depraved habit of body and disorders of the stomach, the taste being vitiated by an unhappy art--that of

---

13 Clement, *The Instructor*, bk. I, chap. 2, in *The Ante-Nicene Fathers*, vol. 2, pp. 209, 210.

14 Clement, *The Instructor*, bk. I, chap. 12, in *The Ante-Nicene Fathers*, vol. 2, p. 234.

cookery, and the useless art of making pastry. . . . There is no limit to epicureanism among men. For it has driven them to sweetmeats, and honey-cakes, and sugar-plums; inventing a multitude of desserts, hunting after all manner of dishes. A man like this seems to me to be all jaw, and nothing else. . . . Wherefore we must guard against those articles of food which persuade us to eat when we are not hungry, bewitching the appetite. For is there not within a temperate simplicity a wholesome variety of eatables? Bulbs, olives, certain herbs, milk, cheese, fruits, all kinds of cooked food without sauces; and if flesh is wanted, let roast rather than boiled be set down.[15]

Dyeing of clothes is also to be rejected. For it is remote both from necessity and truth, in addition to the fact that reproach in manners spring from it. For the use of colors is not beneficial, for they are of no service against cold; nor has it anything for covering more than other clothing, except the opprobrium alone. And the agreeableness of the color afflicts greedy eyes, inflaming them to senseless blindness. But for those who are white and unstained within, it is most suitable to use white and simple garments.[16]

Women are to be allowed a white shoe, except when on a journey, and then a greased shoe must be used. When on a journey, they require nailed shoes. Further, they ought for the most part to wear shoes; for it is not suitable for the foot to be shown naked: besides, woman is a tender thing, easily hurt. But for a man bare feet are quite in keeping, except when he is on military service.[17]

Clement further instructs:

---

15 Clement, *The Instructor*, bk. II, chap. 1, in *The Ante-Nicene Fathers*, vol. 2, pp. 237-241.

16 Clement, *The Instructor*, bk. II, chap. 11, in *The Ante-Nicene Fathers*, vol. 2, p. 265.

17 Clement, *The Instructor*, bk. II, chap. 12, in *The Ante-Nicene Fathers*, vol. 2, p. 267.

Pleasantry is allowable, not waggery. Besides, even laughter must be kept in check; for when given vent to in the right manner it indicates orderliness, but when it issues differently it shows a want of restraint. . . . For the seemly relaxation of the countenance in a harmonious manner. . . is called a smile. So also is laughter on the face of well-regulated men termed. But the discordant relaxation of countenance in the case of women is called a giggle, and is meretricious laughter; in the case of men, a guffaw, and is savage and insulting laughter. . . . We are not to laugh perpetually, for that is going beyond bounds; nor in the presence of elderly persons, or others worthy of respect, unless they indulge in pleasantry for our amusement. Nor are we to laugh before all and sundry, nor in every place, nor to every one, nor about everything. For to children and women especially laughter is the cause of slipping into scandal. And even to appear stern serves to keep those about us at their distance. For gravity can ward the approaches of licentiousness by a mere look.[18]

Also we must abandon a furious mode of walking, and choose a grave and leisurely, but not lingering step.[19]

. . . but the hiccup is to be quietly transmitted with the expiration of breath, the mouth being composed becomingly, . . .[20]

Clement was especially concerned about the problem that sexual desire presents to the Christian. He counseled:

But above all, it seems right that we turn away from the sight of women. For it is sin not only to touch, but to look; and he who is rightly trained must especially avoid them. "Let thine eyes look straight, and thine eyelids wink right." For while it is

---

18 Clement, *The Instructor*, bk. II, chap. 5, in *The Ante-Nicene Fathers*, vol. 2, p. 250.

19 Clement, *The Instructor*, bk. III, chap. 11, in *The Ante-Nicene Fathers*, vol. 2, p. 288.

20 Clement, *The Instructor*, bk. II, chap. 7, in *The Ante-Nicene Fathers*, vol. 2, p. 253.

possible for one who looks to remain steadfast; yet care must be taken against falling. For it is possible for one who looks to slip; but it is impossible for one, who looks not, to lust. For it is not enough for the chaste to be pure; but they must give all diligence, to beyond the range of censure, shutting out all ground of suspicion, . . .[21]

In Clement, we find the beginnings of the continual preoccupation with the sexual life of the married found later among the celibate lawgivers especially in western Christianity. Going far beyond Scripture, Clement dictates:

Yet, marriage in itself merits esteem and the highest approval, for the Lord wished men to "be fruitful and multiply." He did not tell them, however, to act like libertines, nor did He intend them to surrender themselves to pleasure as though born only to indulge in sexual relations. . . . Why, even unreasoning beasts know enough not to mate at certain times. To indulge in intercourse without intending children is to outrage nature, whom we should take as our instructor. . . .

Those whom nature has joined in wedlock need the Educator that they might learn not to celebrate the mystic rites of nature during the day, nor like the rooster copulate at dawn, or after they have come from church, or even from the market, when they should be praying or reading or performing the good works that are best done by day. In the evening, after dinner, it is proper to retire after giving thanks for the good things that have been received. . . .

Intercourse performed licitly is an occasion of sin, unless done purely to beget children, . . . he who seeks only sexual pleasure turns his marriage into fornication.[22]

There are few human activities for which Clement does not have instruction and rules:

---

21 Clement, *The Instructor*, bk. III, chap. 11, in *The Ante-Nicene Fathers*, vol. 2, p. 291.

22 Clement, *Christ the Educator*, bk. 2, chap. 10, in *The Fathers of the Church: Clement of Alexandria* (New York: Fathers of the Church, Inc.) pp. 173-176.

There are, then, four reasons for the bath, for which we frequent it: for cleanliness, or heat, or health, or lastly, for pleasure. Bathing for pleasure is to be omitted. For unblushing pleasure must be cut out by the roots; and the bath is to be taken by women for cleanliness and health, by men for health alone. To bathe for the sake of heat is a superfluity, since one may restore what is frozen by the cold in other ways.[23]

Let the pipe be resigned to the shepherds, and the flute to the superstitious who are engrossed in idolatry. For, in truth, such instruments are to be banished from the temperate banquet, being more suitable to beasts than men, and the more irrational portion of mankind.[24]

The above is a small sample of the rules for living composed by Clement of Alexandria that make up the ninety double-columned pages of an English translation of *The Instructor*." It seems obvious that Clement had little understanding of Paul's counsel to the Colossian Christians:

Therefore let no one pass judgment on you in questions of food and drink . . . Why do you submit to regulations, "Do not handle, Do not taste, Do not touch" (referring to things which all perish as they are used), according to human precepts and doctrines? These have indeed an appearance of wisdom in promoting rigor of devotion and self-abasement and severity to the body, but they are of no value in checking the indulgence of the flesh. (Colossians 2:16-23 RSV)

Clement of Alexandria was one of the foremost Christian teachers of his age. Clement may have had a good understanding of Christian love, but he offended against the freedom of the Christian to make his own behavioral and ethical decisions in matters concerning which the Bible and especially the New Testament are silent. The influence of Clement and of his catechetical school at Alexandria spread widely over the Christian world. The bishop of Jerusalem, Alexander, for example, referred to Clement as "the holy Clement, my teacher, who was to me so greatly useful

---

23 Clement, *The Instructor*, bk. III, chap. 9, in *The Ante-Nicene Fathers*, vol. 2, p. 282.

24 Clement, *The Instructor*, bk. II, chap. 4, in *The Ante-Nicene Fathers*, vol. 2, p. 248.

and helpful."[25]

Origen (185?-254?)

Origen followed Clement as the head of the catechetical school of Alexandria. Clement had been forced to leave Alexandria during the severe persecution of the Church by the Roman Emperor Septimius Severus. Origen was a brilliant, well-educated, and a zealous Christian who when only eighteen became head of the school. Origen also followed Clement in continuing the trend toward a demanding asceticism.

Origen's family had been impoverished when his father was martyred as a Christian, and the family's considerable wealth confiscated by the government. To support himself, Origen sold his valuable library of secular literature and lived frugally on the small pension he received from the proceeds of the sale. Eusebius writes of his sleeping on the floor rather than a bed, owning the barest minimum of clothing, and following Clement's counsel in going for long periods without shoes. In order to avoid temptation and any possible scandal while teaching female students, he castrated himself. This caused him difficulties later when his bishop, Demetrius, refused to ordain him to the priesthood because of the emasculation.[26] Origen was a prodigious worker, teaching during the day and curtailing his hours of sleep in order to make more time for his study, research, and writing at night.[27]

Although there have been many disputes over his teaching and writings, Origen became one of the most influential theologians of the eastern Christian Church especially during his lifetime and in the decades following his death. Because of his fame as a theologian and interpreter of Scripture, his ascetic life also became widely known and was regarded as a model to be followed during the centuries after his life. Along with the austere asceticism of his life, Origen, however, remained faithful to the emphasis in the New Testament on a Christian love expressed in deeds.

Concerning marriage, he taught that the unmarried life was a higher and purer life. In his tract against the pagan philosopher Celsus, he wrote, "But God has allowed us to marry, because all are not fit for the higher, that is, the perfectly pure life; . . ."[28] Unlike the writings of his teacher Clement,

---

25 *The Ante-Nicene Fathers*, vol. 2, p. 166.

26 Will Durant, 1944, *Caesar and Christ* (New York: Simon and Schuster), p. 615.

27 Eusebius, c. 325, transl. by G.A. Williamson, 1965, *The History of the Church from Christ to Constantine*, bk. 6, secs. 1-8 (New York: Dorset Press), pp. 239-248.

28 Origen, *Origen Against Celsus*, bk. VIII, chap. 55, in *The Ante-Nicene Fathers*,

Origen infrequently discusses the Christian way of life in a practical or concrete way in the many writings of his that have been preserved.

Clement and his successor Origen were undoubtedly major factors in the growth of asceticism in the Christian Church. The stress on asceticism as a way of attaining personal purity and perfection was slowly eclipsing the emphasis on a faith active in deeds of love that was taught by the apostles.

Tertullian (160?-230?)

The famous North African theologian Tertullian was born of non-Christian parents in Carthage, Africa. Before his conversion to Christianity, he was trained in law. He was the first major Christian theologian to write in Latin rather than Greek. Tertullian wrote voluminously on many subjects: He defended Christianity to pagan Roman authorities. He disputed the false doctrines of a variety of heresies and argued against the claims of Judaism. He ably wrote in support of such Christian doctrines as the resurrection, the humanity of Christ, the Trinity, and the soul. He wrote especially vehemently concerning church discipline and Christian morality.

Unfortunately, Tertullian in his later life became a follower of the heretic Montanus and grew increasingly legalistic and ascetic in his writings concerning the Christian life. Montanism was a heretical movement in the Church based on the supposed revelations given by the Holy Spirit to the prophet Montanus and his co-workers, the prophetesses Prisca and Maximilla. The movement began in Phrygia in Asia Minor around the middle of the 100s. The movement was called "The New Prophecy" and professed to be a final revelation of the Holy Spirit. The Montanists wanted their revelations to be accepted as equal to the revelation of the Scriptures. They advocated an excessive moral rigor and decried the looseness of the contemporary Church.

Without denying the fullness of the New Testament revelation, Tertullian accepted the validity of the prophetic utterances of the New Prophecy. He was especially attracted to the rigid morality of Montanism. Thus in his later years Tertullian advocated a legalistic asceticism at odds with his views earlier in life. He was dismayed by what he felt was the growing moral laxness of the Church. He wrote a number of tracts that zealously supported his strict ideas on what was the proper way for Christians to live.

As did Clement of Alexandria, Tertullian condemned the dyeing of

---

vol. 4, p. 660.

clothes. He wrote in his treatise *On the Apparel of Women*:

> . . . for what legitimate honour can garments derive from
> adulteration with illegitimate colours? That which He Himself
> has not produced is not pleasing to God, unless He was unable
> to order sheep to be born with purple and sky-blue fleeces! If He
> was able, then plainly He was unwilling: what God willed not, of
> course ought not to be fashioned. Those things, then, are not
> the best by nature which are not from God, the Author of nature.
> Thus they are understood to be from the devil, from the
> corrupter of nature: for there is no other whose they can be, if
> they are not God's; . . . [29]

Neither Clement of Alexandria nor Tertullian comment on the
conversion and baptism of Lydia, the seller of purple goods (Acts
16:14-15). Paul did not exclude her from the Christian fellowship because
of her occupation. Neither is there any indication that she had to give up her
trade.

Tertullian also railed against any use of cosmetics by women,
dyeing the hair, and even against arranging the hair. Lest women think that
he was reproaching only them, he also sarcastically criticized men for using
such "deceptive trickeries" as cutting the beard too sharply, shaving around
the mouth, arranging the hair or dyeing it to conceal the gray hairs, and so
forth.[30] Tertullian condemns many practices such as wearing the laurel
wreath or dressing in the toga rather than the philosopher's cloak. He argues
at great length in his essays to substantiate his legalistic opinions. He
obviously had little understanding of Christian liberty or freedom as taught
by Paul. He would deny the right of a Christian storekeeper to sell
frankincense, arguing that he partakes of idolatry if the frankincense is later
used as an offering to an idol. Tertullian has what he considers the ultimate
argument against any behavior that offends his sense of Christian propriety.
In writing in his work De *Corona* concerning whether a Christian should
ever wear a laurel wreath, he argued:

> For if it shall be said that it is lawful to be crowned [wear a laurel
> wreath] on this ground, that Scripture does not forbid it, it will as

---

29 Tertullian, *On the Apparel of Women*, bk. I, chap. 8, in *The Ante-Nicene Fathers*,
vol. 4, p. 17

30 Tertullian, *On the Apparel of Women*, bk. II, chaps. 5-8, in *The Ante-Nicene
Fathers*, vol. 4, pp. 20-22.

validly be retorted that just on this ground is the crown unlawful, because the Scripture does not enjoin it. What shall discipline do? Shall it accept both things, as if neither were forbidden? Or shall it refuse both, as if neither were enjoined? But [some say] "the thing which is not forbidden is freely permitted." I should rather say what has not been freely allowed is forbidden.[31]

As we shall see in a later chapter, John Calvin and John Knox in their reformation in the 1500s took a similar approach concerning what should remain in Christianity. For example, they forbade the celebration of Christmas because it was not found in Scripture.

Paul in his letter to Timothy counseled concerning young widows, "Therefore I desire that the younger widows marry, bear children, manage the house, give no opportunity to the adversary to speak reproachfully" (1 Timothy 5:14 NKJV). After vacillating over the years on the whether widows or widowers should remarry, Tertullian wrote in his *On Exhortation to Chastity,* "If we look deeply into his [Paul's] meanings, and interpret them, second marriage will have to be termed no other than a species of fornication." Tertullian continues by arguing that a widower when contemplating second marriage must necessarily view his intended spouse with lust in his heart. Thus he is condemned by Christ's words, "But I say to you that whoever looks at a woman to lust for her has already committed adultery with her in his heart" (Matthew 5:28 NKJV). This, Tertullian concludes, also besmirches a first marriage that "consists of that which is the essence of fornication. Accordingly, the best thing for a man is not to touch a woman; and accordingly the life of a virgin is the principal sanctity, because it is free from affinity with fornication." Only grudgingly does Tertullian admit that God has indulged Christians by permitting first and second marriages.[32]

The above are examples of Tertullian's strictures on Christian behavior. It is so easy, however, to fault unfairly the writings of such a wide-ranging and voluminous writer as Tertullian. Much of what Tertullian wrote in the areas of Christian doctrine was very useful to the Christian Church of his day. The later church could well have heeded his words concerning freedom of conscience in religious matters when he wrote in *To Scapula* concerning Christians being forced to offer sacrifices to pagan gods:

---

31 Tertullian, *De Corona*, chap. 2, in *The Ante-Nicene Fathers,* vol. 3, p. 94.

32 Tertullian, *On Exhortation to Chastity*, chap. 9, in *The Ante-Nicene Fathers*, vol. 4, p. 55.

> However, it is a fundamental human right, a privilege of nature, that every man should worship according to his own convictions: one man's religion neither harms nor helps another man. It is assuredly no part of religion to compel religion–to which free-will and not force should lead us–the sacrificial victims even being required of a willing mind. You will render no real service to your gods by compelling us to sacrifice.[33]

Tertullian understood the all-embracing nature of Christian love. He wrote to the Roman authorities, "For our religion commands us to love even our enemies, and to pray for those who persecute us, aiming at a perfection all its own, and seeking in its disciples something of a higher type than the commonplace goodness of the world."[34]

In the essay *An Answer to the Jews,* Tertullian argued at length that with the coming of Christ the Old Testament law was superseded by the new law that had been foretold in the Old Testament.[35] He discusses Christ's ethical teachings in the Sermon on the Mount in his book *Against Marcion*, but he does it more to lend strength to his arguments against the heretic Marcion than to develop an understanding of Jesus' way of life.[36]

In his writings, Tertullian is seldom primarily concerned with the way of life as taught by Christ. His writings are mainly argumentative, written against what he considers the false opinions of others. He obviously, however, understands that Jesus brought a new way of life into existence that emphasized a Christ-like unselfish love. Nonetheless, Tertullian has little understanding of the liberty a Christian has in applying the principle of Christian love to his life. When later in life he writes more directly on how Christians should conduct themselves in the world, it is from the crabbed, rigid, and legalistic asceticism taught by the Montanists.

Cyprian (200-258)

Cyprian was the most prominent of the bishops of the North African church. Born of wealthy pagan parents and well educated by them,

---

33 Tertullian, *To Scapula*, chap. 2, in *The Ante-Nicene Fathers*, vol. 3, p. 105.

34 Tertullian, *To Scapula*, chap. 1, in *The Ante-Nicene Fathers*, vol. 3, p. 105.

35 Tertullian, *An Answer to the Jews*, chaps. 3-6, in *The Ante-Nicene Fathers*, vol. 3, pp. 153-157.

36 Tertullian, *Against Marcion*, bk. IV, chaps. 15-17, in *The Ante-Nicene Fathers*, vol. 3, pp. 365-374.

he was converted to Christianity around 246 A.D. A little more than two years after his conversion, he was elected bishop of Carthage. In 258 A.D., he was beheaded as a martyr for the faith during the persecution under the Roman Emperor Valerian. Cyprian had a high regard for the writings of Tertullian. A secretary of Cyprian commented that Cyprian "was accustomed never to pass a day without reading Tertullian."[37]

The greatest crisis during Cyprian's bishopric came with the repeated persecutions that the Christian Church was undergoing. He therefore wrote much on the need for Christian fortitude under persecution. He also considered at length how to deal with those who fell away from the faith during persecution. As the leader of the numerous North African bishops, he vigorously opposed the decision of Bishop Stephen of Rome who ruled that now penitent, but formerly apostate, clergy, could be returned to their offices. Cyprian also viewed baptism and ordination performed by schismatic or heretical clergy to be clearly invalid and to validate them was a major departure from the faith and practice of Christianity.[38]

Cyprian was an active defender of the prerogatives and dignity of the clergy and especially of the bishops. A curious instance of this is his misquoting Leviticus 19:32. The verse in Hebrew reads, "In the face of gray hairs, you shall rise and honor the face of an old man." Cyprian, however, quotes it as follows: "You shall rise up before the face of the elder, and honor the person of the presbyter." He uses the verse as a proof text to demand in Testimony 85 of his Twelfth Treatise, "That we must rise when a bishop or a presbyter comes."[39]

Upon converting to Christianity, Cyprian abandoned his former affluent and luxurious way of life for that of a rather rigid asceticism. As did Tertullian and Clement of Alexandria, he counseled an austere and grave style of life. The following from his treatise *On the Dress of Virgins* is but one example of many that illustrates his approach to the life of the Christian:

> For God made neither the sheep scarlet or purple, nor taught the juices of herbs and shell-fish to dye and color wool,

---

37 Jerome, *Lives of Illustrious Men*, chap. 53, in *The Nicene and Post-Nicene Fathers*, Second Series, vol. 3, p. 373.

38 Cyprian, *Epistles Sixty-nine to Seventy-four*, in *The Ante-Nicene Fathers*, vol. 5, pp. 375-397.

39 Cyprian, *The Treatises of Cyprian*, Treatise 12, in *The Ante-Nicene Fathers*, vol. 5, p. 553.

nor arranged necklaces with stones set in gold, and with pearls distributed in a woven series or numerous cluster, wherewith you would hide the neck which He made; . . . Has God willed that wounds be made in the ears, . . . that subsequently from the scars and holes of the ears precious beads may hang, heavy, if not by their weight, still by the amount of their cost? All which things sinning and apostate angels put forth by their arts, when, lowered to the contagions of earth, they forsook their heavenly vigour. They taught them also to paint the eyes with blackness drawn round them in a circle, and to stain the cheeks with a deceitful red, and to change the hair with false colours, and to drive out all truth, both of face and head, by the assault of their own corruption.[40]

Nor did he restrict himself to the practices of women, he ruled in Testimony 84, "That the beard must not be plucked." citing Leviticus 19:27, "Ye shall not deface the figure of your beard."[41]

The Church was growing increasingly legalistic during this period. Councils of bishops were gathering to make rules and laws for the governance of the clergy and Christian people. According to a letter from Cyprian to the clergy and people of Furni, a recent council of bishops had declared that no clergy should be named as an executor of a will. If someone did name a clergyman as an executor upon the person's death, "no offering should be made for him, nor any sacrifice celebrated for his repose."[42] This was in keeping with the rule or canon followed by Cyprian that no clergyman was to be involved with secular employment or affairs. Paul's support of himself by making tents was obviously not viewed as a precedent. The concept of Christian freedom and liberty to follow where the Holy Spirit leads in the exercise of Christian love was being lost to the Church.

But for all his ascetic and legalistic tendencies, Cyprian's heart is still full of Christian love and his writings give much evidence of a true pastor's heart. His writings have many quotations from the Old and New Testaments that counsel good works, and that emphasize the love that

---

40 Cyprian, *The Treatises of Cyprian*, Treatise 2, On the Dress of Virgins, par. 14, in *The Ante-Nicene Fathers*, vol. 5, p. 434.

41 Cyprian, *The Treatises of Cyprian*, Treatise 12, in *The Ante-Nicene Fathers*, vol. 5, p. 553.

42 Cyprian, *Epistle 65*, in *The Ante-Nicene Fathers*, vol. 5, p. 367.

Christians should have for their fellowman.[43] He wrote to encourage his people and correspondents to care for the poor, the sick, and strangers in need. He set them an example in his generous aid to the poor as shown in his letter to the clergy of his diocese:

> I request that you will diligently take care of the widows, and of the sick, and of all the poor. Moreover, you may supply the expenses for strangers, if any should be indigent, from my own portion, which I have left with Rogatianus, our fellow presbyter; which portion, lest it should be all appropriated, I have supplemented by sending to the same by Naricus the acolyte another share, so that the sufferers may be more largely and promptly dealt with.[44]

He counsels love for one's enemies and persecutors and that good should be returned for evil.[45] He devotes a major treatise (VIII) to good works and charity. His life exemplified both piety and a faith active in love.

Methodius (260-312)

Methodius was a prominent bishop in Asia Minor. He was a principal opponent of the writings and thought of Origen. However, like Origen, he had a strong inclination towards a life of asceticism. Playing upon the Greek words, he writes that the Greek word for "church," "*ekklesia*," which means, "called out," really means called out in respect to pleasures.[46]   Although he recognized the validity of marriage, in his allegorical discourse *The Banquet of the Ten Virgins,* Methodius exalts virginity by having one of the virgins exclaim:

> Virginity is something supernaturally great, wonderful, and glorious; and, to speak plainly and in accordance with the Holy Scriptures, this best and noblest manner of life alone is the root

---

43 Cyprian, *The Treatises of Cyprian*, Treatise 12, Third Book, Testimonies 1-3, in *The Ante-Nicene Fathers*, vol. 5, pp. 530-533.

44 Cyprian, *Epistle 35*, in *The Ante-Nicene Fathers*, vol. 5, p. 314.

45 Cyprian, *The Treatises of Cyprian*, Treatise 10, pars. 13, 15-17, in *The Ante-Nicene Fathers*, vol. 5, pp. 494-496.

46 Methodius, *Extracts from the Work on Things Created*, VI, in *The Ante-Nicene Fathers*, vol. 6, p. 381.

of immortality, and also its flower and first-fruits; . . . [47]

Another of the virgins at the allegorical banquet asserts:

> They also possess it [chastity] who live chastely with their wives, and do, as it were about the trunk, yield its lowly branches bearing chastity, not being able like us to reach its lofty and mighty boughs, or even to touch them; yet they, too, offer no less truly, although in a less degree, the branches of chastity. But those who are goaded on by their lust, although they do not commit fornication, yet who, even in the things which are permitted with a lawful wife, through the heat of unsubdued concupiscence are excessive in embraces, how shall they celebrate the feast? How shall they rejoice, who have not adorned their tabernacle, that is their flesh, with the boughs of the Agnos, nor have listened to that which has been said; that "they that have wives be as though they had none.[48]

According to Methodius, marriage is permitted; but its sexual side is to be under severe restraint. In Methodius's deprecation of marriage as compared to virginity, we see the continuing trend toward viewing the normal life of Christians as a second-class existence.

Lactantius (260?-325?)

Lactantius, known as the Christian Cicero, experienced the last great persecutions of the Church. He lived on into the age of Constantine when the Church finally became an accepted religion in the Roman Empire. The Emperor Constantine honored him in choosing him to be the tutor of his son, Crispus.

Lactantius was converted in middle age and became an active defender of the truths of Christianity. He possessed a fine Ciceronian grasp of classical Latin. He wrote his *The Divine Institutes* in the attempt to present a systematic overview of Christianity that would win over the intellectuals of the Roman Empire. The work shows a broad and

---

47 Methodius, *The Banquet of the Ten Virgins*, Discourse 1, chap. 1, in *The Ante-Nicene Fathers*, vol. 6, p. 310.

48 Methodius, *The Banquet of the Ten Virgins*, Discourse 9, chap. 4, in *The Ante-Nicene Fathers*, vol. 6, pp. 346, 347.

comprehensive understanding of classical literature and philosophy. Although as a work of theology it has been belittled in the past, many times it exhibits a true grasp of the nature of Christianity as the following excerpt indicates:

> Therefore we are not born for this purpose, that we may see those things which are created, but that we may contemplate, that is, behold with our mind, the Creator of all things Himself. Wherefore, if any one should ask a man who is truly wise for what purpose he was born, he will answer without fear or hesitation, that he was born for the purpose of worshiping God, who brought us into being for this cause, that we may serve Him. But to serve God is nothing else than to maintain and preserve justice by good works.[49]

Lactantius discloses in his writings the struggle many in the Church were experiencing in trying to define the nature of the Christian life. Is the emphasis to be on the avoidance of evil as one strives for perfection through inward personal purity, or is the emphasis to be on serving God by selflessly serving the needs of one's fellowman? He writes, on the one hand, that perfect virtue is obtained through the avoidance of evil and sin:

> The whole duty of virtue is not to sin. . . . The first step of virtue is to abstain from evil works; the second, to abstain also from evil words; the third, to abstain even from thoughts of evil things. He who ascends the first step is sufficiently just; he who ascends the second is now of perfect virtue, since he offends neither in deeds nor in conversation; he who ascends the third appears truly to have attained the likeness of God.[50]

Yet, on the other hand, Lactantius appears unsatisfied with true virtue obtained only by avoiding evil, he also counsels:

> God teaches us never to do evil, but always good. And He also prescribes in what this doing good consists: in affording aid to

---

49 Lactantius, *The Divine Institutes*, bk. 3, chap. 9, in *The Ante-Nicene Fathers*, vol. 7, p. 77.

50 Lactantius, *The Divine Institutes*, bk. 6, chaps. 5, 13, in *The Ante-Nicene Fathers*, vol. 7, pp. 167, 178.

those who are oppressed and in difficulty, and in bestowing food on those who are destitute.[51]

Lactantius may not write about love as the fulfilling of the law, but his writings are faithful to the emphasis upon a faith active in love as taught in the New Testament.

The Pseudo-Clementine Literature

Writings falsely ascribed to Clement of Rome

A number of early Jewish-Christian documents termed the Pseudo-Clementine Literature have been ascribed falsely to the authorship of Clement of Rome, the co-worker of Paul and Peter. In some cases, the ascription is made because perhaps the true author was not known. In other cases, it was probably to obtain the prestige of the revered Clement for the document by attaching his name to it. Pseudepigraphic literature is often written to invent documentary evidence for ideas and concerns of the writers for which there is little valid support from Scripture or other recognized authority. The documents overall are legalistic and foster an ascetic way of life.

Two Epistles Concerning Virginity

The *Two Epistles Concerning Virginity* is an example of a writing that has been implausibly attributed to Clement. A Coptic version of the treatise lists Athanasius, the great Alexandrian archbishop, as its author; but this ascription is also doubtful. It appears to come from the 200s. The first epistle has for its purpose the teaching of an exacting asceticism. Although it commends works of mercy, it is primarily negative in tone and gives long lists of evils to avoid.[52] The second epistle is especially concerned about the separation of the sexes. If night overtakes "Clement" and his party while they journey away from home, they are to seek to lodge with a holy man; and no women may be under the roof. For, as "Clement" wrote:

But with us may no female, whether young maiden or married

---

51 Lactantius, *The Divine Institutes*, bk. 6, chap. 10, in *The Ante-Nicene Fathers*, vol. 7, p. 173.

52 *The First Epistle of the Blessed Clement*, chaps. 8, 13, in *The Ante-Nicene Fathers*, vol. 8, pp. 57, 60.

woman, be there at that time; nor she that is aged, nor she that has taken the vow; not even a maid-servant, whether Christian or heathen; but there shall only be men with men.[53]

If women are present and "Clement" and his party after having spoken words of edification feel the necessity to depart in order to find other lodging, they take their leave and avoid the alluring presence and touch of women as follows:

And then we pray, and salute one another, the men with the men. But the women and the maidens will wrap their hands in their garments; and we also, with circumspection and all purity, our eyes looking upwards, shall wrap our right hand in our garments; and then they will come and give us the salutation on our right hand wrapped in our garments. Then we go where God permits us.[54]

If by chance they come to a place where no consecrated brother is present but only married Christians, they are to say to their hosts:

We holy men do not eat or drink with women, nor are we waited on by women or by maidens, nor do women wash our feet for us, nor do women anoint us, nor do women prepare our bed for us, nor do we sleep where women sleep, so that we may be without reproach in everything, lest any one should be offended or stumble at us.[55]

If "holy men" neither have their feet washed by women nor are they anointed by women, what does that make Jesus whose feet were anointed and washed by a woman (Luke 7:36-38); and who after his head was anointed by a woman rebuked his disapproving disciples by saying "Why do you trouble the woman? For she has done a good work for me" (Matthew 26:10)?

---

53 *The Second Epistle of the Same Clement*, chap. 2, in *The Ante-Nicene Fathers*, vol. 8, p. 61.

54 *The Second Epistle of the Same Clement*, chap. 2, in *The Ante-Nicene Fathers*, vol. 8, p. 61.

55 *The Second Epistle of the Same Clement*, chap. 3, in *The Ante-Nicene Fathers*, vol. 8, p. 62.

After other similar instructions, the epistle concludes by giving many examples from primarily the Old Testament of how women are a temptation to men. Such early literature forecasts the extreme asceticism of a later time when some monastics abhorred as possibly defiling all contact and even the sight of a person of the opposite sex.

Other Pseudo-Clementine Literature

In the 200s, other Clementine forgeries gained circulation produced by Jewish-Christians who were descendants of an extreme group among the Ebionites. This group demanded circumcision for all Christians and observance of the Old Testament Law. They denied both the virgin birth and that Jesus was true God. They viewed Paul as an apostate from the law.

To serve as a cover for the forgeries and perhaps to provide a reason as to why the writings were for so long unknown, a letter supposedly written by Peter to James, the brother of Christ and bishop of Jerusalem, was circulated with the documents. The letter urges James to keep the documents secret and to show them only to those who are "proved and found worthy."[56] This letter also shows the hostility of the Ebionites toward Paul because he taught that the Old Testament law had come to an end. The letter has Peter complaining to James about Paul:

> For some from among the Gentiles have rejected my legal preaching, attaching themselves to a certain lawless and trifling preaching of the man who is my enemy. And these things some have attempted while I am still alive, to transform my words by certain various interpretations, in order to [cause] the dissolution of the law; as though I also myself were of such a mind, but did not freely proclaim it, which God forbid![57]

Two of the major Ebionite documents are: *The Recognitions of Clement* and *The Clementine Homilies.* Very similar in content, they claim to be accounts of episodes in the lives of Peter, Clement of Rome, and Simon Magus, Peter's antagonist. It is noteworthy that the documents completely ignore Paul, counseling their readers:

> Wherefore, above all, remember to shun apostle or teacher or

---

56 *Epistle of Peter to James*, in *The Ante-Nicene Fathers*, vol. 8, p. 215.

57 *Epistle of Peter to James*, chap. 2, in *The Ante-Nicene Fathers*, vol. 8, p. 215.

prophet who does not first accurately compare his preaching with that of James, who was called the brother of my Lord, and to whom was entrusted to administer the church of the Hebrews in Jerusalem, . . ."[58]

The Recognitions of Clement especially received a wide readership among Christians because of its translation from Greek into Latin by Rufinus around 400 A.D. who believed its authorship by Clement of Rome to be authentic.[59]

The Clementine Homilies picture Peter as a faithful follower of the law, and he is quoted as saying to the mother of Clement:

"I wish you to know, O woman, the course of life involved in our religion. We worship one God, who made the world which you see; and we keep His law, which has for its chief injunctions to worship Him alone, and to hallow His name, and to honour our parents, and to be chaste, and to live piously. In addition to this, we do not live with all indiscriminately; nor do we take our food from the same table as Gentiles, inasmuch as we cannot eat along with them, because they live impurely. . . . For not even if it were our father, or mother, or wife, or child, or brother, or any other one having a claim by nature on our affection, can we venture to take our meals with him; for our religion compels us to make a distinction."[60]

In this the Ebionites are carrying on the distinctions and practices between Jew and Gentile taught in Judaism during Jesus' time.

Although the documents possess a favorable view of marriage, the ascetic view is still obvious. Peter is quoted as teaching that in marriage "sexual intercourse must not take place heedlessly and for the sake of mere pleasure, but for the sake of begetting children."[61]

---

58 *The Clementine Homilies*, Homily 11, chap. 35, in *The Ante-Nicene Fathers*, vol. 8, p. 291.

59 Rufinus, *The Preface to the Books of the Recognitions of St. Clement*, in *The Nicene and Post-Nicene Fathers*, Second Series, vol. 3, pp. 563, 564.

60 *The Clementine Homilies*, Homily 13, chap. 4, in *The Ante-Nicene Fathers*, vol. 8, pp. 300, 301.

61 *Recognitions of Clement*, bk. 6, chap. 12, in *The Ante-Nicene Fathers*, vol. 8, p. 155.

At times, the Christian life is viewed primarily in terms of negative strictures as in the following:

> But when you have been regenerated by water, show by good works the likeness in you of that Father who has begotten you. Now you know God, honour Him as a father; and His honour is, that you live according to His will. And His will is, that you so live as to know nothing of murder or adultery, to flee from hatred and covetousness, to put away anger, pride, and boasting, to abhor envy, and to count all such things entirely unsuitable to you.[62]

Nonetheless, the avoidance of evil does not sum up the Christian life entirely. Christians are urged to love all the brethren with grave and compassionate eyes. Repeatedly in these writings, Christians are exhorted to care for widows and orphans, feed the hungry, aid the homeless and strangers, visit the sick and imprisoned, employ the unemployed, and support the incapable.[63]

The Apocrypha of the New Testament

The Nature of the Apocrypha

The New Testament Apocrypha is composed of many gospels, acts of the apostles, and letters that make a pretense of being equal in validity and authority to the canonical writings of the New Testament. Typically, many were written to give support and authority to heretical teachings that opposed the faith of the early Church. At times they were apparently devised to support cherished but unscriptural beliefs such as the perpetual virginity of the Virgin Mary. Some were written to promote an extreme asceticism for which there is little basis in the canonical books of the New Testament. Others were fanciful attempts to fill in periods of time in the life of Christ and his followers about which the New Testament records little, for example, the experiences of Jesus as a young boy. Although some of these books were widely read in the Church, most were never seriously

---

62 *Recognitions of Clement*, bk. 6, chap. 10, in *The Ante-Nicene Fathers*, vol. 8, p. 155.

63 *Epistle of Clement to James*, chaps. 8, 9, in *The Ante-Nicene Fathers*, vol. 8, pp. 219, 220.

considered for inclusion in the New Testament.

The apocryphal gospels go to great lengths to counter the plain statements of the Gospels about the normal married relationship between Mary and Joseph and the later children born to them (see pages 177-179) in order promote the celibate life.

The Protevangelium of James

The apocryphal gospel, *The Protevangelium of James*, enlarges upon the circumstances surrounding the birth of Mary, her espousal to Joseph, and the birth of Jesus. Joseph is made out to be an old man with children from a previous marriage in an obvious attempt to account for the brothers and sisters of Jesus. To underscore the virginity of Mary, after Jesus is born, a friend of the midwife attending Mary intimately examines her and finds that she still has proof of her virginity.[64]

The Gospel of Pseudo-Matthew

A similar account is found in *The Gospel of Pseudo-Matthew*. This account adds, however, that as a young girl Mary had taken a vow of perpetual virginity while being a ward of the Temple. When she becomes of an age to marry, Joseph is chosen by lot to be her guardian. Joseph is then quoted as protesting, "I am an old man, and have children; why do you hand over to me this infant, who is younger than my grandsons?" The children of Joseph are explicitly described as being James, Joseph, and Judah, and Simeon and his two daughters.[65] That Mary should be viewed as the exemplar virgin was obviously of great importance to those who would exalt celibacy and virginity in the Church.

Acts of Paul and Thecla

The apocryphal *Acts of Paul and Thecla* also is an attempt to foster a rigorous asceticism in the church. The book tells the story of a young woman who after listening to Paul is converted by his preaching. She then renounces her engagement to be married in order to devote herself to a life of virginity. Her mother and the intended husband after having failed to discourage her from her new faith arrange for her to be condemned to be

---

64 *The Protevangelium of James*, pars. 9, 19, 20, in *The Ante-Nicene Fathers*, vol. 8, pp. 363, 365.

65 *The Gospel of Pseudo-Matthew*, chaps. 8, 42, in *The Ante-Nicene Fathers*, vol. 8, pp. 372, 382

burned to death. The flames, however, do not touch her; and a thunderstorm puts out the fire. Neither could she be killed though lions, bears, and wild bulls were loosed upon her. Amazed at her invulnerability, the governing authorities release her, and at the age of eighteen she retires to a remote cave to live seventy-two years on a diet of herbs and water.[66]

Acts of the Holy Apostle Thomas

Another example of the extreme asceticism that afflicted the Church, and especially the heretical groups that existed alongside it, is found in the apocryphal *Acts of the Holy Apostle Thomas*. The apostle Thomas, identified in this account as Jesus' brother Judas Thomas, is present at the marriage of a king's daughter in the East. The king asks Thomas to pray in the bridal chamber for the couple, but Jesus takes Thomas's place and instructs the young couple with the following words:

> Keep in mind, my children, what my brother said to you, and to whom he commended you; and this know, that if you refrain from this filthy intercourse, you become temples holy and pure, being released from afflictions and troubles, known and unknown, and you will not be involved in the cares of life, and of children, whose end is destruction; but if you get many children, for their sakes you become grasping and avaricious, plundering orphans, coveting the property of widows, and by doing this you subject yourselves to most grievous punishments. For many children become unprofitable, being harassed by demons, some openly and others secretly: for they become either lunatics, or half-withered, or lame, or deaf, or dumb, or paralytics, or idiots; and even if they be in good health, they will be again good-for-nothing, doing unprofitable and abominable works: for they will be detected either in adultery, or in murder, or in theft, or in fornication, and by all these you will be afflicted. . . .[67]

The couple is persuaded by Jesus. In the morning when the king, her father, is with them, he wonders why she has not covered her face in shame over the happenings of the past night. His daughter says to him:

> For this reason, then, I am no longer covered, since the look of

---

66 *The Acts of Paul and Thecla*, in *The Ante-Nicene Fathers*, vol. 8, pp. 487-492.
67 *Acts of the Holy Apostle Thomas*, in *The Ante-Nicene Fathers*, vol. 8, p. 537.

shame has been taken away from me, and I am no longer ashamed or abashed . . . and because I am in cheerfulness and joy, since the day of joy has not been disturbed; and because I hold of no account this husband, and these nuptials that have passed away from before my eyes, since I have been joined in a different marriage; and because I have had no intercourse with a temporary husband, whose end is with lewdness and bitterness of soul, since I have been united to a true Husband.[68]

The king is angry with Thomas and seeks him, but he has left to continue his journey to India.

Acts of the Holy Apostle and Evangelist John

The type of asceticism found in the above is also found in the *Acts of the Holy Apostle and Evangelist John* who in a prayer of thanksgiving to Christ prays: . . . You who have preserved me also to this present hour pure to Yourself, and free from intercourse with woman, . . . who when I was looking about me, did call even the gazing upon a woman hateful; . . .[69]

When one considers the trends toward asceticism found in the works cited above, the stage is certainly set for a vehement turning toward an excessive asceticism. This finally culminated in the late 200s, especially in Egypt, with Christians fleeing into the desert to live the solitary life of anchoritic hermits, far from what they hoped would be the temptations of the flesh. A little later, some of the hermits began to cluster themselves in relatively close proximity to one another. In a relatively short time, this trend also gave rise to the first monastic communities governed by an abbot.

---

68 *Acts of the Holy Apostle Thomas*, in *The Ante-Nicene Fathers*, vol. 8, p. 538.

69 *Acts of the Holy Apostle and Evangelist John*, in *The Ante-Nicene Fathers*, vol. 8, p. 563.

Chapter Ten

THE ECLIPSE OF JESUS' WAY OF LIFE— ASCETICISM AND MONASTICISM, 300 - 1500 A.D.

The Nature of Asceticism

Striving for Perfection and Salvation through Self-Denial

The overriding concern of the ascetic was his spiritual well-being and the salvation of his own soul, not that of others.[1] The Cappadocian church father, Archbishop Basil the Great (329?-379), who wrote an influential rule[2] for the governance of monastic life, asserted, "The ascetic life has one purpose, the salvation of the soul, and so it is necessary to keep with fear as a divine commandment everything that can contribute to this very purpose."[3]

The ascetic did this by seeking for perfection gained primarily by striving for inner purity. His life would be one long time of continual repentance before God. He would give satisfaction to God for his sins through many acts of penance. He also sought to achieve perfection and purity by renouncing all sources of temptation or bodily pleasure that might hinder his contemplation and worship of God. He would spend his time in silence and devote his mind to meditation on the ineffable nature of his God.

The ascetic's life would be one of renouncing and avoiding the things and pleasures of this world. Through fasting and a very austere diet,

---

1 Kenneth S. Latourette, 1953, *A History of Christianity* (New York: Harper and Bros.), p. 222.

2 A "rule" in monastic life is the name given the book or set of guides and regulations that govern the monastery.

3 W. K. L. Clarke, translator, *The Ascetic Works of Saint Basil* (London: Society for Promoting Christian Knowledge), p. 141.

he would overcome the temptation to have the enjoyment of the table interfere with his devotion to God. It would also free him from the sin of gluttony. By sleeping in a chair or upon a hard bed, by seeking to limit the hours of sleep, and by rising periodically through the night for prayer, he would overcome the temptation to take pleasure in rest. By clothing himself in the simplest and plainest garments, he would overcome any desire for display or dressing for sexual attractiveness. By subjecting his will completely in obedience to his religious superior, the temptation for pride and self-assertion would be overcome. Through giving up all possessions, he would free himself from the temptations of materialism. By avoiding contact with the opposite sex, he hoped to lessen the opportunity of sinning sexually by thought or action. The ascetic believed that these endeavors would aid in achieving the inner purity and perfection that would result in both his entrance to paradise and a greater reward in the heavenly kingdom.

A text often used by monastics to justify the renunciation of possessions and family ties are Christ's words found in the Gospel of Luke, "And there went great multitudes with Him, and He turned and said to them, 'If anyone comes to Me and does not hate his father and mother, wife and children, brother and sister, yes, and his own life also, he cannot be My disciple. . . . So likewise, whoever of you does not forsake all that he has, he cannot be My disciple'" (14:25-26, 33 NKJV). One might ask, however, is Jesus telling the great multitudes that heard these words that they should forthwith break all family and home ties? Or is he telling them that they are to forsake the things that pertain to this world if because of opposition or persecution they are forced to choose between belief in Him and giving up family ties, possessions, and even life itself?

The Ascetic Glorification of Virginity and Celibacy

For many ascetics no sacrifice was too great in the pursuit of their own salvation. To renounce material possessions, to abandon parents, and even wife, and children often with little thought of their welfare was the order of the day in the 300s. Many major church leaders encouraged this flight from responsibility and family life. They urged that God wanted complete and undivided devotion to Himself alone, no matter what the cost. In glorifying the celibate life, they intentionally denigrated married and family life.

The great Bishop of Milan, Ambrose (340-397), mentor of Augustine, was famous for his sermons, ethical discourses, and doctrinal studies. In his treatise *Concerning Virgins* he wrote in comparing marriage to virginity:

Let us compare, if it pleases you, the advantages of married women with that which awaits virgins. Though the noble woman boasts of her abundant offspring, yet the more she bears the more she endures. Let her count up the comforts of her children, but let her likewise count up the troubles. She marries and weeps. How many vows does she make with tears? She conceives, and her fruitfulness brings her trouble before offspring. She brings forth and is ill. How sweet a pledge which begins with danger and ends in danger, which will cause pain before pleasure! It is purchased by perils, and is not possessed at her own will.

Why speak of the troubles of nursing, training, and marrying? These are the miseries of those who are fortunate. A mother has heirs, but it increases her sorrows . . . . Why should I further speak of the painful ministrations and services due to their husbands from wives, to whom before slaves God gave the command to serve. . . . And in this position spring up those incentives to vice, in that they paint their faces with various colors, fearing not to please their husbands; and from staining their faces, come to think of staining their chastity. . . . And next, what expense is necessary that even a beautiful wife may not fail to please? Costly necklaces on the one hand hang on her neck, on the other a robe woven with gold is dragged along the ground. . . . The married woman loves her own perceptions, and does she think that this is to live?

For Ambrose, virginity has no such problems, he continues:

But you, O happy virgins, . . . whose holy modesty, beaming in your bashful cheeks, and sweet chastity are a beauty, you do not, intent upon the eyes of men, consider as merits what is gained by the errors of others. You, too, have indeed your own beauty, furnished by the comeliness of virtue, not of the body. A comeliness which age puts not an end, which death cannot take away, nor any sickness injure. Let God alone be sought as the judge of loveliness, Who loves even in less beautiful bodies the more beautiful souls. You know nothing of the burden and pain of childbearing, but more are the offspring of a pious soul, which esteems all as its children, which is rich in successors, barren of all bereavements, which knows no deaths, but has many heirs.[4]

Ambrose was hardly alone in his disparagement of marriage. The renowned Cappadocian church father, Gregory of Nyssa (330?-395?), also discounted marriage in comparison with virginity. In his work, *On Virginity*, Gregory of Nyssa deplores the problems of the married:

> The more exactly we understand the riches of virginity, the more we must bewail the other life; for we realize by this contrast with better things, how poor it is. . . . Well then, is not the sum total of all that is hoped for in marriage to get delightful companionship? Grant this obtained; let us sketch a marriage in every way most happy; illustrious birth, competent means, suitable ages, the very flower of the prime of life, deep affection, the very best that each can think of the other, that sweet rivalry of each wishing to surpass the other in loving; in addition, popularity, power, wide reputation, and everything else. But observe that even beneath this array of blessings the fire of an inevitable pain is smoldering. . . . They are human all the time, things weak and perishing; they have to look upon the tombs of their progenitors; and so pain is inseparably bound up with their existence, if they have the least power of reflection. This continued expectancy of death, realized by no sure tokens, but hanging over them the terrible uncertainty of the future, disturbs their present joy, clouding it over with the fear of what is coming. If only, before experience comes, the results of experience could be learnt, or if, when one has entered on this course, it were possible by some other means of conjecture to survey the reality, then what a crowd of deserters would run from marriage into the virgin life; what care and eagerness never to be entangled in that retentive snare, where no one knows for certain how the net galls till they have actually entered it! You would see there, if only you could do it without danger, many contraries uniting; smiles melting into tears, pain mingled with pleasure, death always hanging by expectation over the children

4 Ambrose, *Concerning Virgins*, bk. 1, chap. 6, in *The Nicene and Post-Nicene Fathers* (Grand Rapids: Wm. B. Eerdmans Publ. Co.), Second Series, vol. 10, pp. 367-368.

that are born, and putting a finger upon each of the sweetest joys. Whenever the husband looks at the beloved face, that moment the fear of separation accompanies the look. . . . But her time of labour comes upon the young wife; and the occasion is regarded not as the bringing of a child into the world, but as the approach of death; in bearing it is expected that she will die; . . . The danger of childbirth is past; a child is born to them, the very image of its parents' beauty. Are the occasions for grief at all lessened thereby? Rather they are increased; for the parents retain all their former fears, and feel in addition those on behalf of the child, lest anything should happen to it in its bringing up; for instance a bad accident, or by some turn of misfortunes a sickness, a fever, any dangerous disease. Both parents share alike in these; but who could recount the special anxieties of the wife? We omit the most obvious, which all can understand, the weariness of pregnancy, the danger in childbirth, the cares of nursing, . . . Thus even the most favored live, and they are not altogether to be envied; their life is not to be compared to the freedom of virginity. Yet this hasty sketch has omitted many of the more distressing details. . . . So many-sided, then, so strangely different are the ills with which marriage supplies the world. There is pain always, whether children are born, or can never be expected, whether they live, or die. . . . Neither will I do more than mention how sadly and disastrously family jealousies and quarrels, arising from real or fancied causes, end. Who could go completely into all those details? . . .

If only, Gregory of Nyssa suggests, Christians would consider virginity:

But we need no longer show in this narrow way the drawback of this life, . . . none of that evil in life, which is visible in all its business and in all its pursuits, can have any hold over a man, if he will not put himself in the fetters of this course. The truth of what we say will be clear thus. A man who, seeing through the illusion with the eye of his spirit purged, lifts himself above the struggling world, and, to use the words of the Apostle, slights it all as but dung, in a way exiling himself altogether from human life by his abstinence from marriage, -- that man has no fellowship whatever with the sins of mankind, such as avarice, envy, anger, hatred, and everything of the kind. . . . He has raised his own life above the world, and prizing virtue as his only precious possession he will pass his days in painless peace and quiet.[5]

What a contrast to the views concerning married life of Ambrose and Gregory of Nyssa are those of the Bible. The Book of Proverbs gives a very different vision of family life. The focus in the following text is on the life of the blessed and virtuous woman who is the heart of her family:

> A good wife who can find? She is far more precious than jewels. The heart of her husband trusts in her, and he will have no lack of gain. She does him good, and not harm, all the days of her life. She seeks wool and flax, and works with willing hands. She is like the ships of the merchant, she brings her food from afar. She rises while it is yet night and provides food for her household and tasks for her maidens. She considers a field and buys it; with the fruit of her hands she plants a vineyard. She girds her loins with strength and makes her arms strong. She perceives that her merchandise is profitable. Her lamp does not go out at night. She puts her hands to the distaff, and her hands hold the spindle. She opens her hand to the poor, and reaches out her hands to the needy. She is not afraid of snow for her household are clothed in scarlet. She makes herself coverings; her clothing is fine linen and purple. Her husband is known in the gates, when he sits among the elders of the land. She makes linen garments and sells them; she delivers girdles to the merchant. Strength and dignity are her clothing, and she laughs at the time to come. She opens her mouth with wisdom, and the teaching of kindness is on her tongue. She looks well to the ways of her household, and does not eat the bread of idleness. Her children rise up and call her blessed; her husband also, and he praises her: "Many women have done excellently, but you surpass them all." Charm is deceitful, and beauty is vain, but a woman who fears the Lord is to be praised. Give her of the fruit of her hands, and let her works praise her in the gates. (Proverbs 31:10-31 RSV)

---

5 Gregory of Nyssa, *On Virginity*, chaps. 3, 4, in *The Nicene and Post-Nicene Fathers*, Second Series, vol. 5, pp. 345-348.

Jerome (340?-420), famed for his translation of the Bible into Latin, placed the life of the virgin far above that of the married. To a young woman who had taken a monastic vow, Jerome wrote:

> I write to you thus, Lady Eustochium, . . . to show you by my opening words that my object is not to praise the virginity which you follow, and of which you have proved the value, or yet to recount the drawbacks of marriage, such as pregnancy, the crying of infants, the torture caused by a rival, the cares of household management, and all those fancied blessings which death at last cuts short. Not that married women are as such are outside the pale, they have their own place, the marriage that is honorable and the bed undefiled. My purpose is to show you that you are fleeing from Sodom and should take warning by Lot's wife.[6]

It is not that marriage was viewed as a total evil. It just had a status far below the virgin or celibate life. A common way of viewing marriage at this time is seen in the interpretation given to Jesus' parable of the sower and the seed (Matthew 13:3-9). A number of church fathers taught that those who lived as virgins were the ones who bore fruit and yields of hundredfold; those who remained unmarried after their spouse died, sixtyfold; however, the married, only thirtyfold. Jerome (340?-420) writes concerning this in a letter to a widow in which he also condemns second marriages:

> In the gospel parable the seed sown in the good ground brings forth fruit, some an hundredfold, some sixtyfold, some thirtyfold. The hundredfold which comes first betokens the crown of virginity; the sixtyfold which come next refers to the work of widows; while the thirtyfold--indicated by joining together the points of the thumb and forefinger--denotes the marriage-tie. What room is left for double marriages? None. They are not counted.[7]

---

6 Jerome, *Letter 22, to Eustochium*, 2, in *The Nicene and Post-Nicene Fathers*, Second Series, vol. 6, p. 23.

7 Jerome, *Letter 123, to Ageruchia*, 9, in *The Nicene and Post-Nicene Fathers*, Second Series, vol. 6, p. 233. See also Letter 48, p. 67.

Archbishop Athanasius of Alexandria (296?-373), famed for his defense of the orthodox doctrine of the Trinity, similarly wrote:

> For there are two ways in life, as touching these matters. The one the more moderate and ordinary, I mean marriage; the other angelic and unsurpassed, namely virginity. Now if a man choose the way of the world, namely marriage, he is not indeed to blame; yet he will not receive such great gifts as the other. For he will receive, since he too brings forth fruit, namely thirtyfold. But if a man embrace the holy and unearthly way, even though, as compared to the former, it be rugged and hard to accomplish, yet it has the more wonderful gifts: for it grows the perfect fruit, namely an hundredfold.[8]

Another way of comparing the married to the virgin life was to view the virgin life as golden and the married life as silver. Bishop Cyril of Jerusalem (315?-386), wrote in his catechetical lectures:

> Nor again, on the other hand, in maintaining your chastity are you puffed up against those who walk in the humbler path of matrimony? For as the Apostle says, "Let marriage be held in honor among all, and let the bed be undefiled." You too who retain your chastity, were you not begotten of those who had married? Because you have a possession of gold, do not on that account reprobate the silver.[9]

The virgin had a higher standing in part because he or she were considered to be concerned with the things of God rather than those of the world. Paul's words on this in 1 Corinthians 7:32-33 were often cited.

Another major problem, however, with marriage in the minds of the church fathers was the sexual union that takes place in marriage. In Athanasius' *Life of Antony*, who was one of the first ascetics to retire as a hermit to the desert, he quotes Antony instructing his monks with the words ". . . nor shall we retain at all the desire of women or any other foul

---

8 Athanasius, *Letter to Amun*, Letter 48, in *The Nicene and Post-Nicene Fathers*, Second Series, vol. 4, p. 557.

9 Cyril of Jerusalem, *Catechetical Lectures*, Lecture 4, sect. 25, in *The Nicene and Post-Nicene Fathers*, Second Series, vol. 7, p. 25.

pleasure."[10] Sexual intercourse came to be viewed as a filthy, befouling activity. If engaged in at all, it was only to be done reluctantly in order to conceive children.

The great teacher of the Church Augustine (354-430) viewed all sexual desire as concupiscence or lust.[11] He argues in his book, *The City of God*, that the shamefulness of sexual intercourse is seen in that it is always carried out in private:

> Lust requires for its consummation darkness and secrecy; and this not only when unlawful intercourse is desired, but even such fornication as the earthly city has legalized. Where there is no fear of punishment, these permitted pleasures still shrink from the public eye. Even where provision is made for this lust, secrecy also is provided; and while lust found it easy to remove the prohibitions of law, shamelessness found it impossible to lay aside the veil of retirement. For even shameless men call this shameful; and though they love the pleasure, dare not display it. What! does not even conjugal intercourse, sanctioned as it is by law for the propagation of children, legitimate and honorable though it be, does it not seek retirement from every eye? . . . And why so, if not because that which is by nature fitting and decent is so done as to be accompanied with a shameful begetting penalty of sin.[12]

Augustine thus continually confused the yearning of sexual desire with concupiscence.[13] He could not admit that sexual desire could occur without lust, the selfish desire for carnal possession. He denigrated those who disagreed with him on this matter. He argued that because married couples have sexual relations in private it showed the shamefulness of sexual activity. In his treatise *On Marriage and Concupiscence* Augustine

---

10 Athanasius, *Life of Antony*, sec. 19, in *The Nicene and Post-Nicene Fathers*, Second Series, vol. 4, p. 201.

11 Augustine, *On Marriage and Concupiscence*, bk. 1, chaps. 27-40 [24-35]; bk. 2, chaps. 14 [5], 17-18 [7], 34-37 [19-22]; in *The Nicene and Post-Nicene Fathers*, First Series, vol. 5, pp. 274-279, 288-290, 296-298.

12 Augustine, *The City of God*, bk. 14, chap. 18, in *The Nicene and Post-Nicene Fathers*, First Series, vol. 2, pp. 276-277.

13 Augustine, *On Marriage and Concupiscence*, bk. 1, chaps. 22-40, in *The Nicene and Post-Nicene Fathers*, First Series, vol. 5, pp. 273-280.

asserts:

> Shameful lust, however, could not excite our members, except at our own will, if it were not a disease. Nor would even the lawful and honorable cohabiting of husband and wife raise a blush, with avoidance of any eye and desire of secrecy, if there were not a diseased condition about it.[14]

Only intercourse for the sake of conceiving children has no fault for the married couple. In the essay, *On the Good of Marriage,* Augustine wrote:

> For intercourse of marriage for the sake of begetting has no fault; but for the satisfying of lust, but yet with husband or wife, by reason of the faith of the bed, it has venial fault; but adultery or fornication has deadly fault, and, through this, continence from all intercourse is indeed better even than the intercourse of marriage itself, which takes place for the sake of begetting. . . . but to pay the due of marriage is no crime, but to demand it beyond the necessity of begetting is a venial fault, . . . [15]

> It is, however, one thing for married persons to have intercourse only for the wish to beget children, which is not sinful; it is another thing for them to desire carnal pleasure in cohabitation, but with the spouse only, which involves venial sin.[16]

Perhaps the reason for his views is that Augustine only knew lust and never really knew what it meant to fully love a woman. After the sexual escapades in his youth, at nineteen Augustine began to live with a young woman and had a son by her. However, after nine years of cohabitation, he casts her aside as an impediment to his betrothal to a more respectable girl yet too young for marriage. His disowned concubine leaves him vowing never to trust herself to another man. Augustine tells of his racked,

---

14 Augustine, *On Marriage and Concupiscence*, bk. 2, chap. 55 [33], in *The Nicene and Post-Nicene Fathers*, First Series, vol. 5, p. 306.

15 Augustine, *On the Good of Marriage*, sec. 6, in *The Nicene and Post-Nicene Fathers*, First Series, vol. 3, p. 402.

16 Augustine, *On Marriage and Concupiscence*, bk. 1, chap. 17 [15], in *The Nicene and Post-Nicene Fathers*, First Series, vol. 5, pp. 270.

wounded, and bleeding heart upon leaving her, but nonetheless sends her away. As Augustine has two years to wait before marriage to his underage fiancée, he engages an interim mistress. Upon his conversion, he decides to devote himself to the celibate life, and we hear no more of either his forsaken betrothed or of the other women he discarded.

It is of interest that in his *Confessions* Augustine spends more time lamenting over stealing a few pears when he was a boy than the selfish way he sexually used women. He repents and bewails his own lasciviousness but not the destructiveness of his conduct in the lives of the women. In his own words, he was "not so much a lover of marriage, as a slave to lust."[17] Let us then not take too seriously Augustine's judgment that all sexual desire is lust or concupiscence. Augustine was certainly one of Christianity's great theologians, but he too had his blind spots.

Augustine's writings on marriage and virginity unfortunately carried great weight over the succeeding centuries. Augustine became the main authority on sexuality in the Middle Ages according to Thomas Tentler.[18]

Enforcing Celibacy among the Secular Clergy

If the views of the church fathers concerning sexuality had an effect on the laity, they had an even greater impact on the lives of the secular clergy, the bishops, priests, and deacons serving the churches.

Paul obviously envisioned a married clergy. His words to Timothy (3:1-13) and Titus are evidence of this. To Titus he wrote:

> For this reason I left you in Crete, that you should set in order the things that are lacking, and appoint elders in every city as I commanded you--if a man is blameless, the husband of one wife, having faithful children not accused of dissipation or insubordination. For a bishop must be blameless, as a steward of God, not self-willed, not quick-tempered, not given to wine, not violent, not greedy for money, but hospitable, a lover of what is good, sober-minded, just, holy, self-controlled, holding fast the faithful word as he has been taught, that he may be able, by sound doctrine, both to exhort and to convict those who contradict. (Titus 1:5-9 NKJV)

17 Augustine, *The Confessions of St. Augustine*, bk. 6, chap. 15, in *The Nicene and Post-Nicene Fathers*, First Series, vol. 1, p. 100.

18 Thomas N. Tentler, 1977, *Sin and Confession on the Eve of the Reformation* (Princeton: Princeton Univ. Press), p. 168-169.

Although Paul himself was unmarried, he made it evident that he had a right to marriage (1 Corinthians 9:5).

An ancient Christian document called *Didascalia Apostolorum*, the teaching or doctrine of the apostles, also views a married clergy as the norm. The document pretends to have been compiled by the apostles soon after the Council of Jerusalem. It was originally written in Greek but is now only extant in a Syriac and a partial Latin version. It usually is dated around 250 A.D.; however, the church polity it portrays implies an earlier date.

The *Didascalia Apostolorum* describes the family life of the bishop in a way that is closely allied to Paul's instruction in 1Timothy 3:2-7. In a chapter devoted to the requirements for the bishopric, the document adds the following comment to Paul's words:

> But it is required that the bishop be thus: a man that hath taken one wife, that hath governed his house well. And thus let him be proved when he receives the imposition of hands to sit in the office of the bishopric: whether he be chaste, and whether his wife also be a believer and chaste; and whether he has brought up his children in the fear of God, and admonished and taught them; and whether his household fear and reverence him, and all of them obey him.[19]

Obviously, at this time in Christian history it is taken for granted that the clergy will be married.

A later group of documents based upon the *Didascalia Apostolorum* is *The Apostolic Constitutions*. *The Apostolic Constitutions* are a set of eight small books composed from various sources and gathered by unknown author(s) probably early in the 300s. The first six books are primarily based on the *Didascalia Apostolorum*. The seventh book is a revised and expanded version of *The Didache*. The eighth deals primarily with liturgical matters. As in the *Didascalia Apostolorum*, the names of the various apostles are forged to the different mandates in *The Apostolic Constitutions*. So obvious is the forgery that outside of what must have been a rather small following, the vast majority of the Church regarded *The Apostolic Constitutions* as spurious

Appended to *The Apostolic Constitutions*, however, are a set of eighty-five regulations entitled *The Apostolical Canons*, again of unknown authorship. Unlike *The Apostolic Constitutions*, *The Apostolical Canons*

---

19 R. Hugh Connolly, translator, 1929, *Didascalia Apostolorum* (Oxford: Clarendon Press), p. 32.

were highly regarded by the church. All of the eighty-five canons became part of the Canon Law of the Eastern Church, and the first fifty canons were included in a collection of canon law made around 500 A.D. in western Christianity. There is much dispute about the origin of these canons. But they seem to have come into being early in the history of the Church, for they presuppose a married clergy. Canon 40, for example, protects the right of a bishop to will his personal goods to his wife and children. The following two canons also speak of clerical marriage:

> Canon 5: Let not a bishop, presbyter, or deacon, put away his wife under the pretense of religion; but if he put her away, let him be excommunicated, and if he persists, let him be deposed.

> Canon 51: If any bishop, presbyter, or deacon, or any one of the sacerdotal list, abstains from marriage, or flesh, or wine, not by way of religious restraint, but as abhorring them, forgetting that God made all things very good, and that he made man male and female, and blaspheming the work of creation, let him be corrected, or else deposed, and cast out of the Church. In like manner a layman.[20]

The "religious restraint" in regard to marriage mentioned in Canon 51, however, comes to be less a matter of individual choice and more of a requirement of the church authorities. Although anyone admitted to holy orders was to remain married if already married when ordained, only the minor orders could become married once they came into their office. Unmarried persons once ordained as a subdeacon, deacon, or presbyter no longer had the option to become married. Canon 26 of *The Apostolical Canons* states: "Of those who have been admitted to the clergy unmarried, we ordain, that the readers and singers only may, if they will, marry."[21]

Thus, quite early there is a movement among some in the Church to restrict marriage once an individual is ordained. This, you may recall from chapter nine, is why Bishop Hippolytus castigated Callistus, the bishop of Rome (in office from 218-223). Callistus allowed a priest to marry and also some priests even to contract second and third marriages after the death of their wives, a practice referred to in the church as digamy.

---

20 *The Apostolical Canons*, Canons 40, 5, 51, in *The Nicene and Post-Nicene Fathers*, Second Series, vol. 14, pp. 596, 594, 597.

21 *The Apostolical Canons*, Canon 26, in *The Nicene and Post-Nicene Fathers*, Second Series, vol. 14, p. 595.

Some clergy, however, became uncomfortable with the marital privileges of the married clergy. Around 305 A.D. at a synod in Elvira, Spain, Spanish bishops enacted a canon or law that further restricted the rights of the clergy in regard to marriage. Canon 33 states:

> Bishops, presbyters, and deacons and all other clerics having a position in the ministry are ordered to abstain completely from their wives and not to have children. Whoever, in fact, does this, shall be expelled from the dignity of the clerical state.[22]

The Spanish church along with other clergy two decades later tried to extend this canon to the entire church at the First Ecumenical Council of Nicaea in Asia Minor called by the Emperor Constantine in 325 A.D. Bishops attended this council from both western and eastern Christianity. At the council, a number of bishops proposed and supported a canon that would restrict the clergy from having sexual relations with their wives whom they had married before ordination. The revered confessor Paphnutius, a bishop from Egypt, opposed this proposed church law. (A "confessor" was one who suffered persecution for his faith, typically imprisonment or torture.) Paphnutius was noted for his austere and ascetic life and achieved his status as a confessor of the Church during a persecution in which his eye was gouged out. The church historians Socrates and Sozomenus writing in the 400s both record this incident in their accounts of the council. Sozomenus wrote:

> Zealous of reforming the life of those who were engaged about the churches, the Synod enacted laws which were called canons. While they were deliberating about this, some thought that a law ought to be passed enacting that bishops and presbyters, deacons and sub-deacons, should hold no intercourse with the wife they had espoused before they entered the priesthood; but Paphnutius, the confessor, stood up and testified against this proposition; he said that marriage was honorable and chaste, and that cohabitation with their own wives was chastity, and advised the Synod not to frame such a law, for it would be difficult to bear, and might serve as an occasion of incontinence to them and their wives; and he reminded them, that according to the ancient tradition of the

---

22 Samuel Laeuchli, 1972, *Power and Sexuality: the Emergence of Canon Law at the Synod of Elvira* (Philadelphia: Temple Univ. Press), p. 130.

church, those who were unmarried when they took part in the communion of sacred orders, were required to remain so, but that those who were married, were not to put away their wives. Such was the advice of Paphnutius, although he was himself unmarried, and in accordance with it, the Synod concurred in his counsel, enacted no law about it, but left the matter to the decision of individual judgment, and not to compulsion. 23

The argument of Paphnutius carried the day for Christian freedom, and the discussion of the subject ended. The great Nicaean Synod enacted no canon regarding clerical abstinence concerning their wives. Eastern Orthodox Christianity has followed this decision to this day.

In the West, however, the case was different. Western Christianity followed the lead of a number of lesser provincial synods that in the 300s and early 400s made canons requiring continence among married clergy. For example, in *The Code of Canons of the African Church,* enacted in Carthage in 419 A.D., is found:

Canon 4: Faustinus, the bishop of the Potentine Church, in the province of Picenum, a legate of the Roman Church, said: It seems good that a bishop, a presbyter, and a deacon, or whoever perform the sacraments, should be keepers of modesty and should abstain from their wives.

By all the bishops it was said: It is right that who serve the altar should keep pudicity [chastity] from all women.24

In this they were following voices such as that of Epiphanius (c. 315?-403), bishop of Constantia in Cyprus, who avowed:

Nay, moreover, he that still uses marriage, and begets children, even though the husband of but one wife, is by no means admitted by the Church to the order of deacon, presbyter, bishop, or subdeacon. But for all this, he who shall have kept himself from commerce of his one wife, or has been deprived of

---

23 Sozomenus, *Church History from A.D. 323-425*, Book 1, chap. 23, in *The Nicene and Post-Nicene Fathers*, Second Series, vol. 2, p. 256. Socrates, *Church History from A.D. 305-439*, bk. 1, chap. 11, in *The Nicene and Post-Nicene Fathers*, Second Series, vol. 2, p. 18.

24 *The Code of the Canons of the African Church, 419 A.D.*, Canons 3 and 4, in *The Nicene and Post-Nicene Fathers*, Second Series, vol. 14, pp. 444-445.

her, may be ordained, and this is most usually the case in those places where the ecclesiastical canons are most accurately observed.[25]

Ambrose (340-497), bishop of Milan, also ignored the precedent of the Council of Nicaea in that synod's refusal to forbid the married clergy to lead a normal married life. In a treatise entitled, *Duties of the Clergy*, Ambrose maintains:

> But you know that the ministerial office must be kept pure and unspotted, and must not be defiled by conjugal intercourse; you know this, I say, who have received the gifts of the sacred ministry, with pure bodies, and unspoiled modesty, and without ever having enjoyed conjugal intercourse. I am mentioning this, because in some out-of-the-way places, when they enter on the ministry, or even when they become priests, they have begotten children.[26]

Popes Siricius in 385 A.D. and Innocent I, the pope between 401 and 417, issued decrees forbidding sexual relations between the clergy and their wives. Later Pope Leo the Great (390?-461) strove mightily to enforce his policy forbidding sexual relations between deacons, presbyters and even subdeacons and their wives. He wrote to the bishops of Illyricum:

> . . . for the exhibiting of the purity of complete continence, even subdeacons are not allowed carnal marriage: "that both those that have, may be as though they had not," and those who have not, may remain single.[27]

To another bishop Pope Leo wrote:

> The law of continence is the same for the ministers of

---

25 Excursus in the *The Nicene and Post-Nicene Fathers*, Second Series, vol. 14, pp. 366-367.

26 Ambrose, *Duties of the Clergy*, bk. 1, chap. 50, in *The Nicene and Post-Nicene Fathers*, Second Series, vol. 10, p. 41.

27 Pope Leo the Great, *Letter 14*, in *The Nicene and Post-Nicene Fathers*, Second Series, vol. 12, p. 18.

the altar [subdeacons] as for bishops and priests, who when they were laymen or readers, could lawfully marry and have offspring. But when they reached to the said ranks, what was before lawful ceased to be so. And hence, in order that their wedlock may become spiritual instead of carnal, it behooves them not to put away their wives but to "have them as though they had them not," whereby both the affection of their wives may be retained and the marriage functions cease.[28]

That the prohibitions of the popes regarding the clergy having sexual relations with their wives was hard to maintain is seen in the letter Pope Gregory the Great (540?-604) wrote to the bishop of Catana:

We have found from the report of many that a custom has of old obtained among you, for subdeacons to be allowed to have intercourse with their wives. That any one should any more presume to do this was prohibited by the servant of God [the Pope], the deacon of our see, under the authority of our predecessor, in this way; that those who at that time had been coupled to wives should choose one of two things, that is, either to abstain from their wives, or on no account whatever presume to exercise their ministry. . . . for the future let your Fraternity be exceedingly careful, in the case of any who may be promoted to this office, to look to this with the utmost diligence, that, if they have wives, they shall enjoy no licence to have intercourse with them: but you must still strictly order them to observe all things after the pattern of the Apostolic See.[29]

As mentioned previously, Eastern Christianity did not follow the popes of Rome in their stringent laws governing the married life of the clergy. Although the bishops in keeping with ancient practice were chosen among men who were celibate, the lower orders of clergy could be married. A normal married life was allowed to such clergy.

In 692 the Quinisext Council in Constantinople was held, a council viewed by those attending as the continuation of the Fifth and Sixth

---

28 Pope Leo the Great, *Letter 167*, in *The Nicene and Post-Nicene Fathers*, Second Series, vol. 12, p. 110.

29 Pope Gregory the Great, *Epistle 36*, in *The Nicene and Post-Nicene Fathers*, Second Series, vol. 12, pp. 158-159.

Ecumenical Councils. The Quinisext Council was never recognized as an ecumenical council by the Roman church, and its canons were ignored. This was partly because attendance at the council was primarily by eastern bishops, but also because the council passed canons in direct conflict with rulings of the Roman popes. One such was Canon 13 that reads:

> Since we know it to be handed down as a rule of the Roman Church that those who are deemed worthy to be advanced to the diaconate or presbyterate should promise no longer to cohabit with their wives, we, preserving the ancient rule and apostolic perfection and order, will that the lawful marriages of men who are in holy orders be from this time forward firm, by no means dissolving their union with their wives nor depriving them of their mutual intercourse at a convenient time. Wherefore, if anyone shall have been found worthy to be ordained subdeacon, or deacon, or presbyter, he is by no means to be prohibited from admittance to such a rank, even if he shall live with a lawful wife. Nor shall it be demanded of him at the time of his ordination that he promise to abstain from lawful intercourse with his wife: lest we should affect injuriously marriage constituted by God and blessed by his presence, as the Gospel says: "What God has joined together let no man put asunder;" and the Apostle says, "Marriage is honorable and the bed undefiled;" . . . If therefore anyone shall have dared, contrary to the Apostolic Canons, to deprive any of those who are in holy orders, presbyter, or deacon, or subdeacon of cohabitation and intercourse with his lawful wife, let him be deposed. In like manner also if any presbyter or deacon on pretense of piety has dismissed his wife, let him be excluded from communion; and if he persevere in this let him be deposed.[30]

This canon, however, did not hold for bishops. In such places as western Africa and Libya where at times married clergy were chosen for the bishopric, the Quinisext Council forbade the bishops to continue to live with their wives.[31]

---

30 *The Quinisext Council*, A.D. 692, Canon 13, in *The Nicene and Post-Nicene Fathers*, Second Series, vol. 14, p. 371.

31 *The Quinisext Council*, A.D. 692, Canon 12, in *The Nicene and Post-Nicene*

The Quinisext Council in Canon 6, however, reaffirmed Canon 27 of *The Apostolic Canons* in forbidding marriage to those who were unmarried at the time of their ordination to the ranks of subdeacon, deacon, and presbyter.[32]

The Roman church of Western Europe continued to maintain the papal rulings made during the 300s and 400s forbidding sexual relations between the clergy and their wives. Many in the church's hierarchy railed against those married priests who by having children proved their disobedience to the decrees against normal marital relations between the priests and their spouses. But, obviously, from the frequency with which these rulings had to be reissued, there was much opposition among the clergy. Many defied the authority of a church that allowed priests to be married but demanded that the priest and his wife live in celibacy.

After six hundred years, the discrimination against the clergy who had married before ordination finally resulted in the complete banning of clerical marriage. The Roman church decreed that married priests were to separate from their wives. A synod in Rome in 1074 under Pope Gregory VII, Hildebrand (1020?-1085), passed legislation that required married priests either to dismiss their lawful wives or cease to read mass. The same synod forbade the laity to attend a mass conducted by a priest who still lived with his wife. Pope Gregory VII insisted on the strict enforcement of these canons. Contrary to Jesus' words, that what God had joined together, let no man break asunder, Pope Gregory could indeed break asunder (Mark 10:9)![33]

Monasticism, the Ascetic Movement among the Laity

The Rationale of Monasticism

The asceticism that was enforced upon the clergy had its counterpart among the laity in the rise of monasticism. In its origin and for many centuries, monasticism was primarily a lay movement. The definition of monasticism includes both those monks or monastics who take up the life of an anchorite, that is, a solitary hermit, and those who choose to live in a community of monks under the authority of an abbot.

Fathers, Second Series, vol. 14, p. 370.

32 *The Quinisext Council*, Canon 6, in *The Nicene and Post-Nicene Fathers*, Second Series, vol. 14, p. 364.

33 Philip Schaff, 1907, *History of the Christian Church*, vol. 5, The Middle Ages (Grand Rapids: Wm. B. Eerdmans Publ. Co., 1949), pp. 36-45.

The early monastic was one who fled from the temptations of the world in order to strive through self-denial for inner perfection. The monastic lived a life of abstinence in restricting or denying the enjoyment of foods, sleep, bodily comfort, personal property, sex, and status. In committing himself to a life of total obedience and submission to the will of his religious superior, he also gave up the further use of his Christian freedom to act in Christian love as led by the Spirit (Galatians 5:13-25). The monastic's life was to be a perfect one of obedience, penitence, prayer, meditation, and religious devotion. Even today, upon his death he may be declared to be "perfected."

Monasticism was founded on the premise that somehow turning one's back on God's good gifts to humankind would be most pleasing to Him. It appears to have been based on the following assumptions:

1. That a life of total and unquestioning obedience to the will of a religious superior was better than a life of Christian freedom acting in Christian love as led by the Holy Spirit and guided by God's Word.

2. That wearing coarse garments, sleeping on a hard bed, and living an austere, grave, and sober existence in order to remind oneself constantly of one's sinful nature and the need for giving satisfaction through penance for one's sins was most agreeable to God—more agreeable evidently than accepting fully and joyfully God's gift of pardon and forgiveness through faith in the redeeming sacrifice of His Son.

3. That a celibate life of solitude in the desert or a monastic cell was most pleasing to God—more pleasing than a life wherein a maid marries a young man and together they live and work to give their children a happy and joyful childhood and as a family prove a blessing to their community.

4. That spurning God's gift of a bountiful nature to subsist instead on a restricted, severe, and austere diet, often fasting on just bread, salt, and water, was most acceptable to God—more acceptable than with thanksgiving appreciating the wondrous variety of wholesome and satisfying foods that God in His bounty provides.

It is almost as if Paul had never warned:

Now the Spirit expressly says that in later times some will

depart from the faith by giving heed to deceitful spirits and
doctrines of demons, through the pretensions of liars whose
consciences are seared, who forbid marriage and enjoin
abstinence from foods which God created to be received with
thanksgiving by those who believe and know the truth. For
everything created by God is good, and nothing is to be rejected
if it is received with thanksgiving; for then it is consecrated by
the word of God and prayer. (1Timothy 4:1-5 RSV)

The Origin of Monasticism

It is not the intent of this book to give a detailed history of
monasticism; however, the monastics have played a very prominent role in
the history of Christianity. To understand what happened to the way of life
that Jesus taught over the past two thousand years, one has to understand
the tremendous influence monasticism had on the way Christians lived over
the centuries.

Monasticism had its origin in Egypt. One of the first men to go out
into the desert to live the life of a hermit for religious reasons was Antony
(251-356?). The severe austerity of his life and his reputation for holiness
was publicized by Athanasius (293?-373), the archbishop of Alexandria,
when he wrote his influential *Life of Antony*. Towards the end of the third
century and thereafter, many thousands followed the example of Antony.
They left their homes and deserted their wife and children to take up the life
of a religious hermit or anchorite in the vast deserts of Egypt.

The excesses of the religious devotion among the hermits held a
peculiar attraction for many Christians of the day. They were fascinated by
such austerities as fasting to the point of emaciation, eating the poorest of
foods, sleeping on the hard ground, never washing one's body, continual
weeping over one's sins, and suffering from exposure to cold and heat.
Jerome wrote vividly of the years he spent as a hermit:

How often, when I was living in the desert, in the vast solitudes
which gives to hermits a savage dwelling-place, parched by a
burning sun, how often did I fancy myself among the pleasures
of Rome! I used to sit alone because I was filled with bitterness.
Sackcloth disfigured my unshapely limbs and my skin from long
neglect had become as black as an Ethiopian's. Tears and
groans were every day my portion; and if drowsiness chanced to
overcome my struggles against it, my bare bones, which hardly
held together, clashed against the ground. Of my food and drink
I say nothing: for, even in sickness, the solitaries have nothing

but cold water, and to eat one's food cooked is looked upon as self-indulgence. Now, although in my fear of hell I had consigned myself to this prison, where I had no companions but scorpions and wild beasts, I often found myself amid bevies of girls. My face was pale and my frame chilled with fasting; yet my mind was burning with desire, and the fires of lust kept bubbling up before me when my flesh was as good as dead. Helpless, I cast myself at the feet of Jesus, I watered them with my tears, I wiped them with my hair: and then I subdued my rebellious body with weeks of abstinence.[34]

Jerome's description of his life as a hermit is typical of the literature concerning the life of an anchorite of that time. Although one may flee the temptations of society, one cannot flee from one's imagination. Athanasius in his *Life of Antony* wrote of Antony being tempted by Satan who appeared to Antony in the form of a woman and imitated all her acts.[35]

Not all those who fled civilized life for the desert lived as complete solitaries. Some although living apart in their simple caves or dwellings yet lived in proximity to other hermits. They often chose one of their number to be their religious superior. Such a loose association of hermits was called a "laura."

A further development of monastic life came with the highly organized communal living for those who wished to live apart from normal society but not in isolation. In just a relatively few years after many took up the solitary life of the hermit in the desert, others organized the first monasteries.

Pachomius (292?-346?) after his conversion to Christianity spent a few years living as a hermit in Egypt. Finding that the life of a solitary hermit presented many problems, psychological and otherwise, he gathered a group of monks and founded the first monastery. He proved an able organizer. By the time of his death, Pachomius had established nine monasteries containing some three thousand men. He also organized a nunnery for women.

Pachomius devised an extensive rule or set of regulations for his Egyptian monks. Jerome (340?-420) later translated a Greek version of the rule into Latin. *The Rules of St. Pachomius* proved highly influential in the

---

34 Jerome, *Letter 22, to Eustochium*, in *The Nicene and Post-Nicene Fathers*, Second Series, vol. 6, pp. 24-25.

35 Athanasius, *Life of Antony*, sec. 5, in *The Nicene and Post-Nicene Fathers*, Second Series, vol. 4, p. 197.

further development of monasticism. Much of Pachomius's Rule also is preserved in the *Institutes of the Coenobia* written by John Cassian (360?-435?) after his journeys to and visits among the Egyptian monasteries. Cassian relied in part upon *The Rules of St. Pachomius* in establishing monasteries in Western Europe. Benedict of Nursia (480-543) also made use of Pachomius's rules in writing his highly influential *Rule of St. Benedict*. Thus, the regulations of Pachomius laid down early in the fourth century largely determined the character of monasticism down to this present day.

According to Jerome, the monks in each Egyptian monastery were organized into houses of about forty men each. Each monk had his own small cell. Each house was under a master, and one monk was chosen to be spiritual father to the entire monastery.[36] The monastery was fully enclosed, and no monk was allowed to leave its bounds without permission.

Under *The Rules of St. Pachomius* the monks lived a rigid and highly regulated life. They had nothing in their cells except a mat, a goatskin, two hoods, a linen mantle and belt, three sleeveless garments for sleeping or working, and shoes and a staff for journeys. They ate twice a day, the first meal being at noon. The meals were eaten in silence, and the monks were forbidden to look at one another while eating. Neither were they to speak to other monks when either returning to their cells or going to work after the meal. If a monk wished to eat alone, he was served bread, salt, and water in his cell. The monks fasted twice a week, on Wednesdays and Fridays.

When the monks went out to work, they were forbidden to ask where they were going. At work, they were not to sit without the superior's order. No one was to clasp the hand or anything else of his companion and whether sitting, standing, or walking were to keep a forearm's space between themselves. They were not to walk in the monastery fields, walk around within the monastery, or go outside the monastery walls without their housemaster's permission. They slept in a reclining chair covered with one mat. Although the Egyptian monks engaged in farming and other crafts, their major work was plaiting rushes into mats or baskets for sale as a way of furnishing an income for the monastery. They received religious instruction three times a week from their housemasters. They were allowed books to read from the common library; however, their major study was to be the Scriptures. They met several times a day for worship.

The Rules of St. Pachomius is made up of a number of sections. The first section, "The Precepts of our father Pachomius," is composed of 144

---

36 Jerome's Preface to Rules of St. Pachomius in *Pachomian Koinonia*, vol. 2 (Kalamazoo, Michigan: Cistercian Publ. Inc.) p. 142.

primarily negative regulations designed to closely control the behavior and activity of the monks.[37] The second section the "Precepts and Institutes of our father Pachomius." contains seventeen lengthy precepts or regulations followed by the eighteenth precept, itself made up of fifty short commands with almost all beginning with the words, "He shall not. . . ." To give a few examples: "He shall not be quick to utter idle words. He shall not dispute for higher rank. He shall not desire beautiful clothes."[38] *The Rule of St. Pachomius* is thus primarily a set of negative injunctions that tightly regulated the life of the monks. It has much more in common with the negative rules of *The Doctrina* than the life of outgoing Christian love expressed in deeds of service to others taught in the New Testament.

The Rules of St. Pachomius was a severe but fair rule. The punishments for violating the rule were primarily psychological rather than the physical punishments to which monks were subjected later in the history of monasticism. The monks, including their superiors, were all treated alike; and no one whether working as a cook, farmer, orchardist, or baker was allowed to have any advantages over any other brother. Not even fruit fallen to the ground could be picked up and eaten. Only the sick, the old, the very young, and those engaged in heavy labor received a relaxation of the sparse and austere diet. The sick especially were given careful and considerate care. The monks were known for their hospitality to all visitors.

The Spread of Monasticism

The monastic life that began in Egypt quickly spread to other regions. Monasteries and hermits were soon to be found in Palestine, Syria, and Asia Minor. In Asia Minor, Basil the Great (329?-379) composed a book on asceticism and gave a series of rules for monastic life. In it he wrote that complete and unquestioning obedience was the primary requirement of the monastic:

> Now true and perfect obedience of subordinates towards the leader is shown in this, namely, in not only refraining from wrong things according to the counsel of the Superior but not doing even praiseworthy things without his approval.[39]

---

37 "Precepts of our father Pachomius," in *Pachomian Koinonia*, vol. 2, pp. 145-167.

38 "Precepts and Institutes of our father Pachomius," in *Pachomian Koinonia*, vol. 2, pp. 169-174.

39 W. K. L. Clarke, translator, *The Ascetic Works of Saint Basil*, p. 142.

Indicative of the solemnity of the monastic's life is his thirty-first rule:

> XXXI. Must we not laugh at all?
>
> Since the Lord condemns those that laugh it is obvious that
> there is never a time for laughter for the believer, especially
> when there is so great a multitude of those who by transgression
> of the law dishonour God and are dead in sins, for whom one
> should mourn and grieve.[40]

The monks came to be looked upon by most Christians as a spiritual elite. Those monks who undertook especially severe austerities were considered "athletes of God." Some monks seemed to vie with one another in their ascetic excesses. One hermit lived suspended in a cage. Others sought disengagement from the world by living on top of tall pillars. They became known as "pillar saints."

Many of the church leaders of the 300s and thereafter held up the monastic life as exemplary. The bishops of eastern Christianity were often drawn from the ranks of the monks. Many of the prominent church leaders and theologians, such as Jerome, John Chrysostom, and Basil, began their careers as monastics, either solitary or communal. The hermits and monastery monks were considered to live more sanctified, purer, and holier lives than those of the secular priests who served Christian people in the parishes.

The highest Christian ideal, therefore, was no longer serving one's Lord through serving even the least of his brothers and being in but not of the world. The ideal Christian was neither of nor in the world. He was one who fled the world and sought to achieve an inner purity and perfection through celibacy and stringent self-denial. His service to God was to be one of tearful penitence, prayer, meditation, and engaging in periods of devotional worship every few hours. It was the extent of one's piety that counted, not Christian love or goodness.

Monasticism came to western Christianity and Rome largely through Athanasius (296?-373) during his periodic exiles from his bishopric in Alexandria, Egypt. His *Life of Antony* was translated into Latin around the year 370 and made a deep impression. Jerome (340?-420) in one of his letters notes its influence and also writes of an early monastery in Rome that was seemingly based on *The Rules of St. Pachomius*.[41] Ambrose (340-397),

---

40 W. K. L. Clarke, translator, *The Ascetic Works of Saint Basil*, p. 241.

41 Jerome, *Letter 127*, par. 5, in *The Nicene and Post-Nicene Fathers*, Second Series, vol. 6, p. 254-255.

bishop of Milan, also was an early expounder of the virtues of monasticism. Near Milan was one of the first monasteries in the West. Another founder of monasticism in the West was Martin of Tours (315?-399).

John Cassian (360?-435?), who founded the monastery of St. Victor near Marseilles, was highly influential in the development of western monasticism. As a young man, he became a monk in Bethlehem. Later he spent years studying the monasticism of Egypt and Palestine and wrote extensively on his observations in his twelve books gathered under the title: *Institutes for Monasteries and the Eight Remedies against the Eight Capital Vices.* His books detailed the practices, rules, and organization of eastern monasticism. He also published a series of dialogues he had had with various abbots of the desert monasteries in his book called *The Conferences of John Cassian.* The Conferences were also highly influential. The later *Rule of St. Benedict* recommended that Cassian's *Conferences* be read aloud to the monks.[42]

The negation of self in absolute obedience to the religious superior was a primary thrust in Cassian's writings. Cassian, for example, writes approvingly of a young monk in Egypt who as a test of his obedience was ordered by his superior to water each day a dry piece of wood stuck in the ground. For a year, the young man carried water everyday over a distance of two miles in all kinds of weather in order to water the dead stick. At another time, he was ordered to move an enormous boulder. The young monk did not argue with his superior's order but strained at his impossible task until both he and the rock were saturated with perspiration.[43]

The extent to which obedience played a part in monastic life also is indicated by Cassian's story in his *Institutes* of what was considered the remarkable and praiseworthy obedience of a novice monk. Cassian relates the story of a man accompanied by his eight-year-old son who after many entreaties was finally permitted to enter an Egyptian monastery. The account continues:

> . . . And when they were at last admitted they were at once not only committed to the care of different superiors, but also put to live in separate cells that the father might not be reminded by the constant sight of the little one that out of all his possessions and carnal treasures, which he had cast off and renounced, at

---

42 *The Rule of St. Benedict*, Owen Chadwick, trans., in vol. 12, *Western Asceticism* of *The Library of Christian Classics* (Philadelphia: The Westminster Press), p. 319.

43 John Cassian, *The Institutes of John Cassian*, bk. 4, chap. 24, in *The Nicene and Post-Nicene Fathers*, Second Series, vol. 11, pp. 226, 227.

least his son remained to him; and that as he was already taught that he was no longer a rich man, so he might also forget the fact that he was a father. And that it might be more thoroughly tested whether he would make affection and love for his own flesh and blood of more account than obedience and Christian mortification (which all who renounce the world ought out of love to Christ prefer), the child was on purpose neglected and dressed in rags instead of proper clothes; and so covered and disfigured with dirt that he would rather disgust than delight the eyes of his father whenever he saw him. And further, he was exposed to blows and slaps from different people, which the father often saw inflicted without the slightest reason on his innocent child under his very eyes, so that he never saw his cheeks without their being stained with the dirty marks of tears. And though the child was treated thus day after day before his eyes, yet still out of love for Christ and the virtue of obedience the father's heart stood firm and unmoved. For he no longer regarded him as his own son, as he had offered him equally with himself to Christ; nor was he concerned about his present injuries, but rather rejoiced because he saw that they were endured, not without profit; thinking little of his son's tears, but anxious about his own humility and perfection. And when the Superior of the Coenobium [monastery] saw his steadfastness of mind and immovable inflexibility, in order thoroughly to prove the constancy of his purpose, one day when he had seen the child crying, he pretended that he was annoyed with him and told the father to throw him into the river. Then he, as if this had been commanded him by the Lord, at once snatched up the child as quickly as possible, and carried him in his arms to the river's bank to throw him in. And straightaway in the fervour of his faith and obedience this would have been carried out in act, had not some of the brethren been purposely set to watch the banks of the river very carefully, and when the child was thrown in, had somehow snatched him from the bed of the stream, and prevented the command, which was really fulfilled by the obedience and devotion of the father, from being consummated in act and result.[44]

---

44 John Cassian, *The Institutes of John Cassian*, bk. 4, chap. 27, in *The Nicene and Post-Nicene Fathers*, Second Series, vol. 11, pp. 227-228.

Whether this story is true or not is irrelevant to the fact that Cassian included it in his *Institutes* as a model of laudable obedience. The story, however, is also noteworthy in that it tells us about the lack of Christian love that prevailed in the lives of the Egyptian monastics who considered the actions of the father praiseworthy. The abuse of the small boy depicts a hardness of heart that hardly befits a follower of the Christ who welcomed little children into his arms (Mark 10:13-16). The excessive concern for personal perfection that led to such unnatural behavior on the part of the father is seen in that he thought little of either his small son's tears or his life but was "anxious about his own humility and perfection." Perhaps in justification of the cruelty, Cassian further relates that by divine testimony it was afterwards revealed to the father's superior that God found acceptable this copying of the deed of Abraham in regard to Isaac (Genesis 22). The fact that the monastics of the time viewed the father's actions as exemplary and praiseworthy is an excellent example of what a vast difference may exist between piety and goodness.

It is primarily in Cassian's recording of his conferences with the leading abbots of the monasteries of Egypt that Christian love is mentioned. Some of the abbots maintained that love was preeminent over even fasting, vigils, withdrawal from the world, and meditation on Scripture.[45] Abbot Moses, for example, speaks of the futility of seeking perfection without love.[46] Abbots Nesteros and Joseph both stress Jesus' command to love one another.[47] Abbot Chaeremon speaks of love as the most excellent way of all.[48]

Nonetheless, the major emphasis in early monasticism was not on a faith active in deeds of selfless love to one's fellow humans. It stressed rather fleeing from the temptations of the human world. Personal salvation and a hoped for heavenly reward for inner purity and perfection were to be obtained by repentance, a struggle against temptation, self-denial, and devotion to God through prayer, worship, and contemplation. Cassian writes that the object of the monk's profession "is nothing but meditation

---

45 John Cassian, *Cassian's Conferences*, in *The Nicene and Post-Nicene Fathers*, Second Series, vol. 11, pp. 297-298, see also 418-421, 448, 452-455.

46 John Cassian, *First Conference with Abbot Moses*, chap. 6, in *The Nicene and Post-Nicene Fathers*, Second Series, vol. 11, p. 297.

47 John Cassian, *The Second Conference of Abbot Nesteros*, chap. 7, *The First Conference of Abbot Joseph*, chap. 6, in *The Nicene and Post-Nicene Fathers*, Second Series, vol. 11, pp. 448, 452.

48 John Cassian, *The First Conference of Abbot Chaeremon*, chaps. 12, 13, in *The Nicene and Post-Nicene Fathers*, Second Series, vol. 11, pp. 420-421.

and contemplation of that divine purity which excels all things, and which can only be gained by silence and continually remaining in the cell, . . ."[49] In his *Conferences* Cassian quotes Abbot Theonas as saying:

> "Contemplation then, i.e., meditation on God, is the one thing, the value of which all the merits of our righteous acts, all our aims at virtue, come short of. . . . So then the merits of all the virtues, which I enumerated above, though in themselves they are good and precious, yet become dim in comparison of the brightness of contemplation. For they greatly hinder and retard the saints who are taken up with earthly aims even at good works, from the contemplation of that sublime good.[50]

Thus, the contemplative, solitary life of the monk in his cell became the superior way to strive for the perfection to which one may aspire. Even acting in love in doing good works would "greatly hinder and retard the saints" in their meditation upon and contemplation of God, the sublime good. The monk thus is encouraged to become primarily self-centered in his quest for purity and perfection.

Some monks, however, came to doubt that the contemplative life of the monastic was the true road to perfection. If, as Paul wrote in 1 Corinthians 13, love is the greatest Christian virtue and surpasses both faith and hope, how is Christian love to be expressed if one is leading a solitary life in a monastic cell? Even when the monk met for meals not only was silence the rule, they also had to draw their hoods down over their eyelids so that they could see nothing but the food before them. Requests at the table were made by hand signals.[51]

A life so lived gave rise to the grave problem of acedia among the monastics. Acedia was a general apathy, torpor, or additionally a feeling of uselessness and worthlessness that afflicted some monks. Some came to doubt the value of their irrevocable choice of becoming a monk. They began to wonder whether a life almost devoid of meaningful opportunity to serve one's fellow humans was a life that God approved.

Cassian devoted a major section of his *Institutes* to the problem of

---

49 John Cassian, *The Institutes of John Cassian*, bk. 10, chap. 3, in *The Nicene and Post-Nicene Fathers*, Second Series, vol. 11, p. 267.

50 John Cassian, *Third Conference of Abbot Theonas*, chaps. 3, 4, in *The Nicene and Post-Nicene Fathers*, Second Series, vol. 11, pp. 520-521.

51 John Cassian, *The Institutes of John Cassian*, bk. 4, chap. 17, in *The Nicene and Post-Nicene Fathers*, Second Series, vol. 11, p. 224.

acedia. He gave a vivid description of a monk afflicted with acedia:

> . . . he often groans because he can do no good while he stays there, and complains and sighs because he can bear no spiritual fruit so long as he is joined to that society; . . . Then the disease suggests that he ought to show courteous and friendly hospitalities to the brethren, and to pay visits to the sick, whether near at hand or far off. He talks too about some dutiful and religious offices; that those kinsfolk ought to be inquired after, and that he ought to go and see them oftener; that it would be a real work of piety to go more frequently to visit that religious woman, devoted to the service of God, who is deprived of all support of kindred; and that it would be a most excellent thing to get what is needful for her who is neglected and despised by her own kinsfolk; and that he ought piously to devote his time to these things instead of staying uselessly and with no profit in his cell.[52]

Perhaps the problem of Cassian's monk was that he took seriously the words of James that he heard during the regular nightly reading of the Bible: "Religion that is pure and undefiled before God and the Father is this: to visit the orphans and widows in their affliction," as well as "and to keep oneself unstained from the world" (James 1:27 RSV).

In the 500s, Benedict of Nursia compiled a rule for the governance of monastic groups that became a standard in monasticism. He drew on the previous monastic rules of Pachomius, Cassian, Augustine of Hippo, and Basil the Great to produce an austere, but responsible and caring rule for the monasteries.

In Benedict's rule, the lives of the monks primarily were governed by the canonical hours for worship that came at about three hour intervals. Benedict hallowed these times of periodic worship; and called the canonical hours that occurred throughout the day and night "the Work of God."[53] Benedict wrote concerning keeping the canonical hours, "Let nothing be preferred to the work of God." Work, study, prayer, and rest or reading

---

52 John Cassian, *The Institutes of John Cassian*, bk.10, chap. 2, in *The Nicene and Post-Nicene Fathers*, Second Series, vol. 11, p. 267.

53 *The Rule of St. Benedict*, translation by U. J. Schnitzhofer and commentary by the Rev. Basilius Steidle, 1952, (Beurom/Hohenzollern, Deutschland: Beuroner Kunstverlag), p. 212.

consumed the remaining times.

The monasteries were to be self-sufficient. To "travel the hard road of obedience" conforming to the will of one's superior was a major requirement. At a command from his superior, a monk was to instantly respond, dropping whatever he was doing. Everything was to be held in common; no personal possessions were allowed of any kind, not as much as a pen. Food was to be simple and frugal. Usually two meals a day, each with two courses, were considered sufficient. Meat could be given to the sick to aid their recovery, however, "Except the very weak, no one shall eat meat at any time."[54] All were to take their turn in the kitchen. The sick could bathe as necessary, but especially the younger monks were seldom to bathe. Monks were to sleep in individual beds in dormitories by tens or twenties. A lamp was to burn throughout the night. The monks were not to send or receive letters or gifts without the abbot's permission. If the abbot permitted a monk to accept a gift, it was to be given to the abbot that he may dispose of the gift to whom he pleased and in any manner he chose. Monks were not to follow their own good but the good of their brothers. According to the Holy Rule:

> They shall be charitable, with a pure heart, towards their brothers. They shall fear God. They shall love their abbot with a sincere and humble affection. They are to put nothing at all before Christ; whom we pray to lead us together to eternal life.[55]

As the centuries passed, there arose a variety of monastic orders. A few of these groups sought to be more active in the world, although the majority remained cloistered from the world. With the founding of the Franciscan and Dominican orders of friars in the 1200s came an emphasis on service to humanity and to the Christian community. The friars became active in education and caring for those in need. Monasticism remained a dominant aspect of Christianity up to the time of the Reformation.

One should not ignore the considerable fruits and blessings of monasticism. The monasteries were educational centers. They have preserved for us much of our knowledge of the earlier Greek and Roman civilizations. When the barbaric invaders from the north disdained the learning and benefits of the Greek and Roman cultures, the monasteries where lights of education and learning glowing across the Europe in the

---

54 *The Rule of St. Benedict*, Owen Chadwick, translator, in vol. 12, *Western Asceticism* from *The Library of Christian Classics*, p. 317.

55 *The Rule of St. Benedict*, Owen Chadwick, translator, in vol. 12, *Western Asceticism* from *The Library of Christian Classics*, p. 336.

gloom of the dark ages brought on by the northern barbarians. The monks of the West, who copied and recopied many of the ancient writings and so preserved them, have done an inestimable service.[56] In Ireland especially, far removed from the onslaught of the barbaric tribesmen of northern Europe, the monks made noteworthy contributions in preserving the ancient literature. Likewise, far to the east in Mesopotamia the Nestorian Christians similarly translated the Greek philosophers into the Arabic of their overlords. Today many scholars overlook that it was from these translations that the Moslem Arabs came to know many of the writings of the ancient Greek and Roman civilizations. It is thus from eastern Christian sources that the Moslems of Spain later passed this ancient literary heritage into Christian Western Europe.[57]

From the time of their origin, the monasteries have been hospitable to the traveler and those in need. At times hospitals were connected with the monasteries for service to both the monks and the surrounding community. They often had schools for the education both of the monastics and the young people of the area. The monasteries especially have been places from which missionaries went out to Christianize a barbaric world. From the 500s on, monks from both eastern and western Christianity were the chief missionaries to the pagan peoples of Europe and Asia. They reduced pagan languages to writing so that unlettered peoples could read the Scriptures and other literature. Indeed, in the past 1900 years more languages have been given a written form by Christian missionaries than by all other agencies combined.[58] Later, the monks were missionaries to lands far beyond Europe.

The monasteries have been places where many devoted men and women have poured out their hearts and lives for their God. The God who looks at the faith, hearts, and motivations of humans had a multitude of fervent and sincere devotees among many of the monastics of Christianity.

The monastic life, nonetheless, as fostered by the medieval church had a major negative influence on way of life that Jesus taught. The monastics were held up as the spiritual nobility of the Church. Their somber piety and asceticism were regarded as exemplifying the highest Christian virtues. They were people to serve as examples to the laity. The laity might approach the holiness of their celibacy only if they would refrain from sexual relations with their spouses. The monastic's ascetical practices concerning food, clothing, and housing were also to be examples to the laity. As it became the custom in parts of Europe to obtain bishops from the

---

56 Kenneth S. Latourette, 1953, *A History of Christianity*, pp. 349, 357, 552.

57 Kenneth S. Latourette, 1953, *A History of Christianity*, pp. 276, 323, 497.

58 Kenneth S. Latourette, 1953, *A History of Christianity*, p. 100.

monasteries, the monk bishop in his preaching naturally praised asceticism as the highest virtue.

Monasticism divided Christianity into two groups. One group, the monastics, considered themselves an elite group held to a higher standard than the remaining Christians. They believed that what they called the New Testament's "counsels of perfection" such as: returning good for evil, giving away one's possessions, going the second mile, turning the other cheek, and so forth, were meant for just a special group of Christians such as themselves. They were the "religious" ones striving to be perfected. The remaining Christians could also be considered Christian but living in the world meant compromises with the world. Even the "secular" priests serving the parishes were not viewed as coming up to the monastic's high standard of devotion to God. But was it really to just His small group of devoted disciples to whom Jesus said, "Therefore you shall be perfect, just as your Father in heaven is perfect" (Matthew 5:48 NKJV)? No, it was to the great multitude who listened to Him during the Sermon on the Mount.

Thus, it developed that those considered most holy and most revered were men and women who removed themselves from the world and its trials in order to self-centeredly seek out their personal salvation and win for themselves a greater reward in heaven. The reclusive, whining, vitriolic, and irascible Jerome is the one to be elevated by his church to sainthood rather than the faithful woman selflessly giving herself in loving service to her husband, children, and neighbors for Jesus' sake.[59] The stress on one's own inner purity and a striving for personal perfection in monasticism undercut the emphasis of the New Testament on an outgoing faith active in deeds of love. The concern with one's own purity displaced the emphasis of Christ, Paul, and John on Christians being active in the world as they sought ways to serve God by serving the good of their fellowman. The emphasis on lives devoted to the extreme piety found in asceticism far eclipsed lives devoted to goodness and Christian love in the minds of the people of the day.

---

59 If any take exception to this characterization of Jerome's personality, I suggest they read his letters in *The Nicene and Post-Nicene Fathers*, Second Series, vol. 6, pp. 1-294.

Chapter Eleven

CHRISTIAN LOVE AND EARLY RENEWERS OF THE CHURCH: CHRYSOSTOM AND AUGUSTINE

The Endless Endeavor to Remain Faithful to New Testament Christianity

Attempts to reform and renew the Church occurred repeatedly in its long history. The reformer Martin Luther, for example, was hardly alone in trying to bring the Church back to a way of life based on a faith active in Christian love following Jesus' New Commandment. Far earlier in the Church's history there were others who came to realize that a life of self-giving love following the example of Christ's love was the way of life taught by the New Testament. In the late 300s, two of the most prominent of these were John Chrysostom and Augustine.

Both Chrysostom and Augustine, however, were slow to understand the way of life taught in the New Testament. They had been converted to a church saturated with the view that asceticism and withdrawal from the world to seek personal purity and perfection were the highest Christian ideals. For both men it was their intensive study of the New Testament that led them back to the way of life taught by Christ and His apostles. Chrysostom had the greater insight concerning the nature of the Christian way of life. Augustine, after an immoral young manhood, turned in reaction to his former life to an ascetic and celibate way of life. For the rest of his life, he contended that celibacy and asceticism were superior to the normal, married life of Christian people. As happened with Chrysostom and Augustine, throughout history the Bible has served as a corrective to the errors and theological distortions of humans.

John Chrysostom (345?-407)

The Golden-Mouthed Preacher of the Christian Way of Life

What Augustine is to western Christianity his contemporary, John Chrysostom, is to eastern Christianity. John Chrysostom, one of the four most prominent church fathers of the East, was a native of Antioch, Syria. He first took up a career in law; but after his baptism in 370, he retired to life as a monastic. He spent four years under the guidance of an ascetic mentor. For two more years, he lived as a solitary hermit. His health failing under the austere life of a hermit, he returned to Antioch to serve as a deacon and in 386 was ordained a priest. John's gifts as a preacher were soon recognized. In 398, his saintly life and his fame as a preacher resulted in his call to the archbishopric of Constantinople, the new capital city of the Roman Empire.

John was called "Chrysostom" (which in Greek means "golden-mouth") not only for his eloquence and brilliant rhetoric. His greatest strength was his broad knowledge of the Bible, his reliance on a plain, literal, and faithful interpretation of the Scriptures, and the remarkable insight and frankness with which he applied the Bible to life. As he grew older, his constant scholarly study of the Scriptures led him to many deeper insights into the true nature of the Christian way of life. For Chrysostom, "Great is the profit of the divine Scriptures, and all-sufficient is the aid which comes from them".[1] In reviewing many hundreds of his sermons, I found them difficult to scan. His insights are so captivating that one involuntarily stops scanning and starts reading word for word. Especially during the time he was archbishop of Constantinople, he was a preacher of Christ's way of life in a faithful, fearless, and well-balanced manner to all classes of society. He was Christ-like in his preaching and paid the same price for his truthfulness that Christ paid. His preaching against sumptuous self-indulgence so enraged Empress Eudoxia and her courtiers that they exiled him in 404 and later persecuted him to death in 407.

Chrysostom's Changing View of Asceticism

John Chrysostom is noted for his many ascetic treatises written early in his career. For example, he wrote such works as —*On Virginity,* —

---

1 John Chrysostom, *Homilies on St. John*, Homily 37, in *The Nicene and Post-Nicene Fathers* (Grand Rapids: Wm. B. Eerdmans Publ. Co.), First Series, vol. 14, p. 128.

Against Remarriage in which he argued for a celibate life.[2] Chrysostom spoke highly of the monastic life during these years and in his early years as a presbyter preacher in Antioch. This changed, however, especially when Chrysostom became archbishop of Constantinople and took up the bishop's burden as the principal preacher to the people.

If a Christian preacher is to remain faithful to his calling, he must avoid preaching the whims and opinions of men, including his own. He must rather steadfastly strive to apply to the lives of his hearers God's revelation of Himself and His will as they are found in the Scriptures. In this Chrysostom was truly a faithful preacher. He achieved a tremendous grasp and understanding of the Scriptures and obviously was a keen observer of human nature. Thus, as his experience with life broadened and as his understanding from the New Testament of Christ's way of life deepened, he modified his earlier blanket approval of asceticism and the monastic life as the ideal Christian way of life. He came to stress the importance of serving one's fellowman through works of love rather than being apart from the world in ascetic isolation. In a homily on *The Gospel of St. Matthew* while a presbyter in Antioch, Chrysostom preached:

> Let there be then two ways of most holy life, and let the one way secure the goodness only of him that practices it, but let the other way secure also the goodness of his neighbor. Let us see which is the more approved and leads us to the summit of virtue. Surely he, who only seeks his own things, will receive even from Paul endless blame, and when I say from Paul, I mean from Christ, but he who follows the other way wins commendations and crowns. From what is this evident? Hear what His language is to the one, and what He says to the other. "Let no man seek his own, but every man another's wealth." Do you see how he rejects the one, and brings in the other? Again, "Let every one of you please his neighbor for good to edification." Then comes also the praise beyond words with an admonition, "For even Christ pleased not Himself." . . . Fasting then, and lying on the bare ground, and keeping virginity, and a self-denying life, these things bring their advantage to the persons themselves who do them; but those things that pass from ourselves to our neighbors are almsgiving, teaching, charity. . . . let the one fast, and deny himself, and be a martyr,

2 John Chrysostom, —*On Virginity,* —*Against Remarriage,* Sally Rieger Shore, translator, 1983 (New York and Toronto: The Edward Mellen Press), 157 pages.

and be burnt to death, but let another delay his martyrdom for his neighbor's edification; and let him not only delay it, but let him even depart without martyrdom. Who will be more approved after his removal hence? . . . Paul is at hand, giving his judgment, and saying, "To depart and to be with Christ is better, nevertheless to abide in the flesh is more needful for you;" even to his removal unto Christ did he prefer his neighbor's edification. For this is in the highest sense to be with Christ, even to doing His will, but nothing is so much His will, as that which is for one's neighbor's good.[3]

And in another sermon from St. Matthew's Gospel, Chrysostom taught the benefits of both piety and goodness:

And all this I say, not to disparage fasting, God forbid, but rather highly to commend it. But I grieve when other duties being neglected, you think fasting enough for salvation, it having but the last place in the choir of virtue. For the greatest thing is charity, and moderation, and almsgiving; which hits a higher mark even than virginity.[4]

In a homily on Titus also preached while a presbyter at Antioch, Chrysostom instructed:

For he who has learned to give to him that needs, will in time learn not to receive from those who have to give. This makes men like God. Yet virginity, and fasting, and lying on the ground, are more difficult than this, but nothing is so strong and powerful to extinguish the fire of our sins as almsgiving. It is greater than all other virtues. It places the lovers of it by the side of the King Himself, and justly. For the effect of virginity, of fasting, of lying on the ground, is confined to those who practice them, and no other is saved thereby. But almsgiving extends to all, and embraces the members of Christ, and actions that

---

3 John Chrysostom, *The Gospel of St. Matthew*, Homily 77 secs. 5, 6, in *The Nicene and Post-Nicene Fathers,* First Series, vol. 10, pp. 468-469.

4 John Chrysostom, *The Gospel of St. Matthew*, Homily 46, sec. 4, in *The Nicene and Post-Nicene Fathers*, First Series, vol. 10, p. 291.

extend their effects to many are far greater than those which are confined to one.

For almsgiving is the mother of love, of that love, which is the characteristic of Christianity, which is greater than all miracles, by which the disciples of Christ are manifested.[5]

Here in the words of Chrysostom is the insight that a life of self-giving Christian love lived in the world is more approved by the Scriptures than the solitary life of the self-denying ascetic living in the desert or in his monastic cell. Christians may be not of the world, but they are meant to live in the world (John 17:14-18). Chrysostom therefore criticizes the Christian who fleeing the unwholesome life of the city escapes to live an ascetic life in the mountains justifying his action by saying, "lest I perish too and the edge of my goodness be taken off." "Now how much better," says Chrysostom, "were it for you to become less keen, and to gain others, than abiding on high to neglect your perishing brethren?"[6]

Chrysostom spent six years as a monk until his health faltered because of his severe ascetic practices. Later when a presbyter and archbishop, he continued to live an austere and simple style of life. Nonetheless, Chrysostom had great understanding and compassion for those of Christ's people who lived normal lives. During an age when the church allowed only one time of penance for grievous sin during life, Chrysostom taught that Christ's mercy also extended to the relapsing sinner. He allowed for reoccurring penance; only the need for such forgiveness was required.[7]

The Blessing of Marriage and Sex

Although Chrysostom lived a celibate life, he did not disparage marriage as did so many of his contemporaries. His view of sexual life was truly Biblical. To those who would wallow in the wanton pleasures of the theater, Chrysostom said:

You have a wife, you have children; what is equal to this pleasure? You have a house, you have friends, these are the

---

5 John Chrysostom, *Homilies on Titus*, Homily 6, in *The Nicene and Post-Nicene Fathers*, First Series, vol. 13, p. 542.

6 John Chrysostom, *Homilies on First Corinthians*, Homily 6, sec. 8, in *The Nicene and Post-Nicene Fathers*, First Series, vol. 12, pp. 33.

7 Oscar D. Watkins, 1920, *A History of Penance*, vol. 1 (New York: Burt Franklin), pp. 475-476.

true delights: besides their purity, great is the advantage they bestow. For what, I pray you, is sweeter than children? What sweeter than a wife, to him that will be chaste in mind?"[8]

As does the Scriptures, Chrysostom understood that married life was the normal life for men and women. For Chrysostom, "To each man God has assigned a wife, . . ."[9] "For there is nothing that so welds our life together as the love of man and wife."[10] Chrysostom would have Christian love be the mark of marriage. In a beautiful sermon on Paul's description of Christian marriage in Ephesians, Chrysostom counseled husbands, "But the partner of one's life, the mother of one's children, the foundation of one's every joy, one ought never to chain down by fear and menaces, but with love and good temper."[11]

Chrysostom did not condone sexual activity outside of marriage but rather preached, "He who has not learned to commit fornication, will neither know how to commit adultery."[12] Modern sociological studies have shown his insight to be only too true. The divorce rate is significantly higher for those who lived in fornication before marriage.[13] How Chrysostom would have scoffed at the rationalization of many who excuse their fornication by saying that they have to live together before marriage to see if they are sexually compatible. To control the sexual urges of youth, Chrysostom encouraged fathers to see that their sons married early.[14]

Unlike so many theologians of his time who viewed sexual relations in marriage as a necessary evil, Chrysostom in preaching against the

---

8 John Chrysostom, *The Gospel of St. Matthew*, Homily 37, in *The Nicene and Post-Nicene Fathers*, First Series, vol. 10, p. 250.

9 John Chrysostom, *Homilies on Thessalonians*, Homily 5, in *The Nicene and Post-Nicene Fathers*, First Series, vol. 13, p. 345.

10 John Chrysostom, *Homilies on Ephesians*, Homily 20, in *The Nicene and Post-Nicene Fathers*, First Series, vol. 13, p. 143.

11 John Chrysostom, *Homilies on Ephesians*, Homily 20, in *The Nicene and Post-Nicene Fathers*, First Series, vol. 13, p. 144.

12 John Chrysostom, *Homilies on Thessalonians*, Homily 5, in *The Nicene and Post-Nicene Fathers*, First Series, vol. 13, p. 345.

13 *The New York Times*, 7 Dec. 1987, "Ex-Unwed Couples Found More Likely To Have a Divorce."

14 John Chrysostom, *Homilies on Thessalonians*, Homily 5, in *The Nicene and Post-Nicene Fathers*, First Series, vol. 13, pp. 345-346.

widespread prostitution found in the major cities said, "For I neither 'forbid to marry' nor hinder your taking pleasure; but I would have this be done in chastity, not with shame, and reproach, and imputations without end."[15] Chrysostom followed the Scriptures in his view of the marital relationship being the natural outlet of the inherent sexual desire found in humans. He quotes Paul and comments:

> But concerning women he says, "Do not defraud one another, except it be with consent"–and "come together again." And you see him often laying down rules for a lawful intercourse, and he permits the enjoyment of this desire, and allows of a second marriage, and bestows much consideration upon the matter, and never punishes on account of it. But he everywhere condemns him who is fond of money. Concerning wealth also Christ often commanded that we should avoid the corruption of it, but He says nothing about abstaining from a wife."[16]

In this Chrysostom differs from Augustine, who took the same text (1 Corinthians 7:5) and managed laboriously to argue that Paul really meant that married sexual intercourse was still sinful—though only a trivial sin.[17]

Love as the Fulfilling of the Law

Chrysostom taught that the Christian way of life is to be based on the teachings of Jesus and His apostles and not on the law of the Old Testament. In a homily on the Sermon on the Mount, he explains how Jesus in this sermon is introducing a new and higher way of life that His followers are to live. He preached:

> "And here He signifies to us obscurely that the fashion of the whole world is also being changed. Nor did He speak this way without purpose, but in order to arouse the hearer, and indicate, that He was with just cause introducing another

---

15 John Chrysostom, *The Gospel of St. Matthew*, Homily 7, sec. 8, in *The Nicene and Post-Nicene Fathers*, First Series, vol. 10, p. 49.

16 John Chrysostom, *Homilies on Titus*, Homily 5, in *The Nicene and Post-Nicene Fathers*, First Series, vol. 13, p. 536.

17 Augustine, *Enchiridion*, chap. 78, in *The Nicene and Post-Nicene Fathers*, First Series, vol. 3, pp. 262-263.

discipline; . . . and to a higher way of practicing how to live."[18]

The above indicates that Chrysostom understood that Jesus had to teach carefully and somewhat obscurely and ambiguously in the Sermon on the Mount. The Jews would have been highly agitated if they had known the full import of the new way of life that Jesus was introducing. Therefore, Chrysostom points out, "since there seemed to be some suspicion of novelty, He ordered his discourse with reserve."[19] Jesus was setting aside Old Testament civil and ceremonial law and the complex and confusing casuistry that had been built around the interpretation of this law. He was replacing it with the principle of selfless love, a love that extended even to one's enemies in imitation of God the Father who "sends rain on the righteous and the unrighteous" (Matthew 5:45 NASB).

Chrysostom also noted the abundance of confusing law and ethics found in the secular government and among philosophers. He compared this complexity with the way of life that Christ taught in saying:

> But our lessons are not such; rather Christ taught us what is just, and what is seemly, and what is expedient, and all virtue in general, comprising it in few and plain words: at one time saying that, "on two commandments hang the Law and the Prophets;" that is to say, on the love of God and the love of our neighbor: at another time, "Whatsoever you would that men should do to you, do you also to them; for this is the Law and the Prophets."
>
> And these things even to a laborer, and to a servant, and to a widow woman, and to a very child, and to him that appears to be exceedingly slow of understanding, are all plain to comprehend and easy to learn."[20]

Chrysostom thus recognized what Jesus had accomplished. He had taken ethics away from the argumentative and verbose disputations of the legal scholar and the professional ethicist and returned it to the conscience

---

18 John Chrysostom, *The Gospel of St. Matthew*, Homily 16, sec. 4, in *The Nicene and Post-Nicene Fathers*, First Series, vol. 10, p. 106.

19 John Chrsysotom, *The Gospel of St. Matthew*, Homily 16, sec. 5, in *The Nicene and Post-Nicene Fathers*, First Series, vol. 10, p. 106.

20 John Chrysostom, *The Gospel of St. Matthew*, Homily 1, sec. 12, in *The Nicene and Post-Nicene Fathers*, First Series, vol. 10, p. 5.

of the believer. The believer's primary concern need only be to act in self-giving love to his neighbor. Even a man or woman of limited intelligence can understand that he or she is to treat others with the same unselfish and self-denying love that Jesus showed to them. The Christian, being no longer under the Law, is able to walk the way of Christian love for he is empowered and led by the Spirit. Chrysostom wrote in his *Commentary on Galatians*: "For this is the force of the words 'let us walk,' that is, let us be content with the power of the Spirit, and seek no help from the Law."[21]

Chrysostom understood that through living Christ's way of life the moral law of the Old Testament is fulfilled. In a sermon on John 15:11-12, in which he comments on Jesus giving His New Commandment, he cites Paul in writing:

> And, "love is the fulfilling of the Law." (Rom. 13:10.) Which He says also here; for if to abide proceeds from love, and love from the keeping of the commandments, and the commandment is that we love one another, then abiding in God proceeds from love towards each other. And He does not simply speak of love, but declares also the manner, "As I have loved you."[22]

That love would fulfill the mainly negative commands of the Ten Commandments was only the beginning of the Christian life. Chrysostom followed Jesus in emphasizing that the Christian should spend his life not only avoiding evil but also seeking the good of his neighbor. In a sermon on a text from Thessalonians, Chrysostom taught that Christians should not stop at the limit of the commandments, but go beyond them abounding in good works more and more, he sums up—"For virtue is divided into these two things, to decline from evil, and to do good."[23]

Chrysostom argues that the greatest of all Christian gifts is that of Christian love—the love that imitates the selfless love of Christ who gave His life for us. If we are to be imitators of Christ's love, we are to love even those who do us evil, just as did Jesus:

---

21 John Chrysostom, *Commentary on Galatians*, Homily 5, v. 25, in *The Nicene and Post-Nicene Fathers*, First Series, vol. 13, p. 42.

22 John Chrysostom, *Homilies on St. John*, Homily 77, sec. 1, in *The Nicene and Post-Nicene Fathers*, First Series, vol. 14, p. 282.

23 John Chrysostom, *Homilies on Thessalonians*, Homily 5, vv. 1-3, in *The Nicene and Post-Nicene Fathers*, First Series, vol. 13, p. 344.

> For Christ too so loved his enemies, having loved the obstinate,
> the injurious, the blasphemers, them that hated Him, them that
> would not so much as see Him; them that were preferring wood
> and stones to Him, and with the highest love beyond which one
> cannot find another. "For greater love has no man than this," He
> says, "that one lay down his life for his friends."[24]

According to Chrysostom, to love one another means that Christian love should be shown to all persons whether or not they are our Christian brothers and sisters. Even for those considered vile or unprofitable we are to pity and weep—"heretics and Heathen and Jews." He adds, "Herein we shall be like God if we love all men, even our enemies; not, if we work miracles."[25]

Serving Christ through Serving Those in Need

John Chrysostom taught that especially those who are poor or suffering should be aided and enveloped by Christian love. He is passionate in preaching that we are not to inquire whether people are worthy but only respond to their evident need. In homilies based on the Book of Hebrews, he demolishes every rationalization and excuse that people make to avoid helping those in need.[26] I do not think anyone can read his words without a feeling of shame.

Chrysostom first preached in Antioch, Syria and later as archbishop in Constantinople. Both large cities were renowned for their opulent culture and wealthy citizens. On the other hand, the cities also had large under classes composed of the poor and the slaves. Chrysostom was especially uneasy about Christians who lived sumptuous, self-indulgent lives and neglected caring for those less fortunate than themselves. Repeatedly, he reproached the rich for their coldness and indifference toward those in need:

> For I am greatly ashamed, I own, when I see many of the rich
> riding upon their golden-bitted chargers with a train of domestics
> clad in gold, and having couches of silver and other [luxuries]

---

24 John Chrysostom, *The Gospel of St. Matthew*, Homily 61, sec. 3, in *The Nicene and Post-Nicene Fathers*, First Series, vol. 10, p. 375.

25 John Chrysostom, *Homilies on Hebrews*, Homily 3, sec. 11, in *The Nicene and Post-Nicene Fathers*, First Series, vol. 14, p. 381.

26 John Chrysostom, *Homilies on Hebrews*, Homily 10, secs. 7-9; Homily 11, secs. 7-10, in *The Nicene and Post-Nicene Fathers*, First Series, vol. 14, pp. 416-417, 421-422.

and more pomp, and yet when there is need to give to a poor man, becoming more beggarly than the very poorest.[27]

He excoriates those who furnish their table with gold and silver; and who even have chamber pots of silver, and yet are "unable to give relief to even one poor person."[28] His unvarnished words about the selfishness and self-indulgence of many of the rich were deeply resented.

Nor is Chrysostom impressed by those who give large but really only token gifts when compared with their wealth:

> But why do I trifle in saying these things to men who do not even choose to disregard riches, but hold fast to them as though they were immortal? And if they give a little out of much, think they have done all. This is not almsgiving. For almsgiving is that of the widow (Mark 12:41-44) who emptied out "all her living." But if you do not go on to contribute so much as the widow, yet at least contribute the whole of your superfluity: keep what is sufficient, not what is superfluous.[29]

How different is Chrysostom's view of giving compared to even the most eminent of the previous pagan Roman society. The great Roman statesman Cicero (106-43 B.C.) advocated aiding those in need. He cautioned, however, that self-denial or giving when it might reduce one's own standard of living was going too far:

> The good man is to perform even to a stranger all the service that he can, and to harm no one even when provoked by injustice; but the helping whom he can is to be limited by this, that he shall not himself suffer injury thereby.[30]

---

27 John Chrysostom, *Homilies on First Corinthians*, Homily 21, sec. 10, in *The Nicene and Post-Nicene Fathers*, First Series, vol. 12, p. 124.

28 John Chrysostom, *Homilies on Colossians*, Homily 7, in *The Nicene and Post-Nicene Fathers*, First Series, vol. 13, p. 292-293.

29 John Chrysostom, *Homilies on Hebrews*, Homily 28, sec. 9, in *The Nicene and Post-Nicene Fathers*, First Series, vol. 14, p. 495.

30 Gerhard Uhlhorn, 1879, *The Conflict of Christianity with Heathenism* (New York: Charles Scribner's Sons), p. 193.

Sacrificial giving as taught by Christianity was not a virtue in Roman times.

To those who exploited the poor and yet made a show of philanthropy, Chrysostom preached:

> For to this intent you have wealth, to relieve poverty, not to make a gain of poverty; but you with a show of relief [for the poor] make the calamity greater, and sell benevolence for money.[31]

It is obvious that it is not only in our own time that there are robber barons that become wealthy by exploiting their fellowman and then buy back their reputations by making a show of philanthropy.

Although Chrysostom was preaching in the cathedral in Antioch, he exclaimed against those who would bedeck the altar with gold and silver and expensive hangings and yet neglect the poor. Keeping in mind Jesus' words, "inasmuch as you did not do it to one of the least of these, you did not it to Me" (Matthew 25:45 NKJV), Chrysostom preached:

> Would you do honor to Christ's body? Neglect Him not when naked; do not, while here you honor Him with silken garments, neglect Him perishing without of cold and nakedness. . . . Even so honor Him with this honor, which He ordained, spending your wealth on poor people. Since God has no need at all of golden vessels, but of golden souls. . . . For what is the profit, when His table indeed is full of golden cups, but He perishes of hunger? First fill Him, being hungry, and then abundantly deck out His table also. Do you make Him a cup of gold, while you do not give Him a cup of cold water? What is the profit? Do you furnish His table with cloths bespangled with gold, while to Himself you do not afford even the necessary covering? And what good comes of it? For tell me, should you see one at a loss for necessary food, and omit appeasing his hunger, while you first overlaid his table with silver; would he indeed thank you, and not rather be indignant? What, again, if seeing one wrapped in rags, and stiff with cold, you should neglect giving him a garment, and build golden columns, and say, "you were doing it in his honor." would he not say that you were mocking, and account it an insult, and that the most extreme? . . . Do not therefore while adorning His

---

31 John Chrysostom, *The Gospel of St. Matthew*, Homily 56, sec. 9, in *The Nicene and Post-Nicene Fathers*, First Series, vol. 10, p. 350.

house overlook your brother in distress, for he is more properly a temple than the other.[32]

The piety of the clergy and wealthy laymen displayed in their love of taking part in glorious and grandiose liturgies and worship services performed in richly ornamented temples cut no ice with Chrysostom either in Antioch or later when he was archbishop of Constantinople. He understood only too well what was the service of love which his Lord asked of His followers.

Righteousness before God Is Through Faith Not Works

With all his stress on living a life of Christian love expressed in serving the needs of one's fellowman, Chrysostom remains careful in his evaluation of good works done in love. A man does not become righteous before God because of his good works; his righteousness comes from faith in Christ, a faith that is a gift of God. In a sermon on Philippians, he summed up this righteousness as being:

> That (righteousness) which is from the faith of God, that is, it too is given by God. This is the righteousness of God; this is altogether a gift. And the gifts of God far exceed those worthless good deeds, which are due to our own diligence."[33]

But although the Christian's good works are truly worthless when it comes to his salvation, Chrysostom sees them intimately tied up with the Christian's faith in Christ. After emphasizing that a Christian is saved only by his faith which is a gift given to him by the grace of God, Chrysostom then stresses that a life of good works is to follow from faith. In a homily on Ephesians 2, Chrysostom explained:

> But no one, he [Paul] says, is justified by works, in order that the grace and loving-kindness of God may be shown. He did not reject us as having works, but as abandoned of works He has saved us by grace; so that no man henceforth may have whereof to boast. And then, lest when you hear that the whole work is accomplished not of works but by faith, and you would become

---

32 John Chrysostom, *The Gospel of St. Matthew*, Homily 50, secs. 4, 5, in *The Nicene and Post-Nicene Fathers*, First Series, vol. 10, p. 313.

33 John Chrysostom, *Homilies on Philippians*, Homily 11, in *The Nicene and Post-Nicene Fathers*, First Series, vol. 13, p. 235.

idle, observe how he continues, "For we are His workmanship, created in Christ Jesus for good works, which God before prepared that we should walk in them."[34]

Along with James, Chrysostom knew that a faith without good works is not a true faith. The Christian's work is the care of his neighbor:

> Again, if we do all things ever so rightly, and yet do our neighbor no service, neither in that case shall we enter the kingdom. From where is this evident? From the parable of the servants entrusted with the talents [Matthew 25:14-30]. For, in that instance, the man's virtue was in every point unimpaired, and there had been nothing lacking, but forasmuch he was slothful in his business, he was rightly cast out.[35]

It is obvious that Chrysostom was aware that the parable of the talents was followed immediately by Jesus' vision of the Last Judgment in which Jesus said, "Then they themselves also will answer, saying, 'Lord, when did we see You hungry, or thirsty, or a stranger, or naked, or sick, or in prison, and did not take care of you?' Then He will answer them, saying, 'Truly I say to you, to the extent that you did not do it to one of the least of these, you did not do it to Me.' And these will go away into eternal punishment, but the righteous into eternal life" (Matthew 25:44-46 NASB).

The Primacy of Christian Love

The love of which Chrysostom speaks is seen as based both on the old commandment from Leviticus of loving our neighbor as ourselves and on Jesus' new commandment of loving one another as He loved us. In a homily on First John, Chrysostom explains the relationship in saying:

> But how does He call that a new commandment which is contained also in the Old Testament? He made it new Himself by the manner in which they were to love; therefore He added, "As I have loved you." "I have not paid back to you a debt of good

---

34 John Chrysostom, *Homilies on Ephesians*, Homily 4, vv. 8-10, in *The Nicene and Post-Nicene Fathers*, First Series, vol. 13, p. 68.

35 John Chrysostom. *Homilies on Ephesians*, Homily 4, in *The Nicene and Post-Nicene Fathers*, First Series, vol. 13, p. 68.

deeds first done by you, but I Myself began," He says. "And so ought you to benefit your dearest ones, though you owe them nothing"; and omitting to speak of the miracles which they should do, He makes their characteristic, love. And why? Because it is this which chiefly shows men holy; it is the foundation of all virtue; by this mostly we are all even saved. For "this" He says, "is to be a disciple; so shall all men praise you, when they see you imitating My Love."[36]

In a homily, Chrysostom commented on Paul's paraphrase of Christ's New Commandment in Ephesians. Paul had written: "Therefore be imitators of God, as beloved children; and walk in love, just as Christ also loved you, and gave Himself up for us, an offering and a sacrifice to God as a fragrant aroma" (Ephesians 5:1-2 NASB). Chrysostom explained the passage by pointing out that Christ voluntarily gave Himself up for us out of love, not because of compulsion. He then counseled his hearers:

As your Master loved you, love also your friend. . . . "as beloved children," he says. You have yet another cogent reason to imitate Him, not only in that you have received such good at His hands, but also in that you are called His children. And since not all children imitate their fathers, but those which are beloved, therefore he says, "as beloved children." "Walk in love." Behold, here is the groundwork of all.[37]

The cardinal guideline, therefore, for living the Christian life of selfless service is a Christian love lived in imitation of Christ's love for us, for as Chrysostom states, "For nothing is good which is not done through love."[38] In a sermon on Paul's letter to the Galatians, Chrysostom points out that we are to examine our motivations so that non-worthy motivations do not creep in:

Here he [Paul] shows that we ought to be scrutinizers of our

---

36 John Chrysostom, *Homilies on St. John*, Homily 72, sec. 5, in *The Nicene and Post-Nicene Fathers*, First Series, vol. 14, p. 266.

37 John Chrysostom, *Homilies on Ephesians*, Homily 17, in *The Nicene and Post-Nicene Fathers*, First Series, vol. 13, p. 129.

38 John Chrysostom, *Homilies on Hebrews*, Homily 19, sec. 3, in *The Nicene and Post-Nicene Fathers*, First Series, vol. 14, p. 456.

lives, and this not lightly, but carefully to weigh our action; as for example, if you have performed a good deed, consider whether it was not from vainglory, or through necessity, or malevolence, or with hypocrisy, or from some other human motive.[39]

Only those actions which flow from Christian love have value in God's eyes. Nonetheless, Chrysostom also taught that working for a heavenly reward might also be a motivation for some Christians.[40] In this instance, Augustine has a better understanding of reward as shall be seen later in this chapter.

Christian Freedom

Chrysostom counsels that Christians are to lead a quiet and moderate life. A life in which the simpler pleasures and gifts of God such as family, friends, holy places, and natural beauty as found in flowing rivers, lakes, the loveliness of gardens, and even the singing of grasshoppers are enjoyed.[41] He is not a bluenose who would deny all enjoyment. To those who would condemn drinking wine because it may lead to excesses such as drunkenness and immoral behavior, Chrysostom remains Biblically sound in preaching:

When other men sin, do you find fault with God's gifts? . . . Wine was given, that we might be cheerful, not that we might behave ourselves unseemly; that we might laugh, not that we might be a laughing stock; that we might be healthful, not that we might be diseased; that we might correct the weakness of our body, not cast down the might of our soul. God honored you with the gift, why disgrace yourself with the excess thereof. . . . For wine was given for gladness, "Yes, wine," so it is said, "makes glad the heart of man." But you mar even this excellence in it.[42]

---

39 John Chrysostom, *Commentary of Galatians*, chap. 6, v. 3, in *The Nicene and Post-Nicene Fathers*, First Series, vol. 13, p. 44.

40 John Chrysostom, *Homilies on St. John*, Homily 25, sec. 3, in *The Nicene and Post-Nicene Fathers*, First Series, vol. 14, p. 89.

41 John Chrysostom, *The Gospel of St. Matthew*, Homily 37, sec. 9. in *The Nicene and Post-Nicene Fathers*, First Series, vol. 10, p. 250.

42 John Chrysostom, *The Gospel of St. Matthew*, Homily 57, sec. 5, in *The Nicene and Post-Nicene Fathers*, First Series, vol. 10, p. 356-357.

Chrysostom would not allow the legalistic and moralistic judgments of humans to impinge upon Christian freedom by ruling out what the Bible in Psalm 104:14-15 calls a gift of God to humankind.

That the Christian has freedom to make his own moral choices based on Christian love is an insight of Chrysostom's. In a commentary on Paul's letter to the Galatians, he writes:

> Christ has delivered us, he says, from the yoke of bondage, He has left us free to act as we will, not that we may use our liberty for evil, but that we may have ground for receiving a higher reward, advancing to a higher philosophy. . . . Thus Paul says that Christ has removed the yoke from you, not that you may prance and kick, but that though without the yoke you may proceed at a well-measured pace. And next he shows the mode whereby this may be readily effected; and what is this mode? He says "But through love be servants one to another."[43]

The Slave as Our Christian Brother

In contrast to the dominant culture, Chrysostom extended the love of God to the numerous slaves at that time. To those Christians who mistreated their slaves, and especially female slaves, Chrysostom urged them to rather treat their slaves with thoughtful concern and Christian love. To those who protested, "What am I to be her keeper? How absurd!" Chrysostom rejoined, "And why are you not to be her keeper? Has she not the same kind of soul as yourself? Has she not been promised the same privileges by God? Does she not partake of the same [communion] table? Does she not share with you the same high birth?"[44] These were astonishing words to be heard in a culture in which a slave suffered under much more severe laws than non-slaves. Concerning such laws in a homily on Ephesians, Chrysostom preached:

> Think not, he [God] would say, that what is done towards a slave, He will therefore forgive, because done to a slave. Heathen laws indeed, as being the laws of men, recognize a

---

43 John Chrysostom, *Commentary of Galatians*, chap. 5, verse 13, in *The Nicene and Post-Nicene Fathers*, First Series, vol. 13, pp. 39-40.

44 John Chrysostom, *Homilies on Ephesians*, Homily 15, in *The Nicene and Post-Nicene Fathers*, First Series, vol. 13, p. 124.

difference between these kinds of offenses. But the law of the common Lord and Master of all, as doing good to all alike, and dispensing the same rights to all, knows no such difference.[45]

Because of such views of slavery, it is evident why the conditions of the slaves ameliorated as time passed. Chrysostom remained faithful to Paul's words: "There is neither Jew nor Greek, there is neither slave nor free, there is neither male nor female, for you are one in Christ Jesus" (Galatians 3:28).

Christianity: Faith and Love

Chrysostom looks back to an earlier period of Christianity and sees a time when a people whose lives were lived in accordance with their faith influenced the growth of the Church. He suggests in a homily on First Corinthians, "And if the same were done now, we would convert the whole world, even without miracles." He decries how Christianity has degenerated among so many in his own day. He sees a love of luxury, comfort, ease, and careless virtue replacing a life of Christian service and good works.[46]

Chrysostom understood the true nature of Christianity. He followed Paul who wrote: "So faith, hope, love abide, these three, but the greatest of these is love" (1 Corinthians 13:13 RSV). Chrysostom summed up his view of Christianity in saying:

There are many things characteristic of Christianity: but more than all, and better than all, Love towards one another, and Peace. Therefore Christ also says, "My peace I give unto you." (John 14:27) And again, "By this shall all men know that ye are my disciples, if ye love one another." (John 13:35)[47]

A life of Christian love is a most powerful testimony to the truth of Christianity according to Chrysostom. Christians are to let the light of their good works shine forth before men to the glory of God (Matthew 5:16):

---

45 John Chrysostom, *Homilies on Ephesians*, Homily 22, verse 9, in *The Nicene and Post-Nicene Fathers*, First Series, vol. 13, p. 159.

46 John Chrysostom, *Homilies on First Corinthians*, Homily 6, sec. 8, in *The Nicene and Post-Nicene Fathers*, First Series, vol. 12, pp. 32-33.

47 John Chrysostom, *Homilies on Hebrews*, Homily 31, sec. 1, in *The Nicene and Post-Nicene Fathers*, First Series, vol. 14, p. 506.

There were no need of words, if we so shone forth in our lives, there were no need of Teachers, did we but exhibit works. There would be no Heathen, if we were such Christians as we ought to be. If we kept the commandments of Christ, if we suffered injury, if we allowed advantage to be taken of us, if being reviled we blessed, if being ill-treated we did good (1 Corinthians 4:12); if this were the general practice among us, no one would be so brutal as not to become a convert to Godliness.[48]

In his preaching Chrysostom calls all Christians to live Christ's way of life. He exhorted his congregation:

Let us show forth then a new kind of life. Let us make earth, heaven; let us hereby show the Greeks, of what a great blessing they are deprived. For when they behold in us good behavior, they will look upon the very face of the kingdom of heaven. Yes, when they see us gentle, pure from wrath, from evil desire, from envy, from covetousness, rightly fulfilling all our other duties, they will say, "If the Christians are become angels here, what will they be after their departure thence?" . . . I say nothing burdensome. I say not, do not marry. I say not, forsake cities, and withdraw yourself from public affairs; but by being engaged in them, show virtue. Yes, and such as are busy in the midst of cities, I would rather have more approved than such as have occupied mountains [the monks and hermits]. Why? Because great is the profit thence arising. "For no man lights a candle and sets it under a bushel." . . . And tell me not, "I have a wife, and children belonging to me, and am master of a household, and cannot practice all this." . . . For there is but one thing that is wanted, the preparation of a generous mind; and neither age, nor poverty, nor wealth, nor reverse of fortune, nor anything else, will be able to impede you. Since in fact both old and young, and men having wives, and bringing up children, and working at crafts, and serving as soldiers, have duly performed all that is enjoined. For so Daniel was young, and Joseph a slave, and Aquila worked at a craft, and the woman who sold purple was over a workshop, and another was a keeper of a

---

48 John Chrysostom, *Homilies on Timothy*, Homily 10, in *The Nicene and Post-Nicene Fathers*, First Series, vol. 13, p. 440.

prison, and another a centurion, as Cornelius; and another in ill health, as Timothy; and another a runaway, as Onesimus; but nothing proved an hindrance to any of these, but all were approved, both men and women, both young and old, both slaves and free, both soldiers and people.[49]

Chrysostom was more than a great preacher. He was a true reformer and renewer of the Church. Without fear or favor he preached the way of life that Jesus and His apostles taught. By his life, he showed there need not be a difference between piety and goodness. The common people recognized the truth of his words. When the rich and powerful who took offense at his preaching forced him from his archbishopric into exile, the common people compelled his return.

Those in the church, however, who had reached an easy accommodation with their Christianity—the opulent and wealthy among the laity; the lovers of luxury, power, and prestige among the clergy; and those who enjoyed the luxuriousness of life in the Emperor's court—could not abide Chrysostom's attempt to bring back the Christian way of life. Once more he was sent into exile as a result of the scheming between the Emperor's court and the clergy. This time he was persecuted to his death, dying while forced by a guard of soldiers to travel to one more place of exile, a remote village high in the Caucasus Mountains.

John Chrysostom paid the price usually exacted from earnest and fearless reformers of a corrupted Christendom. He suffered the martyrdom visited upon reformers such as Savonarola, John Hus, William Tyndale, and narrowly escaped by such as Wycliffe and Luther. Chrysostom is too often viewed only as a golden-mouthed orator. What was golden about his mouth was his fearless and faithful teaching of the true way of life taught by Christ and His apostles.

Augustine, Bishop of Hippo, N. Africa (354-430)

Love, the Basis of Christianity

Augustine, as did Chrysostom, saw love as the very core of Christianity—God's love for humans, our love for God and our neighbor. Unfortunately, his scanty knowledge of Greek, the original language of the New Testament, hindered his struggle to more fully understand the nature of

---

49 John Chrysostom, *The Gospel of St. Matthew*, Homily 43, sec. 7, in *The Nicene and Post-Nicene Fathers*, First Series, vol. 10, pp. 277-278.

love taught by the New Testament. In his *Confessions,* he states that during his boyhood he loved Latin but heartily disliked the study of the Greek language and literature.[50] In his work with the New Testament, he therefore used Latin translations of the Greek text.

The problem that results from his reliance on a Latin translation rather than the Greek original is seen in his discussion of Jesus' dialogue with Peter on the shores of the Sea of Galilee after Jesus' resurrection (John 21:15-18). Augustine does a word study on the different words for love in the dialogue. He struggles with the Latin words for love that were used to translate the Greek. He attempts to bolster his argument by citing a Latin word used to translate both a Hebrew word for love from the Psalms as well as a Greek word for love in John's Gospel, a rather questionable exercise.[51] Augustine's quest to understand accurately the concept of Christian love, *agape*, as found in the New Testament was obviously hindered by his dependence on Latin translations that often poorly translated the Greek verb *agapao*. Nonetheless, Augustine achieved a remarkable understanding of the nature of Christian love. The term he often used for his understanding of Christian love was "Charity," in Latin, *Caritas*.

Scripture: The Primary Authority

As did Chrysostom, Augustine had a high regard for the authority of Scriptures. Before coming to the Christian faith, Augustine achieved a broad education in the literature and philosophies of his time. He also was well-acquainted with the writings of the earlier church fathers. It is to Scripture, however, that he accords preeminence. In a letter to Jerome, Augustine wrote:

> For I confess to your Charity [Jerome] that I have learned to yield this respect and honor only to the canonical books of Scripture: of these alone do I most firmly believe that the authors were completely free from error. And if in these writings I am perplexed by anything which appears to me opposed to truth, I do not hesitate to suppose that either the manuscript is faulty, or the translator has not caught the meaning of what was said, or I myself have failed to understand it. As to all other

---

50 Augustine, *The Confessions*, bk. 1, chap. 13, in *The Nicene and Post-Nicene Fathers*, First Series, vol. 1, p. 51.

51 Augustine, *The City of God*, bk. 14, chap. 7, in *The Nicene and Post-Nicene Fathers*, First Series, vol. 2, p. 266.

writings, in reading them, however great the superiority of the authors to myself in sanctity and learning, I do not accept their teaching as true on the mere ground of the opinion being held by them; but only because they have succeeded in convincing my judgment of its truth either by means of these canonical writings themselves, or by arguments addressed to my reason.[52]

In another context Augustine wrote, "But we wished to show that the Scriptures of our religion, whose authority we prefer to all writings whatsoever, make no distinction . . . ."[53] Augustine places the authority and teachings of the writings of earlier church fathers markedly subservient and subordinate to that of the authority of the Old and New Testament Scriptures. Thus, he placed the oral tradition of the church that came to be written as time passed as inferior in authority to the Bible.

Augustine also saw that those who would substitute their own opinions and ideas for the inspired teachings of Scripture resented the authority of the Bible. They were people who felt impelled to attack the authority and integrity of the Bible, for they knew that the authoritative revelation of God as found in the Scriptures eventually would prove their undoing. They defended their own theological novelties by attempting to undermine the integrity of the Scriptures. Augustine contended with those who attempted to discredit the authority of the New Testament. How modern sound the attacks upon Scripture against which Augustine protested. He wrote in 388 A.D. to the Manichaean heretics:

> But it is folly to discuss passages of Scripture with you; for you both mislead people by promising to prove your doctrines, and those books which possess authority to demand our homage you affirm to be corrupted by spurious interpolations.[54]

In an argument around the year 400 with the heretic Faustus, Augustine protests:

---

52 Augustine, *Letter 82*, sec. 3, in *The Nicene and Post-Nicene Fathers*, First Series, vol. 1, p. 350, see also p. 358.

53 Augustine, *The City of God*, bk. 14, chap. 7, in *The Nicene and Post-Nicene Fathers*, First Series, vol. 2, p. 266.

54 Augustine, *On the Morals of the Manichaeans*, chap. 14, sec. 35, in *The Nicene and Post-Nicene Fathers*, First Series, vol. 4, p. 79.

But in your inability to find a reason for not receiving what is written in the New Testament, you are obliged, as a last resource, to pretend that the passages are not genuine. This is the last gasp of a heretic in the clutches of truth; or rather it is the breath of corruption itself.

You are so hardened in your errors against the testimonies of Scripture, that nothing can be made of you; for whenever anything is quoted against you, you have the boldness to say that it is written not by the apostle, but by some pretender under his name.[55]

There is indeed nothing new under the sun. It is amusing to see that the types of attacks against the trustworthiness of the New Testament 1600 years ago are essentially the same as those by liberal Biblical "scholars" today, who, as did Augustine's opponents, maintain:

Somebody at a later time added (interpolated) words into the Biblical text for their own doctrinal reasons.

Jesus really did not say these words; somebody in the church later put them into his mouth.

St. Paul could not have written Ephesians, Titus, etc.; somebody for doctrinal reasons wrote them later and attached St. Paul's name to the letters.

Many of the liberal Biblical scholars today may exhibit more sophistication and subtilty in their pretensions, but under the guise of academic objectivity the purpose is the same: an attempt to destroy the authority of the New Testament by attacking its integrity. If you want to be accepted by this group and be published by the academic media they largely control, you must subscribe wholeheartedly to their dictum that no book in the New Testament could possibly be written by the writer ascribed to it by the early Church, except a few of Paul's letters.[56] Sadly, many such

---

55 Augustine, *Reply to Faustus the Manichaean*, bk. 11, sec. 2 and bk. 33, sec. 6, in *The Nicene and Post-Nicene Fathers*, First Series, vol. 4, pp. 177, 343.

56 For a good example of such literature, try reading the acclaimed *From Jesus to Chrisianity: How Four Generations of Visionaries & Storytellers Created the New Testament and the Christian Faith,* by Univ. of Texas, Austin, professor L. Michael White, 2004, 508 pages. If you have had any scientific

"scholars" and their faddish followers are found in denominational seminaries as well as in university schools of religion or theology. Certainly, there were forgeries as was noted earlier in the discussion of the apocryphal gospels. The early Christians, however, had relatively little difficulty in distinguishing the authentic from the false and spurious. After all, they had first hand knowledge as either disciples of the apostles, or, for example, in the case of Irenaeus (130?-202?), as a disciple of a disciple of an apostle. The oral tradition and memory of the Church in the earliest years of Christianity was alive and well.

Love as the Fulfilling of the Law

Augustine was greatly influenced in his theology by Ambrose, the virile, bluff bishop of Milan. The fame of Ambrose as a preacher drew Augustine to the Milan cathedral. Later Augustine was baptized by Ambrose. Ambrose's life was marked by great generosity. Upon becoming bishop, he gave all that he had to the poor, setting aside only what was necessary for the maintenance of his sister. During a time when an invading army occupied Milan, Bishop Ambrose melted down the gold and silver vessels of the cathedral and sold the metals for the relief of the suffering populace. His writings urge generous giving flowing from true Christian love to those in need. He also counsels on how this giving might be done wisely. Ambrose may have had his legalistic and censorious tendencies, but Augustine was undoubtedly influenced by such of Ambrose's teaching as:

> Kindness to exist in perfection must consist of these two qualities. It is not enough just to wish well; we must also do well. Nor, again, is it enough to do well, unless this springs from a good source, even from a good will. "For God loves a cheerful giver."[57]

Ambrose is an excellent example of a Christian who united in a holy life both a sincere piety and a life of goodness.

Augustine saw the new way of life of the New Testament prefigured in the Old. In his commentary on Psalm 96 concerning the first

---

training in mentally assigning levels of probability to weakly supported arguments and speculations, and to speculations built on speculations, you will have as much trouble finishing the book without dismay as did I.

57 Ambrose, *Duties of the Clergy, Book 1* chap. 30, par. 143, in *The Nicene and Post-Nicene Fathers*, Second Series, vol. 10, pp. 24, 25.

verse, "O sing to the Lord a new song; sing to the Lord, all the earth!" he wrote, "Hear why it is a new song: The Lord says, 'A new commandment I give unto you, that you love one another.' The whole earth then sings a new song; there the house of God is built."[58]

Augustine viewed the New Testament as fulfilling the prophecy found in Jeremiah 31:31-34 concerning the new covenant that God would make with His people, and that He would write the law upon their hearts. Concerning what Jesus taught about love and how this love fulfills the Old Testament law, Augustine in his *On the Spirit and the Letter* explains:

> What then is God's law written by God Himself in the hearts of men, but the very presence of the Holy Spirit, who is "the finger of God," and by whose presence is shed abroad in our hearts the love which is the fulfilling of the law, and the end of the commandment?[59]

Augustine in *On Grace and Free Will* follows Paul in seeing Christian love as the fulfilling of the moral commandments of the Old Testament. Paul cites Jesus' use of Leviticus 19:18, "You shall love your neighbor as yourself," in writing of love fulfilling the law (Romans 13:8-10). Augustine uses both Christ's New Commandment as well as the Leviticus reference in referring to love fulfilling the law.[60] And at times he uses only the New Commandment as in the following example from *On Baptism, Against the Donatists*:

> But who are true Christians, save those of whom the same Lord said, "He that has my commandments, and keeps them, he it is that loves me?" But what is it to keep His commandments, except to abide in love? Whence also He says, "A new commandment I give unto you, that you love one another;" and again, "By this shall all men know that you are my disciples, if you have love for one another." . . . For He came not to destroy

---

58 Augustine, *On the Psalms*, Psalm 96, sec. 2, in *The Nicene and Post-Nicene Fathers*, First Series, vol. 8, p. 470.

59 Augustine, *On the Spirit and the Letter*, chaps. 29, 33-36, in *The Nicene and Post-Nicene Fathers*, First Series, vol. 5, pp. 95, 97-99.

60 Augustine, *On Grace and Free Will*, chap. 33, in *The Nicene and Post-Nicene Fathers*, First Series, vol. 5, pp. 457-458.

the law, but to fulfill. But the fulfilling of the law is love.[61]

In keeping with the majority of the fathers of the Church, Augustine believed that only the moral law, the Ten Commandments, remained of the codes of Old Testament law. The great number of other civil and ceremonial laws found in the Old Testament he viewed as having meaning only for the times before the coming of Christ.[62]

The Influence of St. John and the New Commandment upon Augustine

It was Augustine's study of the writings of John, and especially of his letters, that brought him to realize the primacy of Christian love and Jesus' New Commandment in a Christian's life. In his treatise *On Grace and Free Will*, he sums up John's teaching in writing:

> So also the Apostle John says, "He that loves his brother abides in the light;" again, in another passage, "Whosoever does not righteousness is not of God, neither he that loves not his brother; for this is the message which we have heard from the beginning, that we should love one another." Then he says again, "This is His commandment, that we should believe on the name of His Son Jesus Christ, and love one another." Once more: "And this commandment have we from Him, that he who loves God love his brother also." Then shortly afterwards he adds, "By this we know that we love the children of God, when we love God, and keep His commandments; for this is the love of God, that we keep His commandments: and His commandments are not grievous." While, in his second Epistle, it is written, "Not as though I wrote a new commandment unto you, but that which we had from the beginning, that we love one another."[63]

---

61 Augustine, *On Baptism, Against the Donatist*, bk. 3, sec. 26, in *The Nicene and Post-Nicene Fathers*, First Series, vol. 4, pp. 444-445. See also *Reply to Faustus the Manichaean*, bk. 17, sec. 6, ibid., Vol. 4, p. 236, 250.

62 Augustine, *Reply to Faustus the Manichaean*, bk. 10, sec. 2, in *The Nicene and Post-Nicene Fathers*, First Series, vol. 4, p. 177.

63 Augustine, *On Grace and Free Will*, chap. 35, in *The Nicene and Post-Nicene Fathers*, First Series, vol. 5, p. 459.

Augustine explains to what degree we should love one another in his homily on Jesus' giving the New Commandment as recorded in the Gospel of John:

> The Lord, beloved brethren, has defined that fullness of love which we ought to bear to one another, when He said: "Greater love has no man than this, that a man lay down his life for his friends." Inasmuch, then, as He had said before, "This is my commandment, that you love one another, as I have loved you;" and appended to these words what you have been just hearing, "Greater love has no man than this, that a man lay down his life for his friends;" there follows from this as a consequence, what this same Evangelist John says in his epistle, "That as Christ laid down His life for us, even so we also ought to lay down our lives for the brethren;" loving one another in truth, as He has loved us, who laid down His life for us.[64]

Many church bodies today make the Ten Commandments their main focus as they attempt to teach Christian ethics. Therefore, many present-day Christians have the Ten Commandments so ingrained in them that whenever they see the word "commandment" in the New Testament they immediately think it refers to the Ten Commandments. Augustine obviously also recognized the problem that Christians had in this regard. In his homilies on the First letter of St. John, he repeatedly emphasizes that when John speaks of commandments, he means the New Commandment. In regard to 1 John 2:3-5, Augustine preached:

> "And in this," says he [St. John], "we do know Him, if we keep His commandments."
> What commandments?
> "He that says, I know him, and keeps not His commandments, is a liar, and the truth is not in him."
> But still you ask, What commandments?
> "But whoso," says he, "keeps His word, in him truly is the love of God perfected."
> Let us see whether this same commandment is not called love. For we were asking, what commandments? And he says, "But

---

64 Augustine, *On the Gospel of John*, Tractate 84, sec. 1, in *The Nicene and Post-Nicene Fathers*, First Series, vol. 7, p. 349.

whoso keeps His word, in him truly is the love of God perfected."
Mark the Gospel [John 13:34], whether this is not the
commandment: "A new commandment," says the Lord, "give I
unto you, that you love one another.–In this we know that we are
in Him, if in Him we be perfected." Perfected in love, he calls
them: what is the perfection of love? To love even enemies, and
love them for this end, that they may be brethren.[65]

Augustine became impatient with those who would not recognize
that when John in his letter writes of commandments he means the New
Commandment. Vexed with the denseness of his congregation concerning 1
John 3:21-22, Augustine chides:

"What are 'His commandments'? Must we be always repeating?
'A new commandment give I unto you, that you love one
another!'"[66]

For Augustine the New Commandment extends not only to one's
fellow Christians but also to all people, even one's enemies. Augustine
reasoned that as we are to love our enemies, it follows that our fervent wish
for them is that they also might enjoy the gift of eternal life. If we do not
wish this boon for them, then we can hardly be said to love our enemies.
Thus, we love all, for they are all potential brothers. Augustine preached,
"We say that God loved sinners: for he [Jesus] says, 'They that are whole
need not the Physician, but they that are sick.' Did He love us sinners to the
end we should still remain sinners?" Augustine is insistent upon his hearers
viewing all men as does God:

Show mercy then, as men of merciful hearts; because in loving
enemies also, you also love brethren. Think not that John has
given no precept concerning love of our enemy, because he has
not ceased to speak of brotherly love. . . . And let no man say
that John the apostle has admonished us somewhat less, and
the Lord Christ somewhat more. John has admonished us to
love the brethren; Christ has admonished us to love even

---

65 Augustine, *Ten Homilies on the First Epistle of John*, Homily 1, sec. 9, in *The Nicene and Post-Nicene Fathers*, First Series, vol. 7, p. 465. See also pp. 497, 519, 521, 522-523.

66 Augustine, *Ten Homilies on the First Epistle of John*, Homily 6, sec. 4, in *The Nicene and Post-Nicene Fathers*, First Series, vol. 7, p. 495.

enemies. Mark to what end Christ has bidden you to love your enemies. That they may always remain enemies? If He asked it for this end, that they should remain enemies, you would be hating, not loving. Mark how He Himself loved, for example, because He would not have them still be the persecutors they were, He said, "Father, forgive them, for they know not what they do." Whom He willed to be forgiven, them He willed to be changed: whom He willed to be changed, of enemies He deigned to make brethren, and did in truth make them so.[67]

In his epistle, John states that he is writing no new commandment but the old commandment which they had from the beginning and yet, on the other hand, he is writing a new commandment (1 John 2:7-8). Augustine explains in a homily that John in speaking of the old commandment is actually referring to the New Commandment that Jesus gave around sixty years previously. John is making clear that the emphasis on Christian love in his epistle is not a novelty but is based on the New Commandment given so many decades before.[68]

Acts of Love, Not Just Avoidance of Evil, Make Up Christian Life

As did Chrysostom, Augustine in his homilies urges his hearers to do good works. He is especially concerned that those who have an abundance beyond their needs share their surplus with those who lack what is necessary.[69] In keeping with Christ, he preaches that we are to transfer our treasures in this life to the treasuries of heaven by giving to those in need. In a homily based on Christ's Sermon on the Mount in which Jesus exhorts his hearers to store up their treasure in heaven where neither moth nor rust consumes and thieves do not break in and steal, Augustine urges:

> If our possessions are to be carried away, let us transfer them to a place where we shall not lose them. The poor to whom we give alms! With regard to us, what else are they but porters through

---

67 Augustine, *Ten Homilies on the First Epistle of John*, Homily 8, sec. 10, in *The Nicene and Post-Nicene Fathers*, First Series, vol. 7, pp. 510-511. See also p. 524.

68 Augustine, *Ten Homilies on the First Epistle of John*, Homily 1, sec. 10, in *The Nicene and Post-Nicene Fathers*, First Series, vol. 7, pp. 465-466.

69 Augustine, *Sermons on New Testament Lessons*, Sermons 10, 11, 35, 36, in *The Nicene and Post-Nicene Fathers*, First Series, vol. 6, pp. 290-298, 366-373.

whom we transfer our goods from earth to heaven? Give away your treasure. Give it to a porter. He will bear to heaven what you give him on earth. But you will say to me:" How does he bear it to heaven, for I see that he consumes it by eating?" Certainly, he eats it. It is by eating it, and not keeping it, that he bears it to heaven. Have you forgotten the words, "Come, blessed of my Father, take possession of the kingdom. . . For I was hungry and you gave me to eat. . . When you did it for one of these, the least of my brethren, you did it for me?" . . . What I ask you does this imply? I understand its import with regard to those who are to take possession of the kingdom. They are to possess the kingdom because, like good and faithful Christians, they did not disregard the Lord's words, but gave alms, and did so with the confident hope of receiving the promised rewards. For, even if they had not done this, their moral life could still not rightly be called barren. Indeed, they may have been chaste, they may not have been drunkards or defrauders, they may have kept themselves free from evil deeds, but, if they had not added almsgiving, their lives would have remained fruitless. In that case, they would indeed have observed the command, "Turn away from evil," but they would not have observed its complement, "And do good." Yet, not even to such as those does He say: "Come, take possession of the kingdom; for you have lived chastely, you have defrauded no man, you have not oppressed any poor man, you have not plundered any man's property, you have deceived no one by an oath." That is not what He said. Here are his words: "Take possession of the kingdom, for I was hungry and you gave me to eat." Since the Lord made no mention of other commandments, but named only this one, how much greater than all the others must this one be! And now, with regard to those to whom it was said: "Depart unto the everlasting fire which was prepared for the devil and his angels." Of how many sins could he accuse the ungodly, if they were to ask Him: "Why are we departing into everlasting fire?" He could have retorted: "Adulterers, murderers, defrauders, impious, blasphemers, unbelievers, why do you ask the reason?" But He said none of those things; He said merely: "Because I was hungry, and you did not give me to eat."[70]

---

70 Augustine, *Commentary on the Lord's Sermon on the Mount with Seventeen*

Christian Love to Motivate All Our Actions

Augustine stresses that good works are to flow from true Christian love. He realizes that good works may also be done for selfish reasons. He recognizes that those who do good works out of pride or vainglory may be doing the same good deeds as that of a Christian whose actions flow from love. However, it is the motivation that inspires the good deed that is of vital consequence. Good works are to be the fruit of faith working through love. Augustine quotes Paul in this regard, "If I distribute all my goods to the poor, and if I deliver up my body to be burned, and have not charity, it profits me nothing.[71]

Love is to motivate all our actions even when severe action is taken in correcting another. Augustine uses the illustration of a father who chastises his son in contrast with the child-stealer who entices with caresses and blandishments. He asks, "Who would not choose the caresses and decline the punishment?" Augustine points out, however, that in this case it is love that chastises, and evilness that caresses. It is by the motivation of the heart that deeds are judged.[72]

Thus, love is to be the root of all our actions. Whatever we do is to be done out of love. Augustine emphasized:

> Once for all, then, a short precept is given you: Love, and do what you will: Whether you hold your peace, through love hold your peace; whether you cry out, through love cry out; whether you correct, through love correct; whether you spare, through love do you spare. Let the root of love be within, out of this root can nothing spring but good.[73]

Christian Liberty to Act in Christian Love

With his precept, "Love, and do what you will," Augustine

Selected Sermons, Sermon 60, in the *The Fathers of the Church* (New York: The Fathers of the Church, Inc.). p. 268-269.

71 Augustine, *Ten Homilies on the First Epistle of John*, Homilies 6 and 8, in *The Nicene and Post-Nicene Fathers*, First Series, vol. 7, pp. 494, 510.

72 Augustine, *Ten Homilies on the First Epistle of John*, Homily Seven, secs. 8, 11, in *The Nicene and Post-Nicene Fathers*, First Series, vol. 7, pp. 504, 505.

73 Augustine, *Ten Homilies on the First Epistle of John*, Homily 7, sec. 8, in *The Nicene and Post-Nicene Fathers*, First Series, vol. 7, p. 504.

proclaimed his understanding of Christian liberty. The Christian is to make his own moral decisions on the basis of Christian love as he goes through life. Augustine notes how Paul used his Christian freedom in circumcising Timothy in order to avoid offending the Jews. However, in other circumstances, it was also an exercise of Paul's Christian freedom in having Titus remain uncircumcised to avoid giving the impression that circumcision was necessary for salvation.[74] In a letter to Jerome, Augustine argued that Christian freedom should be exercised also concerning the ceremonies and religious observances of the Church. He disagreed with Jerome's habit of seeing issues only in black and white.[75]

Augustine also discusses Christian liberty in regard to food and drink concerning which Paul writes in Romans 12 and 1 Corinthians 6:12. He sums up his views on Christian freedom in a treatise *On the Morals of the Catholic Church* by using as an illustration a class of Christian men who in the cities lived a communal life apart from other people:

> Those, then who are able, and they are without number, abstain both from flesh and from wine for two reasons: either for the weakness of their brethren [who believe drinking wine and eating meat is sinful], or from their own liberty. In this way charity is principally attended to. There is charity in the choice of diet, charity in their speech, charity in their dress, charity in their looks. Charity is the point where they meet, and the plan by which they act. To transgress against charity is thought criminal, like transgressing against God.[76]

When Augustine preached, "Love, and do what you wish," did he mean that he would carry love to the extreme of violating one of the Ten Commandments in the name of love? Hardly, rather Augustine understands fully that love is the fulfilling of the law. If a commandment is violated under the pretext of love, one scarcely can say that love fulfills the law. In a sermon emphasizing love as the fulfilling of the law, Augustine preached:

---

74 Augustine, *On Lying*, sec. 8, in *The Nicene and Post-Nicene Fathers*, First Series, vol. 3, p. 461. See also *Letters of St. Augustine, Letter 82*, sec. 12, *ibid*, vol. 1, p. 353.

75 Augustine, *Letters of St. Augustine, Letter 82*, secs. 12-14, in *The Nicene and Post-Nicene Fathers* (Grand Rapids: Wm. B. Eerdmans Publ. Co.), First Series, vol. 1, pp. 353-354.

76 Augustine, *On the Morals of the Catholic Church*, chap. 33, secs. 70-73, in *The Nicene and Post-Nicene Fathers*, First Series, vol. 4, p. 61.

Now who is he that fulfills the Law, but he that has charity? Ask the Apostle, "Charity is the fulfilling of the Law. For all the Law is fulfilled in one word, in that which is written, You shall love your neighbor as yourself." But the commandment of charity is twofold; "You shall love the Lord your God with all your heart, and with all your soul, and with all your mind. This is the great commandment. The other is like it; You shall love your neighbor as yourself." They are the words of the Lord in the Gospel: "On these two commandments hang all the Law and the Prophets." Without this twofold love the Law cannot be fulfilled. . . . "A new commandment I give unto you, that you love one another." And because He came to give charity, and charity fulfills the Law, with good reason said He, "I came not to destroy the Law, but to fulfill."[77]

Augustine, for example, considered Scriptures as teaching that telling a lie was sinful under any and all circumstances. In his treatise *On Lying* Augustine taught that telling a lie was wrong even if the lie was used to save an innocent person's life from murderers or a woman from rape.[78] For Augustine, therefore, the Christian freedom signified by his precept, "Love, and do what you will," applied only to moral decisions in those situations concerning which he believed the moral code of the Ten Commandments was silent.

The Christian's freedom to follow where an unselfish and self-denying love would lead is not, however, a major emphasis in Augustine's writings. In keeping with the tenor of the times, he too had his legalistic tendencies. Augustine, for example, in contrast to Chrysostom, held the prevailing view that sexual intercourse in marriage was sinful except when attempting to conceive a child.[79] It did not disturb him to use his own judgment of what was right to make laws and bind consciences where God had not bound them. He therefore denied any use by a married couple of contraceptive measures. To use contraceptive measures meant that they were having sex only for pleasure and that he considered sinful. He

---

77 Augustine, *Sermons on New Testament Lessons*, Sermon 75, sec. 10, in *The Nicene and Post-Nicene Fathers*, First Series, vol. 6, p. 480-481.

78 Augustine, *On Lying*, secs. 9, 10, in *The Nicene and Post-Nicene Fathers*, First Series, vol. 3, pp. 462, 463.

79 Augustine, *Enchiridion*, chap. 78, in *The Nicene and Post-Nicene Fathers*, First Series, vol. 3, p. 263.

scoffed at the Manichaeans who encouraged their followers to use the rhythm method of contraception in writing:

> Is it not you who used to counsel us to observe as much as possible the time when a woman, after her purification, is most likely to conceive, and to abstain from cohabitation at that time, lest the soul should be entangled in flesh? This proves that you approve of having a wife, not for the procreation of children, but for the gratification of passion. In marriage, as the marriage law declares, the man and woman come together for the procreation of children.[80]

We Are Justified and Saved by Faith in Christ, Not by Good Works

Augustine is in harmony with Paul in understanding that it is faith that saves and not works. In an essay entitled *On the Spirit and the Letter*, he writes:

> Now, having duly considered and weighed all these circumstances and testimonies, we conclude that a man is not justified by the precepts of a holy life, but by faith in Jesus Christ, –in a word, not by the law of works, but by the law of faith; not by the letter, but by the spirit; not by the merits of deeds, but by free grace.[81]

Both Faith and Good Works Are God's Gifts

In his catechetical instruction book for those entering the Church, Augustine similarly teaches:

> And before this redemption is wrought in a man, when he is not yet free to do what is right, how can he talk of the freedom of his will and his good works, except he be inflated by that foolish pride of boasting which the apostle restrains when he says, "By grace are you saved, through faith." [Ephesians 2:8]

---

80 Augustine, *On the Morals of the Mainichaeans*, chap. 18, sec. 65, in *The Nicene and Post-Nicene Fathers*, First Series, vol. 4, p. 86.

81 Augustine, *On the Spirit and the Letter*, chap. 22, in *The Nicene and Post-Nicene Fathers*, First Series, vol. 5, p. 93.

And lest men should arrogate to themselves the merit of their own faith at least, not understanding that this too is the gift of God, this same apostle, who says in another place that he had "obtained mercy of the Lord to be faithful," here also adds: "and that not of yourselves; it is the gift of God: not of works, lest any man should boast." And lest it should be thought that good works will be wanting in those who believe, he adds further: "For we are His workmanship, created in Christ Jesus unto good works, which God has before ordained that we should walk in them."[82]

Nor does Augustine see Christians reveling in their own good works, for the good works done by Christians flow from their faith and are themselves a gift of God. Thus, both the faith of the Christian and his good works are due to the pure grace of God toward us. Just as God's gift of eternal life is also due to His grace. There is no room for the Christian to boast either of his faith or his good works; all are a free gift given by the grace of God.[83] Augustine understands that a true faith will be active in love. He explains that it is impossible for a person who says that he has faith but leads a bad life and has no good works truly to have faith. In *On Grace and Free Will,* he writes concerning such persons:

Therefore they possess not the faith by which the just man lives, –the faith which works by love in such wise, that God recompenses it according to its works with eternal life. But inasmuch as we have even our good works from God, from whom likewise comes our faith and our love, therefore the selfsame great teacher of the Gentiles has designated "eternal life" itself as His gracious "gift."[84]

Faith without Works Is Dead

Augustine rejected the idea held by some that because they claimed

---

82 Augustine, *Enchiridion*, chaps. 30, 31, in *The Nicene and Post-Nicene Fathers*, First Series, vol. 3, pp. 247-248.

83 Augustine, *On Grace and Free Will*, chaps. 17-21, in *The Nicene and Post-Nicene Fathers*, First Series, vol. 5, pp. 450-452.

84 Augustine, *On Grace and Free Will*, chap. 18, in *The Nicene and Post-Nicene Fathers*, First Series, vol. 5, p. 451.

to be Christians and had been baptized they could choose to live in gross sin. They believed that at most they would be punished in proportion to their misdeeds before attaining heaven. To these Augustine applied the words of James in writing:

> I have written a book on this subject, entitled *Of Faith and Works*, in which, to the best of my ability, God assisting me, I have shown from Scripture, that the faith which saves us is that which the Apostle Paul clearly enough describes when he says: "For in Jesus Christ neither circumcision avails anything, nor uncircumcision, but faith which works by love." But if it works evil, and not good, then without doubt, as the Apostle James says, "it is dead, being alone."[85]

In keeping with Paul and James, Augustine taught that a Christian is saved by God's gift of faith, if, however, it is a true faith of the heart, a faith working by love, and not just an assertion of the mouth. Good works will be the natural fruit of such a faith.

Asceticism and Christian Love

Augustine approved of the life of the anchoritic hermit who benefited his fellow Christians through his prayer.[86] He also praised the communal life of the monasteries in their pursuit of perfection but emphasized that a true community of Christian love, concord, and harmony was to exist within their walls. He wrote a "Rule" for the governing of monasteries, and Rule Eight read: "Let there radiate over everything the love that is eternal."[87] And at the close of his rule he prayed that the Lord might grant that the monks observe all these things with love and that their good lives radiate the sweet fragrance of Christ as free persons living in grace.[88] For Augustine, the monastery was to be a model of the ideal Church

---

85 Augustine, *Enchiridion*, chap. 67, in *The Nicene and Post-Nicene Fathers*, First Series, vol. 3, p. 259.

86 Augustine, *On the Morals of the Catholic Church*, chap. 31, par. 66, in *The Nicene and Post-Nicene Fathers*, First Series, vol. 4, p. 59.

87 *The Rule of St. Benedict*, translation by U. J. Schnitzhofer and commentary by the Rev. Basilius Steidle, 1952, (Beurom/Hohenzollern, Deutschland: Beuroner Kunstverlag), p. 23.

88 Agatha Mary, S.P.B., 1992, *The Rule of St. Augustine* (Villanova, Pennsylvania: Augustinian Press), p. 331.

on earth. There was to be both the contemplation of the divine and service to others. He extols and praises a monasticism in which both work and contemplation are followed. Augustine especially commends those monasteries in which when after the basic needs of the monks are met, whatever remains of the produce or profit from the work of the monks is given to the poor.[89]

The Christian Life and the Opposition of the World

Augustine stands in a long line of Christian teachers going back to Christ in his warning against loving the things and values of the world. He warns against following the world in its lust of the flesh, the lust of the eyes, and the pride of life.[90] However, in his lectures on the Gospel of John, he taught that rejecting the values of the worldly and striving to live according to an unselfish and self-denying Christian love exacts a price:

> But alongside of this love we ought also patiently to endure the hatred of the world. For it must of necessity hate those whom it perceives recoiling from that which is loved by itself. But the Lord supplies us with special consolation from His own case, when, after saying, "These things I command you, that you love one another," He added, "If the world hate you, know that it hated me before [it hated] you."[91]

The Impact of Chrysostom and Augustine

These two great Christian thinkers and teachers, Chrysostom and Augustine, worked to bring back into Christianity the way of life taught in the New Testament by Jesus and His Apostles. In their lives, there was no vast difference between piety and goodness; both were united in a holiness of life that coupled a pious life with a faith working through Christian love. Although finally rejected in his own time, John Chrysostom came to be

---

89 Augustine, *On the Morals of the Catholic Church*, chap. 31, in *The Nicene and Post-Nicene Fathers*, First Series, vol. 4, pp. 59-60. See also *The City of God*, bk. 19, chap. 19 (ibid.), First Series, vol. 2, pp, 413-414.

90 Augustine, *Ten Homilies on the First Epistle of John*, Homily 2, secs. 8-14, in *The Nicene and Post-Nicene Fathers*, First Series, vol 7, pp. 472 475.

91 Augustine, *Lectures or Tractates on the Gospel According to John*, Tractate 87, sec. 2, in *The Nicene and Post-Nicene Fathers*, First Series, vol. 7, p. 355.

honored as the foremost church father by the Eastern Orthodox Church. He, however, was honored in name, but not necessarily by his church being observant of his teachings concerning asceticism and the Christian way of life. Augustine's stress on charity and Christian love did have a degree of influence over succeeding centuries.

In regard to monastic life, neither Augustine's emphasis on monasteries as centers of vital Christian love serving others, nor Chrysostom's reevaluation of relative worth of the monastic life prevailed. When Benedict of Nursia (480-543) composed his famous Rule, it took more after the regulations of the compassionless John Cassian than those of the more humane and charitable Augustine. The Benedictine Rule was to hold sway for many centuries in western Christianity. It fostered an austere but not extreme asceticism.

Therefore, the teachings of Chrysostom and Augustine concerning Christ's way of life cannot be said to have greatly influenced Christendom. As was seen in the previous chapter, slowly fading was the Christian ideal of a Christian who lived in the world and served his Lord by serving his fellow humans with the same self-denying love that Jesus did. The church instead came to hold up as the ideal Christian the ascetic who lived apart from the world and struggled to attain perfection before God by striving for personal purity. The church encouraged the laity to avoid guilt and purgatory by obediently conforming their lives to the growing new codes of church law. These multiplying and manifold codes of church law will be the topic of the next chapter.

Chapter 12

THE ECLIPSE OF JESUS' WAY OF LIFE:
CHURCH LAW
200 - 1500 A.D.

Canon Law and Penitential Manuals

In addition to asceticism and monasticism, there was another trend that resulted in undercutting and obscuring the way of life taught by Christ and His apostles. This was the growing legalistic regulation of the church through church law. Church law attempted to govern the lives of Christians both through codes of Canon Law and later through manuals for priests called "penitentials." Penitentials set forth rules, canons, and laws that governed the behavior of Christians in a wide variety of situations. Each canon or law was accompanied by a suitable penance to be imposed by the priest during private confession if the canon or law had been violated. The penances compelled a variety of imposed actions or restrictions on the penitent in order that he might show his sorrow and repentance over committing a given sin.

Already in the 200s, the development of Canon Law in the church was taking place. About two centuries later, the monks of the church in Ireland began writing a variety of penitential manuals. The penitentials later spread from Ireland and came to be widely used over Europe in the Middle Ages.

In this chapter on the legalistic developments within the medieval church, a discussion of the views of such church theologians as Thomas Aquinas and others who wrote during the age of Scholasticism (c. 800-1600) is omitted. This is done for the following two reasons: First, this chapter is concerned with church law as it affected the lives and behavior of the people of the church. The academic and learned writings of the Latin scholars on church law and ethics had little effect on the Christianity of the clergy and the laypeople. The local clergy were typically poorly trained and often semi-literate. The posts of the higher clergy, such as bishops and archbishops, during this period were often reserved for the sons of the nobility. These were second and later sons placed in a clerical calling through the influence of their families primarily to insure an affluent and prestigious way of life in keeping with their noble birth, not because they necessarily had a particular interest in Christianity. The day of the bishops being chosen from the monks of the monastery was passing. Thus, the writings of the scholastic theologians may have been read by their scholarly colleagues, but they had little influence on the lives of the people. A similar situation exists today in which the papers and tomes of the professional philosophers in the universities are typically read only by their colleagues and have practically no effect on the general population. In the area of scientific research, I have noted that the academic philosophers of science are almost ignored by the physical and natural scientists who might work in the same university. Second, to have discussed the views of the Schoolmen, the scholastic theologians, concerning the Christian way of life would have enlarged this study to an undue degree. This would be undue in regard to the number of pages, but also undue in that it implied an importance to their writings far beyond that experienced in the life of the average Christian.

The Early Growth of Canon Law

By the 300s, Canon Law became the attempt to regulate the life of the church and Christian people through laws set forth by a bishop, a council of bishops, or the mandates and decisions from the bishop of Rome.[1] The word "canon" is derived from a similar Greek word meaning a norm, rule, or measure. Roman Catholic literature defines Canon Law as "a binding norm of action, not merely a counsel or directive."[2] The growth of

---

1 The bishop of the city of Rome, as bishop of the capital city of the Roman Empire, was early viewed by some and came to view himself as having precedence and primacy over all other bishops of the empire. As a metropolitan was the leading bishop of a Roman province by virtue of his being bishop of the province's capital city, the bishop of Rome, as bishop of the empire's capital city, came to claim for himself the position of leading bishop over the empire. As time went on, a theological justification for this view was developed based on regarding Peter as the supposed first bishop of Rome and on a very strained interpretation of Matthew 16:13-19. Peter, after having served mainly in Asia Minor as well as in Palestine, had spent a few years in Rome before his martyrdom in the sixties; but there is no record of what his status was in Rome during those years. In addition, when Paul wrote his letter to the Christians in Rome in 56 A.D., it is significant that he does not mention Peter among the many people he greets in the closing chapter. The term "pope" (Latin "Papa") was a title of affection given to some bishops and priests from the 200s through the 400s. Since the 800s, the title has been exclusively reserved for the bishop of Rome.

2 *New Catholic Encyclopedia*, 1967, vol. 3 (New York: McGraw-Hill Book Co.), p. 31.

Canon Law finally resulted in extensive legal documents and legalistic interpretations of the documents. Canon Law scholars have debated these laws of the church over the centuries in a manner reminding one of the lengthy arguments of the rabbinical scholars in the Jewish Talmud. However, even before the more formal legislating of Canon Law by the hierarchy of the church took place, regulations and rules for Christian people are found in early church documents whose origins and authors are lost to history. That a love for law and its interpretations was already present among early church members is seen in the comment of Paul to Timothy:

> But the goal of our instruction is love from a pure heart and a good conscience and a sincere faith. For some men, straying from these things, have turned aside to fruitless discussion, wanting to be teachers of the Law, even though they do not understand either what they are saying or the matters about which they make confident assertions." (1 Timothy 1:5-7 NASB)

Paul was writing about those disputing about Old Testament law, but his warnings are appropriate also for those who would foster a new legalism in the church.

In chapter five, it was pointed out that from the very beginning there were those who were enamored with a legalistic approach to Christian life. The Circumcision Party, which wanted to place all Christians under the law of the Old Testament, had to be combated by Paul. About fifty years later, John emphasized Christ's New Commandment in his Gospel. In his first letter, he reduced God's commandments to two in writing, "And whatever we ask we receive from Him, because we keep His commandments and do those things that are pleasing in His sight. And this is His commandment: that we should believe on the name of His Son Jesus Christ and love one another, as He gave us commandment" (1 John 3:22-23 NKJV). John evidently opposed such trends toward a new legalism as found in *The Didache* that commanded "you must fast on Wednesday and Friday."[3] Also, as previously mentioned, the *Shepherd of Hermes* was legalistic in many respects.

A very early document of unknown origin, the *Didascalia Apostolorum* (c. 175-250), which was discussed previously in reference to

---

3 Edgar J. Goodspeed, 1950, *The Apostolic Fathers* (New York: Harper and Bros., Publ.), p. 14-15.

the marriage of the clergy (see pages 228-229), also had its legalistic requirements. The *Didascalia* instructs that hair should not be combed or adorned, neither fine raiment nor shoes worn, nor golden rings, lest women be enticed to sin.[4]

Much of the *Didascalia Apostolorum* was incorporated into a later and larger document, *The Apostolic Constitutions*, probably early in the 300s (see page 229). *The Apostolic Constitutions*, also of unknown origin, illustrates well the transitional period in the life of the early church when the ethic of Christian love taught by Christ and His apostles was being slowly supplanted by an ethic based on law.

The Apostolic Constitutions still shows a high regard for a Christian love active in deeds by its real concern for the poor and those in need. Christians are especially urged to be charitable to widows and orphans, but they are also to respond generously to all who may be in want.[5]

In *The Apostolic Constitutions*, the Ten Commandments are differentiated from the civil and ceremonial law of the Old Testament.[6] Although the Mosaic civil and ceremonial laws are considered abrogated, the Ten Commandments, which are termed the law of nature, are viewed as still valid. The Ten Commandments are understood as being fulfilled by Christ's New Commandment as Book Six of *The Apostolic Constitutions* instructs:

> How Christ became a fulfiller of the Law, and what parts of it He put a period to, or changed, or transferred:

> XXIII. For He did not take away the law of nature, but confirmed it. For He that said in the law, "The Lord thy God is one Lord"; the same says in the Gospel, "That they might know Thee, the only true God." And He that said, "Thou shalt love thy neighbor as thyself," says in the Gospel, renewing the same precept, "A new commandment I give unto you, that you love one another." He

---

4 R. Hugh Connolly, introduction and notes, 1929, *Didascalia Apostolorum* (Oxford: Clarendon Press), p. 10f.

5 *Constitutions of the Holy Apostles*, bk. 3, sec. 1, par. 4; bk. 4, sec. 1, pars. 2, 9; in *The Ante-Nicene Fathers* (Grand Rapids: Wm. B. Eerdmans Publ. Co.), vol. 7, pp. 427, 433, 435.

6 *Constitutions of the Holy Apostles*, bk. 6, sec. 4, pars. 19, 20, in *The Ante-Nicene Fathers*, vol. 7, pp. 458, 459.

who then forbade murder, does now forbid causeless anger. He that forbade adultery, does now forbid all unlawful lust. He that forbade stealing, now pronounces him most happy who supplies those that are in want out of his own labors. He that forbade hatred, now pronounces him blessed that loves his enemies.[7]

The tendency, however, toward a legalistic and ascetic way of life is strong in *The Apostolic Constitutions*. Sexual intercourse in marriage, for example, is only permissible when the intent is for the conception of a child and not for its own sake as the following text counsels husbands:

Nor, indeed, let them frequent their wives' company when they are with child. For they do this not for the begetting of children, but for the sake of pleasure. Now a lover of God ought not be a lover of pleasure.[8]

Rules for the adornment of men and women are also laid out. Under the title, "Commandments to Men," men are directed to avoid "over-fine" garments, stockings, or shoes. They are rather to wear only those articles of apparel that are suited to decency and usefulness. Nor should men wear gold rings, "for all these ornaments are the signs of lasciviousness, . . ."[9]

The Apostolic Constitutions directs Christians "to abstain from all the books of those that are out of the church." If Christians wish to read history, they can read the Old Testament books of Kings. If they want poetry or books of wisdom, they have the books of the prophets. If they desire something to sing, they can sing the psalms.[10] There is also a return to the negative Golden Rule of pre-Christian times, "Do not that to another which you hate that another should do to you."[11]

---

7 *Constitutions of the Holy Apostles*, bk. 6, sec. 4, par. 23, in *The Ante-Nicene Fathers*, vol. 7, p. 460.

8 *Constitutions of the Holy Apostles*, bk. 6, sec. 5, par. 28, in *The Ante-Nicene Fathers*, vol. 7, p. 463.

9 *Constitutions of the Holy Apostles*, bk. 1, sec. 2, in *The Ante-Nicene Fathers*, vol. 7, p. 392.

10 *Constitutions of the Holy Apostles*, bk. 1, sec. 2, par. 6, in *The Ante-Nicene Fathers*, vol. 7, p. 393.

11 *Constitutions of the Holy Apostles*, bk. 1, sec. 1, par. 1, in *The Ante-Nicene Fathers*, vol. 7, p. 391.

An expanded version of *The Didache* with its numerous and predominantly negative prohibitions composes the seventh of the eight books of *The Apostolic Constitutions*. In this book the positive and outgoing way of life based on Christian love and Christian liberty taught in the New Testament is hemmed in by a multiplicity of Old Testament and non-Biblical laws. Our Lord's instruction (Matthew 5:39) is also undermined when a quotation from Jesus is explained as follows:

> "If any one gives you a stroke on your right cheek, turn to him the other also." Not that revenge is evil, but that patience is more honorable.[12]

This counsel from the expanded version of *The Didache* is in direct contradiction with an earlier paragraph in Book One of *The Apostolic Constitutions* entitled, "That We Ought Not to Return Injuries, Nor Revenge Ourselves on Him that Does Us Wrong." In this section, Jesus' words concerning loving one's enemies are extensively quoted.[13]

Book Seven also has regulations concerning Christian giving. Christians are required to give to the priests the first fruits of their farms that thereby their storehouses and the production of their farms may be blessed and increased. In particular, they are commanded to give to the priests all the first fruits of their hot bread, barrels of wine, oil, honey, nuts, or "other things," but those items of silver, garments, "and of all sort of possessions, [are given] to the widow and orphan." They are also commanded, "You shall give the tenth of your increase to the orphan, and to the widow, and to the poor, and to the stranger."[14] This regulation from the early 300s concerning the tithe is an early mention of the tithe as a requirement for Christians in early Christian literature. Note that the tithe is given for the support of those in need, not for the use of the church. The requirement, however, is in conflict with Irenaeus' (130?-202?) comment that the tithe was abrogated along with the other such laws of the Old Testament (see page 168). How very different are these regulations from the New Testament counsel to give voluntarily and cheerfully as the Lord has

---

12 *Constitutions of the Holy Apostles*, bk. 7, sec. 1, par. 2, in *The Ante-Nicene Fathers*, vol. 7, p. 465.

13 *Constitutions of the Holy Apostles*, bk. 1, sec. 1, par. 2, in *The Ante-Nicene Fathers*, vol. 7, p. 392.

14 *Constitutions of the Holy Apostles*, bk. 7, sec 2, par. 29, in *The Ante-Nicene Fathers*, vol. 7, p. 471.

prospered one and as one sees the need.

The *Apostolic Canons* form the final part of Book Eight of *The Apostolic Constitutions* (see page 229-230). *The Apostolic Canons* form a body of law for the regulation of the church especially in regard to its bishops and clergy. They are almost totally legalistic in tone as they set up new, non-Biblical laws that curtail Christian freedom. Canon 7, for example, forbids the clergy to engage in any secular work. Canon 20 forbids the clergy to be co-signers of notes. Canon 69, under the threat of deprivation of office for clergy or suspension from communion for laity, commands the observance of the fast of forty days (Lent), the fourth day of the week, and the day of the preparation.[15]

As the authors and source of the *Didascalia Apostolorum* and *The Apostolic Constitutions* are unknown, the nature of the authority of those who wrote the documents cannot be determined. The attempt by the writers to mask their authorship by ascribing the writing of the documents to the apostles Jesus causes one to be skeptical concerning the trustworthiness of the documents. The two documents, however, enable us to gain some insight into the legalistic tendencies of some Christians early in the life of the Church.

Church Law:
One Result of the Rise of the Hierarchical Church

The Origin and Growth of Hierarchical Church Government

The development of Canon Law in the church is also partially a result of the trend toward an ever more powerful hierarchical system of church governance that began evolving shortly after the apostolic age. As a result of this trend, the bishops became the lawmakers for the church. In order, therefore, to understand how Canon Law came to be such a force over the lives of Christians, one has to understand how the authoritarian and autocratic hierarchical structure of the early and medieval church came into being.

Jesus did not set forth a plan for the organization of His Church. What He did was to commission His apostles to preach the good news of God's love and forgiveness, baptize those who came to have faith in God's love for them, and teach those who believed in Him as their Savior to live a life of self-giving love for others just as He had loved them (Matthew

---

15 *Constitutions of the Holy Apostles*, Ecclesiastical Canons, in *The Ante-Nicene Fathers*, vol. 7, pp. 500, 501, 504.

28:18-20). He also envisioned His followers coming together to form groups of believers who would partake of His supper under leaders who would not dominate them but be as those who humbly serve (Luke 22:24-27). He gave the members of His Church the privilege of forgiving or retaining sins (John 20:23). He foresaw the immense growth of His Church in His parables (Matthew 13:31-33). By His constantly calling Himself the Son of Man, He made it evident that He saw Himself as the One to whom "was given dominion, glory and a kingdom, that all peoples, nations, and men of every language might serve Him." It would be an everlasting kingdom, never to pass away or be destroyed (Daniel 7:13-14 NASB, see Appendix 1). Faith and love were to be hallmarks of Jesus' New Covenant Church. He taught that the way His people were to serve Him was by serving even the least of His brethren (Matthew 25:34-40). The presence of the Church in the world was to be found in the lives of its people; for as Jesus said, "By this all will know that you are My disciples, if you have love for one another" (John 13:35 NKJV).

Those who believed in Jesus in the first days of Christianity drew close to one another and gathered to form groups of believers. They gathered "to stir up one another to love and good works" and to "offer to God acceptable worship, with reverence and awe, for our God is a consuming fire" (Hebrews 10:24; 12:28-29 RSV). At their Sunday evening *Agape* or Love Suppers, they came together for a common meal that involved prayer, fellowship, instruction, and for the partaking of the Eucharist, the Lord's Supper.

The apostles either appointed or had such groups of Christians choose leaders to watch over the welfare of the congregations. The New Testament does not clearly define the various offices of leadership within the church. There is only mention of such offices as deacon (*diakonos*), elder (*presbyteros*), and overseer or bishop (*episkopos*). Christians who performed various services in the early church in additional roles are mentioned by Paul in 1 Corinthians 12:8-10, 28-29.

Luke in the Acts of the Apostles describes the office of deacon as created by the apostles for the purpose of administering and caring for the physical and material needs of people within the Church (Acts 6:1-6). The deacons, however, obviously also carried on other activities. Luke writes of the deacon Philip going into Samaria and proclaiming Christ to the people (Acts 8:4-5). The deacon Stephen also was engaged in evangelism (Acts 6:8-10).

One, however, cannot differentiate the offices of elder (presbyter) and bishop (overseer). Luke writes in Acts 20:

> And from Miletus he [Paul] sent to Ephesus and called to him
> the elders (*presbyterous*) of the church. And when they had

come to him, he said to them, . . . "Be on guard for yourselves and for all the flock, among which the Holy Spirit has made you overseers (*episkopous*), to shepherd the church of God which He purchased with His own blood." (Acts 20:17-18, 28 NASB).

In the above, the terms for bishop or overseer (*episkopous*) and elder (*presbyterous*) are applied to the same individuals.

Paul in his letter to Titus also uses the terms elder (presbyter) and bishop (overseer) interchangeably:

> For this reason I left you in Crete, that you should set in order the things that are lacking, and appoint elders (*presbyterous*) in every city as I commanded you–if a man is blameless, the husband of one wife, having faithful children not accused of dissipation or insubordination. For a bishop (*episkopon*) must be blameless, . . . (Titus 1:5-7a NKJV)

The Didache, coming from the late first century and which pretends and professes to be the teaching of the apostles, directs the following concerning the officers of the church:

> Appoint, therefore, for yourselves, bishops and deacons worthy of the Lord, men meek, and not lovers of money, and truthful and proved; for they also render to you the service of prophets and teachers. Despise them not therefore, for they are your honoured ones, together with the prophets and teachers.[16]

Elders (presbyters) are not mentioned, but that only indicates the early date of the document when the distinction between the elder (presbyter) and bishop (overseer) had not yet been made. Note also that the congregation appoints the church officers.

In Clement of Rome's letter to the Corinthians (96 A.D.), again the various offices are mentioned; but the roles of elder and bishop are not differentiated.

Thus, in the first century Christian Church the terms elder and bishop appear to be synonymous. Jerome (340?-420) recognized this in arguing in a letter to Evangelus that in the New Testament the offices of

---

16 *The Didache, The Teaching of the Twelve Apostles*, chap. 15, in *The Ante-Nicene Fathers*, vol. 7, p. 381.

bishop and elder (presbyter) were the same.[17] A recent article on the formation of the early church by a Roman Catholic author, a member of the Jesuits, states:

> . . . it must be admitted that the New Testament does not clearly distinguish between *episkopoi* (overseers) and *presbyteroi* (elders), both terms being employed seemingly for the same hierarchical office (cf. Acts 20:17, 28; Tit 1:5-7; 1 Tim 3:1-5 and 5:17). It should also be recalled that the term *hiereus* (priest), while predicated of the glorified Christ (Heb 5:5 et passim) and of the whole Christian people (Apoc [Revelation] 1:6; 5:10; 20:6), is never used in the New Testament to designate an officer in the Church.[18]

Early in the 100s, however, the terms presbyter and bishop come to be used for officers in the church who have differing functions. The letters of Ignatius (c. 107) considered earlier (see pages 149-153) indicate that the polity of the church had in just a few years evolved to a more definite form. The term bishop (*episkopos*) is now reserved for the office of the presiding and primary overseer of the congregation. The presbyters or elders are differentiated as officers who form a council to advise the bishop. The deacons remain a group devoted to serving the material needs of the people of the church.

In the letters of Ignatius, the bishop of Antioch, the place of the bishop is supreme. To the church at Ephesus, Ignatius wrote: "It is manifest, therefore, that we should look upon the bishop even as we would upon the Lord Himself."[19] Repeatedly, Ignatius counsels that everything in the church should be done with the knowledge and approval of the bishop. To the church at Philadelphia, he wrote: "Do nothing without the bishop, . . ."[20]

---

17 Jerome, *Letter 146*, in *The Nicene and Post-Nicene Fathers* (Grand Rapids: Wm. B. Eerdmans Publ. Co.), Second Series, vol. 6, pp. 288, 289.

18 David Stanley, S.J., 1967, *Discerning the Permanent and Transitory: The Experience of the Apostolic Church*, in *Law for Liberty: The Role of Law in the Church Today*, James E. Beichler, ed. (Baltimore: Helicon Press, Inc.), pp. 25-26.

19 Ignatius, *Epistle of Ignatius to the Ephesians*, chap. 6, in *The Ante-Nicene Fathers*, vol. 1, pp. 51-52.

20 Ignatius, *Epistle to the Philadelphians*, chap. 7, in *The Ante-Nicene Fathers*, vol. 1, p. 84.

Thus at the time of Ignatius, the three separate offices of bishop, presbyter, and deacon appear established as the following two citations from Ignatius also indicate:

> Since therefore I have, in the persons before mentioned, beheld the whole multitude of you in faith and love, I exhort you to study to do all things with a divine harmony, while your bishop presides in the place of God, and your presbyters in the place of the assembly of the apostles, along with your deacons, who are most dear to me, and are entrusted with the ministry of Jesus Christ, who was with the Father before the beginning of time, and in the end was revealed.[21]

> In like manner, let all reverence the deacons as an appointment of Jesus Christ, and the bishop as Jesus Christ, who is the Son of the Father, and the presbyters as the sanhedrim of God, and assembly of the apostles. Apart from these, there is no Church.[22]

From the letters of Ignatius, therefore, we see the church being organized with the bishop as the presiding officer, the presbyters or elders as a council advising the bishop, and the deacons distributing aid those in need.

The *Didascalia Apostolorum* also reflects the polity of the early church. This church order or manual is usually dated around 250 A.D. The church organization it describes, however, sounds much more like that of the late 100s than the 200s.

It teaches that as Christ is to God the Father, so is the deacon to the bishop. The bishop preaches, teaches, and administers the sacraments, and the deacon ministers to the people. The presbyters or elders have no clearly defined role except as councilors to the bishop. Relevant texts from the *Didascalia Apostolorum* are as follows:

> But concerning the bishopric, hear ye. The pastor who is appointed bishop and head among the presbytery in the Church

---

21 Ignatius, *Epistle to the Magnesians*, chap. 6, in *The Ante-Nicene Fathers*, vol. 1, p. 61.

22 Ignatius, *Epistle of Ignatius to the Trallians*, chap. 3, in *The Ante-Nicene Fathers*, vol. 1, p. 67.

in every congregation, it is required of him that he be blameless,
. . .

He (the bishop) is minister of the word and mediator; but to you
a teacher, and your father after God, who begot you through the
water [of baptism]. This is your chief and your leader, and he is
your mighty king. He rules in the place of the Almighty: but let
him be honoured by you as God, for the bishop sits for you in the
place of God Almighty. But the deacon stands in the place of
Christ; and do you love him. And the deaconess shall be
honoured by you in the place of the Holy Spirit; and the
presbyters shall be to you in the likeness of the Apostles; . . .

Now in like case is also the bishop. . . . so now does the bishop
also take for himself from the people those whom he accounts
and knows to be worthy of him and of his office, and appoints
him presbyters as counsellors and assessors, and deacons and
subdeacons, as many as he has need of in proportion to the
ministry of the house.[23]

This certainly sounds like the Christianity of the 100s in which the
Christians of each town or city gathered as one congregation under a bishop
as reflected in the letters of Ignatius (c. 110 A.D). In addition, worthy of
note is that the bishop now is the only one who chooses and ordains
individuals from his diocese to the diaconite or presbyterite. No longer are
they chosen by the people of the congregation. This episcopal prerogative
came to be jealously guarded. Origen (185?-254?), for example, enraged his
own bishop Demetrius of Alexandria by allowing himself to be ordained a
presbyter by the bishops of Caesarea and Jerusalem while on a journey in
Palestine. When Origen later returned to Alexandria, he was defrocked by
an Egyptian synod called by Bishop Demetrius.

The *Didascalia Apostolorum* thus appears to describe the
organization of the church before the growth of the number of Christians in
a city required additional parishes or congregations. When this increase in a
city's parishes later took place, in order to staff these additional
congregations the bishop apparently assigned a presbyter from his council

---

23 R. Hugh Connolly, introduction and notes, 1929, *Didascalia Apostolorum*, pp. 28,
86-88, 96.

of advisors to serve the new parish as a presbyter-priest. The presbyter-priest thus existed as the bishop's agent in the parish. The term presbyter is still used for parish priests in the 1983 Roman Catholic Church's *Code of Canon Law*, and presbyterial councils in that church still exist to advise the bishop.

The *Didascalia Apostolorum* also seems to imply the greater stature and importance of the deacons over the presbyters. The deacons are in the place of Christ while the presbyters are like the apostles. This obviously changes later when the bishop places the presbyters in charge of the spiritual life of the parishes with deacons then appointed to care for the material needs of the members in a parish. The document thus appears to describe a Christian polity between that shown in the letters of Paul and the later polity of the church of the 200s.

The first bishops were primarily in the major urban centers of the Roman Empire as these were usually the first areas into which Christianity spread. Bishops in the early church had oversight of only one city. *The letters of Ignatius* and the *Didascalia Apostolorum* know nothing of metropolitans or of archbishops, the later important bishops of the leading cities or capitals of the Roman provinces.

Christianity, however, slowly spread to the rural areas and more minor cities. When the bishop of a large urban center recognized an outlying city as worthy of having its own bishop, in concert with at least two other bishops, he would ordain a bishop for that city or town. This was in keeping with the practice of having a bishop the leader of each municipality. If the size of a village did not warrant a bishop, a presbyter would be assigned to the hamlet. In addition, there was a period of time when a city bishop might institute the office of *chorepiscopos* through whom he governed an adjacent rural area.

One of the reasons that bishops of the provincial capitals in the 200s came to become known as metropolitans and later archbishops is that they had the authority to ordain bishops in new places of growth. The power of these metropolitans in the provincial capitals grew until each came to have a degree of authority over the other bishops in the Roman province. Thus, whether by thoughtful design or by happenstance, the government of the church came to reflect and mainly coincide with the government and provincial jurisdictions of the Roman Empire.

The Autocracy of the Hierarchy

Among the prerogatives and major responsibilities of the bishops in the early centuries was teaching and especially preaching. The bishops in particular reserved the preaching office for themselves. It appears that most priests or presbyters did not preach unless appointed to this task by their bishop, and then typically only in the bishop's cathedral church. John Chrysostom, for example, was such a presbyter preaching in his bishop's cathedral in Antioch, Syria. Preaching remained the peculiar prerogative of the bishop for many centuries. In an age when books were handwritten and therefore beyond the purse of most people and when literacy was minimal, the spoken word was too powerful a means of communication to be shared by the bishop even with his own presbyter-priests.

In the early days of Christianity, the bishop had a close relationship with his people when he was the leader of the one congregation in a city. As related above, however, the Church grew to the point that one congregation for a city became unwieldy; and additional parishes had to be established in the city. With the bishop's presbyters being appointed to staff such parishes, the bishop was thus a step removed from familiar interaction with the people of the parishes. No longer did the bishop have a personal and knowledgeable relationship with the Christian people under his care as seen in the *Didascalia Apostolorum* where he is described as being "well acquainted with those who are in distress."[24] However, lack of close personal knowledge of the parishes did not mean that the bishop wished to give up his personal control or authority over the parishes. The presbyter-priests of the parishes were his appointees from his council of presbyters. He continued his authority over his jurisdiction by becoming a governor who set the rules for the parishes under his control.

As the bishop set the rules, he became in effect the legislator for his diocese. As he could no longer guide his people directly through personal contact, he governed them by setting forth laws and regulations to be administered by the presbyter-priests he appointed in the parishes of his district or diocese.[25] The bishop may have listened to his presbyterial councilors, but his was the final word.

In a later attempt to make the governance and the laws of the church more uniform, bishops from a given geographic area or a province met in council in order to legislate and make policy pronouncements and rulings for their territory. The North African church was among the first to hold such regional councils. The council of Spanish bishops at Elvira in

---

24 R. Hugh Connolly, introduction and notes, 1929, *Didascalia Apostolorum*, p. 88.

25 The Latin word "diocese" for a bishop's area of jurisdiction is a carryover from the administrative restructuring of the Roman Empire under Emperors Diocletion (245-315) and Constantine (272-337) who divided the Roman prefectures into districts called dioceses. By the 1200s, the term "diocese" settled down to mean a bishop's area of jurisdiction in the Roman church. In the Orthodox Eastern Church, it is the area under the jurisdiction of a patriarch.

309? A.D., mentioned earlier, gathered for the purpose of formulating laws or canons for the Spanish church. Such canons, however, were still only regional in effect. It was only in 325 A.D., at the church-wide, First Ecumenical Council at Nicaea in Asia Minor that bishops from almost all of Christendom gathered to enact canons or laws for the entire church.

Such were developments that resulted in the Canon Law of the churches. Canon Law in part grew out of the legalistic tendencies found in some of the early literature of the church. Canon Law also came into being as the result of the increasing preeminence of the bishops who over time gathered to themselves exclusively the prerogatives of appointment, doctrinal oversight, preacher, administrator, and lawgiver. Once attained, these prerogatives were zealously guarded from all challenge from lower clergy or lay people. Some, like the Montanists, a group in Asia Minor later deemed heretical, rebelled at the autocracy of the bishops; but the bishops prevailed. Seldom has the maxim that power accrues to those who possess it been more amply illustrated.

The above is not to imply that the bishops were self-aggrandizing individuals, eager for power and control. For most of them, it undoubtedly was for the good and welfare of the Church that they wanted the reins of power firmly in their hands. In the perilous times of early Christianity, as on a ship during a storm, many may have felt it best to have one captain with absolute powers. Whether the evolution of the New Testament overseer or bishop, the *episkopus,* into an all-powerful autocrat was a God-pleasing development, however, is open to question.

Over the centuries, the people even lost their ancient right to choose the bishop who would rule over them. Pope Leo the Great (390?-461), for example, in resisting this development found it necessary to write to Anastasius, bishop of Thessalonica, to insist that only a person elected by the people and the clergy should be ordained bishop.[26] In another letter, Leo wrote, "He who is to govern all, should be chosen by all."[27] In the later history of the Roman church, Pope Leo's words did not prevail. Today, Pope Leo's successor in Rome alone makes all appointments to the bishopric.

---

26 Leo the Great, *Letter 14*, sec. 6, in *The Nicene and Post-Nicene Fathers*, Second Series, vol. 12, p. 18.

27 Leo the Great, *Letter Ten*, sec. 6, in *The Nicene and Post-Nicene Fathers*, Second Series, vol. 12, p. 11.

The Canon Law of the Church

The Imposition of Canon Law upon the Life of the Church

It was especially the bishops of Rome who sought to rule the church through Canon Law. Pope Leo the Great admonished a group of bishops:

> . . . so are we saddened with no slight sorrow whenever we learn that anything has been taken for granted or done contrary to the ordinances of the canons and the discipline of the Church: and if we do not repress such things with the vigilance we ought, we cannot excuse ourselves to Him who intended us to be watchmen, . . .[28]

To the bishop of Thessalonica, Pope Leo also wrote, "The sanctions of God's law must be respected, and the decrees of the canons should be more especially kept."[29]

Pope Gregory the Great (540?-604) was equally insistent on ruling the church by means of codes of church law. He threatened the bishop of Larissa with whom he was quarreling:

> For this we lay down as a rule, agreeably to the teaching of the holy fathers, that whosoever knows not how to obey the holy canons, neither is he worthy to minister or receive the communion at the holy altars.[30]

One of the first comprehensive collections of the laws of the western church was made by Dionysius Exiguus in about 500 A.D. Included in his collection were the first fifty canons of *The Apostolic Canons*, the canons of the ecumenical councils, the canons of the more important provincial councils, and papal decretal letters, that is, letters containing

---

28 Leo the Great, *Letter 4*, sec 1, in *The Nicene and Post-Nicene Fathers*, Second Series, vol. 12, pp. 2-3.

29 Leo the Great, *Letter 6*, sec. 3, in *The Nicene and Post-Nicene Fathers*, Second Series, vol. 12, p. 5.

30 Gregory the Great, *Epistle 7*, in *The Nicene and Post-Nicene Fathers*, Second Series, vol. 12, Second Section, p. 126.

decrees or orders from the pope often given in reply to a question concerning ecclesiastical law.

In the Eastern Church, John Scholasticus about fifty years later made a similar collection. In his collection, he includes all eighty-five canons of *The Apostolic Canons.* The collections of Canon Law made by the Roman church and those patriarchies around the eastern end of the Mediterranean Sea thus differ from one another. Later, for example, Pope Sergius of Rome summarily rejected the 102 canons of the Quinisext Council of Constantinople (692). As previously mentioned, Canon 13 of the council was especially objectionable; for it stated that the Roman church deviated from ancient and apostolic rule in forbidding the clergy to live fully with their wives.[31]

Collections and revisions of Canon Law gathered from various church councils and the pronouncements and writings of prominent bishops and popes were made many times in the long history of Canon Law. For the Roman church the latest collection and revision is the *Codex Iuris Canonici* promulgated by Pope John Paul II in 1983, the Latin-English edition containing 668 pages.

The strongly legalistic nature of Canon Law is especially seen in that it is patterned after the law codes of the Roman Empire. The bishops took Roman law as their guide even to the extent of following its parliamentary procedures in producing church law.[32] The church not only adopted the basic organization of the Roman government, it also took its legal system as a guide to the point at times of incorporating secular Roman law into Canon Law.[33] The *New Catholic Encyclopedia* states: "In actual fact the history of Canon Law is the history of continual borrowing and adaptation from various legal systems, and especially from that of the Roman Empire."[34] This incorporation of secular civil law into the Canon Law of the church has continued to modern times.[35]

---

31 *The Second Council in Trullo, the Quinisext Council,* Canon 13, in *The Nicene and Post-Nicene Fathers,* Second Series, vol. 14, p. 371.

32 Hamilton Hess, 1967, *The Early Expression of Ecclesiastical Authority* in *Law for Liberty: The Role of Law in the Church Today,* James E. Biechler, ed. (Baltimore: Helicon Press), p. 35.

33 Constant Van De Wiel, 1991, *History of Canon Law* (Louvain: Peeters Press, Eerdmans), pp. 108, 129.

34 *New Catholic Encyclopedia,* 1967, vol. 3, p. 30, see also pp. 50-53.

35 Constant Van De Wiel, 1991, *History of Canon Law,* p. 20.

Much of Canon Law concerns itself with the organization, administration, and functioning of the church establishment. However, a good deal goes beyond such concerns and at times severely infringes upon the Christian freedom of Christ's people. Contrary to Paul's warning, "Stand fast therefore in the liberty with which Christ has made us free, and do not be entangled again with a yoke of bondage" (Galatians 5:1 NKJV). Canon Law bound Christians to a new yoke of bondage, codes of law that are the tradition of men rather than the counsel of God. They are codes of law that too often go against the clear words of Paul to let no one pass judgment on you according to human precepts (Colossians 2:16-23). For example, Paul had warned that there would come those who would forbid marriage and abstinence from foods that God created to be received with thankful hearts (1 Timothy 4:1-5).

In the development of Canon Law, the leaders of the church departed from the principle of Christian liberty and freedom taught in the New Testament. The bishops legislated conduct in areas where the Scriptures were silent. They at times enacted laws that were in direct contradiction to the words of the New Testament. In earlier chapters, some of these canons were reviewed in regard to the marriage of the clergy. There are, however, many more areas where the legislators of the church trespassed on the Christian freedom of their people. The liberty of Christians to be led by the Spirit as they endeavored to live by the New Commandment of loving others as Christ loved was often ignored. The net result was to bind the consciences of Christians with codes of law that came from the minds and traditions of men and not from the Word of God. Church law bound Christians even to the extent of threatening eternal damnation if the laws were not obeyed. The bishops enacted codes of conduct, as did Clement of Alexandria with his *The Instructor* (see page 194), that attempted to put divine authority behind the pronouncements of men. The warning of God in Jeremiah went unheeded: "I am against the prophets, says the Lord, who concoct words of their own and then say, 'This is his very word'" (Jeremiah 23:31 NEB).

The trend toward legalism in the Church that was fought by Paul and John in their day thus finally led to the establishment of new legalistic codes of conduct, the Canon Law of the eastern and western churches. The freedom of Christians to live in accordance with Christ's New Commandment as guided by the Holy Spirit and informed by the New Testament became submerged in a sea of Canon Law. A number of such examples from the Canon Law of both western and eastern Christianity are given below.

A previous chapter (see page 230) discussed the canons of the Spanish Council of Elvira that in 305 A.D. passed laws restricting the married life of the clergy. The legalistic bent of this gathering and its infringement on Christian freedom is also seen in the following canons. The Spanish bishops felt empowered to make such canons as:

> Canon 67. It is forbidden for a woman, whether baptized or a catechumen, to have anything to do with long-haired men or hairdressers; any who do this shall be kept from communion.

> Canon 81. Women shall not presume on their own, without their husbands' signatures, to write to lay women who are baptized, nor shall they accept anyone's letters of peace addressed only to themselves.[36]

Concerning a weekly holy day, Paul had written concerning the liberty of Christians to the church at Rome:

> One person esteems one day above another; another esteems every day alike. Let each be fully convinced in his own mind. He who observes the day, observes it to the Lord; and he who does not observe the day, to the Lord he does not observe it. (Romans 14:5-6a NKJV)

In direct contradiction of Paul's counsel concerning Christian freedom about a holy day, the Spanish bishops passed the following canon:

> Canon 21. If anyone living in the city does not go to church for three Sundays, he shall be kept out for a short time in order that his punishment be made public.[37]

A later council of bishops from various provinces meeting at Sardica (343-344), a city north of the Aegean Sea, referred approvingly to the above canon.[38] In 692, the Council in Trullo meeting in Constantinople, better known as the Quinisext Council, also stated:

---

36 Samuel Laeuchli, 1972, *Power and Sexuality* (Philadelphia: Temple Univ. Press), pp. 134, 135.

37 Samuel Laeuchli, 1972, *Power and Sexuality*, p. 129.

38 *The Canons of the Council of Sardica*, Canon 11, in *The Nicene and Post-Nicene Fathers*, Second Series, vol. 14, p. 426.

Canon 80. If any bishop, or presbyter, or deacon, or any of those who are enumerated in the list of the clergy, or a layman, has no very grave necessity nor difficult business so as to keep him from church for a very long time, but being in town does not go to church on three consecutive Sundays--three weeks--if he is a cleric let him be deposed, but if a layman let him be cut off.[39]

Paul's instruction concerning the liberty of the Christian concerning a holy day was also ignored in the 300s by the Synod of Laodicea, a council of the bishops of Asia Minor, which legislated:

Canon 29. Christians must not judaize by resting on the Sabbath [Saturday], but must work on that day, rather honoring the Lord's Day [Sunday]; and, if they can, resting then as Christians. But if any be found to be judaizers, let them be anathema [accursed and excommunicated] from Christ.[40]

In 506, the provincial council of Agde in Gaul (modern France) promulgated a canon that decreed that anyone who did not receive Holy Communion on Christmas, Easter, and Pentecost was guilty of apostasy, that is, falling away from the faith.[41]

Binding consciences with laws where God has not bound them, the Quinisext Council in Canon 50 dictated:

No one at all, whether cleric or layman, is from this time forward to play at dice. And if any one hereafter shall be found doing so, if he be a cleric he is to be deposed, if a layman let him be cut off.[42]

---

39 *The Canons of the Council in Trullo*, Canon 80, in *The Nicene and Post-Nicene Fathers*, Second Series, vol. 14, p. 400.

40 *The Synod of Laodicea*, Canon 29, in *The Nicene and Post-Nicene Fathers*, Second Series, vol. 14, p. 148.

41 *Saint Caesarius of Arles, Sermons*, vol. 1 (New York: The Fathers of the Church, 1956), p. xiii.

42 *The Canons of The Council in Trullo, the Quinisext Council*, Canon 50, in *The Nicene and Post-Nicene Fathers*, Second Series, vol. 14, p. 388.

Paul had written, "Therefore let no one pass judgment on you in questions of food and drink . . ." (Colossians 2:16). In a law regulating fasting the provincial council of Gangra in northern Asia Minor (meeting sometime between 325-381) decreed in Canon 18, "If any one, under the pretense of asceticism, shall fast on Sunday, let him be anathema."[43]

Abstaining from flesh foods during Lent was required on the Sabbath and the Lord's Day. Hearing that some in the Armenian church were eating eggs and cheese on these days, the Quinisext Council in 692 decreed that hereafter any cleric who ate of these foods would be deposed from office, if a layman he would be excommunicated[44]

Archbishop Peter of Alexandria, who died a martyr under the persecution of the Emperor Diocletian in 311, set forth canons that declared Wednesday and Friday were to be days of fasting. In his sermon on penitence, he decreed:

> Canon 15: Wednesday is to be fasted, because then the Jews conspired to betray Jesus; Friday, because he suffered for us. We keep the Lord's Day as a day of joy, because then our Lord rose. Our tradition is, not to kneel on that day.[45]

Archbishop Timothy of Alexandria, one of the 150 bishops who attended the Ecumenical Council of Constantinople in 381, gave canonical answers to eighteen questions. Half of the questions are concerned with whom should be allowed to partake of Holy Communion. In Timothy's answers, we see the beginning of the trend that resulted in later centuries of married couples being forbidden to engage in conjugal love on various days of the week:

> Question 5. Can a man or woman communicate [take Holy Communion] after performing the conjugal act over night? Answer. No. 1 Corinthians 7:5.

---

43 *The Council of Gangra*, Canon 18, in *The Nicene and Post-Nicene Fathers*, Second Series, vol. 14, p. 99.

44 *The Council in Trullo, the Quinisext Council*, Canon 56, in *The Nicene and Post-Nicene Fathers*, Second Series, vol. 14, p. 391.

45 *Canons of Peter of Alexandria*, Canon 15, in *The Nicene and Post-Nicene Fathers*, Second Series, vol. 14, p. 601.

Question 13. When are a man and wife to forbear the conjugal act? Answer. On Saturday, and on the Lord's Day; for on those days the spiritual sacrifice is offered.

Archbishop Timothy was also concerned with the acceptability of women at religious rites during their periods of menstruation:

Question 6. The day appointed for the baptism of a woman; on that day it happened that the custom of women was upon her; ought she then to be baptized? Answer. No, not till she be clean. Question 7. Can a menstruous woman communicate [take Holy Communion]? Answer. Not until she be clean.[46]

Peter's canons and Timothy's canonical answers are representative of a bishop's right to legislate and decree canons for his people. They illustrate how a bishop thus can use his legislative prerogative to make laws that bind consciences of Christians where God has not bound them. Peter's canons and Timothy's Canonical Answers were confirmed and ratified for the entire church by the Quinisext Council in 692[47] and also by the Seventh Ecumenical Council of Nice in 787.[48]

As time went on Canon law became in part a penal code with all sorts of penalties and penances laid out for various infractions. One of the major problems addressed by Canon Law was what to do with those Christians who had denied their Christianity during the ten periods of intermittent persecution the Church suffered during it first 300 years. Should they be forgiven and once more admitted to full membership in the church after the time of persecution had ended?

The Apostates, Defectors from the Church during Persecution

The Roman Empire typically tolerated the great variety of religions in its vast domain. It normally allowed the people over which it held sway

---

46 *The Canonical Answers of Timothy, etc.*, in *The Nicene and Post-Nicene Fathers*, Second Series, vol. 14, p. 613.

47 *The Council in Trullo, the Quinisext Council*, Canon 2, in *The Nicene and Post-Nicene Fathers*, Second Series, vol. 14, p. 361.

48 *The Second Council of Nice*, Canon 1 in *The Nicene and Post-Nicene Fathers*, Second Series, vol. 14, p. 555.

to practice their own peculiar religions. It might even include their deities in the Pantheon in Rome, a building in which were represented many of the diverse religions of the Empire. Christianity, however, was not content to be one of many religions.

The early Christians took seriously the words of Christ, "I am the way, the truth, and the life. No one comes to the Father except through Me" (John 14:6 NKJV). Christ's view of the Biblical faith being an exclusive faith was in keeping with such Old Testament texts as found in Isaiah:

> Thus says the Lord, the King of Israel
>   and his Redeemer, the Lord of hosts:
> "I am the first and I am the last;
>   besides me there is no god. . . .
> Is there a God besides me?
>   There is no Rock; I know not any." (Isaiah 44:6-8 RSV)
>   see also 43:10, 11; 45:20-21; Exodus 34:14;
>   Jeremiah 10:1-10; Hosea 13:3)

Peter also witnessed to the exclusiveness of Christianity as the way to God and salvation. The assembled leaders of Judaism upon learning that Peter had healed a man lame from birth asked him, "By what power, or in what name, have you done this?" Peter responded:

> " . . . let it be known to all of you, and to all the people of Israel, that by the name of Jesus Christ the Nazarene, whom you crucified, whom God raised from the dead--by this name this man stands before you in good health. He is the stone which was rejected by you, the builders, but which became the very corner stone. And there is salvation in no one else; for there is no other name under heaven that has been given among men, by which we must be saved" (Acts 4:11-12 NASB).

John also emphasized that the only way given by God for salvation was through His Son, Jesus Christ. In his letter to the churches, John wrote:

> If we receive the witness of men, the witness of God is greater; for this is the witness of God which He has testified of His Son. . . . And this is the testimony: that God has given us eternal life, and this life is In His Son. He who has the Son has life; he who does not have the Son of God does not have life. (1 John 5:9-12 NKJV)

Nor did Christianity accommodate itself to Judaism. Rather it held that Christ was the Messiah for so long foretold in the Old Testament, and that the Old Covenant had passed away with Christ's life and resurrection. The author of the New Testament book of Hebrews wrote, "In that He [Jesus] says, 'A new covenant,' He has made the first obsolete. Now what is obsolete and growing old is ready to vanish away" (Hebrews 8:13 NKJV). The gifts and the calling of God to Israel were indeed irrevocable, but God's gift of salvation to His beloved people was now to be mediated through the Jesus, the Messiah of the New Covenant (Romans 9-11).

Because of its exclusiveness, Christianity was resented as an intolerant religion. It denied the existence of the ancient gods and goddesses of the Greeks and Romans and even ridiculed the many stories of their ignoble behavior that had grown up around them. The Christians also rejected the validity of the many other religions in the Roman Empire. It was viewed as an unaccommodating religion.

Because of its forthright denial of the many deities and religions of the Empire, Christianity was accused of atheism. When the Christians would not even take part in a minor ritual involved with the worship of the Roman emperor, they were charged with treason. Such an obstinate and stiff-necked people had to have their necks bent to the yoke or else. Concerning the obstinacy of the Christians, Pliny the Younger, the governor of the Roman province of Bythinia in Asia Minor, around 110 A.D. wrote to the Emperor Trajan:

> . . . the method I have observed toward those who have been brought before me as Christians is this: I asked them whether they were Christians; if they admitted it, I repeated the question twice, and threatened them with punishment; if they persisted, I ordered them to be at once punished: for I was persuaded, whatever the nature of their opinions might be, a contumacious and inflexible obstinacy certainly deserved correction. . . . An anonymous information was laid before me containing a charge against several persons, who upon examination denied they were Christians, or had ever been so. They repeated after me an invocation to the gods, and offered religious rites with wine and incense before your statue; . . . and even reviled the name of Christ: whereas there is no forcing, it is said, those who are really Christians into any of these compliances: I thought it

proper, therefore, to discharge them.[49]

Trajan answered that he agreed with Pliny's procedures except that acting on anonymous information was "quite foreign to the spirit of our age."[50]

The punishments inflicted upon the Christians ranged from flogging, torture, imprisonment, to martyrdom inflicted under often excruciatingly painful circumstances. Up to the time of the conversion of the Emperor Constantine to Christianity and his edict granting toleration to Christianity in 313 A.D., the Church endured ten episodes of either local or empire-wide persecution. There has been a tendency to denigrate and play down the severity of these persecutions by recent writers. No one, however, in the least familiar with the numerous contemporary accounts of these persecutions could possibly do so. The holocaust deniers are not alone in their revision of history.

After each period of persecution, the church was faced with the problem of receiving once more into membership those who under the threat of persecution had denied that they were Christians to the Roman authorities. In the 300s, a large number of the canons of the church councils dealt with these apostates who once the time of persecution had passed desired to renew their membership in the Church. Forgiveness for defection from Christianity was not easy to obtain. Those who had kept the faith and had suffered for it did not look kindly upon those who escaped persecution by denying their faith. The church demanded a long period of penance to expiate the sin of apostasy. Various church councils enacted graduated penances in keeping with the degree to which people denied their faith.

Canon Law and its Penalties—Penance and Purgatory

A penance is a penalty or reparation imposed by churchly authority for a spiritual offense. The offender might come to the notice of the church through voluntary confession, or he may have caused a public scandal that brought his offense to the attention of the church. A penance can take many forms such as prayer, almsgiving, exclusion from religious rites, enforced abstinence from certain foods or drinks, denial of marital intercourse, commitment to a monastery, pilgrimages, and so forth. The sinner's

---

49 *Correspondence of Pliny with the Emperor Trajan*, Letter 47, in the *Harvard Classics* (New York: Collier and Son), vol. 9, p. 426.

50 *Correspondence of Pliny with the Emperor Trajan*, Letter 48, in the *Harvard Classics*, vol. 9, p. 428.

observance of a penance is taken as a sign of his sorrow for his sin. As his working out of his penance was public; his reconciliation with the church upon being absolved of his sin by the bishop was also public.

The development of the concept of penance came from the erroneous but growing belief among many in the church that baptism only forgave sins committed before baptism. This is a belief taught by some churches even to this day.[51] Clement of Alexandria (c. 160-230) was one of the first to write of the necessity of subjecting to discipline those who needed to be purged of their sins committed after baptism.[52] Tertullian (c. 160-230) wrote of true repentance and baptism that washed away previous sins. However, in the unfortunate event that grave sins were committed after baptism there was one further opportunity for repentance. This was the severe discipline of repentance or penance, a discipline that involved confession, sackcloth and ashes, prostration, fasting, and so forth. This was to be available only once in a lifetime. [53]

Grave sins committed after baptism thus posed a major problem. Minor sins were not the subject of much concern. Augustine taught that they could be forgiven through prayer, such as the fifth petition of the Lord's Prayer. Grave sins, however, such as adultery, murder, or relapsing back to idolatry were of great concern. These were not to be blotted out by prayer, but only "by the greater humility of penance."[54]

One way that some tried to solve the problem of the threat of having to undergo a harsh penance was to wait until close to death before being baptized. As baptism forgave all previous sins, no penance need be exacted. The Emperor Constantine (280?-337) is an example of one who so delayed his baptism. Tertullian, for similar reasons, advised that baptism be deferred until after marriage because of the greater danger of falling into grave sexual sin by the unmarried.[55]

The doctrine of penance was considered to be based on the Church's

---

51 *Catechism of the Catholic Church*, 1994, sec. 1486 (Liguori Missouri: Liguori Publ.), p. 373.

52 Clement, *The Stromata,*, bk. 4, chap. 24, in *The Ante-Nicene Fathers*, vol. 2, p. 438.

53 Tertullian, *On Repentance*, chaps. 7-12, in *The Ante-Nicene Fathers*, vol. 3, pp. 662-666.

54 Augustine, *On the Creed*, sec. 15, in *The Nicene and Post-Nicene Fathers*, First Series, vol. 3, pp. 374, 375.

55 Tertullian, *On Baptism*, chap. 18, in *The Ante-Nicene Fathers*, vol. 3, p. 678.

power given to it by Christ to forgive or retain sins (John 20:22-23; Matthew 16:19 and 18:15-18). But the time came when the bishops would no longer readily offer Christ's forgiveness even to the truly repentant for what they considered grievous sins. They believed that the grave sins after baptism demanded that the sinner make reparations. A satisfaction had to be offered to the Lord. The bishops legislated into Canon Law what satisfaction to the Lord for gross and mortal sins was required of the repentant sinner. Today this is still the teaching of the Roman Catholic Church as is stated in their official catechism:

> Raised up from sin, the sinner must still recover his full spiritual health by doing something more to make amends for the sin: he must "make satisfaction for" or "expiate" his sins. This satisfaction is also called "penance."[56]

Among those who hold this view, there is little understanding of the continual state of baptismal grace and forgiveness in which a Christian lives. It is true faith in the redeeming sacrifice of Christ that cleanses from all sins committed in the weakness of human flesh. The purging was done once for all by Christ. John had written in this regard:

> . . . the blood of Jesus his Son cleanses us from all sin. If we say we have no sin, we deceive ourselves, and the truth is not in us. If we confess our sins, he is faithful and just, and will forgive our sins and cleanse us from all unrighteousness. If we say we have not sinned, we make him a liar, and his word is not in us.
> My little children, I am writing this to you so that you may not sin; but if any one does sin, we have an advocate with the Father, Jesus Christ the righteous; and he is the expiation for our sins, and not for ours only but also for the sins of the whole world. (1 John 1:7b-2:2 RSV)

There is no suggestion in the New Testament of any need for the sinner to offer reparation or satisfaction. The atonement made by Jesus Christ alone "cleanses us from all sin" and "is the expiation for our sins."

Paul, for example, had written to the Corinthian congregation that they should excommunicate the young man who was living incestuously with his father's wife (1 Corinthians 5:1-5). Evidently, the excommunication

---

56 *Catechism of the Catholic Church*, 1994, sec. 1459, p. 366.

had the desired effect of impressing on the young man the enormity of his sin. Upon his repentance, both the congregation and Paul forgave and reaffirmed their love for him (2 Corinthians 2:5-11). There is nothing here of years of prostration and penance. The church was as ready to forgive the young man as Christ was when He forgave the woman caught in adultery (John 8:1-11).

Paul had written, "Therefore, having been justified by faith, we have peace with God through our Lord Jesus Christ, through whom also we have access by faith into this grace in which we stand, and rejoice in hope of the glory of God" (Romans 5:1-2 NKJV). The Church at the end of the first century offered the peace and grace spoken of by Paul by the practice of a general confession and absolution. *The Didache* at that time instructed, "But every Lord's day [Sunday] do ye gather yourselves together, and break bread, and give thanksgiving, after having confessed your transgressions, that your sacrifice may be pure."[57] By this means, the early church put into practice Christ's words to His assembled disciples after His resurrection, "Receive the Holy Spirit. If you forgive the sins of any, they are forgiven them; and if you retain the sins of any, they are retained" (John 20:22b-23 NKJV).

In the 300s and 400s, penance for grave sin was available only once in a lifetime as a rule. Even after the period of penance was completed and the person was reconciled to the church severe disabilities remained. Especially in the Roman church, those admitted once more to fellowship and communion after penance had to submit to further restrictions. They were required to refrain from military service, not to engage in trade, not attend the games of the circus, and were expected to remain unmarried or if married to refrain from sexual relations with their spouses for the rest of their lives.[58]

The concept of a purgatory slowly evolved from the first speculations in the 200s and through the centuries thereafter. The idea of purgatorial punishment after death was seen as solving the problem concerning non-mortal sins for which the satisfaction had not been given or for which there was no time or opportunity in this life for giving satisfaction or reparation. The late development of this novel doctrine is seen in that Augustine (354-430) was of two minds about the emerging teaching of purgatory. In *The City of God,* he appears to accept the existence of a

---

57 *The Didache, The Teaching of the Twelve Apostles*, chap. 14, in *The Ante-Nicene Fathers*, vol. VII, p. 381.

58 Oscar D. Watkins, 1920, *A History of Penance*, Vol. 1 (New York: Burt Franklin, 1961), p. 482.

purgatory.[59] However, in his *Enchiridion*, a handbook of Christian doctrine, in discussing what Paul means when he speaks of fire consuming a man's work (1 Corinthians 3), Augustine wrote:

> And it is not impossible that something of the same kind may take place even after this life. It is a matter that may be inquired into, and either ascertained or left doubtful, whether some believers shall pass through a kind of purgatorial fire, and in proportion as they have loved with more or less devotion the goods that perish, be less or more quickly delivered from it.[60]

Pope Gregory the Great finally established the doctrine of purgatory in 604. It became one of the causes of the break between eastern Christianity and the Roman church, for the Orthodox churches of the East remained catholic in rejecting the doctrine of purgatory, deeming it a non-Biblical novelty.

The church's emphasis and focus on sin and penance and the danger of prolonged suffering in purgatory had a deleterious effect on the life of Christians. Those committing grave sins were often counseled to confine themselves to a monastery and endure a life-long remorse for their sins and thereby hope to regain the good graces of their God. The specter of unforgiven sin or the lack of sufficient satisfaction given for past sins haunted the lives of many. There was no "peace with God through our Lord Jesus Christ" as taught by Paul.

A pall therefore hung over the lives of many sincere Christians. No longer did the Christian live the joyous life of one who in a state of grace was secure in the knowledge that his faith in the redeeming death of Jesus Christ overcame his sinfulness. No longer was the Christian's life one of loving gratitude to the Lord who redeemed him and freed him completely from his sin and rebellion towards God. Thus no longer could the focus of his life be one of a love and gratitude towards God expressed in serving his fellow humans in keeping Christ's teaching of loving others as Christ loved him. His God became One who demanded that he pay a price for his sins, a price whose greatness he could never know. It was a price to be paid either

---

59 Augustine, *The City of God*, bk. 20, chap. 25; bk. 21, chaps. 13, 24; in *The Nicene and Post-Nicene Fathers*, First Series, vol. 2, pp. 445-446, 464, 470,

60 Augustine, *Enchiridion*, chap. 69, in *The Nicene and Post-Nicene Fathers*, First Series, vol. 3, p. 260.

by penitential suffering in this life or after death by undergoing the pangs of purgatory.

Canon Law and the Grave Sin of Apostasy

After every time of persecution, the Church was faced with what to do with the individuals who to escape persecution had denied that they were Christians but later wished to return to the faith. The sin of apostasy was considered grave, and the penance was severe. For example, the First Ecumenical Council of Nicaea in 325 A.D. concerned itself with those who fell away from the faith during the persecution under the reign of the Emperor Licinius (co-emperor 308 to 324). Canon 11, to give an example, dealt specifically with people who left the faith even though they were in no immediate danger of being persecuted. Canon 11 decreed that these apostates upon their repentance were to undergo a penance that would curtail their participation during the church service as follows:

> First, for three years as "hearers" they had to stand in the narthex or vestibule outside the nave [the church proper] during the liturgy [the church service].
>
> Second, for the next seven years as "prostrators" they could stand only in the rear of the nave. Before leaving they had to prostrate themselves before the bishop to receive his blessing. Both hearers and prostrators had to leave the church with the unbaptized catechumens halfway through the liturgy and before the start of the Eucharist, the Lord's Supper.
>
> Third, for two years more as "co-standers" they could remain for the whole service standing among the communing members of the congregation but could not receive communion themselves.
>
> Finally, after twelve years of penance they were received once more into full communion with the congregation.[61]

It is evident that the example set by Christ who a short time later compassionately forgave the repentant Peter his vehement denial of Him obviously was not considered a precedent to follow (Mark 14:66-72, John

---

61 *The First Council of Nice*, Canon 11, in *The Nicene and Post-Nicene Fathers*, Second Series, vol. 14, p. 24.

21:15-19).

Penance for Other Grave Sins

The canons of the church councils also set up penal codes for those who committed grave crimes such as adultery, murder, and other gross sins. To give an example, the provincial Council of Ancyra, the capital city of Galatia in Asia Minor, in 314 legislated:

> Canon 22. Concerning wilful murderers let them remain prostrators; but at the end of life let them be indulged with full communion.[62]

Canon 1 of the Fourth Ecumenical Council, meeting in Chalcedon near Constantinople in 451, ratified the canons of Ancyra and other provincial synods.[63]

Basil the Great (329?-379), Archbishop of Caesarea in Cappadocia of Asia Minor, wrote three canonical epistles comprising eighty-five canons. These canons were confirmed and ratified by the Quinisext Council in 692,[64] and also by the Seventh Ecumenical Council of Nice in 787.[65] A number of the canons deal with grave crimes and the penances exacted for them. The following are some examples:

> Canon 56, He that willfully commits murder, and afterwards repents, shall for twenty years remain without communicating of the Holy Sacrament. Four years he must mourn without the door of the oratory (church), and beg of the communicants that go in, that prayer be offered for him; then for five years he shall be admitted among the hearers, for seven years among the

---

62 *The Council of Ancyra*, Canon 22, in *The Nicene and Post-Nicene Fathers*, Second Series, vol. 14, p. 74.

63 *The Council of Chalcedon*, Canon 1, in *The Nicene and Post-Nicene Fathers*, Second Series, vol. 14, p. 267. See also p. 361 for the ratification by Canon 2 of the Quinisext Council in 692.

64 *The Council in Trullo, the Quinisext Council*, Canon 2, in *The Nicene and Post-Nicene Fathers*, Second Series, vol. 14, p. 361.

65 *The Second Council of Nice*, Canon 1, in *The Nicene and Post-Nicene Fathers*, Second Series, vol. 14, p. 555.

prostrators; for four years he shall be a co-stander with the communicants, but shall not partake of the oblation [the Lord's Supper]; when these years are completed, he shall partake of the Holy Sacrament.

Canon 57, The involuntary murderer for two years shall be a mourner, for three years a hearer, for four years a prostrator, one year a co-stander, and then communicate.

Canon 58, The adulterer shall be four years a mourner, five a hearer, four a prostrator, two a co-stander.

Canon 59, The fornicator shall be a mourner two years, two a hearer, two a prostrator, one a co-stander.

Canon 61, The thief, if he discover himself, shall do one year's penance, if he be discovered [by others] two; half the time he shall be a prostrator, the other half a co-stander.

Canon 62, He that abuses himself with mankind [homosexuality], shall do the penance of an adulterer.[66]

Thus, there developed in the 300s a rigorous system of public penance that grave sinners had to undergo in order to get back into the good graces of the church. In some cases, the penitent's bishop could reduce the severity of the penance. Only after the penance was accomplished would full absolution come from the bishop. With the imposition of the bishop's hands in blessing upon the head of the kneeling penitent, the offender would be finally reconciled with the church and once more be allowed to partake of the Holy Sacrament.

The Later Relaxation of Penance

After the conversion of the Emperor Constantine and his edict of toleration in 313, the rate of influx of people into especially the Eastern Church grew rapidly. But these people often were of a different stripe than the previous Christians. They were not a people who had had their faith tested by persecution. The church became more worldly as it achieved dominant status, and there were those that entered it because from a worldly point of view it now became advantageous to do so.

---

66 *The Canons of St. Basil*, Canons 56-59, 61, 62, in *The Nicene and Post-Nicene Fathers*, Second Series, vol. 14, p. 608. See also: St. Basil, *Letter 217, To Amphilochius, on the Canons*, Canons 56-59, 61, 62, ibid, vol. 8, pp. 256-257.

The western church additionally was faced with inroads into its territory by barbaric Germanic and other northern peoples through both migration and military invasion. Many of these, if they had any allegiance to Christianity at all, were heretical Arian Christians.[67] Their assimilation into non-Arian Christianity was a long process. The penitential discipline of the church had much less influence on these invaders from the north.

Thus, as time went on the severe penances of earlier centuries came to be more and more ignored in various parts of the church. The oftentimes-worldly church of the eastern Roman Empire and the church struggling for its survival in the West were not places where the Canon Law concerning penance could be rigorously observed.

The Penitentials

The Origin and Spread of the Penitentials

Isolated far to the northwest, a steadfast Celtic Christianity arose in Ireland, Scotland, and Wales unaffected by the turmoil of the invading barbaric peoples that was troubling Christianity in continental Europe. While Italy and Gaul were entering the dark ages, Greek and Latin scholarship in the Irish church flourished.

The monasteries were strong in Ireland and dominated Christianity on the island. They developed their own brand of monastic discipline. Following an ancient Egyptian tradition transmitted to the western monasticism by the writings of John Cassian, private confession of sins was part of the regular practice of the monks.[68]

Private confession was made typically to a priest although other holy persons were sometimes used, and the imposition of penances by a priest was basic to the Irish discipline. This was a novel feature in that a priest instead of the bishop gave absolution. The Irish practice of penance also allowed recurring confessions and penances. This was unlike the earlier discipline of Mediterranean Christianity where penance and absolution was

---

67 Arian Christianity followed the heretical opinions of Arius, a presbyter in the church of Alexandria who died in 336. Arius taught that God was alone and absolute and that Jesus Christ was created by God and thus not eternal or equal to God. He taught that Jesus was neither true God nor true man. The Nicene and Athanasian Creeds were formulated in sharp distinction to the views of Arius.

68 John Cassian, *The Twelve Books of John Cassian*, bk. 4, chap. 9, in *The Nicene and Post-Nicene Fathers*, Second Series, vol. 11, p. 221. Also *The Second Conference with Abbot Moses*, chaps. 10-13, vol. 11, pp. 312-315.

possible only once or at most twice in a lifetime.

As an aid to the priests who heard the confessions of the monks and nuns, during the 500s small books known as penitentials were written. These manuals were composed of canons that classified the various sins that might be committed by the monastics. They also gave the penances that were to be imposed by the confessor for the various sins. The earliest penitential manuals came from the Celtic church in Ireland, Wales, and Scotland.

The Anglo-Saxon church in England, established by the missionaries sent by Pope Gregory I in 597, never instituted the public canonical system of penance legislated by the church councils of the 300s and 400s. Therefore, it was easy for them to follow the pattern of private confession between priest and penitent used by the Celtic church; and they developed their own penitential books for use of the priest.

Celtic and Anglo-Saxon missionaries and monks made numerous missionary journeys to continental Europe around the beginning of the 600s. They founded many monasteries in the lands they visited. The penitentials that they had used in their homelands were carried along with them. From this beginning, the penitentials became widely used over the following centuries, especially in the non-Mediterranean lands of Europe.

Quite early the discipline of recurring private confession, penance, and absolution practiced by the monks became available also to the general Christian population. One of the earliest of the penitentials, *The Penitential of Finnian* (c. 525-550) indicates this. Although most of the canons are for monks, a considerable number deal with the sins of lay people. A few examples of canons from *The Penitential of Finnian* follow:

> 6. If anyone has started a quarrel and plotted in his heart to strike or kill his neighbor, if [the offender] is a cleric, he shall do penance for half a year with an allowance of bread and water and for a whole year abstain from wine and meats, and thus he will be reconciled to the altar.
> 7. But if he is a layman, he shall do penance for a week, since he is a man of this world and his guilt is lighter in this world and his reward less in the world to come.
>
> 25. If a cleric commits theft once or twice, that is, steals his neighbor's sheep or hog or any animal, he shall do penance an entire year on an allowance of bread and water and shall restore fourfold to his neighbor.
>
> 36. If any layman defiles his neighbor's wife or virgin daughter,

he shall do penance for an entire year on an allowance of bread and water, and he shall not have intercourse with his own wife; after a year of penance he shall be received to communion, and shall give alms for his soul.[69]

The Penitentials and the Married Christian

The perennial interest of the celibate clergy in regulating the sexual lives of the married laity is often evident in the penitentials. There were many canons in the penitentials that restricted the Christian freedom of married couples and sought to bind their consciences with law made by humans and not God. *The Penitential of Finnian* decreed:

> 46. We advise and exhort that there be continence in marriage, since marriage without continence is not lawful, but sin; and [marriage] is permitted by the authority of God not for lust but for the sake of children, as it is written, "And the two shall be in one flesh," that is, in the unity of the flesh for the generation of children, not for the lustful concupiscence of the flesh. Married people, then, must mutually abstain during the three forty-day periods in each single year, by consent for a time, that they may be able to have time for prayer for the salvation of their souls; and on Sunday night or Saturday night they shall mutually abstain, and after the wife has conceived he shall not have intercourse with her until she has borne her child, . . . [70]

Concerning the forty-day fast periods, a later English penitential, *The Confessional of Egbert*, (c. 950-1000) defined the three fast periods as follows:

> 37. . . . There are three lawful fasts in the year; one for all the people, namely, the one in the forty days before Easter, when we pay the yearly tithe, and the one in the forty days before the

---

69 John T. McNeill and Helena M. Gamer, 1938, *The Penitential of Finnian*, in the *Medieval Handbooks of Penance* (New York: Columbia U. Press, reprinted 1965 Octagon Books, Inc.), pp. 88, 92, 94.

72 John T. McNeill and Helena M. Gamer, 1938, *The Penitential of Finnian*, in the *Medieval Handbooks of Penance*, p. 96.

nativity, when all the people pray for themselves and read prayers, and the one in the forty days after Pentecost.[71]

Compiled in Ireland or Scotland around 650 and circulated in the domains of the Franks (modern France and much of adjacent Germany) in the 700s, *The Penitential of Cummean* ruled concerning the married:

> 28. In the case of one whose wife is barren, both he and she shall live in continence [without sexual intercourse].
>
> 30. He who is in a state of matrimony ought to be continent during the three forty-day periods and on Saturday and on Sunday, night and day, and in the two appointed week days [the fast days of Wednesday and Friday], and after conception, and during the entire menstrual period.
> 31. After a birth he shall abstain, if it is a son, for thirty-three [days]; if a daughter, for sixty-six [days].
> 32. A man whose child dies on account of neglect without baptism [shall do penance] for three years; in the first with bread and water, in the other two without delicacies and without the married relationship.[72]

Many other penitentials sought to regulate the marriage relationship of the laity, for example, *The Penitential of Theodore,* thought to be taken down from the rulings of Theodore of Tarsus, the Archbishop of Canterbury (in office c. 668-690). For about four hundred years, the penitential was widely used in the English church and in time also had wide usage on the continent. Theodore ruled:

> 20. He who has intercourse on the Lord's day shall seek pardon from God and do penance for one or two or three days.
> 21. In case of unnatural intercourse with his wife [anything other than the position of the man above the woman], he shall do penance for forty days the first time.

---

71 John T. McNeill and Helena M. Gamer, 1938, *The Confessional of Egbert*, in the *Medieval Handbooks of Penance*, p. 248.

72 John T. McNeill and Helena M. Gamer, 1938, *The Penitential of Cummean*, in the *Medieval Handbooks of Penance*, p. 105.

22. For a graver offense of this kind [the man behind the woman] he ought to do penance as one who offends with animals.

23. For intercourse at the improper season [Lent and others], he shall fast for forty days.

31. A husband ought not to see his wife nude.[73]

Regino's Ecclesiastical Discipline (c. 906) similarly ruled concerning the sexual life of married couples:

cccxl. Of Lent.--He who has intercourse with his wife during the forty days before Easter and refuses to abstain from her shall do penance for one year, or he shall pay to the church his own value, namely, twenty-six solidi, or distribute it to the poor. If it happened through drunkenness, not habitually, he shall do penance for forty days.[74]

Not only the motives for sex in marriage were in question; there were also numerous summaries of unnatural and sinful acts in marital sex. Only the position of the man on top facing the woman was considered permissible. All other positions were normally considered to be sinful to a lesser or greater degree.[75]

The emphasis above on sexual conduct found in the penitentials is not overstated. A scholar of the Sacrament of Penance recently wrote:

Yet sexuality holds a special place in medieval religion. For while it is true that the medieval church could excoriate all kinds of vices and all kinds of sins, it was inordinately concerned with the sexual. From the age of the Fathers, in fact, sex was disparaged and condemned in such excessive language that it is

---

73 John T. McNeill and Helena M. Gamer, 1938, *The Penitential of Theodore*, in the *Medieval Handbooks of Penance*, pp. 195-197, 211.

74 John T. McNeill and Helena M. Gamer, 1938, *Regino's Ecclesiastical Discipline*, in the *Medieval Handbooks of Penance*, p. 318.

75 Thomas N. Tentler, 1977, *Sin and Confession on the Eve of the Reformation* (Princeton, N.J.: Princeton U. Press), pp. 186-208.

difficult to acquit some of the most prominent Catholic theologians of a heretical dualism.[76]

For example, the influential Raymond of Peneforte (c. 1185-1275), a Spanish Dominican friar, in a treatise on Canon Law gives four motives for marital sex. They are: First, for the generation of offspring; Second, for rendering the debt, that is, fulfilling one's marital obligation [in accordance with 1 Corinthians 7:3-5]; Third, to avoid fornication; Fourth, to satisfy sexual desire. The first two are viewed as sinless, the third a venial sin, and the fourth a mortal sin. In respect to the fourth motive, Raymond cites Huguccio, a theological mentor of Pope Innocent III (1161-1216), who wrote, "Either coitus is a sin or it is not; but it can never be completely without sin because it always occurs with excitement and pleasure, which cannot be without sin."[77]

There were others, however, such as the noted French theologian Jean Gerson (1363-1429) and Albert the Great (1206-1280), the teacher of Thomas Aquinas, who were much more lenient in their views of marital sex. Gerson viewed intercourse between a married couple either sinless or only a venial sin.[78] Albert the Great saw no sin at all in marital intercourse.[79]

To sum up, during the Middle Ages the Roman church came to lay many restrictions on married love. The priests were to regard sexual relations between husband and wife as sinful during the following times: the forty days of Advent (before Christmas); the forty days of Lent; the Easter Week; the forty days after Pentecost; on a feast day; on a special fast day; during Saturday and Sunday, as it was too close to the time of going to Mass; during Wednesday and Friday, as they were fast days; when the wife was menstruating, pregnant, or nursing a child; during daylight hours; not while naked; and never for pleasure but only when trying to conceive a child. Before sexual intercourse, there was to be no fondling, and only the position

---

76 Thomas N. Tentler, 1977, *Sin and Confession on the Eve of the Reformation*, p. 165.

77 Thomas N. Tentler, 1977, *Sin and Confession on the Eve of the Reformation*, pp. 169, 175.

78 Thomas N. Tentler, 1977, *Sin and Confession on the Eve of the Reformation*, p. 180.

79 Vern L. Bullough and James Brundage, 1982, *Sexual Practices and the Medieval Church* (Buffalo New York: Prometheus Books), p. 64.

of the male face to face upon the female was normally considered permissible.[80]

The married life of Christians was burdened, therefore, with a host of churchly canons that closely regulated married love. If one as a sincere Christian took all the rules of the western Christian church seriously, a guilty conscience over one's relationship with one's spouse was undoubtedly an ever-present burden. The emphasis was on obeying church law rather than on living in Christian love with one's mate. The confession of one's supposed marital sins to the prying questions of the priest-confessor must have been a stressful time for the medieval Christian up through the time of the Reformation. The penitentials expected the priest to ask such questions.

The Far-ranging Canons of the Penitentials

The penitentials had canons that assigned penances for a multitude of real and imagined misdeeds other than the supposed sexual sins of a married couple. For example, *The Penitential of Cummean* (c. 650) mandated:

I. Of Gluttony:
> 2. He who compels anyone, for the sake of good fellowship, to become drunk shall do penance in the same manner as one who is drunk.

II. Of Fornication:
> 1. A bishop who commits fornication shall be degraded and shall do penance for twelve years.

> 23. A layman who defiles his neighbor's wife or virgin [daughter] shall do penance for one year with bread and water, without his own wife.

III. Of Avarice:
> 1. He who commits theft once shall do penance for one year; if [he does it] a second time, for two years.

---

80 James A. Brundage, 1987, *Law, Sex, and Christian Society in Medieval Europe*, pp. 154-164.

IV. Of Anger:

      7. But he who does this [murder] through anger, not from premeditation, shall do penance for three years with bread and water and with alms and prayers.

      8. But if he kills his neighbor unintentionally, by accident, he shall do penance for one year.[81]

The following canons are examples from a penitential known as *The Irish Canons* (c. 675):

      1. The penance of a parricide[82] is fourteen years, or half as long if [he commits the deed] on account of ignorance, on bread and water and with satisfaction.

      2. This is the penance of a homicide: seven years shall be served, on bread and water.

      13. The penance for eating horseflesh, four years on bread and water.

      20. The penance for the illicit drinking of what has been contaminated by the dead body of a mouse, seven days on bread and water.[83]

The influential *The Penitential of Theodore* cited previously decreed:

Book One, I. Of Excess and drunkenness

      6. Whoever is drunk against the Lord's command, if he has taken a vow of sanctity, shall do penance for seven days on bread and water, or twenty days without fat, laymen, without beer.

---

81 John T. McNeill and Helena M. Gamer, 1938, *The Penitential of Cummean*, in the *Medieval Handbooks of Penance*, pp. 101, 102, 104, 105, 107.

82 One who kills his parent(s)

83 John T. McNeill and Helena M. Gamer, 1938, *The Irish Canons*, in the *Medieval Handbooks of Penance*, pp. 118-121.

VII. Of Many and Diverse Evils

> 1. He who has committed many evil deeds, that is, murder, adultery with a woman and with a beast, and theft, shall go into a monastery and do penance until his death.

> 6. He who eats unclean flesh or a carcass that has been torn by beasts shall do penance for forty days. But if the necessity of hunger requires it, there is no offense, since a permissible act is one thing and what necessity requires is another.

XI. The Lord's Day

> 1. Those who labor on the Lord's day, the Greeks [Eastern Christianity] reprove the first time; the second, they take something from them; the third time, [they take] the third part of their possessions, or flog them; or they shall do penance for seven days.

> 4. But if he despises a fast appointed in the church and acts contrary to the decrees of the elders, not in Lent, he shall do penance for forty days. But if it is Lent, he shall do penance for one year

XII. Of the Communion of the Eucharist, or the Sacrifice

> 5. He who receives the sacrament after food shall do penance for seven days.[84]

The Judgment of Clement (c. 700-750), an early penitential, was in use in Western Europe. Among its 20 canons are the following:

> 6. If anyone unwittingly gives to another drink or food in which

---

84 John T. McNeill and Helena M. Gamer, 1938, *The Penitential of Theodore*, in the *Medieval Handbooks of Penance*, pp. 184-197.

there was a dead mouse or household beast, he shall perform three special fasts.

7. If through negligence anyone does work on Sunday, either bathes himself, or shaves, or washes his head, he shall do penance for seven days; if he does it again, he shall do penance for forty days; . . .

9. If anyone eats and afterwards takes communion, he shall do penance for seven days on bread and water. Boys shall be beaten for this.

17. No spoil [booty or loot] shall be received in the church before he who took the spoil does penance.

20. If during any festival anyone coming to the church sings outside it or dances or sings amatory songs, he shall be excommunicated by the bishop or presbyter or cleric and shall remain excommunicate so long as he does not do penance.[85]

A Spanish penitential, *The Penitential of Silos*, written around 800 illustrates the tight reign the priest had over the laity:

If anyone unintentionally swallows a drop of water while he is washing his face and his mouth to take communion, he shall sing a hundred psalms; nevertheless, he shall take the sacred elements. . . . Those who work on the Lord's day--something shall be taken from them; those who walk shall do penance for seven days. . . . If anyone commits perjury, he shall do penance for seven years. . . . Christians must not sing or dance when going to marriages. . . . He who in a rage speaks evil to a brother shall make satisfaction and thereafter do penance for seven days. . . . If anyone is known to be absent from church on solemn festival days, he shall be excommunicated.[86]

---

85 John T. McNeill and Helena M. Gamer, 1938, *The Judgment of Clement*, in the *Medieval Handbooks of Penance*, pp. 272-273

86 John T. McNeill and Helena M. Gamer, 1938, *The Penitential of Silos*, in the *Medieval Handbooks of Penance*, pp. 286-289.

In 830 the Frankish Bishop Halitgar of Cambrai was asked by the archbishop of Reims to produce a penitential that would end the discrepancies over penance found in many penitentials then in use. He produced what became known as *The Roman Penitential,* because he said that he found the penitential in a book repository of the Roman church. The Roman origin of the book has been disputed as many of the canons appear to be of Celtic origin. Halitgar begins his penitential with a discussion of how a bishop or priest ought to receive penitents. Then follow 105 canons of which the following are examples:

> 4. If any layman intentionally commits homicide he shall do penance for seven years, three of these on bread and water.
>
> 14. If anyone begets a child of the wife of another, that is, commits adultery and violates his neighbor's bed, he shall do penance for three years and abstain from juicy foods and from his own wife, giving in addition to the husband the price of his wife's violated honor.
> 15. If anyone wishes to commit adultery and cannot, that is, is not accepted, he shall do penance for forty days.
> 16. If anyone commits fornication with women, that is, with widows or girls, if with a widow, he shall do penance for a year; if with a girl, he shall do penance two years.
>
> 46. If anyone intentionally brings about abortion, he shall do penance for three years, one year on bread and water.
> 47. If anyone exacts usury from anybody, he shall do penance for three years, one year on bread and water.
>
> 65. He who eats the flesh of animals whose [manner of] death he does not know, shall do penance for a third part of a year.
>
> 89. If through necessity anyone steals articles of food or a garment or a beast on account of hunger or nakedness, pardon shall be given him. He shall fast for four weeks. If he makes restitution, thou shalt not compel him to fast.

100. If a hen dies in a well, the well is to be emptied. If one drinks knowingly of it, he shall fast for a week.[87]

As in Scripture and the early Church, homosexual practices were viewed as sinful throughout the medieval period. The outstanding medieval scholar Albert the Great viewed homosexual practices as especially sinful for the following reasons: "(1) it proceeded from a burning frenzy that subverted the order of nature; (2) the sin was distinguished by its disgusting foulness and yet was more likely to be found among persons of high degree than of low; (3) those who became addicted to such vices seldom succeeded in freeing themselves; (4) and, lastly, such vices were as contagious as any disease and spread rapidly from one to another."[88] *The Roman Penitential* of Bishop Halitgar ruled: "13. If any layman commits fornication as the Sodomites did, he shall do penance for seven years."[89]

The Laurentian Penitential (c. 1200) bound the Christian's conscience with non-Biblical church law that tightly regulated the observance of Sunday. It commanded:

47. We decree the observance with all reverence of all Lord's days from evening until evening, and abstinence from illicit work, [that] is, that there be no gainful trade, . . . that men shall neither carry on rural labors--the cultivation of vineyards, or planting of hedges, or the setting out of groves or the felling of trees--nor assemble to the tribunals; nor shall trading take place, nor hunting be engaged in. . . . Women shall not make woven work on the Lord's day; they shall not wash the head; they shall not sew garments together, nor pluck wool. . . . But they shall come together from all sides to the celebration of masses and shall praise God for the benefits which he has deigned to bestow upon us in that day. On the Lord's day it is not permissible to sail and ride for business in connection with any tasks, nor to make bread, nor to bathe, nor to write; for if anyone projects or carries

---

87 John T. McNeill and Helena M. Gamer, 1938, *The So-called Roman Penitential of Halitgar*, in the *Medieval Handbooks of Penance*, pp. 302-313.

88 Vern L. Bullough and James Brundage, 1982, *Sexual Practices and the Medieval Church*, pp. 64, 65.

89 John T. McNeill and Helena M. Gamer, 1938, *The So-called Roman Penitential of Halitgar*, in the *Medieval Handbooks of Penance*, p. 303.

on work, he shall do penance for seven days. . . .[90]

The penitentials were often more than just a list of sins and their prescribed penances. At times, there were instructions as to how the priest should ferret out the sins of the penitent. The famous French theologian Jean Gerson (1363-1429) in his treatise, *On the Confession of Masturbation*, for example, gives explicit and detailed instructions on how a priest during the confessional might guilefully get a boy to confess that he masturbates. Gerson instructs the priest to ask: "Friend, do you remember when you were young, about ten or twelve years old, your rod or virile member ever stood erect?" If the answer is yes, then the priest is to ask in a calm and non-threatening manner: "Friend, wasn't that thing indecent? What did you do, therefore, so that it wouldn't stand erect?" If the boy does not answer, the priest then asks: "Friend, didn't you touch or rub your member the way boys usually do?" If the penitent admits to this, the priest then asks for how long did he rub it. If he answers that he did it until the erection ceased, the act of masturbation is considered established.[91]

Even as late as 1700, penitentials were still in use within the Roman church. *The Milan Penitential* sets forth the following canons:

On the Third Commandment:

> 1. He who does any servile work on the Lord's day or on a feast day shall do penance for seven days on bread and water.
> 2. If anyone violates fasts set by Holy Church, he shall do penance for forty days on bread and water.
> 3. He who violates the fast in Lent shall do a seven-day penance for one day.
> 4. He who without unavoidable necessity eats flesh in Lent shall not take communion at Easter and shall thereafter abstain from flesh.

---

90 John T. McNeill and Helena M. Gamer, 1938, *The Laurentian Penitential*, in the *Medieval Handbooks of Penance*, pp. 352 353.

91 Thomas N. Tentler, 1977, *Sin and Confession on the Eve of the Reformation*, pp. 91, 92.

On the Fourth Commandment:

> 5. If anyone despises or derides the command of his bishop, or of the bishop's servants, or of his parish priest, he shall do penance for forty days on bread and water.

On the Sixth Commandment:

> 7. If any woman paints herself with ceruse or other pigment in order to please men, she shall do penance for three years.

On the Seventh Commandment:
> 3. He who retains to himself his tithe or neglects to pay it, shall restore fourfold and do penance for twenty days on bread and water.[92]

The use of a penitential as an aid to a priest hearing confession presented its own peculiar problems. The priest had to make careful use of a penitential to avoid giving the penitent insight into sins about which he was ignorant. In a capitulary or ruling by Bishop Theodulf of Orleans (c. 798), the following is found:

> But he who makes confession shall bend his knees with the priest before God and then confess whatever he is able to recall from his youth--his behavior in all particulars. And if he cannot recall all his misdeeds, or if perchance he hesitates, the priest ought to ask him whatever is set down in the penitential--whether he has fallen into this offense or another. But, nevertheless, not all the offenses ought to be made known to him, since many faults are read in the penitential which it is not becoming for the man to know. Therefore the priest ought not to question him about them all, lest perchance, when he has gone away from him, at the devil's persuasion he fall into some

92 John T. McNeill and Helena M. Gamer, 1938, *The Milan Penitential*, in the *Medieval Handbooks of Penance*, p. 366-367.

one of those offenses of which he previously did not know.[93]

Some who disputed their authority opposed the growing use of the penitential books. The ancient canons discussed earlier in this chapter concerning public penance had never been completely ignored, and the penitentials were thought to be both of much lesser authority and contradictory to them. Unlike the ancient canonical penance, the penitentials allowed repeated penance and absolution and had no restrictions on the life of the penitent after his penance was completed. The provincial Council of Chalon in 813 completely repudiated the penitentials as did the provincial Council of Paris in 829. On the other hand, the provincial Council of Tours in 813 suggested that the bishops should give careful thought to what penitential book they should recommend to their presbyter-priests.[94]

The usefulness of the penitentials to the clergy of the medieval church cannot be denied. If the laity had to come to their clergy for confession and absolution, it gave the clergy great control over their lives. It gave the clergy a practical way of forcing compliance with the canons and laws of the church. If absolution was withheld by a priest from a recalcitrant layman, the layman was given to understand that his eternal salvation was in jeopardy.

The spiritual benefits of the proper use of confession and absolution, on the other hand, are also not to be denied. Christ did give His Church the authority to loose or retain sins. And the announcement of absolution can be of great comfort to the Christian. However, to use the Sacrament of Penance as a club over the laity to force compliance with the new codes of law with which the bishops saddled the church was a grievous sin against the Christian liberty of Christ's people.

The use of the penitentials had spread rapidly in especially the non-Italian European churches. Pope Innocent III (in office from 1198-1216), perhaps both for spiritual and practical reasons, realized their usefulness to the church. In 1215, the practice of private confession, penance, and absolution became a requirement in the Roman church. The Fourth Lateran Council under Innocent III decreed the following canon:

---

93 John T. McNeill and Helena M. Gamer, 1938, in the *Medieval Handbooks of Penance*, p. 397.

94 John T. McNeill and Helena M. Gamer, 1938, in the *Medieval Handbooks of Penance*, pp. 401, 402.

xxi. Every Christian of either sex, after attaining years of discretion, shall faithfully confess all his sins to his own priest at least once a year, and shall endeavor to his ability to fulfill the penance enjoined upon him, reverently receiving the sacrament of the Eucharist at least at Easter, . . . Otherwise he shall both be withheld from entrance to the church while he lives and be deprived of Christian burial when he dies. . . .[95]

With this canon, the voluntary nature of the confession of one's sins to God or to another human was legislated away. Confession of one's sins had to be to the Christian's own parish priest. There was to be no shopping around for a more lenient priest. Only with permission granted from his parish priest was a Christian allowed to confess to another priest. Upon pain of excommunication, the Christian had to make confession at least once a year. The freedom of the Christian to practice his faith as led by the Holy Spirit and informed by the New Testament was once more overridden by church law. The Christian liberty that Paul taught in his letter to the church at Colossae was ignored. It was as if Paul had never written:

See to it that no one takes you captive through philosophy and empty deception, according to the tradition of men, according to the elementary principles of the world, rather than according to Christ. . . . Therefore let no one act as your judge in regard to food or drink or in respect to a festival or a new moon or a Sabbath day-- . . . If you have died with Christ to the elementary principles of the world, why, as if you were living in the world, do you submit yourself to decrees, such as, "Do not handle, do not taste, do not touch!" (which all refer to things destined to perish with the using)--in accordance with the commandments and teachings of men? These are matters which have, to be sure, the appearance of wisdom in self-made religion and self-abasement and severe treatment of the body, but are of no value against fleshly indulgence. (Colossians 2:8, 16, 20-23 NASB)

The preoccupation with sinfulness that is found in the penitentials

---

95 John T. McNeill and Helena M. Gamer, 1938, in the *Medieval Handbooks of Penance*, p. 413.

and in the Roman church's Sacrament of Penance necessarily had a debilitating effect on the Christian's life. The focus of the Christian's life was not on following Christ's example of a life of selfless and self-denying love and goodness. It was rather centered on the avoidance of evil, both real and those evils that sprang from the imagination of the clergy.

In questioning the Christian, the priest in following the guidance of his penitential was not likely to inquire about whether the Christian was living a faith active in love. There was no casuistry of love as there was an almost endless casuistry of sin. The emphasis was once more on avoidance of sin and evil rather than on a life that fulfilled the moral law of the Ten Commandments through Christian love expressed in unselfish service to one's fellowman.

The confessional was not a place where the Christian shared with his priest his joys of service to Christ through serving even the least of Christ's brethren. It was a place where a Christian was to scour his conscience aided by the questioning of the priest for every evidence of sin, sins truly against God and sins as determined by the churchly codes of canon law.[96] It resulted in a piety motivated by fear rather than love.[97] It produced a guilt-ridden church where too often good deeds were not done out of gratitude and love for God but rather from the necessity of paying the penalties of the assigned penance or out of fear of the pangs of purgatory.

The use of penitentials to aid the priests in hearing confessions and assigning penances continued to the time of the Reformation in the 1500s and beyond. Among the more prominent later penitentials were the *Summa Angelica* written by the Franciscan Angelus do Clavasio and the *Sylvestrina* written at the time of the Reformation by the Dominican Sylvester Prierias Mazzolina. One of the main aspects of the later penitentials was the growing use of lenient penances. The *Summa Angelica* is especially noted for this.[98]

At the time of the Reformation, therefore, the legalistic strictures of the penitentials of the Roman church were still very much in evidence. An enormous and entangling body of constantly growing church law bound the

---

96 Thomas N. Tentler, 1977, *Sin and Confession on the Eve of the Reformation*, pp. 135, 139.

97 Lewis W. Spitz, 1974, "Further Lines of Inquiry for the Study of Reformation and Pedagogy," in *The Pursuit of Holiness in Late Medieval and Renaissance Religion*, Charles Trinkaus with Heiko Oberman, eds. (Leiden: E.J. Brill), p. 296.

98 Thomas N. Tentler, 1977, *Sin and Confession on the Eve of the Reformation*, pp. 336-339.

conscience of the Christian. The Christian's God-given liberty to be guided by God's Spirit as he sought to live in accordance with Christ's New Commandment was severely eroded. It was time to hear once more the words of Paul who, highly irritated by those Judaizers who insisted that gentile Christians had to submit to the laws of the Old Testament, wrote to the Galatians: "For freedom Christ has set us free; stand fast therefore, and do not submit again to a yoke of slavery" (Galatians 5:1 RSV).

Nevertheless, Church Law Eclipsed but Did Not Extinguish Christian Love in the Medieval Church

This is not to say that Christian love disappeared from the medieval church. One should not paint too grim a picture of the place of Christian love during the medieval period. Following the first beginnings mentioned in a previous chapter, hospitals, especially for the poor, spread throughout Europe, many attached to monasteries.

For all his legalistic tendencies, the great preacher and Archbishop, Caesarius of Arles (470-542), whose sermons were published and republished throughout the Middle Ages, could also proclaim:

> When you assemble in church, let each one give in offering to the poor whatever he can. Moreover, entertain strangers in your dwelling with great kindness; do what you can for them, and wash their feet. Above all, visit the sick, and, if any people are in disagreement, with all your might recall them to peace and harmony. Thus, at the day of judgment that desirable word may be addressed to you: "I was hungry, and you gave me to eat, . . ."[99]

Caesarius of Arles is hardly alone in this. The strong-minded bishop of Milan, Ambrose, modified his strict legalistic temperament with many acts of Christian love.

Although hardly one of his emphases, Thomas Aquinas (1225-1274) wrote, "The New Law consists chiefly in the grace of the Holy Ghost, which is shown forth by faith working through love." He could write also of the Christian liberty that prevails in the many deeds wrought by faith working through love that canon law left to the discretion of each

---

99 Caesarius of Arles, *Sermons*, Vol. 1, pp. 80-81.

individual.[100]

In keeping with the teaching of the Roman church, many unquestionably engaged in charitable deeds in order to gain merit before God for themselves to avoid temporal punishment in this life or purgatory or to attain for themselves a higher degree of eternal reward. Nonetheless, undoubtedly many others were led by the Spirit to do acts of Christian love and mercy with the pure heart commended by Jesus and primarily out of love and gratitude to their Savior. God's Holy Spirit is ever active sanctifying the lives of His faithful people, both laity and clergy. The acts of love and mercy of a multitude of medieval Christians remain nameless and unrecorded. They followed the counsel of their Lord that when you give alms you are not to let your left hand know what your right hand is doing (Matthew 6:3). The effect of the gentleness and love in their lives is seen in how they changed the fierceness of many of the barbaric tribes who moved in among them.

---

100 Thomas Aquinas, *The Summa Theologica*, Vol. 2, (Chicago: Encyclopedia Brittanica, Inc.), p. 331.

Chapter Thirteen

LUTHER AND THE RETURN TO
JESUS' WAY OF LIFE

Luther and the Protestant Reformation

Luther's Break with the Roman Catholic Church

It was on a late fall day in 1520, that Martin Luther (1483-1546), the founder of the Protestant Reformation, cast onto a bonfire in Wittenberg Germany the papal bull, *Exsurge Domini*, to the cheers of his students and the townspeople.[1] This document, signed by Pope Leo X, threatened Luther with excommunication if he did not disown and recant his teachings within sixty days.

Also upon the fire, Luther cast the books of Canon Law of the Roman Catholic Church and one of the most recent and popular of the Roman church's penitentials, the *Summa Angelica*.[2] This last was a widely-used penitential that treated in alphabetical order all possible cases of conscience and sin with which priests might deal as they listened to the confessions of their parishioners. The penitential gave penances for each violation. With these symbolic actions, Luther signaled his attempt to break the heavy yoke of church law fastened on the necks of Christian people. They foretold his endeavor to restore to Christ's people their Christian liberty to follow a life based on a faith active in Christian love as taught in the New Testament apart from the dictates of a legalistic church.

---

1 Henry S. Lucas, 1934, *The Renaissance and the Reformation* (New York: Harper and Bros. Publ.) p. 444.

2 Thomas N. Tentler, 1977, *Sin and Confession on the Eve of the Reformation* (Princeton, N.J.: Princeton U. Press), p. 35.

Luther's Early Years

Martin Luther's father, a successful miner, had sacrificed to give his son an education in law. After Martin Luther's attainment of a Master of Arts degree, however, he underwent a profound religious experience. It caused him to leave his studies at the University of Erfurt. To the displeasure of his father, in 1505 at age twenty-two Luther entered a strict Augustinian monastery in Erfurt. Two years later, he was ordained a priest and celebrated his first mass.

His religious superiors soon recognized the new monk's brilliance of mind and dedication. However, it was over Luther's protests that he was directed by them to work for a doctorate in theology. This he obtained in 1512. To Luther's further unhappiness, they directed him to move from Erfurt to the monastery at Wittenberg. There he was to teach at the University of Wittenberg recently founded by Frederick the Wise, the Duke of Electoral Saxony. At first, he had to teach Aristotelian philosophy. Soon, however, he was required to teach courses on the books of the Bible. His training as a priest, his education for the doctorate in theology, and his study of the Bible as a professor led him deeply into both the Old and New Testament Scriptures.

Luther as Scholar, Teacher, and Preacher

Luther was a prodigious scholar, writer, and preacher. The German Weimar edition of his works fills over 100 large volumes. An abbreviated edition of his works in English fills fifty-four volumes. And even these volumes include few of the sermons found in what is known as his *Church Postil*, a collection of Luther's sermons written for the clergy as a source for and examples of Christian preaching.

Of all Luther's sermons, the most important are those of the *Church Postil*. A postil can be either a single sermon based on one of the Scripture readings for a given day or a collection of such sermons. Luther wrote his *Church Postil*, comprising in English an eight-volume edition of around 3200 pages, at the request of Duke Frederick the Wise in whose domains Luther lived. Duke Frederick knew that many clergy had little training in either theology or in writing sermons. He therefore asked Luther to write sample sermons to serve as models for the clergy as to what constitutes good Christian preaching.

The *Church Postil* is composed of studies and sermons that are carefully worked out in terms of what Luther felt should be preached to God's people. If one wants to see what is important in Luther's understanding of Christian preaching, his carefully written sermons in the *Church Postil* are an excellent source. In these he preached those truths that he felt should be primary for the life and understanding of Christian people. Starting in 1520 and over a period of many years, he continued to write the sermons based mainly on the traditional Bible texts that were read during worship on the various Sundays and days of the Church Year. Luther considered the sermons that make up the *Church Postil* to be, "The best of all his books."[3]

The sermons also show Luther's intellectual development as he continued his evaluation of medieval theology and practice during the 1520s. For example, Luther's early sermons in the *Church Postil* often end with a discussion of the spiritual, that is, the allegorical interpretation of the Scripture text. Luther soon realized, however, the unwarranted speculation that resulted from forcing an allegorical interpretation on each text. Although treating texts allegorically was a time-honored and standard method in medieval preaching going back to the time of Origen (185?-254?), Luther in his *Church Postil* soon discards this often illegitimate way of interpreting a text.

Other than the sermons he wrote in the *Church Postil*, many of Luther's sermons come only from notes taken down by various listeners; for he usually preached from just a brief outline. Luther also at times preached long series of sermons based on a particular book of the Bible. Some of these sermons were later combined and edited by Luther and others to form an extended commentary on the book.

Luther's View of the Bible

The Holy Scriptures were for Luther the primary authority in understanding the teachings of the Christian faith. Luther often cited the writings of the church fathers in his lectures; however, as did Augustine (see pages 271-272), Luther gave preeminence to the books of Scripture. He accepted the opinions of the church fathers only insofar as they agreed with Holy Scripture. Concerning those who would deny the authority of the Bible, Luther advised in a sermon on First Peter:

> Therefore if people refuse to believe, you should keep silence; for you have no obligation to force them to regard Scripture as God's Book or Word. It is sufficient for you to base your proof on Scripture.[4]

---

3 *Sermons of Martin Luther*, the *Church Postil* (Grand Rapids: Baker Book House), vol. 1, p. 3.

4 Martin Luther, *Sermons on the First Epistle of St. Peter*, in *Luther's Works* (Philadelphia and St. Louis: Fortress Press and Concordia Publ. Hse.), vol. 30, p. 107.

Luther identified the Word of God with the Holy Scriptures. In discussing the Biblical basis for the doctrine of the Trinity in a sermon on John's Gospel, Luther taught:

> So be governed by this fact and say: "I believe and confess that there is one eternal God and, at the same time, three distinct Persons, even though I cannot fathom and comprehend this. For Holy Scripture, which is God's Word, says so; and I abide by what it states."[5]

Luther fully understood that the infinite mind of God far surpassed the finite brain of man with its limited human reasoning. In this he differed from some of other Protestant reformers who too often tried to subject the mysteries of God that are revealed in Scripture to the logic of human reasoning. Luther in a sermon on John's Gospel explained his approach to the Word of God and its teachings as follows:

> First of all, John warns all those who hear this doctrine of Christ not to pry and to question when God's Word and spiritual matters are concerned, and not to ask how this can be reconciled with reason. Whoever wants to be a Christian and apprehend the articles of the Christian faith must not consult reason and mind how a doctrine sounds and whether it is consistent with reason. He must say forthwith: "I do not care whether it agrees with reason or not. All I must know is whether or not it is supported by God's Word. This I ask: Did God say it? That decides it for me." [6]

Although a university professor himself, Luther looked with dismay at the scholarship of the doctors of theology in the universities. As is still often the case today, their struggles to constantly come up with some new insight often led them to poorly supported, trendy, and speculative ideas and concepts, speculations whose low levels of probability they ignored. Thus, things never seem to change. If one looks back, for example, over the past one hundred years of university Biblical scholarship, Luther's comments in his *Exhortation to All Clergy* are obviously as appropriate

---

5 Martin Luther, *Sermons on the Gospel of St. John*, in *Luther's Works*, vol. 22, p. 6.

6 Martin Luther, *Sermons on the Gospel of St. John*, in *Luther's Works*, vol. 23, pp. 78-79.

today in many instances as when he wrote:

> Even at that, the doctors in the universities helped along [with
> the downfall of theology]. They had nothing else to do than to
> devise new "opinions," one after another. One could not be a
> doctor with special honors unless one had brought forth
> something new. They were at their very best, however, in that
> they despised the Holy Scriptures and let them lie under the
> bench. "What? The Bible? The Bible?" they said, "The Bible is a
> heretics' book! You must read the doctors! There you find what
> is what."[7]

Luther had little respect for those who preferred the opinions of men to the
revelation of God in the Holy Scriptures.

Luther's Major Insight: Salvation by Faith Alone

It was out of his profound study of the Bible that Luther achieved
insight into his major spiritual problem. He had agonized over whether a
Christian could ever be confident of his salvation if it were partly dependent
on the merits of his good works. This uncertainty had long troubled him.
His years as a monk in a strict monastery had not overcome his anxiety.
Finally, through his study of the letters of Paul, he came to the answer—
Man cannot earn salvation by working his way up into God's good graces.
Rather, it is God who out of steadfast love and pure grace must descend to
man with His offer of forgiveness of sins and eternal salvation. Salvation
depends solely on a Christian's faith in the merits of Jesus Christ and in
Jesus' sacrificial death on the cross. Through faith alone in Christ's work of
salvation comes forgiveness of sins and the promise of eternal life with
God. The good works a person might accomplish either before or after his
conversion play no part in his salvation. It is faith alone in the saving power
of the blood of Jesus Christ that cleanses man from all sins (1 John 1:7-10).
Luther had come to understand the full meaning of the words Paul
had written:

> For I am not ashamed of the gospel of Christ, for it is the power
> of God to salvation for everyone who believes, for the Jew first
> and also for the Greek. For in it the righteousness of God is
> revealed from faith to faith; as it is written, "The just shall live by

---

7 Martin Luther, *Exhortation to All Clergy*, in *Luther's Works*, vol. 34, p. 27.

faith" (Romans 1:16-17 NKJV).

Paul further explained:

> For there is no difference; for all have sinned and fall short of the glory of God, being justified freely by His grace through the redemption that is in Christ Jesus, . . . Where is boasting then? It is excluded. By what law? Of works? No, but by the law of faith. Therefore we conclude that a man is justified by faith apart from the deeds of the law. . . . Therefore, having been justified by faith, we have peace with God through our Lord Jesus Christ. (Romans 3:22b, 27-28, 5:1 NKJV).

No longer did fears of the agony of hell or the pangs of purgatory assail Luther. He had received "peace with God" through his faith in the love of God as revealed in the life, death, and resurrection of God's Son Jesus. There was no need to make further satisfaction for his sins. Luther in his study of Scripture thus came to the same conclusion as did Augustine[8]—we are not saved by our good works, but through our faith in Jesus Christ, a faith that is a gift of God. Salvation through faith alone became the watchword of those who followed Luther in his reformation of the Roman Catholic Church.

Luther's Second Major Teaching:
A True Faith Is Active in Deeds of Christian Love

The Neglect of Luther's Emphasis on Love and Good Works

The doctrine of salvation by faith alone, however, came to loom so large in the minds of Luther's followers that another major emphasis of Luther's became obscured. Luther's stress on salvation by faith alone did not mean that he had no interest in a Christian's living a life of Christian love expressed in good works. Luther almost equally stresses that while good works play no part in one's salvation because all is due to God's grace alone, good works are a natural outcome of a true faith.

This major emphasis of Luther's on a faith active in love that results in a life of good works is not sparsely but repeatedly found throughout his writings. It is found in his major theological writings, in his commentaries, and especially in his *Church Postil* and other sermons. To see the emphasis

---

8 see pages 284-286

and the connection that Luther makes between faith and good works, one need but read the very first sermon of his *Church Postil*.[9] The first section of the sermon concerns faith and the second section good works. Luther then states that these two "constitute a true and complete Christian life."

Luther's greatest stress in his sermons is on the good news of God's love and forgiveness as exemplified in the life, death, and resurrection of Jesus Christ. Through this preaching, the Holy Spirit could work the gift of faith in the hearer (Romans 10:17). However, a theme that also runs throughout his sermons is that a true faith will be active in deeds of Christian love.

In the following pages, Luther's own words will be extensively quoted concerning the many ways in which faith is to be active in love. For two reasons this is done:

> First, that you may read Luther's words first hand. There is no substitute for the primary documents. The extensive and full footnotes will easily allow you to go back to the entire document if you wish to check further. The quotations are sometimes long in order to give the context of a given point. Luther should not be made to say what he never intended.

> Second, that you may better understand the founder of the Protestant Reformation as you experience the vigorous vitality of Luther's outspoken, salty, good-natured personality. If chronic illnesses such as the agony of kidney stones at times abraded his naturally ebullient temperament in his later years, they still could not stifle his joy in people, life, and his Lord.

Faith Active in Love

Faith, Luther repeatedly emphasizes, is active in Christian love. The fruit of faith is a life of good works in serving one's neighbor. Good works are to follow faith, Luther taught, as rays of light accompany the rising of the sun. Jesus did not come as a new lawgiver. His New Commandment is the fulfilling of the commandments. It is the principle by which a Christian lives and written by God's Spirit on the Christian's heart. One does not order an apple tree to bear fruit. As it is the nature of apple trees to bear apples, so also it is the nature of true Christian faith to be active in deeds of love.[10] In his preface to Paul's letter to the Romans, Luther explains the close

---

9 Martin Luther, *Sermons of Martin Luther*, the *Church Postil*, vol. 1, pp. 19-41.

10 Ida Walz Blayney, 1957, *The Age of Luther* (New York: Vantage Press), p. 415.

connection between saving faith and a life of good works:

> Faith is a living, daring, confidence in God's grace, so sure and certain that a man would stake his life on it a thousand times. This confidence in God's grace and knowledge of it makes men glad and bold and happy in dealing with God and with all His creatures; and this is the work of the Holy Ghost in faith. Hence a man is ready and glad, without compulsion, to do good to everyone, to serve everyone, to suffer everything, in love and praise of God, who has shown him this grace; and thus it is impossible to separate works from faith, quite as impossible as to separate heat and light from fire.[11]

Good Works Do Not Save but Flow from Faith

Again, however, Luther does not allow God's saving gift of faith to be confused with the life of love and good works that flowed from that faith. He made that clear in his *Lectures on Galatians*:

> Therefore we conclude with Paul that we are justified solely by faith in Christ, without the Law and works. But after a man is justified by faith, now possesses Christ by faith, and knows that He is his righteousness and life, he will certainly not be idle but, like a sound tree, will bear good fruit (Matthew 7:17). For the believer has the Holy Spirit; and where He is, He does not permit a man to be idle but drives him to all the exercises of devotion, to the love of God, to patience in affliction, to prayer, to thanksgiving, and to the practice of love toward all men. Therefore we, too, say that faith without works is worthless and useless.[12]

God's Judgment on the Basis of Works

Luther was concerned that Christians should not be led astray when the Scriptures speak of God's judgment according to works. In a sermon on

---

11 Martin Luther, *Preface to the Epistle to the Romans*, 1522, in the *Works of Martin Luther*, Phila. Ed. (Grand Rapids: Baker Book House), vol. 6, p. 452.

12 Martin Luther, *Lectures on Galatians*, 1535, in *Luther's Works*, vol. 26, p. 154-155.

1 Peter 1:27 he explained:

> Since we say that God saves us solely through faith and without
> regard to works, why, pray, does St. Peter say that God does not
> judge according to the person, but that He judges according to
> the works? Answer: What we have taught, that faith alone
> justifies before God, is undoubtedly true, since it is so clear from
> Scripture that it cannot be denied. Now what the apostle says
> here, that God judges according to the works, is also true. But
> one should maintain with certainty that where there is no faith,
> there can be no good works either, and, on the other hand, that
> there is no faith where there are no good works. Therefore link
> faith and good works together in such a way that both make up
> the sum total of the Christian life. As you live, so you will fare.
> God will judge you according to this. Therefore even though God
> judges us according to our works, it nevertheless remains true
> that the works are only the fruits of faith. They are the evidence
> of our belief or unbelief. Therefore God will judge and convict
> you on the basis of your works. They show whether you have
> believed or have not believed, . . . God will not judge according
> to whether you are called a Christian or have been baptized. No,
> He will ask you: "If you are a Christian, then tell Me: Where are
> the fruits with which you can show your faith?"[13]

As James Writes, Faith without Works is Dead

Luther repeatedly instructs that good works are the natural fruit of
faith. He also, as in the above, many times makes it explicit that if a life of
Christian love does not follow, true faith is not present. In his *Church Postil*
Luther liked to cite the letter of James on this point:

> Even those who gladly hear and understand the doctrine of pure
> faith do not proceed to serve their neighbor, as though they
> expected to be saved by faith without works: they see not that
> their faith is not faith, but a shadow of faith, just as the picture
> in the mirror is not the face itself, but only a reflection of the
> same, as St. James so beautifully writes, saying, "But be ye

---

13 Martin Luther, *Sermons on the First Epistle of St. Peter*, in *Luther's Works*, vol.
30, p. 34-35.

doers of the word, and not hearers only, deluding your own selves. . . "[14]

And in another sermon:

This is what St. James means when he says in his Epistle, 2:26: "Faith without works is dead." That is, as the works do not follow, it is a sure sign that there is no faith there; but only an empty thought and dream, which they falsely call faith.[15]

Luther had his reservations about James' Epistle. In considering the edifying depiction of Christ and the teachings of Christianity found in St. John's Gospel and his First Epistle, the Epistles of St. Paul, and St. Peter's first Epistle, he wrote that "St. James' Epistle is really an epistle of straw, compared to them; for it has nothing of the nature of the Gospel about it."[16]

Pastors Are to Urge their People to Good Works

Luther in lecturing to his students on Galatians 6:8 instructed the future Christian pastors to encourage their people to a life of good works:

It is extremely necessary, following Paul's example, to exhort believers to do good works, that is, to exercise their faith through good works; for unless these works follow faith, this is the surest possible sign that the faith is not genuine.[17]

Luther, however, instructed that preachers should be very careful not to confuse faith and good works in the minds of the people:

It is difficult and dangerous to teach that we are justified by faith without works and yet to require works at the same time. Unless the ministers of Christ are faithful and prudent here and are 'stewards of the mysteries of God' (1 Cor. 4:1), who rightly divide

---

14 Martin Luther, *Sermons of Martin Luther*, the *Church Postil*, vol. 1, p. 112-113.

15 Martin Luther, *Sermons of Martin Luther*, the *Church Postil*, vol. 4, p. 308.

16 Martin Luther, *Preface to the New Testament*, 1545 (1522), in the *Works of Martin Luther*, Phila. Ed., vol. 6, p. 444.

17 Martin Luther, *Lectures on Galatians*, 1535, in *Luther's Works*, vol. 27, p. 127.

the Word of truth (2 Tim. 2:15) they will immediately confuse faith and love at this point. Both topics, faith and love, must be carefully taught and emphasized, but in such a way that they both remain within their limits. Otherwise, if works alone are taught, as happened under the papacy, faith is lost. If faith alone is taught, unspiritual men will immediately suppose that works are not necessary.[18]

Unfortunately, it is my experience that Luther's counsel has too many times gone unheeded in the preaching of many pastors.

The Relationship between Faith and Love

Faith and love are the two services and works asked of us by our God—faith in the redemption wrought for us by Christ, love expressed in service to our neighbor. Luther commented on these in his interpretation of John's account of the people asking Jesus, "'What shall we do, that we may work the works of God?' Jesus answered and said to them, 'This is the work of God, that you believe in Him whom He has sent.'" (John 6:28-29 NKJV). In his *Lectures on Galatians,* Luther explained:

> For the true service of God consists in faith in Him whom the Father sent, namely, Jesus Christ. . . . Therefore if you want to serve God, bear in mind that you must believe in Him whom the Father sent. If you want to know how to obtain God's grace and how to approach God, how to render satisfaction for your sin, and how to escape death, then this is truly God's will and true service, that you believe in Christ. . . . For faith is a divine work which God demands of us; but at the same time He Himself must implant it in us, for we cannot believe by ourselves. . . . "After that follow the external good works toward your neighbor, and this is a service also demanded of you by God. This service to man will not fail after we first render God the service we owe Him. In this way you and God will be at one."[19]

---

18 Martin Luther, *Lectures on Galatians, in Luther's Works,* 1535, v. 27, pp. 62-63.

19 Martin Luther, *Sermons on the Gospel of St. John,* in *Luther's Works*, vol. 23, pp. 22, 23, 27.

Luther's writings are filled with a continued emphasis on a faith that expresses itself in love and service to one's neighbor. As mentioned above, in his eight volume *Church Postil* he underscored the importance of faith and love by making them the first two topics he discusses in his first sermon. After a discussion of saving faith, Luther continued:

> We have said enough of faith. We now come to consider good works. We receive Christ not only as a gift by faith, but also as an example of love toward our neighbor, whom we are to serve as Christ serves us. Faith brings and gives Christ to you with all his possessions. Love gives you to your neighbor with all your possessions. These two things constitute a true and complete Christian life, then follow suffering and persecution for such faith and love; and out of these grows hope in patience. . . . Thus it is not your good work that you give alms or that you pray, but that you offer yourself to your neighbor and serve him, wherever he needs you and every way you can, be it with alms, prayer, work, fasting, counsel, comfort, instruction, admonition, punishment, apologizing, clothing, food, and lastly with suffering and dying for him. . . . A good work is good for the reason that it is useful and benefits and helps the one for whom it is done; why else should it be called good![20]

Luther follows the emphasis of Jesus in pointing out that the way we are to serve our God is to serve our neighbor. He takes to heart Christ's words in His vision of the Last Judgment, "Truly I say to you, to the extent that you did it to one of these brothers of Mine, even the least of them, you did it to Me" (Matthew 25:40 NASB). Therefore, following Jesus' stress on serving even the least of one's fellowman, Luther wrote in a sermon in his *Church Postil* for the Advent season:

> Christ teaches us rightly to apply the works and shows us what good works are. All other work, except faith, we should apply to our neighbor. For God demands of us no other work that we should do for him than to exercise faith in Christ [John 6:28-29]. With that he is satisfied, and with that we give honor to him, as to one who is merciful, long-suffering, wise, kind, truthful and the like. After this think of nothing else than to do to your

---

20 Martin Luther, *Sermons of Martin Luther*, the *Church Postil*, vol. 1, pp. 34-35.

neighbor as Christ has done to you, and let all your works together with all your life be applied to your neighbor. Look for the poor, sick and all kinds of needy, help them and let your life's energy here appear, so that they may enjoy your kindness, helping whoever needs you, as much as you possibly can with your life, property and honor. . . . But know that to serve God is nothing else than to serve your neighbor and do good to him in love, be it a child, wife, servant, enemy, friend; without making any difference, whoever needs your help in body or soul, and wherever you can help in temporal or spiritual matters. This is serving God and doing good works. O, Lord God, how do we fools live in this world, neglecting to do such works, though in all parts of the world we find the needy, on whom we could bestow our good works; but no one looks after them nor cares for them. But look to your own life. If you do not find yourself among the needy and the poor, where the Gospel shows us Christ, then you may know that your faith is not right, and that you have not yet tasted of Christ's benevolence and work for you. . . . In love we stumble, because we are not mindful of the poor and needy, do not look after them, and yet we think we satisfy the demands of faith with other works than these. Thus we come under the judgment of Christ, who says: "For I was hungry, and you did not give me to eat, I was thirsty, and yet you gave me no drink," Matthew 25:42. Again: "Inasmuch as you did it not unto one of these least, you did it not unto me. Matthew 25:45.[21]

To Do Good Works Also Means Answering Spiritual Needs

Luther has a constant emphasis on the obligation of a Christian to respond to the physical needs of his neighbor. This, however, does not mean that the Christian should neglect his neighbor's spiritual needs. He taught in a sermon that discussed faith and good works:

He who does not firmly believe in God's grace assuredly will not extend kindness to his neighbor, but will be tardy and indifferent in aiding him. . . . But the fact is, all Christian doctrines and works, all Christian living, is briefly, clearly and completely

---

21 Martin Luther, *Sermons of Martin Luther*, the *Church Postil*, vol. 1, p. 111-112.

comprehended in these two principles, faith and love. . . . Thus the Christian becomes a vessel, or rather a channel, through which the fountain of divine blessings continuously flows to other individuals. . . . Your first desire will be that all men may obtain the same knowledge of divine grace. . . . Note this: the truly Christian life is that which does for others as God has done for itself.[22]

In his *Treatise on Good Works*, Luther similarly wrote:

For Christ at the last day will not ask how much you have prayed, fasted, pilgrimaged, done this or that for yourself, but how much good you have done to others, even the very least. Now without doubt among the "least" are also those who are in sin and spiritual poverty, captivity and need, of whom there are at present far more than of those who suffer bodily need. Therefore take heed: our own self-assumed good works lead us to and into ourselves, that we seek only our own benefit and salvation; but God's commandments drive us to our neighbor, that we may thereby benefit others to their salvation.[23]

Who, Then, Is My Neighbor?

Even Those Who Consider Themselves Our Enemy

When Jesus was asked by the lawyer, "And who is my neighbor?" (Luke 10:29), Jesus responded by telling the parable of the Good Samaritan. He made the point that even a man who considers himself my enemy is my neighbor. Luther followed Jesus in this expansive view of who is my neighbor in saying:

Now our neighbor is any human being, especially one who needs our help, as Christ interprets it in Luke 10:30-37. Even one who has done me some sort of injury or harm has not shed his humanity on that account or stopped being flesh and blood, a creature of God very much like me; in other words, he does not

---

22 Martin Luther, *Sermons of Martin Luther*, the *Church Postil*, vol. 6, p. 145-148.

23 Martin Luther, <u>Treatise</u> *on Good Works*, the Third Commandment, in the *Works of Martin Luther*, Phila. Ed., vol. 1, p. 240.

stop being my neighbor.[24]

Even The Unworthy

As did John Chrysostom (see page 260), Luther realized that Christian love is not to be restricted to the "worthy":

> Love, however, is greater than brotherhood; for it extends also to enemies, and particularly to those who are not worthy of love. For just as faith is active where it sees nothing, so love should also not see anything and do its work chiefly where nothing lovable but only aversion and hostility is seen. Where there is nothing that pleases me, I must put up with it for this very reason. And this, says St. Peter, should be done fervently and with all one's heart, just as God loved us when we were unworthy of love.[25]

Even Those Who Might Take Advantage of Us

Paul had written, "To the pure all things are pure, but to the corrupt and unbelieving nothing is pure; their very minds and consciences are corrupted" (Titus 1:15 RSV). Luther well understood this saying, and he applied it to those who do good works in living the Christian life. He was aware that the corrupt and unbelieving might take advantage of those who live a Christian life, but no matter—he wrote in his interpretation of 1 Corinthians 13:7:

> ... love "believes all things." Paul does not here allude to faith in God, but to faith in men. His meaning is: Love is of a decidedly trustful disposition. The possessor of it believes and trusts all men, considering them just and upright like himself. He anticipates no wily and crooked dealing, but permits himself to be deceived, deluded, flouted, imposed upon, at every man's pleasure, and asks, "Do you really believe men so wicked?" He measures all other hearts by his own, and makes mistakes with utmost cheerfulness. But such error works him no injury. He

---

24 Martin Luther, *Lectures on Galatians*, 1535, in *Luther's Works*, vol. 27, p. 58.

25 Martin Luther, *Sermons on the First Epistle of St. Peter*, in *Luther's Works*, vol. 30, p. 43.

knows God cannot forsake, and the deceiver of love but deceives himself. The haughty, on the contrary, trust no one, will believe none, nor brook deception.[26]

Christian Love Therefore Extends to All Humans

"Just as God loved us when we were unworthy of love," this phrase of Luther's sums up the New Commandment of loving others as Christ loved us. It also tells us to what extent we are to love our neighbor and just who is our neighbor. For example: In a sermon commenting on the text, "Love your neighbor as yourself" as used by Paul (Romans 13:9), Luther stated:

> The commandment of our text, however, requires of us free, spontaneous love to all men, whoever they may be, and whether friend or foe, a love that seeks not profit, and administers only what is beneficial. Such love is most active and powerful in serving the poor, the needy, the sick, the wicked, the simple-minded and the hostile; among these it is always and under all circumstances necessary to suffer and endure, to serve and do good. Note here, this commandment makes us all equal before God, without regard to distinctions incident to our stations in life, to our persons, offices and occupations. Since the commandment is to all—to every human being—a sovereign, if he be a human being, must confess the poorest beggar, the most wretched leper, his neighbor and his equal in the sight of God.[27]

To show Christian love to our neighbor, whoever he might be, is a constant refrain in Luther's sermons and teaching:

> You have often heard that it is our duty, for love's sake, to serve our neighbor in all things. If he is poor, we are to serve him with our goods; if he is in disgrace, we are to cover him with the mantle of our honor; if he is a sinner, we are to adorn him with our righteousness and piety. That is what Christ did for us.

---

26 Martin Luther, *Sermons of Martin Luther*, the *Church Postil*, vol. 7, pp. 127-128.

27 Martin Luther, *Sermons of Martin Luther*, the *Church Postil*, vol. 7, p. 71-72.

(Philippians 2). He who was so exceedingly rich did, for our sake, empty himself and become poor. He served us with his goods, that we in our poverty might become rich. He was made to be sin on our behalf, that we might become the righteousness of God in him.[28]

Aiding Others Does Not Mean Impoverishing Our Own Family

Luther does not intend, however, for a person to neglect the needs of his family as the result of aiding his neighbor. Ours is to be a discerning Christian love. In his lectures on the First Letter of St. John, he advised:

> Furthermore, there are several degrees of love: an enemy must not be offended, a brother must be helped, a member of one's own household must be supported. You know Christ's commandment concerning love for one's enemies. But you owe more to a brother who loves you in return. He who has nothing to live on should be aided. If he deceives us, what then? He must be aided again. But you owe most to those who are yours. "If anyone does not provide for his relatives, and especially for his own family, he has disowned the faith and is worse than an unbeliever," says 1 Timothy 5:8. It is a common rule that he who has goods and yet is not moved does not have love [1 John 3:17].[29]

The New Commandment and Works of Love

The Preeminence for Luther of Jesus' New Commandment

Jesus' New Commandment (John 13:34-35, 15:12-13) is basic to Luther's understanding of the way of life taught by Jesus. For Luther it is the foremost commandment that Christ gave. In a sermon in his *Church Postil,* he taught:

> Therefore since you have received enough and become rich, you have no other commandment to serve Christ and render

---

28 Martin Luther, *Sermons of Martin Luther*, the *Church Postil*, vol. 4, p. 58-59.

29 Martin Luther, *Lectures on the First Epistle of St. John*, in *Luther's Works*, vol. 30, p. 278.

obedience to him, than so to direct your works that they may be of benefit to your neighbor, just as the works of Christ are of benefit and use to you. For this reason Jesus said at the Last Supper: "This is my commandment that you love one another; even as I have loved you." John 13:34. Here it is seen that he loved us and did every thing for our benefit, in order that we may do the same, not to him, for he needs it not, but to our neighbor; this is his commandment, and this is our obedience.[30]

In his preface to the New Testament, Luther similarly wrote:

That is what Christ meant when He gave, at last, no other commandment than love, by which men were to know who were His disciples and true believers. For where works and love do not break forth, there faith is not right, the Gospel does not take hold, and Christ is not rightly known. See, then, that you so approach the books of the New Testament as to learn to read them in this way.[31]

For Luther a life of Christian love is the natural response of the believer to Jesus' great love for him. In a sermon on St. John's Gospel, Luther expands upon Jesus' New Commandment (John 13:34-35) by imagining Jesus saying to his disciples:

"It would please Me, and I would be satisfied, if you, as members of one body under one Head, show one another fidelity and benevolence, friendship, service, and assistance; if you do not stir up factions and schisms among one another and thus destroy love. This is the entire commandment I am giving you and asking you to observe in return for My great and ineffable love, if you want to be recognized and regarded as My disciples."

Luther then commented:

---

30 Martin Luther, *Sermons of Martin Luther*, the *Church Postil*, vol. 1, p. 145.

31 Martin Luther, Preface *to the New Testament*, 1545, in the *Works of Martin Luther*, Phila. Ed., vol. 6, p. 443.

He who refuses to obey this commandment is hereby informed that he is not a Christian, even though he may be called a Christian. For where there is no love but its opposite manifests itself, there certainly is no faith. And although the works of love do not justify and save, they should follow as fruits and signs of faith.[32]

The New Commandment Sums Up the Christian Way of Life

For Luther the New Commandment summed up the Christian way of life. It was the guiding principle by which a Christian lived a faith working through love. To the Christian enriched beyond measure by the forgiveness of his sins and the promise of eternal life that Christ had gained for him, Luther preached:

Love does to our neighbor as it sees Christ has done to us, as he says in John 13:15: "For I have given you an example, that you also should do as I have done to you." And immediately afterwards he says in verse 34: "A new commandment I give unto you, that you love one another; even as I have loved you, that you also love one another. By this shall all men know that you are my disciples, if you have love one to another." What else does this mean than to say: Through me in faith you now have everything that I am and have; I am your own, you are now rich and satisfied through me; for all I do and love I do and love not for my but only for your sake, and I only think how to be useful and helpful to you, and accomplish whatever you need and should have. Therefore consider this example, to do to each other as I have done to you, and only consider how to be useful to your neighbor, and do what is useful and necessary for him. Your faith has enough in my love and grace; so your love shall also give enough to others.

Luther continued

Behold, this is a Christian life, and in brief it does not need much doctrine nor many books, it is wholly contained in faith and love.

---

32 Martin Luther, *Sermons on the Gospel of St. John*, in *Luther's Works*, vol. 24, pp. 251-252.

. . . Again, love naturally teaches him how to do good works. For they alone are good works which serve your neighbor and are good. . . . Thus, Christ speaks in John 15:12-13:"This is my commandment, that you love one another, even as I have loved you. Greater love has no man than this, that a man lay down his life for his friends." As though he would say: So completely have I done all my works for your benefit, that I also gave my life for you, which is the greatest of all love, that is, the greatest work of love. If I had known a greater love, I would have manifested it to and for you. Therefore you should also love each other, and do all good deeds to one another. I require no more of you. I do not say you are to build for me churches, make pilgrimages, fast, sing, become monks or priests, or that you are to enter into this order or rank; but you do my will and service when you do good to each other, and no one cares for himself but for others, on this all entirely depends.[33]

The New Commandment Is Not Restricted to Fellow Christians

As did Chrysostom and Augustine (see pages 259-260 and 278), Luther does not see Christ's New Commandment only restricted to His disciples and followers. Luther adds to the quotation above by writing in a *Church Postil* sermon:

And these he calls "friends." By this he does not mean that we should not love our enemies. For he says clearly: "Who lays down his life for his friends." "His friends" are more than mere "friends." It may come to pass that you are my friend, and yet I am not your friend, or I may love you and receive you as a friend and offer you my friendship, and yet you may hate me and remain my enemy. Just as Christ says to Judas in the garden: "Friend, do that for which you are come." Matthew 27:50. Judas was his friend, but Christ was Judas' enemy, for Judas considered him his enemy and hated him. Christ loved Judas and esteemed him as his friend. It must be a free, perfect love and kindness toward every one.[34]

---

33 Martin Luther, *Sermons of Martin Luther*, the *Church Postil*, vol. 5, pp. 69-71.

34 Martin Luther, *Sermons of Martin Luther*, the *Church Postil*, vol. 5, p. 71.

Jesus Did Not Come as a New Lawgiver

Although on the night before He died Jesus gave to His disciples the New Commandment of loving one another as He loved them, Luther taught that He did not come as a new lawgiver. The New Testament does not contain a body of law as does the Old Testament. Luther in his Lectures *on Galatians* explained this in writing:

> Christ did not establish a new Law to follow the old Law of Moses but abrogated it and redeemed those who were being oppressed by it. Therefore it is a very wicked error when the monks and sophists portray Christ as a new lawgiver after Moses, not unlike the error of the Turks, who proclaim that their Mohammed is a new lawgiver after Christ. Those who portray Christ in this way do Him a supreme injury. He did not come to abrogate the old Law with the purpose of establishing a new one; but, as Paul says here [Galatians 4:5], He was sent into the world by the Father to redeem those who were being held captive under the Law.[35]

The Motivation for Christian Love and Good Works

The Holy Spirit is the Source of Faith and Good Works

The Holy Spirit who gives the gift of faith to the individual also provides the sanctifying power to live the life of love toward one another that Jesus taught. Concerning this Luther in his S*ermons on the Epistle of St. Jude* preached:

> Faith is the foundation on which one should build. But to build up means to increase from day to day in the knowledge of God and Jesus Christ. This is done through the Holy Spirit. Now when we are built up in this way, we should not do a single work in order to merit anything by it or to be saved; but everything must be done for the benefit of our neighbor.[36]

---

35 Martin Luther, *Lectures on Galatians*, 1535, in *Luther's Works*, vol. 26, pp. 367-368.

36 Martin Luther, *Sermons on the Epistle of St. Jude*, 1523, in *Luther's Works*, vol. 30, p. 214.

Luther in the *Treatise on Christian Liberty* used one of Augustine's favorite verses (Romans 5:5) in underscoring how the Holy Spirit grants us the gift of love as we strive to be Christs to one another:

> Therefore, if we recognize the great and precious things which are given us, as Paul says, there will be shed abroad in our hearts by the Holy Ghost the love which makes us free, joyful, almighty workers and conquerors over all tribulations, servants of our neighbors and yet lords of all. . . . Just as our neighbor is in need and lacks that in which we abound, so we also have been in need before God and have lacked His mercy. Hence, as our heavenly Father has in Christ freely come to our help, we also ought freely to help our neighbor through our body and its works, and each should become as it were a Christ to the other, that we may be Christs to one another and Christ may be the same in all; that is, that we may be truly Christians.[37]

Our Love is a Response to God's Love

Christian love wells up in a believer as a result of his faith in God's great love for him. Luther preached in his *Church Postil*:

> For if your heart is in the state of faith that you know your God has revealed himself to you to be so good and merciful, without your merit, and purely gratuitously, while you were still his enemy and a child of eternal wrath; if you believe this, you cannot refrain from showing yourself so to your neighbor; and do all out of love to God and for the welfare of your neighbor.[38]

For Luther, therefore, the Christian's life was a response to God's love. In a comment on the First Letter of St. Peter, he wrote:

> Now if God has dealt this way with us, has given us everything that is His, and has become our own, so that we have all blessings and enough of everything through faith, what are we to

---

37 Martin Luther, *Treatise on Christian Liberty*, 1520, in the *Works of Martin Luther*, Phila. Ed., vol. 2, p. 338.

38 Martin Luther, *Sermons of Martin Luther*, the *Church Postil*, vol. 4, p. 101.

do now? Are we to be idle? To be sure, it would be best for us to die. Then all this would be ours. But since we are still living here, we should do for our neighbor as God has done us and give ourselves to him as God has given Himself to us. Thus it is faith that saves us. But it is love that prompts us to give ourselves to our neighbor, now that we have enough. That is, faith receives from God, love gives to the neighbor.[39]

All Is To Be Done Out of Unselfish Christian Love

A life of Christian love is the way that Christ's people are to live. All that we do is to be done in love. Luther in his *Church Postil* follows Paul in urging Christians to follow love by writing:

"Walk in love," [Ephesians 5:1], counsels the apostle. He would have our external life all love. But not the world's love is to be our pattern, which seeks only its own advantage, and loves only so long as it is the gainer thereby; we must love even as Christ loved, who sought neither pleasure nor gain from us but gave himself for us, not to mention the other blessings he bestows daily—gave himself as a sacrifice and offering to reconcile God unto ourselves, so that he should be our God and we his children.

Thus likewise should we give, thus should we lend, or even surrender our goods, no matter whether friends claim them or enemies. Nor are we to stop there; we must be ready to give our lives for both friends and enemies, and must be occupied with no other thought than how we can serve others, and how both our life and property can be made to minister to them in this life, and this because we know that Christ is ours and has given us all things.[40]

We Are Led by God's Spirit, Guided by the Scriptures

To have God's love abide in us means to allow ourselves to be

---

39 Martin Luther, *Sermons on the First Epistle of St. Peter*, in *Luther's Works*, vol. 30, p. 67.

40 Martin Luther, *Sermons of Martin Luther*, the *Church Postil*, vol. 7, p. 151-152.

under the guidance of God's Holy Spirit and God's will as revealed in the Holy Scriptures. Luther explained this in preaching:

> To be "led by the Spirit of God" [Romans 8:12-17] means, then, to be given a heart which gladly hears God's Word and believes that in Christ it has grace and the forgiveness of sins; a heart which confesses and proves its faith before the world; a heart which seeks, above all things, the glory of God, and endeavors to live without giving offense, to serve others and to be obedient, patient, pure and chaste, mild and gentle; a heart which, though at times overtaken in a fault and it stumble, soon rises again by repentance, and ceases to sin. All these things the Holy Spirit teaches one if he hears and receives the Word, and does not willfully resist the Spirit.[41]

Faith and Love Sum Up the Christian's Life

Thus for Luther it is a God-given faith through which we are led by the Holy Spirit to be active in deeds of love that sums up the Christian's life. In commenting upon Galatians 5:6 in which Paul writes of "faith working through love," Luther lectured:

> But in brief summary he draws a conclusion about the Christian life, saying: "In Christ Jesus neither circumcision nor uncircumcision is of any avail, but faith working through love," that is, a faith that is neither imaginary nor hypocritical but true and living. This is what arouses and motivates good works through love. . . . Paul is describing the whole of the Christian life in this passage: inwardly it is faith toward God, and outwardly it is love or works toward one's neighbor. Thus a man is a Christian in a total sense: inwardly through faith in the sight of God, who does not need our works; outwardly in the sight of men, who do not derive any benefit from faith but do derive benefit from works or from our love. . . . here stands Paul in supreme freedom and says in clear and explicit words: "That which makes a Christian is faith working through love." He does not say: "That which makes a Christian is a cowl or fasting or vestments or ceremonies." But it is true faith toward God, which loves and

---

41 Martin Luther, *Sermons of Martin Luther,* the *Church Postil,* vol. 8, p. 173.

helps one's neighbor—regardless of whether the neighbor is a servant, a master, a king, a pope, a man, a woman, one who wears purple, one who wears rags, one who eats meat, or one who eats fish. Not one of these things, not one, makes a man a Christian; only faith and love do so.[42]

Good Works Are To Be Gratuitous and Spontaneous

As the Christian lives enveloped in the flood of God's unmerited love and sanctified by God's Holy Spirit, so also the works of love that flow from the Christian's life are to be as full of grace and loving kindness as is God's steadfast love for him. Luther wrote that good works are to be done gratuitously and spontaneously toward our neighbor. A life doing good works "must be practiced until it becomes a second nature with us."[43] For Luther, "The Christian's mind and heart should be constantly devoted to merciful deeds, with an ardor so intense as to make him unaware he is doing good and compassionate acts."[44] Christian love, therefore, should not be a case of being compelled to love, or having to make a conscious decision in a given situation that one ought to love. A Christian is to grow in Christian love until the natural and spontaneous orientation of his mind is that of selfless love towards his neighbor. Luther repeatedly emphasizes that Christian love is to flow liberally in doing good to one's neighbor. Referring to his own sermons, he declared in the *Church Postil*:

> For as we have often heard it is characteristic of Christian love to do all freely and gratuitously, to the praise and honor of God, that a Christian lives upon the earth for the sake of such love, just as Christ lived solely for the purpose of doing good; as he himself says: "The Son of man came not to be ministered unto, but to minister." Matthew 20:28."[45]

---

42 Martin Luther, *Lectures on Galatians*, 1535, in *Luther's Works*, vol. 27, pp. 30-31.

43 Martin Luther, *Sermons of Martin Luther*, the *Church Postil*, vol. 4, p. 342.

44 Martin Luther, *Sermons of Martin Luther*, the *Church Postil*, vol. 7, p. 78.

45 Martin Luther, *Sermons of Martin Luther*, the *Church Postil*, vol. 2, p. 96.

Neither the Commands of Law, Fear of Punishment, nor Hope for Reward Are Motivations for Christian Love

Luther was concerned that Christians understand the true nature of the Christian life. Christians were not to act in love toward their neighbor because Christ so commanded. One cannot command love; one can only guide its direction as Christ did. Christ came to show us how to fulfill the law, and it is a cheerful, willing spirit of unselfish and self-denying Christian love that fulfills the law. What was once done under constraint and compulsion is now done cheerfully and willingly. The Holy Spirit's gift of faith and his work of sanctification in our lives allows us to love in a way that truly fulfills the Law of the Ten Commandments as Paul taught (see page 104). Luther explained this in preaching:

> Observe, no one is able to fulfill the Law until he is first liberated from it. . . . All who perform good works simply because commanded, and from fear of punishment or expectation of reward, are under the Law. Their piety and good deeds result from constraint, and not from a willing spirit. . . . when the Law with its threats and its promises interposes, man abstains from evil and endeavors to do good; not from love of good and hatred of evil, but through fear of punishment or hope of reward. . . . But they who are liberated from the Law do good and avoid evil, regardless of the threats and promises of the Law—not from fear of punishment or expectation of reward. They act voluntarily, from love for the good and hatred of the evil, because they delight in the Law of God. Even were there no Law, they would not have it otherwise, and be prompted by the same spirit to do good and abstain from evil. . . . The blessing of Christ gives the willing disposition. Willingness is the result of his grace and of the influence of the Holy Spirit. Therefore, "not under the Law" does not mean liberty to do evil and neglect good as we feel inclined. It means doing good and avoiding evil, not in consequence of fear, not from the restraints and requirements of the Law, but from pure love and a willing spirit. Freedom from the Law involves a spirit which would voluntarily do only good, as if the Law did not exist and our nature were prone to do good. . . . Having faith, we too shall perform the requirements of the Law voluntarily, unfettered and liberated from the prison of the Law. The two chains, fear of punishment and hope of reward, will no

longer restrain us. All our acts will be spontaneous, prompted by pure love and a cheerful spirit.[46]

Thus, Luther teaches that Christians do good works neither from fear of punishment in hell nor hope for reward in heaven. These are basically selfish motivations, and they hardly flow from a love for God. As Luther in a sermon observed, "those who do not know faith, only speak and think of the reward."[47]

The Nature of "Reward" as found in the New Testament

Luther rebelled against the idea that God's grace and the sacrifice of Christ were not sufficient to fully atone for all the sins of men. In *The Magnificat* he took to task those who taught that the works of men contributed to their salvation or were to be done to merit a greater reward in heaven by writing:

> They exalt good works to such a height that they imagine they can merit heaven thereby. But the bare goodness of God is what ought rather to be preached and known above all else, and we ought to learn that, even as God saves us out of pure goodness, without any merit of works, so we in our turn should do the works without reward or self-seeking, for the sake of the bare goodness of God. We should desire nothing in them but His good pleasure, and not be anxious about a reward. That will come of itself, without our seeking. . . . A son serves his father willingly and without reward, as his heir, solely for the father's sake. But a son who served his father merely for the sake of the inheritance would indeed be an unnatural child and deserve to be cast off by his father.[48]

Luther, however, recognized that the New Testament often tells of God's beneficence in rewarding the good works of his faithful people. Luther discussed this fully, for example, in a postscript to his long series of

---

46 Martin Luther, *Sermons of Martin Luther*, the *Church Postil*, vol. 6, p. 251-252, 255.

47 Martin Luther, *Sermons of Martin Luther*, the *Church Postil*, vol. 4, p. 310.

48. Martin Luther, *The Magnificat* 1520-21, in the *Works of Martin Luther*, Phila. Ed., vol. 3, pp. 143-144.

homilies on *The Sermon on the Mount*. But he always kept in mind the words of Christ: "So likewise you, when you have done all those things which you are commanded, say, 'We are unprofitable servants. We have done what was our duty to do'" (Luke 17:10 NKJV).[49] Thus in his postscript, Luther wrote:

> Learn to give this answer regarding the passages that refer to merit and reward: "Of course I hear Christ saying (Matthew 5:3): 'Blessed are the poor, for they shall have the kingdom of heaven'; and (Matthew 5:11, 12): 'Blessed are you when you suffer persecution for My sake, for your reward is great in heaven.' But by these statements He is not teaching me where to build the foundation of my salvation, but giving me a promise that is to console me in my sufferings and in my Christian life... . It does not say that I can merit this and that I do not need Christ and Baptism for it. Rather, those who are Christ's pupils, those to whom He has been preaching here and who have to suffer many things for His sake, should know how to console themselves. Because people refuse to tolerate them on earth, they will have everything that much more abundantly in heaven; and he who does the most work and endures the most suffering will also get the most glorious recompense."
>
> In Christ, as I have said, they are all alike. Grace is granted equally to all and brings full salvation to each individual, as the highest and most common possession; thus whoever has Christ has everything. And yet there will be a distinction in the glory with which we shall be adorned, and in the brightness with which we shall shine. In this life there is a distinction among gifts, and one labors and suffers more than another. But in that life it will all be revealed, for the whole world to see what each one has done from the degree of glory he has; and the whole heavenly host will rejoice.[50]

---

49 Martin Luther, *The Sermon on the Mount*, in *Luther's Works*, vol. 21, p. 289.

50 Martin Luther, *The Sermon on the Mount*, in *Luther's Works*, vol. 21, pp. 293-294.

Good Works Are Not Done to Earn the Gratitude of the Recipient

Nor should our motivation in doing good works be the gratitude or thankfulness of those who receive our aid. Luther discussed this in the *Treatise on Christian Liberty*:

> Lo, thus from faith flow forth love and joy in the Lord, and from love a joyful, willing and free mind that serves one's neighbor willingly and takes no account of gratitude or ingratitude, of praise or blame, of gain or loss. For a man does not serve that he may put men under obligations, he does not distinguish between friends and enemies, nor does he anticipate their thankfulness or unthankfulness; but most freely and most willingly he spends himself and all that he has, whether he wastes all on the thankless or whether he gain a reward.[51]

Works Done Out of Christian Love Are the Only Good Works

The motivation is what counts for Luther. And the only motivation that God desires is that of Christian love. It is not the greatness of the deed that counts but the faith active in unselfish love that inspires it. In his discussion of monasticism, Luther wrote:

> In the first place, we make no distinction between one work and another. They are all equal in the sight of God. It is only as we see them, or in relation one to another, that some seem important and others unimportant. Everything is given according to the measure of faith, as Paul says in Romans 12 [:3]. It is not the man who has done many great things who is approved, but the man who has acted in greater faith and love.[52]

---

51 Martin Luther, *Treatise on Christian Liberty*, 1520, in the *Works of Martin Luther*, Phila. Ed., vol. 2, p. 338.

52 Martin Luther, *The Judgment of Martin Luther on Monastic Vows*, 1521, in *Luther's Works*, vol. 44, p. 348.

Christian Love and the Secular Government

Government is Instituted by God

The Christian is to serve his neighbor, and this includes those by whom he is governed. Following Paul (Romans 13:1-7), Luther recognized that government was instituted by God and that even an unworthy government was to be obeyed. Luther believed that anarchy was the worst of conditions under which to live.[53] Yet there were times when Christians should refuse to obey their governing authorities.

Christians Should Refuse To Serve In an Unjust War

Luther cautioned in his *Treatise on Good Works* that a Christian should not take part in an unjust war:

> But if it should happen, as it often does, that the temporal power and authorities, as they are called, should urge a subject to do contrary to the Commandments of God, or hinder him from doing them, there obedience ends, and that duty is annulled. . . . Thus, if a prince desired to go to war, and his cause was manifestly unrighteous, we should not follow nor help him at all; since God has commanded that we shall not kill our neighbor, nor do him injustice. Likewise, if he bade us bear false witness, steal, lie or deceive and the like. Here we ought rather give up goods, honor, body, and life, that God's Commandments may stand.[54]

One wonders to what degree the history of the Twentieth Century would have been changed if the German people had taken to heart Luther's counsel to soldiers in his essay, *Whether Soldiers, too, Can Be Saved*:

> A second question: "Suppose my lord were wrong in going to war." I reply: If you know for sure that he is wrong, then you should fear God rather than men (Acts 4), and not fight or serve,

---

53 Martin Luther, *Secular Authority: To What Extent It Should Be Obeyed*, 1523, in the *Works of Martin Luther*, Phila. Ed., vol. 3, pp. 236-237.

54 Martin Luther, *Treatise on Good Works*, in the *Works of Martin Luther*, Phila. Ed., vol. 1, p. 271.

for you cannot have a good conscience before God. 'Nay,' you say, "my lord compels me, takes my fief [his farm], does not give me my money, pay, and wages; and besides, I am despised and put to shame as a coward, nay, as a faith-breaker in the eyes of the world, as one who has deserted his lord in need." I answer: You must take that and, with God's help, let go what goes; He can restore it to you a hundredfold, as He promises in the Gospel, "He that leaves house, home, wife, goods, for my sake, shall get it back a hundredfold." In all other works, too, we must expect the danger that the rulers will compel us to do wrong; but since God will have us leave even father and mother for his sake, we must certainly leave lords for his sake.[55]

It is no wonder that Adolf Hitler and his National Socialist Party had no use for Christianity and its teachings but rather tried to build a national cult in part by glorifying the old Germanic myths.

It Is Better To Obey God than the Government

There is a limit to the obedience we owe governing authorities. When the government demands us to do what is contrary to God's will, it should not be obeyed. In his *Treatise on Good Works* Luther discusses this as follows:

In all this we are to regard that which St. Peter bids us regard, namely, that its [the government's] power, whether it do right or wrong, cannot harm the soul, but only the body and property; unless indeed it should try openly to compel us to do wrong against God or men; as in former days when the magistrates were not yet Christians, and as the Turk is now said to do. For to suffer wrong destroys no one's soul, nay, it improves the soul, although it afflicts loss upon the body and property; but to do wrong, that destroys the soul, although it should gain all the world's wealth.[56]

---

55 Martin Luther, *Whether Soldiers, Too, Can Be Saved*, 1526, in the *Works of Martin Luther*, Phila. Ed., vol. 5, p. 68.

56 Martin Luther, *Treatise on Good Works*, in the *Works of Martin Luther*, Phila. Ed., vol. 1, p. 263.

Luther has often been accused of teaching a blind obedience to government. As the above quotations indicate, just the opposite is the case. Luther saw governments as ordained by God. Citizens, however, could work to change their government but only through peaceful means. When governments tried to force their citizens to violate their conscience, Luther advised civil disobedience as in his sermon on First Peter:

> We should be subject to power [government] and do what they order, so long as they do not bind our conscience and so long as they give commands that pertain to external matters only, even though they deal with us as tyrants do. For if anyone takes our coat, we should let him have our cloak as well (Matthew 5:40). But if they want to encroach on the spiritual rule and want to take our conscience captive where God alone must sit and rule, one should by no means obey them and should sooner let them have one's life. Secular domain and rule do not extend beyond external and physical matters. . . . Therefore a Christian can surely be obedient to such a prince, provided that the prince does not give any commands that do violence to a Christian's conscience. A Christian does this without compulsion, since he is free in all things.57

Although he taught obedience to authority, Luther was hardly the obsequious subject. Repeatedly he rebuked governing authorities and even his own lord. He attacked the privileges of the rulers in writing in his *Lectures on Romans*:

> On the basis of what authority do secular princes and secular leaders act when they keep for themselves all the animals and the fowl so that no one besides them may hunt them? By what right? If anyone of the common people would do that, he would justly be called thief, robber, or swindler, because he would take away from common use what does not belong to him. But because the ones who do these things are powerful, therefore they cannot be thieves. . . . Along the same lines they exact taxes from the people without urgent reason and exploit them by changing and devaluating the money, but they fine their subjects for greed and avarice. What is this but stealing and robbing

---

57 Martin Luther, *Sermons on 1 Peter*, in *Luther's Works*, vol. 30, p. 80.

those things which do not belong to us? Indeed, who will finally absolve of theft people who collect regular tribute and rightful compensation and yet do not fulfill their duties owed to the people by giving them protection, health, and justice? For their eyes are only on tyranny, on collecting riches, and on boasting with empty show of the possessions which they have acquired and kept.[58]

As the above shows, in the defense of the neighbor who is being exploited, Christian love may call for strong words. Surely, it was out of love for God's people who were being exploited that Jesus cleansed the Temple. The moneychangers and those who sold animals for sacrifice within the precincts of the Temple, he called robbers (Mark 11:15-17). Not for self, but in the defense of others, Christians out of Christian love are to oppose exploitation and oppression.

Luther and Those Who Corrupt Christianity

Luther's Strong Words in Defense of the Faith

It was also with strong, biting words that Luther opposed those who would distort the Christian faith to the point that the salvation of God's people was in danger:

It is not right that my charity be liberal enough to tolerate unsound doctrine. In the case of false faith and doctrine there is neither love nor patience. Against these it is my duty earnestly to contend and not to yield a hair's breadth. Otherwise—when faith is not imperiled—I must be unfailingly kind and merciful to all notwithstanding the infirmities of their lives.[59]

In this Luther was acting as a true pastor, that is, a shepherd of God's flock. As David in the Twenty-third Psalm depicts, on the one hand, a shepherd is one who tenderly guides, feeds, and cares for his sheep. With his staff he comforts his flock. When Luther as a pastor is writing or preaching to his Christian people, his words show this great love,

---

58 Martin Luther, *Lectures on Romans* in *Luther's Works*, vol. 25, p. 172-173.

59 Martin Luther, *Sermons of Martin Luther*, the *Church Postil*, vol. 7, p. 80; see also p. 81.

tenderness, and care for Christ's people.

However, on the other hand, as David writes in the psalm, the shepherd also carries a rod, a club. With it he defends his sheep as did David who killed both bears and lions in defense of his flock (1 Samuel 17:34-36). Luther also took this aspect of his pastorate seriously. He vigorously defended the Christian liberty of his people against the unbiblical church laws of the medieval church. He contended forcefully with those who endangered the salvation of his flock; especially those who were teaching people to trust their own righteousness rather than the true righteousness gained for them by Christ. He opposed those who would fleece his flock by selling them indulgences to remove the temporal punishment of their sins when Christ already had gained for them full satisfaction for their sins.

To those who criticized his use of strong and at times indelicate language, Luther cited the words Jesus and Paul used against those who would distort the faith. Concerning churchmen who would endanger the salvation of others, Luther wrote in a letter to Pope Leo X:

> I have indeed sharply inveighed against ungodly teachings in general, and I have not been slow to bite my adversaries, not because of their immorality, but because of their ungodliness. And of this I repent so little that I have determined to persevere in that fervent zeal, and to despise the judgment of men, following the example of Christ, Who in His zeal called His adversaries a generation of vipers, blind, hypocrites, children of the devil. And Paul arraigned the sorcerer as a child of the devil full of all subtility and mischief, and brands others as dogs, deceivers and adulterers. If you will allow those delicate ears to judge, nothing would be more biting and more unrestrained than Paul. Who is more biting than the prophets?[60]

One also should remember that Luther lived in a rather vulgar and unrefined age. His language toward those who in his view were in league with Satan as they distorted Christianity may sound coarse to our ears, but such language was quite common among the scholars of his day. Thomas More, for example, often used scurrilous and drastic epithets, such as "the devil's stinking pot, swine, apes that dance for the pleasure of Lucifer," and

---

60 Martin Luther, "Letter to Pope Leo X" 1520, in the *Works of Martin Luther*, Phila. Ed., vol. 2, p. 302.

so forth, in his writings against those he considered heretics.[61] In addition, many of Luther's writings are directed not to the theologians but rather to the common people, who would have little ear for refined, scholarly speech. Coming from peasant stock rather than the aristocracy, Luther knew how to communicate effectively with the German people.[62] Nonetheless, when he writes against those who endanger the spiritual life of God's people, Luther's invective at times sounds extreme to our ears. He has little toleration or patience for those who put in jeopardy the salvation of his flock. Luther was no cold fish; he had a passionate and, perhaps too often, an impulsive nature. His intense feelings and the mood of the moment seem to carry him away in some of his writings against those who would corrupt the faith of the people.

Luther and the Jews of Germany

As a defender of the faith of his flock, late in his life Luther became unhappy with the Jews who he viewed as guests living among the Christian German people. They were guests, who in Luther's view, abused the hospitality of their hosts by attempting "to lure to themselves even us, that is, the Christians."[63] Jewish proselytizing in the Germany of Luther's time was about as welcome as Christian evangelistic efforts are in the state of Israel today.[64] Luther's scathing, grossly intemperate, and reprehensible essay on the Jews came about when a friend sent him a Jewish pamphlet and asked him to refute the writer's arguments against Christianity with which, as the ailing and aged Luther wrote, "he thinks he can destroy the basis of our faith."[65]

Earlier in his life, Luther had argued that the Jews should be left to live in peace. In an exposition of Mary's Magnificat, Luther counseled:

---

61 David Schaff, 1910, *The Middle Ages*, vol. 6, in Philip Schaff's *History of the Christian Church* (Grand Rapids, Mich.: Wm B. Eerdmans Publ. Co., reprint of 1949), p. 654, 655.

62 Heiko A. Oberman, 1982, *Luther: Man between God and the Devil* (New York: Doubleday), pp. 106-109.

63 Martin Luther, *On the Jews and their Lies*, 1543, in *Luther's Works*, vol. 47, p. 137.

64 For an example of the antipathy toward freedom of religious expression in Israel today see: "Groups halt Israel missionary work," [Jerusalem (AP)] in *The Oregonian*, March 31, 1998, p. A3.

65 Introduction to *On the Jews and their Lies*, 1543, in *Luther's Works*, vol. 47, pp. 133, 137.

We ought, therefore, not to treat the Jews in so unkindly a spirit, for there are future Christians among them, and they are turning every day. Moreover, they alone, and not we Gentiles, have this promise, that there shall always be Christians among Abraham's seed, who acknowledge the blessed Seed, who knows how or when? As for our cause, it rests upon pure grace, without a promise of God. If we lived Christian lives, and led them with kindness to Christ, there would be the proper response. Who would desire to become a Christian, when he sees Christians fdealing with men in so unchristian a spirit? Not so, my dear Christians. Tell them the truth in all kindness; if they will not receive it, let them go. How many Christians are there who despise Christ, do not hear His word, and are worse than Jews or heathen! Yet we leave them in peace, and even fall down at their feet and well-nigh adore them as gods.[66]

Luther was not among those who blamed the Jews for the death of Jesus. Just the opposite, he told his congregation that although the Jews had judged and banished Jesus, "they have still been the servants of your sins, and you are truly the one who strangled and crucified the Son of God through your sins, as has been said."[67]

Christian Love in our Everyday Life

The All-pervasiveness of Christian Love

Luther counseled that Christ's way of life was to be lived in the everyday affairs of a man or woman's life. He taught that we are called to that station of life in which we find ourselves, whether farmer, burgher, husband, child, prince, bishop, and so forth. He preached that in truly serving in these capacities we are found on the road to heaven:

What a glorious state of things would reign, if it were thus that each tended to his own affairs and yet thereby served others, and thus traveled together to heaven in one flock in the right road. . . . Hence there is no doubt it is Satan's own doings that

---

66 Martin Luther, *The Magnificat*, 1520-21, in the *Works of Martin Luther*, Phila. Ed., vol. 3, p. 197.

67 Martin Luther, *Sermons of Martin Luther*, the *Church Postil*, vol. 2, p. 187.

divine worship is confined only to churches, altars, masses, singing, reading, offerings and the like, as if all other works were vain or of no use whatever. How could Satan mislead us more completely from the right way than when he confines God's worship within such narrow limits, only to the church and whatever is done in it?[68]

In commenting on James 1:23-24, one of the many in which James stresses the necessity of good works as well as faith, Luther wrote in a sermon in his *Church Postil*:

This passage in James deceivers and blind masters have spun out so far, that they have demolished faith and established only works, as though righteousness and salvation did not rest on faith, but on our works. To this great darkness they afterwards added still more, and taught only good works which are no benefit to your neighbor, as fasting, repeating many prayers, observing festival days; not to eat meat, butter, eggs and milk; to build churches, cloisters, chapels, altars; to institute masses, vigils, hours; to wear gray, white and black clothes; to be spiritual; and innumerable things of the same kind, from which no man has any benefit or enjoyment; all which God condemns, and that justly. But St. James means that a Christian life is nothing but faith and love. Love is only being kind and useful to all men, to friends and enemies. And where faith is right, it also certainly loves, and does to another in love as Christ did to him in faith.[69]

All Vocations Are Equal in God's Sight

For Luther, therefore, there was no difference in the various vocations men and women might pursue. If they could be done to the glory of God through service to others, they were equal in the sight of God. In his discussion of the commandment in Galatians 5:14, "You shall love your neighbor as yourself," Luther commented:

---

68 Martin Luther, *Sermons of Martin Luther*, the *Church Postil*, vol. 1, pp. 244-245.

69 Martin Luther, *Sermons of Martin Luther*, the *Church Postil*, vol. 5, pp. 72-73.

But those who accept the doctrine of faith and, in accordance with this commandment of Paul's, love one another do not criticize someone else's way of life and works; but each one approves the way of life of another and the duties which the other performs in his vocation. No godly person believes that the position of a magistrate is better in the sight of God than that of a subject, for he knows that both are divine institutions and have a divine command behind them. He will not distinguish between the position or work of a father and that of a son, or between that of a teacher and that of a pupil, or between that of a master and that of a servant; but he will declare it as certain that both are pleasing to God if they are done in faith and in obedience to God.[70]

All Tasks, Even the Humblest, Can Be Done To God's Glory

Martin Luther certainly ranks among the most courageous and stalwart men in history. Against the advice of friends, he left the safety provided by Duke Frederick of Electoral Saxony to go to his trial before Emperor Charles V in the city of Worms. He knew well and actually expected that he might die as did the reformer John Hus who 100 years earlier was burned at the stake during the Council at Constance despite the promise of safe conduct. At the conclusion of Luther's trial, Emperor Charles V published the "Edict of Worms" which proclaimed that once Luther's safe conduct had elapsed all citizens of the Holy Roman Empire were ordered:

". . . not to take the aforenamed Martin Luther into your houses, not to receive him at court, to give him neither food nor drink, not to hide him, to afford him no help, following, support, or encouragement, either clandestinely or publicly, through words or works. Where you can get him, seize him and overpower him, you should capture him and send him to us under tightest security."[71]

It was only because he was taken by friends and hidden for months

---

70 Martin Luther, *Lectures on Galatians*, 1535, in *Luther's Works*, vol. 27, pp. 60-61.

71 Heiko A. Oberman, 1982, translated by Eileen Walliser-Schwarzbart, *Luther: Man between God and the Devil*, p. 203.

in the Wartburg Castle that Luther was preserved from perishing under the Emperor's ban.

For all his personal courage, Luther spurned the facade of machismo, the false manliness, assumed by so many weak and insecure males. A true man sees no need to prove or show off his manhood, only the self-doubting do. A mature man shows his courage when it is purposeful and needed. The immature, unsure of their manhood, attempt to prove their manliness by engaging in activities that are merely foolhardy. Luther pointed out it was not beneath the self-regard of a man to rock a baby, make its bed, and wash its dirty diapers. He praises such a father in writing:

> Now you tell me, when a father goes ahead and washes diapers or performs some other mean task for his child, and someone ridicules him as an effeminate fool—though that father is acting in the spirit just described and in Christian faith—my dear fellow you tell me, which of the two is most keenly ridiculing the other? God, with all his angels and creatures, is smiling—not because that father is washing diapers, but because he is doing so in Christian faith. Those who sneer at him and see only the task but not the faith are ridiculing God with all his creatures, as the biggest fool on earth. Indeed, they are only ridiculing themselves; with all their cleverness they are nothing but devil's fools.[72]

It at times takes great courage for a man or woman to live a life of Christian love and ignore the consequent disdain of the world.

Humans may belittle the work of others, but God only looks to see if the works are done in Christian love and in service to one's neighbor. In a homily on the Biblical text: "are grapes gathered from thorns or figs from thistles," Luther commented:

> When a pious hired man is hauling a wagonload of manure to the field, he is actually hauling a wagonload of precious figs and grapes—but in the sight of God, not in our own sight, . . .[73]

---

72 Martin Luther, *The Estate of Marriage*, in *Luther's Works*, vol. 45, pp. 40-41.

73 Martin Luther, *The Sermon on the Mount*, in *Luther's Works*, vol. 21, pp. 266, 269.

Luther knew that the world would scorn the Biblical view of the Christian life. In a letter to a friend, he wrote:

> The world does not know the hidden treasures of God. It cannot be persuaded that the maid working obediently and the servant faithfully performing his duty, or the woman rearing her children are as good as the praying monk who strikes his breast and wrestles with his spirit.[74]

All vocations that can serve one's fellow humans are equally true ways to serve our God.

And now may we conclude this chapter on Luther's teaching by quoting from the close of one of Luther's sermons:

> This is now enough on today's Gospel. May God grant us grace that some day we may also even put it into practice! May the Gospel remain not only in our ears and on our tongues, but come into our hearts and break forth fresh into loving deeds![75]

---

74 Preserved Smith, 1911, *The Life and Letters of Martin Luther* (London: John Murray), p. 339.

75 Martin Luther, *Sermons of Martin Luther*, the *Church Postil*, vol. 5, p. 117.

Chapter Fourteen

LUTHER AND THE RETURN TO CHRISTIAN FREEDOM

The Freedom of the Christian

Three Aspects of Christian Freedom

A major emphasis in Luther's reformation of the Roman Catholic Church was his endeavor to bring back Christian love and Christian freedom as taught in the New Testament. Luther held that every Christian is to have Christian liberty in his effort to lead a life of Christian love as led by the Holy Spirit and guided by the Bible, the Word of God, as understood and interpreted by the New Testament.

Luther struggled to free his fellow Christians from the entangling and distressing morass of non-Biblical laws that had been laid upon them by the church hierarchy since the 300s. This crushing burden of church laws was composed of the Canon Law, the Penitentials, and the laws continually being added through the decrees of popes, bishops, and councils. Luther with a degree of exasperated hyperbole observed:

> There is today established by the Pope and the clergy a world-wide system of human devices in regard to meats and drinks, apparel and place, days and seasons, persons and orders, customs and performances, so elaborate that one can scarce eat a morsel, drink a drop, or open his eyes even, but there is a law concerning the act. Thus is our liberty usurped.[1]

Luther understood Christian freedom as taught in the New Testament in three ways: freedom from the condemning accusations of the

---

1 Martin Luther, *Sermons of Martin Luther*, the *Church Postil* (Grand Rapids: Baker Book House), vol. 6, pp. 31-32.

Law, freedom from Old Testament Law as a way of life and salvation, and freedom from human-contrived church laws in order for the Christian to follow Christian love through the leading of the Holy Spirit and the guidance of God's Word.

Christian Freedom from the Accusations of the Law

Luther's greatest emphasis was on freedom from the accusations of the Law that put in danger the Christian's salvation. Luther wrote in his commentary on the letter of Paul to the Galatian churches:

> Let us remember this well in our personal temptations, when the devil accuses and terrifies our conscience to bring it to the point of despair. He is the father of lies (John 8:44) and the enemy of Christian freedom. At every moment, therefore, he troubles us with false terrors, so that when this freedom has been lost, the conscience is in continual fear and feels guilt and anxiety. When that "great dragon, the ancient serpent, the devil, the deceiver of the whole world, who accuses our brethren night and day before God" (Revelations 12:9-10)–when, I say, he comes to you and accuses you not only of failing to do anything good but of transgressing against the Law of God, then you must say: "You are troubling me with the memory of past sins; in addition, you are telling me that I have not done anything good. This does not concern me. For if I either trusted in my performance of good works or lost my trust because I failed to perform them, in either case Christ would be of no avail to me. Therefore whether you base your objections to me on my sins or on my good works, I do not care; for I put both of them out of sight and depend only on the freedom for which Christ has set me free. Therefore I shall not render Him useless to me, which is what would happen if I either presumed that I shall attain grace and eternal life because of my good works or despaired of my salvation on account of my sins."[2]

For Luther the freedom from the curse of the law was the greatest of the freedoms given by God. It is "the freedom before God, the freedom we have

---

2 Martin Luther, *Lectures on Galatians*—1535, in *Luther's Works* (Philadelphia and St. Louis: Fortress Press and Concordia Publ. Hse.), vol. 27, p. 11.

when God pronounces us free from sin."[3]

Christian Freedom from Old Testament Law as a Way of Life and Salvation

It was Christ who ended the Law of the Old Testament. Luther in his *Lectures on Galatians* cites Jesus concerning this:

> You may understand the duration of the time of the Law either literally or spiritually. Literally: The Law lasted until Christ. "The Law and the prophets," Christ says, "prophesied until John [the Baptist]. From the days of John until now the kingdom of heaven has suffered violence, and men of violence take it by force" (Matthew 11:13, 12). At that time Christ was baptized and began to preach, when in a literal way the Law and the whole Mosaic system of worship came to an end."[4]

Christian Freedom from Church Law

Luther urged Christian people to free themselves and their consciences from the enormous body of non-Biblical and human-created church law that had built up over the centuries. Luther maintained in a sermon based on Peter's first letter:

> The pope did wrong by attempting to force and compel the people with laws. For in a Christian people there should and can be no compulsion, and if one begins to bind consciences with external laws, faith and the Christian way of life soon perish. For Christians must be guided and governed only in the Spirit, so that they know that through faith they already have everything by which they are saved, that they need nothing else for this, that they are not obligated to do anything more than serve and help their neighbor with everything they have, just as Christ helped them. All their works are performed without compulsion and for nothing; they flow from a happy and cheerful heart,

---

3 Martin Luther, *Sermons on the Gospel of St. John* in *Luther's Works*, vol. 23, p. 404.

4 Martin Luther, *Lectures on Galatians*, 1535, in *Luther's Works*, vol. 26, p. 317.

which thanks, praises, and lauds God for all the good things it has received from Him.[5]

In a sermon on the Gospel of John, Luther challenged the arrogance and presumption of the medieval church to call sin what God had not called sin:

The church has no power to justify sin and to exact obedience in matters not commanded by Scripture. When the pope declares: "When a priest marries, he is a sinner and will be damned," he brands as sin what God Himself did not make a sin. Furthermore, he calls a man a "digamist" if he marries a second time or marries a woman who is not a virgin; and he will not tolerate such a person in an ecclesiastical office. Tell me, what kind of a sin is that? "Oh," he says, "it is a violation of the prohibition of the holy Christian Church." Then you must answer: "Who ordered the church to call that sin which God Himself did not make a sin?"[6]

In his influential treatise, *The Babylonian Captivity of the Church*, Luther states:

Therefore I say: Neither pope nor bishop nor any other man has the right to impose a single syllable of law upon a Christian man without his consent; and if he does, it is done in the spirit of tyranny. Therefore the prayers, fasts, donations, and whatever else the pope decrees and demands in all of his decretals, as numerous as they are iniquitous, he demands and decrees without any right whatever; and he sins against the liberty of the Church whenever he attempts any such thing.[7]

---

5 Martin Luther, *Sermons on the First Epistle of St. Peter*, in *Luther's Works*, vol. 30, p. 77.

6 Martin Luther, *Sermons on the Gospel of St. John*, in *Luther's Works*, vol. 22, p. 451-452.

7 Martin Luther, *The Babylonian Captivity of the Church*, 1520, in the *Works of Martin Luther*, Phila. Ed. (Grand Rapids: Baker Book House), vol. 2, p. 233, see also pp. 235-236.

Christian Liberty to be Led by the Holy Spirit

Freedom to Live by the Spirit and the Word

In Luther's view, the Scriptures teach that the Christian is to live a life under the grace of God with the freedom to follow promptings of the Holy Spirit as He guides him by the Word of God. Luther in the *Church Postil* explained this in the following way:

> A Christian is set up in the liberty of the Spirit, rid of the Law and all its bonds. He cannot be bound and made captive by any sort of laws, rules or works that may be proposed to him with a view of his becoming righteous through their efficacy in the sight of God. . . . Hence, by faith in the Word and in his baptism he remains a free man, superior to all laws, because he has through Christ forgiveness of sin, the grace of God and the Holy Spirit, and governs his entire life accordingly. Through the Holy Spirit, who operates in his heart, he is now become righteous, and has been quickened into life, and, except as the Holy Spirit by the Word guides and directs him, he does not look for other teaching regarding works of holiness.[8]

Paul's Use of Christian Freedom

For Luther the letters of Paul were especially influential in understanding Christian freedom as it related to a Christian's life. He wrote in his *Treatise on Christian Liberty*:

> St. Paul also circumcised his disciple Timothy, not because circumcision was necessary for his righteousness, but that he might not offend or despise the Jews who were weak in the faith and could not yet grasp the liberty of faith. But on the other hand, when they despised the liberty of faith and insisted that circumcision was necessary for righteousness, he withstood them and did not allow Titus to be circumcised, (Galatians 2). For as he was unwilling to offend or to despise any man's weak faith, and yielded to their will for the time, so he was also unwilling that the liberty of faith should be offended against or

---

8 Martin Luther, *Sermons of Martin Luther*, the *Church Postil*, vol. 3, p. 441.

despised by stubborn work-righteous men. He chose a middle way, sparing the weak for a time, but always withstanding the stubborn, that he might convert all to the liberty of faith. What we do should be done with the same zeal to sustain the weak in faith, as Romans 14 teaches; but we should firmly withstand the stubborn teachers of works.[9]

The Jerusalem Council and Christian Freedom

Very early in the history of the Church the apostles and elders gathered in Jerusalem to discuss whether the Old Testament laws had to be observed by non-Jewish Christians (see page 101). James, the brother of Jesus who was the leader of the Jerusalem church, summed up the meeting by giving his judgment that non-Jewish Christians need not be circumcised or follow the law of Moses. But he nonetheless added that they should "abstain from what has been sacrificed to idols and from blood and from what is strangled and from unchastity" (Acts 21:25 RSV and Acts 15:20).

Paul realized that James overstepped himself in this, for later in a letter to the Corinthian church Paul wrote, "Hence, as to the eating of food offered to idols, we know that 'an idol has no real existence,' and that 'there is no God but one.'. . . Food will not commend us to God. We are no worse off if we do not eat, and no better off if we do. Only take care lest this liberty of yours somehow become a stumbling-block to the weak" (1 Corinthians 8:4, 8-9 RSV). Luther concurs with Paul's defense of Christian liberty in respect to James' rules for the non-Jews by writing, "Later on Paul abrogated this rule, contrary to the decree of the apostolic council, saying (1 Corinthians 8:4), 'An idol has no real existence.'"[10]

In a later treatise, *On the Councils and the Churches*, 1539, in which Luther documents how often church councils erred or contradicted themselves, he discusses the errors of this first Jerusalem council. He points out that three of the four decrees were contrary to Christian liberty and that the Christian Church finally followed only the decree concerning abstaining from unchastity.[11]

---

9 Martin Luther, *Treatise on Christian Liberty*, 1520, in the *Works of Martin Luther*, Phila. Ed., vol. 2, pp. 339-340.

10 Martin Luther, *Lectures on Titus*, in *Luther's Works*, vol. 29, p. 40.

11 Martin Luther, *On the Councils and the Churches*, 1539, in the *Works of Martin Luther*, Phila. Ed., vol. 5, pp. 150ff, 193-197.

Christian Liberty and the Sabbath and Holy Seasons

It is always a temptation of church leaders to attempt to regulate the lives of the people by church law and regulations. Many churchmen think it easier to operate an institution by such ordinances and rules rather than by Christian love. At the dedication of a church in Torgau, Luther spoke on the freedom of the Christian concerning holy days:

> But now that this Christ, our Lord, has come and a new kingdom has been inaugurated throughout the whole world, we Christians are no longer bound to such external, particular conduct, but rather have the freedom, if the sabbath or Sunday does not please us, to take Monday or any other day of the week and make a Sunday of it; though this must be done in an orderly way. . . . We Christians receive this freedom through the teaching of today's Gospel [Luke 14:1-11] and we should insist that we are the lords of the sabbath and of other days and places and not attribute special holiness or service of God to a particular day, as the Jews or our papists do.[12]

In commenting on Galatians 4:10 in which Paul writes disapprovingly, "You observe days, and months, and seasons, and years," Luther observed:

> For Moses had commanded the Jews to observe religiously the Sabbath, the new moon, the first and seventh month, three set seasons or festivals--namely, Passover, the Feast of Weeks, and the Feast of Booths--the Sabbatical Year, and the Year of Jubilee. Now the Galatians had been forced by the false apostles to observe these same rites as something necessary for righteousness. This is why he says that they have lost grace and Christian liberty, and have turned back to the slavery of the weak and beggarly elements. They had been persuaded by the false apostles that these laws had to be observed; that when they were observed, they granted righteousness; but that when they were neglected, they brought damnation. But Paul does not permit consciences to be bound by the Mosaic Law in any way,

---

12 Martin Luther, *Sermon at the Dedication of the Castle Church in Torgau*, 1522, in *Luther's Works*, vol. 51, pp. 336-339.

but everywhere he sets them free from the Law. "Now I, Paul," he says later on, in chapter five [v. 2], "say to you that if you receive circumcision, Christ will be of no advantage to you." In Colossians 2:16 he says: "Let no one pass judgment on you in questions of food and drink or with regard to a festival or a new moon or a Sabbath." Thus Christ says (Luke 17:20): "The kingdom of God does not come by observance." Much less should consciences be burdened and ensnared by human traditions. Here someone may say: "If the Galatians sinned in observing days and seasons, why is it not sinful for you to do the same?" I reply: we observe the Lord's Day, Christmas, Easter, and similar holidays in a way that is completely free. We do not burden consciences with these observances; nor do we teach, as did the false apostles and as do the papists, that they are necessary for justification or that we can make satisfaction for our sins through them.[13]

Christian Freedom and Confession

Pope Innocent III (1161-1216) established through an act of the Fourth Lateran Council the following canon:

> Let every believer of either sex, after arriving at the years of discretion, faithfully confess all his sins alone at least once a year to his own priest, and endeavor with all his strength to observe the penance enjoined upon him, receiving at least at Easter the sacrament of the eucharist. . . . Let the priest be discreet and cautious. . . inquiring diligently as to the circumstances of both the sinner and the sin, from which he may prudently judge what counsel he ought to give to him, and what kind of remedy he ought to impose.[14]

The priest, aided by his penitential manual, thus carefully sought out the sins of the penitent. Absolution from these sins was dependent on

---

13 Martin Luther, *Lectures on Galatians*, 1535, in *Luther's Works*, vol. 26, p. 410-411.

14 Reinhold Seeberg, 1898, *Textbook of the History of Doctrines*, trans. by Charles E. Hay (Grand Rapids: Baker Book House), vol. 2, p. 93.

performing the works of penance assigned as satisfaction by the priest. Such works of penance might be giving alms, works of mercy, prayer, fasting, gifts to the church, pilgrimages, and so forth.

Luther also taught that Christians were to confess their sins. According to Luther, there were three ways to confess one's sins: a person could confess to God, to one's neighbor, or privately to one's spiritual leader. What he opposed was church law that made private confession to a priest compulsory, as is still the case in the Roman church.[15] In his *Church Postil* Luther wrote:

> The third kind of confession is that ordered by the pope, which is privately spoken into the ears of the priest when sins are enumerated. This confession is not commanded by God; the pope, however, has forced the people to it and, in addition, has invented so many kinds and varieties of sin that no one is able to keep them in mind; thus consciences have been troubled and tortured in a manner that is pitiful and distressing.[16]

Luther saw it as a violation of Christian freedom for church authorities to regulate by law the manner in which Christians were to confess.

Christian Liberty and Fasting

Church law also violated Christian freedom when it prescribed when and how fasting periods had to be observed as is still required today in the Roman church.[17] Luther did not deny that fasting at times could be helpful in keeping under control the body with its appetites and lusts. In commenting on the Sermon on the Mount, he explained:

> Everyone must impose or adjust the fasting in relation to his own strength and to his feelings about how much his own flesh requires. For this fasting is directed only against the lust and the passions of the flesh, not against nature itself. It is not confined to any rule or measure, to any time or place. If necessary, it should be practiced continually, to hold a tight rein on the body

---

15 *Catechism of the Catholic Church*, secs. 1457, 2042 (Liguori Mo.: Liguori Publ.), pp. 365-366, 493.

16 Martin Luther, *Sermons of Martin Luther*, the *Church Postil*, vol. 2, p. 196.

17 *Catechism of the Catholic Church*, sec. 2043, p. 494.

and to get it used to enduring discomfort, in case it should become necessary to do so. It should be left up to the discretion of every individual, and no one should take it upon himself to apportion it by rules, as the pope has done.[18]

Luther would not deny the use of fasting and other works of discipline if done for keeping in check the appetites and lusts of the body so that works of love may proceed. Fasting should be a disciplining of the body, however, and not a good work to please God. He wrote, "We only reject hypocritical and spurious good works. Fasting, praying, going to church are good works, if they are done in the right spirit."[19] He commented also on this in a homily based on "*The Sermon on the Mount:*"

> But above all, you must see to it that you are already pious and a true Christian and that you are not planning to render God a service by this fasting. Your service to God must be only faith in Christ and love to your neighbor, simply doing what is required of you. If this is not your situation, then you would do better to leave fasting alone. The only purpose of fasting is to discipline the body by outwardly cutting off both lust and the opportunity for lust, the same thing that faith does inwardly in the heart.[20]

Christian Liberty in Prayer and Giving

Nor should the church violate the Christian's liberty concerning prayer or in giving gifts to charity. Luther continued the above quotation by writing:

> It is likewise impossible to apportion praying, but it must be left free, according to what each individual's devotion or need may suggest or require. Almsgiving cannot be legislated or forced either, to whom or when or how much we are to give.[21]

---

18 Martin Luther, *The Sermon on the Mount*, in *Luther's Works*, vol. 21, p. 162.

19 Martin Luther, *Sermons of Martin Luther*, the *Church Postil*, vol. 1, p. 280.

20 Martin Luther, *The Sermon on the Mount*, in *Luther's Works*, vol. 21, p. 162.

21 Martin Luther, *The Sermon on the Mount*, in *Luther's Works*, vol. 21, p. 162.

Luther returned to the New Testament in stressing that gifts were to be given cheerfully, out of Christian love, and not because of any type of constraint or pressure.

Where the New Testament Is Silent, Christian Liberty Prevails

The New Testament and Freedom of Choice

Christian liberty involves the total life of the Christian. On matters upon which the New Testament is silent, the Christian is to be guided by Christian love in making his moral decisions. Luther insisted that the freedom that Paul so vigorously advocated should be returned to Christian people:

> Already, at an early date, we have taught Christian liberty from [the writings] of St. Paul. There is to be freedom of choice in everything that God has not clearly taught in the New Testament, for example, in matters pertaining to various foods, beverages, attire, places, persons, and various forms of conduct (Romans 14:2-6; 1 Corinthians 8:8-10). We are obligated to do nothing at all for God, except believe and love.[22]

Christian Freedom to Enjoy the Good Gifts of God

In the long history of Christianity, there have always been some who feel that a true Christian must maintain a sober, reverential, and grave conduct. For example, as was discussed earlier, laughter and humor had no place in monasteries. Many who followed ascetic practices often frowned with disapproval upon the Christians who enjoyed with merry and cheerful hearts the good gifts God had given His people. Often they made laws and regulations to restrict behavior or activities that they personally regarded as sinful or possibly leading to sin. In their eyes, too often anything pleasurable was undoubtedly sinful. Their understanding of Christian liberty was almost non-existent. Luther would have none of this dour and sour view of Christian life that so often resulted in the violation of Christian liberty.

In a sermon on Jesus' attendance at the Wedding in Cana (John 2), Luther spoke of the freedom of the Christian to enjoy the festivities of a wedding celebration as long as decency and moderation prevailed:

---

22 Martin Luther, *Against the Heavenly Prophets in the Matter of Images and Sacraments*, 1525, in *Luther's Works*, vol. 40, p. 127.

Here too Christ indicates that he is not displeased with a marriage feast, nor with the things belonging to a wedding such as adornments, cheerfulness, eating and drinking, according to the usage and custom of the country; which appear to be superfluous and needless expense and a worldly matter; only so far as these things are used in moderation and in keeping with a marriage. For the bride and groom must be adorned; so also the guests must eat and drink to be cheerful. . . . so that in these things no one need pay attention to the sour-visaged hypocrites and self-constituted saints who are pleased with nothing but what they themselves do and teach, and will not suffer a maid to wear a wreath or to adorn herself at all. . . . All this Christ allows to pass, as we likewise should let it pass and not make it a matter of conscience. They were not of the devil, even if a few drank of the wine a little beyond what thirst required, and became merry; else you would have to blame Christ for being the cause by means of his presence, and his mother by asking for it; so that both Christ and his mother are sinners in this if the sour-visaged saints are to render judgment. . . . Now is it a sin to play and dance at a wedding, inasmuch as some declare great sin is caused by dancing? Whether the Jews had dances I do not know; but since it is the custom of the country, like inviting guests, decorating, eating and drinking and being merry, I see no reason to condemn it, save its excess when it goes beyond decency and moderation. That sin should be committed is not the fault of dancing alone; since at a table or in church that may happen; even as it is not the fault of eating that some while so engaged should turn themselves into swine. Where things are decently conducted I will not interfere with the marriage rites and customs, and dance and never mind. Faith and love cannot be driven away either by dancing or by sitting still, as long as you keep to decency and moderation. Young children certainly dance without sin; do the same also, and be a child, then dancing will not harm you. Otherwise were dancing a sin in itself, children should not be allowed to dance.[23]

In a sermon on First Peter, Luther notes that Peter (4:3-4) warned

---

23 Martin Luther, *Sermons of Martin Luther*, the *Church Postil*, vol. 2, pp. 57-61.

the Greek Christians not to follow the pagan sensualists who loved reveling and carousing with overindulgence in food and drink. Luther remarked that "we Germans are accused of the same excess; not without some reason either."[24] However, he continued:

> At the same time the apostle does not forbid appropriate and respectable recognition of the things of physical well-being, in keeping with each individual's station in life, even including those things ministering pleasure and joy. For Peter would not have filthy, rusty, greasy monks nor sour-faced saints, with the hypocrisy and show of their simulated austere and peculiar lives, wherein they honor not their bodies, as Paul says (Colossians 2:23), but are ever ready to judge and condemn other people—the maiden, for instance, who chances to join in a dance or wears a red dress. If you are a Christian in other respects, God will easily allow you to dress and to adorn yourself, and to live with comfort, even to enjoy honor and considerable pleasure, so long as you keep within proper bounds; you should, however, not go beyond the limits of temperance and moderation.[25]

If Luther's description of monks as filthy, rusty, and greasy sounds offensive, keep in mind that since the earliest days of monasticism bathing or being too concerned with personal cleanliness was to be avoided as a worldly affectation.

Christian Liberty and One's Standard of Living

The Christian also has freedom concerning the standard of living he might choose. Luther discussed this in a sermon based on Jesus' words, "The eye is the lamp of the body. So, if your eye is sound, your whole body will be full of light; but if your eye is not sound, your whole body will be full of darkness" (Matthew 6:22-23 RSV). He commented:

> For example, you may have an idea like this: "I intend to work and accomplish something so that I can earn enough to support myself with my wife and children in a godly and honest way. And

---

24 Martin Luther, *Sermons of Martin Luther*, the *Church Postil*, vol. 7, p. 304.

25 Martin Luther, *Sermons of Martin Luther*, the *Church Postil*, vol. 7, p. 313.

if God makes it possible for me to use it in serving and helping my neighbor as well, I shall gladly do so." You see, this is the light or spiritual eye from the Word of God, showing you what is appropriate to your station and pointing out to you how you should administer it and live in it. Since the body lives here, it is right and necessary that everyone should do something to support himself and to maintain a household. But be careful that this eye does not become a villain and deceive you. Be sure that you are doing this from a single motivation and with the one purpose of working and doing what your station requires to satisfy your needs and those of your neighbor, and that you are not using it as a pretext to seek something else, namely, the gratification of your own greed. . . . Now, no one can see into your heart and judge you, but you yourself must take care that your eye is not a villain. . . . He [Christ] seeks to warn us and to require of every man's conscience that he watch the condition of his mind and heart. He must not tell himself the lovely lie that he has a good, honest reason and a genuine right to be so grasping and greedy.[26]

According to Luther, it is not up to us to criticize a fellow Christian concerning his standard of living. One person may feel that the comfortable home and lifestyle that he has chosen for his family is in keeping with his desire to follow a life of Christian love. Another person may well have guilt feelings over that same standard of living. He may feel that in view of the poverty to be found in the world, he would be overindulging himself if he lived at that standard of living. But as Luther above states, "Now, no one can see into your heart and judge you, but you yourself must take care that your eye is not a villain." It is up to each Christian to decide for himself what standard of living is in keeping with a life of Christian love.

In Situations where the New Testament Is Silent, the Christian Is Free to Follow Love

The Christian thus has broad freedom to decide for himself what it means to live as a Christian. Or, in the words of Luther quoted above, "There is to be freedom of choice in everything that God has not clearly

---

26 Martin Luther, *The Sermon on the Mount* in *Luther's Works*, vol. 21, pp. 179-181.

taught in the New Testament, for example, in matters pertaining to various foods, beverages, attire, places, persons and various forms of conduct (Romans 14:2-6; 1 Corinthians 8:8-10)."

What this means is that various Christians may have different views of what Christian love requires in a given instance or situation. One man may view a certain action as selfish and sinful, another man may regard the same action as an act of Christian love. Concerning this in his *Lectures on Romans,* Luther taught:

> Because of the difference of consciences, in the selfsame permissible work one man sins, and the other does a good work. Thus he [Paul] says: "Let everyone be fully convinced in his own mind," that is, let him be certain and quiet; and the strong should not change his faith because of the scruples of the weak, nor should the weak because of the strong act against his own judgment; he should let them do as they want, and he himself should act in accord with his own conscience.[27]

It is up to the individual Christian to decide what Christian love requires in a given situation. In the *Church Postil,* Luther wrote concerning this plainly and frankly:

> Paul says we should be "righteous" in our lives. No work, however, nor particular time, is here designated as the way to righteousness. In the ways of God is universal freedom. It is left to the individual to exercise his liberty; to do right when, where and to whom occasion offers.[28]

Are Paul and Luther teaching a type of situation ethics—an ethic in which a person has the liberty to respond in Christian love as he sees fit to the moral concerns involved in a situation in which he might find himself? Of course they are. The last three quotations above make it clear that "in everything that God has not clearly taught in the New Testament" a Christian is "to exercise his liberty, to do right when, where, and to whom the occasion offers;" and he is to realize "because of the difference of consciences, in the selfsame permissible work one man sins, and the other does good work."

---

27 Martin Luther, *Lectures on Romans*, in *Luther's Works*, vol. 25, p. 500.

28 Martin Luther, *Sermons of Martin Luther*, the *Church Postil*, vol. 6, pp. 124-125.

The Difference between Christian and Secular Situation Ethics

However, there is a great difference between the situation ethics taught by Paul and Luther and the situation ethics espoused by some others in the past decades. The difference is one of motivation; what is the source of the love that guides our actions. The over-arching and governing motivation in making moral decisions for the New Testament and Luther is *agape*, Christian love. All is to be done in the self-less, self-denying love taught in the Christ's words, "A new commandment I give to you, that you love one another; even as I have loved you, that you love one another" (John 13:34 RSV). Or in the words of John, "We (are able to) love, because he first loved us" (1 John 4:19).

A Christian views the world with eyes of love that are both dispassionate and compassionate. Christian love is dispassionate because it is not an emotionally charged love. It is a calm, composed, serene, fair, and impartial love. Christian love is compassionate because it is a benevolent, kindhearted, merciful love that impels one to work with good will for the benefit of all. Our motivation to live Christian love is the gratitude and thankfulness in our hearts for the love that Jesus showered on us and which He asks we show to our neighbors.

Some situational ethicists who write and talk of love as being the bases of ethical decisions teach, however, that the love about which they speak can be lived by non-Christians as well as Christians.[29] Thus, their writings make it evident that the love about which they write could not possibly be *agape*, or Christian love. How can a person who does not believe in Jesus' redeeming love have as his example and motivation the love that brought Jesus to lay down His life for his sins? If a person has denied and rejected Jesus as his Savior, how can he live a life based on imitating the love of Jesus? How can his love be one of response to the love of Christ for him? It is difficult to understand the type of love of which these secular or quasi-religious situational ethicists speak, but it is very plainly not Christian love, *agape*. They teach a love uninspired by God's love through whom, "we have redemption through his blood, the forgiveness of our trespasses, according to the riches of his grace which he lavished upon us" (Ephesians 1:7-8). It is not a Christian love enlightened and generated by the Holy Spirit and guided by God's Word.

---

29 John A. T. Robinson, 1963, *Honest to God* (Philadelphia: The Westminster Press), p. 110.

Christian Liberty and Giving Offense to the Weak Brother

Paul wrote to the Roman church, "Owe no one anything but to love one another" (Romans 13:8 RSV). Luther echoes Paul in writing:

> In sum: We owe nobody anything but to love (Romans 13:8) and to serve our neighbor through love. Where love is present, there it is accomplished that no eating, drinking, clothing, or living in a particular way endangers the conscience or is a sin before God, except when it is detrimental to one's neighbor. In such things one cannot sin against God but only against one's neighbor. . . . All things are free to you with God through faith; but with men you are the servant of everyman through love.[30]

There are times, as Luther says above, when the exercise of one's Christian liberty may prove harmful and detrimental to one's neighbor. To give an example: Early in the Reformation at a time when Luther was confined in the Wartburg Castle in order to escape the Emperor's ban, some people in Wittenberg insisted on their Christian freedom to radically revise the liturgy, adornments, and practices of the parish church. In doing this, they offended the consciences of many who did not agree with their revisions. Luther returned to Wittenberg and gently reproved the people:

> And here, dear friends, one must not insist upon his rights, but must see what may be useful and helpful to his brother, as St. Paul says, "All things are lawful for me, but not all things are expedient." We are not all equally strong in faith; some of you have a stronger faith than I. Therefore we must not look upon ourselves, or our strength, or our rank, but upon our neighbor, . . . I would not have gone so far as you have done, if I had been here. What you did was good, but you have gone too fast. . . . Take note of these two things, "must" and "free." The "must" is that which necessity requires, and which must ever be unyielding; as, for instance, the faith, which I shall never permit any one to take away from me, but which I must always keep in my heart and freely confess before every one. But "free" is that in which I have choice, and may use or not, yet in such wise that it profit my brother and not me. Now do not make a "must" out of

---

30 Martin Luther, *Commentary of 1 Cor. 7*, in *Luther's Works*, vol. 28, pp. 46-47.

what is "free," as you have done, so that you may not be called to account for those who were led astray by your exercise of liberty without love. For if you entice any one to eat meat on Friday, and he is troubled about it on his deathbed, and thinks, Woe is me, for I have eaten meat and I am lost! God will call you to account for that soul. . . . Therefore, let us show love to our neighbors, or our work will not endure. We must have patience with them for a time, and not cast out him who is weak in the faith; much more should we regulate our doing and not doing according to the demands of love, provided no injury is done to our faith.[31]

Thus, on the one hand, a Christian may well resist those who violate his Christian liberty by inflicting their codes of conduct upon him. On the other hand, there are times when a Christian should not insist upon his Christian liberty. If using our Christian liberty results in offending and harming the faith of another, in Christian love we ought to refrain from exercising our freedom. In our use of Christian liberty, Paul's words take precedence, "Let all that you do be done in love" (1 Corinthians 16:14 NASB).

Christian Liberty and the Ten Commandments

The Ten Commandments Serve as a Guide in Living Christian Love

Luther understood how readily an individual can rationalize Christian love to justify self-serving purposes, to use one's Christian freedom to act in love as pretext for evil. Humans have an endless capacity to justify to themselves their selfish desires and actions. Luther especially protested concerning those situations in which one tried to convince oneself that Christian love required breaking the moral law of one of the Ten Commandments. The moral code found in the Ten Commandments is not to be broken according to Luther. Luther gives two examples as illustrations of the authority of the Commandments. In the first, he urges that we are not to steal, no matter how great our distress, but rather to trust God:

Take an example: If I were a man who had a wife and children, and had nothing for them and no one gave me anything; then I

---

31 Martin Luther, *The Eight Wittenberg Sermons, The First Sermon*, in the *Works of Martin Luther*, Phila. Ed., vol. 2, pp. 393-396.

should believe and hope that God would sustain me. But if I see that it amounts to nothing and I am not helped with food and clothing, what takes place? Then, as an unbelieving fool, I begin to doubt, and go and take whatever is at hand, steal, deceive, cheat the people and make my way the best I can and may. See this is what shameless unbelief does. But if I am a believer then I close my eyes and say: O God, I am your creature and your handiwork and you have from the beginning created me. I will depend entirely upon you who cares more for me, how I shall be sustained, than I do myself; you will indeed nourish me, feed, clothe and help me, where and when you know best.[32]

In a second illustration from his *Commentary on 1 Corinthians 7*, he condemns the situation, so beloved of the novelists and playwrights, wherein a woman sacrifices her virtue out of love for her husband or family:

From this it follows that those cases were wrong where we read how certain wives, with the consent of their husbands, committed adultery in order to save their husbands from death or prison. For one should keep God's commandments, even though it may cost us husband or wife, life or property. And no one has the right, for any reason whatever, to permit his wife to commit adultery.[33]

The illustrations above show the limits to what Luther means when he writes, "Therefore we conclude that all law, divine and human, treating of outward conduct, should not bind any further than love goes. Love is to be the interpreter of the law."[34] He continues by saying that it is better for a priest to forego participating in a worship service than to neglect a man on his deathbed asking for the priest's prayers. Luther gives the example of Jesus healing on the Sabbath and observes in the *Church Postil*:

As Christ here treats of the law relating to the Sabbath and makes it subserve the needs of man, so we should treat laws of that kind and keep them only so far as they accord with love. If

---

32 Martin Luther, *Sermons of Martin Luther*, the *Church Postil*, vol. 4, pp. 205-206.

33 Martin Luther, *Commentary on 1 Corinthians 7*, in *Luther's Works*, vol. 28, p. 34.

34 Martin Luther, *Sermons of Martin Luther*, the *Church Postil*, vol. 5, p. 161.

laws do not serve love, they may be annulled at once, be they God's or man's commands. . . . If you are a Christian you have power to dispense with all commandments so far as they hinder you in the practice of love, even as Christ here teaches. He goes right on, although it is the Sabbath day, helps this sick man and gives a satisfactory and clear reason for his Sabbath work.[35]

Note, it is the "laws of that kind" that are to give way to the needs of man as we respond to those needs in Christian love.

Therefore, does Luther really mean that all law, all commandments can be set aside by Christian love? The two illustrations concerning stealing and adultery cited above would indicate otherwise. Also in other writings, Luther makes it clear that the laws referred to above that can be set aside do not include the moral code of the Ten Commandments. Luther, rather, is in harmony with the early church fathers who agreed that the setting aside of the civil and ceremonial laws of the Old Testament did not include the Ten Commandments. He makes this distinction in writing in his *Introduction to the Old Testament*:

> For unbelief and evil desire are, in their nature, sin, and worthy of death; but not to eat leavened bread on Easter, and to eat any unclean beast, to make no sign on the body, and all those things that the Levitical priesthood deals with as sin,--these things are not, in their nature, sinful or wicked, but they become sins because they are forbidden by the law. This law can be done away; but the Ten Commandments cannot be done away, for sin against the Ten Commandments would be sin, even though there were no commandments, or they were not known; just as the unbelief of the heathen is sin, even though they do not know or think that it is sin.[36]

Paul wrote that our Christian love is to be the fulfilling of the Commandments (Romans 13:8-10). It can hardly be the fulfilling of them if it leads to violating one of the moral laws of the Ten Commandments.

---

35 Martin Luther, *Sermons of Martin Luther*, the *Church Postil*, vol. 5, pp. 164-165.

36 Martin Luther, *Introduction to the Old Testament*, 1545, in the *Works of Martin Luther*, Phila. Ed., vol. 6, p. 375.

The Commandment Regarding the Sabbath

In keeping, however, with the teachings of Paul (Romans 14:5-6), Luther makes an exception concerning the commandment dealing with the Sabbath. Luther concurs with Paul's annulment of this commandment:

> For St. Paul (Colossians 2 [:16-17]), speaks frankly and clearly, "Therefore let no one pass judgment on you in questions of food and drink or with regard to a festival or a new moon or a sabbath. These are only a shadow of what is to come." Here Paul expressly abrogates the sabbath and calls it a shadow now past since the body, which is Christ himself, is come. Also, Galatians 4 [:10-11], "You observe days, and months, and seasons, and years! I am afraid I have labored over you in vain." Here Paul calls it lost labor to observe days and seasons, among which is also the sabbath.[37]

The Augsburg Confession, the primary statement of the teachings of the Lutheran church, not written by but approved by Luther, also maintains Christian liberty concerning the Sabbath Commandment. Article Twenty-eight states:

> For those who judge that by the authority of the Church the observance of the Lord's Day [Sunday] instead of the Sabbath-day was ordained as a thing necessary, do greatly err. Scripture has abrogated the Sabbath-day; for it teaches that, since the Gospel has been revealed, all the ceremonies of Moses can be omitted. And yet, because it was necessary to appoint a certain day, that the people might know when they ought to come together, it appears that the Church designated the Lord's Day for this purpose; and this day seems to have been chosen all the more for this additional reason, that men might have an example of Christian liberty, and might know that the keeping neither of the Sabbath nor of any other day is necessary.[38]

---

37 Martin Luther, *Against the Heavenly Prophets in the Matter of Images and Sacraments*, 1525, in *Luther's Works*, vol. 40, p. 93.

38 *The Augsburg Confession*, Art. 28, in the *Concordia Triglotta*, pp. 91, 93.

The Ten Commandments Show Our Need for a Savior

The Law, Luther writes, is still active spiritually in its role of showing non-Christians their sin before God, and their need for forgiveness and a Savior from sin.[39] In this sense, Luther preached that even mature Christians still need the Law:

> But besides, we must bear in mind that the doctrine of the Law is not to be entirely done away with, even in the case of those who are Christians, inasmuch as Christians must exercise themselves in daily repentance, because they still live in the flesh which is moved by sinful lusts. Hence they must be so taught and admonished, after they have received the forgiveness of sins, that they do not fall back again into a state of security, or give the flesh occasion to war against the Spirit. Galatians 5:13.[40]

Christian Liberty and Libertinism

As did Paul (Romans 6:15), Luther had to defend himself against the charge that Christian liberty would lead people into libertinism and licentiousness. Luther realized a Christian might use his freedom from the church law to act in selfish ways, therefore he taught in a sermon:

> Our conscience has been rescued and liberated from the human [papal church] laws and all the compulsion they imposed on us, so that we are not obligated to do what they have commanded us to do on pain of losing salvation. To this freedom we must now cling firmly, and we must never let ourselves be torn from it. In addition, however, we must also be very careful not to make this freedom a pretext for evil.[41]

The Ten Commandments and Luther's Catechisms

As has been documented above, Luther had a great deal to say

---

39 Martin Luther, *Lectures on Galatians*, 1535, in *Luther's Works*, vol. 26, p. 317.

40 Martin Luther, *Sermons of Martin Luther*, the *Church Postil*, vol. 4, p. 161.

41 Martin Luther, *Sermons on 1 Peter*, in *Luther's Works*, vol. 30, p. 77.

about Jesus' way of life in his sermons, commentaries, and many of his other writings. In most of these writings, the way of life that Jesus taught is portrayed in a manner that reminds us of the writers of the New Testament.

Luther, however, at times used the Ten Commandments as a framework to explain how Christian love was to be lived in a Christian's life. He used the commandments in this way in his *A Treatise on Good Works*[42] and in his Small and Large Catechisms as well as in other documents.

Luther's first "catechism" published in 1520 included only the Ten Commandments, the Creed, and the Lord's Prayer. This was similar to an instructional booklet first printed in 1498 and used by the Brethren of the Common Life with whom Luther had lived for a time. Their booklet covered the same three topics as Luther's first "catechism": faith, the Creed; hope, the Lord's Prayer; and love, the Ten Commandments. Many such handbooks for lay instruction dealing with the Commandments, the Creed, and the Lord's Prayer had been produced during medieval times in Europe.[43] Later Luther added other topics to his catechisms: Baptism, Confession and the Office of the Keys, and the Lord's Supper.

In attempting, however, to teach Christian love by using the Ten Commandments as a framework, Luther did not follow the manner in which the New Testament teaches Christ's way of life. Neither Christ nor his apostles use the Ten Commandments as the basis or framework for teaching Christian love. In fact, the Ten Commandments make up a very small part of the great many passages in the New Testament that present the life of love that Jesus would have his followers live. The Ten Commandments are not set aside or abolished; they are superceded by way of life that Jesus and his apostles taught and through which the Ten Commandments are fulfilled.

Luther used the Ten Commandments as a framework to teach the Christian way of life as he had a very expansive way of interpreting the Ten Commandments. This was a common practice used by some earlier in the medieval church. Although the commandments are for the greater part succinctly negative, Luther, and later also John Calvin,[44] read into them far-ranging, positive connotations and implications. For example, in the brief explanations to each of the Ten Commandments found in his

---

42 Martin Luther, *A Treatise on Good Works*, 1520, in the *Works of Martin Luther*, Phila. Ed., vol. 1, pp. 173-285.

43 John Calvin, 1559, *Institutes of the Christian Religion*, 2 vols., in the *Library of Christian Classics* (Philadelphia: Westminster Press), vol. 1, p. 367 footnote.

44 John Calvin, 1559, *Institutes of the Christian Religion*, 2 vols., in *The Library of Christian Classics*, vol. 1, pp. 374 to 421.

catechisms, Luther always concluded with a strongly positive statement based on the Christian's awe, respect, and love for God. In this way he endeavored to teach how Christian love should undergird a believer's life. To give examples: in his short explanation of the commandment, "You shall not murder," Luther wrote, "We should fear and love God that we may not hurt nor harm our neighbor in his body, but help and befriend him in every need and danger of life and body." In regard to the commandment, "You shall not bear false witness against your neighbor," Luther explained its meaning by writing, "We should fear and love God that we may not deceitfully belie, betray, slander, or defame our neighbor, but defend him, think and speak well of him, and put the best construction on everything." The explanation to the commandment, "You shall not commit adultery," reflected Luther's high regard for the institution of marriage in his writing: "We should fear and love God that we may lead a chaste and decent life in words and deeds, and each love and honor his spouse."[45]

Luther's catechisms were his heartfelt attempt to teach the Christian way of life in a simple way to the average Christian in his country. Whether his departure from the way the New Testament teaches Christian love succeeded, however, is another matter. Too often many Lutheran Christians forget the short explanations appended to each of the commandments of how Christian love fulfills the commandment and only the "Thou shall nots . . ." remain. As a consequence, the primarily negative commands of the Ten Commandments unfortunately sum up the Christian way of life for many Lutherans rather than Jesus' positive New Commandment of loving others as selflessly as He loved them. In my experience, it has made Lutherans a respectable people who avoid the gross sins of the Ten Commandments, but not a people who noted for following the example of Jesus as He expressed His love in service to those who needed His aid: the guilt-stricken, the bereaved, the sick, the hungry, and the oppressed.

Christian Freedom Concerning Marriage

In Luther's view, the medieval church belittled the institution of marriage in comparison with the celibate life. In contrast, Luther in a sermon from the *Church Postil* on Jesus' attendance at the wedding at Cana (John 2:1-11) remarks:

> In the first place, it is indeed a high honor paid to married life for Christ himself to attend this marriage, together with his mother

---

45 Martin Luther, *The Small Catechism*, 1529, in the *Concordia Triglotta*, p. 541.

and his disciples. . . . Now the second honor is his giving good wine for the poor marriage by means of a great miracle, making himself the bride's chief cup-bearer; . . . for by this miracle he confirms marriage as the work and institution of God, no matter how common or how lowly it appears in the eyes of men, God nonetheless acknowledges his own work and loves it. Even our Caiaphases themselves have often declared and preached that marriage was the only state instituted by God. . . . yet they shun, reject and revile this state, and deem themselves so holy that they not only themselves avoid marriage—though they need it and ought to marry—but from excess of holiness they will not even attend a marriage, being much holier than Christ himself who as an unholy sinner attends a wedding."[46]

Nor did Luther have any patience with the ancient interpretation of Jesus' parable of the Sower and the Seed (Luke 8:4-15) which had persisted up to his time. This interpretation found in the Church Fathers (see page 224) viewed marriage as bearing fruit only thirty-fold; widowhood, sixty-fold; but virginity a hundred-fold. Luther rebuked the Church Fathers for such an interpretation. For Luther marriage, virginity, and widowhood were neither fruits, virtues, nor good works, but rather three stations in life created and ordained by God. For Luther there were not three kinds of chastity, that of the virgin, the widowed, and the married; but three God-approved stations in life in which Christians might live chaste and honorable lives.[47] The Roman Catholic Church responded to Luther at the Council of Trent in 1563 by declaring in Canon 10, "If any one saith, . . . that it is not better and more blessed to remain in virginity, or in celibacy, than to be united in matrimony; let him be anathema."[48]

Luther also held that there were some, who as Jesus said, made themselves eunuchs for the sake of the kingdom of heaven (Matthew 19:12).[49] In harmony with Jesus and Paul, he taught that the ability to live a celibate life was a special gift from God (1 Corinthians 7:7). It was a gift, however, in Luther's view, given to few. And as it was a gift of God, it was

---

46 Martin Luther, *Sermons of Martin Luther*, the *Church Postil*, vol. 2, pp. 55-56.

47 Martin Luther, *Sermons of Martin Luther*, the *Church Postil*, vol. 2, pp. 119-122.

48 *The Canons and Decrees of the Council of Trent*, J. Waterworth, translator (Chicago: The Christian Symbolic Publ. Soc.), p. 195.

49 Martin Luther, *Sermons of Martin Luther*, the *Church Postil*, vol. 6, p. 90.

no more a reason for spiritual pride than any other of the charismatic gifts of the Holy Spirit.[50] To attempt to live the celibate life without this gift of the Spirit was to subject oneself to unjustifiable distress and frustration. He agreed with Paul that "because of the temptation to immorality, each man should have his own wife and each woman her own husband. . . . For it is better to marry than to be aflame with passion" (1 Corinthians 7:2,9 RSV).

Luther was a student of history. He knew of the innumerable clergy, the many popes, bishops, and countless priests, who not having the gift of continence had descended into immorality because of the church laws forbidding clerical marriage. Pierre Dubois, a French layman and lawyer, in the early thirteen hundreds lamented that few clergymen kept their vows, yet they were retained while ordination was denied to married men.[51] It has been a problem that continually embarrassed the Roman church, as it does to this day. Luther wrote vehemently against this denial of the Christian freedom for the clergy to marry that resulted from the non-Biblical, legalistic strictures of the Canon Law of the Roman Catholic Church.[52] He opposed requiring vows of celibacy when God had not given the gift of continence. He suggested that if men want to make vows that they can keep, then let them vow not to bite off their own noses.

Luther strongly opposed the Penitentials that sought to govern married life. He decried in his famous treatise to the Christians of his day, *The Babylonian Captivity of the Church*, the eighteen hindrances to marriage found in the then popular penitential, the *Summa Angelica*:

> There is circulating far and wide and enjoying a great reputation, a book whose contents have been poured together out of the cesspool of all human traditions, and whose title is "The Angelic Sum," though it ought rather to be "The More than Devilish Sum." Among endless other monstrosities, which are supposed to instruct the confessors, while they most mischievously confuse them, there are enumerated in this book eighteen hindrances to marriage. If you will examine these with the just and unprejudiced eye of faith, you will see that they belong to those things which the Apostle foretold: "There shall be those

---

50 Martin Luther, *Commentary on 1 Corinthians 7*, in *Luther's Works*, vol. 28, pp. 47-50.

51 Philip Schaff, 1910, *History of the Christian Church*, vol. 6, pp. 41-42.

52 Martin Luther, *An Open Letter to the Christian Nobility*, 1520, in the *Works of Martin Luther*, Phila. Ed., vol. 2, pp. 118-123.

that give heed to spirits of devils, speaking lies in hypocrisy, forbidding to marry." What is forbidding to marry if it is not this--to invent all those hindrances and set those snares, in order to prevent men from marrying or, if they be married, to annul their marriage? Who gave this power to men? Granted that they were holy men and impelled by godly zeal, why should another's holiness disturb my liberty? Why should another's zeal take me captive? Let whoever will, be a saint and a zealot, and to his heart's content; only let him not bring harm upon another, and let him not rob me of my liberty!

Luther then goes on to comment on the supposed hindrances to marriage.[53]

In the *Shepherd of Hermas* (see pages 156-157) and in the writings of Tertullian (see page 203) as well as in others, even giving a woman an admiring look and contemplating her as a possible marriage partner was considered lusting after her and therefore sinful. Luther in his *An Open Letter to the Christian Nobility* takes up this question in writing:

This argument and inquiry has come from some: "Is it sinful for a man and a woman to desire each other for the purpose of marriage?" This is ridiculous, a question that contradicts both Scripture and nature. Why would people get married if they did not have desire and love for each other? Indeed, that is just why God has given this eager desire to bride and bridegroom, for otherwise everybody would flee from marriage and avoid it. In Scripture, therefore, He also commanded man and woman to love each other, and He shows that the sexual union of husband and wife is also most pleasing to Him. Hence this desire and love must not be absent, for it is a good fortune and a great pleasure, . . .[54]

Luther was aware that involuntary, lustful thoughts might arise in one's mind. Such spontaneous thoughts he did not consider sin in themselves; the sin was to dwell on them:

53 Martin Luther, *The Babylonian Captivity of the Church*, 1520, in the *Works of Martin Luther*, Phila. Ed., vol. 2, pp. 261-271.

54 Martin Luther, *The Sermon on the Mount*, in *Luther's Works*, vol. 21, p. 89.

It is impossible to keep the devil from shooting evil thoughts and lusts into your heart. But see to it that you do not let such arrows (Ephesians 6:16) stick there and take root, but tear them out and throw them away. Do what one of the ancient fathers counseled long ago: "I cannot," he said, "keep a bird from flying over my head. But I can certainly keep it from nesting in my hair or from biting my nose off."[55]

In a medieval church that all too often viewed sexual love as bestial and filthy, Luther had a much more Biblical view. In a sermon in his Postil, he counseled:

Dear youth, do not be ashamed that you desire a girl, and that the girl desires a boy; only let this result in marriage, not unchastity, and then it is no more a disgrace than eating and drinking. Celibacy ought to be a virtue which happens among God's miracles, as the instance of a man who neither eats nor drinks. It is beyond healthy nature, not to mention sinful, fallen nature.[56]

Luther had little use for Augustine's view that all sexual desire was shameful concupiscence (see pages 225-227). Nonetheless, David's confession in Psalm 51:5, "Behold, I was brought forth in iniquity, and in sin did my mother conceive me," had long been used in the church as a proof text for the sinfulness of sexual intercourse. Luther in his treatise *The Estate of Marriage* also makes the unwarranted assumption that this text applies to all marital sexuality in writing:

With all this extolling of married life, however, I have not meant to ascribe to nature a condition of sinlessness. On the contrary, I say that flesh and blood, corrupted through Adam, is conceived and born in sin, as Psalm 51 [:5] says. Intercourse is never without sin, but God excuses it by his grace because the estate of marriage is his work, and he preserves in and through the sin all that good which he has implanted and blessed in marriage.[57]

---

55 Martin Luther, *The Sermon on the Mount*, in *Luther's Works*, vol. 21, p. 88.

56 Martin Luther, *Sermons of Martin Luther*, the *Church Postil*, vol. 1, p. 441

57 Martin Luther, *The Estate of Marriage*, 1522, in *Luther's Works*, vol. 45, p. 49.

For Luther, it is only in marriage that the sexual drive of humans is to be fulfilled. Luther, however, was aware that perfect bliss was not to be found this side of heaven. He knew that a married man might have a roving eye. Therefore, in his commentary, *The Sermon on the Mount*, he counseled that a husband look upon his wife:

> . . . as the one whom God gives him and whom He blesses, . . . And if he saw another woman, even one more beautiful than his own wife, he would say: "Is she beautiful? As far as I am concerned, she is not very beautiful. And even if she were the most beautiful woman on earth, in my wife at home I have a lovelier adornment, one that God has given me and has adorned with His Word beyond the others, even though she may not have a beautiful body or may have other failings. Though I may look over all the women in the world, I cannot find any about whom I can boast with a joyful conscience as I can about mine: 'This is the one whom God has granted to me and put into my arms.' I know that He and all the angels are heartily pleased if I cling to her lovingly and faithfully. Then why should I despise this precious gift of God and take up with someone else, where I can find no such treasure or adornment?"[58]

Luther's View of True Saintliness

Both Clergy and Laity Can Equally Serve God

Luther took issue with the idea that the lives of the monks and other clerics were more saintly by their very nature than the lives of lay people. Thomas Aquinas (1225-1274), the premier theologian of the Roman church, for example, discussed seriously and at length as to which church office had the innately greater sanctity and merit among the lay brothers, monks, deacons, archdeacons, parish priests, and bishops.[59] Luther took a decidedly different view in the *Church Postil* by preaching:

> Good works are imperative, and we should extol them in others; but no one is to be judged, justified or preferred because of

---

58 Martin Luther, *The Sermon on the Mount*, in *Luther's Works*, vol. 21, p. 87.

59 Thomas Aquinas, *Summa Theologica*, vol. 2 (Chicago: Wm. Benton, Publ.), p. 638.

them. The farmer at his plow sometimes may be better in God's sight than the chaste nun. . . . It is impossible for us mortals to discern the relative merits of individuals and the value of their works; we ought to praise all, giving equal honors and not preferring one above another. . . . Then we are to leave it to God to judge who ranks first. . . . Who would have become a priest, who a monk, yes, who a pope and bishop, had he realized that in such capacity his position and its works are no more meritorious than those of the poorest nurse maid who rocks children and washes swaddling clothes?[60]

In his treatise *The Babylonian Captivity of the Church*, Luther counseled:

Therefore I advise no one to enter any religious order or the priesthood--nay, I dissuade everyone--unless he be forearmed with this knowledge and understand that the works of monks and priests, be they never so holy and arduous, differ no whit in the sight of God from the works of the rustic toiling in the field or the woman going about her household tasks, but that all works are measured before Him by faith alone; . . .[61]

Faith and Love Sums Up the Christian's Life

Luther realized that true saintliness might well be found in an otherwise quite ordinary Christian. He summed up the Christian life in writing, "To believe in Christ and do to your neighbor as you believe Christ did to you, is the only true way to godliness and salvation. There is none other."[62] All Christians are called by God to serve their neighbor in whatever vocation they find themselves. In his work *On the Councils and the Churches,* Luther recognized that a true saint could be:

. . . a Christian burgher or peasant who has a true, pure Christian faith toward Christ and practices the true, old, good

---

60 Martin Luther, *Sermons of Martin Luther*, the *Church Postil*, vol. 6, pp. 86-88.

61 Martin Luther, *The Babylonian Captivity of the Church*, 1520, in the *Works of Martin Luther*, Phila. Ed., vol. 2, p. 241.

62 Martin Luther, *Sermons of Martin Luther*, the *Church Postil*, vol. 6, p. 300.

works, such as humility, patience, mildness, chastity, love, and faithfulness to his neighbor, and diligence and care in his work, office, calling, and station,--such a man is a real old saint and Christian; . . . "[63]

He preached that it makes no difference in what station of life one finds oneself:

> The Christian faith bids each person in his life, and all in common, to be diligent in the works of love, humility, patience. It teaches that one be not intolerant of another, but rather render him his due, remembering that he whose condition in life is the most insignificant can be equally upright and blessed before God with the occupant of the most significant position. Again, it teaches that man must have patience with the weakness of his fellow, being mindful of how others must bear with his own imperfections. In short, it says one must manifest to another the love and kindness he would have that other extend to him. . . . Let him confine himself to his own sphere; let him serve God in his vocation, remembering that God makes him, too, his instrument in his own place.[64]

The Christian, however, is to keep in mind that all is to be done in faith and selfless love to the glory of God:

> For just as Christ with all his works did not merit heaven for himself, because it was his before; but he served us thereby, not regarding or seeking his own, but these two things, namely our benefit and the glory of God his Father; so also should we never seek our own in our good works, either temporal or eternal, but glorify God by freely and gratuitously doing good to our neighbor.[65]

A primary point in the above is that the Christian should not live for

---

63 Martin Luther, *On the Councils and the Churches*, 1539, in the *Works of Martin Luther*, Phila. Ed., vol. 5, p. 245.

64 Martin Luther, *Sermons of Martin Luther*, the *Church Postil*, vol. 8, pp. 287-288.

65 Martin Luther, *Sermons of Martin Luther*, the *Church Postil*, vol. 4, p. 309.

himself no more than did Jesus Christ. Luther explained in his *Church Postil* that as Jesus lived a life of fulfilling the will of the Father, so a Christian is to live a life pleasing to the Father:

> Christ the Lord had also sufficient; what the world had was his. He might have passed us by, but it is not the nature of true life to do so. Nay, cursed be that life into perdition that lives for self; for to so live is heathenish and not Christian. Then those who have at present their sufficiency from Christ, must follow the example of Christ and with utter sincerity do good to their neighbors, as Christ did to us; freely, without the least thought of obtaining anything thereby, only with the desire that it be pleasing to God.[66]

In Luther's writings, faith and love go hand in hand. The piety found in the formal worship of a forgiving and loving God has its counterpart in the worship of God through a life involved in acts of love and goodness toward all with whom one comes in contact. In the life of a true Christian there is not to be that difference between piety and goodness of which Blaise Pascal wrote (see page 42-43).

The Christian as Simultaneously Saint and Sinner

Paul encouraged Christians in his letter to the Galatians to follow a life of faith working through love (Galatians 5:6). He exhorted these Christians to abide by the guidance of the Holy Spirit and avoid the temptations of the flesh in writing, "But I say, walk by the Spirit, and do not gratify the desires of the flesh. For the desires of the flesh are against the Spirit, and the desires of the Spirit are against the flesh; for these are opposed to each other, to prevent you from doing what you would" (Galatians 5:16-17 RSV). Luther followed Paul in warning that leading a Christian life could be hindered by appetites of one's own body. He felt it necessary for Christian preachers to warn against such fleshly desires. He knew such lusts might otherwise overwhelm the motivations of Christian love and the sanctifying power of God's Spirit. Luther therefore warned:

> For although the Spirit truly is present and, as Christ says, willing and effective in those that believe, on the other hand, the flesh is weak and sluggish. Besides, the devil is not idle, but seeks to

---

66 Martin Luther, *Sermons of Martin Luther*, the *Church Postil*, vol. 3, p. 349.

seduce our weak nature by temptations and allurements. So we must not permit the people to go on in their way, neglecting to urge and admonish them, through God's Word, to lead a godly life. Indeed, you dare not be negligent and backward in this duty; for, as it is, our flesh is all too sluggish to heed the Spirit and all too able to resist it. Paul says (Galatians 5:17): "For the flesh lusts against the Spirit, and the Spirit against the flesh . . . that you may not do the things that you would."[67]

Thus Luther, as Paul, was ever the realist. The Christian's love for his God may well seek to overflow into the lives of his neighbors. God's sanctifying Spirit may truly be at work in the Christian. The Christian, nonetheless, must be constantly encouraged to follow the way of God and to resist the allurements of world, the blandishments of the devil, and the too often immoral or selfish desires of his own fleshly nature.

Luther was aware of the variety of impure motivations that crowded in to dilute the purity of Christian love that he endeavored to live. He confessed in his *Treatise on Baptism*:

"I know full well that I have not a single work which is pure, but I am baptized, and through my baptism God, Who cannot lie, has bound Himself in a covenant with me, not to count my sin against me, but to slay it and blot it out."[68]

Christians live simultaneously as saints and sinners. They are saints in that they live in a state of grace in which, as Luther wrote, God "forgives daily and richly all sins to me and all believers."[69] They are also sinners as Luther explained in a postil:

It is true of Christ's kingdom that his Christians are not perfectly holy. They have begun to be holy and are in a state of progression. There are still to be found among them anger, evil desire, unholy love, worldly care and other deplorable infirmities, remains of the old Adam. . . . But whoso recognizes Christianity

---

67 Martin Luther, *Sermons of Martin Luther*, the *Church Postil*, vol. 8, p. 305.

68 Martin Luther, *Treatise on Baptism*, 1519, in the *Works of Martin Luther*, Phila. Ed., vol. 1, p. 63.

69 Martin Luther, *The Small Catechism* in the *Concordia Triglotta* p. 545.

as a progressive order yet in its beginning, will not be offended at the occasional manifestation of ungentleness, unkindness and impatience on the part of a Christian; for he remembers that Christians are commanded to bear one another's burdens and infirmities.[70]

Living the Christian life is one of becoming, one of striving to imitate Christ in a life of selfless love. The Christian never fully succeeds; the frailty of his human nature pulls him down. However, he knows he lives in a state of grace in which God forgives his sins of weakness. He looks forward to the time when God will call him to Himself, and the weakness of his flesh will be no more. This is the view of the Christian life that Luther tried to bring back in his attempt to reform the Roman Catholic Church. He summed up this view of the total Christian life in his *Lectures on Galatians* by teaching:

> You cannot produce anyone on earth who loves God and his neighbor as the Law requires. In the life to come, when we shall be completely cleansed of all our faults and sins and shall be as pure as the sun, we shall love perfectly and shall be righteous through our perfect love. But in this present life such purity is hindered by our flesh, to which sin will cling as long as we live. And thus our corrupt love of ourselves is so powerful that it greatly surpasses our love of God and of our neighbor. Meanwhile, however, to make us righteous also in this present life, we have a Propitiator and a mercy seat, Christ (Romans 3:25). If we believe in Him, sin is not imputed to us. Therefore faith is our righteousness in this present life. In the life to come, when we shall be thoroughly cleansed and shall be completely free of all sin and fleshly desire, we shall have no further need of faith and hope.[71]

Only God Can Judge Who is the True Saint

It is only God who knows who will be His in the life to come, the true saints whom he will not forsake. Luther was grieved at the arrogance

---

70 Martin Luther, *Sermons of Martin Luther*, the *Church Postil*, vol. 7, p. 83-84.

71 Martin Luther, *Lectures on Galatians*, 1535, in *Luther's Works*, vol. 27, p. 64.

and presumption of church authorities who took upon themselves the prerogative of deciding who should be canonized as a Saint, upon whom they would confer Sainthood, he wrote in his *An Open Letter to the Christian Nobility*:

> I would that the dear saints were left in peace, and the poor folk not led astray! What spirit has given the pope the authority to canonize the saints? Who tells him whether they are saints or not? Are there not already sins enough on earth, that we too must tempt God, interfere in His judgment and set up the dear saints as lures for money?[72]

It is impossible for humans to judge true saintliness, for it is only God who can look into the heart and discern the faith and Christian love in one's life. It is on the basis of faith in Jesus and the purity of Christian love that flows from that faith that God judges. In these terms Luther writes, "Now there is no greater service of God than Christian love which helps and serves the needy, as Christ himself will judge and testify at the Last Day, Matthew 25 [:31-46]."[73] He further instructs in *Secular Authority: to What Extent Should It Be Obeyed*:

> For perfection and imperfection consist not in works and do not establish a distinct external order among Christians; but they exist in the heart, in faith and love, so that they who believe and love the most are the perfect ones, whether outwardly they be male or female, prince or peasant, monk or layman. For love and faith produce no sects or outward differences.[74]

The True Worship of God is also Service to One's Neighbor

For Benedict of Nursia (480?-543?) as seen in his guide to monastic living, the *Holy Rule*, the monk's true work of God was to participate in communal worship as observed during the seven canonical hours

---

72 Martin Luther, *An Open Letter to the Christian Nobility*, 1520, in the *Works of Martin Luther*, Phila. Ed., vol. 2, p. 131.

73 Martin Luther, *Ordinance of a Common Chest*, 1523, in *Luther's Works*, vol. 45, p. 172.

74 Martin Luther, *Secular Authority: To What Extent Should It Be Obeyed*, 1523, in the *Works of Martin Luther*, Phila. Ed., vol. 3, pp. 233-234.

throughout the day. When the signal for one of the times of worship was given, the monks had to immediately leave whatever they were doing and with haste and gravity go to the chapel. In Benedict's words, "Let nothing, therefore, be preferred to the work of God."[75]

For Luther "the work of God" desired by God was selfless service to one's neighbor. Luther suggested that to minister to the necessities of a neighbor was 600 times more meritorious than saying one of the canonical hours.[76]

Peter Damianus (1007-1072) was a zealous and highly regarded reformer of the lives of the clergy and of the monks in the monasteries. In his zeal for asceticism, among the many recommendations he advocated was that during the recital of each psalm a monk should flagellate himself with a hundred strokes of a leather thong on his bare back. He did seek, however, to check excess among his many followers by directing that no one should be forced to scourge himself and that at any one time forty psalms and 4000 strokes should be sufficient. This penance became a rage among monks and some flogged themselves to death.[77] Luther also scourged himself in his early years as a monk in the attempt to placate what he then thought was an angry God. Later in life, however, when Luther realized that it was his faith in the blood of Christ that cleansed him from all sin, he counseled in his lectures on Titus:

> Godliness means to serve God and to worship Him. The worship of God among Christians is not the sort of trumpery which wears out the body by chanting at night, fasting, and torturing the body. God knows nothing of such worship; but where His Word is diligently used, there He is being worshiped purely. Souls are aroused to faith, love for God and one's neighbor is taught. To believe in Christ, to be moved to compassion for the poor and the weak, and to persist in these things--this is our religion, that is, the Christian religion. And if a cross follows, this is perfect Christianity. Godliness is to believe in Jesus Christ and to love

---

75 Benedict of Nursia, *The Rule of St. Benedict*: A Commentary, translated into German with commentary by Basilius Steidle, translated into English by Urban J. Schnitzhofer, O.S.B., 1952 (Germany: Beuroner Kunstverlag), p. 212.

76 Martin Luther, *A Discussion of Confession*, 1520, in the *Works of Martin Luther*, Phila. Ed., vol. 1, p. 94.

77 Philip Schaff, 1910, *History of the Christian Church*: Medieval Christianity, vol. 4 (Grand Rapids: Wm. B. Eerdmanns Publ. Co.), pp. 788-789.

one's brother.[78]

The Way to Faith and True Saintliness Is the Gospel

For Luther the preaching of the Gospel was the way one came to have faith in Jesus Christ and to have love for one's neighbor. The Gospel, the announcement of the good news of God's love expressed in the life, death, and resurrection of Jesus Christ for the sins of men, is for Luther the heart and soul of the Church's life. It is the Gospel through which the Holy Spirit works faith and brings humans to love, trust, and hope in God. Luther was impatient with the excesses and trivialities in churchly activity that so often obscured the priority of the preaching of the Gospel in the church of his time. This theme is often found in Luther's sermons, as, for example:

> Briefly in two words, to live godly is to fear and trust God. As it is written, "but the Lord takes pleasure in those who fear him, in those who hope in his steadfast love" (Psalm 147:11). . . . The individual yields to God when he gives himself wholly to God, attempting nothing of himself but permitting the Lord to work in and to rule him; . . . The way of God does not require us to build churches and cathedrals, to make pilgrimages, to hear mass, and so on. God requires a heart moved by his grace, a life mistrustful of all ways not emanating from grace. Nothing more can one render God than such loyalty. . . . Note, such obedience to God is real, divine service. For this service we need no bells nor churches, no vessels nor ornaments. Lights and candles are not necessary; neither are organs and singing, images and pictures, tables and altars. We require not bald pates nor caps, not incense nor sprinkling, not processions nor handling of the cross; neither are indulgences nor briefs essential. All these are human inventions, merely matters of taste. God does not regard them, and too often they obscure with their glitter the true service of God. Only one thing is necessary to right service--the Gospel. Let the Gospel be properly urged; through it let divine service be made known to the people.[79]

The life and teaching of the Church according to Luther thus should

---

78 Martin Luther, *Lectures on Titus*, in *Luther's Works*, vol. 29, pp. 9-10.

79 Martin Luther, *Sermons of Martin Luther*, the *Church Postil*, vol. 6, pp. 126-128.

be centered upon the Gospel, the proclamation of God's steadfast love as shown in the life of his Son. But for Luther the Gospel was more than words concerning God's love shown in the life of Christ. The Gospel is also preached through the works of love shown by Christians who are following Christ's example. He explained this in his *Church Postil* by writing:

> These are the two things in which a Christian is to exercise himself, the one that he draws Christ into himself, and that by faith he makes him his own, appropriates to himself the treasures of Christ and confidently build upon them; the other that he condescends to his neighbor and lets him share in that which he has received, even as he shares in the treasures of Christ. . . .
>
> The other mystery, or spiritual teaching, is, that in the churches the Gospel only should be preached and nothing more. Now it is evident that the Gospel teaches nothing but the foregoing two things, Christ and his example and two kinds of good works, the one belonging to Christ by which we are saved through faith, the other belonging to us by which our neighbor receives help. Whosoever therefore teaches any thing different from the Gospel leads people astray; and whosoever does not teach the Gospel in these two parts, leads people all the more astray and is worse than the former who teaches without the Gospel, because he abuses and corrupts God's Word, as St. Paul complains concerning some. 2 Corinthians 2:17. . . .
>
> Therefore let us beware of all teaching that does not set forth Christ. What more would you know? What more do you need, if indeed you know Christ, as above set forth, if you walk by faith in God, and by love to your neighbor, doing to your fellow man as Christ has done to you. This is indeed the whole Scripture in its briefest form, that no more words or books are necessary, but only life and action.[80]

When Jesus gave His New Commandment He was not setting forth a new law. He was encouraging His people to let their lives show forth the Gospel, thus after giving the New Commandment He said, "By this all will know that you are My disciples, if you have love for one another" (John

---

13:35 NKJV). For Luther, therefore, to encourage people to deeds of Christian love was not a preaching of the law. He, as did Christ, was urging them to preach the Gospel through the acts of goodness and love in their lives. The New Commandment is no more "law" than is the Great Commission, "Go therefore and make disciples of all nations, . . ." (Matthew 28:19). To preach the Gospel is both to tell and to live God's love. It is to abide by our Lord's instruction, "Let your light shine before men in such a way that they may see your good works, and glorify your Father who is in heaven" (Matthew 5:16 NASB).

The good works a Christian performs is a living witness to the Gospel. As happened in the early Church, Luther wishes Christians to advance the Gospel through the loving kindness of their lives as seen in a sermon at Weimar:

> When we have Christ by true faith, then he causes us to live in such a way that we are strengthened in faith, in such a way that I do these works which I do for the benefit and the good of my neighbor. For my Christian name would not be sufficient, despite my baptism and my faith, if I did not help my neighbor and draw him to faith through my works in order that he may follow me.[81]

Serving the Institutional Church
Is No Substitute for a Life of Christian Love
Serving One's Neighbor

Good Works are Service to One's Neighbor not the Institution

Luther protested against the idea that churchly activities, activity centered upon serving the institution of the church, could take the place of Christian love expressed in deeds with which we serve our neighbor. In his lectures on Romans, he taught:

> He has shown above how we ought to conduct ourselves toward God, namely, through the renewal of our mind and the sanctification of our body, so that we may prove what is the will of God. At this point, and from here to the end of the epistle, he teaches how we should act toward our neighbor and explains at length this command to love our neighbor. But it is remarkable

---

81 Martin Luther, *Two Sermons at Weimar*, 1522, in *Luther's Works*, vol. 51, p. 116.

how such a clear and important teaching of such a great apostle, indeed of the Holy Spirit Himself, receives no attention. We are busy with I don't know what kind of trifles in building churches, in increasing the wealth of the church, in piling up money, in multiplying ornamentation and gold and silver vessels, in installing organs, and in other forms of visible display.[82]

Yet Luther also understood that Christian liberty applied in this area also. Concerning vestments used in public worship, he counseled in *An Order of Mass and Communion for the Church at Wittenberg:*

We have passed over the matter of vestments. But we think about these as we do about other forms. We permit them to be used in freedom, as long as people refrain from ostentation and pomp. For you are not more acceptable for consecrating in vestments. Nor are you less acceptable for consecrating without vestments. But I do not wish them to be consecrated or blessed–as if they were to become something sacred as compared with other garments–except that by general benediction of word and prayer by which every good creature of God is sanctified.[83]

Luther also did not argue that it was wrong to build churches. His point was that it was wrong to emphasize the building of churches and their adornment at the expense of the good works that God desired:

We must not, however, be led to conclude it is wrong to build and endow churches. But it is wrong to go to the extreme of forfeiting faith and love in the effort, presuming thereby to do good works meriting God's favor. . . . There is no other reason for building churches than to afford a place where Christians may assemble to pray, to hear the Gospel and to receive the sacraments; if indeed there is a reason.[84]

Luther does not protest against the work of the ministry. He many

---

82 Martin Luther, *Lectures on Romans*, in *Luther's Works*, vol. 25, pp. 444-445.

83 Martin Luther, 1523, *An Order of Mass and Communion for the Church at Wittenberg*, in *Luther's Works*, vol. 53, p. 31.

84 Martin Luther, *Sermons of Martin Luther*, the *Church Postil*, vol. 6, pp. 197-199.

times urged his followers to support fully the work of their pastors and teachers.[85] Christians are to assemble for communal prayer, to partake of the sacraments, be taught the faith, and hear the Gospel. The primary place, however, for the Christians to serve their Lord is not within the walls of the church but outside in the world.

To avoid the problem of people serving the institution of the church, the expense of its upkeep, and its adornment, Luther in the sermon quoted above went as far as to suggest, "it would be well to overthrow at once all the churches of the world, and to utilize ordinary dwellings or the open air for preaching, praying, and baptizing, and for all Christian requirements."[86] In his *Treatise on Usury* Luther further explained his views:

> We would not prevent the building of suitable churches and the adornment of them, for we cannot do without them, and the worship of God ought rightly be conducted in the finest way; but there should be a limit to it, and we should have a care that the appointments of worship should be pure, rather than costly. It is pitiable and lamentable, however, that by these clamorous goings-on we are turned away from God's commandments and led only to the things that God has not commanded, and without which God's commandments can be well kept. It would be sufficient, if we gave the smaller portion to churches and the like, and let the real stream flow toward God's commandment, so that among Christians good deeds done to the poor would shine more brightly than all the churches of stone or of wood. To speak out boldly, it is sheer trickery, dangerous and deceptive to the simple-minded, when bulls, breves, seals, banners, and the like are hung up for the sake of dead stone churches, and the same thing is not done a hundred times more for the sake of needy, living Christians. Beware, therefore, O man! God will not ask you, at your death and at the Last Day, how much you have left in your will, or whether you have given so much or so much to churches; but He will say to you, "I was hungry and you fed me not; I was naked and you clothed me not." Let these words go to your heart, dear man! Everything will depend on whether you

---

85 Martin Luther, *Sermons of Martin Luther*, the *Church Postil*, vol. 2, p. 400.

86 Martin Luther, *Sermons of Martin Luther*, the *Church Postil*, vol. 6, p. 199.

have given to your neighbor and done him good. Beware of show and glitter and color that draw you away from this![87]

In the sermons of his *Church Postil,* Luther often urged his followers to keep the proper emphasis on what constitutes a true Christian life. He was not interested in religiosity. Instead, he stresses a Church composed of Christians going about fulfilling the wishes of its founder, Jesus Christ. How much like John Chrysostom Luther sounds (see pages 262-263) when he exhorted and warned:

Observe now from this how far those have gone out of the way who have united good works with stone, wood, clothing, eating and drinking. Of what benefit is it to your neighbor if you build a church entirely out of gold? Of what benefit to him is the frequent ringing of great church bells? Of what benefit to him is the glitter and the ceremonies in the churches, the priests' gowns, the sanctuary, the silver pictures and vessels? Of what benefit to him are the many candles and much incense? Of what benefit to him is the much chanting and mumbling, the singing of vigils and masses? Do you think that God will permit himself to be paid with the sound of bells, the smoke of candles, the glitter of gold and such fancies? He has commanded none of these, but if you see your neighbor going astray, sinning, or suffering in body or soul, you are to leave every thing else and at once help him in every way in your power and if you can do no more, help him with words of comfort and prayer. Thus has Christ done to you and given you an example for you to follow.
    These are the two things in which a Christian is to exercise himself, the one that he draws Christ into himself, and that by faith he makes him his own, appropriates to himself the treasures of Christ and confidently builds upon them; the other that he condescends to his neighbor and lets him share in that which he has received, even as he shares in the treasures of Christ. He who does not exercise himself in these two things will receive no benefit even if he should fast unto death, suffer torture or even give his body to be burned, and were able to do all miracles, as St. Paul teaches, 1 Corinthians 13ff.[88]

---

87 Martin Luther, *Treatise on Usury,* 1520, in the *Works of Martin Luther,* Phila. Ed., vol. 4, pp. 48-49.

In a subsequent homily, Luther defined what it means to do good works:

> It is not necessary to inquire what outward works you can perform. Look to your neighbor. There you will find enough to do, a thousand kind offices to render. Do not suffer yourself to be misled into believing you will reach heaven by praying and attending church, by contributing to institutions and monuments, while you pass by your neighbor. If you pass him in this life, he will lie in your way in the life to come and cause you to go by the door of heaven as did the rich man who left Lazarus lying at his gate.[89]

In the view of the medieval church, the building of great cathedrals and beautiful churches, the endowment of monasteries, going on pilgrimages were the true works for God. Luther, steeped in Christ's teaching as found in the Gospels, understood that these works were not those that Christ asked. Therefore, Luther remonstrated, ".... God, having no need for our works and benefactions for himself, bids us to do for our neighbor what we would do for God."[90] And in another sermon he preached, "Therefore observe here what a perversion it is for man to exercise himself in doing works to God, which should be done to his neighbor; and then centers his faith in men and saints, which he should center alone in God."[91] Luther urges Christians to follow the teachings of Christ concerning how their faith should be active in Christian love. He wrote in an early *Church Postil*:

> Hear then how Christ explains good works, "Whatsoever you would that men should do to you, even so do you unto them; for this is the law and the prophets" (Matthew 7:12). [Luther continues by envisioning Jesus as saying] "Do you hear now what are the contents of the whole law and of all the prophets? You are not to do good to God and to his dead saints, they are not in need of it; still less to wood and stone, to which it is of no

88 Martin Luther, *Sermons of Martin Luther*, the *Church Postil*, vol. 1, p. 146.

89 Martin Luther, *Sermons of Martin Luther*, the *Church Postil*, vol. 6, pp. 125-126.

90 Martin Luther, *Sermons of Martin Luther*, the *Church Postil*, vol. 7, p. 69.

91 Martin Luther, *Sermons of Martin Luther*, the *Church Postil*, vol. 4, p. 98.

use, nor is it needed, but to men, to men, to men. Do you not hear? To men you should do everything that you would they should do to you. I would not have you build me a church or tower or cast bells for me. I would not have you construct for me an organ with fourteen stops and ten rows of flute work. Of this I can neither eat nor drink, support neither wife nor child, keep neither house nor land. You may feast my eyes on these and tickle my ears, but what shall I give to my children? Where are the necessaries of life?" . . .

Keep in mind, that you need not do any work for God nor for the departed saints, but you ask and receive good from him in faith. Christ has done and accomplished everything for you, atoned for your sins, secured grace and life and salvation. Be content with this, only think how he can become more and more your own and strengthen your faith. Hence direct all the good you can do and your whole life to the end that it be good; but it is good only when it is useful to other people and not to yourself. You need it not, since Christ has done and given for you all that you might seek and desire for yourself, here and hereafter, be it forgiveness of sins, merit of salvation or whatever it may be called. If you find a work in you by which you benefit God or his saints or yourself and not your neighbor, know that such a work is not good. A man is to live, speak, act, hear, suffer and die for the good of his wife and child, the wife for the husband, the children for the parents, the servants for their masters, the masters for their servants, the government for its subjects, the subjects for the government, each one for his fellowman, even for his enemies, so that one is the other's hand, mouth, eye, foot, even heart and mind. This is a truly Christian and good work, which can and shall be done at all times, in all places, toward all people.[92]

Be Warned of Self-serving Clergy

Luther warned repeatedly of the dangers of following the counsel of self-serving churchmen instead of the counsel of God. He wrote in the Postil:

---

92 Martin Luther, *Sermons of Martin Luther*, the *Church Postil*, vol. 1, p. 36-37.

Many a man passes by his poor neighbor who has a sick child or wife, or is otherwise in need of assistance, and makes no effort to minister to him, but instead contributes to endow some church. Or else while health remains he endeavors to heap up treasures, and when he comes at last to his deathbed makes a will bequeathing his estate to some certain institution. He will be surrounded by priests and monks. They will extol his act, absolve the religious man, administer the Sacrament and bury him with honors. They will proclaim his name from the pulpit and during mass, and will cry: "Here is worthy conduct indeed! The man has made ample provision for his soul. Many blessings will hereafter be conferred upon him." Yes, hereafter but, alas, eternally too late. But no one while he is living warns of the man's sins in not administering to the wants of his neighbor when it lies in his power to relieve; in passing him by, and ignoring him as the rich man did Lazarus in the Gospel.[93]

The Christian and the World

"Enlightened" Reason Scoffs at Lives of Faith and Love

Lives of faith and Christian love that please God, however, do not necessarily win the applause of the world. This is true especially of the worldly types who vaunt themselves as the intellectually superior and look down disdainfully upon such ordinary lives. But as Luther points out in *Lectures on Galatians*, the Word of God judges otherwise:

Reason, of course, is offended at this stinginess and paucity of words, when it is stated so briefly "Believe in Christ" and "You shall love your neighbor as yourself." Therefore it despises both the doctrine of faith and the doctrine of truly good works. To those who have faith, however, this stingy and paltry phrase "Believe in Christ" is the power of God (Romans 1:16), by which they overcome sin, death, and the devil, and obtain salvation. So also serving another person through love seems to reason to mean performing unimportant works such as the following: teaching the erring; comforting the afflicted; encouraging the weak; helping the neighbor in whatever way one can; bearing

93 Martin Luther, *Sermons of Martin Luther*, the *Church Postil*, vol. 6, pp. 200-201.

with his rude manners and impoliteness; putting up with annoyances, labors, and the ingratitude and contempt of men in both church and state; obeying the magistrates; treating one's parents with respect; being patient in the home with a cranky wife and an unmanageable family, and the like. But believe me, these works are so outstanding and brilliant that the whole world cannot comprehend their usefulness and worth; indeed, it cannot estimate the value of even one tiny truly good work, because it does not measure works or anything else on the basis of the Word of God but on the basis of a reason that is wicked, blind, and foolish.[94]

The Necessity of Civil Laws

Because of the nature of the world, Luther recognized that the Christian way of life could never take the place of the laws of civil government. He taught that there were two kingdoms under which Christians were to live—the kingdom of civil government as well as the kingdom of God. To those who argued that there was no need for civil laws in a Christian nation, Luther responded in his treatise on secular authority:

> . . . but first take heed and fill the world with real Christians before ruling it in a Christian and evangelical manner. This you will never accomplish; for the world and the masses are and always will be unchristian, although they are all baptized and are nominally Christian. Christians, however, are few and far between, as the saying is. Therefore it is out of the question that there should be a common Christian government over the whole world, nay even over one land or company of people, since the wicked always outnumber the good.[95]

The Opposition of the World to the Christian Way of Life

As was noted in earlier chapters, there is a natural tension between the materialistic, hedonistic, and pleasure-seeking values of the world and

---

94 Martin Luther, *Lectures on Galatians*, 1535, in *Luther's Works*, vol. 27, p. 56.

95 Martin Luther, *Secular Authority, To What Extent It Should Be Obeyed*, 1523, in the *Works of Martin Luther*, Phila. Ed., vol. 3, p. 237.

the values of Christianity. Jesus, Paul, John, James, Peter, Ignatius, Bishop Soter (2 Clement), Chrysostom, and Augustine among others, all warned against the antagonism and false values of the world. Luther certainly recognized the same dangers to the faith of Christians.

As did Jesus (John 12:31, 16:11) and Paul (2 Corinthians 4:4), Luther acknowledged Satan as the prince and god of this world. Luther in the *Lectures on Galatians* told his students:

> But pay careful attention to what Paul says. Out of his words you may boldly and freely pronounce this sentence against the world: that the world, with all its wisdom, righteousness, and power, is the devil's kingdom, out of which only God is able to deliver us by His only Son.[96]

Also in his *Sermons on the Gospel of St. John,* he preached that one should never expect the world to become Christian:

> Just as the devil, who is the god and lord of the world, will never become pious, so it will never be possible to make the whole world pious. And no matter how much one says to the world, it grows defiant and does all the more in opposition. It takes this as a provocation to be even worse. Because these people refuse to hear and to believe, we let them go their way until they find and experience the truth, not only in eternity but also here in this temporal life.[97]

The world is incensed that it is to be judged by God's commandments. Luther did not mince words when he stated:

> Hence you see pictured here what the world is, nothing but a great company of wicked, stubborn people, who will not believe Christ, but despise God's Word, praise and accept the seduction of the devil, and defiantly run counter to all of God's commandments. They receive all the favors and benefits of God only to repay him with ingratitude and blasphemy. And yet in all this they are unwilling to be convicted or reproved, but wish to

---

96 Martin Luther, *Lectures on Galatians*, 1535, in *Luther's Works*, vol. 26, p. 41.

97 Martin Luther, *Sermons on the Gospel of St. John*, in *Luther's Works*, vol. 24, p. 249.

be called excellent, pious and saintly people.[98]

Nor do the people of the world fear the wrath of God. They feel that they are immune from God's anger even though they spurn him and the way of life he would have them live. Luther pointed out, "The old man [unregenerate man] believes that God will not be moved to vengeance though he does as he pleases, even to decorating vices with the names of virtues.[99]

"Decorating vices with the names of virtues" has a long history among mankind. The Roman historian Tacitus" wrote in the time of the Emperor Nero, "Many people liked this very license, but they screened it under respectable names."[100] It is no different in our own day with "adult films" used to describe pornographic films, "exotic dancing" for the gyrations of nude or semi-nude dancers, "living together" for living in fornication, "gay" for those who practice the sexual perversions of homosexuality, "love" child for an infant conceived in lust, and, "gaming" for gambling.

The world, however, does not appreciate its pretenses to virtue being pointed out. Moreover, there are many who resent those who live decent, honest, and unselfish lives. It makes their own lives suffer too much in comparison. Christians may well find themselves ill-treated by those who take offense at their lives. To avoid this subtle or overt persecution, Luther points out that there are many lukewarm Christians who get on in the world by compromising their Christianity. On Titus 2:13 (2:11-14), he remarked:

> The words of this verse afford comfort to all who live soberly, righteously and godly. . . . On the other hand, the words of this verse are terrible to the worldly-minded and wicked who are unwilling to endure, for the sake of godliness, the persecutions of the world. They prefer to make their godliness go no farther than to live without friction in the world and thus avoid incurring enmity and trouble.[101]

---

98 Martin Luther, *Sermons of Martin Luther*, the *Church Postil*, vol. 3, p. 142.

99 Martin Luther, *Sermons of Martin Luther*, the *Church Postil*, vol. 8, p. 307.

100 *The Complete Works of Tacitus*, transl. by A.J. Church and W.J. Brodribb (New York: The Modern Library), Annals 14:21, p. 332.

101 Martin Luther, *Sermons of Martin Luther*, the *Church Postil*, vol. 6, p. 132.

In discussing Jesus' words, "Blessed are those who are persecuted for righteousness' sake, for theirs is the kingdom of heaven. Blessed are you when men revile you and persecute you and utter all kinds of evil against you falsely on my account. Rejoice and be glad, for your reward is great in heaven" (Matthew 5:10-12 RSV), Luther taught:

> But here is what it says: "If you do not want to have the Gospel or be a Christian, then go out and take the world's side. Then you will be its friend, and no one will persecute you. But if you want to have the Gospel and Christ, then you must count on having trouble, conflict, and persecution wherever you go."[102]

The same applies to the preaching and teaching of Christianity by those who seek to please men instead of being to God's Word:

> Hence the Lord says in Luke 6:26, "Woe to you when all men speak well of you; for so their fathers did to the false prophets." Therefore, to be cursed, abused, reproved is the pathway to safety; to be blessed, praised, approved is the way of danger and destruction."[103]

Luther summed up his discussion on the opposition of the world to Christianity by composing the following comparisons:

> The righteous man has peace with God but affliction in the world, because he lives in the Spirit.
> The unrighteous man has peace with the world but affliction and tribulation with God, because he lives in the flesh.
>
> But as the Spirit is eternal, so also will be the peace of the righteous man and the tribulation of the unrighteous.
> And as the flesh is temporal, so will be the tribulation of the righteous and the peace of the unrighteous.[104]

---

102 Martin Luther, *The Sermon on the Mount*, in *Luther's Works*, vol. 21, p. 51.

103 Martin Luther, *Lectures on Romans*, in *Luther's Works*, vol. 25, p. 237.

104 Martin Luther, *Lectures on Romans*, in *Luther's Works*, vol. 25, p. 286.

God Is Our Refuge and Strength

For Luther the trials of this life are not to vex a Christian, for his life is cradled in the hand of God's love. Luther from his own experience well knew that the only peace and security that this world affords comes from God. He encourages and comforts his hearers with the words:

> "In nothing be anxious." Take no thought for yourselves. Let God care for you. He whom you now acknowledge is able to provide for you. It is the heathen, unknowing he has a God, who takes thought for himself. Christ says: "Be not therefore anxious, saying, What shall we eat? or, What shall we drink? or, Wherewithal shall we be clothed? For after all these things do the Gentiles seek; for your heavenly Father knows that you have need of all these things."[105] Then, let the whole world grasp, and deal unrighteously, you shall have enough. . . . We have no reason to take thought for ourselves when we have a Father and Protector who holds in his hands all things, even them who, with all their possessions, would rob or injure us. Our duty is to rejoice ever in God and be forbearing toward all men, as becomes those assured of ample provision for body and soul; especially in that we have a gracious God. They without him may well be concerned about themselves. It should be our concern not to be anxious, to rejoice in God alone and to be kind to men. On this topic the Psalmist says (Psalm 37:25): "I have been young, and now am old; yet have I not seen the righteous forsaken, nor his seed begging bread."[106]

---

105 Matthew 6:31-32

106 Martin Luther, *Sermons of Martin Luther*, the *Church Postil*, vol. 6, pp. 104-105.

Chapter Fifteen

CALVIN AND THE CHRISTIAN WAY OF LIFE

John Calvin as Reformer

John Calvin's Road to Reformation

John Calvin (1509-1564), born twenty-six years after Luther, was the most noted of the second generation church reformers. Calvin came from a middle class family. His father was secretary to the Bishop of Noyon and attorney for the cathedral chapter. His mother was born into the family of a prosperous innkeeper.

As a boy, John Calvin was educated in the home of a neighboring noble family. At the age of twelve, he was appointed to the chaplaincy of the cathedral of Noyon. It was the first of the church benefices that supported his education. When the plague threatened Noyon, Calvin at age fourteen left the city to attend the University of Paris. His career studying theology at the university went well. He was highly regarded and soon achieved the Master of Arts degree. After earning his degree, at his father's suggestion he left Paris in 1528 for Orleans to take up the study of law. Along with law, Calvin also studied Greek, Hebrew, and the humanities at the University of Orleans and other academic institutions.

After achieving his doctorate at Orleans, Calvin in 1533 returned to Paris where he became a close friend of the new rector of the university. With what is thought to have been Calvin's aid in its composition, the rector delivered his initial sermon at the university that included such Lutheran teachings as justification by faith alone. In the uproar that followed over such Lutheran sentiments, the rector and Calvin had to flee Paris. Calvin resigned his benefices in 1534 having come to a full acceptance of the theology of the reformation.

Calvin changed his residence a number of times in the next years. During this period, he wrote the first edition of his famous *Institutes of the Christian Religion*. It was a book sent to the king of France that set forth

Calvin's defense of the teachings of the reformation.

Calvin in Geneva

The year 1536 found Calvin in Geneva aiding the reformer Farel in the religious reformation of the city. Their insistence on a strictly enforced moral discipline, however, caused Farel and Calvin to be banished from the city by the city council in 1538.

Political and religious chaos followed in Geneva. After three years of such disturbances, the Genevan civil authorities urged Calvin to return and resume his pastorate and the work of reformation in Geneva. With often the full support of the magistrates, Calvin completed his work of reforming the theology, clergy, and morality of the city. For the rest of his life, Calvin continued to be Geneva's dominant religious figure. He founded an academy in Geneva that in time became the University of Geneva. From that institution there went out young men trained in Calvin's theology and discipline who spread his teaching into many countries of Europe. John Calvin died in 1564 at age fifty-five from the cumulative result of a number of chronic illnesses.

Calvin and Luther, Similarities Between and as Students of Scripture

After having spent a year studying over 10,000 pages of Luther and then reading Calvin's 1559 edition of his voluminous *Institutes of the Christian Religion*, I was struck by the truth of the words in the Encyclopedia Britannica, ". . . Calvin built his theology on the foundations laid by the earlier reformers, and especially by Luther and Bucer, . . ."[1] When the total theology of Calvin is considered, one realizes how the past emphasis on the theological differences between Luther and Calvin has obscured their remarkable similarities. In many instances, when one reads Calvin one gets a feeling of *deja vu*; it sounds so much like what one has just read in the works of Luther.

This is not to say that Calvin followed Luther's theology slavishly. John Calvin was also a faithful and enduring student of the Scriptures. Calvin, as did Luther, taught that the Scriptures alone were the guide to true Christianity. The thorough Biblical scholarship of the two men would quite naturally lead them to similar conclusions. One area, however, where Luther and Calvin differed, especially in regard to practice, was their views on the Christian way of life. One wonders, however, to what degree that

---

1 *The Encyclopedia Britannica*, 14th Edition (New York: Encyclopedia Britannica, Inc.), vol. 4, p. 633.

was due to the difference between their personalities. Could the austere, dour John Calvin ever see eye to eye with the exuberant, jovial Luther on how Christians were to live?

Calvin's View of the Christian Way of Life

Calvin's Emphasis on a Purity of Life

John Calvin, as Luther, was very much interested in the way Christians lived their Christianity. Unlike Luther, however, his emphasis was more on the avoidance of evil than a life of doing good. He was concerned that his followers strive for perfection in living upright lives. For Calvin, however, in the words of eminent Yale University church historian Roland Bainton "The upright life was interpreted in the sense of austere and stern behavior, and abstaining from dancing, card playing, gambling, obscenity, and drunkenness."[2]

Salvation by faith alone in Jesus Christ was also a major theme of John Calvin. Good works played no part in the justification of the sinner. Nor were good works to be pursued to gain greater reward in heaven. But despite his understanding of the place of good works in Christian theology, doing good works was not the major priority of Calvin in his understanding of the Christian life.

In the section of his *Institutes* devoted to "The Life of the Christian Man," John Calvin described the major motivation for the conduct of Christian life as follows:

> But Scripture draws its exhortation from the true fountain. It not only enjoins us to refer our life to God, its author, to whom it is bound; but after it has taught that we have degenerated from the true origin and condition of our creation, it also adds that Christ, through whom we return into favor with God, has been set before us as an example, whose pattern we ought to express in our life. What more effective thing can you require than this one thing? Nay, what can you require beyond this one thing? For we have been adopted as sons by the Lord with this one condition: that our life express Christ, the bond of our adoption. Accordingly, unless we give and devote ourselves to righteousness, we not only revolt from our Creator with wicked

---

2 Roland H. Bainton, 1952, *The Reformation of the Sixteenth Century* (Boston: The Beacon Press), p. 116.

perfidy but also abjure our Savior himself.

Calvin then carefully described how we are to "devote ourselves to righteousness":

> Then the Scripture finds occasion for exhortation in all the benefits of God that it lists for us, and in the individual parts of our salvation. Ever since God revealed himself Father to us, we must prove our ungratefulness to him if we did not in turn show ourselves his sons [Mal. 1:6; Eph. 5:1; I John 3:1]. Ever since Christ cleansed us with the washing of his blood, and imparted this cleansing through baptism, it would be unfitting to befoul ourselves with new pollutions [Eph. 5:26; Heb. 10:10; I Cor. 6:11; I Peter 1:15,19]. Ever since he engrafted us into his body, we must take especial care not to disfigure ourselves, who are his members, with any spot or blemish [Eph. 5:23-33; I Cor. 6:15; John 15:3-6]. Ever since Christ himself, who is our Head, ascended into heaven, it behooves us, having laid aside love of earthly things, wholeheartedly to aspire heavenward [Col. 3:1 ff.]. Ever since the Holy Spirit dedicated us as temples to God, we must take care that God's glory shine through us, and must not commit anything to defile ourselves with the filthiness of sin [I Cor. 3:16; 6:19; II Cor. 6:16]. Ever since both our souls and bodies were destined for heavenly incorruption and an unfading crown [I Peter 5:4], we ought to strive manfully to keep them pure and uncorrupted until the Day of the Lord [I Thess. 5:23; cf. Phil. 1:10]. These, I say, are the most auspicious foundations upon which to establish one's life.[3]

One cannot help notice the difference here between Calvin and Luther. Calvin placed his emphasis on a life concerned with one's own personal purity. He stressed the negatives in writing of avoiding or befouling ourselves with pollutions, disfiguring ourselves with any spot or blemish, defiling ourselves with the filthiness of sin. We are rather to strive to keep ourselves pure and uncorrupted. Luther's emphasis, as we have seen, does not stress the negatives but accents a positive life of active Christian

---

3 John Calvin, 1559, *Institutes of the Christian Religion*, bk. 3, chap. 6, sec. 3, in *The Library of Christian Classics* (Philadelphia: The Westminster Press), vol. 20, pp. 686-687.

love involved in working for the benefit of one's neighbor. It is a life of love and gratitude in response to God's great gift of love in sending His Son to this earth for our salvation.

This does not mean, however, that Luther is unconcerned about the Christian living a pure life or that Calvin is not concerned with good works done to one's neighbor. Rather the difference is in what the two reformers emphasized.

It is noteworthy that in Calvin's primary and extensive theological work, *Institutes of the Christian Religion*, the New Commandment that Jesus gave (John 13:34-35; 15:12-13, 17) goes almost unmentioned. Nor is the verse that contains Paul's insistence on a life based on "faith working through love" (Galatians 5:6b) treated other than in passing when discussing other subjects. This is in keeping with Calvin's greater concern and emphasis that a Christian's life be free from evil rather than a Christian be active in deeds of Christian love.

Self-denial is a basic concern of Calvin. He would have Christians renounce self and devote themselves wholly in service to God. This means fleeing the vices, avarice, and passions of human nature. It means avoiding the irreligion and temptations of the world and its lusts. He quotes Paul in urging Christians to live sober, upright and godly lives. Self-denial for Calvin, nonetheless, also means that we apply ourselves wholly to doing good to our fellowman. It means not esteeming ourselves above him, not putting down others and their gifts, and not exaggerating their faults but overlooking them.

Calvin's Teaching Concerning Christian Love and One's Neighbor

True self-renunciation means seeking to benefit our neighbor in Christian love. Calvin wrote in the *Institutes*:

> No surer rule and no more valid exhortation to keep it could be devised than when we are taught that all the gifts we possess have been bestowed by God and entrusted to us on condition that they be distributed for our neighbors' benefit [cf. I Peter 4:10].[4]

Calvin taught that we are stewards of our possessions; and they are to be used to benefit others, even before ourselves. It should not matter what kind of men the recipients are. All men are made in God's image. Even the

---

4 John Calvin, 1559, *Institutes of the Christian Religion*, bk. 3, chap. 7, sec. 5, in *The Library of Christian Classics*, vol. 20, p. 695.

least worthy are to be aided, for they too partake of the image of God. Even those who have provoked us by unjust acts and curses are to be embraced in love and be beneficiaries of our acts of Christian love. In "The Lausanne Articles" Calvin proclaimed:

> Further this same Church denies all other ways and means of serving God beyond that which is spiritually ordained by the Word of God, which consists in love of himself and of one's neighbor.[5]

Calvin wrote that God looks at the intention that motivates our acts of love, not only at the act itself. He taught that alms are not to be given contemptuously with a proud countenance and insolent words but rather with a cheerful countenance and friendly words. Nor should aiding another person in any way place him or her in our debt. Also, when a man has once given aid, he should not consider himself relieved from further acts of charity:

> Rather, each man will so consider with himself that in all his greatness he is a debtor to his neighbors, and that he ought in exercising kindness toward them to set no other limit than the end of his resources; these, as widely as they are extended, ought to have their limits set according to the rule of love.[6]

Calvin recognized that there was no law needed to encourage one's love of self. Self-love, Calvin saw, was part of the nature of humankind and was already excessive in many. He remarked that Jesus also recognized this in His use of the Old Testament's teaching that one should love one's neighbor as oneself. Self-love could be taken for granted. However, excessive self-love, Calvin instructs, is to be overcome if we are to live as Christians:

> Hence it is very clear that we keep the commandments not by loving ourselves but by loving God and neighbor; that he lives the best and holiest life who lives and strives for himself as little

5 John Calvin, "The Lausanne Articles," art. 6, in *Calvin: Theological Treatises*, a volume of *The Library of Christian Classics*, vol. 22 (Philadelphia: Westminster Press), p. 36.

6 John Calvin, 1559, *Institutes of the Christian Religion*, bk. 3, chap. 7, sec. 7, in *The Library of Christian Classics*, vol. 20, p. 698.

as he can, and that no one lives in a worse or more evil manner than he who lives and strives for himself alone, and thinks about and seeks only his own advantage.[7]

In writing about Jesus' counsel to lay up treasures in heaven, Calvin asks, "But how shall we transmit them?" Calvin provides the answer, "Surely, by providing for the needs of the poor; whatever is paid out to them, the Lord reckons as given to himself [cf. Matt. 25:40]."[8]

Calvin cited the parable of the Good Samaritan to show that the Christian must regard as his neighbor even the person most remote from him. Certainly, he taught, our first responsibility is to be toward our family, friends, and neighborhood; but the whole human race is also to be embraced by our love; and this includes also the blameworthy:

Therefore, if we rightly direct our love, we must first turn our eyes not to man, the sight of whom would more often engender hate than love, but to God, who bids us extend to all men the love we bear to him, that this may be an unchanging principle: whatever the character of the man, we must yet love him because we love God.[9]

Calvin took strong exception to the Roman church's teaching that such uncompromising sayings of Christ as: do not take vengeance, love your enemies, and turn the other cheek, need not be taken seriously by the average Christian. The Roman church had taught that such sayings were to be regarded as "Evangelical Counsels" that need be observed only by such fully committed Christians as the monks. Both Calvin and Luther saw these teachings applying to all Christians.

Calvin and His Use of the Ten Commandments

As did Luther, Calvin has an expansive view of the Ten Commandments. He taught that if the commandments forbid an action, it

---

7 John Calvin, 1559, *Institutes of the Christian Religion*, bk. 2, chap. 8, sec. 54, in *The Library of Christian Classics*, vol. 20, p. 417.

8 John Calvin, 1559, *Institutes of the Christian Religion*, bk. 3, chap. 18, sec. 6, in *The Library of Christian Classics*, vol. 20, p. 827.

9 John Calvin, 1559, *Institutes of the Christian Religion*, bk. 2, chap. 8, sec. 55, in *The Library of Christian Classics,* vol. 20, p. 419.

follows that the opposite of the action pleases God.[10] Thus, in a way similar to Luther, Calvin expands on the commandment, "Thou shalt not steal," in writing:

> On the other hand, let this be our constant aim: faithfully to help all men by our counsel and aid to keep what is theirs, in so far as we can; but if we have to deal with faithless and deceitful men, let us be prepared to give up something of our own rather than to contend with them. And not this alone: but let us share the necessity of those whom we see pressed by the difficulty of affairs, assisting them in their need with our abundance.[11]

Thus, as did Luther, Calvin attempted to teach Christ's new way of life under the Ten Commandments of the Old Testament.

Calvin and Christian Freedom

The Three Aspects of Christian Freedom

Christian freedom was also one of Calvin's concerns. Calvin taught that there were three parts to Christian freedom. First, Christians were free from the necessity of attempting to attain righteousness before God through the works of the Law. If Christians are to be justified before God, it is through His mercy and through looking in faith to Christ for salvation. Second, Christians observe the Law not through compulsion and necessity as a yoke laid upon them, but freely and willingly in order through love to strive to obey God's will. Third, Christians have freedom to choose concerning outward things that are in themselves "indifferent," that is, morally neutral. Calvin recognizes this third freedom is plainly taught in the New Testament. He understood that "it makes no difference in God's sight whether they eat meat or eggs, wear red or black clothes."[12] Calvin, however, seems uncomfortable with the concept. He spent more words in warning against the abuse of Christian liberty than in rejoicing in its use.

---

10 John Calvin, 1559, *Institutes of the Christian Religion*, bk. 2, chap. 8, sec. 8, in *The Library of Christian Classics*, vol. 20, p. 375.

11 John Calvin, 1559, *Institutes of the Christian Religion*, bk. 2, chap. 8, sec. 46, in *The Library of Christian Classics*, vol. 20, p. 410.

12 John Calvin, 1559, *Institutes of the Christian Religion*, bk. 3, chap. 19, sec. 10, in *The Library of Christian Classics*, vol. 20, p. 842.

Christian Freedom from Man-made Law

In reviewing his understanding of Christian liberty concerning indifferent things, Calvin wrote:

> To sum up, we see whither this freedom tends: namely, that we should use God's gifts for the purpose for which he gave them to us, with no scruple of conscience, no trouble of mind. With such confidence our minds will be at peace with him, and will recognize his liberality toward us. For here are included all ceremonies whose observance is optional, that our consciences may not be constrained by any necessity to observe them but may remember that by God's beneficence their use is for edification made subject to him.[13]

But will not people abuse such freedom? Calvin was afraid that indeed they would, especially in pursuit of luxury and gluttony. He therefore admonished:

> There is almost no one whose resources permit him to be extravagant who does not delight in lavish and ostentatious banquets, bodily apparel, and domestic architecture; . . . And all these things are defended under the pretext of Christian freedom. . . . Surely ivory and gold and riches are good creations of God, permitted, indeed appointed, for men's use by God's providence. And we have never been forbidden to laugh, or to be filled, or to join new possessions to old or ancestral ones, or to delight in musical harmony, or to drink wine. True indeed. But where there is plenty, to wallow in delights, to gorge oneself, to intoxicate mind and heart with present pleasures and be always panting after new ones—such are very far removed from a lawful use of God's gifts.[14]

Calvin would have God's gifts be used in decency and moderation.

---

13 John Calvin, 1559, *Institutes of the Christian Religion*, bk. 3, chap. 19, sec. 8, in *The Library of Christian Classics*, vol. 20, p. 840.

14 John Calvin, 1559, *Institutes of the Christian Religion*, bk. 3, chap. 19, sec. 9, in *The Library of Christian Classics*, vol. 20, p. 841.

Giving Offense and Resisting New Law-givers

Above all, Calvin urged that the Christian out of Christian love avoid giving offense to the weak in the exercise of his Christian liberty. Calvin, however, was also mindful that there are those who are pharisaical in their quickness to take offense. Calvin would restrain his use of Christian freedom to avoid giving offense to the weak; but he would oppose with rigor, ignore, and disregard those who would attempt to restrict his freedom with their decisions of what was right.

The Need for Decency and Order in the Reformed Church

Calvin taught that a Christian thus should oppose those who would make rules, regulations, and constitutions that restrict Christian liberty. Calvin, however, sees a danger here. Is that freedom also to be exercised by the uneducated Christian concerning the discipline and rules of the Reformed church? Calvin takes up this question in writing:

> But many unlettered persons, when they are told that men's consciences are impiously bound by human traditions, and God is worshiped in vain, apply the same erasure to all the laws by which the order of the church is shaped.

The impious human traditions of which Calvin wrote are obviously meant to be those of the Roman church. Calvin would not have such a judgment applied to the laws of the Reformed church of Geneva. He therefore explains why the Reformed church and its constitution and discipline are legitimate. He philosophizes that in all human society some form of organization is necessary in the interest of maintaining peace, concord, and public decency. Because of this need for organization and rules, he continues:

> This ought especially to be observed in churches, which are best sustained when all things are under a well-ordered constitution, and which without concord become no churches at all. Therefore, if we wish to provide for the safety of the church, we must attend with all diligence to Paul's command that "all things be done decently and in order"[I Cor. 14:40].[15]

---

15 John Calvin, 1559, *Institutes of the Christian Religion*, bk. 4, chap. 10, sec. 27, in *The Library of Christian Classics*, vol. 21, p. 1205.

Under this maxim, that "all things be done decently and in order," Calvin would justify the constitution, laws, and discipline of the Reformed church. Calvin explains that because of the diversity of customs and variety in the minds of men, it is necessary for the churches to have definite laws and set forms. If this were not done, as he often repeats, the very sinews of the churches would disintegrate.

Are Observing the Rules of the Reformed Church Necessary for Salvation?

Thus, the church needs constitutions and rules, but their authority can be carried too far. Calvin warned:

> But in these observances one thing must be guarded against. They are not to be considered necessary for salvation and thus bind consciences by scruples; nor are they to be associated with the worship of God, and piety thus be lodged in them.[16]

Unfortunately, however, as will be shown, this is what indeed happened in Calvin's Geneva and in other Calvinistic jurisdictions. Christians who would not abide by Calvin's and the Reformed church's ecclesiastical laws and were steadfast in maintaining their Christian freedom were often finally excommunicated and thus regarded as cut off from salvation.

Christian Liberty for Reformed Church Leaders to Make Law

Christians, according to Calvin, are to distinguish between the impious church constitutions, that is, those of the Roman Catholic Church that obscure Christianity and bind consciences, and legitimate church constitutions. Legitimate church constitutions and their laws can be recognized in that they insure that things be done in the church with decency and dignity. Such decorum in the rites of the church will promote reverence and piety toward sacred things. Calvin also answers the question as to who is to set up such constitutions and laws:

> The first point in order is that those in charge know the rule and law of good governing, but that the people who are governed become accustomed to obedience to God and to right

---

16 John Calvin, 1559, *Institutes of the Christian Religion*, bk. 4, chap. 10, sec. 27, in *The Library of Christian Classics*, vol. 21, pp. 1205-1206.

discipline.[17]

The clergy and elders are to set up the discipline and laws of the church. The task of the laity is to be obedient.

Calvin's Mistrust of Christian Freedom for the Laity

Calvin is not willing to allow Christian freedom to be fully exercised by every Christian. He has a jaundiced view of his fellow Christian. In a passage quoted above (p. 438) he had written, "There is almost no one whose resources permit him to be extravagant who does not delight in lavish and ostentatious banquets, bodily apparel, and domestic architecture; . . . And all these things are defended under the pretext of Christian freedom." Therefore, in his *Institutes* Calvin forecasts how he would deal with those whom he considered to be overindulging themselves. He warns:

> But many today, while they seek an excuse for the intemperance of the flesh in its use of external things, and while they would meanwhile pave the road to licentious indulgence, take for granted what I do not at all concede to them: that this freedom is not to be restrained by any limitation but to be left to every man's conscience to use as far as seems lawful to him.[18]

Calvin then goes on to say, "consciences neither ought to nor can be bound here to definite and precise legal formulas." But, again, this is just what occurred in Geneva under Calvin's oversight. At the instigation of the Reformed church, legal formulas abounded that restricted the Christian liberty of the individual Christians as well as other citizens.

As the Calvin scholar Harro Hopfl notes concerning freedom for the Christian, "Calvin seems constantly to be giving with one hand and taking away with the other." Christians are to have freedom, but that freedom is limited for individuals. The full exercise of Christian freedom is reserved

---

17 John Calvin, 1559, *Institutes of the Christian Religion*, bk. 4, chap. 10, sec. 28, in *The Library of Christian Classics*, vol. 21, p. 1206.

18 John Calvin, 1559, *Institutes of the Christian Religion*, bk. 3, chap. 10, sec. 1, in *The Library of Christian Classics*, vol. 20, p. 720.

for the churches not individuals.[19] And who of the church is to decide? —as quoted above, "those in charge know the rule and law of good governing." It was sufficient "that the people who are governed become accustomed to obedience to God and to right discipline."

In the governance of the Genevan church, Calvin was as good as his word. The Christian freedom of the laity was not left to every man's conscience. Calvin did not concede that they could properly use such freedom. Nor was ecclesiastical power sufficient for Calvin. The regulations of the church would ideally also be the regulations of the civil government.

The Civil Government as the Arm of the Reformed Church

Civil government was to be supportive of the church. The civil government was to be one that "prevents idolatry, sacrilege against God's name, and blasphemies against his truth, and other public offenses against religion from arising and spreading among the people; . . ." Calvin further wrote:

> Let no man be disturbed that I now commit to civil government the duty of rightly establishing religion, which I seem above to have put outside of human decision. For, when I approve of a civil administration that aims to prevent the true religion which is contained in God's law from being openly and with public sacrilege violated and defiled with impunity, I do not here, any more than before, allow men to make laws according to their own decision concerning religion and the worship of God.[20]

It is to be the duty of civil government to support and defend the church. However, not the civil government but the church leaders are to make the decisions concerning religion and the worship of God. The civil authorities are to follow the lead of the church.

Supervision of Christian Life in Geneva

The Church of Geneva under Calvin set up a quasi-religious, supervisory organization to oversee the discipline of the church and city. It

---

19 Harro Hopfl, 1982, *The Christian Polity of John Calvin* (Cambridge: Cambridge Univ. Press), p. 37.

20 John Calvin, 1559, *Institutes of the Christian Religion*, bk. 4, chap. 20, sec. 3, in *The Library of Christian Classics*, vol. 21, p. 1488.

was called "The Consistory" and was composed of six of Geneva's pastors and twelve lay elders chosen from and by the civil governing councils of Geneva. The elders were chosen from all parts of the city.

The pastors and elders of the Consistory were to watch over the life of every individual in Geneva. Each home in Geneva was to be visited by an elder at least once a year. The elder was to investigate the morals, religious knowledge, opinions, and the family life of each home. The Consistory also employed many spies and informers to serve as sources of information about the lives of the citizens. The elders and clergy members of the Consistory met weekly in their effort to oversee and correct the behavior and morals of the citizens of the city. They were in a friendly way to admonish and warn those who deviated from the discipline and regulations of the church and city. Those, however, who proved stubborn or whose offenses were grave could be remanded to the civil magistrates for punishment. If a citizen was summoned to appear before the Consistory and refused to come, a civil officer was sent to bring him.[21] The Consistory was meant to be remedial not a punishing institution, but its powers of correction finally came also to include full excommunication.

Calvin viewed the task of the Consistory to be primarily the reformation of the sinner. The church was to use persuasion to bring the sinner to repent his sin. If necessary, however, public censure of the individual was also used. At times humbling acts, such as kissing the ground after having uttered a blasphemy, were used to reform the sinner. If moderate approaches failed or if the sin was sufficiently severe, the sinning individual was excluded from taking communion until he promised reformation. Only as a last resort was full excommunication imposed.

Full excommunication meant that the individual was pronounced not only excluded from Christ's Church but also from any hope of salvation. It also meant that no Christian could have anything to do with the one under full excommunication, including talking to him, doing business with him, feeding him, and so forth. Because of the severity of full excommunication, Calvin and the pastors had a continual argument with the civilian authorities concerning the church's insistence that the Consistory have the right to impose full excommunication. No sin, nonetheless, was so great that excommunication could not be rescinded upon the sinner's repentance and the sinner received back into the church.

This did not mean, however, that punishment for such a sin as adultery or other grave offense ended with the church's forgiveness. The Consistory did not have the power of the sword. It could refer, however,

---

21 *The Cambridge Modern History*, vol. 2, *The Reformation*, 1903 (Cambridge: the University Press), p. 375.

cases involving grave offense to the civil authorities. A banker, for example, was executed for repeated adultery even after he turned penitent.[22] Thus in cooperation with the church, the civil magistrates through their judicial procedures might add their own punishments of fines, incarceration, corporal or capital punishment, or banishment from the city. In Geneva, the laws of the church did not only apply to recognized members of the church; they applied to all citizens within the confines of the Genevan city-state.

Thus many laws of the church, seconded by the civil authorities, came to be saddled upon the citizenry of Geneva during Calvin's lifetime. Not only were these laws on the books; but unlike many similar laws passed by other cities at that time, Geneva's laws were strictly enforced by church and city authorities. There also was no respect of persons or position in Geneva. The laws were applied equally to all.

The Church Laws Governing All Citizens of Geneva

Attendance at church and listening to sermons was required of everyone. The fine for not attending the church service and preaching was three sols[23]. Watchmen were assigned to tour the city and see that the people went to church.[24] Homes of those not attending church could be entered during the time of service. Those found within could be remanded to prison. Visitors to the city were expelled from the city if after three warnings they did not attend church. Church attendance was also required on Wednesday morning, and the police were to check the shops for those not attending. There was to be no card playing on Sunday.[25] Calvin forbade all normal work on Sunday.

Calvin also severely reduced the number of religious holidays and saint's days. Any observance of the forbidden holy days resulted in punishment. Along with the suppression of the saint's days, the celebration and keeping of Christmas were also prohibited under pain of both fine and

---

22 Philip Schaff, 1910, *History of the Christian Church*, vol. 8 (Grand Rapids: Wm. B. Eerdmans Publ. Co.), pp.491-492.

23 A sol was a medieval French coin, and its value was nominally one-twentieth of a livre. The livre was a monetary unit originally of a troy pound of silver. However, because of the practice of debasing the coinage by adding base metals to the silver and because of inflation, etc., an accurate determination of the value of the sol at Calvin's time in Geneva's history is difficult to ascertain.

24 Philip Schaff, 1910, *History of the Christian Church*, vol. 8, p. 490.

25 Georgia Harkness, 1931, *John Calvin: The Man and His Ethics* (New York: Abingdon Press), pp. 26-27, 50-51.

imprisonment. Fasting on Good Friday was also forbidden.[26] There were also penalties for misbehavior in church, such as laughing.

Considered as serious offenses in Calvin's Geneva of the 1550s were those of citizens who still prayed or said the Creed in Latin or who kept altars or images in their rooms. Caught up by the authorities was a woman who said "rest in peace" in Latin over her husband's grave. Similarly apprehended was a barber who tonsured a priest, a goldsmith who made a Catholic chalice, and a citizen who made the error of saying that the pope was a fine man.[27] To deny Calvin's theory of predestination meant banishment from the city.[28] Banished also was a young woman who sang profane songs; scourging was the punishment of another woman who sang secular songs to psalm-tunes.[29]

In 1546, a minister in Geneva at the baptism of a child tried to give the name Abraham to the child instead of the popular name "Claude" chosen by the parents. The Genevan Council backed up the minister in his choice of the name Abraham. To forestall further problems, they asked Calvin to make up a list of objectionable first names. On the list of forbidden names were most of the names of the saints revered by the medieval church. This list of outlawed given names then became law upon the action of the council.[30] Names taken from the Old Testament were preferred as baptismal given names.

Dancing was prohibited by the church and city ordinances even when done in connection with weddings and betrothal celebrations. In 1546, one of the heads of the Genevan government was imprisoned for a short time along with others when caught dancing at a betrothal festivity.[31] Besides dancing, also attendance at plays and at times card playing were prohibited by church and city.[32]

---

26 Preserved Smith, 1920, *The Age of the Reformation* (New York: Henry Holt and Co.), p. 171.

27 E. William Monter, 1967, *Calvin's Geneva* (Huntington, New York: R. E. Krieger Publ. Co.), pp. 137-138.

28 Roland H. Bainton, 1952, *The Reformation of the Sixteenth Century* (Boston: The Beacon Press), p. 120.

29 *The Cambridge Modern History*, vol. 2, *The Reformation*, 1903, p. 375.

30 Williston Walker, 1906, *John Calvin* (New York: Schocken Books), p. 299.

31 Williston Walker, 1906, *John Calvin*, p. 301.

32 Preserved Smith, 1920, *The Age of the Reformation*, p. 172.

At Calvin's request, the Council in 1546 closed the taverns of Geneva. In their place five "abbayes" were opened. Innkeepers of the abbayes were required to see that all patrons prayed before and after meals; otherwise they were not to be served. They also were to see that their guests did not dawdle over their meals. It was required of the innkeepers to report any guest who used blasphemous, insulting, indecent, or profane language. They were also to forbid dancing, card playing for more than one hour, and dice games. Nine o'clock was bedtime, and the innkeeper was to allow only the Consistory's spies to sit up past that time.[33] After three months, the abbayes were closed for lack of patronage; and the taverns reopened.[34]

Calvin and those who after his death led the Church of Geneva were much concerned about the proper food, drink, and apparel of the Genevans. Clothes were to be sober and decent and certainly not luxurious; color and quality were specified. The way women did up their hair was also regulated.[35] Calvin became very aggravated during a festival at which some male contestants in a shooting match wished to wear slashed hose and doublets.[36] After Calvin's death, stringent sumptuary codes were enacted that closely regulated supposed excesses in clothing and eating, even specifying the number of dishes to be served at a meal. One had to live in accordance with one's station in life. A widow was fined and spent four days in prison for repeating her offense of wearing a fine silk kerchief. Curled hair was forbidden for women as was long hair for men. A craftsman's wife was forbidden to have a ring with a jewel. A woman was fined for owning a silk dress. People were punished for being both underdressed and overdressed.[37] One should note, however, that similar sumptuary codes and laws enacted by the civil authorities were common in other cities of late medieval times, and also in cities of Germany that became Lutheran, as, for example, in Magdeburg. In Geneva, however, unlike the case in many other civil jurisdictions, church and state saw that the codes were strictly enforced.

Punishments in Geneva were often severe. A thirteen year old girl was publicly beaten with rods because she said she wanted to be a Catholic.[38] To show reverence for the commandment concerning honoring

33 Preserved Smith, 1920, *The Age of the Reformation*, p. 172-173.

34 Georgia Harkness, 1931, *John Calvin: The Man and His Ethics*, p. 28.

35 Preserved Smith, 1920, *The Age of the Reformation*, p. 172.

36 Harro Hopfl, 1982, *The Christian Polity of John Calvin*, p. 197.

37 E. William Monter, 1967, *Calvin's Geneva*, p. 216-217.

38 Preserved Smith, 1920, *The Age of the Reformation*, p. 175.

one's father and mother, a child was condemned to be whipped for calling her mother a she-devil. In Geneva, a city of around 16,000 during the years 1542 to 1546, there were fifty-eight executions and seventy-six banishments from the town.[39] In 1545 during a time of pestilence, over twenty men and women were burnt alive for witchcraft. It was thought they were conspiring to spread the disease.[40] Torture of those under suspicion, as in the rest of Europe, was commonly used in Geneva to ascertain the "truth."

After Calvin's death in 1564, the laws governing the Geneva city-state became even more repressive and severe. Clergy and magistrates kept the city under a tight rein. Christian freedom for the people of the church became ever more extinguished under a growing body of legalistic regulations. Once more the emphasis in living as a Christian became avoiding any real or imagined evil rather than on a life of doing good.

Calvin's Partial Reformation of the Christian Way of Life

The reformation of John Calvin concerning the Christian life was thus a partial reformation. Although a life of Christian love in the service of God and neighbor was taught, numerous church laws severely violated the Christian freedom of the people. Geneva under Calvin's tutelage merely substituted the Reformed church's offenses against Christian liberty for those of the Roman church. Both Rome and Geneva from different vantage points limited and denied the freedom of the Christian so clearly taught by Paul in Romans, Galatians and Colossians (see pages 105-115). Once more the people were not to be trusted to live by Paul's words when he wrote, "Therefore let no one act as your judge in regard to food or drink or in respect to a festival or a new moon or a Sabbath day— . . . If you have died with Christ to the elementary principles of the world, why, as if you were living in the world, do you submit yourself to decrees, such as, 'Do not handle, do not taste, do not touch!'" (Colossians 2:16-21 NASB).

In Calvin's view, Christ's people for their own good were to be encased with binding laws and regulations. They were restricted in the use of their God-given freedom to act in Christian love as led by the Holy Spirit and guided by God's Word. The overwhelming emphasis in Calvin's Geneva was upon a strict piety, although not to the exclusion of love and goodness.

---

39 Preserved Smith, 1920, *The Age of the Reformation*, p. 171.

40 Philip Schaff, 1910, *History of the Christian Church*, vol. 8, p. 492.

Calvinism and Christian Liberty in France

The discipline to which Calvin subjected the people of Geneva was exported to a greater or lesser degree to the countries which followed Calvin's rather than Luther's reformation. In France, the Reformed church was never dominant except in certain localities, but the church authorities in those areas nevertheless subjected their members to a rather severe discipline.

The *Discipline of the Reformed Churches of France* was adopted in 1559 by the first national Synod. It threatened excommunication upon those who persisted in dancing or in attending events where dancing occurred.[41]

The Reformed church's governing authorities in France, the Consistories, warned individuals that failure to pay their assessed "contribution" for the support of the pastor and other church activities would subject them to exclusion from the Lord's Supper, the minor excommunication. In some jurisdictions, this threat was carried out. One could also be suspended from Holy Communion for declining a church office.[42]

The consistories of the churches also oversaw even minor infractions of what they considered proper Christian behavior. In Saint-Amans, the consistory deplored a lack of respect for her recently deceased father when a woman wore an intricate hair arrangement. They suspended her from the Lord's Supper for the offense.

In Nimes, France, a city in which the Reformed church predominated, the local consistory exercised tight control over the lives of those in the town. There was to be no playing of athletic games on Sunday. Merchants were not to sell playing cards. Jugglers and tumblers were condemned.[43] Violins used at dances were seized and broken; carnival masks confiscated and burned.[44] Immodest or extravagant dress could bring censure. Long hair on men, hoops for extending skirts, and the wearing of rouge were among the many forbidden practices.[45]

This not to say that the Nimes Consistory acted only in a negative and censorious fashion. They considered their purpose to be that of

---

41 Raymond A. Mentzer, ed., 1994, *Sin and the Calvinists* (Kirksville, Mo.: Sixteenth Century Journal Publishers), p. 88.

42 Raymond A. Mentzer, ed., 1994, *Sin and the Calvinists*, p. 116.

43 Raymond A. Mentzer, ed., 1994, *Sin and the Calvinists*, pp. 91-92.

44 Raymond A. Mentzer, ed., 1994, *Sin and the Calvinists*, p. 66.

45 Raymond A. Mentzer, ed., 1994, *Sin and the Calvinists*, pp. 86-87.

promoting a quiet, peaceful, and sober society. In their many actions concerning family and sexual matters, for example, their obvious purpose was to aid families to live together in a harmonious manner. But, then again, all the acts of the Calvinistic consistories that trampled upon the Christian freedom of individuals might be similarly defended. Calvin's overall rationale for his suspension of the individual's Christian freedom, "that things be done decently and in good order," was highly elastic.

Calvinism in Scotland

The church discipline that Calvin insisted upon in Geneva that so violated the Christian liberty was transported also to the Netherlands and especially to Scotland. John Knox (1505-1572), the leader of the Calvinistic reformation in Scotland, was a worthy protégé of John Calvin. Excluded from Scotland for a period of years, he spent some of those years with Calvin in Geneva.

John Knox had no more regard for the Christian freedom of the individual Christian than did John Calvin. He insisted upon strict church attendance in Scotland enforced by fines for non-attendance. No golf or other games were to be played on Sunday.[46] He not only forbade the observance of Christmas; he made it illegal to abstain from work on Christmas Day.[47] Also forbidden was the making of pilgrimages. As in Geneva, the discipline of the church was in league with and enforced by the civil government in many areas.

There was no more Christian freedom concerning the financial support of the church under John Knox than there was in the previous Roman Catholic times.[48] The *First Book of Discipline* written by Knox and others enforced the collection of tithes for the work of the church.[49]

Punishment was also meted out for too elaborate a wedding celebration or for spending too much money on a wedding.[50] Dancing and piping were forbidden at wedding celebrations. Indeed, dancing at any time

---

46 Madeleine Bingham, 1971, *Scotland under Mary Stuart*, (New York: St. Martin's Press), pp. 181, 231.

47 Madeleine Bingham, 1971, *Scotland under Mary Stuart*, pp. 194-195.

48 Madeleine Bingham, 1971, *Scotland under Mary Stuart*, p. 126.

49 Kenneth Scott Latourette, 1953, *A History of Christianity* (New York: Harper and Bros.), p. 771.

50 Raymond A. Mentzer, ed., 1994, *Sin and the Calvinists*, p. 145.

was considered sinful.[51] The church was especially irritated by what they considered the vanity of women's clothing, and the preachers assailed such vanity.[52]

After the death of John Knox, the legalistic control of the lives of the Scots did not diminish. Laws of church and state continued to multiply, and for the next hundreds of years the Scots lived under the careful and rigorous discipline of the Church of Scotland. The typical Scotsman was to attend church twice on Sundays and on Tuesday morning. Church attendance and catechetical instruction was required on Thursday. The General Assembly of the Church of Scotland in 1600 required the entire family plus servants to attend the doctrinal instruction given on Thursdays.[53] A magistrate, an elder, and two deacons patrolled the town of St. Andrew in 1574 during church services to catch those who were not in church. Sabbath breaches such as sleeping in the fields during church services, selling or drinking ale except for thirst, fishing, harvesting crops or other breaches of the sanctity of Sunday resulted in a summons and fine.[54]

Although under pressure from the church, the Parliament of Scotland in 1560 nonetheless refused to make the Church of Scotland's *Book of Discipline* the law of the land. In later decades, however, blasphemy was made an offense against the state; and a series of laws were passed that concerned the breach of the Sabbath.[55] Sexual offenses and other grave offenses were often punished by both church and state.

Considered to be worthy of rebuke and admonition by the church were minor offenses such as: "wanton and vain words, uncomely gestures, negligence in hearing the preaching, abstaining from the Lord's Table when it is administered, suspicion of avarice or pride, and superfluity or riotousness in jollity or raiment." Nor were such admonitions allowed to be ignored. If after repeated attempts at reformation, the offender was still unrepentant and stubborn, he could be excommunicated. "And thus a small offense or slaunder [sic] may justly deserve excommunication, by reason of the contempt and disobedience of the offender."[56] Punishments administered

51 Madeleine Bingham, 1971, *Scotland under Mary Stuart* (New York: St. Martin's Press), pp. 76, 250.

52 David Calderwood, 1843, *The History of the Kirk of Scotland* (Edinburgh: The Wodrow Society), vol. 2, p. 216.

53 Madeleine Bingham, 1971, *Scotland under Mary Stuart*, p. 196.

54 Raymond A. Mentzer, ed., 1994, *Sin and the Calvinists*, pp. 183-184.

55 Raymond A. Mentzer, ed., 1994, *Sin and the Calvinists*, p. 166.

56 David Calderwood, 1843, *The History of the Kirk of Scotland*, vol. 2, pp. 71-73.

by the church authorities might include a private rebuke from the church court session, public rebuke during the sermon, and payments of fines to the church's poor box. A public repentance could also be ordered that might involve being clothed in sackcloth and seated prominently on a "stool of repentance." The stool was at times six feet high and placed in the midst of the congregation for one or more Sundays during the services.[57]

Calvinism in Colonial America

The Calvinistic Puritans of England and the American colonies continued the practices of the Scottish church. The Sabbath observance started Saturday afternoon at three and continued all Sunday in the Massachusetts Bay Colony. Physical labor, all play, and even recreational walking in the streets was disallowed. Sabbath breaking was punished by fines and whipping. In Connecticut, punishment was meted out for leaving one's house on Sunday except for church attendance or necessity. Even in more liberal New York, a law was passed in 1659 that outlawed all "travel, labor, shooting, fishing, playing, horse-racing, frequenting ale-houses, etc., on the Lord's Day."[58] The predominance of Old Testament given names in old New England is also the heritage of John Calvin's preference for such names.

The fact that the Christmas celebration of Christ's birth with services of worship is often confined primarily to Orthodox, Roman Catholic, Lutheran, and Episcopal churches in the United States shows the staying power of Calvin's and Knox's outlawing the religious observance of Christ's birth, even among Protestant churches that would deny Calvin's influence in their church's history.

Christian Love and Christian Liberty
in the Calvinistic Churches

Nonetheless, did the strict discipline of the Calvinistic churches mean that Christian love was not present? Not at all. The consistories and church court sessions were meant to be more remedial and reformatory than punishing. They were meant to be agents of counsel and reconciliation between Christians and to be healers of families. The plight and needs of the poor and weak were never far from the thoughts of Calvin and Knox. Calvin may have outlawed begging in Geneva, but he also saw to it that

---

57 Raymond A. Mentzer, ed., 1994, *Sin and the Calvinists*, p. 180.

58 Georgia Harkness, 1931, *John Calvin: The Man and His Ethic*, p. 118.

those in need were cared for so that there was no necessity for begging. In his "Ecclesiastical Ordinances" he set up the order of deacons. The deacons were charged with looking after the hospitals and the sick, dispensing charity, and in general caring for the poor. People in want of the necessities of life had their needs met in Calvin's Geneva.[59] The many hospitals and charitable institutions that were founded by the Christians who were heir to Calvin's teachings show that his teachings concerning serving one's neighbor in Christian love had their effect.

---

59 Henry S. Lucas, 1934, *The Renaissance and the Reformation* (New York: Harper and Bros.) p. 586.

Chapter Sixteen

JESUS' WAY OF LIFE IN THE WORLD TODAY

Legalistic Tendencies in the Churches Today

The way of life that Jesus taught and that Paul and John so ably defended has not fared too well in the years since the Reformation.

The Puritans of England and those Puritans who immigrated to America continued the strict church discipline of Calvin and Knox. There are still many church denominations influenced by John Calvin's insistence on a discipline that violates the Christian liberty of the individual. Although Calvin drank wine as a food and beverage all his life, his later followers added the use of alcoholic beverages to Calvin's strictures on clothing, recreations, food, and the observance of Sunday. In some denominations and in parts of the United States being Christian primarily means abstinence from alcohol, tobacco, no card playing, dancing, attending plays, or doing anything else on Sunday other than attending church. In many churches, the negative stress on what Christians should avoid has almost obliterated the emphasis of the New Testament on a positive and active life of Christian love selflessly lived for others.

Although the Roman Catholic Church no longer teaches many of the legalistic rules formerly governing human behavior in the Penitentials, the Canon Law still reigns. The Canon Law, for example, still decrees, "On Sundays and other holy days of obligation the faithful are bound to participate in the Mass."[1] It is still a grave sin to be absent from mass on Sunday except for a serious reason.[2] On the other hand, in many parts of the Roman Catholic Church, especially in the past decades, I have noticed there an increasing emphasis on Christian love.

---

1 *Code of Canon Law*, Latin-English Edition, 1983 (Washington D.C.: Canon Law Society of America), p. 445.

2 *Catechism of the Catholic Church*, 1994 (Liguori, Mo.: Liguori Publications), p. 527.

The Greek Orthodox Church also is not averse to making rules that infringe on Christian freedom as taught in the New Testament. Its catechism for North and South America admonishes that playing cards, drinking, and other activities that the church deems sinful are a profanation of the Sabbath day. Quoting Exodus 20:8, "Six days shalt thou work," the catechism teaches that being idle during the six days is a flagrant violation of the Sabbath commandment.[3]

When one considers how often Luther emphasized that a true faith is to be followed by Christian love shown in good works done to one's neighbor, one would think that Lutherans would be renowned for their works of love and generosity of spirit. Especially one would think this would be the case since Luther restored the New Testament's teaching that the Christian has freedom to follow Christian love as guided by the Holy Spirit and informed by the New Testament. But, unhappily, this is not the case. In my experience, the emphasis in so many of his writings that Luther placed on faith working through Christian love is almost unknown to many Lutheran pastors and seminary professors, let alone the lay people.

This is not to say that Christian love is never taught in the sermons and current literature of the Lutheran churches. But the strong emphasis that Luther put on Christian love selflessly serving one's neighbor as the primary way of serving one's Lord is seldom found. For most Lutheran people, their understanding of the Christian way of life does not go much beyond the Ten Commandments as was taught to them in Sunday School and in their youthful confirmation instruction.

Neither is the Christian freedom that Luther taught an emphasis of the churches. Luther's teaching that Christians have the liberty to follow their own understanding of what Christian love requires in a given situation about which the New Testament is silent is seldom heard. It is as if the reformation of the church initiated by Luther had never occurred when one considers how those that profess to follow a Lutheran interpretation of Christianity have ignored Luther's teachings concerning the Christian way of life.

Today in Lutheran churches, one finds the piety of worshiping God with services filled with the Word, sacrament, prayer, praise, and singing. However, one does not find to the same degree the goodness that God equally desires—the members of the congregation reaching out in Christian love and goodness to all who are in need. The Lutheran order of worship in its solemnity and piety is almost indistinguishable from that described by Justin Martyr around 150 A.D. (see page 2); however, unlike in Justin's

---

3 Constantine N. Callinicos, 1953, *The Greek Orthodox Catechism* (New York: Greek Archdiocese of N. and S. America), p. 63.

time, it is a very minor portion of the contributions of the church members rather than the major portion that "takes care of all that are in need."[4]

It is not that teaching Christian love is absent in Lutheran and other Christian churches. It is just lost and obscured by the emphasis on other teachings and concerns of the churches. Also, the emphasis placed on the Old Testament Ten Commandments by churches serves to diminish the way of life taught in the New Testament. It is an emphasis that overshadows the New Testament way of life that is based on a Christian love that supersedes and fulfills the moral code of the Commandments.

There are also church bodies and clergy who find it easier to govern and control their members through ecclesiastical law and regulations rather than to shepherd and lead Christ's people through Christian love. Unfortunately, on the other hand, there are Christian people who are more than willing to allow their clergy to make their moral decisions for them. They find it more comfortable to be told what to do rather than to work out for themselves what Christian love requires in their life. The result is that in the teaching of many churches the new way of life that Jesus and His apostles taught does not have the prominent position given to it in the New Testament. Jesus' way of life is no longer ascendant.

Accommodating Our God

Two major conclusions result from this study of the Bible's teachings concerning the way of life that God wished His people to lead and how God's Old Testament and New Testament people have responded to these teachings :

First: God's people are usually willing to offer Him pious behavior in ritual and devotional activities. For many, however, when God asks in the Old Testament that His people also act toward their neighbor with *chesed* (loving kindness, goodness, steadfast love, mercy) or in the New Testament with *agape* (unselfish, self-denying Christ-like acts of love), God is viewed as just asking too much.

Second, there is a constant tendency for God's people to prefer to live guided by restrictive laws which primarily limit their behavior rather than by outgoing love, *chesid* and *agape,* which frees it.

---

4 Justin Martyr, *The First Apology of Justin*, chap. 67, in *The Ante-Nicene Fathers* (Grand Rapids: Wm. B. Eerdmans Publ. Co.), vol. 1, p 186.

God's Old Testament and New Testament peoples have sought to reach a comfortable and easy accommodation with their God. People may be willing to acknowledge God and His concern for them, but many who consider themselves religious people still insist on their own plans and goals, not God's, for their lives. They are willing to accommodate the will of God only if it does not interfere too much with their own agenda of what they want out of life.

They do not mind obeying the moral code of the Ten Commandments that primarily deals with not harming one's neighbor. The Commandments still allow plenty of room for working out one's own selfish purposes in life. However, on the other hand, to follow the teachings of the Old and New Testament that encourage a life of kindliness and unselfish love towards one's neighbor is considered far too open-ended. Such teachings obviously will get in the way of attaining that which is of prime importance, the accumulation and enjoyment of the things and pleasures of this world. Also, one can usually devise ways to rationalize and circumvent the letter of a given law; but if we are to live a life of steadfast love to our neighbor, there is no letter of the law to evade. If we are to love our neighbor as ourselves or to love one another as Christ loved us there is only the spirit of the law to fulfill. People do not want to be that religious. And this is seen among the descendants of the Judao-Christian tradition today.

It is obvious, therefore, why the Jews of today value the debates over the law in their Talmudic studies much more than the counsel of God in their Bibles that asks them to act in loving kindness toward the poor, the needy, the widow and orphan, and the non-Jew among them. It is also obvious why the Christians of today prefer to teach the Ten Commandments and almost ignore instructing their children about the New Commandment which if followed results in a life of unselfish and self-denying love and goodness. Both God's Old and New Testament peoples live as if God should be satisfied and pleased that we accommodate Him by avoiding the gross evils outlined in the Ten Commandments. And they seem to feel that if they do not live the positive and outgoing life of love and goodness toward their neighbor that He asks, they will at least accommodate Him by offering to Him the life of piety entailing temple, synagogue, or church ritual and activity that He also asks.

The mark of the truly religious Jews today seems to be to what extent they are willing to carry on the practice of their piety. Do they avoid forbidden non-kosher foods? Do they keep a truly kosher house by having two sets of tableware, dishes, and pot and pans to avoid the possibility of ever boiling a kid in it mother's milk (Exodus 23:19, 34:26)? Do they honor the Sabbath by quietly remaining in their place (their homes) on the Sabbath

(Exodus 16:29)?[5] Thus in present times, as also in the time of Jesus, the observant Jews offer to God lives of meticulous piety. One should not deny, however, that there are also a great many Jews who offer to their God lives of true goodness. To give just one example, Julius Rosenwald, who did so much to aid the black citizens of the American South.[6] None-the-less., is the Israeli of today more known for his forbearance, love, and goodness towards others. Or is he known for his dislike of ever being viewed as a "*freier*," "a sucker" who puts others before himself?[7] Can we say that the religious Jews of today are known equally for both their piety toward God and also lives of *chesed*, mercy, loving kindness, and goodness, toward both Jews and Gentiles, "the nations"?

The most influential Jew who ever lived, Jesus of Nazareth, came to this earth not only to bring His people forgiveness of their sin through His sacrificial death, but also to free the people from their formal, rigid, and pedantic attachment to the Law. Speaking with the authority of the Son of Man prophesied in Daniel 7:13-14, He set aside the laws concerning clean and unclean foods by declaring it was the evil that came out of the heart that defiled a man, not the food that went into him.[8] He was criticized for healing on the Sabbath; and when His disciples were faulted for plucking and eating grain on the Sabbath, quoting from Hosea 6:6 He declared, "But if you had known what this means, 'I desire mercy and not sacrifice,' you would not have condemned the guiltless. For the Son of Man is Lord even of the Sabbath" (Matthew 12:7-8 NKJV).

Jesus and His disciples were faulted for not following the tradition of the Jews in ritually washing their hands before eating. In one instance, He responded:

> "You Pharisees are fond of cleaning the outside of your cups and dishes, but inside yourselves you are full of greed and wickedness! Have you no sense? Don't you realize that the one

---

5 This is ameliorated by rabbinical teaching which allows making simulated walls of the home by means of a rope (an *eruv*) that can be stretched around the entire community, for example, the rope stretched from telephone pole to telephone pole around some New York City suburbs. In Jerusalem, the rope stretches for eighty miles thus turning the city into a single dwelling and therefore making it easier to fulfill the ban against carrying anything outside one's house on the Sabbath.

6 "A Model of Philanthropy," The Wall Street Journal, February 24, 1998, p. A22.

7 "Letting oneself be a 'freier' in Israel is really blowing it," by Marjorie Miller of the *Los Angeles Times* as reported in the *Seattle Times*, July 27, 1997, p. A3.

8 Mark 7:14-23.

who made the outside is the maker of the inside as well? If you would only make the inside clean by doing good to others, the outside things become clean as a matter of course! But alas for you Pharisees, for you pay out your tithe of mint and rue and every little herb, and lose sight of the justice and the love of God. Yet these are the things you ought to have been concerned with--it need not mean leaving the lesser things undone. Yes, alas for you Pharisees, who love the front seats in the synagogues and having men bow down to you in public! Alas for you, for you are like unmarked graves--men walk over your corruption without ever knowing it is there."9

Jesus also upbraided the scribes for their pretended and showy piety in saying, "Beware of the scribes, who desire to go around in long robes, love greetings in the marketplaces, the best seats in the synagogues, and the best places at feasts, who devour widows' houses, and for a pretense make long prayers. These will receive the greater condemnation."[10] A piety not coupled with goodness was a false piety in the eyes of the long-awaited Messiah as it also had been to the ancient prophets (see pages 42-48). If Jesus and the New Testament are to be considered anti-Semitic for such words, then so also must be the words and books of Isaiah, Jeremiah, Ezekiel, Amos, Micah, Hosea, and others down to Malachi; for Jesus' words are almost mild compared to theirs.

With perhaps the exception of the first few centuries, have people who call themselves Christian done any better? Many Christians try to accommodate their God in such a way that what they consider of greater importance, their money, leisure, possessions, and living standard, are not unduly diminished? They are willing to offer to God the piety of church-going, taking part in church activities, building churches, and supporting the clergy. They may even be tithers, giving a tenth of their income to the church. Their active participation in the affairs of the congregation is what they offer to their God, and with that He should be pleased. Their attention paid to the institution of the church should be sufficient to demonstrate their belief in God and their hope in His promise of life eternal. But after such pious activity they want to get on with their life—living as they see fit.

However, do we expect that God should be pleased with the

---

9 Luke 11:39-44, J.B. Phillips, *The New Testament in Modern English.*

10 Mark 12:38-40 NKJV.

accommodation that people make with Him on their terms? The piety of activity in Christ's Church is certainly a part of the Christian's life, but followers of Jesus are also to live lives of goodness that show forth their true love of God. And what is the true love of God? It is the love that we have for Christ in giving us so great a salvation. It is the love that He redirects to our neighbor. It is the Christian love that is to pervade our lives the entire seven days of our week. Our Lord wants both piety and goodness.

Christ asks us to remember His death for us by gathering to partake of His Holy Supper (1 Corinthians 11:23-26). He also that same evening gave His New Commandment that directs that as He has loved us so we are to love one another (John 15:121-13). In our piety we are to meet together to offer to God acceptable worship, with reverence and awe (Hebrews 12:28). But we also are to meet in order that we might stir each other to love and good works (Hebrews 10:23-25). Paul urges us to let the word of Christ dwell in us richly, as we gather to teach and admonish one another in all wisdom; and as we sing psalms and hymns and spiritual songs with thankfulness in our hearts to God (Colossians 3:16). But Paul also tells us that what avails before God is a faith working through love, not growing weary in doing good, but pleasing our Lord by being fruitful in every good work, for we were created in Christ Jesus for good works, which God prepared beforehand that we should walk in them.[11] Our piety is to be coupled with acts of Christian love for others: our spouses, parents, children, employees or employers, our customers or clients, and for our neighbors whoever they may be. We are to be known as friendly, helpful, kindly, and considerate individuals in all our human relations. We are to give of ourselves unstintingly in spontaneous Christian love.

In previous chapters various aspects of Jesus' way of life were discussed as we reviewed the history of The Way over the past millennia. Perhaps it would be well to review and sum up just what living the "**still more excellent way**" involves.

The Still More Excellent Way

Jesus' New Way of Life

As was earlier discussed in chapter four, Jesus followed His Father's will in bringing to this earth a revolutionary and distinctively new way of life by which His followers were to live. He summed up this way of life with the words:

---

11 Galatians 5:6, 6:9; Colossians 1:10; Ephesians 2:10.

"As the Father loved Me, I also have loved you; continue in My love. If you keep My commandments, you will abide in My love, just as I have kept My Father's commandments and abide in His love. . . . This is My commandment, that you love one another as I have loved you. Greater love has no one than this, that he lay down his life for his friends." (John 15:9-13 NKJV)

As we have seen, this was the way of life that His apostles taught, the early Church lived, Augustine and Chrysostom sought to renew, and Luther and Calvin in their reformation of the church sought diligently to bring back. It was a way of life that made Christian love preeminent in the Church in keeping with Paul's words:

And I will show you a **still more excellent way.**
If I speak in the tongues of men and of angels, but have not love, I am a noisy gong or a clanging cymbal. And if I have prophetic powers, and understand all mysteries and all knowledge, and if I have all faith, so as to remove mountains, but have not love, I am nothing. If I give away all I have, and if I deliver my body to be burned, but have not love, I gain nothing. Love is patient and kind; love is not jealous or boastful; it is not arrogant or rude. Love does not insist on its own way; it is not irritable or resentful; it does not rejoice at wrong, but rejoices in the right. Love bears all things, believes all things, hopes all things, endures all things. Love never ends; . . . So faith, hope, love abide, these three; but the greatest of these is love.
Make love your aim.
(1 Corinthians 12:31b-14:1a RSV)

Throughout the passage, the Greek word for love that Paul uses is *agape*, Christian love.

The Importance of the New Commandment

The New Commandment of loving others as Jesus loved us is not a new law whereby humans can earn their way into God's favor. Jesus did not bring a new set of commands that humans were required to follow. The New Commandment is rather the basic principle by which Christians live. Luther rightly understood that to live a life of Christian love following the New Commandment in loving others as Christ loved us is part of the preaching of the Gospel (see pages 416-418).

Christian love is what flows from our faith in Jesus Christ, and both faith and love are the gifts of the Holy Spirit. It is the Holy Spirit that guides our love to the need of our neighbor. We do not show Christian love to our neighbor out of a sense of conforming to a law; we do it because our love for Jesus wells up in us and we would strive to do that which is pleasing to Him. Our Lord does not compel us by law, for an obedience that stems from compulsion does not come from love. Our obedience to our Lord flows from a loving, willing, and cheerful heart. For as Paul instructs us, when we do merciful deeds, let them be done cheerfully (Romans 12:8b).

Forming the basis of all Christian life are our Lord's words, "that you love one another as I have loved you. Greater love has no one than this, that he lay down his life for his friends" (John 15:12-13). These words are not a legal injunction. We are not to look at anyone with the grudging thought, "the Lord says I must love him." That is not Christian love. Rather the New Commandment gives us a distinctive way of looking at the world. It is an orientation of the Christian's mind toward the world.

On the one hand, Christian love is a dispassionate love. It is not a love that is present only when we are stimulated and wrought up. It does not have the driving passion and urge of erotic love; it does not have fraternal love's compelling sense of commitment towards one's friend. Rather, being reconciled with God, the Christian possesses a deep sense of inner peace that allows him or her to look calmly and impartially upon the world with loving and benevolent eyes.

Yet, on the other hand, Christian love is also a compassionate love. It views the world with same kindhearted love that our Lord had when He came to this earth to suffer and die for us to render us righteous and holy before His Father. It looks upon the world with steadfast goodwill. It is a way of looking at all our fellow humans with eyes of charity and loving-kindness that would do them good if it was in our power to do so.

Jesus had a compassionate heart for those in need. He rose to the need of the newlyweds, embarrassed at the wedding at Cana when the wine for their guests was running out (John 2:1-11). He had compassion for the sick (Matthew 14:14), for the widow whose only son had died (Luke 7:11-15), and for the crowd who had been with Him three days and had nothing to eat (Mark 8:2-3). In Jesus' parable of the Good Samaritan, it was compassion that led the man of Samaria to tend to the needs of a Jew who had been mugged (Luke 10:33-34). In the Greek of the New Testament, the word for Christ's compassion could be literally translated "His bowels yearned" for them. In English we would say, "His heart went out to them."

And that is the way it is with the Christian when he or she sees people or a person in need. As did Jesus' heart, so also the Christian's heart goes out to those in need of our aid. Many times because of limited means, the Christian cannot meet the needs of those whom he or she would wish to aid. The Spirit's gift of faith and Christian love, however, still causes the Christian to yearn to be of help. For the compassion that Jesus showed during His years on earth is also to be ours when we, as imitators of God and as His beloved children, walk in love, as Christ loved us and gave Himself up for us (Ephesians 5:1-2). Our heart goes out to our neighbor's need, whether he is living near us or whether he lives on a distant continent.

Hating the Sin but Loving the Sinner

It is with eyes of compassionate love that we also view those who sin grievously against their God. Christians follow their God in His hatred of the sin but love for the sinner. This is indeed the very crux of Christianity. Christ repeatedly said that He came to save the sinner not those who considered themselves "the righteous." It is a mark of the Biblical ignorance of our pagan culture that a great metropolitan newspaper can scoff at the idea, for example, of Christians loving the homosexual but deploring his sexually perverse practices. This, however, has long been the teaching of Christianity. A portion of the *Rule of St. Augustine* reads, "and that with love of the persons and hatred of the offenses."[12] Augustine insisted that a just war, a war for the punishment of injustice or to restore the peace, is to be waged without vindictiveness or unnecessary violence and with inward love for the aggressors.[13] Pope Leo the Great in the 400s wrote, "Not men, but their sins, must be hated."[14] Luther preached:

> "A truly Christian work is it that we descend and get mixed up in the mire of the sinner as deeply as he sticks there himself, taking his sin upon ourselves and floundering out of it with him, not acting otherwise than as if his sin were our own. We should rebuke and deal with him in earnest; yet we are not to despise but sincerely to love him. If you are proud toward the sinner and despise him, you are utterly damned."[15]

---

12 Sister Agatha Mary, S.P.B., 1991, *The Rule of St. Augustine: An Essay in Understanding* (Villanova, Pa.: Augustinian Press), p. 190.

13 Kenneth S. Latourette, 1953, *A History of Christianity* (New York: Harper and Bros.), p. 244.

14 *Letters of Leo the Great* in *The Nicene and Post-Nicene Fathers* (Grand Rapids: Wm. B. Eerdmans Publ. Co.), Second Series, vol. 12, p. 109.

15 Martin Luther, *Sermons of Martin Luther*, the *Church Postil* (Grand Rapids: Baker Book House), vol. 4, p. 61.

Christian Love Supersedes the Ten Commandments

It is the love of Christ that controls the Christian and he lives no longer for himself but for Christ who died and rose for him (2 Corinthians 5:14-15). It is through living by Christian love that the Ten Commandments are superseded in Christianity. In living for Christ, the Christian lives as his Savior directs—giving himself even for the least of Christ's brethren. If the Christian's main concern is to serve his neighbor in a selfless and self-giving way, he will obviously not violate the commandments concerning murdering or stealing from him. If he looks upon his neighbor with eyes of Christian love that wish him well, he will rejoice with him in any good fortune the neighbor enjoys and thus hardly covet his belongings or attempt to obtain them under false pretenses.

If a young man looks upon his girl friend with eyes of Christian love, he will not violate the commandment concerning chastity and defile her by attempting her seduction. It will be especially reprehensible to him to act so selfishly and lovelessly that he would take even the slightest risk of imposing upon a child the ignominy of a lifetime of illegitimacy, all so that he could have an hour of sexual pleasure. An illegitimate child is not a "love child"; it is a "lust child." So often what the world calls love in its songs, plays, and books is really only lust, a selfish desire for carnal possession.

Christian Love Is Guided by the Scriptures as Understood in the New Testament

Trying to determine what is the Christian thing to do in a given instance is often a difficult task. But there is one approach that is helpful. Try to look at a given problem through the eyes and minds of Jesus, Paul, Peter, James, or John and also the prophets of the Old Testament. As Paul said to the Corinthian Christians, "Be imitators of me, as I am of Christ" (1 Corinthians 11:1).

Now the way to do this is to read the Gospel accounts of the life of Christ, the letters of the apostles, and the words of God's Old Testament prophets so often that their ways of observing the world become second nature to you. Paul advised the Christians at Colossae, "Let the word of Christ dwell in you richly, as you teach and admonish one another in all wisdom" (Colossians 3:16a RSV). And to the church at Corinth he wrote that we are to learn "to live according to Scripture" (1 Corinthians 4:6 RSV). We come to really know both Old and New Testaments when they color and change our thinking just as tea colors and changes a cup of hot water. Our minds are to be steeped in the Word of God. When our attitudes become like the attitudes and ways of thinking exhibited by Jesus and His apostles and the Old Testament prophets, then living the Christian way of life becomes a more natural way of life. Does this mean that you will lose your own personality? No, it only means that you will become more Christ-like.

Christian Love is an Orientation of the Mind

Christian love is an inclination and orientation of the mind that looks at the world through the eyes of Jesus Christ. Christian love means to live in the world with the same spontaneous, selfless love as did Jesus Christ. Paul explains this in his letter to the Christians of Philippi. He first describes what it means to live as a Christian:

> Therefore if there is any consolation in Christ, if any comfort of love, in any fellowship of the Spirit, if any affection and mercy, fulfill my joy by being like-minded, having the same love, being of one accord, of one mind. Let nothing be done through selfish ambition or conceit, but in lowliness of mind let each esteem another better than himself. Let each of you look out not only for his own interest, but also for the interests of others. (Philippians 2:1-4 NKJV)

Paul then tells how this is to be done:

> Let this mind be in you which was also in Christ Jesus, who, being in the form of God, did not think equality with God something to be grasped, but emptied Himself by taking the form of a servant, and coming in the likeness of men. And being found in appearance as a man, He humbled himself and became obedient to the point of death, even the death of the cross. (Philippians 2:5-8 NKJV)

"Let this mind be in you"—Christian love is a mind-set that wars against our natural inclination to act selfishly toward our fellowman when our own interests are involved. Unfortunately, for too many years we have lived in a willful, self-centered culture whose sense of freedom is often license. Thus, the Christian way of viewing the world is not achieved overnight. Satan and our own selfish and demanding flesh will not give up so easily the fight to command our behavior. Paul understood this in writing, "For the flesh sets its desire against the Spirit, and the Spirit against the flesh; for these are in opposition to one another, so that you may not do the things that you please" (Galatians 5:17 NASB). Thankfully, we have the power of the Holy Spirit working through the guidance given to us in God's Word that can aid us in our striving to show the same selfless and self-giving love for others that Jesus showed to us. Thus no longer are we to live as we please, but we are to please God as we live.

To Live as a Christian Means to Live "The Way"

Jesus' way of life is a gift to the people of His Church. Luke in the Book of Acts relates that earliest Christianity was called "The Way."[16] It is the way of life to which Paul referred when he wrote, "And I will show you a still more excellent way. . . . Make love your aim."[17]

"Make love your aim." These words are basic to the way of life of the Christian. Everything that we do is to be done in Christian love. Especially should Christian love be our aim concerning those persons who are the closest to us, our own spouse and children. Within our immediate family we spend a major portion of our lives. Let us consider this most significant relationship that we have with other humans.

Christian Love in Marriage and the Family

The Bible views marriage as a gift of God. It was God who in the Genesis story gave Eve to Adam as a helper comparable to him. Therefore, Scripture instructs a man to leave his father and mother and cleave to his wife and become one flesh with her (Genesis 2:18-24).

Paul in the New Testament underscored this profound bond made by God between the husband and his wife. He encouraged the husbands:

> Husbands, love your wives, just as Christ also loved the church and gave Himself up for her; that He might sanctify her, having cleansed her by the washing with the word, that He might present to Himself the church in all her glory, having no spot or wrinkle or any such thing; but that she should be holy and blameless. So husbands ought also to love their own wives as their own bodies. He who loves his own wife loves himself; for no one ever hated his own flesh, but nourishes and cherishes it, just as Christ also does the church, because we are members of His body. For this cause a man shall leave his father and

---

16 Acts 9:2, 19:9, 19:23, 22:4, 24:22.

17 1 Corinthians 12:31b, 14:1a

> mother, and shall cleave to his wife; and the two shall become one flesh. This mystery is great; but I am speaking with reference to Christ and the church. Nevertheless let each individual among you also love his own wife even as himself; and let the wife see to it that she respect her husband. (Ephesians 5:25-33 NASB)

A husband is to love his wife to the extent that he would willingly go to his death for her, just as Jesus Christ did for the salvation of His Church. As Christ cares for His Church, so also husbands are to nourish and cherish their wives.

Paul also counsels above that husbands are to love their wives as their own bodies. In marriage we are no longer separate individuals. We have given up our insistence on our own separateness and identity. Jesus underscored this oneness in marriage when He said, "Have you not read that He who made them at the beginning 'made them male and female,' and said, 'For this reason a man shall leave his father and mother and be joined to his wife, and the two shall become one flesh'? So then, they are no longer two, but one flesh. Therefore what God has joined together, let not man divide" (Matthew 19:4-6 NKJV). Although there may be good reasons for remaining single, men and women normally were not meant to live their lives as only self-determining, detached individuals. They were meant to merge their lives with their spouses.

The Christian husband does not have to be ordered to do the above. To be Christian means to walk in the way of Christian love. If Christians are to show love to one another, certainly their own family should be in the first circle of that love. Paul encouraged the Christians of Colossae to live this life of love in their families when he wrote:

> And so, as those who have been chosen of God, holy and beloved, put on a heart of compassion, kindness, humility, gentleness and patience; bearing with one another, and forgiving each other, whoever has a complaint against anyone; just as the Lord forgave you, so also should you. And beyond all these things put on love, which is the perfect bond of unity.[18] . . . Wives, submit and yield yourselves in love to your husbands, as is becoming in the Lord. Husbands, love your wives, and be not bitter against them. Children be obedient to your parents in everything, for this is well-pleasing to the Lord. Fathers, do not

---

18 Colossians 3:12-14

harass your children, lest they become disheartened.[19]

Thus, the relationship of love that exists between Christ and His Church is the model for that which should exist between husband and wife. To the couple Paul wrote:

> Submit and yield yourself in love to one another out of reverence for Christ.

And to the wives especially, he continued:

> Wives, submit and yield yourself in love to your husbands, as to the Lord. For the husband is the head of the wife as Christ is the head of the church, his body, and is himself its Savior. As the church submits and yields itself in love to Christ, so let wives also submit and yield themselves in love to their husbands in everything.[20]

The Christian wife's relationship to her husband is one of voluntarily submitting and yielding herself in love. It is a love that does not have to be commanded or demanded; it is a love that flows from her heart to the man she loves. It is not a coerced or forced relationship. It is a voluntary relationship. As Christ is the natural head of His Church, in the economy of God the husband is the natural head of the family. Note too, that although the headship of the husband in the family is recognized by Paul, in Ephesians 5:21 he tells both husband and wife to yield themselves in love to one another out of reverence for Christ.

Indeed, no Christian husband should ever use the texts above to insist that his wife recognize his place as head of the family. We are not to use the words of Scripture as clubs over one another. When our Lord gave His New Commandment that we should love one another as He loved us, He did not intend that anyone should ever say to another, "You would do that for me if you really loved me and lived by the New Commandment." The New Commandment is given to each of us individually to apply to our own lives in our relationships to others. It was not meant to be used as a way of compelling the behavior of another. So also in regard to marriage, the husband's love for his wife even to the point of giving his life for her

---

19 Colossians 3:18-21, author's translation

20 Ephesians 5:21-24, author's translation

does not have to be demanded. It is his free gift to her. The wife's yielding and submitting herself in love to her husband is not to be regarded as his right and due. It is a willing gift of the wife to her beloved and is to be as openhearted as the Church's love for Christ.

Even when the husband is not Christian, the Christian wife should live with him as God ordained as we read in Peter's first letter:

> Likewise you wives, submit and yield yourself in love to your husbands, in order that if any do not obey the word, by their wives' conduct without a word they may be won, having witnessed your chaste and respectful conduct.[21]

It is worth noting in the texts cited above both Peter and Paul ask the wife not only to love but also to respect her husband. In many marriages it may happen that the wife turns out to be the more capable, or more intelligent, or the more strong-minded one of the couple. Let not that bring her to lose her respect for her husband or for his position as head of the family. Once a woman allows herself to lose her respect for her husband, it soon results in her losing her love for him; and the marriage has a poor future. Either the woman may cast him off, or the man may separate himself from his domineering spouse. There are few women who do not deeply feel the need to be protected, cared for, nurtured, and enfolded by the man to whom they yield and give themselves in marriage. If a woman finds that she can dominate her husband, she will wonder why she ever married him. Without even being conscious of what she is doing, a woman may at times test her man; but gratified and pleased she will be if she finds she has a husband whom she can trust to be the strong man she had hoped to marry. One wonders to what degree the high divorce rate among modern Western marriages is due to ignoring Peter and Paul's advice that women are to not only love but also respect their husbands.

Where a Christian husband is concerned, Peter in his first letter cautioned:

> Likewise you husbands, live together according to Christian understanding, conferring honor on the woman as the more delicate sex, as you are joint heirs of the grace of life, that your prayers may not be cut off.[22]

---

21 1 Peter 3:1-2, author's translation

22 1 Peter 3:7, author's translation

In other words, the God who throughout Scripture is the defender of the orphan, the widow, the sojourner, and the oppressed will also turn a deaf ear to the prayers of those husbands who fail to treat their wives with Christian love.

Can living the way that Peter and Paul teach result in one spouse taking advantage of the other? Of course it can. A husband who loves his wife with a true Christian love, who serves his wife as Christ did His Church, may find that his less-than-Christian wife takes advantage of him. Similarly, a wife who yields and submits herself in love to an unchristian husband may find that he just exploits her love for him. But here again is where a Christian returns good for evil. We may be regarded as fools by our unchristian spouse; but, in the same way as Paul viewed himself, we are fools for Christ's sake (1 Corinthians 4:10). It is for Christ's sake that we live as true Christians in our marriages, in the hope that some, though they do not obey the word, may be brought to the faith without a word by our behavior.

The words of Peter and Paul concerning the relationship between husbands and wives are hardly popular today. This is partly because the world thinks that the Bible teaches that the wife is her husband's inferior. This is not the Biblical view. In God's plan for the family, there is a difference in roles; but there also is an equivalence of worth in the sight of God.

The idea of equality between the sexes as we speak of it today just does not fit into the Biblical thought patterns concerning the relationship between men and women. This is because Scripture views men and women to be in a complementary relationship and not a symmetrical one. The roles in life that men and women are to live are quite different from one another's. And both sexes are considered normally to be psychologically and biologically suited for their roles. Any attempt by either sex to usurp the other's role in life would be viewed as foolhardy and contrary to nature. For greatest happiness each is to fulfill to the utmost his or her own role.

Scripture indeed speaks of a subordination of roles, the woman's to the man's, but never of an inferiority of roles. Paul writes that woman was made for man and not man for woman (1 Corinthians 11:8, 9); but this gives only the order of God's creation not a superior, inferior relationship. Paul makes it plain that all humans are the same in the sight of God. He wrote, "There is neither Jew nor Greek, there is neither slave nor free, there is neither male nor female; for you are all one in Christ Jesus" (Galatians 3:28 NKJV).

The role of woman is seen as being very much tied up with her sexual nature. She is to be the lover, companion, and child bearer to her husband. Because she is the one who has the leading role in bringing children into the world, she will need the protection and support of her husband during the years she is involved with pregnancies and child nurturing. After the fall of man into sin, God tells the woman, "I will greatly multiply your pain in childbearing; in pain you shall bring forth children, yet your desire shall be for your husband, and he shall rule over you" (Genesis 3:16 RSV). The woman in this verse does not undergo the discomforts of childbirth only to propagate the race, but rather because her desire is for her husband. She loves him and wants him even if this brings her distress in childbearing. It is a distress, however, that is soon replaced, as Jesus said, by "joy that a child has been born into the world" (John 16:21 NASB).

The woman's role is thus seen to be closely tied up with the home. She is to marry, bear and nurture children, rule the household,[23] and be a comfort and joy to her husband. In these roles she will find greatest happiness, for this purpose she was made according to Scriptures. To understand the high value the Bible puts on the wife, one has only to read Proverbs 31:10-31 (see pages 223-224).

The pagan world often derisively puts down the view of the woman's life as depicted in Proverbs 31 as merely devoted to *kuche, kirche, und kinder*, or in English: cooking, church, and children. The decadent world may scorn; but you may be assured, the Good Lord does not. Women, as described in Proverbs 31, are the foundation of any culture. Their care and nurture of the children is crucial to the well-being of the next generation. Upon the noble, virtuous, and stalwart character of its women, the society stands or falls. Any society that does not value and recognize this is self-destructive.

This is not to say that being a married homemaker is to be the only way of life open to women. The Scriptures speak highly of the prophetess, Deborah, a judge in ancient Israel.[24] Phoebe, a deaconess, is praised by Paul.[25] Jesus showed his high regard for the unmarried sisters, Mary and Martha. It is no act of love to discriminate against a woman in education or a career. She also has the Christian freedom to serve her Lord as she is led by the Spirit of God.

The wife is normally the homemaker, one concerned with the quality of life of her family. She makes the home pleasant and comfortable, a joy for the children to grow up in, and a pleasure for her husband to return to. She realizes a great sense of fulfillment when she does her job well as a quality of life engineer. The role of the husband is typically concerned with

---

23 1 Timothy 5:14

24 Judges 4:4-5

25 Romans 16:1

functions outside the home. As the wife is to be his lover and companion, so is the husband to love and befriend. As he has the greater muscularity, so is he to labor to support and protect his family. To Adam God said, ". . . In the sweat of your face you shall eat bread till you return to the ground, . . ." (Genesis 3:19 NKJV).

How foolish is the view that the roles of fathers and mothers in the family are to be the same. Children in a family need both a mother and a father, and mothers and fathers will quite naturally relate to the children in different ways. Is a man to envy his wife because she has the unique role as child bearer in the family? Is he to be jealous of the very special bond that is built between mother and child during the many months she cuddles and nurses the child at her breast? What a fool he would be if he were to do so. When a child skins a knee, is he to be put out because the child runs to mother for comfort instead of father? Why should a man envy his wife because she is the living heart of the house, while he is only the head? Rather let him and the children, as planets around the sun, bask in the warmth and love that radiate from her. The New King James Version of the Bible rightly translates verse three of Psalm 128 as the wife being the "very heart" of the home. A Christian father will work out his own special relationship with his children. Many studies have shown that girls especially need a caring father to relate to if they are to grow up with healthy personalities and a sound outlook on life. Children need both a mother and father who will love and care for them in their own ways if they are to grow up in a wholesome fashion and especially in order to furnish them models to follow when they have their own families.

"By love serve one another," counseled Paul (Galatians 5:13 KJV). That is how Christians are to live in their marriages. They are not to count the cost of love. They are not to worry if the other is doing his or her part. They are to show Christian love wholeheartedly in service to one another. Christian love is to reinforce the natural human love the couple have for one another. The hallmark of Christian love is that it is given selflessly, self-forgetfully, without thought of return or reward. **Once again, if you are a Christian, how a person treats you is irrelevant as to how you treat them.** We live a life of Christian love because we strive to follow our Lord's instruction to love one another as self-givingly as He loved us. In marriage such love can truly be lived to the fullest.

Therefore, we are not to go into marriage for what we can get out of it. We are to enter marriage because it is the will of God that we enter into such a relationship of self-giving love. As our Creator said, "It is not good that man should be alone; I will make him a helper comparable to him" (Genesis 2:18 NKJV), and "Therefore a man shall leave his father and mother and be joined to his wife, and they shall become one flesh" (Genesis 2:24 NKJV). We are to be one flesh, as if we were of one body. We are no longer our own person; we belong to the other. Paul put it this way, "The wife does not have authority over her own body, but the husband does. And likewise also the husband does not have authority over his own body, but the wife does" (1 Corinthians 7:4 NKJV).

True oneness in marriage comes through complete commitment and trust. There is no honorable way out of a marriage. Jesus said, "What therefore God has joined together, let no man put asunder" (Matthew 19:6 RSV). Scripture gives only two reasons whereby a divorce might be countenanced by God: adultery and malicious desertion (Matthew 19:9; 1 Corinthians 7:10-15). Marriage is to be as the vows indicate, "for better or for worse, for poverty or wealth, for sickness or health, until death do you part." Your marriage partner is to be the one person in this world that you should be able to completely trust. Your spouse is to be the one person in whom you can completely confide, to be the person that you can count on no matter what the circumstances. How shallow and weak is the marriage in which such trust and commitment is not found.

The oneness of marriage is founded on a total commitment of the couple to each other. It is a total giving of each to the other. Nothing is to be held back. There should be no talk of what is mine and what is yours. All should be held in common when the two have become one. Keep in mind the words of John Chrysostom, who in the 300s protested:

> After marriage you are no longer two, but have become one flesh. And then are your possessions two, and not one? Oh! this love of money! You are both become one person, one living creature; and do you still say "My Own"?[26]

To the degree that a person insists on his or her own in marriage, to that degree the chance of experiencing the full joy and contentment of the marriage relationship is destroyed. It is only through complete trust and commitment that married love will grow ever deeper.

When we enter marriage as Christians, we take upon ourselves the responsibility for our partner's happiness, contentment, and fulfillment. If our spouse is to live a full and complete life, it is very much dependent on us. Our commitment to our mate's total well-being is one of our primary responsibilities in life.

So often the reason a marriage breaks up is that one person thinks they are not getting out of it all that they should. This can never be a reason for a Christian. It is completely contrary to the Christian way of life. The

---

26 John Chrysostom, *Homily 20*, in *The Nicene and Post-Nicene Fathers*, First Series, vol. 13, p. 152.

husband's concern should not be whether he is getting out of marriage all that he expected or wanted. Rather, his concern is how he can make his wife's experience in marriage as full and complete, as happy and joyful, and as contented and satisfying as possible. Leaving her is obviously not the way of fulfilling such a commitment. So also with the wife, her concern is to make her husband's marriage to her as pleasant as possible. His happiness, contentment, and fulfillment are her basic responsibility. We should keep in mind that the service of gratitude we offer to our God occurs in part by serving our spouse and our family to the best of our ability. If in our careers we find that in fulfilling our calling we are neglecting our service of love to our spouse and family, we should not expect God to be pleased.

Marriage is not to be regarded as a fifty/fifty proposition. It is to be a one hundred percent giving of the each to the other. We are not to sit around wondering whether we are getting out of marriage as much as we are giving to it. That is a recipe for disaster. We are to give and keep on giving. When two people live with one another in such a way, each giving one hundred percent of themselves to the other, marriage will indeed be the blissful estate that the good Lord meant it to be.

Our Creator ordained marriage to be the basic relationship in which most men and women are to live. He fostered marriage as one of the mainstays of human happiness and fulfillment. He designated marriage as the institution in which children are to be nurtured in an atmosphere of security and love.

Too often our society sacrifices the interests of the children in its stress on the individual adult's goals, desires, and self-realization. Many who would be cultural leaders in our society decree that children are not in any way to be an obstacle to one's own self-realization and fulfillment. Such selfishness is an abomination to God. The Savior, who reprimanded His disciples for trying to keep the children from Him, desires that children live happy and secure lives growing in the nurture and admonition of the Lord and guided by both their parents.

When individuals indulge in alternative life styles that are not in keeping with the sanctity and stability of family life, they set examples that contribute to attitudes destructive to the well-being of the culture. Attitudes are fostered that result in the miseries of abuse and abandonment or to the enduring pain of being defenseless victims of a divorce that so many children now experience. It is for this reason that God does not condone homosexual practices, sexual activity between the unmarried, adultery, and unwarranted divorce. Such self-centered behavior that decays the basic values and institutions of the community is repugnant to the God who calls children "the heritage of the Lord" and who took up children into His arms and blessed them (Psalm 127:3 and Mark 10:16). As cited earlier (page 47), the Old Testament prophet Malachi summed up God's attitude toward the selfishness of His people:

> Another thing you do: You flood the Lord's altar with tears. You weep and wail because he no longer pays attention to your offerings or accepts them with pleasure from your hands. You ask, "Why?" It is because the Lord is acting as the witness between you and the wife of your youth, because you have broken faith with her, though she is your partner, the wife of your marriage covenant. Has not the Lord made them one? In flesh and spirit they are his. And why one? Because he was seeking godly offspring. So guard yourself in your spirit, and do not break faith with the wife of your youth. "I hate divorce," says the Lord God of Israel, . . . (Malachi 2:13-16a NIV)

It is of interest that while our society decries the physical and sexual abuse of children, it ignores the great evil of the suffering inflicted on helpless children by their parents' abandonment of their well-being in divorce. These children are typically psychologically scared and often suffer even physical deprivation of some of life's necessities when the home is broken up. In the writer's experience of seventeen years as a pastor, this latter abuse of children is much greater than the comparatively rare cases of sexual and physical abuse. However, as long as personal selfishness (disguised as self-fulfillment and self-realization) is trumpeted and exalted by the media and by those who consider themselves to be our culture's intellectual leaders , do not expect our society any time soon to rise to the defense of the children who so often suffer miserably during and after a divorce.

Where the welfare of children is concerned, all alternatives to the nuclear family composed of father, mother, and children are poor substitutes. A child needs much more than food, clothing, and housing. The child also needs a model to follow in later life of what constitutes a healthy, loving, normal family life, and that includes the special married relationship that exists between a man and a woman. Homosexual couples cannot provide that. A good model exemplifying how a husband and wife relate to each other and to their children is the best predictor for a child's own later married happiness. There are excellent cultural reasons why almost all cultures in the past have viewed "gay marriage" as an oxymoron.

Many individuals may unfortunately end up as a single parent, and they may strive to do well by their child. For the overall welfare of all the members of the culture, an intelligent society endeavors to keep such situations at a minimum. If not, there are many prices to be paid; for example, recently it has been documented that unmarried teenage girls have a much higher rate of pregnancy when there is no father in the home.

This then is Christian marriage. It is a Christian woman giving herself in love to her husband as does the Church to Christ. It is the husband loving his wife as selflessly and as fervently as Christ loved His Church; not demanding for himself his prerogatives as head of the family, but rather seeing himself as one who serves, remembering Jesus' words that he is to serve "just as the Son of Man did not come to be served, but to serve, and to give His life a ransom for many" (Matthew 20:28 NASB).

Certainly, it takes a great deal of trust, commitment, and love to live in a true Christian marriage. But one will never really experience what marriage was meant to be unless one gives oneself completely over to full commitment and love in marriage. Too many cheat themselves out of experiencing the joy, serenity, and bliss that God meant marriage to be by selfishly or fearfully holding themselves back. To the degree that they do, they will diminish their own marriage and destroy their chance to experience true wedded happiness and the great depth of married love that our God intended.

The non-Christian world may scoff at the possibility of achieving such married happiness, but when did it ever understand what it meant to be truly married? Self-styled authorities in the media often consider Christian marriage as portrayed above to be a chimera, a hopeless ideal, a nostalgic looking back to a time that never was. They vaunt such writers as Sinclair Lewis who project their own warped and dysfunctional personalities on the rest of society. But the great host of Christian people who have experienced the blessings and bliss of such a marriage would argue otherwise.

The Problem of Overindulging Our Families

If, on the one hand, we are to love our neighbors as ourselves, certainly one's family and extended family relationships are our closest "neighbors." To neglect the needs of those closest to us would hardly be in keeping with Christian love. On the other hand, to indulge one's family with all that we possess is also not in keeping with Christian love. The over-indulgence of one's family can be a besetting sin. A great many fall into this trap. We may well make our lives a stench in the nostrils of our God if we use the resources God has given us to house our families in as palatial a home as we can afford, and to indulge our families similarly with expensive food, abundant and costly clothing, opulent jewelry, posh vacations, and luxurious and over-priced cars; just because we can afford them. John Calvin (see page 438) concerning this commented:

There is almost no one whose resources permit him to be

extravagant who does not delight in lavish and ostentatious banquets, bodily apparel, and domestic architecture; who does not wish to outstrip his neighbors in all sorts of elegance; who does not wonderfully flatter himself with his opulence. And all these things are defended under the pretext of Christian freedom.[27]

In our Christian freedom, no one but God can be our judge if we indulge our families in the above ways. But we should keep in mind God's words explaining His fiery destruction of the wicked city of Sodom:

"Behold, this was the guilt of your sister Sodom: she and her daughters had arrogance, abundant food, and careless ease, but she did not help the poor and needy. Thus they were haughty and committed abominations before Me. Therefore I removed them when I saw it" (Ezekiel 16:49-50 NASB).

Good Works Are Those Which Are Pleasing to God

Christian Faith Active in Christian Love

It is not only to the poor or those who need our aid upon whom we look with Christian love. The Christian looks with Christian love upon all with whom he or she lives upon this earth. There is no portion of life that is partitioned out as charitable acts. The Christian life is one of selfless service to all with whom he or she comes in contact. Christians, as did Jesus, do not live to be served, but to serve (Matthew 20:25-27). Our service does not aid in our salvation, but it is for a life of good works that we are saved by faith. Paul made this clear when he wrote:

For by grace you have been saved through faith, and that not of yourselves; it is the gift of God, not of works, lest anyone should boast. <u>For we are His workmanship, created in Christ Jesus for good works, which God has prepared beforehand that we should walk in them.</u> (Ephesians 2:8-10 NKJV)

Created for and walking in good works, that is the life of the Christian. The Christian lives his life in imitation of the life of Jesus Christ, and Jesus lived

---

27 John Calvin; 1559, *Institutes of the Christian Religion*, bk. 3, ch. 19, sec. 8, in *The Library of Christian Classics* (Philadelphia: The Westminster Press), vol. 20, p. 841

a life that aimed to please His Father. To the Jews who demanded to know who He was, Jesus said:

> "When you have lifted up the Son of Man, then you will know that I am He, and that I do nothing of Myself; but as My Father has taught Me, I speak these things. And He who sent Me is with Me. The Father has not left Me alone, for I always do those things that please Him. (John 8:28-29 NKJV)

As Jesus lived to please His Father, so we also live to please our God. Paul prayed that the Colossian Christians would live in a way that pleased God in writing to them:

> For this reason also, since the day we heard of it [their faith], we have not ceased to pray for you and to ask that you may be filled with the knowledge of His will in all spiritual wisdom and understanding, so that you may walk in a manner worthy of the Lord, to please Him in all respects, bearing fruit in every good work and increasing in the knowledge of God; . . . (Colossians 1:9-10 NASB)

The writer of the Book of Hebrews wrote similarly, "And do not neglect doing good and sharing; for with such sacrifices God is pleased" (Hebrew 13:16 NASB).

Philosophers who deal with ethics have long discussed what is "good," and any study of their works will show that their answers have been many, varied, and often at odds with each other. In this regard, one cannot help but think of Cicero's observation as quoted by the philosopher and mathematician Blaise Pascal, "Nothing can be said so absurd that it may not be said by some philosopher."[28]

The Christian also has a definition of the "good." For the Christian, that is "good" which is pleasing to His Creator, for God, not man, is the measure and takes the measure of all things. If we would know what is pleasing to God, He has given us a revelation of Himself and His will for us in the Scriptures. If we would know what good work is pleasing to God, we need but turn to the Scriptures as they are interpreted by the New Testament. There we will find that a good work is one which is motivated by Christian love and done for the benefit of others.

---

28 *Pascal's Thoughts and Minor Works*, no. 363, in *The Harvard Classics* (New York: P. F. Collier and Son), vol. 48, p. 123.

A good work can be one of bringing the good news of God's love to your neighbor by words or through benefiting him by aiding him in material ways. A good work can be one of keeping oneself healthy, mentally and physically, so that one is capable of being of service to others. A good work can be as small as that of opening a door for a person burdened with packages; and it can be as large as giving away the majority of one's wealth in endowing a hospital, both acts flowing from the motivation of Christian love. A good work can be a child helping a younger sister with her homework, or a mother unstintingly seeking to provide nourishing and appetizing food for her family. Good works can be done by the rich and poor alike. One does not have to be wealthy to benefit one's neighbors by deeds of Christian love. Jesus said concerning this, "And whoever gives to one of these little ones even a cup of cold water because he is a disciple, truly, I say to you, he shall not lose his reward" (Matthew 10:42 RSV).

Rural folk perhaps have a better understanding that a good deed does not have to be a grand gesture rather than those who live in the anonymity of urban centers. For example, seldom does a farmer who has a severe accident or illness in the Midwest of the United States have to worry about planting or harvesting his crops. His neighbors will be quick to do it for him. If his wife is seriously ill, meals prepared by his neighbor's wives will soon be arriving.

Above all, deeds of Christian love are to be done in Christian freedom. Each Christian must decide for himself what Christian love requires when seeing a need to be filled. Christians may well differ on the course of action to follow in a given instance. If the motivation is one of Christian love, we are to respect each other's deeds even when perhaps disagreeing on the course of action. Our good works that flow from Christian love are done in Christian liberty as we are led by the Holy Spirit and under the guidance of God's Word.

Christian Love in Our Daily Work

It is especially in the Christian's daily work that one may serve in Christian love. Christian love is not something that is to be exercised only during one's leisure hours. One cannot exclude Christian love the major activity of our lives, the work-a-day world in which we earn our living.

All of us are called by God to serve in the vocation in which we find ourselves. It does not matter what our occupation is as long as it is a benefit and not a detriment to the welfare of our fellowman. For example, to speak first of a vocation that I know well, that of a university professor, for fourteen years my calling as a geology professor primarily was to serve my students to the best of my ability. During the many years I taught, they were a major reason for my being. They came to me for knowledge and training.

I failed them and my Lord if I did not do my best for them. Through my students, I served the greater community. No dam should fail because I did not train them properly to be able as geologists to evaluate carefully the placement of its footings. My call was also to serve the greater community through research, but this was not to be done at the expense of neglecting my students. My call also included serving the needs of the educational community, the university, in which I worked. Thus my daily work as a professor was a primary way in which I served my neighbor in Christian love. True enough, I supported my family through my work. The opportunity, however, to serve my neighbors, the entire university community in all its worthier endeavors, had to be primary, my salary secondary.

The businessman or woman also has a valid calling. He or she also in Christian love weighs the many ways to serve the neighbor. He tries to see that those who invested in the firm earn a good return. There may well be many people who are dependent on the dividends his company pays.

However, the Christian businessman is not to enrich his investors by exploiting his employees. The Christian employer knows well the Word of God concerning those who work for him. He does not need to be compelled by the words of his Lord in Malachi (3:5), where God promises to be a swift witness against those who oppress the employee in his wages, or by Deuteronomy 24:14 and James 5:4 that tell of the cries of the exploited workman coming straight to the ears of the Lord. Nor is it Christian to pay one's employees as little as possible during a period of recession and unemployment. Christian love will bring the Christian businessperson to strive to pay a living wage, a wage upon which an employee may support his or her family. And the above also applies to the owners or shareholders in a business who might be tempted for their own financial benefit to put pressure on the management of a firm to exploit the employees. Shareholders are to use their power of ownership to bring pressure upon management and the board of directors so that the company is conducted in a just and fair manner.

Nor can the needs of the customer of the business be neglected. The goal of the Christians whether investors, management, or employees is to see that the business firm serves its customers by putting out a good product at a fair price. It is not an act of Christian love to charge all that the traffic will bear just because a product is in short supply. On the other hand, neither is it an act of Christian love to exploit another person by paying for goods or services well below their true value just because it is a time of extremity for a producer or business. Jesus' Golden Rule of doing for others as you would have then do for you is operative under these conditions also (Luke 6:31). A fair price for fair value works in both directions. And don't worry if no one else seems to see it this way. A Christian can expect his or her values to be different from those of the world.

The above does not make the life of the Christian businessman or employer an easy one. He or she must contend with the demands of the investors, the employees, and the customers. As he lives in a non-Christian environment, he will be hard-pressed to satisfy everyone; for few will be satisfied until they get their fair share, plus more. No one, however, ever said the Christian way of life was an easy one. Jesus, indeed, said just the opposite, "Whoever desires to come after Me, let him deny himself, take up his cross and follow Me. For whoever desires to save his life will lose it, but whoever loses his life for My sake and the gospel's will save it" (Mark 8:34b-35).

If one is an employee, there is also abundant opportunity to serve in Christian love. The employee is doing much more than just serving the demands of his employer in return for his pay. If the product or service of his employer meets the needs of the community, through his work the employee also is serving. The worker on the assembly line in the auto factory is serving his community by making much needed transportation. The nurse, the clerk, the custodian in a hospital is serving the patients as well as the doctor. Whatever one does as an employee, as long as the product or service of the organization enhances the general welfare of the community, the work can be done in true Christian love in service to one's neighbor.

Only if the service or product of the organization for which one works does not serve the general welfare of the community does the Christian have a problem. One can hardly serve one's neighbor in Christian love if one sees that what one does degrades the general welfare, health, or morality of the society. However, here again, Christian liberty must reign. One man might give up tobacco farming, for he has come to realize the health hazards of tobacco use. Another Christian may truly feel that the relaxation, enjoyment, and relief from stress that many feel they receive from smoking outweigh the unhealthy aspects of tobacco use.

"Let all that you do be done in love." The farmer does not produce food only for the support of his family; in Christian love through his farming he produces food and products for the needs of his neighbor. The owner of a computer store sees more than just a chance for profit when a customer walks through the door. That customer is his chance in Christian love to serve the needs of his neighbor to the best of his ability, only secondarily should his profit be a consideration. His task is not to sell the most expensive computer, but rather to find that computer which would best serve the needs of his customer. The stockbroker sees more than his commission coming into his office. He sees rather his chance to insure the financial needs of his neighbor. He prostitutes himself if his concern is only to gain the greatest commission possible from his advice to his client. The sanitation man collecting the refuse of his community can be serving his fellowman in Christian love in as worthy a manner in the eyes of his Lord as the most eminent Christian surgeon. Our Lord evaluates both on the purity of the Christian love with which they serve. The greatest saint living today is probably not some churchman; but perhaps a woman living in the highlands of Mexico serving her husband, her children, and her neighbors with a purity of Christian love that eclipses all others.

Neither is the argument valid that says when each individual or group within an economy strives only for their own self-interest is the general welfare and prosperity of all the people best served. In any objective reading of the history of civilization over the past thousands of years, time and again just the opposite is the case. Small wealthy classes of people through the power of their money or property have repeatedly caused much misery to the many through their rapacity, selfishness, and callous indifference. Just consider the economic conditions in so many of the world's countries today in which the vast majority of people endure a bare subsistence while the wealthy few enjoy the fruits of the land through their control of the nation's resources and property. One cannot find a period in history that is not replete with such instances. Over 2500 years ago, the aggrandizement of the wealthy and unscrupulous was condemned by God who declared, "Woe to those who join house to house, who add field to field, until there is no more room, and you are made to dwell alone in the midst of the land" (Isaiah 5:8 RSV).

How the world would change if Christians lived as Christ taught. As Chrysostom said, "There would be no more heathen if we would be true Christians."[29] What a difference it would make if one could count on Christians to live by Christian love. When a child saw a cross on her teacher's necklace, the child would know that the teacher had only her best interests at heart. When you bargained for a new car with a Christian new car dealer, you knew he would strive to arrive at a fair price for both you and the dealership; and especially he would not take advantage of your ignorance about autos and their financing. When you came to a Christian medical doctor, you knew that she would care for you as a true professional to whom your welfare would be her highest concern. She would not demean the honorableness of the profession by seeing it as only a business for self-enrichment. Too often today in the U.S.A., the medical establishment may indeed save a patient's life but by its fees so impoverish the patient that his life is scarcely worth living. What a relief it would be when you walked into a lawyer's office and seeing the cross on his lapel, you knew that his foremost concern would be to aid you in your legal problem to the best of

---

29 Kenneth Scott Latourette, 1953, *A History of Christianity* p. 99.

his ability. And for his work he would only ask a reasonable recompense. The proverb from the ancient Roman dramatist Plautus, "A man is a wolf to a man whom he does not know,"[30] should never be said of a Christian. As Christ showed His love for all by dying for all, so His followers imitate His love by showing unselfish and self-giving behavior to both friend and stranger.

The Christian as a Citizen

It is not only in our day-to-day interactions with our fellowman that Christian love is to prevail. As citizens of a nation, Christians will attempt to uphold their government by recognizing, as Paul taught in Romans 13, that governments are ordained by God to serve the good of their people.

Christians have a special responsibility if they live in a democracy. A democracy can only be good and just if the citizens take seriously their responsibility to work at being well-informed so that they may elect good leaders and lawmakers. It is no act of Christian love toward their fellow citizens for Christians in a democracy to read and watch the worst and most sensational of the news media. An ignorant and misinformed citizen will hardly be in a position to act or vote intelligently to enhance the welfare of his neighbor.

Nor should a Christian voter, leader, or lawmaker be afraid to act and vote in accord with his Christian conscience. The Christian has as much right to vote and act according to his ethics as does any other. If the electorate does not approve of a politician who operates from Christian principles, they need not vote for him. A democratic government should be the reflection of its constituents. If the government acts in ways that a Christian disapproves, so be it. Unless his government forces him to act contrary to the teachings of his faith, his task is to uphold it even as he may simultaneously try to change its policies.

There is also nothing wrong with a Christian statesman conducting the nation's affairs from Christian principles. No more than a private citizen should a nation act immorally or self-centeredly. Certainly, the interests of one's own nation should always be kept in mind, but the policies of a nation that attempts to prosper by exploiting other nations or peoples should be opposed by its citizens.

Perhaps one of the best examples of the Christian way of life being lived out in the life of a Christian statesman is that of the former Secretary-General of the United Nations, Dag Hammarskjold. His

---

30 Gerhard Uhlhorn, 1879, *The Conflict of Christianity with Heathenism* (New York: Charles Scribner's Sons), p. 192.

autobiography, *Markings*, showed the influence of his Christian faith as he struggled in his role as peacemaker in the world. His death in serving people and nations as peacemaker was a true martyrdom for his faith.

Another excellent example of the work of Christian statesmen is the Marshall Plan carried out by the United States after World War II. Certainly, the Christian consciences of George C. Marshall, Harry Truman, and other Christian leaders played a part in the formation of the plan to rebuild the economies of both friendly and former enemy countries. Undoubtedly, many Christians in the United States from a Christian perspective approved of their legislators voting to fund the Marshall Plan.

When the history of the Twentieth Century is definitively written, the most surprising event of the century will not be the invention of the atomic bomb or the many technological innovations of the century. Rather future historians will come to realize that the most astounding event of the century occurred when one country, the sole nuclear power in the years after 1945, did not use its overwhelming power to dominate or subjugate the world. Nor did it attempt to wring reparations from the defeated countries. Instead, it offered freedom to its colony, the Philippines. And it set up programs to distribute large amounts of its wealth both to allies impoverished by the war and also to its former enemies to enable them to reestablish themselves economically so that their citizens might prosper.

This was a complete reversal of history. The French, British, Germans, Italians, Dutch, Belgians, Spanish and others in past centuries used their power to build empires and subjugate other nations and peoples for mainly their own benefit. Think also of the subjugation of Eastern Europe and the reparations exacted by the Soviet Union after World War II. The mark of greatness among nations from even before the time of the Roman Empire was the extent of their colonial empires or the amount of their neighbor's land that they could either control or include within their boundaries.

The United States made a new standard of greatness. It was not the amount of wealth that a nation could take from others, but rather it was the amount of aid a nation could give to weaker and poorer nations that made a nation great. Since the Second World War, this has become established as a new mark of national greatness. Many nations take pride in giving a larger percentage of their income in foreign aid than does the United States.

Unfortunately, the amount of aid to less fortunate nations has declined in the United States. One reason for this decline has been the constant refrain from many in the academic community and the cynical media that the Marshall Plan was established for self-serving reasons, instituted mainly because the U.S. economy needed nations with which to trade. The evaluation of America's foreign aid given in the preceding paragraphs is rejected as merely jingoistic. The view that the Marshall Plan was set up also because it was the right thing to do and was in keeping with the ethic of the nation's predominant Christian religion is ridiculed as naive. It is to the shame of the United States that this unceasing propaganda on the campus and in the media finally succeeded in convincing the populace that the Marshall Plan and later foreign aid was really just a selfish ploy on the part of the United States. What an excellent example of Paul's observation that to the minds of the corrupt all is corrupt and nothing is pure.[31] After thirty-three years in academia as a student and geology professor, I cannot help but feel that if Jesus would come back today it is among the ranks of the professors that He would find the new "Pharisees," people so certain of the purity of their own motives and so certain that others operate from disguised, ulterior, and self-serving motivations.

Christian Freedom

The Freedom of the Christian to Act in Christian Love

To live a life of Christian love the New Testament has given us Christian freedom. Each Christian enlightened and led by the Holy Spirit and guided by God's Word has the freedom to act in Christian love toward his neighbor according to his own determination of what Christian love asks. To each is given his or her own responsibility of deciding what is called for by Christian love in any given situation. This is the Christian's own responsibility and liberty, and it is not to be relegated to another.

On issues where the Bible as it is interpreted and understood by the New Testament is silent, the Christian is free to make his or her own moral decisions based on Christian love. We are not to make rules for one another based on our own viewpoints. For example, one Christian may feel that spending a few dollars at a gambling casino is a harmless recreation. His wife, however, may feel very uncomfortable in gambling casinos where often considerable sums are lost. She feels such sums could be put to worthier purposes. She may dislike being in a place where some people ruin their families through addiction to gambling. She does not want her presence to imply her approval of gambling. Christians are to respect each other's decisions in situations where God's Word has not clearly spoken. We should resist those who insist that all gambling is a sin, and who try to bind our consciences with their dictums. We should also, however, not offend the faith of Christians who feel gambling is sinful by luring them to gamble and thus offend their conscience to their spiritual harm (Romans 14:22-23).

If one lived in a community where drinking alcoholic beverages

---

31 Titus 1:15

was considered sinful, a man might decide not to sit on his front porch drinking a glass of beer in the summertime. That does not mean that he could not have wine or beer in his refrigerator for more private refreshment. Is he being a hypocrite? No, in keeping with Romans 14 and out of Christian love he is trying to avoid offending the weaker faith of those for whom Christ died.

Infringements by the Clergy on Christian Freedom

It is a violation of Christian liberty for one person to try to force another Christian to conform to what he thinks in a given situation where God's word is silent. One may seek to influence another's decision through discussion and persuasion. Each, however, must answer to God for their own decision as to what it means to act in a purity of Christian love in a given situation.

When a Christian comes to his clergyman for aid in making a moral decision in a situation concerning which God's Word is silent, it is not the place of the spiritual leader to tell the Christian what to do. To do so would be an offense against the Christian liberty of his parishioner. The clergy's task is to aid the parishioner in understanding the principles of Christian love with which the person will make his or her own decision. The clergy may discuss with the person the various ways Christian love might be involved in the case. The Christian himself, however, must decide based on Christian love what course he should take in the given situation. When the Christian makes his decision based on unselfish Christian love, it is the clergyman's responsibility to respect and uphold the Christian in his decision even if he would judge the matter differently.

In the tumultuous years on campus during the Vietnam War, I was a college chaplain in New York City. One student in keeping with Christian love might feel that he could not take part in what he considered an unjust war and therefore might decide to move to Canada to avoid the draft. Another student out of Christian love and in keeping with 1 John 3:16 might feel he should join the army to defend those Christians who had fled religious persecution in North Vietnam and now were endangered by the North's invasion of South Vietnam. It was not my place as their chaplain to decide between them when their actions flowed from Christian love. It was my responsibility to support them both and give my blessing to each of them. I had my own personal feelings about the war, but I would offend against the student's Christian freedom by withholding my pastoral support from a student who disagreed with my personal views. This did not mean that I as a private citizen could not join in the debate over the war, but it did mean that I honored all those who acted out of Christian love regardless of their decision.

Another infringement of individual Christian liberty is when the leaders of a church body seek to speak for all the members of their church on a given social or moral issue on which the Bible is silent. They may well have members who in true Christian love judge the issue quite differently. It is arrogant and presumptuous for a church gathering or church leaders to try to give the impression that they speak for their entire membership on such issues. It is an offense against the Christian liberty of members who think otherwise. There is no reason why such leaders or representative groups may not speak for themselves, but they should make it plain that it is their own opinion and not necessarily that of the entire membership.

Once more, it is the task of the church leader to teach the members how to act, live, and make their moral decisions on the basis of Christian love. It is the responsibility of the individual member to act on social or moral issues in accordance with how he or she might see the situation in the light of Christian love. The media and others often hound church leaders to make pronouncements for their church bodies on social issues concerning which Christians may legitimately differ. They may scorn and declare the churches to be irrelevant if they do not make such pronouncements. Let church leaders resist such pressures and temptations to offend against the Christian freedom of their members to make up in their own minds as to what Christian love requires.

Nothing has hampered Christian liberty in the Church more than the feeling of many of the clergy that the layperson is unfit to make moral decisions for himself on the basis of Christian love. John Calvin was a prime example of one who evidently fully understood the nature of Christian liberty but could not bring himself to allow the laypeople this freedom. Indeed, as the previous chapters of this book has established, the whole history of the Christian church is full of such sins by the clergy against the Christian liberty of God's people. Such clergy feel that as lay Christians cannot be trusted to live by Christian love, it is therefore incumbent upon the clergy to make extra-Biblical regulations, laws, and canons to control their behavior. Fallen upon deaf ears are the words of Scripture that declare: "I am against the prophets, says the Lord, who concoct words of their own and then say, 'This is his very word'" (Jeremiah 23:31 NEB); and "But the prophet who shall speak a word presumptuously in My name which I have not commanded him to speak, or which he shall speak in the name of other Gods, that prophet shall die. (Deuteronomy 18:20, NASB). It is a most grievous fault for the clergy to bind consciences where God has not bound them. And yet, as has been many times documented in previous chapters, often in contradiction to the plain words of the New Testament; this has occurred numerous times in the history of Christendom.

The Tithe as an Infringement on Christian Liberty

One law of the Old Testament that many clergy have been loathe to give up is the tithe. They value the legalistic teaching of the tithe because it works so well in bringing in funds for the support of their churches.

When the twelve tribes of Israel first subdued and occupied the Holy Land, the land was divided and distributed to only eleven of the twelve tribes. The tribe of Levi was not given any farmland for their support as they were charged with the care of the sanctuary. This being the case, each of the other eleven tribes was required to set aside a tithe, a tenth, of their produce to be given to the Levites for their support. In turn, of the eleven-tenths the Levites received, one tenth was to be given by them to the priests for their maintenance (Numbers 18:21-28).

As the New Testament Church did not have a tribal polity, and as the law concerning the tithe also came to an end along with the other ceremonial and civil laws of the Old Testament, no mention of the tithe is to be found in the New Testament. The early theologian Irenaeus (130?-202?) was faithful to the New Testament when he wrote, "and instead of the law enjoining the giving of tithes, (He told us) to share all our possessions with the poor; . . . " A few pages later Irenaeus comments:

> And for this reason they (the Jews) had indeed the tithes of their goods consecrated to Him, but those (the Christians) who have received liberty set aside all their possessions for the Lord's purposes, bestowing joyfully and freely not the less valuable portions of their property, since they have the hope of better things (hereafter); as that poor widow acted who cast all her living into the treasury of God.[32]

An early example of the tithe being required in the Christian Church comes from the early 300s. The *Apostolic Constitutions*, a legalistic Syrian document purporting to come from the time of the apostles, decreed that while the first-fruits were to be given for the maintenance of the clergy, a tenth of one's increase shall be given to the widows, orphans, poor, and needy strangers.[33] Over the next two centuries the requirement to give the tithe spread through Christendom and became compulsory. But now it was

---

32 *Ireneaus Against Heresies*, bk. IV, 13:3 and bk. IV, 18:2, in *The Ante-Nicene Fathers*, vol. 1, p. 477 and p. 485.

33 *Constitution of the Holy Apostles*, bk. 7, sec. 2:29 in *The Ante-Nicene Fathers*, vol. 7, p. 471.

to be given for the maintenance of the church, not necessarily to the poor. Archbishop Caesarius of Arles in the early 500s preached on the necessity of giving the tithe.[34] Charlemagne made the giving of the tithe to the bishops an imperial law.

In response to Luther's teaching that the law concerning the tithe was set aside along with the other Old Testament law, the Roman church's Council of Trent in 1563 ordered the faithful to give the tithe or suffer excommunication.[35] John Knox, as noted in a previous chapter (see page 449), continued the Roman church's practice of an enforced collection of the tithe with a similar requirement in the Protestant Church of Scotland.

Today, despite Luther and the Lutheran Confessions, there are still some Lutheran clergy who continue to speak about the tithe in a way that gives the impression that it is the law of God and obligatory. In other instances, although not presented as a law of God, the tithe is discussed in a manner that is nonetheless designed to make people feel guilty if they do not give ten percent to the church. Again, this is in direct contradiction of Luther's teachings concerning giving and the tithe.[36] It also contravenes Article 28 of the Augsburg Confession which states that if bishops require the tithe, it is by human civil law and not by divine right. The venerable Lutheran theologian Francis Pieper also repudiated those who taught the tithe as pertaining to Christian giving in writing:

> "The obligation to pay the tithe has been abolished in the New Testament. While the New Testament Scripture inculcates the obligation of generous and untiring giving, it leaves the exact amount and the details of the contributions to Christian insight and freedom."[37]

It is not wrong to suggest the tithe as an example of giving as did, for example, John Chrysostom.[38] It is an offense against Christian liberty,

---

34 Caesarius of Arles, *Sermons*, vol. 1 (New York: The Fathers of the Church), pp. 76, 81, 160-166.

35 *The Canons and Decrees of the Council of Trent*, J. Waterworth, trans. (Chicago: The Christian Symbolic Publ. Soc.), p. 269.

36 Martin Luther, *Sermons on the First Epistle of St. Peter* in *Luther's Works* (Philadelphia and St. Louis: Fortress Press and Concordia Publ. Hse.), vol. 30, p. 54. See also *Lectures on 1 Timothy*, chap. 5, vs. 18, in the same series, Vol. 28, p. 349.

37 Francis Pieper, 1924, *Christian Dogmatics*, vol. 3 (St. Louis: Concordia Publishing House, 1953), p. 50.

38 John Chrysostom, *Homilies on First Corinthians*, Homily 43, sec. 7, in *The*

however, to suggest that the tithe is a requirement of God or to give the impression that it is somehow sinful not to tithe. The only motivation for a Christian to give either to his church or to his fellowman is Christian love. According to the New Testament, Christian giving is to be done cheerfully and willingly as one sees the need and as God has prospered one.[39] One Christian may feel that because of his circumstances he can only give three percent of his income; another may well feel that sixty percent is what he is led by Christian love to give. Another problem with the tithe is that many feel that once they have given their ten percent they are perfectly free to indulge themselves with the remainder of their income. This is hardly a New Testament point of view.

Because of the legalistic abuse of the tithe in Christianity over the past centuries, it would probably be best to view the tithe as does the New Testament and the Church's literature during the first three hundred years, that is, the tithe finds no place in a discussion of Christian giving. If a church wishes to be considered Christian, then let it be Christian!

Christian Love Does Not Violate the Law, It Fulfills It

The moral code of the Ten Commandments serves to restrain sinful behavior that claims it flows from Christian love. If a commandment of the moral code of the Ten Commandments is violated by some act, then love is obviously not the fulfilling of the Commandments (Romans 13:8-10).

A Christian businessman, for example, may feel that he has drifted over the years into a loveless marriage with both he and his wife going their own ways. He notices, however, that his secretary looks upon him with adoring and longing eyes. As his present marriage seems meaningless, would not it be an act of Christian love to end his empty marriage; and in Christian love unselfishly fulfill the desires of his devoted secretary? The commandment, "You shall not commit adultery," however, will stand in his way as an iron gate. Humans have a great capacity for rationalizing their selfish desires to make them more acceptable to their minds and consciences. The moral code of the Ten Commandments stands as a wall to guide a person's behavior away from such self-deluding selfishness.

God Wants Our Complete Trust as We Live "The Way"

No need or necessity can ever be so great that it would lead us to

---

Nicene and Post-Nicene Fathers, First Series, vol. 12, p. 262.

39 2 Corinthians 9:7, 1 John 3:17, 1 Corinthians 16:2

steal, murder, or commit adultery to attain our ends. Even when things look completely hopeless, our task is to depend upon the God, our Rock. To trust God means to trust Him also when there appears to be no way out. Too often we are willing to trust God only when we can see our own way clear. That is not trusting God. One should keep in mind the words of the book of Isaiah:

> Who among you fears the Lord and obeys the word of his servant? Let him who walks in the dark, who has no light, trust in the name of the Lord and rely on his God.
> But now, all you who light fires and provide yourselves flaming torches, go, walk in the light of your fires and of the torches you have set ablaze.
> This is what you shall receive from my hand: You will lie down in torment. (Isaiah 50:10-11, NIV).

Our God wants our total trust. And those who have spent their lives in trusting Him know from their own experience the truth of Isaiah's words:

> You will keep in perfect peace him whose mind is steadfast,
>   because he trusts in you.
> Trust in the Lord forever, for the Lord, the Lord,
>   is the Rock eternal. (Isaiah 26:3-4, NIV).

Does this mean that we will be rescued from every situation in a way that we might like it to happen? Not at all. Think of all the martyrs of both the Old and New Testament. Death, however, holds no terrors for those who put their trust in God, their Savior. Death is God's way of ending our suffering and bringing us home to Him. In Isaiah we find:

> The righteous perishes.
> And no man takes it to heart;
> Merciful men are taken away,
> While no one considers
> That the righteous is taken away from evil.
> He shall enter into peace;
> They shall rest in their beds,
> Each one walking in his uprightness. (Isaiah 57:1-2 NKJV)[40]

---

40 Isaiah 57:1-2 are among the most mistranslated verses of the Scriptures in most versions. The King James Version and the New King James version are closest to the

And where will each one be walking? A few verses later we read:

> For thus say the High and Lofty One
> Who inhabits eternity, whose name is Holy:
> "I dwell in the high and holy place,
> With him who has a contrite and humble spirit,
> To revive the spirit of the humble,
> And to revive the heart of the contrite ones."
> (Isaiah 57:15 NKJV)

The Church: Christ's Agency on Earth

To aid Christians in living such a life of total trust in the goodness of their God, Jesus established His Church. Christ's Church is composed of all those who accept Him as their Lord and Savior. His kingdom on earth is made up of all whom in true faith in His redeeming death come into His kingdom through baptism and place their lives under His reign.

Before his ascent into heaven, Jesus appointed His disciples to be His apostles. The apostles were sent out to preach the Gospel, the good news of God's love for humans. They proclaimed that God so loved humankind that He sent His Son into the world that all who believe in Christ's redeeming sacrifice would have everlasting life. The apostles gathered those who did not reject the Holy Spirit's gift of faith into believing communities. To be overseers of these communities, the apostles ordained undershepherds, the presbyter/overseers, to lead, teach, and watch over those called into the believing community. In this way, Christian churches were established over the world.

The Christians that make up the local churches are the very core of Christianity. In such gatherings, worship and prayer are offered to God, the Scriptures are taught and studied, the visible Gospel of the Lord's Supper is shared, baptism is administered, and the members encourage one another to do good works.[41] From Christ's Church the members go out into the world to extend Christ's Kingdom by means of the Gospel communicated by their words and acts of Christian love. Into such communities, new Christians are brought for instruction and baptism. It is through the Means of Grace—the

---

literal translation of the Hebrew original that reads: "The righteous one perishes and no man lays on heart. And men of *chesid* (mercy, loving kindness, steadfast love) are gathered with none discerning that from the face of evil the righteous is gathered. He shall enter peace. They shall rest on their couches, walking his uprightness."

41 Hebrews 10:23-25

Holy Spirit of God working faith through the preaching and teaching of the gospel, through the sacrament of Holy Communion, and through the sacrament of Holy Baptism that the Christian receives forgiveness for sin and is strengthened and empowered to live a life of Christian love.

To attempt to live as a solitary Christian, never joining fellow Christians in worship, disregarding Christ's command that we partake of His Holy Supper, refusing the spiritual care of a pastor, and choosing to live apart from the fellowship of fellow believers is contrary to New Testament Christianity. Christians are to be part of a believing, worshiping, teaching, and evangelizing community, a congregation of the faithful, a church.

Public worship, gathering for times of fellowship, and taking part in the necessary activities and tasks of the local church are a natural but rather minor part of the Christian's life. This pious activity should not overshadow what is an even more important worship of our God, the homage we offer Him by living His way of life each day out in the world. Too often people consider their activity in the affairs of the local congregation as satisfying their obligation to serve the Lord of the Church. The supposed success of a local church in the U.S. is often judged by the degree it succeeds in involving its members in its many functions and activities. Our piety that involves Christians in the activities of the congregation, however, is only a small part of the service our Lord asks. In fact, it can be a major distraction to serving our Lord. Too often what some churches foster is a personal piety that is active in the affairs of the local congregation rather than an active faith out in the world working through love and good works. Even worse is when churches devise merely man-made rituals, practices, and observances and then expect their members to spend their time performing such acts of religiosity which they, not God, have decided should be pleasing to Him.

Christians are to be concerned with serving the Lord of the Church as He Himself asks and not with their own self-devised requirements. They are to serve Him as He bids them to serve. They are to serve Him especially by responding to His call to serve in Christian love even the least of His brethren in every contact that they have with their fellowman in the world. Christians are to serve in the world, not seclude themselves from the world within the confines of their church's walls. They are to act in keeping with James' summation, "Pure and undefiled religion before God and the Father is this: to visit orphans and widows in their trouble, and to keep oneself unspotted from the world" (James 1:27 NKJV).

The Christian and the World

Christians Are in the World, But Not of the World

The term "world" has a variety of meanings in the Scriptures but is primarily used in two ways. The term "world" often refers to the good creation of God, the universe in which we live. It also can mean the world of ungodly humans over which Satan reigns. Jesus called Satan the ruler of this world (John 12:31; 14:30; 16:11), Paul called him the god of this world (2 Corinthians 4:4).

Christians are not to withdraw from the world. On the night before Jesus was crucified he prayed to his Father concerning his disciples, "I have given them Your word; and the world has hated them because they are not of the world, just as I am not of the world. I do not pray that You take them out of the world, but that You keep them from the evil one" (John 17:14-15 NKJV). Paul makes the point that Christians are in the world; and if Christians were to avoid associating with the immoral men of the world, they would have to leave the world (1 Corinthians 5:9-10). The idea of Christians withdrawing and hiding from the world to preserve their personal sanctity is not a New Testament concept.

Jesus' followers are to live in the world. They are to be the salt of the earth, the light of the world, showing forth the light of the good news of God's love through the works of love they do (Matthew 5:13-16). But Christians should not expect the applause of the world but rather the opposite. Paul wrote, "Yes, and all who desire to live godly in Christ Jesus will suffer persecution" (2 Timothy 3:12 NKJV). We should always keep in mind Jesus' words from the Sermon on the Plain:

> Blessed are you when men hate you, and ostracize you, and cast insults at you, and spurn your name as evil, for the sake of the Son of Man. Be glad in that day, and leap for joy, for behold, your reward is great in heaven; for in the same way their fathers used to treat the prophets. (Luke 6:22-23 NASB)

In fact, Jesus said that to be praised by the world is a warning that you are not living the Christian life. He cautions, "Woe to you when all men speak well of you! For in the same way their fathers used to treat the false prophets" (Luke 6:26 NASB). Or recall His words to His disciples at that last supper:

> "If the world hates you, you know that it hated Me before it hated you. If you were of the world, the world would love its own. Yet because you are not of the world, but I have chosen you out of the world, therefore the world hates you. Remember the word that I said to you, 'A servant is not greater than his master.' If they have persecuted Me, they will also persecute you." (John 15:18-20a NKJV)

The world cannot stand the Christian, for he will not partake of its sinful ways. Recollect what Peter had to say:

> For it should be sufficient that we did the will of the Gentiles in the former time of our lives--when we walked in licentiousness, lusts, drunkenness, revelry, drinking parties, and abominable idolatries, in which they think it strange that you do not run with them in the same flood of dissipation, speaking evil of you. They will give an account to Him who is ready to judge the living and the dead. (1 Peter 4:3-5 NKJV)

John had a similar insight. When after writing about Abel's murder by Cain because of Cain's resentfulness over Abel's righteousness, John concluded, "Do not marvel, my brethren, if the world hates you" (1 John 3:11-13 NKJV).

Jesus understood full well why so many rejected His message. He said to Nicodemus:

> "And this is the judgment, that the light is come into the world, and men loved the darkness rather than the light; for their deeds were evil. For everyone who does evil hates the light, and does not come to the light, lest his deeds should be exposed." (John 3:19-20 NASB)

In view of the warnings given above from Scripture, Christians should not be surprised that they may be unappreciated by the world. A person who strives to live in keeping with unselfish Christian love is by his very existence a rebuke to those who live selfishly. His life is not to be believed. People think that there must be hypocrisy in such a life. Those who justify their sin by rationalizing that everybody does it will be resentful of those who willingly pay their full taxes, treat the opposite sex with consideration and respect, put in a full day's work as if serving their Lord rather than men, and attempt to give fair value.

Neither will the world believe that Christians strive to live a life of Christian love only from motives of pure love and gratitude to their God. The rationalist philosopher Thomas Hobbes (1588-1679) viewed charity that aids a stranger as only a bribe to buy peace or a contract to buy service. Also, those who have not experienced the joy that comes from the Holy Spirit's gift of faith often put down Christians as living a life of doing good primarily out of fear of hell, hope for heaven and its rewards, or as a bribe to their God for benefits in this life. This is pure nonsense! Christians are already Christ's own both in this life and the life to come. Hell holds no terrors, for life forever with God is already theirs. And they take seriously Jesus' promise that His Father will take care of the physical needs of those who seek first the Kingdom and the righteousness that comes from God (Matthew 6:31-33).

Christians realize that they lose nothing by serving their neighbor in Christian love. They have a broad perspective of their total life with their Lord. The only problems Christians have are small temporal ones pertaining to this life. As Paul said, "For I consider that the sufferings of this present time are not worthy to be compared with the glory which shall be revealed in us" (Romans 8:18 NKJV). Such passing troubles do not disturb the deep peace with God and their fellow humans that pervades their lives. Their lives of service to others come from the love of God that they experience and which overflows from their lives to enrich the lives of others.

The World Views "The Way" as Too Idealistic, Impractical

The New Testament's teaching that unselfish and self-denying Christian love is to guide the lives of Christ's followers is viewed by many as impractical and far too idealistic. The world is amused by people who would try to live this way. They are considered foolish and pushovers. But again, the words of Paul come to mind, "We are fools for Christ's sake."[42] Jesus made no apologies for His way of life that was scoffed at by those Pharisees who loved money more than God.[43] Christ knew that His way of life went right to the roots of the ills of the world. Therefore, He brooked no compromises. In the Sermon on the Mount after Jesus spoke of loving even one's enemies, He ended by saying, "Therefore you are to be perfect, as your heavenly Father is perfect" (Matthew 5:48 NASB). Unfortunately, even among some Christians Jesus' teachings as found in Matthew 5:38-47 are viewed as being too extreme for average Christians. As mentioned earlier, in the Roman church these words were considered a counsel of perfection to be attempted only by the monks and nuns.

The New Testament asks us to live our faith twenty-four hours a day. It means taking sincerely Paul's words, "Let all that you do be done in love" (1 Corinthians 16:14 NASB). Years ago I had a serious, very bright, and quite admirable young woman in one of my geology classes. Later when visiting a congregation, I met her and she mentioned that she had read a previous work of mine that discussed Christ's way of life. I asked her what she thought of the way of life the book presented. She replied, "I don't want

---

42 1 Corinthians 4:10a

43 Luke 16:13-15

to be that Christian." Her answer was in keeping with the response of the majority of the Jews and Christians to the way of life presented by Scripture over the past three plus millennia. We applaud such great teachers as Isaiah, Hosea, Micah, Amos, Malachi, Jesus, Paul, John, Augustine, Chrysostom, Luther, and Calvin for their words, but we do not intend to live according to them. Recall again what God said about His people's response to Ezekiel's message:

> . . . your people who talk together about you by the walls and at the doors of the houses, say to one another, each to his brother, 'Come, and hear what the word is that comes forth from the Lord.' And they come to you as people come, and they sit before you as my people, and they hear what you say but they will not do it; for with their lips they show much love, but their heart is set on gain. And, lo, you are to them like one who sings love songs with a beautiful voice and plays well on an instrument, for they hear what you say, but they will not do it. When this [retribution] comes--and come it will!--then they will know that a prophet has been among them." (Ezekiel 33:30-33 RSV)

And that, I'm afraid may be the response of many who read this book also. They will prefer the Christianity in which they grew up. It promised the sweet hope of eternal life and asked for little difference in their lives—just avoid grave sin, be in church on Sunday, and support your church and its activities. If you do these things, you can indulge yourself with the rest of your life as you please. It may be an easy religion to live, but it is not Christianity!

Christianity Exists Where Christ Truly Reigns

Christianity does not reside in the grandeur of architecturally magnificent churches, or in the sumptuousness of the vestments of the clergy or the elegance of the liturgies, nor in the organization and power of a church's hierarchy. Nor does it reside in the emotional high that might come from an hour in church more gauged to be entertaining than in keeping with gratefully offering "to God acceptable worship, with reverence and awe; for our God is a consuming fire" (Hebrews 12:28 RSV). That Christians are to gather for worship, and that worship is a natural part of the Christian's life is a given. Public worship, however, is not the reason for the church's existence despite what was recently stated by a canon law scholar of the Roman Catholic Church who wrote:

As a community, the Church is organized by disciplinary measures. Its reason for existence, which can be found in Holy Scripture, with the Apostles, and in the pseudo-apostolic writings, is the public worship of God, which should be organized according to certain rules. It is for the bishops to issue these rules.[44]

The true worship of God is when Christ the King reigns over the heart of Christians as they live a life of Christian love in response to the great love that God has given to them. The Christian life is a faith active in love. It is a wholehearted acceptance of the gift of faith and not just an intellectual agreement. The faith of a Christian is based on a full realization of God's love for one. Faith alone saves, but the evidence of that faith is a life of Christian love led by the Holy Spirit. To be led by the Spirit is to manifest the fruits of the Spirit. It means being controlled, filled, and impelled by the Spirit. It is not a law that we live by *agape*. The kingdom of God is realized in our lives when the love of God overflows our life and through us passes to the lives of others. As Christ said, "The Kingdom of God does not come with observation; nor will they say, 'See here!' or 'See there!' For, indeed, the kingdom of God is within you" (Luke 17:20b-21 NKJV).

Martin Franzmann, a New Testament scholar of the past century, wrote an insightful description of the conversion and the life of a Christian:

> This is not a mystic's dream of being absorbed into the life of God; it is conscious, waking, responsible life in the presence and in the service of God. This transformation therefore involves a perpetual renewal of the mind, a making-new of the religious intellect for the life in the new age. In every case, as each case may arise, the child of God is called upon to "prove" the will of God, that is, to weigh and ponder and decide what the revealed will of his Father God is asking of him now. The child knows that will; it asks of him that what he says and does be "good," that it be a kindly, gracious furthering of the welfare of the man whom God has set beside him as his neighbor. It asks of him that what he says and does be "well-pleasing," well-pleasing to God, who is the measure of all things in the transformed life of the renewed mind. No blind

---

44 Constant van de Wiel, *History of Canon Law* (Louvain: Peeters Press), p. 62.

sentimental love, which ignores God's will and word and in the last analysis works harm, can be of a service done to Him, a sacrifice with which He will be well pleased. The Father's will asks of the child that what he says and does be "perfect," that it go all the way and reach its goal, like God's love for His enemies (Matt. 5:43-48), regardless of the worth of the recipient, regardless of the kind of answer it finds.[45]

The Christian Daily Strives for Purity of Motivation

Not that the Christian will ever achieve perfection, any more than did Paul. But, like Paul, we strive after the upward call of God in Christ Jesus.[46] The Christian life is one of constantly attempting to purify one's motives so that all is done in spontaneous Christian love. Each evening during our prayers, we look at the past day and grieve for the many times we did not act in Christian love. We never succeed in living a pure Christian love. Other sub-Christian motivations always seem to creep in: a little bit of pride; perhaps a feeling of superiority, smugness, or conceit; a degree of self-satisfaction; and so forth. In a sense, the Christian daily falls on his face into the mud of his own sin; but also he daily brushes off that dirt and strives once more to live the life to which his Lord calls him. All that is not done in Christian love he knows to be imperfect.

Paul's confession, "For the good that I wish, I do not do; but I practice the very evil that I do not wish,"[47] pertains to all who are honest with themselves. We are simultaneously saints and sinners. The devil is leashed but still can tempt. The world and the Christian's own flesh lure him to thoughts and acts of selfishness. The Christian's sins, however, are sins of weakness, not of *hubris*, arrogant insolence, against God.

The non-Christian psychologist might expect the world to be full of neurotic, frustrated Christians who are constantly striving to live by Christian love but constantly failing in the attempt. But this is not the case—just the opposite. The Christian knows that he lives in a state of grace. His sins do not stem from unbelief; they are sins of weakness, of succumbing to the temptations of Satan, the world, and his own flesh. He is truly contrite in his daily repentance. Nonetheless, the Christian trusts that

---

45 Martin H. Franzmann, copyright 1968, *Concordia Commentary, Romans* (St. Louis: Concordia Publ. Hse.), p. 218. Used with permission.

46 Philippians 3:12-14

47 Romans 7:19 NASB

God daily forgives for Christ's sake. He lives constantly bathed in the love of God's forgiveness. The words of John are a constant reassurance to the Christian:

> And this is the message which we have heard from Him and declare to you, that God is light and in Him is no darkness at all. If we that say we have fellowship with Him, and walk in darkness, we lie and do not practice the truth. But if we walk in the light as He is in the light, we have fellowship with one another, and the blood of Jesus Christ His Son cleanses us from all sin. If we say that we have no sin, we deceive ourselves, and the truth is not in us. If we confess our sins, He is faithful and just to forgive us our sins and to cleanse us from all unrighteousness. (1 John 1:5-9 NKJV)

The Christian therefore never stops striving to be perfect even as his heavenly Father is perfect. If he willfully lives a sinful life because of Christ's promise to forgive, he obviously has ceased to be a Christian. If he feels he has attained perfection in Christian love in this life, how he has deceived himself. The life of the Christian is one of constantly being in the state of becoming. It is a life-long process of seeking to purify one's motivations so that Christian love reigns over one's life to the greatest degree. The essence of the Christian way of life lies in constant striving to act in Christian love. The Christian knows he will not achieve perfection of motivation. Christian men and women achieve a perfect righteousness and holiness before God only through their faith in the forgiveness gained by the sacrifice of Jesus. And they realize it is not their own righteousness; it is Christ's righteousness that covers them and veils their sin from the Father.

The non-Christian may view such a life of striving to live in Christian love as onerous. To a Christian it is a life of joy and happiness. Paul wrote of his working together with God (2 Corinthians 5:20-6:1), the Christian is called to be a co-worker with God in His salvation and providence for the world. Certainly many Christians can point to times that God guided those who needed help to them, whether spiritual or material. God oftentimes works out His providence through humans. The Scriptures have many instances of such occurrences: Elijah and the Sidonian widow; Naomi, Ruth, and Boaz; Philip and the Ethiopian eunuch, to name just a few. What greater honor can a person have than to be part of the providence of God for the benefit of others. Christ is the vine; we are the branches to the purpose that we bear much fruit (John 15:1-5). How a Christian is delighted to have such a relationship with his God!

The Wholeness of the Christian's Life

The faith of the Christian is a powerful integrative force in his life. The Christian, for example, has no enemies. People may view themselves as the enemy of the Christian, but the Christian only looks upon such people with eyes of Christian love. No hatred erodes the psyche of the Christian no matter how great the provocation. If Christ can forgive even those who nailed Him to the cross, so can the Christian live by the Lord's Prayer in which he prays that God will forgive him as he forgives others.

The Christian's life has meaning and purpose. His or her faith in Jesus as Lord and Savior fulfills the purpose and plan made by God the Father before the foundation of the world. The Christian is made holy before God through his faith in the redeeming sacrifice of Christ. Redeemed and forgiven, he is part of God the Father's plan for the fullness of time. He will be united with all in heaven and on earth in the Kingdom of God's Son to the praise of His Glory. His eternal life with God is sealed by the promise of the Holy Spirit. The Christian knows his place in the greatest scheme of things. How beautifully Paul summed this up in Ephesians 1:3-14 (see page 11).

Christians know what to do with their life as they await the blessed death that will bring them to live blissfully in the presence of their Lord. They are to serve their fellow humans with the same self-denying and unselfish love that their Savior had when He came into the world to serve, not to be served.

God gave humans dominion over this planet and its animal life; but it is the dominion of a caretaker of God's garden, for God placed man on this earth "to cultivate and keep it."[48] It is a world to be kept, to be used but not abused. As Scripture states, "A righteous man has regard for the life of his beast, but the compassion of the wicked is cruel" (Proverbs 12:10 NASB). God also cares for the animal life on this earth. According to Psalm 104, He sends forth springs in the valley to give drink to every beast of the field. He gives grass to the cattle; even the young lions seek their food from God. The whole of the animal world waits upon God to give them their food in due season.[49] Humans are to work along with their God in the care of His world. The Christian thus is one who is at peace—at peace with God, his neighbor, the world, and himself. That peace will be seen in his or her face and eyes. There will be no hunted, anxious look. It will not be a face that smiles with the mouth, only to have the smile betrayed by disenchanted,

---

48 Genesis 2:15

49 Psalm 104:10-28

disillusioned, and dispirited eyes, eyes that have experienced too much of the evil of the world. It will be the face of one who truly knows the "peace of God that surpasses all understanding" (Philippians 4:7 NKJV). It is the peace promised by the angels at Christ's birth, when they announced, "Glory to God in the highest, and on earth peace to men of goodwill" (Luke 2:14).[50]

The Power of Christianity to Make a Difference

Christianity, Always the Faith of the Minority

As did Jesus, the Christian views the world with realistic eyes. No Christian will ever expect the world to become predominantly Christian. Jesus taught just the opposite in His Sermon on the Mount, "Enter in through the narrow gate, for wide is the gate and broad is the way that leads to destruction, and many are those who enter through it. For the gate is narrow, and the way is restricted that leads to life, and few are they who find it."[51] Christians are to be the salt of the earth; they make the food palatable, but they are not the whole dinner (Matthew 5:13). Christ taught that His followers would be a minority on the earth. If one argues that there were times in past history when Christians were in the majority, for example, in medieval times, just read Robert Southey's *The Chronicle of the Cid* or the documents on which he based his book to cure oneself of such a notion. Christians can and have made a significant difference in the world; but as Jesus and Paul affirm, the world still remains Satan's kingdom.

The Insufficiency of Civil, Rational, and Philosophical Ethics

Still it is Christianity that can fundamentally change the world. For Christianity changes the heart of humans. Laws cannot change the heart; they can only coerce behavior. Many in the world view laws only as rules to be evaded, obstacles to obtaining one's selfish desires. The man or woman who lives by Christian love needs no law to enforce his or her behavior, for Christian love fulfills the law.

In 1949, Albert Einstein refused to renew his relationship with the Kaiser Wilhelm Institute, renamed the Planck Institute, and justified his

---

50 For the justification of the translation "and on earth peace to men of goodwill" see: William F. Arndt and F. Wilbur Gingrich, 1952, trans. and adaptors of Walter Bauer's *A Greek-English Lexicon of the New Testament* (Chicago: Univ. of Chicago Press), p. 319.

51 Matthew 7:13-14, author's literal translation

refusal by writing:

> "The crime of the Germans is truly the most abominable ever to be recorded in the history of the so-called civilized nations. The conduct of the German intellectuals–seen as a group–was no better than that of the mob. And even now there is no indication of any regret or any real desire to repair whatever little may be left to restore after the gigantic murders."[52]

What an indictment of the intelligentsia of a nation that before World War II possessed the world's finest universities and was a world leader in the sciences. It was a nation that had a philosophical and humanistic tradition that included such great names as Kant, Fichte, Hegel, Schopenhauer, Nietzsche, Schiller, and Goethe. It was a nation that was at the very center of the so-called "Age of Enlightenment."

It appears, however, that it is not enough to have a well-worked out philosophical or rational ethic, no matter how idealistic, if there is little motivation to live that ethic. Shortly after the Second World War, I asked a young German woman visiting the U.S. why more Germans did not oppose Hitler and his evil regime. Her response was frank: to do so meant that you were in danger, as the saying went in Nazi Germany, "of going up the chimney."

At a departmental Christmas party while I was a graduate student at Columbia University, I discussed the nature of ethics with one of my professors. He told me that he saw no need for a religious ethic. He could live by a completely rational and secular ethic of what was good. Then I asked him what motivated him to live by his ethic. He was somewhat surprised by the question and for a time was silent. Finally, he answered that if he and others lived by his ethic it would make for a better world in which to live for him and his family. My reply was that his motivation was really one of expediency. It perhaps would suffice for good times. But what if living his ethic meant that he and his family would suffer or be executed as happened in Nazi Germany? What if he were a businessman and that if he did not fraudulently cover up an honest but unfortunate business mistake, all for which he worked in his life would be destroyed? How then could living his ethic be expedient in making a better life for himself and his family? If abiding by his ethic were obviously inexpedient in extreme times or situations, what would then motivate him to live by it during such times?

---

52 Banesh Hoffman and Helen Dukas, 1972, *Albert Einstein: Creator and Rebel* (New York: Viking Press), p. 237.

And that is the problem of non-religious philosophical or rational ethics. The basic motivation when all the verbiage is cleared away boils down to one of expediency. For example, in his book, *Search for a Rational Ethic*, George Snell, the Nobel Prize winning biologist, after explaining the utility of his universal rational ethic argues that self-interest, rightly understood, will bring us to live in a socially responsible manner. But again, his ethic is thus only one for good times. If to live Snell's ethic brings death or ruin, "self-interest" can hardly be a source of motivation. Socrates held that if humans had the right knowledge of the good and virtue, right conduct would spontaneously flow from such knowledge. Human history has shown how false those ideas were. The philosophers can always devise an elegant and rational ethic that instructs a person how to act ethically and morally. Their problem is how to motivate that person to live the ethic under any and all conditions.

Only a religious ethic can bring a person to live by his ethic under all conditions. The religious person is not all that concerned with what happens to him in this life. Among some non-Christian religions, their adherents believe that by living by its religious principles they gain their God's approval and eternal favor. They believe that God will reward them for their works of righteousness.

The Christian has no problem in living by his ethic of unselfish and selfless Christian love. His motivation to live a life of Christian love is his grateful response to the unmerited grace and love of God in granting to him the gift of faith in the saving work and death of Jesus Christ. Neither fear of hell or reward in heaven is part of his motivation. Death holds no fears for a Christian; it is just a passing from the reign of God in this life to living forever in God's heavenly kingdom. When one is already endowed with all the gifts of God, what loss in this life, including life itself, could possibly make a meaningful difference? Therefore, more important than having an ethic is to have the motivation to live that ethic unflinchingly even in the face of death.

The Difference the Christian Ethic Has and Can Make

The eminent Yale Professor of Missions and Oriental History, Kenneth Scott Latourette in his prescient and far-seeing 1940 book, *Anno Domini*, after showing the difference Christianity has made in past centuries, he then rehearses the reasons why Christianity is the one religion that can transform the world. He mentions the challenges the human race faces in the growth of technology and knowledge of the physical universe that may either bless or curse mankind. He points out how nationalism can be directed either to the spiritual enrichment or the degradation of humans. He notes that the demands of the underprivileged peoples of the world for a greater share in this world's goods may lead either to a better life or be followed by strife which will impoverish the world and blot out much of civilization. To meet these challenges and ameliorate the problems Latourette counsels:

> What is required is an ideal high enough and sufficiently in accord with the facts of human nature and of the universe and a dynamic potent enough to direct and control these forces in such fashion that they may become ancillary [an aid] to the best interests of men. The existing non-Christian systems are not equipped for this task. Buddhism is too despairing and too sceptical of this world. At its core are a denial of the reality of human personality and the belief that all striving for food and shelter arises from a misunderstanding of the nature of man and of the apparent universe. Confucianism is too moribund and, even in its heyday, had too little faith in God and did not face in adequate fashion the problem of evil. Hinduism is too monistic and gives insufficient recognition to the reality of evil. Islam is too fatalistic and has in it no incarnation, no entry of God into human life as saviour. Shinto, in its revived form in the intense nationalism and emperor-worship of modern Japan, breeds war and must impoverish both Japan and those neighbors with whom Japan fights. . . . It is from Christianity that the most hopeful efforts are arising to cope with war and with blind materialism. . . . Non-theistic humanism is too blind to the weaknesses and deep-rooted urges towards evil in human nature and too weak in regenerative power to cope with our age. . . . It would be dodging the plainest facts to assert that the influences originating in Jesus have yet eliminated or are even clearly the victor over the forces which menace mankind. Yet from no other source have so many movements arisen which are struggling to save mankind from destruction and to build a better order.[53]

In my own life, I have observed the truth of these insights of Professor Latourette concerning non-Christian religions. When at Purdue University in the late summer of 1956, I came to befriend a new Moslem

---

53 Kenneth Scott Latourette, 1940, *Anno Domini: Jesus, History, and God* (New York: Harper and Bros.), pp. 200-202.

student who was somewhat at a loss. He had arrived from Iran to find an empty campus two weeks before the start of the fall semester. We soon became friends, and I asked him one day what he found most noteworthy about the United States. I expected that he would speak of the towering buildings he had seen in New York City. No, what he found so astounding was that he saw no one sick or dying on the streets. Where were the diseased, the destitute, and the starving children with distended stomachs? In Iran, he told me, one's social responsibility encompassed only one's extended family, the clan. One had no responsibility or concern for those who suffered in the streets.

In this same vein, a geology professor at Washington University in St. Louis once discussed with me the major factor that impelled him to consider and finally become a convert to Christianity. In his wide travels as an intelligence officer in the Second World War, it struck him that only in countries that had experienced Christianity was there a deep respect for all human life. He came to realize that in countries little touched by Christianity human life was viewed as cheaply expendable.

Harrison E. Salisbury of the New York Times a number of years ago had an article on the insights concerning Chinese culture held by Deng Pufang, the son of China's leader Deng Xaioping. Deng Pufang while a university student had been caught up by the Red Guards during the madness of the Cultural Revolution. He was beaten and tortured in the attempt to force from him evidence against his father. Finally he fell(?) from a fourth floor and breaking his back became a permanent cripple confined to a wheel chair. This one-time brilliant physics student pondered long about China and its 2500 year history of cruelty. Salisbury wrote, "His analysis suggests that the restraining philosophy of humanitarianism is absent or nearly absent in Chinese tradition. . . . He believes that much of Chinese violence stems from a lack of humanity and humaneness. He believes China has no tradition of helping the misfortunate. Too often, lepers or cripples were simply clubbed to death as a burden on society. China developed no great philosophy of charity, aid to the downtrodden or an obligation to help the less fortunate."[54]

This is not to say that countries influenced by Christianity have a pristine record. That is hardly the case! It plainly is true, however, that in the countries influenced by Christianity there is a respect for human life that is not to be found in those countries in which Christianity has had few followers. Any unbiased study of world history will bear that out. And, at

---

54 Harrison E. Salisbury, Op-Ed editorial, "In China, 'A Little Blood,'" *The New York Times*, June 13, 1989

the present time, ask yourself in what countries is slavery still a practice, female infanticide still a besetting problem; and the starvation of the poor during times of famine viewed as of little concern to the wealthy members of the nation?

The world is in desperate need of a faith that can turn humans around and in a fundamental way change their outlook on life. Christianity has demonstrated hundreds of millions of times over that it is such a faith. The philosopher Lord Shaftsbury described the selfish man as one who is morose, rancorous and malignant, ill-humored, sour and disquieted, suspicious and jealous. The Christian faith has the power to change the heart of such a man so that he becomes joyful, forbearing, loving, good-natured, friendly and at peace, and one who puts the best interpretations on another's actions and rejoices with those who have good fortune. There is no other power on earth that can so change hearts other than that of the Holy Spirit with His gifts of faith and the fruits of faith, a life of Christian love. The world may scoff, but far too many Christians have experienced the Spirit at work in their own lives and the lives of others to obscure such a truth.

We Christians can make a difference in the world. We can strive to live the way of self-denying and unselfish love that Jesus taught. We can make a difference in our families, our neighborhoods, our workplace, our community, our nation, and even our world. We may not all be in the position to work as peacemaker on the scale of Dag Hammarskjold. But we can make a difference where we are. Christianity is primarily active on a one to one basis. You are not called to remake the whole world. You probably cannot do much to change the world. But one aspect of the world you can change. You can see to it that where you are there is an oasis of Christian love, that those whose lives touch you truly experience a Christ-like love. You can strive to make true your prayer, "Thy will be done on earth as it is in heaven" by living the **"still more excellent way**," a life of Christian love in keeping with Jesus' words:

> A new commandment I give to you, that you love one another; as I have loved you, that you also love one another. By this all will know that you are My disciples, if you have love for one another. . . . Greater love has no one than this, that he lay down his life for his friends. (John 13:34, 35, 15:13 NKJV)

Appendix One

Jesus' Use of "Son of man" and its Reference to Daniel 7:13-14

An excellent example of the attempt of liberal Christianity to obscure Christian belief is to be found in the translation of Daniel 7:13 of the Hebrew words, *bar enash*, as " one like a human being" rather than as "one like a Son of man. This translation can be found in a number of recent Bible translations. Liberal Christianity in its attempt to debunk messianic prophecy has long tried to maintain that when Jesus referred to Himself as the Son of man it was just His way of saying that He was a human being. Translating the Hebrew *bar enash* as "one like a human being," however, although a possible translation, completely obscures for the general reader of the Bible the chance of seeing Jesus' reference to this messianic prophecy in Daniel when He calls Himself "Son of man."

For example, the NRSV translates Daniel 7:13 as: "I saw one like a human being coming with the clouds of heaven." The NRSV relegates their alternate translation, "one like a son of man," to an easily overlooked footnote among a slew of others at the bottom of the page. For the translators of the NRSV to translate *bar enash* as "one like a human being," even though this is a possible alternate translation, is to act with theological bias.

To avoid such liberal skewing of the Bible, one has to choose one's translation of the Bible carefully. And the way Daniel 7:13 is translated is as good a guide as any to the theological bias that may pervade a translation. Such translations should be shunned by Christians who would avoid the hidden agendas of those who attempt to obscure the truths of Scripture.

Now the term *bar enash* is found in the Old Testament book of Daniel as part of a definite messianic prophecy.[1] The prophecy in the RSV, the more faithful and less theologically skewed predecessor to the NRSV, is translated:

> I saw in the night visions, and behold, **with the clouds of heaven there came one like a Son of man,** and he came to the Ancient of Days and was presented before him. And to him was given dominion and glory and kingdom, that all peoples, nations, and languages should serve him; his dominion is an everlasting dominion, which shall not pass away, and his kingdom one that

---

1 Edersheim, Alfred, 1886, *The Life and Times of Jesus the Messiah*, II vol., Appendix IX, List of Old Testament Passages Messianically Applied in Ancient Rabbinic Writings (Chicago: W.P. Blessing Co.), pp. 733-734.

shall not be destroyed. (Daniel 7:13-14 RSV)

This prophecy from Daniel lived in the minds of Jews at Jesus' time. When Jesus referred to Himself as the Son of man, it surely caught the attention of the people. Was He claiming the Messiahship for Himself? In around ninety verses, the four Gospels record Jesus calling Himself the Son of man. These occur from the start to the finish of His three-year ministry. It was hardly because He wanted people just to think of Him as a "human being." His constant reference to Himself as the Son of Man had strong messianic implications.

The religious leaders of the Jews understood that all too well. When at Jesus' trial before the Council the high priest asked Jesus, "I adjure you by the living God, tell us whether you are the Christ, the Son of God?" Jesus replied to the question, "You have said so. But I tell you, hereafter you shall see the **Son of man** seated at the right hand of Power, and **coming on the clouds of heaven"** (RSV). Upon hearing this the high priest threw himself into high dudgeon, for he obviously recognized Jesus' answer as referring to Daniel's ancient prophecy. An ordinary "human being" does not usually refer to himself as **coming on the clouds of heaven.** Jesus' obvious identification of Himself with this Danielic prophecy of the Messiah caused the high priest to tear his robes in anger and accuse Jesus of blasphemy. The Council responded to Jesus' words by judging Him as deserving of death and rising up vented their rage upon Him by spitting in His face, slapping Him, and beating Him with their fists (Matthew 26:63-68).

That Jesus is referring to the Danielic prophecy is also seen in His description of the close of the age in Matthew 24. It is hard to believe that Jesus did not know what He was saying when He describes Himself as coming on "the clouds of heaven":

> "Immediately after the tribulation of those days the sun will be darkened, and the moon will not give its light, and the stars will fall from heaven, and the powers of the heavens will be shaken; then will appear the sign of the Son of man in heaven, and then all the tribes of the earth will lament, and they will see the **Son of man coming on the clouds of heaven with power and great glory**; and he will send his angels with a loud trumpet call, and they will gather his elect from the four winds, from one end of heaven to the other." (Matthew 24:29-31 RSV)

That the Jews knew what the term "Son of man" implied is also seen in their reaction to Stephen's words at his trial:

Now when they heard these things they were enraged, and they ground their teeth against him. But he, full of the Holy Spirit, gazed into heaven and saw the glory of God, and Jesus standing at the right hand of God; and he said, "Behold, I see the heavens opened, and the Son of man standing at the right hand of God." But they cried out with a loud voice and stopped their ears and rushed together upon him. (Acts 7:54-57 RSV)

When our Lord Jesus Christ, the very Creator of this universe (John 1:1-5,14), used the term "Son of man" in His translation of *bar enash* in His obvious use of Daniel 13:13-14, it is a act of presumptuous arrogance for modern translators to deviate from His usage and replace His use of the term "Son of man" with "human being." It obscures for the modern reader what was the obvious intention of Jesus in calling Himself, the Son of man. But perhaps such modern translations were not really made to edify the faithful of Christ's Church.

Early Christian scholars has no such problems understanding that when Jesus called Himself the Son of man He was referring to Daniel 7:13-14. From the very beginnings of Christian literature, it was taken as a given that Daniel 7:13-14 referred to Christ. A few examples follow:

An early 100s an expanded version of Ignatius' *Epistle to the Magnesians* identifies Jesus with the prophecy of the Son of man in Daniel:

He, being begotten of the Father before the beginning of time, was God the Word, the only-begotten Son, and remains the same forever; for "of His kingdom there will be no end," says Daniel the prophet.[2]

Justin Martyr around 155 also identified Jesus with the Daniel 7 prophecy. Justin, however, mistakenly cites Jeremiah rather than Daniel in his quotation:

And how also He again should come again out of heaven with glory, hear what was spoken in reference to this by the prophet Jeremiah. "Behold, as the Son of man He cometh in the clouds of heaven, and His angels with him."'[3]

---

[2] *Epistle of Ignatius to the Magnesians*, chap. 4, in *The Ante-Nicene Fathers* (Grand Rapids; Wm. B. Eerdmans Publ. Co.), vol. 1, p. 61.

[3] *The First Apology of Justin*, chap. 51, in *The Ante-Nicene Fathers*, vol. 1, p. 180.

Irenaeus (130?-202?) in his voluminous *Against Heresies* wrote in reference to Daniel 7:13-14:

> Then, too, is this same individual [Jesus] beheld as the Son of man coming in the clouds of heaven, and drawing near to the Ancient of Days, and receiving from Him all power and glory, and a kingdom. "His dominion," it is said, "is an everlasting dominion, and His kingdom shall not perish."[4]

The lives of the previous three writers overlapped with either those of the apostles or the disciples of the apostles. I think it is good evidence that the apostolic age understood well that Jesus was referring to Daniel 7:13 when He described Himself as the Son of man coming on the clouds of heaven.

Tertullian (160?-230?) in his *Five Books Against Marcion* wrote of the second advent of Christ. "Of this advent the same prophet (Daniel) says, "Behold, one like the Son of man came with the clouds of heaven, and came to the Ancient of Days, . ."[5] He also refers this same text from Daniel to Christ in his work, *An Answer to the Jews,* "Of which second coming of the same (Chirst) Daniel has said: 'And behold, as it were a Son of man, coming with the clouds of heaven, came unto the Ancient of days, and was present in his sight; . . '[6]

Hippolytus (died 236?) in his *Treatise on Christ and Antichrist* wrote of the second coming of Christ in connection with Daniel 7:13-14:

> But His second coming is announced as glorious, when He shall come from heaven with a host of angels, and the glory of His Father, as the prophet saith, "Ye shall see the King in glory;" and "I saw one like the Son of man coming with the clouds of heaven; and He came to the Ancient of days, . . "[7]

---

[4] *Irenaeus Against Heresies*, Book 4, chap. 20, par. 11, in *The Ante-Nicene Fathers*, vol. 1, p. 491.

[5] Tertullian, *Five Books Against Marcion*, Book 3, chap. 7, in *The Ante-Nicene Fathers*, vol. 3, p. 326.

[6] Tertullian, *An Answer to the Jews*, chap. 14, in *The Ante-Nicene Fathers*, vol. 3, p. 172.

[7] Hippolytus, *Treatise on Christ and Antichrist*, sec. 44, in *The Ante-Nicene Fathers*, vol. 5, p. 213.

The Treatises of Cyprian (200-258) also identify Jesus with the Danielic prophecy in writing:

"That after He had risen again He should receive from His Father all power, and His power should be everlasting. In Daniel: 'I saw in a vision by night, and behold as it were the Son of man, coming in the clouds of heaven, and so forth to the end of verse 14'"[8]

In his *The City of God,* Augustine (354-430) wrote:

But of His [Christ's] power and glory he [Daniel] has thus spoken: "I saw in a night vision, and, behold, one like the Son of man was coming with the clouds of heaven . . ."[9]

John Chrysostom (345?-407) in a homily on First Corinthians cites Daniel 7:14 to show that Christ's kingdom was to be eternal, and that He would not cease to exist through merging with the Father at the end of this age as Marcellus of Ancyra was teaching:

How then, first of all, concerning the Father doth the Son Himself say, "My Father worketh hitherto, and I work: "(John v. 17.) and of Daniel, "That His Kingdom is an everlasting kingdom, which shall not pass away?" (Dan. vii. 14)[10]

Against the same error of which Chrysostom wrote, Cyril of Jerusalem (315?-386) in his *Catechetical Lectures* wrote:

"And shouldest thou ever hear any say that the kingdom of Christ shall have an end, abhor the heresy; it is another head of the dragon, lately sprung up in Galatia. . . Listen to the testimony of Daniel in the text; 'I saw in a vision of the night, and behold, one like the Son of Man came with the clouds of

---

[8] Cyprian, *Treatise 12, Three Books of Testimonies Against the Jews,* second bk, chap. 26, in *The Ante-Nicene Fathers,* vol. 5, p. 525.

[9] Augustine, *The City of God,* Book 18, chap. 34, in *The Nicene and Post-Nicene Fathers* (Grand Rapids: Wm. B. Eerdmans Publ. Co.), First Series, vol. 2, p. 380.

[10] John Chrysostom, *Homilies on First Corinthians,* Homily 39, sec. 6, in *The Nicene and Post-Nicene Fathers,* First Series, vol. 12, p. 237.

heaven, and came to the Ancient of Days, . .' for thou hast heard most plainly of the endless kingdom of Christ."[11]

And finally, Luther quoted Daniel 7:14 and saw it speaking of Jesus and applied it in attesting to the everlasting kingdom of Christ:

Thus we read in Isaiah 9[:7], "Of peace there will be no end." And in Daniel [7:14], "His dominion is an everlasting dominion . . . and his kingdom one that shall not be destroyed." This is eternal not before men, who do not live eternally, but before God, who lives eternally.[12]

[11] Cyril of Jerusalem, *The Catechetical Lectures*, Lecture 15, in *The Nicene and Post-Nicene Fathers*, Second Series, vol. 7, p. 113.

[12] Martin Luther, *The Jews and Their Lies*, in *Luther's Works* (Philadelphia and St. Louis: Fortress Press and Concordia Publ. Hse.), vol. 47, p. 206.

Index

522

Messiah, sacrifice for sin in Isaiah 53, 19, universal Savior, 19
Messiahship, Jesus', introduced slowly, 79-80
Messianic Prophecies, 28-31; 507-512
Methodius, Bishop, exalted celibacy and virginity over marriage, 207-208
Metropolitan, 301
Micah, goodness not sacrifice, 45
Molech, human sacrifice to, 22
Monasticism, 236-250; Cassian on, 242-246; in Celtic lands, 321; its negative effect on Jesus' way of life, 249-250; its origin, 237; its rationale and purpose, 236-237, 245; its self-centered emphasis on personal purity and perfection, 236, 249; its spread, 241; Jerome's experiences as a monastic, 238; Pachomius on, 239-240; the Franciscan and Dominican friars active in education and service to humanity, 248; the many positive benefits of, 248-249, 321; the problem of acedia, 245-246; the variety of monastic orders, 248
Montanism, 201, rebelled against autocracy of the bishops, 303
Mosaic Law, *see* Old Testament Law
Nazarenes, Jewish Christians, 173
Nazarites, allowed marriage, 175
New Commandment, 3, 36-37, 459-460; *Apostolic Constitutions* on, 292; Augustine on, 276-279; basis of Christian way of life, 34-35; Chrysostom on, 264-265, 268-269; cited by Clement of Alexandria, 194; cited by Ignatius(?), 152; culminates Jesus' ethical teaching, 78-79; giving of 36-37; John's recording of, 127; John on, 128-130; key to Jesus' ethical teachings, 77; lack of Paul's citing, 85-86; Luther on, 356-359; not accented in early

church, 170; not a new law, 360, 417-418, 460-461
New Covenant, fulfillment of, 16; promise of, 16, 28-31, 34-35
New Testament, guide to understanding Old Testament, 463-464; *see also* New Covenant
Nicaea, Council of, canons concerning apostasy, 318, first ecumenical council, 303; refused to deny clergy marital intercourse, 230-231
Nimes, France, Calvinism in, 448-449
Old Testament Law, 37-42; a model for the nations, 23-24; benevolence and justice toward others, 25; 38-42; Christian love as its fulfilling, 59-60; Christians no longer under, 99-103, 167-169, 292, 382; no longer accuses, 381
Old Testament People, keeping of Mosaic Law, 42-47; *see also* Israel
Old Testament, *see* Covenant with Israel
Onanism, 176
Origen, 200-201; on marriage, 200
Pachomius, his life, 239; his Rule, 239-240; *see also Rules of St. Pachomius*
Pantaenus, 192-193
Papacy, *see* Bishops of Rome and Roman Catholic Church
Paphnutius, Bishop, argued against celibacy for married priests, 231
Papias, Bishop, on Mark's Gospel, 121-122; on Matthew's Gospel, 121; Peter, source of Mark's Gospel, 121-122
Pascal, Blaise, on piety and goodness, 42-43
Paul, the Apostle, 85-120; and lawful government, 89-90; at Jerusalem Council, 101; Christians being led by the Spirit, 114; Christian use of the courts, 97-98; Christians no longer under OT law, 99-103,

Order Form
for
The More Excellent Way:
2000 Years of Jesus'
New Way of Life

Price of Book $24.95

Number of copies_____

Number of copies ____ times 24.95 is   _____

Domestic Shipping and handling for
first book. $4.50

           $2.25 for each added book   _____

International shipping and handling for
first book $8.85

Total Price   _____

Shipping will be by U.S. Postal Service

Send a check or money order made out to **Crucifer Press** to

Crucifer Press
P.O. Box 205
Independence, OR 97351

To keep the cost of the book as reasonable as possible, we do not accept credit cards.

You may return the book(s) for any reason for a full refund for the cost of the books(s), less shipping and handling.